1898

1898

Visual Culture and U.S. Imperialism in the Caribbean and the Pacific

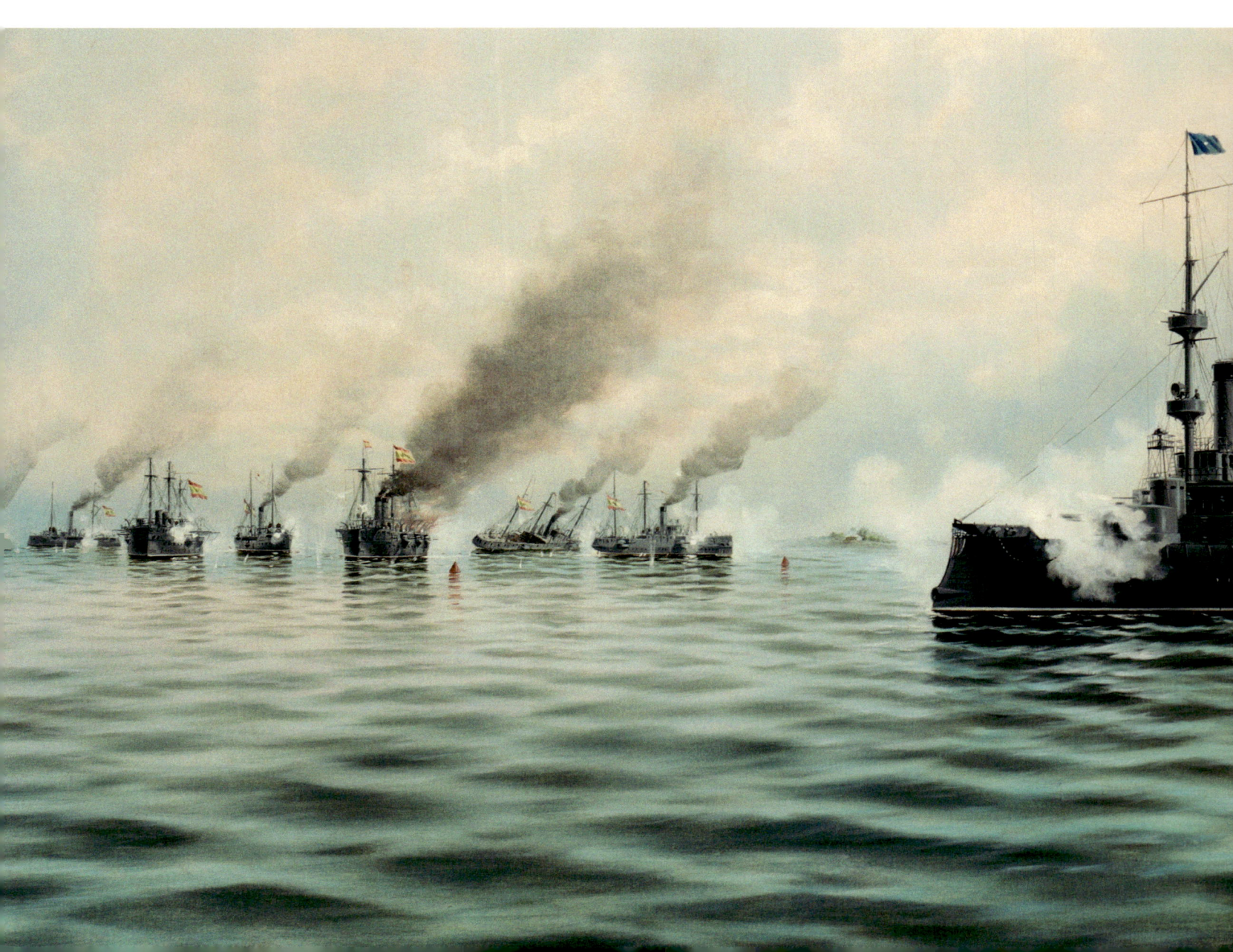

Taína Caragol and **Kate Clarke Lemay**

WITH Jorge Duany, Theodore S. Gonzalves,
Kristin Hoganson, Healoha Johnston, Paul A. Kramer,
Carolina Maestre, and Neil Weare

National Portrait Gallery,
Smithsonian Institution,
Washington, DC

In association with
Princeton University Press,
Princeton and Oxford

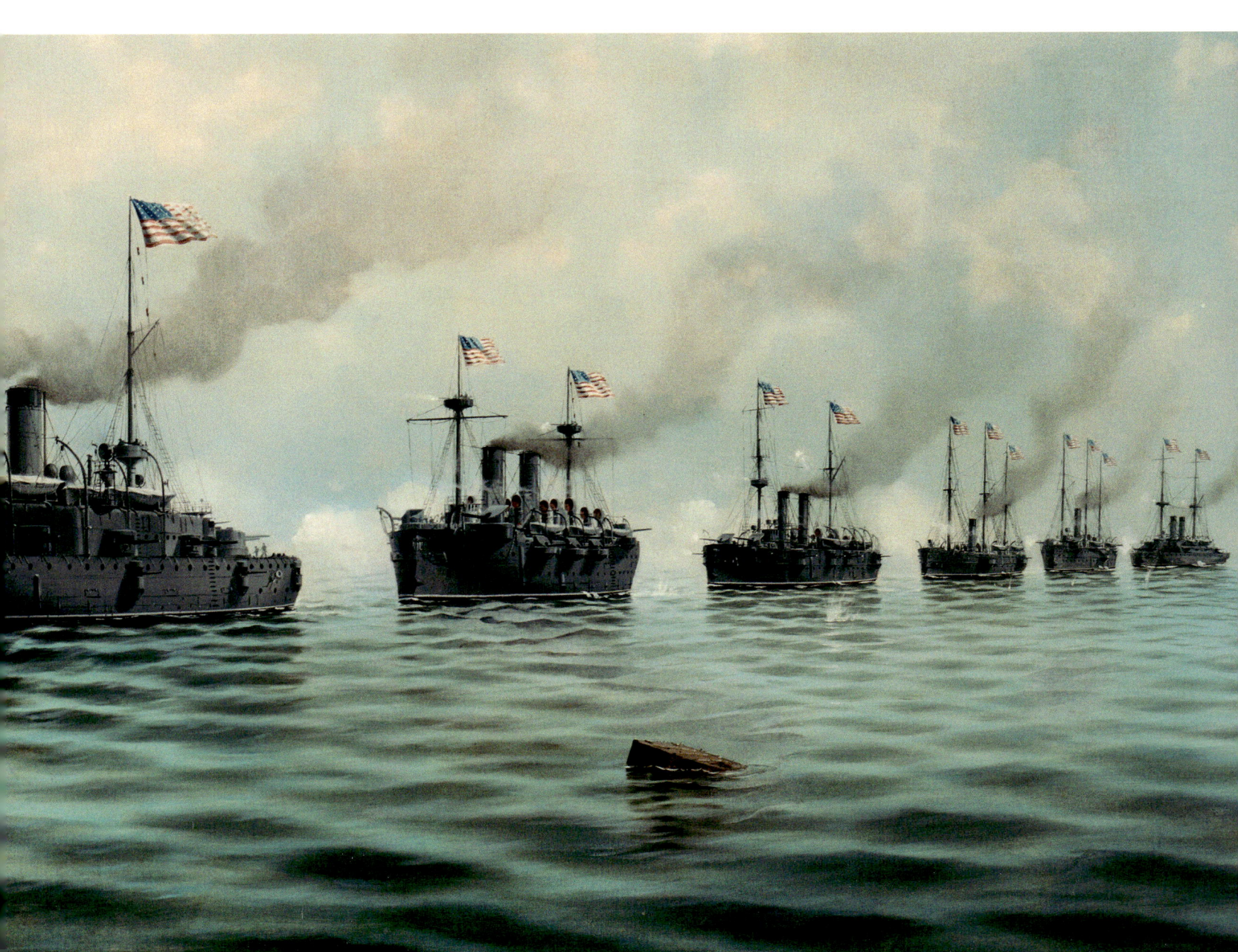

Donors

1898: Visual Culture and U.S. Imperialism in the Caribbean and the Pacific and the exhibition *1898: U.S. Imperial Visions and Revisions* have been made possible through the generous support of:

The Andrew W. Mellon Foundation
Ann S. and Samuel M. Mencoff
Luis Miranda, Jr., the Miranda Family Foundation
Terra Foundation for American Art
Ann E. Roulet, Laura Roulet, and Rafael Hernández
Kate Kelly and George Schweitzer
Gretchen Sierra-Zorita and Peter B. Hutt II
M. Salomé Galib y Duane McLaughlin

Furthermore: a program of the J. M. Kaplan Fund

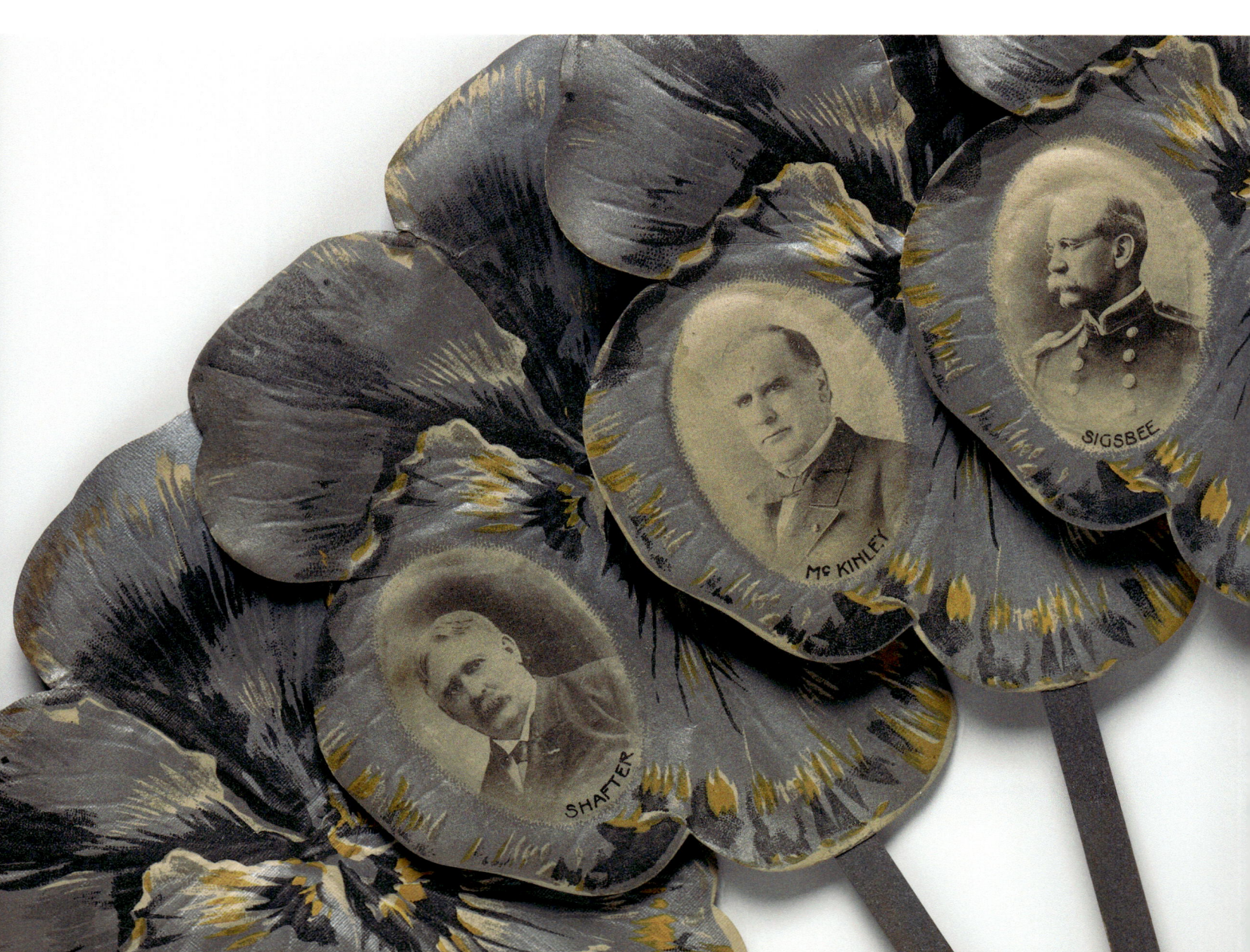

This publication has been supported by Fred M. Levin and Family, The Shenson Foundation, in memory of Nancy Livingston Levin.

The project received federal support from the Latino Initiatives Pool, administered by the National Museum of the American Latino, and the Asian Pacific American Initiatives Pool, administered by the Smithsonian Asian Pacific American Center.

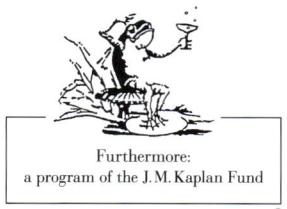

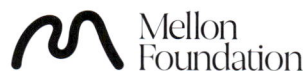

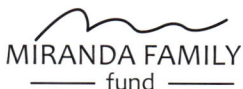

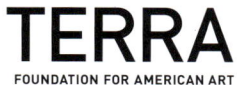

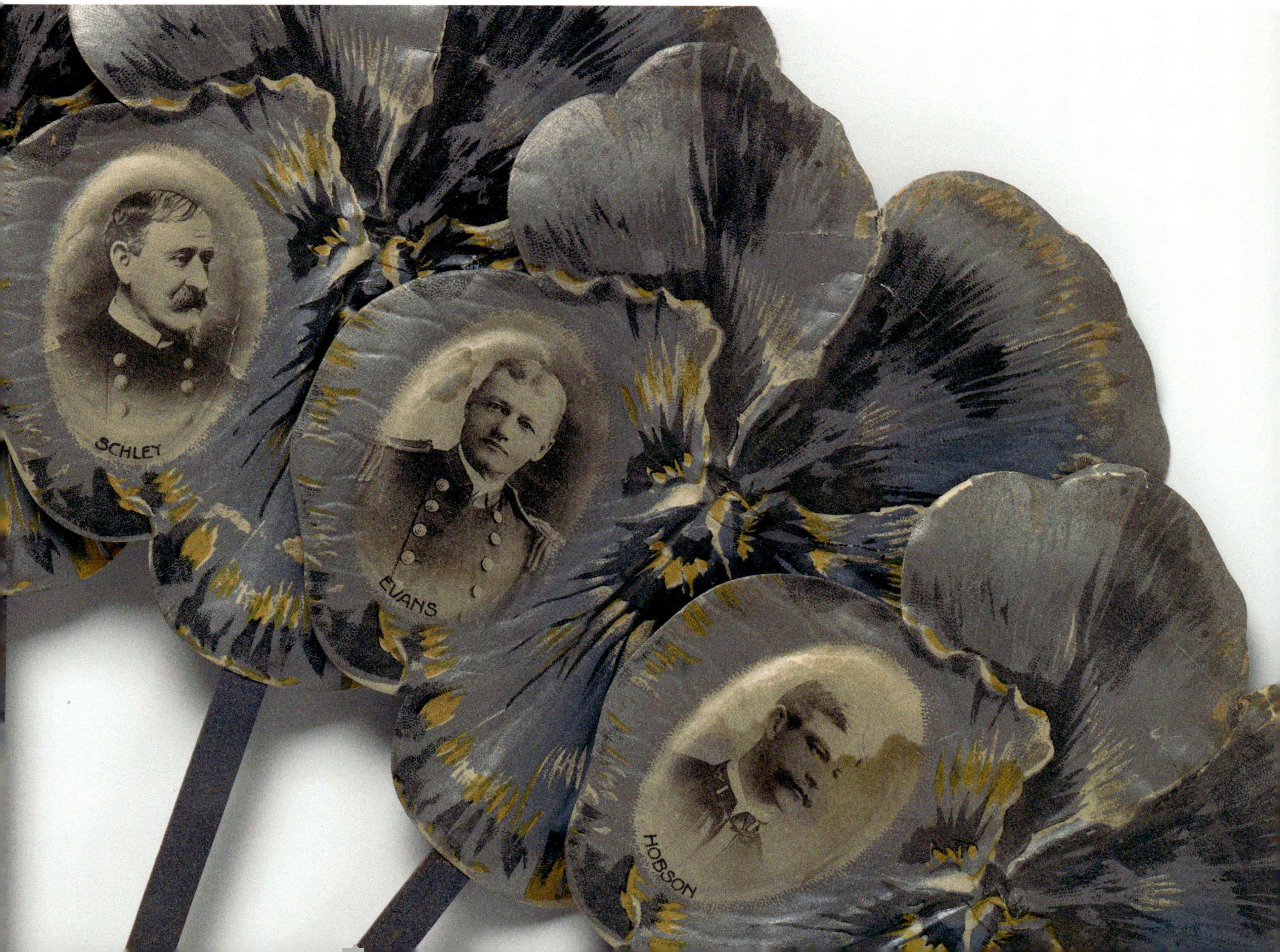

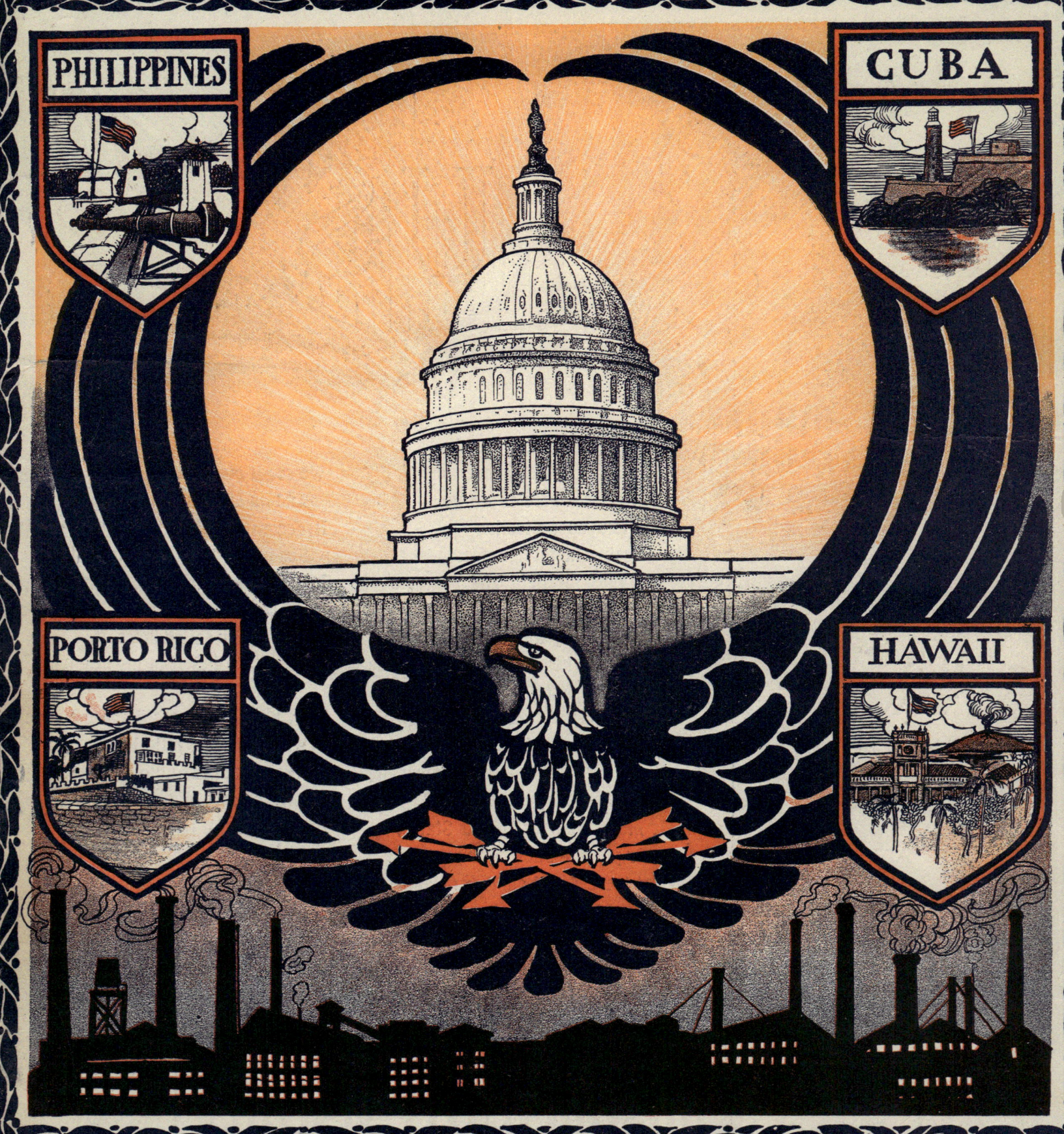

PHILIPPINES

CUBA

PORTO RICO

HAWAII

INAUGURATION NUMBER

Contents

Catalogue

TAÍNA CARAGOL and KATE CLARKE LEMAY
with CAROLINA MAESTRE

Foreword

The atmosphere must have been tense around the Washington, DC-area hotel where the representatives of Cuba, the Philippines, and Puerto Rico gathered to have their picture taken in early February 1899. Crowded together in a nondescript room, the men sat on plain wooden chairs, with their supporters hastily standing behind them in a doorway, ill at ease. They could barely make themselves look toward the camera, let alone each other. Nonetheless, they were frozen in time by the photographer who recorded the consequential event (see p. 179).

While a sudden, fierce snowstorm had frozen everything around the Capitol, tempers were rising over whether Congress would grant sovereignty to the former Spanish colonies, make them part of the United States with all the attending rights of citizenship, or deem them vassals to be governed at the conclusion of the War of 1898.

These representatives had come to ask President William McKinley, in person, to be included in discussions, but they instead found themselves rebuffed from the halls of power. The Treaty of Paris, signed less than two months earlier, had included worrisome language about having their civil rights and political status controlled, and while

the French artist Théobald Chartran was busily creating a large historic painting to commemorate the U.S. victory, the grainy photograph uncovered in Eugenio María de Hostos's undigitized papers in the Library of Congress provides important evidence that their struggles were just beginning.

The question of visual memory—who makes it, who is memorialized by it, who retains it—lies at the heart of this book and its accompanying exhibition, *1898: U.S. Imperial Visions and Revisions.* While we often mark the passage of time by recording events and their dates, it is equally, if not more, important to focus on the people who have played a part in those events or been affected by them.

Representation matters. This is the case for the peoples of Hawai'i, who attained statehood in 1959; for those in Cuba and the Philippines, who would eventually gain independence despite a protracted and bloody war; and for those in Guam and Puerto Rico, who were denied the right to vote in the presidential election, even after the United States retained their land as territories.

Of particular importance in this moment of visualizing—and personalizing—history that has been forgotten or ignored is the full-length royal portrait of Queen Liliʻuokalani, painted around 1891–92 by the artist William Cogswell. Until now, this painting had never left the Iolani Palace on the island of Oʻahu. Remarkable in scale and holding its own near the museum's portraits of Presidents George Washington and Abraham Lincoln, one cannot help but wonder whether events might have unfolded differently if such an imposing picture had been better known. Queen Liliʻuokalani ruled, after all, in the same era as Queen Victoria of England and Isabella II of Spain, so to see a classical painting of a strong female monarch would not have been entirely surprising to the public. While one would like to think that such an oversight might have been avoided had the National Portrait Gallery already existed (we would not open our doors for another seven decades), the truth is that the queen is still only represented in our collection today by several small and fragile pictures on paper.

Marking the one hundred and twenty fifth anniversary of the War of 1898, this exhibition and book provide the National Portrait Gallery with an opportunity to question how we, as an institution, have recognized people in the past. What personal stories have we omitted because they were judged to be of secondary importance? Whose art did we not show because it was deemed too provincial? Understanding that every person leaves an impression on the world around them, how should we, as an organization, acknowledge individual contributions?

We would be wise to apply the principles of "forbearance, forgiveness, and peace," suggested by Queen Liliʻuokalani at her military tribunal, as she urged the United States to create a united people. We should also present, I would argue, the many fascinating stories of the people and communities who have made us what we are today. *1898: Visual Culture and U.S. Imperialism in the Caribbean and the Pacific* offers a glimpse into this complex history through essays that express a variety of perspectives. It is our hope that the art and artifacts gathered here will inspire further debate in the years to come.

—Kim Sajet, Director, National Portrait Gallery, Washington, DC

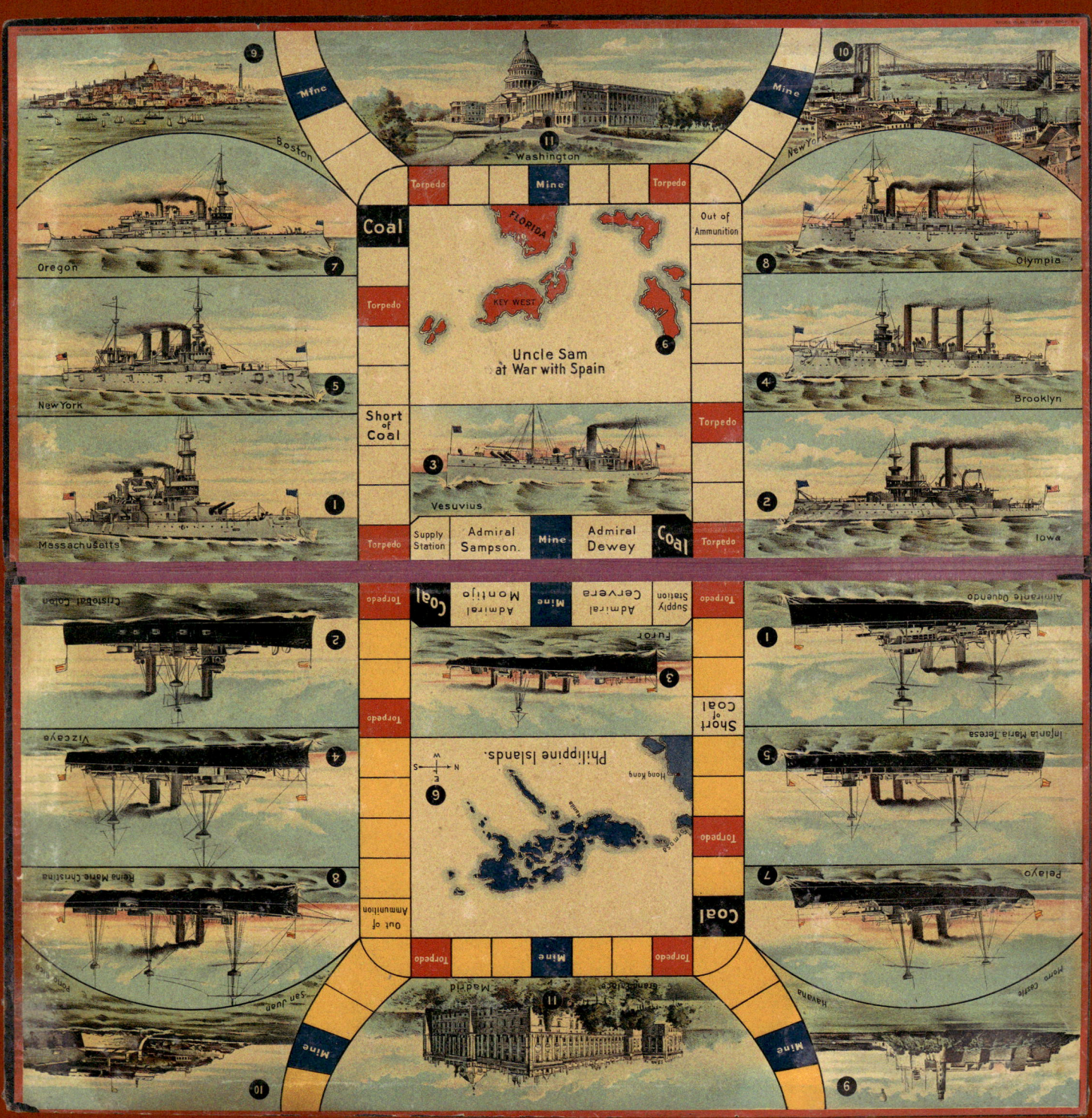

Introduction

1898: U.S. Imperial Visions and Revisions

TAÍNA CARAGOL AND KATE CLARKE LEMAY

In 1898, the Rhode Island Game Company introduced *Uncle Sam at War with Spain*, a board game featuring drawings of famous ships from the U.S. Naval fleet and the Spanish Armada (fig. 1). Starting in the capital city of Madrid or Washington, DC, players move their soldiers and ships as they seek to capture the men and territories of the "enemy" and encounter important sites in the ongoing War of 1898.[1] The board includes architectural landmarks representing Boston; New York City; Santiago, Cuba; and San Juan, Puerto Rico, as well as maps of Key West and the Philippine Islands. Unlucky players face setbacks if they land on any box in enemy territory marked "Mine," "Torpedo," "Short of Coal," or "Out of Ammunition." *Uncle Sam at War with Spain* was advertised as displaying pictures "taken from correct photographs" and claimed to be "the most instructive" game on the market. Underneath the title, the box cover reads, "Let the Americans show what they would have done had they been on the Spanish War Vessels."[2] With its strategic

Fig. 1 *Uncle Sam at War with Spain*, Rhode Island Game Company, 1898. Cardboard, metal, and printed paper; board (open): 52.1 × 52.1 × 0.3 cm (20½ × 20½ × ⅛ in.). Collection of Emilio Cueto

events of battle and real sites of combat, the game tapped into a zeitgeist for war.

All games aside, conflicts during 1898 brought about profound geopolitical changes. Three contentious incidents heralded this sea change: the War of 1898 (commonly known in the United States as the Spanish-American War), the Joint Resolution to annex Hawai'i, and the Philippine-American War. The year's events constitute a critical flashpoint in global history. Due to their foundational role in forging the U.S. overseas empire, this book refers to them jointly as the conflicts of 1898.

The War of 1898 grew out of Cuba's third and final war of independence against Spain (1895–1898). The explosion of the USS *Maine* in Havana Harbor on February 15, 1898, propelled the United States to declare war on Spain on April 25, under the pretext of assisting the Cubans in their fight for freedom. On July 7, as the war continued, the United States annexed Hawai'i as a territory, ignoring Queen Lili'uokalani's (1838–1917) pleas for her kingdom, which included petitions from her people. By the end of the summer, the United States upended what remained of the Spanish empire in the Caribbean and the Pacific, and secured Hawai'i as part of its dominion.[3] After a cease-fire on August 12, the war officially ended with the Treaty of Paris, signed on December 10, 1898. In it, the United States claimed sovereignty over Puerto Rico, the Philippines, Guam, and temporarily occupied Cuba. However, a loose coalition of Filipinos led by Emilio Aguinaldo (1869–1964), who had supported the United States in its fight against Spain, declared the Philippines to be independent. The U.S. refusal to recognize Aguinaldo's claim of independence triggered the Philippine-American War, which lasted officially from 1899 until 1902, although hostilities continued until 1913.

The overseas territorial expansion of the United States presents a paradox. Although the values of freedom, equality, and justice were central to the country's founding, these principles have consistently been at odds with its trajectory of territorial and political expansion. If we understand westward expansion as the displacement and subjugation of Native nations, then the process culminated in 1898 with the imposition of U.S. rule beyond the Atlantic and Pacific coasts.

Through a presentation of portraits of major proponents of U.S. expansionism and empire and portraits of individuals from Cuba, Guam, Hawai'i, the Philippines, and Puerto Rico who negotiated and defended their right to govern themselves, this exhibition puts human faces on the events of 1898, using the platform of our national museum of history and portraiture. On the 125th anniversary of these conflicts, the time is ripe for an examination of this period at the National Portrait Gallery. There are many reasons for addressing this history. The War of 1898 established the United States as an overseas empire and initiated its international positioning as a guardian of democracy. The expansionist spirit that fueled such a vast military intervention contributes to the ongoing discourse of American exceptionalism. This ideology continues to permeate geopolitical thought and international relations in the United States.[4] It also ushered unprecedented political growth over the first decade of the twentieth century, spurring the entry of the United States into the circle of world powers and preparing its ascendency as a global leader.[5]

While the War of 1898 resulted in relatively few U.S. combat casualties and lasted less than four months, by 1913, the ensuing Philippine-American War cost the lives of at least 100,000 Filipino civilians (with some scholars arguing that a more realistic estimate would fall between 250,000 and 300,000).[6] Today, as we reckon with

historical U.S. legacies that have resulted in structural racism against people of color, it is important to understand the assumptions of white Anglo-Saxon superiority underlying the conflicts of 1898. These assumptions defined the expansionist political discourse of the time. As museums contend with their role in supporting and validating histories of colonialism through their collections and exhibitions, *1898: Visual Culture and U.S. Imperialism in the Caribbean and the Pacific* illuminates how the Smithsonian Institution served as a repository for the spoils of war and for cultural objects that were collected as a result of the conflicts of 1898. The military conflicts of 1898 also had significant social and cultural consequences. Colonization implies an outward movement, but it often creates a boomerang effect in migrations that outlast colonial bonds. Since 1898, the movement of U.S. Americans to Cuba, Guam, Hawai'i, Puerto Rico, and the Philippines, as well as that of islanders to the continental United States, has intensified socioeconomic and cultural exchanges. The conflicts have also created a circuit of migration within the territories of the United States.

Given the imbrication of history between all the lands mentioned, it is pertinent to ask: how present are the conflicts of 1898 at the National Portrait Gallery? Until recently, the museum had only sparse references to the conflicts of 1898 in the wall labels for the portraits of expansionist leaders. The texts for Theodore Roosevelt (1858–1919) and George Dewey (1837–1917), both lauded as heroes of the war in the United States, for example, focused on the adoration they received, excluding an acknowledgment of oppositional views of these conflicts, or the political subordination of the territories they helped acquire.[7] The label for the portrait of Leonard Wood (1860–1927), who served in both the Cuban and Filipino campaigns of the war, described the transition between the U.S. military government to the Cuban Republic as "a peaceful turnover of authority." It ignored the Cubans' intense protests over the Platt Amendment— even outside of the Governor Wood's residence—which turned Cuba into a *de facto* protectorate.[8]

These public-facing texts promoted a history of military achievement, heroism, global power, and U.S. benevolence. Until now, this teleological narrative has stood as the definitive word on this historical chapter at the National Portrait Gallery. The mere facts of the war's events—and the resulting vast territorial acquisitions—reduced the narrative to a *fait accompli*. This attitude does not adequately query the arrogant notion of the "Splendid Little War," which is how Secretary of State John Hay (1838–1905) referred to the United States' quick victory over Spain. As we know, U.S. expansionism found both supporters and detractors at home and abroad. Consider, for example, how Ida B. Wells (1862–1931) denounced the hypocrisy implied by the U.S. government's defense of Cuba's right to liberty while it remained silent about the abuse African Americans suffered under Jim Crow laws. Separately, in her role as a member of the Anti-Imperialist League, Jane Addams (1860–1935) decried the Philippine-American War. For the first time at the Portrait Gallery, this catalogue and its accompanying exhibition, *1898: U.S. Imperial Visions and Revisions*, give voice to these important stories.

Taking into consideration the celebratory narratives that have already been told about the conflicts of 1898, this endeavor highlights the voices of dissent and other perspectives that have been overshadowed by exalting stories regarding proponents of imperialism, such as Roosevelt, Dewey, and Wood. Addressing the void in the existing accounts by exhibiting the portraits and biographies of the peoples who came under U.S. control or its sphere of influence in 1898 is crucial to presenting a more complete history.

As curators working in a federal institution, we feel an enormous responsibility toward the research and scholarship representing the points of view of the different territories, states, and countries addressed in this exhibition. We are aware that some people in these places are highly suspicious of federal institutions. Moreover, because the constitutional legacy of U.S. imperialism continues to be contested, many residents of these places are protective and critical of the historical narrative, and of who tells it. Throughout our research and writing, we consulted members of Indigenous communities, as well as scholars and curators living in Cuba, Guam, Hawai'i, Puerto Rico, the Philippines, and Spain. As part of our research for this exhibition, we visited seventy-four archives and collections of art in these locations. With the aim of highlighting the perspectives of peoples from the islands and including their cultures and contexts, we have placed the portraits of previously marginalized figures at the center of the narrative. Whereas federal institutions like the National Portrait Gallery have traditionally elided these figures and their historical roles, today we bring them forth. Furthermore, because the Smithsonian

Institution played a noteworthy role in collecting and disseminating knowledge about the new territories during the birth of the U.S. colonial system in the Caribbean and the Pacific, it has the responsibility of addressing histories of U.S. imperialism.[9]

Curatorial Method

The ways in which we understand history are not static. The language and concepts we use to comprehend its course evolve over time. We intentionally selected the exhibition title, *1898: U.S. Imperial Visions and Revisions*, to signal how we are debating traditional histories of 1898 as a U.S. triumph. Our aim is to yield a critical analysis of this historical juncture, beginning with the name of that year's central conflict in U.S. historiography. The name with which the United States christened the central conflict of 1898—the Spanish-American War—points to the world hierarchy it established through its military intervention. When the United States intervened in the third and final Cuban War of Independence, Cuban involvement in the conflict was obliterated by a stroke of the pen, and the Cubans were denied the credit for their own anti-colonial struggle. Since 1945, Cuban scholars have worked to undo this erasure, reclaiming their centrality in the conflict by calling it the Spanish-Cuban-American War.[10] To recognize all the arenas of war, the conflict might also, awkwardly, be referred to as the Spanish-American-Cuban-Philippine-Puerto Rican War.[11] Even this name is not quite right, for, although the United States captured Guam without military engagement, it would also deserve inclusion in the conflict's name given the ongoing impact of the war on its political status.[12] While there are different ways of perceiving this history and its outcome, we have strived for a comparative view that promotes inclusivity. In this spirit, we have made the decision to refer to these military events as the War of 1898. The date 1898 also signals the annexation of Hawai'i that was the culmination of the overthrow of the Hawaiian Kingdom by white businessmen and landowners that occurred in 1893. Because the War of 1898 immediately preceded and provoked the Philippine-American War, we consider them together in this volume.

Until World War I, empires were the dominant political system around the world. The race for colonization escalated in the mid-to-late nineteenth century. Powerful states, such as Britain, France, Spain, the Austro-Hungarian Empire, Russia, the Ottoman Empire, and Japan, among others, exerted political rule over large expanses of territory over ground or overseas.[13] It is, therefore, not surprising that the words "empire," and its derivatives "imperial" and "imperialism," as well as the word "colony," were in common use at this time. However, the power hierarchies within them were also contested. For example, *The Republican Campaign Text Book* of 1900 cites a speech by William McKinley (1843–1901), the U.S. president during the War of 1898, in which he proclaimed that his party had bravely met the supreme opportunity, referring to the Philippines, "to liberate tens of millions of the human family from the yoke of imperialism."[14] That same textbook liberally uses the word colony to refer to the non-contiguous, revenue-generating territorial possessions of France and England. The very name of the strongest group opposing territorial expansion in 1898, the multitudinous Anti-Imperialist League, exemplifies the circulation and critique of these political terms. At the same time, it is telling that the U.S. government avoided the use of the words "empire" and "colony" as it charted new governmental systems for these acquisitions, which it preferred to call "territories" or "new possessions."[15] In addition to these terms, we use the words "imperialist" and "expansionist" almost interchangeably, as adjectives characterizing the attitudes of political leaders of the era. When describing the military campaigns of the War of 1898, we also use the word "invasion" as a technical term employed by the U.S. military to describe their incursions into foreign lands.

"Empire" and "colony" also allude to the contemporary political realities of lands that do not have full autonomy or equal constitutional rights. Through the conflicts of 1898, the United States claimed sovereignty over archipelagoes in the Caribbean and the Pacific, establishing political control over them.[16] The term "sovereignty" is used through this catalogue and exhibition to refer to the exercise of political power within a limited sphere. Political sovereignty can be exercised by an imperial power, such as Spain or the United States, over a colony. It might be sought after through decolonizing struggles, such as that of the Cubans fighting their third War of Independence, and likewise, the Philippine struggle for independence from Spain and then from the United States. Puerto Rican liberals in the 1890s sought

autonomy from Spain to attain a degree of sovereignty. Under U.S. rule, the Puerto Rican and Guamanian/ CHamoru struggles for more political rights through the twentieth and twenty-first centuries have also been struggles for sovereignty. In the Kingdom of Hawai'i, sovereignty was violently revoked through the dethroning of Queen Lili'uokalani.

"Self-government" is another term we use throughout this catalogue and exhibition. Around the turn of the twentieth century, it was often invoked by the United States in the negative form, as a political capacity that the "new possessions" allegedly lacked, but that they could eventually achieve through colonial tutelage.[17] At the same time, "self-governance" was also invoked as a political model associated with the political relationship between Canada and England, by Puerto Rican advocates of autonomy. Within those same circles, "self-government" was also understood as an admirable trait of the United States that was worthy of emulation.[18]

Until the present, few efforts have been made to address the history and repercussions of the U.S. empire with the inclusivity that we propose. The centennial of the War of 1898 introduced a short-lived moment of heightened awareness about U.S. imperialism. However, in the aftermath, to our knowledge, only niche academic publications and forums have addressed this history. Our exhibition, *1898: U.S. Imperial Visions and Revisions*, as well as this book, intend to bring the conflicts of this period back into public consciousness and prompt reflections on the legacy of the U.S. empire. Our goal is twofold. First, through examining the turn-of-the-century vision—as expressed by powerful portraits of people such as Dewey, Roosevelt, Henry Cabot Lodge (1850–1924), and Alfred Thayer Mahan (fig. 2)—we shed light on how the United States positioned itself as a global power with influence in the Eastern and Western Hemispheres. Second, the word "revisions" from our title refers to our amending the historical narrative by considering those voices that were subsumed by the canonical triumphalist narrative. Most importantly, this book and exhibition bring to the fore conversations about why this history matters.

Curatorial work relies on an economy of space, and we had to make tough decisions regarding our selection.

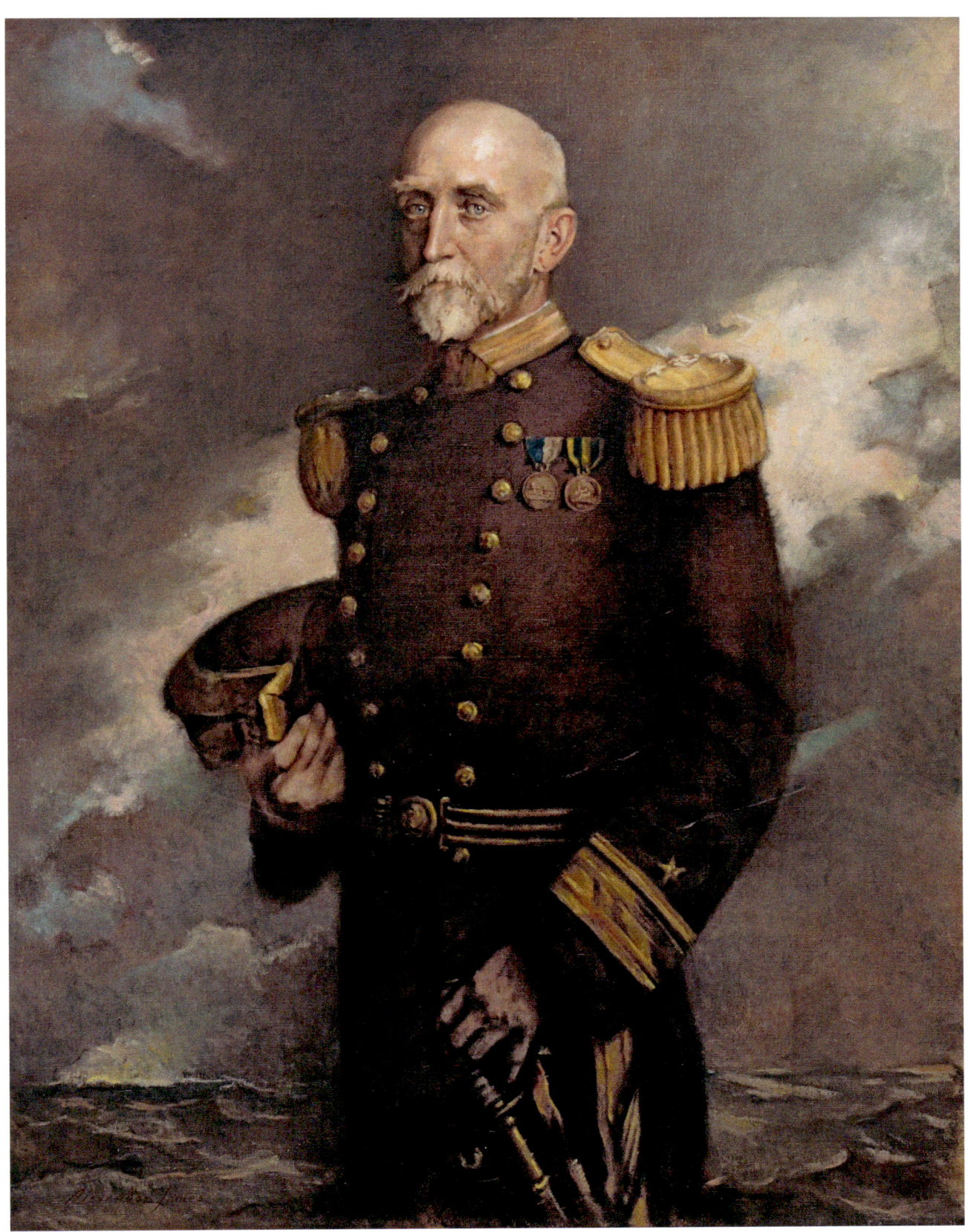

Given our emphasis on an expanded narrative, we chose to prioritize the histories of Spain's former colonies Cuba, Guam, the Philippines, and Puerto Rico over the impact of the war on Spain, and also relate the annexation of Hawai'i to this history of expansion. After enduring a brutal occupation by the Japanese during World War II, the Philippines secured its independence in 1946. Puerto Rico and Guam remain U.S. territories to this day, while Hawai'i became a state in 1959.[19] After the U.S. military government in Cuba ended in 1902, the island gained independence, but until 1934 it was subject to U.S. intervention in its politics and economy through the Platt Amendment. Residents of Guam endured military rule from 1899 through 1950 and could not elect their own governor until 1970.

In this vast geographic span, each archipelago has its own cultural specificity. The perception of the U.S. presence in each of them elicits a variety of responses, sometimes contradictory, that range from U.S. military patriotism, to pride in belonging to one of the strongest world economies, to disapproval of the territorial occupation, and contempt for the lack of full U.S. constitutional protections for the territories.[20] For example, many Kānaka Maoli (Native Hawaiians) consider the "joint resolution for annexation" illegal and question the legitimacy of Hawaiian statehood, calling it an occupation.[21] Since 1967, Puerto Rico has conducted six referendums, considered non-binding by the U.S. Congress, to decide the island's political status. In most of them, no clear majority has emerged for any of the status alternatives proposed by the local board of elections, pointing to the divided opinion of voters regarding the island's relationship to the United States.[22] Guam has a strong sense of U.S. military identity and one of the highest recruitment levels in the country. Yet Guam's Indigenous groups protest the U.S. military-industrial complex, which owns 28 percent of the 212 square-mile island and continues to expand. The presence of the military and its exercises, such as live fire practice, also cause friction with the island's inhabitants.[23]

We curated this show to be inclusive of each archipelago in order to start a more nuanced conversation about their individual histories. Finding portraits of all those who played important roles in the conflicts of 1898 proved challenging, however. For example, portraits of key CHamoru figures, such as Padre José Torres Palomo (1836–1919) and Atanasio Taitano Perez (1874–1950), were

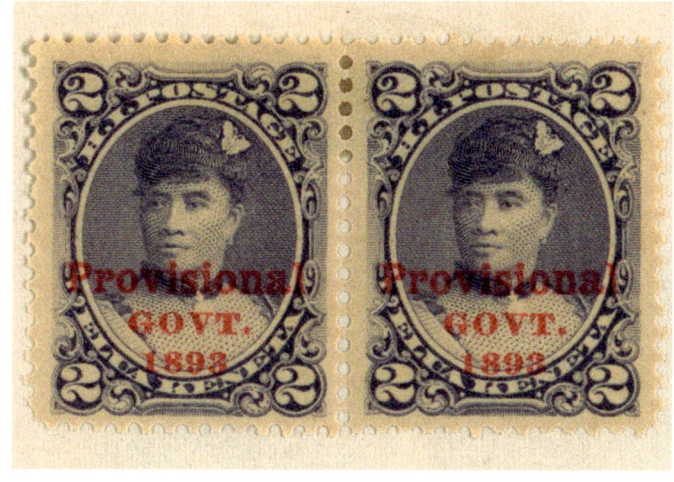

Fig. 3 This Hawaiian postage stamp, valued at 2 cents (Elua Keneta), features a portrait of Queen Lili'uokalani with "Provisional Government 1893" printed over her likeness; 2.9 × 2.2 cm (1⅛ × ⅞ in.). Hawai'i State Archives

almost impossible to find.[24] This may be due, in part, to the difficulties of preserving archives in tropical conditions, but largely results from the ravaging of Guam during World War II. We also had difficulty locating portraits of the many women involved in these conflicts. To our knowledge, women such as the insurgent Paulina Ruiz Gonzáles (life dates unknown) who became a lieutenant in the Cuban Revolutionary Army, or Filipina Gregoria "Gloria" P. Montoya (1863–1896), who commanded several units of the Army of Revolution of the Philippines, never had portraits made.[25] In this book, regrettably, their histories cannot be studied through visual materials, if only because portraiture is imperfect as a tool of inquiry. These instances reinforce for us that portraiture is flawed and exclusive, leaving many figures "out of the picture." Portraiture made in traditional media, like oil painting or marble sculptures, skews toward wealthy elites and male leaders because it demanded such great resources. One exception is the portrait of Queen Lili'uokalani (1838–1917) by William Cogswell (1819–1903). Queen Lili'uokalani recognized the power of portraiture when she wielded it to reinforce her sovereignty. By purchasing a grand-scale portrait of herself in 1893, she carried out one of her most successful acts of resistance against the overthrow led by Anglo-American missionary descendant Lorrin Thurston (1858–1931). Oil on canvas portraiture often reveals the power dynamics of this era, but the rise of photography helped give an opportunity to those who fought for their people's right to govern themselves, like the Filipino insurgent leader Emilio Aguinaldo, or the Cuban *mambí*, Antonio Maceo Grajales (1845–1896).

Despite its flaws, portraiture rallied morale and created an iconography that was indisputably empowering for leaders like Lili'uokalani and proponents of Cuban independence like José Martí (1853–1895) and Maceo. Portraits of these figures, in particular, relied on visual power to create an iconography of resistance and nation-building that their detractors could never defeat. The power of portraiture was so great that agents of the empire often enacted iconoclasm. In one example, after the overthrow of the Hawaiian sovereign government, Thurston's puppet government obscured the portrait of Queen Lili'uokalani in a postal stamp by marking "provisional government" over her face (fig. 3).

Contents and Organization

As co-curators and co-authors studying this history, it has been paramount for us to include the voices of experts from the many lands involved in this history. To that end, the five authors of the book's prefaces have either personal connections to the land or an academic expertise on the topic, or both. These essays point to the contemporary relevance of the history of the conflicts of 1898 and take into consideration the ongoing, unresolved questions pertaining to U.S. imperialism. Kristin Hoganson addresses the expansion of the United States before 1898; Healoha Johnston argues that Hawaiian culture is the core of their resistance; Jorge Duany discusses the diverging political experiences of Cuba and Puerto Rico in the twentieth century; Theodore Gonzalves exposes the suppression of the U.S. history of colonialism and calls for new narratives centered on the perspectives of people from the Philippines and Guam; and Neil Weare sheds light on ongoing debates regarding the *Insular Cases* of the territories in the aftermaths of the War of 1898. Accompanying these essays are the first five chapters of this book, organized as narrative histories driven by portraiture and biography, which trace the show's chronological and geographic structure. Importantly, these chapters present the history of each land through the lens of portraiture and visual culture.

After presenting the exhibition in narrative essays organized according to geography, this exhibition catalogue includes three essays on themes related to 1898. Paul A. Kramer focuses on the Smithsonian's role in surveying the Philippines and representing the new colonial subjects in its collections. Kate Clarke Lemay addresses the end of the Spanish empire, the beginning of the Cuban nation, and the emergence of the United States as an imperial power through the art of Winslow Homer (1836–1910) and Armando García Menocal (1863–1942). Taína Caragol analyzes contemporary artistic interpretations of the conflicts and the legacy of 1898 in the work of Puerto Rican Miguel Luciano, Filipinx Americans Maia Cruz Palileo and Stephanie Syjuco, and CHamoru Gisela McDaniel. She explores how these artists reimagine the genre of portraiture to subvert racialized and disempowering images of colonial subjects.

Chapter one, "Prelude to Empire: Indian Wars and Sea Power," situates the conflicts of 1898 within the desire for territorial expansion that began soon after the United States became an independent state.[26] The notion that U.S. power should extend throughout the Americas went back to Thomas Jefferson (fig. 4). As early as 1786, Jefferson had expressed interest in acquiring the New World territories belonging to Spain, an empire he saw as feeble, and ready to be taken "peice by peice" [*sic*] by the United States in due time.[27] Portraits, such as those of James Monroe by Chester Harding (fig. 5), Alfred Thayer Mahan by Alexander Robertson James (see fig. 2), Theodore Roosevelt by Charles Dana Gibson (see p. 103), and Nelson Miles by David Frances Barry (see p. 33), point to the men in power during the development of U.S. expansionism, from the articulation of the Monroe Doctrine establishing the Americas as a sphere of U.S. influence in 1823, to the displacement and state violence enacted by the United States against Native Americans during the Indian Wars of the 1870s, 1880s, and 1890s, to the development of a vision for overseas expansion in the Atlantic and the Pacific.[28]

Chapter two, "Hawaiian Resistance and U.S. Imperialism," outlines the settler colonialism of Christian missionaries from New England in Hawai'i, beginning in the 1820s, and the subsequent erosion of the Hawaiian monarchy and ultimate dethroning of Queen Lili'uokalani in 1893 by Anglo-American businessmen. They facilitated a coup, which led to the annexation of the archipelago in 1898, an action protested by tens of thousands of Kānaka Maoli who remained loyal to their queen. The royalists, united in a resistance movement, made cultural objects, such as the flag quilt, to symbolize their political loyalties. They also organized petitions of protest throughout the first decade of the 1900s.

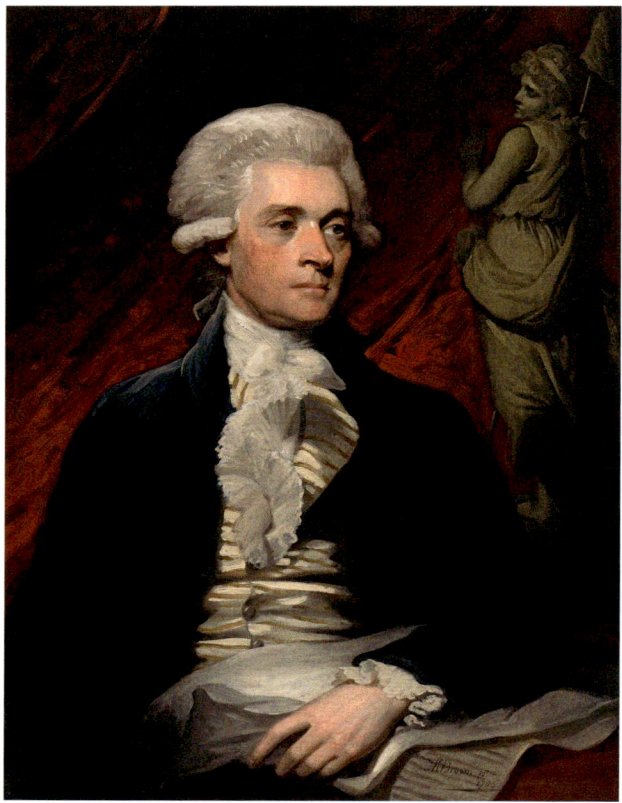

Fig. 4 *Thomas Jefferson* (1743–1826), Mather Brown (1761–1831), 1786. Oil on canvas; 90.8 × 72.4 cm (35¾ × 28½ in.). National Portrait Gallery, Smithsonian Institution; bequest of Charles Francis Adams; frame conserved with funds from the Smithsonian Women's Committee

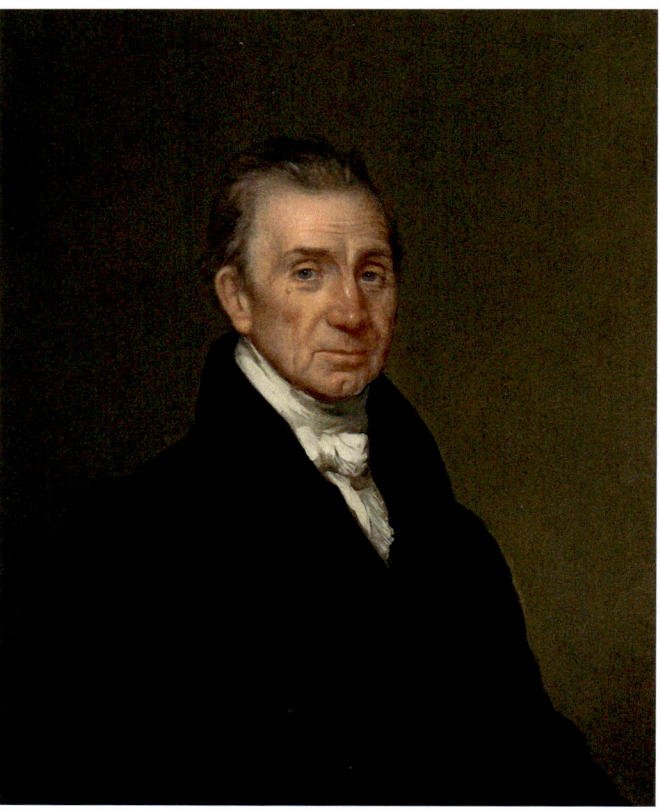

Fig. 5 *James Monroe* (1758–1831), Chester Harding (1792–1866), 1829. Oil on canvas; 76.2 × 63.5 cm (30 × 25 in.). National Portrait Gallery, Smithsonian Institution; gift of John L. and Ann Beal Sanders in honor of their children, Tracy Elizabeth Sanders Justus, Jane Nesbit Sanders, and William Hardy Sanders

Chapter three, "On the Verge of Sovereignty: Cuba and Puerto Rico at the Turn of the Twentieth Century," addresses the political development of Cuba and Puerto Rico in the nineteenth century. This chapter outlines the conditions that ensured the longevity of the Spanish colonial system on these two islands and their interlinked decolonial struggles after 1868. Eventually, Cuban independence and Puerto Rico's autonomy were delayed or thwarted by the intervention of the United States following the explosion of the USS *Maine* in 1898, after which the northern power declared war against Spain. Through contrasting depictions of the U.S. invasion, we explore the mixed outlooks of Puerto Ricans at the prospect of seeing the United States arrive on its shores after decades of repressive Spanish rule.

Chapter four, "Cutting a Path to Sovereignty: The Complex Political Landscapes of the Philippines and Guam" addresses the complicated turn of events

in the Philippines as the United States engaged in war against Emilio Aguinaldo and his soldiers after he declared the Philippines an independent state. Anti-imperialists raged against either the anti-democratic rule or the premise of granting more Brown and Black people U.S. citizenship. The island of Guam was quietly seized, made into a coaling station, and placed under military rule.

The last chapter of the book, "1898: A Contest in Memory," outlines how collective memory has overlooked the nuances of the War of 1898 and ignored the complicated narratives of the annexation of Hawai'i and the Philippine-American War. It explores the colonial politics implicit in the signing of the Treaty of Paris, an accord reached by Spain and the United States, with no representation from the territories that changed hands with the agreement. Following the treaty, the United States was no longer circumscribed to its continental boundaries. It encompassed archipelagoes in the Caribbean Sea and the Pacific Ocean, and, with that, acquired new territorial jurisdictions and peoples to govern. The seizing of Puerto Rico, the Philippines, Guam, and Hawai'i, and the establishment of a protectorate over Cuba, combined with the building of the interoceanic passage of the Panama Canal (inaugurated in 1914), consolidated U.S. economic and political influence. The decisions that the United States made over the political administration of these lands introduced constitutional debates that continue today. The holdings of the United States in the Americas also inaugurated a new era of U.S. interventionism in the continent.

This exhibition and catalogue do not intend to present a definitive history of 1898. As co-curators, we have aspired to provide a panoramic narrative that will help audiences grasp the significance of these pivotal events. Yet, the story of 1898 is one of complexity and overlooked primary sources from native points of view. We are indebted to the many scholars of Cuba, Guam, Hawai'i, the Philippines, Puerto Rico, and Spain who have spent decades researching in archives, often introducing nuance or undoing historical readings that privilege the U.S. perspective. We hope to open a window into their work, as we attempt to bring this chapter of history into the public consciousness of the United States.

The outcome of the war and the U.S. presence in the lands that it claimed are multilayered, and impossible to describe in unequivocal terms, as it often brought improvements in public infrastructure, education, and public works. Certainly, 1898 was a defining year for all these lands, and its legacy endures today. Puerto Rico and Guam, for example, remain unincorporated territories of the United States. Despite the bodies of water between the continental United States and these islands, they are part of the U.S. domestic realm. Just as in 1898, Guam and Puerto Rico remain under the purview of the U.S. Congress, without a voting representative in that political body or the right to vote for the U.S. president. The legacy of U.S. colonialism is also alive in the state of Hawai'i, where low incomes, high unemployment rates, and poor health conditions disproportionately affect Kānaka Maoli.[29]

One hundred and twenty-five years after 1898, the power dynamics at play in the board game *Uncle Sam at War with Spain* remain relevant. Aimed at middle-class white residents of the United States, this game was designed to integrate them into the imperial story as wielders of power, capable of moving the ships and armies that would determine the fate of faceless nations. *1898: Visual Culture and U.S. Imperialism in the Caribbean and the Pacific* puts faces to these nations and helps us understand these conflicts from multiple perspectives, especially those whose sovereignty was assailed, or those who were subjected to the exercise of U.S. power. Through portraiture and biography, this exhibition brings to light the individual stories as well as the cultural richness of this history. By reckoning with these difficult histories, we might hope for a future of equality.

1

"The Portraits in the Gallery Have Never Been Only National"

KRISTIN HOGANSON

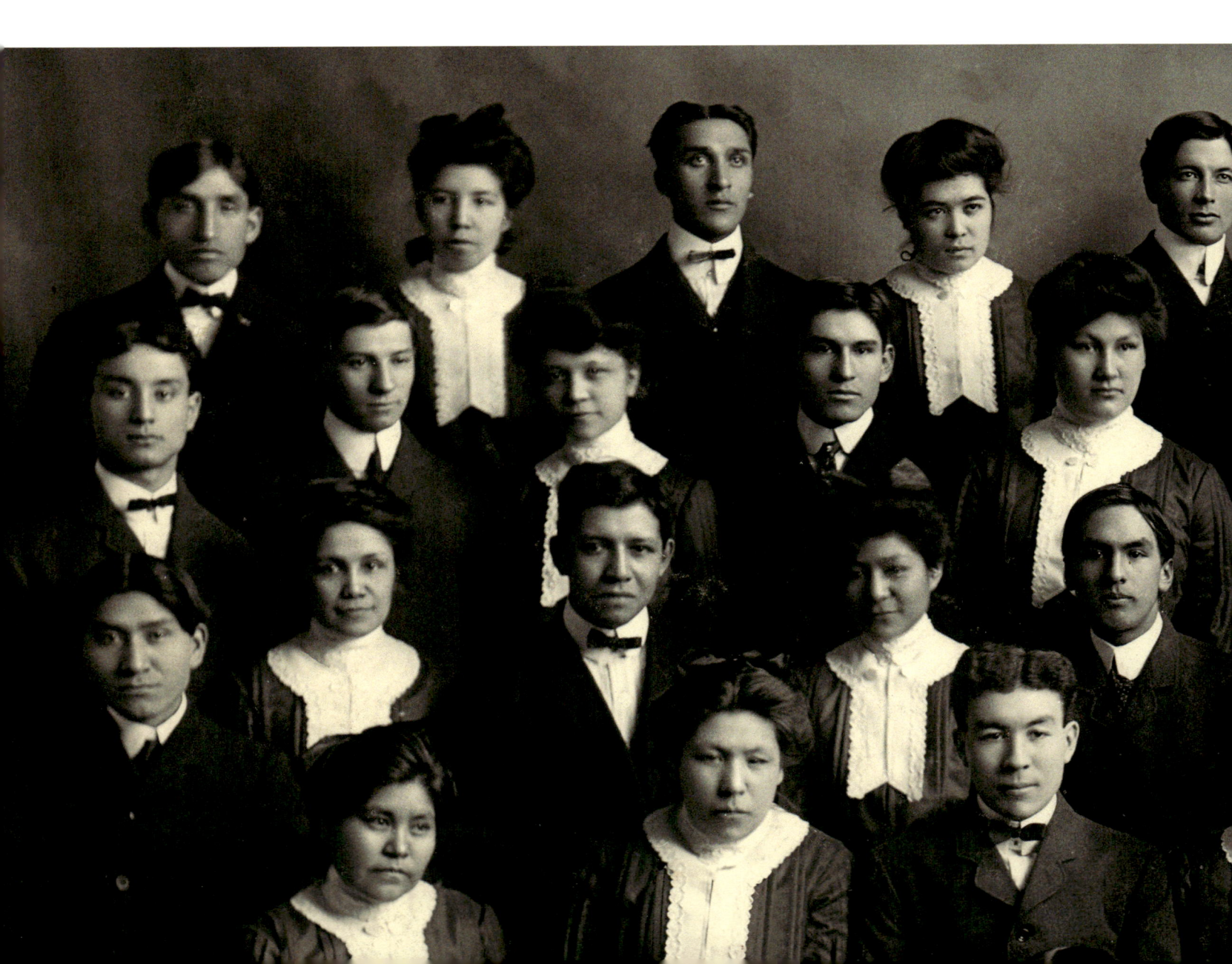

Fig. 1. Carlisle Indian Industrial School class of 1904. (detail of fig. 10, p. 314). Gelatin silver print; 16.5 × 30.5 cm (6 ½ × 12 in.). Cumberland County Historical Society, Carlisle, Pennsylvania

One of the ways that U.S. policymakers linked continental and insular expansion was by channeling Puerto Rican students to the Carlisle Indian Industrial School, a boarding school for Native American youth founded with the intent of destroying their cultural identities. This photograph of the graduating class of 1904 includes Puerto Rican student Zoraida Valdezate, who is seen on this page (second row, fourth from the right). Carlisle officials listed "Porto Rico" as among the "tribes" represented at the school.[2]

The United States came into being as a colonizing nation. Its emergence as an independent state through a war for independence did not suddenly reverse the trajectory of Euro-American colonialism in North America. To the contrary, national independence removed the barriers to expansion across the Appalachians that the British had erected in the settlement-prohibiting Proclamation of 1763. The continent-spanning map of the present-day United States, with remnant pockets of once-vast Indigenous land bases now reduced to approximately 326 Indian land areas, reminds us of the significance of colonialism to U.S. and Native American history.[1]

Although the United States was colonial from its inception, prior to the Vietnam War and concurrent civil rights movement, U.S. history textbooks held up 1898 as an exceptional moment in national history. The U.S. intervention in the Cuban War for Independence from Spain and its launch of another war against Filipino nationalists appeared to be the imperialist exception that proved the more general anti-imperialist rule.

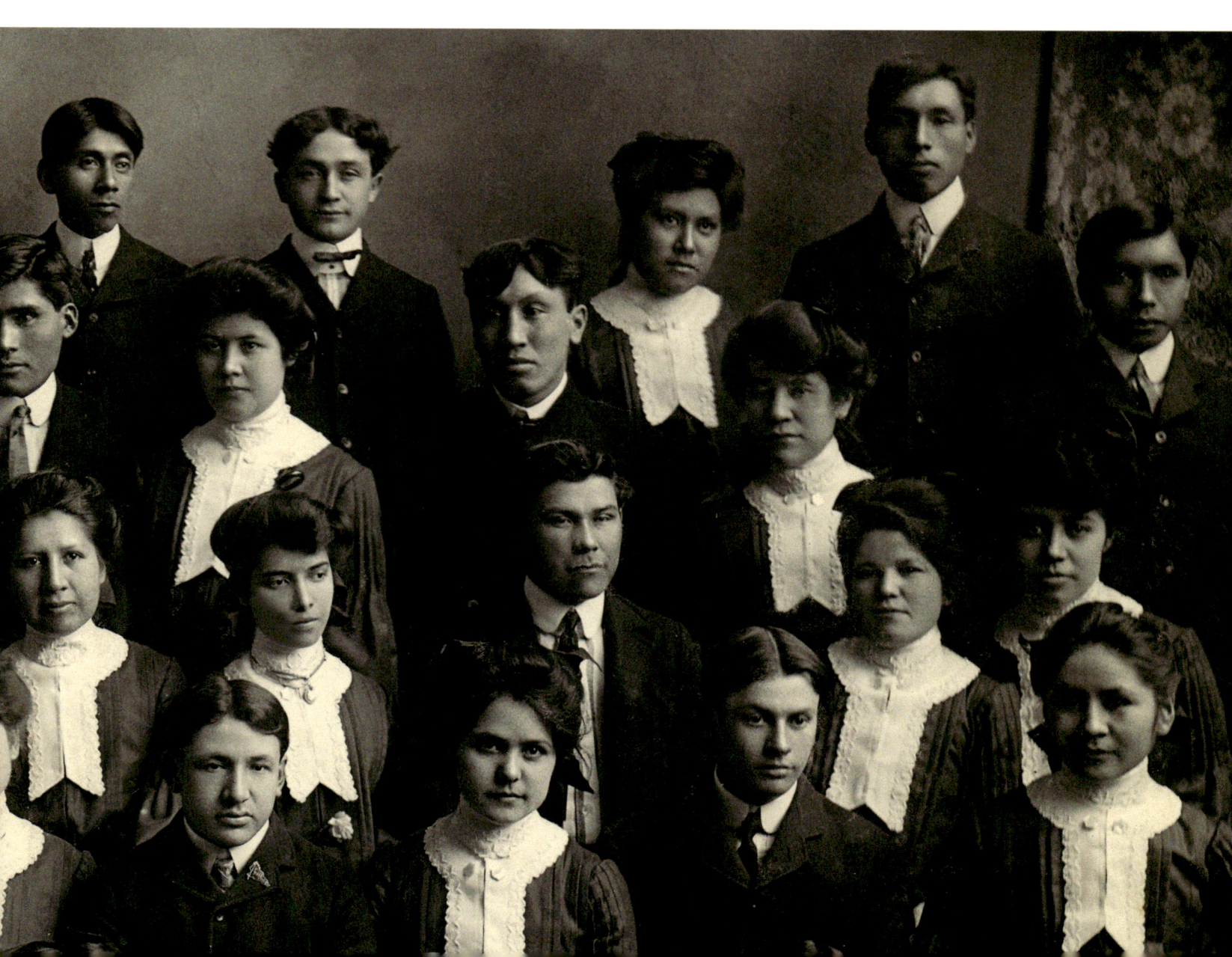

These wars seemed to be a singular moment in national history in part because they involved the annexation of non-contiguous territory. Yet the United States already had a long record of annexing distant land. California, for example, was not readily reachable from the eastern United States overland across Native American homelands until the 1869 linking of the Union Pacific and Central Pacific Railroads. The geographic divide between the Midwest and Pacific Coast caused many gold rushers to travel to California via the Isthmus of Panama. The annexation of offshore islands was not new in 1898 either: the United States had claimed minor Caribbean, Pacific, Atlantic, and Indian Ocean islands under the terms of the 1856 Guano Islands Act, and it acquired a vast arc of Aleutian islands in 1867.

A second reason for regarding the wars of 1898 as exceptional also merits reconsideration. Observers at the time regarded 1898 as a significant departure from past practice because it resulted in the annexation of territory deemed unassimilable due to large non-white populations. In contrast to earlier expansion, which had generally resulted in national incorporation, the wars of 1898 yielded territory that U.S. policymakers expected to govern as colonies. The sense that the United States had suddenly abandoned its principles of democratic self-government for a European-style project of conquest and imperial rule gave rise to an anti-imperialist movement that vigorously protested the Philippine-American War.

Looking back, this sense of departure seems exaggerated: U.S. democracy had never been fully inclusive (despite significant steps toward equality during the Reconstruction period), and indeed exclusionary practices had animated both the antebellum African colonization movement that turned Liberia into a U.S. client state and the mistreatment of Mexicans drawn into the United States through territorial annexation.[3] The turn-of-the-twentieth-century United States already had plenty of disenfranchised colonial subjects from prior expansion in North America (fig. 1).[4] White settlers had already acquired substantial land and power in Hawai'i. In hindsight, it appears that turn-of-the-century imperialists and "antis" alike—and the scholars who followed their cues—saw a divide between past and present because they comprehended settler colonialism only as settlement, not as colonialism.

Looking forward from 1898, the wars in the Caribbean and Asia might seem to be a flash in the pan, for the United States did not vigorously pursue additional territory (exceptions being American Samoa, the U.S. Virgin Islands, and the Northern Marianas, a post–World War II Pacific Trust Territory). Having learned a lesson during the Philippine-American War, in its aftermath U.S. policymakers preferred to wield power via short-term occupations, local leaders who could be relied upon to support U.S. strategic and business interests, U.S.-trained national guards, a network of bases, economic clout, and the soft power tools of positive image and principles.

Although the United States reached peak territory in 1902, the year it granted Cuba its independence, the conflicts of 1898 should nonetheless be construed as part of an ongoing history of power projection. The deployments of 1898 sped the capacity of the United States to wield force in both the Atlantic and Pacific. Upon the outbreak of the war, the U.S. Navy secretary commanded the USS *Oregon* to sail from California to the Caribbean. The ensuing 66-day journey around Cape Horn amplified calls for a shortcut. The subsequent construction of the Panama Canal added to the strategic value of the Caribbean footholds acquired in 1898 (fig. 2).[5] Military victories in Cuba and the Philippines also paved the way for bases at Pearl Harbor and Guantánamo Bay, the landing of troops in China as part of a multi-imperial anti-Boxer campaign, interventions in Central America and the Caribbean during the "bad neighbor" era, and ultimately the unsurpassed global power exercised by the United States from the 1940s through the end of the Cold War.

Positioning the events of 1898 in a larger historical context does not diminish their significance. But it does change our understandings of their exceptionality and thus of U.S. history more generally. Rather than letting 1898 overshadow larger histories of colonial expansion and U.S. global power, we should regard 1898 as an illuminating window into the wider landscape of the past.

Visual materials are a vital part of this landscape. Images serve as important forms of historical documentation. They provide insights into the world views of their creators and enable us to better picture people, places, things, and events. Photographs in particular seem to speak to us in an unmediated way. But images must also be approached with care, with a critical eye on the perspectives they convey and on the stories they hide. This can be seen, for example, in the depictions of imperialism at world's fairs. The government agents, anthropologists, and entrepreneurs who placed colonial subjects on

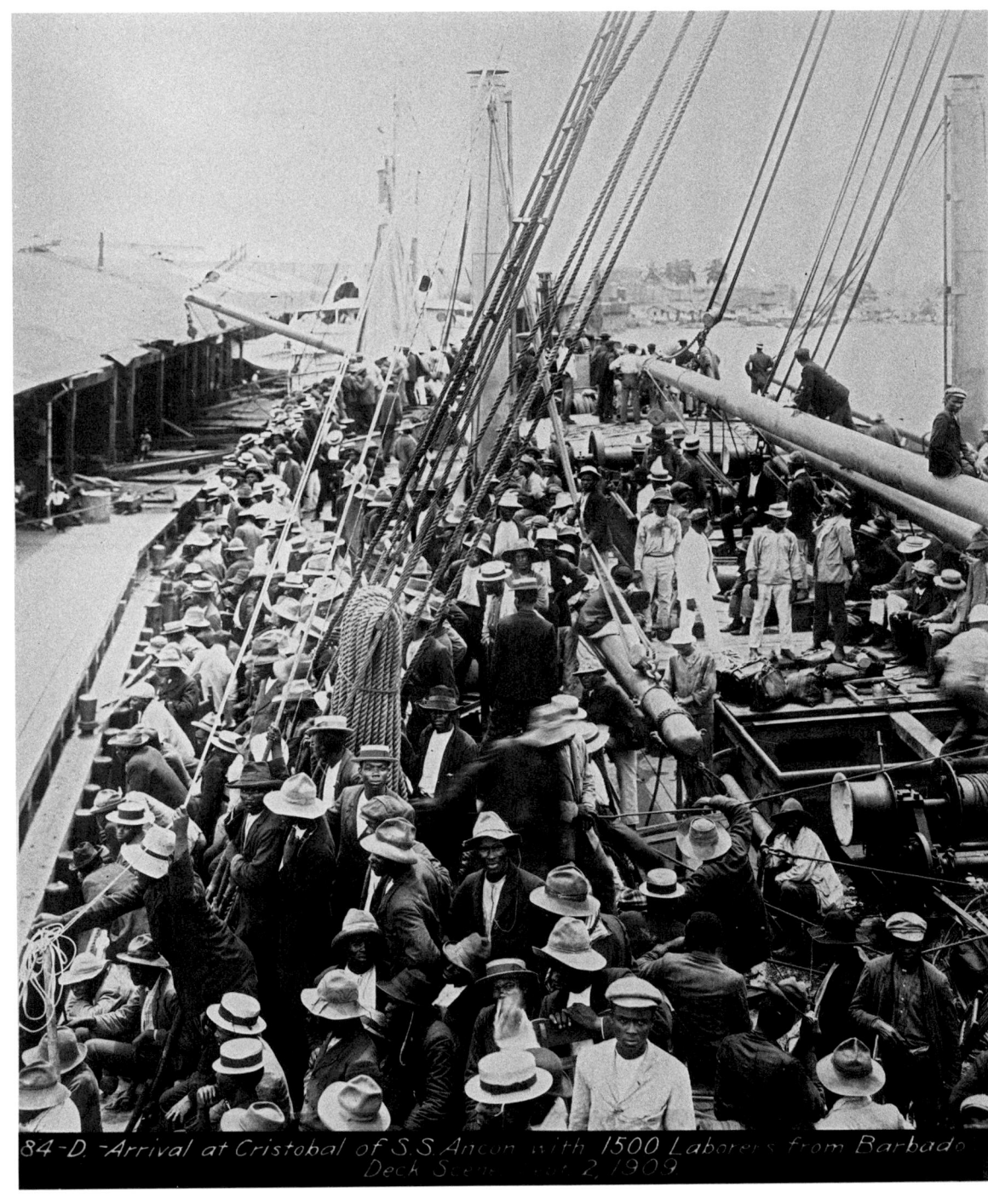

84-D. -Arrival at Cristobal of S.S. Ancon with 1500 Laborers from Barbado[s]
Deck Scene[...] 2, 1909

Fig. 2 Arrival at Cristobal of SS *Ancon* with 1,500 laborers from Barbados, Sept. 2, 1909. National Archives and Records Administration, Washington, DC

U.S. engineers have long been lauded for their technological achievements in building the Panama Canal, but Chief Engineer George Washington Goethals regarded his ability to govern workers—the majority of them West Indians—as his greatest challenge. This photograph documents Barbadians arriving in Panama in 1909 to work on the Canal. In contrast to white workers, paid in gold currency, these men would have been paid in silver currency, which advanced the segregationist practices of the Canal Zone by excluding them from gold-only commercial establishments.[6]

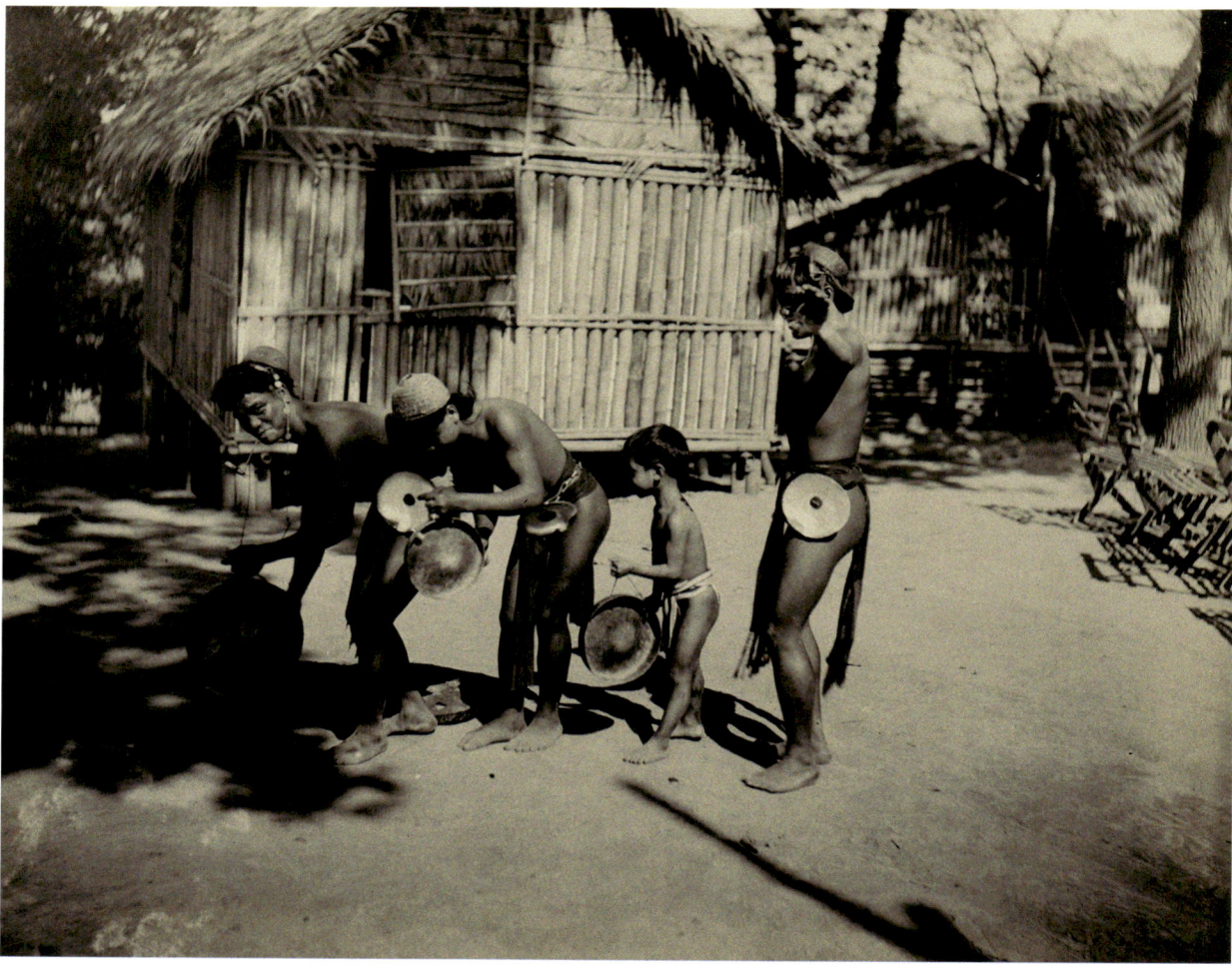

Fig. 3 *Igorrote Dance*, Jessie Tarbox Beals (1870–1942), 1904. Gelatin silver print; 18.1 × 23.3 cm (7⅛ × 9³⁄₁₆ in.). National Portrait Gallery, Smithsonian Institution; gift of Joanna Sturm

This photograph, by Jessie Tarbox Beals, depicts Igorot men from the northern Philippine highlands performing a dance on the "Philippine Reservation" at the 1904 St. Louis World's Fair. These men attracted so much prurient attention that a U.S. Army officer, worried that they would signal shortcomings in the U.S. civilizing mission, proposed clothing them in pants. This matter made it up to the highest level of government and was ultimately settled by President Theodore Roosevelt's endorsement of loincloths for the performers. Igorot men photographed around 1904 in their home province of Benguet typically wore button-down shirts.[7]

display required them to dress and perform in ways that would reinforce fairgoers' assumptions about the need for colonial uplift (fig. 3).

Viewers should also reflect on the perspectives relayed through depictions of military heroism. Contemporaries regarded the U.S. entry into the Spanish-Cuban War as a significant step toward national reconciliation, as men from the former Confederacy served in common cause with men from Union states. The celebration of national unity served exclusionary purposes, however, for white Americans at the time typically disparaged the military service of African American men. By picturing their military heroes solely as white men, white Americans advanced an exclusionary white nationalism that was all the more insidious for not being explicitly labeled as such.

Imperialism is often visually signified via depictions of power-wielding men, but ordinary men and women are

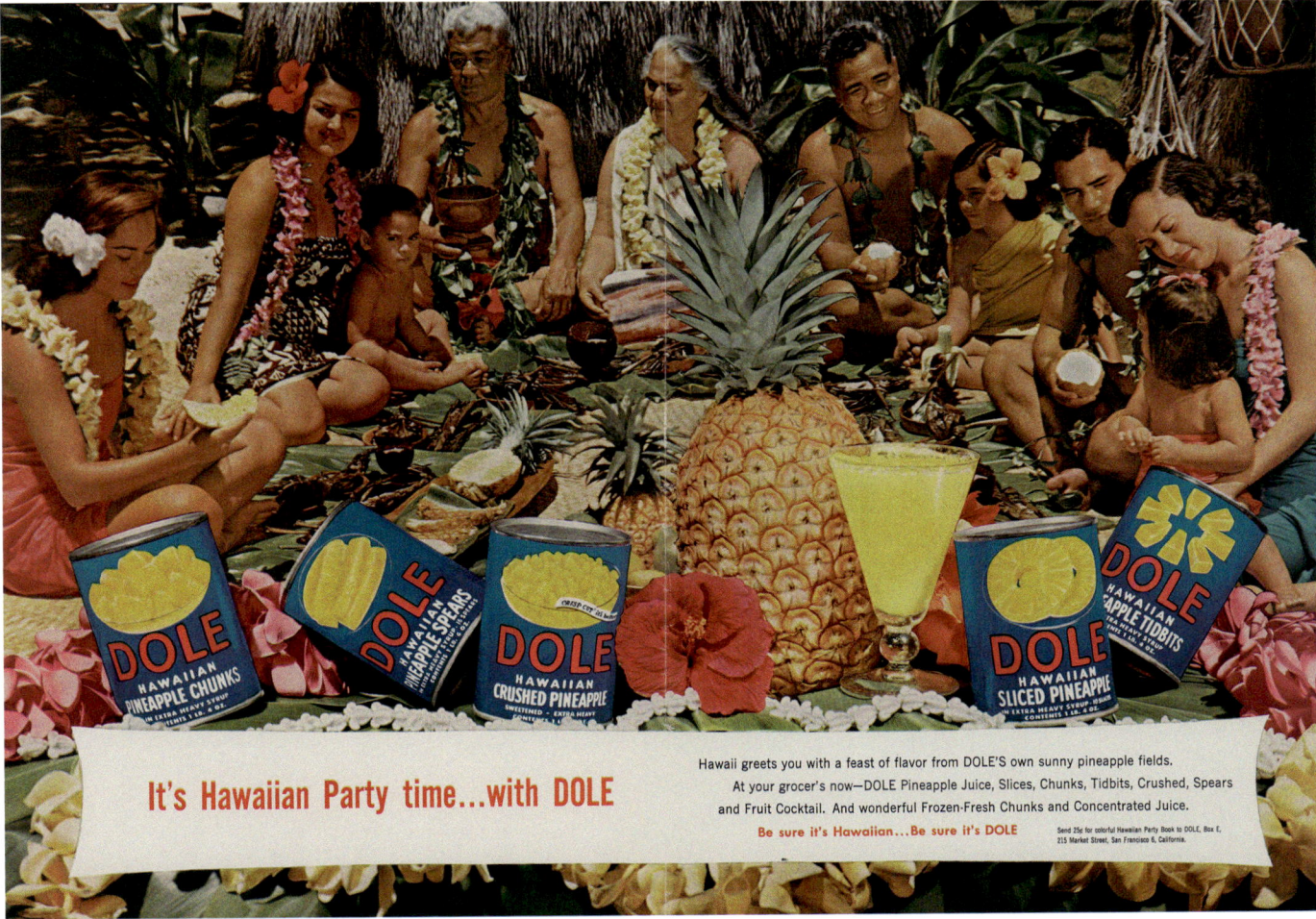

It's Hawaiian Party time...with DOLE

Hawaii greets you with a feast of flavor from DOLE'S own sunny pineapple fields.
At your grocer's now—DOLE Pineapple Juice, Slices, Chunks, Tidbits, Crushed, Spears
and Fruit Cocktail. And wonderful Frozen-Fresh Chunks and Concentrated Juice.

Be sure it's Hawaiian...Be sure it's DOLE

Send 25¢ for colorful Hawaiian Party Book to DOLE, Box E,
215 Market Street, San Francisco 6, California.

Fig. 4 Anton Bruehl for Dole Hawaiian Pineapple Company, Dole Pineapple ad, 1954. Printed paper; 35.6 × 54.6 cm (14 × 21½ in.). Dole Corporation Archives, Hawaiian and Pacific Collections, University of Hawai'i at Mānoa Library

This 1954 advertisement hawks pineapples as a form of Hawaiian greeting that could be enjoyed by distant consumers. It depicts Hawaiians not as agricultural workers but as partygoers who willingly offer up their bounty. The staged Hawaiian-ness of the photo reinforces popular tropes of carefree islanders, thus adding to the appeal of the territory as a tourist destination.[8]

an essential part of the story. Whereas the privileged citizens of imperial centers rarely grasp the full magnitude of their footprint, the colonial subjects of imperial peripheries rarely escape it. The former may see themselves as central figures, but the latter have their own family stories and rosters of heroes and villains. The images that bring hidden histories to light in one context might, from a different perspective, be seen as providing

only a partial lens into histories that have always been palpable, marked on bullet-pocked walls, gravestones, and street signs.

As the war-themed board games of the era reveal, the events and legacies of 1898 played out stateside as well as in the Caribbean and Pacific. By extending U.S. nationality to residents of Hawai'i, Puerto Rico, Guam, and the Philippines, the territorial acquisitions of the 1890s facilitated human mobility, leading, for example, to large mainland Puerto Rican communities. The expanded U.S. presence in the Caribbean and Pacific opened up trade and investment opportunities, with ripple effects for the U.S. standard of living. Affluent U.S. consumers, among them food-secure individuals with the wherewithal to sit for portraits, benefited from expanded access to tropical goods such as bananas, coconuts, pineapples, sugar, and coffee (fig. 4).[9] These consumers gained greater access to cruises and warm-weather resorts, to Cuban musical forms and hula performances, to the colonial subjects on display in world's fairs. Visual reminders of these wars and their legacies can be found across the United States by those disposed to look for them, with one starting point being the statues honoring veterans found in public parks.

By helping us to see histories of empire-building that are all too often hidden, the conflicts of 1898 open our eyes to the U.S. exercise of power in the world. The visual materials that have shaped U.S. perceptions of these conflicts rarely depict this power in its bluntest, most deadly forms (fig. 5).[10] Yet by rendering U.S. imperialism more tangible, even portraits of carefully posed men and dry-docked ships can prompt us to acknowledge that the portraits in the gallery have never been only national.

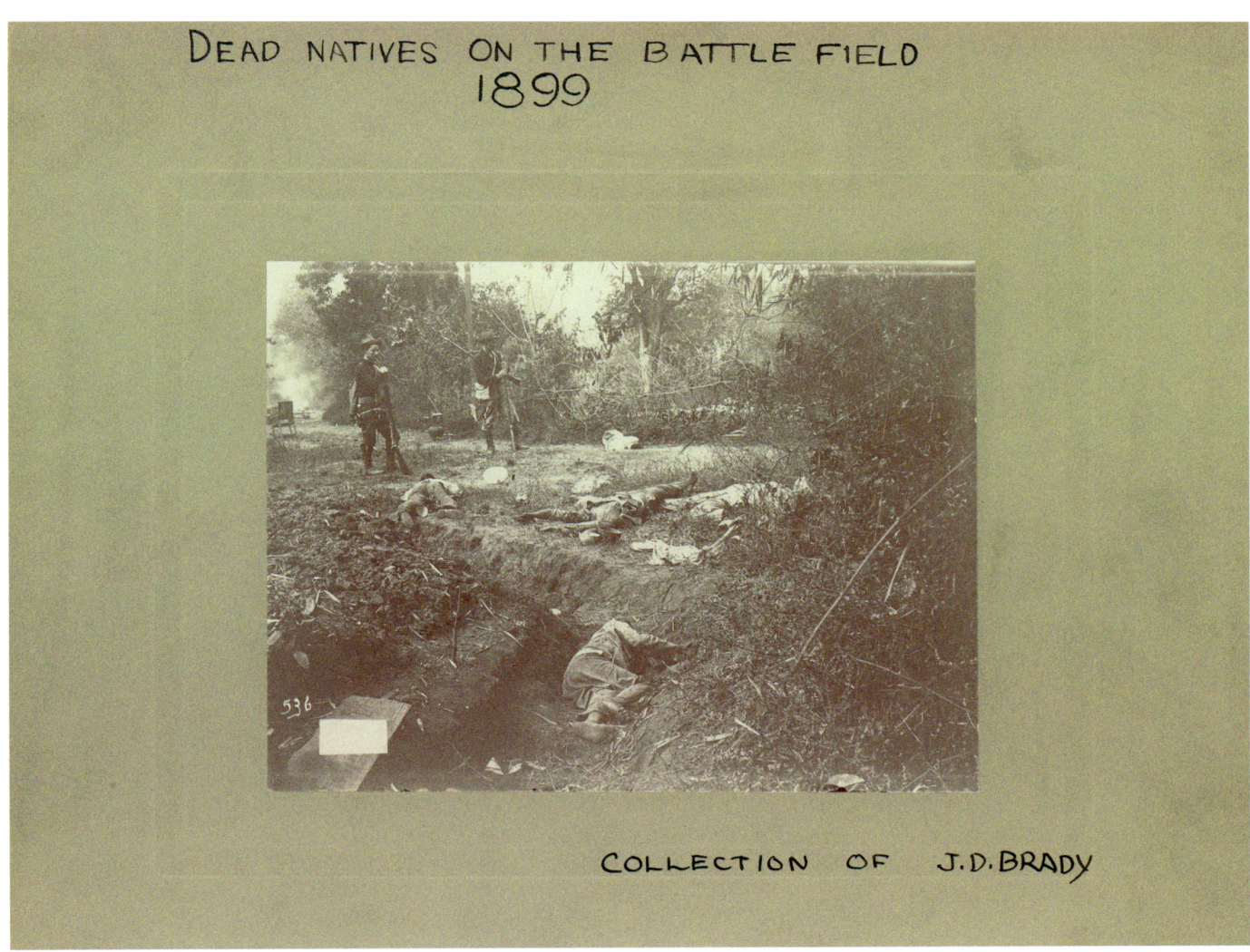

Fig. 5 Photograph from the John D. Brady scrapbook, 1899; 12.5 × 17 cm (4⅞ × 6¾ in.). History Nebraska

Among the exceptions to the general tendency to repress the most horrific scenes of imperialist violence are the depictions of torture and war dead circulated by anti-imperialists. This photograph comes from the scrapbook of John D. Brady, who enlisted in the First Nebraska Infantry Regiment, United States Volunteers, expecting to revenge the *Maine* and fight for freedom in Cuba. Instead, he was deployed to the Philippines, where he became increasingly critical of the war. Brady captioned this photograph: "DEAD NATIVES ON THE BATTLE FIELD 1899," providing no names or other identifying information for the men who have been killed or the U.S. soldiers who stand over them, guns at hand.[11]

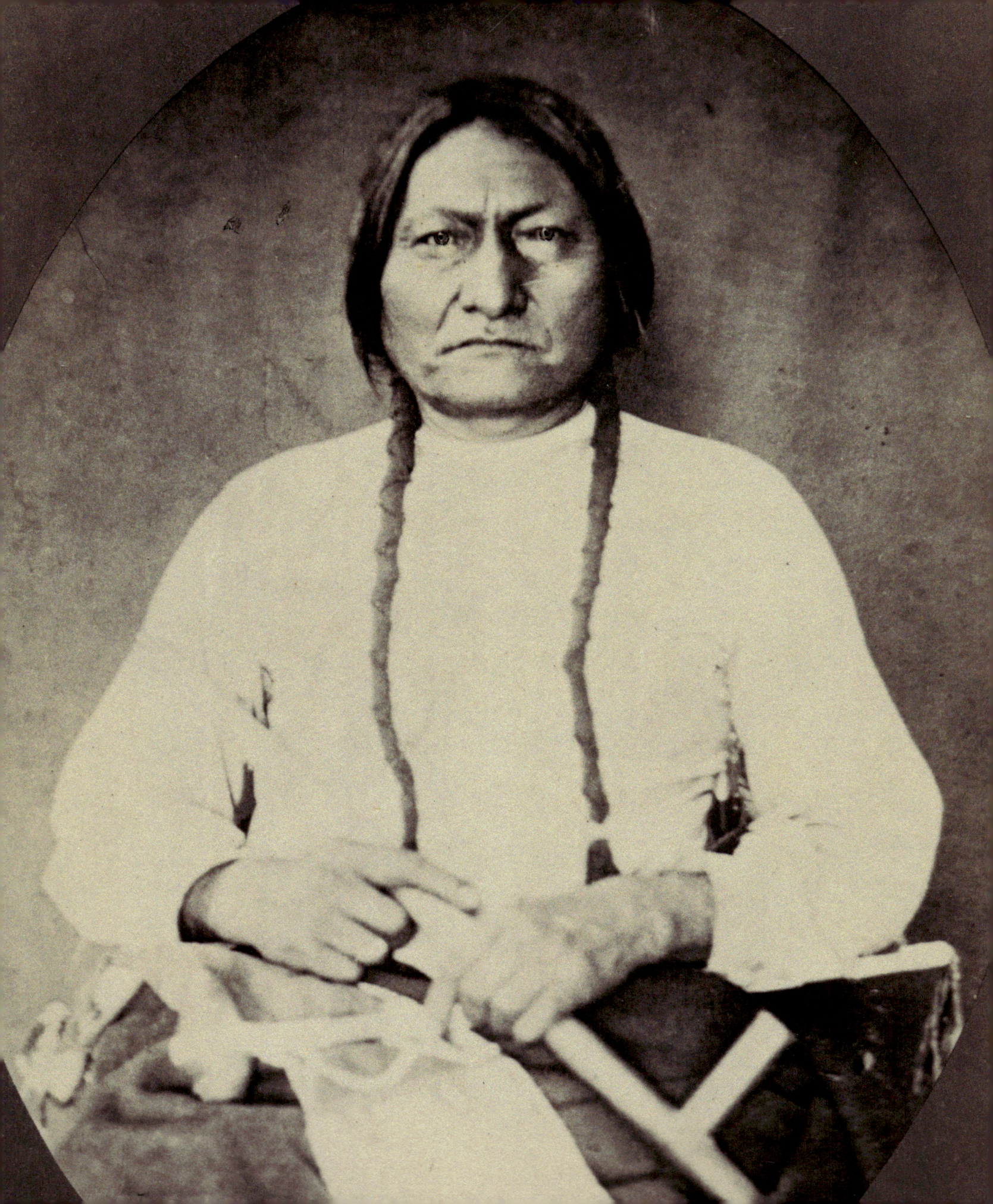

Prelude to Empire
Indian Wars and Sea Power

TAÍNA CARAGOL AND KATE CLARKE LEMAY

"Imperialism, the extension of national authority over alien communities, is a dominant note in the world-politics of today."
—Alfred Thayer Mahan, 1902.[1]

A New World Order

The nineteenth century is often referred to as "the century of nationalisms."[2] As the ramifications of the French Revolution, the anti-monarchical revolutions of 1848, and the U.S. Civil War rippled through Europe, the Americas, and beyond, communities with a shared language, history, ethnicity, and religion began to unite politically against dynastic or colonial rule.[3] However, the same century also witnessed a rise in imperialist ambitions, and as Europe raced to claim colonial outposts abroad, the United States followed. A portrait of President William McKinley holding in his right hand a partly unfurled map of Puerto Rico, inscribed with the date July 25, 1898, crystalizes this transformational moment of the interplay between nation and empire for the United States, Puerto Rico, and Spain (see pp. 48–49). The date references the U.S. invasion of Puerto Rico, led by General Nelson Miles (1839–1925), through the Bay of Guánica. This incursion ended 390 years of Spanish colonialism in Puerto Rico, upended the island's 1897 achievement of an autonomic charter, and established a new system of government controlled by the United States.[4] But even as the most concrete pictorial expression of U.S. claims to Puerto Rico, the map that McKinley

holds can signify that other lands, such as Cuba, the Philippines, Guam, and Hawai'i, also lay in the hands of this U.S. leader.

The Continental Expansion of the United States

The impulse for territorial expansion predated the establishment of the United States and can be traced back to the colonial era.[5] The country grew through various means, most notably a long and violent process of displacement and subordination of Indigenous populations that began in the colonial period and continued through the nineteenth century. Thomas Jefferson's (1743–1826) purchase of Louisiana from Napoleon in 1803 doubled the size of the country and opened the west to Euro-American settlers.[6] Jefferson imagined a United States that would extend through the continent, a dream he still harbored in 1823, when he was a key advisor to President James Monroe, who announced the Monroe Doctrine that year (see pp. 17 and 18).[7] Formulated toward the tail end of the wars of liberation in Latin America (1809–1826), the Monroe Doctrine warned European powers not to intervene in the affairs of the Western Hemisphere or recolonize countries

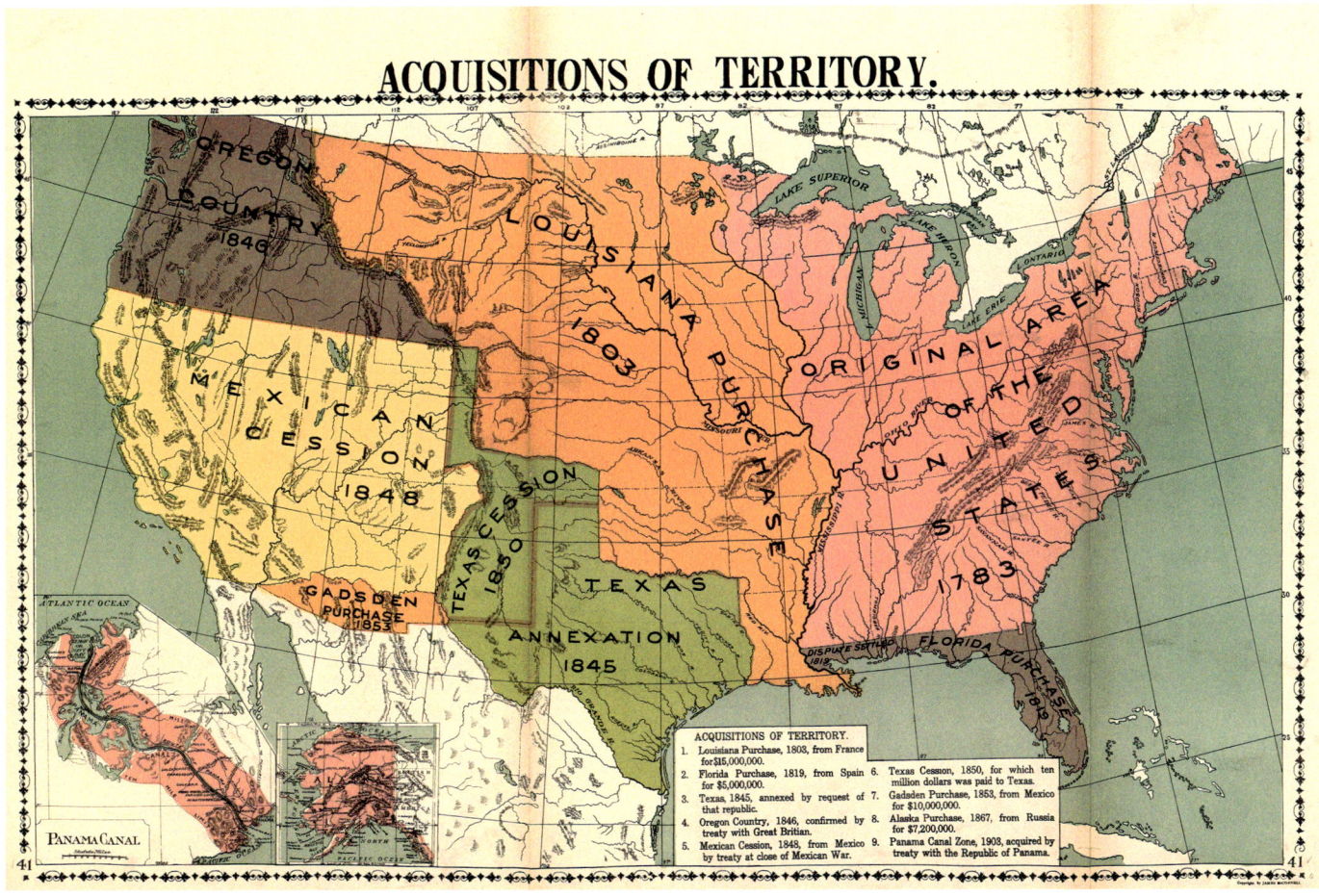

Fig. 1 "Acquisitions of Territory" in *McConnell's Historical Maps of the United States*, McConnell Map Co., 1919. Printed paper; 82 × 113 cm (32¼ × 44½ in.). Library of Congress, Geography and Map Division, Washington, DC

whose independence the United States had recognized. While the Monroe Doctrine was a mere statement of U.S. foreign policy and not a treaty, it launched the process of demarcating Latin America as the United States' sphere of influence.[8]

One of the most infamous examples of expansionist policy was the Indian Removal Act of 1830, which enabled President Andrew Jackson to grant Native American lands west of the Mississippi to settlers in exchange for land within existing state borders. From 1830 to 1838, the U.S. government forced the removal of the Cherokee, Chickasaw, Chocktaw, Creek, and Seminole Nations from their homelands and pushed them west of the Mississippi, in what became known as the Trail of Tears.[9] This tragic event was part of a much wider process of displacing

American Indians from their homelands, with parallel stories unfolding, for example, in what is now the U.S. Midwest. In the 1840s, the U.S. government opened Indian Territory west of the Mississippi to white settlers, confining Native American nations within smaller reservations. The growth of the economy and population continued to drive the country's frontier westward, encouraged by the ideology of Manifest Destiny, which proclaimed that the United States was destined by God to expand its dominion (fig. 1). In 1845, Texas became part of the United States through a joint resolution of Congress.[10] The next year, President James Polk (1795–1849) settled disputes with Canada over the boundary of the Oregon Territory. Polk also offered to buy from Mexico what is today California and New Mexico, and upon their refusal, he launched the

Mexican-American War (1846–1848).[11] The war cost Mexico its northern half: more than 500,000 square miles of its territory became part of the United States, whose boundaries now reached the Pacific Coast.[12] In 1867, the United States made another important land acquisition when it purchased Alaska, a territory two-and-a-half times larger than the size of Texas, from Russia for $7.2 million.

White settlers acquired more land between 1870 and 1900 than they had in the previous three hundred years combined, and through a series of wars, they developed a crushing federal force to violently displace Native Americans. Expansionists found ways to justify the bloodshed. In 1893, the historian Frederick Jackson Turner (1861–1932) published his thesis on the U.S. frontier, arguing that westward expansion distinguished the U.S. populace from its European ancestors. According to Turner, the experience of the frontier made an indelible mark on the U.S. character, forging traits like independence, individuality, and ingenuity. His friend Theodore Roosevelt (1858–1919) (see p. 103) stated in 1889: "It was our manifest destiny to swallow up the land of all adjoining nations who were too weak to withstand us."[13]

Roosevelt rose to power as a consistent advocate of expansionism. Between 1889 and 1897, while he climbed the career ladder up to the position of assistant secretary of the Navy, he published a four-volume history, *The Winning of the West*. Its narrative of U.S. expansionism served as a boilerplate for Roosevelt's theories of imperialism, including empire-building and the strenuous life. In his prose, Roosevelt was blind to the perspective of Indigenous Americans, and he was not alone. Federal policy led to brutal practices in soldiering—ones that later would be used in U.S. overseas imperialist strategies.[14]

Nelson Miles, who fought in the U.S. Civil War and the Indian Wars, led successful campaigns against Native Americans, defeating or capturing notable figures, such as Geronimo (Apache) and Chief Joseph (Nez Perce). The photograph of Miles that served as the frontispiece of his 1895 biography was taken by David Francis Barry, who photographed the U.S. frontier (fig. 2). Miles wears the dress uniform for lieutenant general officers of the period and holds a presentation sword in his left hand. Three military medals decorate his chest: the Badge of the Grand Army of the Republic, a medal of the Union II Corps, and the Military Order of the Loyal Legion of the United States. During the Indian Wars, Miles played a key role in both negotiations with the Plains Indians

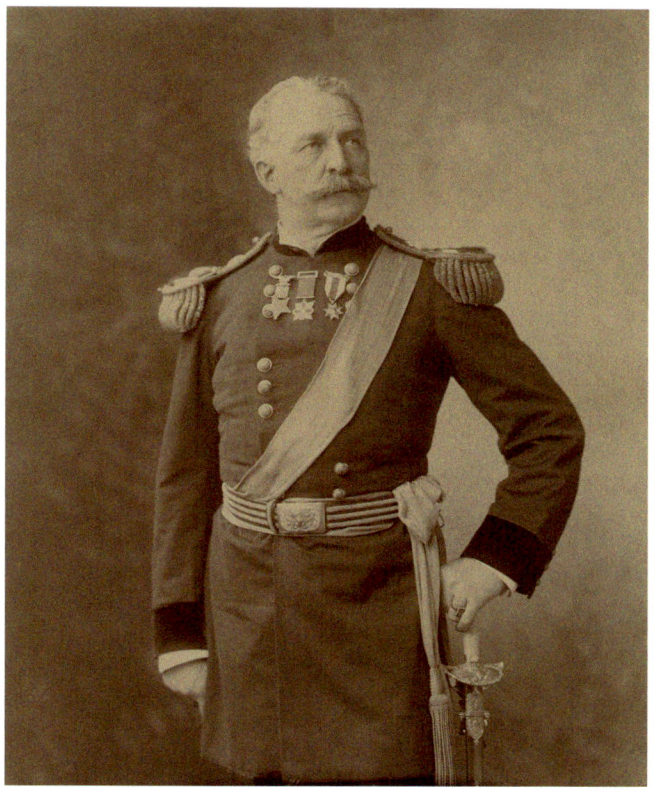

Fig. 2 *Nelson A. Miles* (1839–1925), David Francis Barry (1854–1934), c. 1895. Albumen silver print; 48 × 39.8 cm (18⅞ × 15¹¹⁄₁₆ in.). National Portrait Gallery, Smithsonian Institution

and their displacement. He especially negotiated with Tatanka Iyotanka (Buffalo Bull Who Sits Down), known as Sitting Bull (fig. 3).

A spiritual leader, Sitting Bull was Hunkpapa Lakota, one of the Lakota Sioux tribes.[15] Members of his family believe that he was born on Yellowstone River, near Miles City, Montana.[16] In the 1860s and 1870s, he and others led major Sioux factions to confront federal forces displacing them on the Great Plains.[17] Reacting to the federal government's order that would displace Native Americans and force them onto reservations, thousands of Lakota, Cheyenne, and some Arapaho gathered together along the banks of the Greasy Grass River (Little Bighorn River) in 1876. On June 25 of that year, George Armstrong Custer (1839–1876) led the Seventh Cavalry in an attack against the Native encampment during the Battle of Greasy Grass. In response, Crazy Horse (Oglala Sioux, 1840–1877) and approximately two thousand warriors annihilated Custer and his men, inflicting a stunning defeat on the U.S.

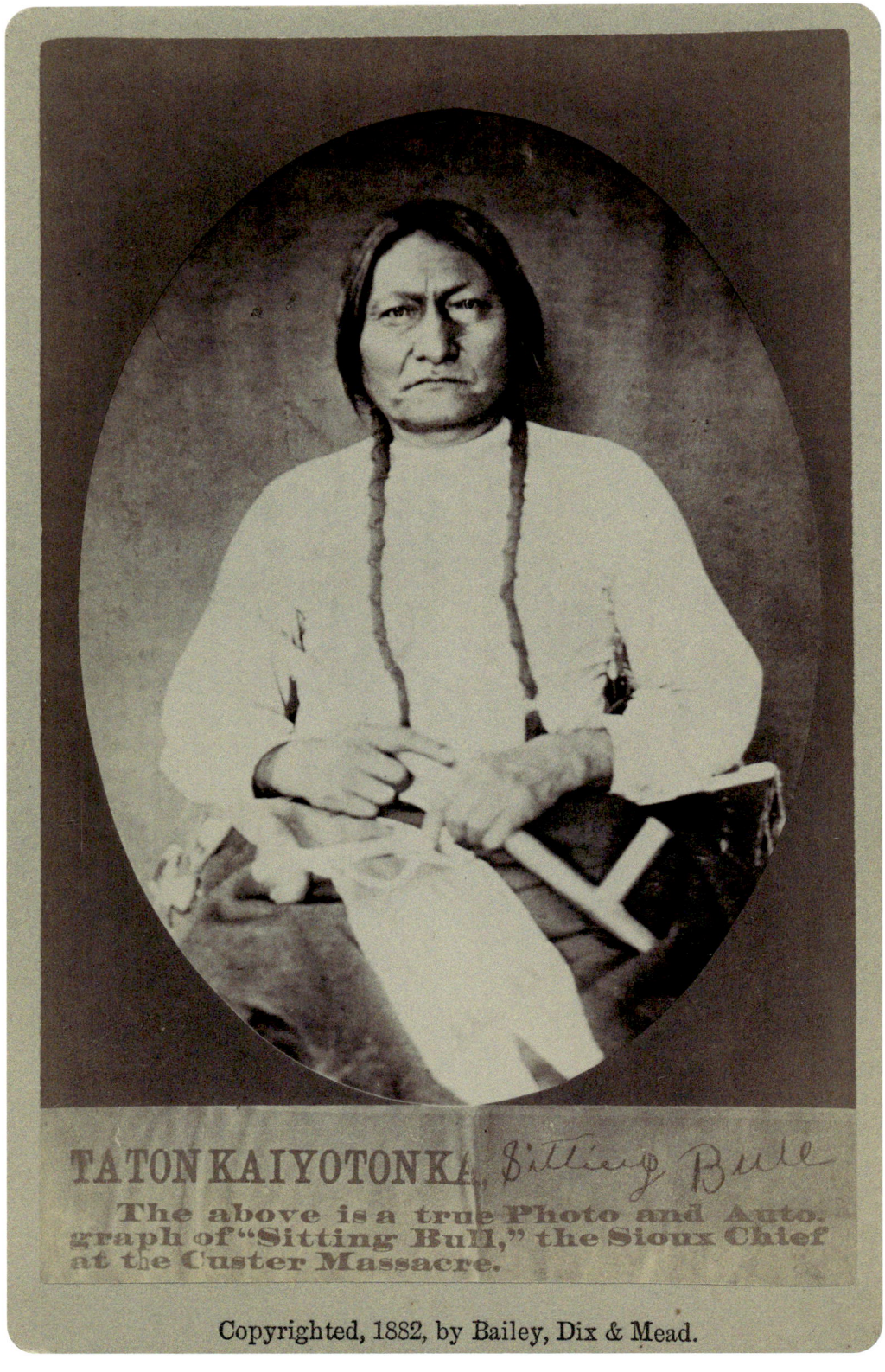

Fig. 3 *Chief Tatanka Iyotanka (Sitting Bull)* (c. 1831–1890), Attributed to William R. Cross (1839–1907), Copyrighted by Bailey, Dix, and Mead (active 1880s), 1882. Albumen silver print; 12.2 × 9.1 cm (4¹³⁄₁₆ × 3⁹⁄₁₆ in.). National Portrait Gallery, Smithsonian Institution

Army that shocked the entire United States.[18] Afterward, Miles pursued the Lakota, who had followed Sitting Bull into Canada to hunt buffalo. Due to the dwindling buffalo population, however, famine forced the Lakota, including Sitting Bull, to return to the United States and surrender in 1881.

This photograph pictures Sitting Bull holding a pipe and a dance club—symbols of peace and warriors' exploits. The pipe, for Native people of the Plains, expresses relationships both sacred and social.[19] As a spiritual leader, Sitting Bull probably used the pipe for personal and communal prayer and rituals.[20] This portrait was reportedly one of twenty-four taken by the Nebraskan photographer William R. Cross while the Hunkpapa leader was imprisoned at Fort Randall, Dakota Territory between 1881 and 1883.[21] In 1885, Sitting Bull began performing in Buffalo Bill's Wild West, an entertainment show that traveled to Europe in the late 1880s.[22] In 1889, federal officials feared that Sitting Bull would be seen as the Native messiah prophesied by the Ghost Dance religious movement. He was seized by members of the Indian police force and was shot and killed during what may have been an attempted rescue by Sioux warriors on December 15, 1890.[23]

As the muslin painting of the Battle of Greasy Grass demonstrates, many Plains Indian artists preserved their history through art (fig. 4). Painted by an Oglala Lakota, Amos Bad Heart Bull (1869–1913), this distant view of the battle represents both sides of the fight. Using strong outlines with overlapping figures to convey depth, the artist depicted sixty individual warring figures.[24]

Bad Heart Bull sourced subject matter from the oral histories of his elders. He alternated between making meticulous drawings in ledger books with ruled, numbered pages, and painting on expansive surfaces, such as buffalo hide, lengths of muslin, and canvas.[25] His images document Oglala daily life and tradition, as well as particular historic events, such as his well-known series, *Battle of the Little Bighorn*.[26] Only a child during the 1876 battle, Bad Heart Bull and his family followed Sitting Bull to Canada before they surrendered. The artist became a scout for the U.S. Army in 1890 and worked as a cowboy. Later, he became the tribal historian for the Oglala Sioux.[27]

Muslin painting carries on a long tradition of painting on hides of buffalo and other animals. Traditionally, representational art was made exclusively by male artists and focused on biographical narratives that celebrated the deeds of living men. This work, however, also incorporates references to spiritual objects that facilitate a man's success, such as medicine shields and headdresses. Frontier military officers often purchased or commissioned

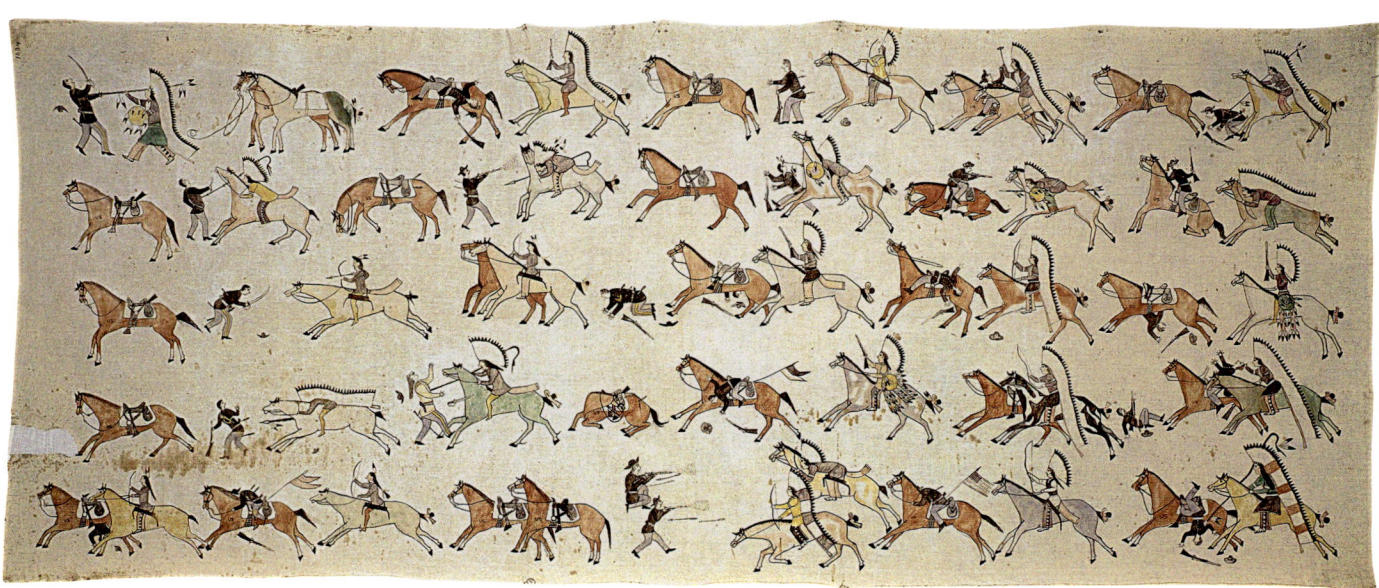

Fig. 4 *Battle of Greasy Grass (Battle of Little Bighorn)*, Amos Bad Heart Bull (1869–1913), c. 1900–1910. Paint on muslin; 89 × 216 cm (35 × 85 in.).

Department of Anthropology, National Museum of Natural History, Smithsonian Institution muslin and canvas paintings, which was probably the case in this instance.[28]

In the 1890s, the United States established an empire with overseas possessions in a series of quick and decisive events. Through warfare as well as executive and congressional action, the United States intervened in foreign affairs, stifling burgeoning nationalist movements in the Caribbean and the Pacific. In 1893, Anglo-American settlers dismantled the Hawaiian monarchy, launching a dedicated campaign to annex the archipelago as a territory of the United States. Five years later, after intervening in Cuba's final war of independence against Spain, the United States annexed Hawai'i and seized Puerto Rico, the Philippines, and Guam. That same year, Anglo-American sugar planters feared the control they held over the Hawaiian economy was threatened by Japan and other nations. Amidst war fever and urgent expansionism, they argued successfully for the U.S. annexation of Hawai'i as a military necessity for the continuation of an open-door policy with China. The building of the Panama Canal beginning in 1904 would ensure the future of the United States as an imperial power. Cumulatively, these events established a new global geopolitical order in the twentieth century.

Cuba and William McKinley's Economic Conundrum

In 1897, the newly inaugurated Republican president of the United States, William McKinley, walked into the center of this maelstrom. An expert on tariffs and business, McKinley had a record of navigating domestic financial concerns, such as taxes and industrialization. His economic acumen was critical as U.S. markets emerged from the financial crisis of 1893, when the Treasury's gold reserve fell short of its obligations and banks failed.[29] The struggling U.S. economy inflamed imperialists, who clamored to access markets beyond North America to help bolster the nation's coffers. McKinley had his eye on sugar and had, in fact, designed the 1890 Tariff Act, which eliminated tariffs on sugar, molasses, tea, and coffee.[30] Between 1891 and 1894, the Cuban economy flourished, mostly due to favorable trade agreements with the United States. Then, in 1895, the United States—which had its own substantial sugar production in the South and in Colorado—imposed tariffs on sugar, thereby keeping the sale of Cuban sugar out of mainstream U.S. markets.[31] Yet for decades, the proximity of Cuba, just ninety miles from U.S. shores, had drawn U.S. business interests, which particularly benefitted from its sugar production. Some businessmen in the United States urged McKinley to annex the island.

Businessmen invested in Cuban plantations, and they often owned factories and land there. This 1894 painting, *Ingenio con carruaje* (Sugar mill with carriage), by Cuban artist Armando García Menocal, depicts bourgeois travelers in a horse-drawn carriage, presumably leaving the sugar plantation in the background (fig. 5). The connection between this painting, which was owned by the Pyne family, and the vested U.S. business interests in Cuban sugar and politics is revealing. Percy Pyne (1820–1895) was a partner at Moses Taylor & Co., which specialized in the sale and importation of Cuban sugar.[32] When the United States instated new tariffs, the Spanish retaliated by implementing levies and taxing Cubans. Unemployment in Cuba rose as essential commodities became unaffordable. Hoping to improve their political and economic situation, Cubans waged their third War of Independence from 1895 to 1898.

By the end of 1896, the situation in Cuba was dire. The leader of the Cuban Liberation Army, Máximo Gómez (1836–1905), had his soldiers set fire to the land, destroying sugar plantations, factories, and railroads. Their strategy of *la tea* (the torch) endorsed total warfare and was meant to obliterate the Cuban economy, thereby denying the Spanish Crown and foreign investors any revenues and profits. Spain responded by appointing the ruthless General Valeriano Weyler y Nicolau (1838–1930) as governor of Cuba in 1896. Weyler retaliated against the Cuban Liberation Army by ordering the burning of more villages and farms, and the slaughtering of animals to destroy any resources for the rebels. To suppress support from rural populations for the Cuban Liberation Army, Spanish colonial authorities forced rural villagers to relocate and "reconcentrated" them in continuously surveilled, fortified areas, without adequate food or sanitation.[33] The Spanish regime rounded up approximately three hundred thousand Cuban civilians, placing them into camps that were little more than prisons.[34] One illustration, published in the *San Francisco Examiner*, was one of countless images reproduced in U.S. newspapers and journals about the Cuban crisis (fig. 6).[35]

Before reconcentration was officially ended in November 1897, tens of thousands of people starved or died of disease. One artist captured the chaotic aftermath of the reconcentration camps. William Glackens, working for

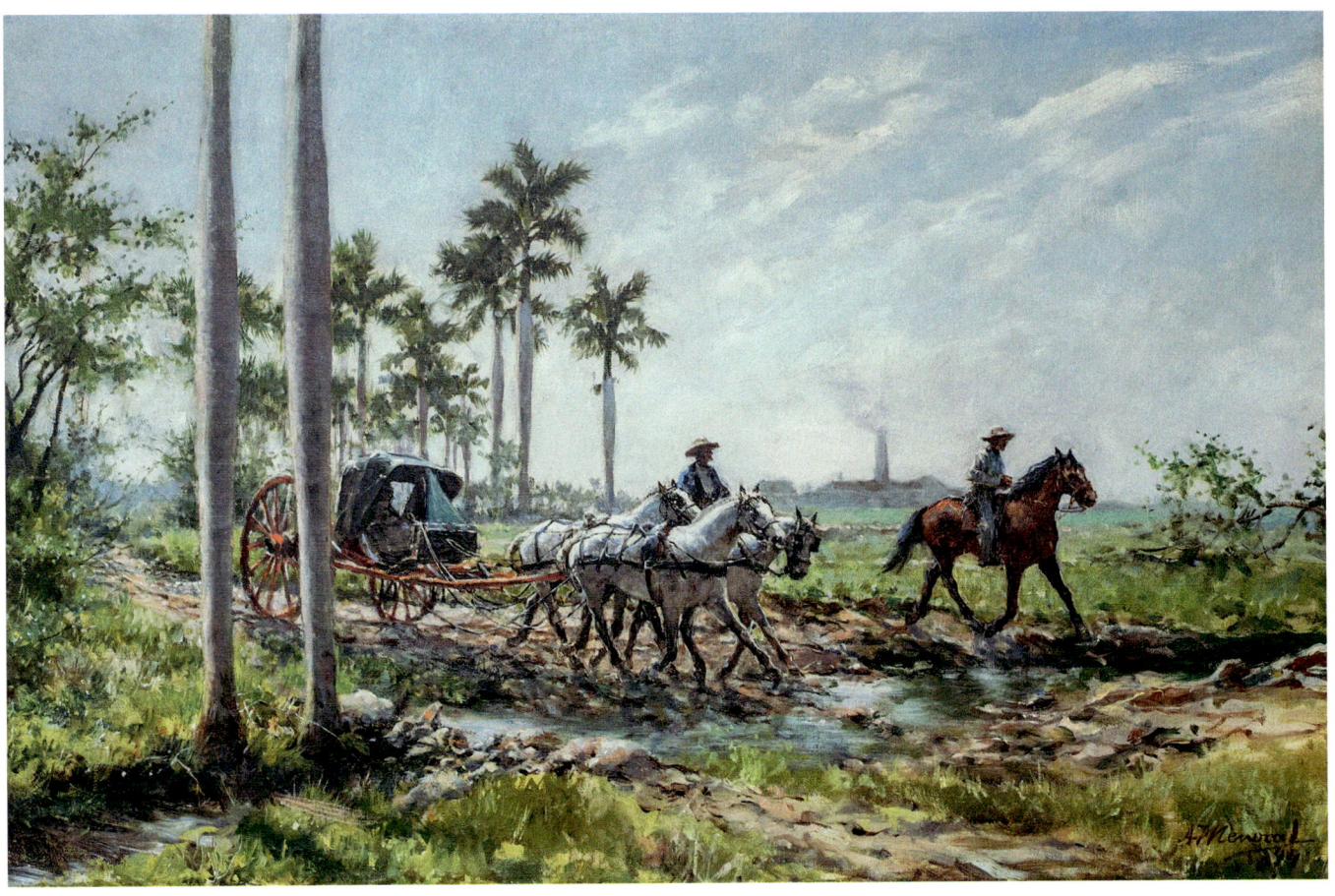

Fig. 5 *Ingenio con carruaje* (Sugar mill with carriage), Armando García Menocal (1863–1942), 1894. Oil on canvas; 43.2 × 64.8 cm (17 × 25½ in.). Collection of Emilio and Sylvia M. Ortiz

McClure's Magazine in June and July 1898, followed U.S. troops from Tampa to Santiago, Cuba, making sketches and reporting back. However, few of his thirty-six sketches made it to press (fig. 7).[36] In this pen-and-ink drawing, hungry refugees from the eastern town of Santiago, spotlessly clean and non-violent, gather around the cathedral of El Caney. Respectably dressed women hold babies while children carry food pails. A *mambí* soldier, or member of the Cuban revolutionary army, stands to the right. This scene probably depicts one of the "protective juntas" organized by Ramón Blanco, the Spanish governor who ended reconcentration camps in November 1897. The "protective junta" was intended to administer emergency rations and medicines to the ill and malnourished citizens who were too weak to be simply turned out of the camps. However, the protective juntas had no resources, and their efforts at food distribution were often chaotic.[37] Glackens captured the desperation of the densely packed crowd, their hands extending upward, waving empty bowls. Yet this scene was deemed

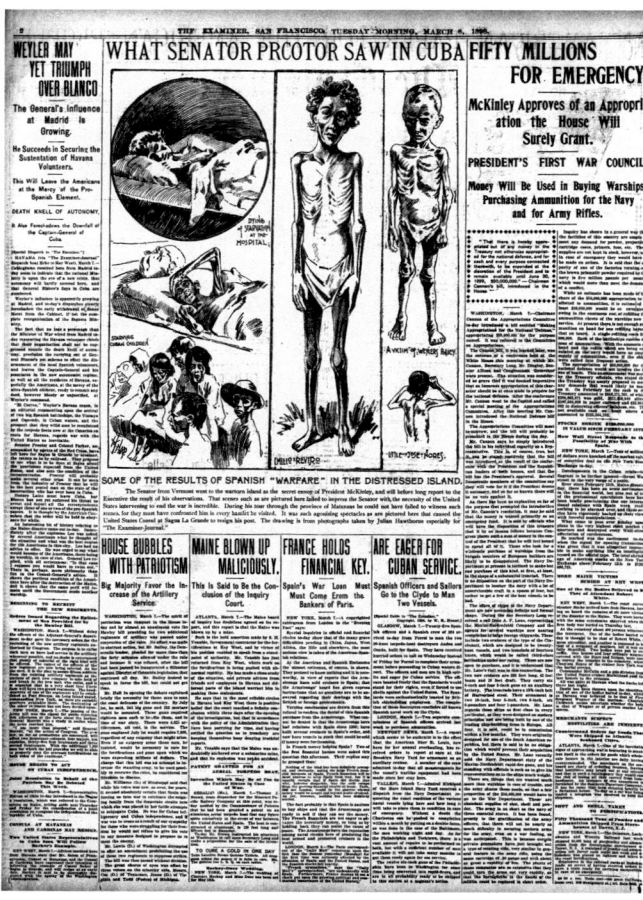

Fig. 6 "What Senator Proctor Saw in Cuba," *San Francisco Examiner*, March 8, 1898

unpublishable in a society magazine like *McClure's*, perhaps because it foregrounds the plight of helpless women and children.[38]

Around this time, William J. Calhoun (1848–1916), a former congressman, traveled at McKinley's bequest to observe conditions in Cuba. He reported:

> I travelled by rail from Havana to Matanzas. The country outside the military posts was practically depopulated. Every house had been burned, banana trees cut down, cane fields swept with fire, and everything in the shape of food destroyed. It was as fair a landscape as mortal eye ever looked upon; but I did not see a house, man, woman or child, a horse, mule, or cow, nor even a dog. I did not see a sign of life, except an occasional vulture or buzzard sailing through the air. The country

was wrapped in the stillness of death and the silence of desolation.[39]

McKinley was moved by the long succession of reports on the catastrophe in Cuba. In 1897, he personally contributed $5,000 to a Red Cross fund that aided imperiled U.S. citizens living in Cuba who needed repatriation.[40] Even so, McKinley may have felt it fiscally irresponsible to recognize the Cuban revolutionaries, as that would have relieved the Spanish government's duty to protect $50 million of U.S. investments in Cuba.[41]

Nevertheless, these scenes were familiar to McKinley. The last Civil War veteran to be elected to the presidential office, McKinley said, "I have been through one war; I have seen the dead piled up, and I do not want to see another."[42] As a Civil War veteran, he deeply understood how racism divided the nation. But McKinley knew that the possible annexation of Cuba would upset the balance of power in terms of white hegemony. U.S. intervention in Cuba was a delicate matter.

Before the Civil War, some political attempts were made by U.S. Southerners to annex Cuba, where chattel slavery remained legal until 1886.[43] In the antebellum era, especially the 1850s, admitting a new slave territory would have upset the precarious equilibrium struck by U.S. politicians over the issue of enslavement.[44] Race dynamics continued to influence U.S.–Cuban relations in 1898, when racism against Cubans of African descent, who comprised one-third of the population, and the idea of mixed races, prevented serious consideration of U.S. annexation of Cuba as a state.[45] Neither McKinley nor the U.S. Congress moved to annex Cuba because in addition to concerns about race relations, it would mean war with Spain. Even in November 1897, when Cuban businessmen and property holders petitioned McKinley to annex Cuba, or at the very least, to make it a protectorate, he declined.[46] During the first year of his presidency, McKinley steadfastly maintained the position he set forth in his first inaugural address of March 4, 1897: "We want no wars of conquest; we must avoid the temptation of territorial aggression. War should never be entered upon until every agency of peace has failed; peace is preferable to war in almost every contingency."[47] His hesitation to intervene in Cuba and aid civilians enduring Spain's punitive measures during the third Cuban War of Independence (1895–1898) prompted criticism from Democrats and Republicans alike.[48]

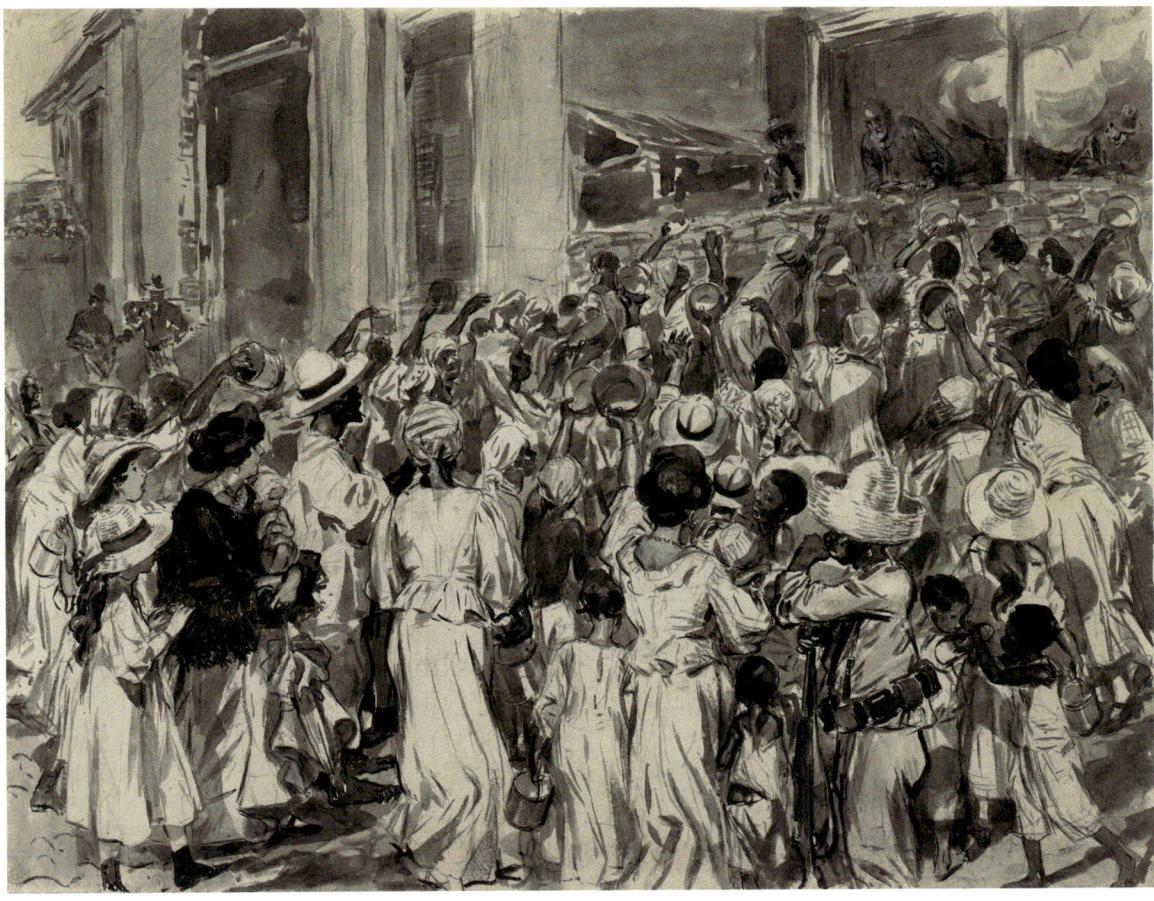

Fig. 7 *Starving Refugees from Santiago Congregating at El Caney*, William Glackens (1870–1938), c. 1898. Pen, ink, watercolor, Chinese white, and crayon on paper; 40.9 × 53.3 cm (16⅛ × 21 in.). Library of Congress, Prints and Photographs Division, Washington, DC

Escalating Crises: The USS *Maine* and the de Lôme Letter

Despite his efforts to remain neutral, McKinley was soon caught in a crisis. When riots broke out across Havana in late 1897, "disturbances, anti-American in character" increased the urgency of addressing U.S. relations with Cuba.[49] With McKinley's permission, Secretary of the Navy John Davis Long sent the battleship USS *Maine* to patrol Havana's waters in January 1898, with the mission to harbor and protect U.S. citizens if necessary. Constructed in 1888 and commissioned in 1895, the *Maine* was a second-class battleship. It was intended as the first armored vessel of the new, modernized U.S. Navy.[50]

The *Maine* incorporated innovations in naval architecture made during the 1870s and 1880s. However, by the time it was commissioned, naval designs had improved, and the *Maine* was therefore not as efficient as planned, even if it was still regarded as a tool of naval power. The concentration of heavy guns on the ship's bow caused unnecessary strain by blast and concussion during maneuvering.[51] In 1895, readying the ship in Norfolk, Virginia, Captain Charles Dwight Sigsbee (1845–1923) discovered barnacles on the boat's bottom and seaweed growth plastering its waterline, so he requested a new coat of the red, antifouling paint.[52] Carlton Theodore Chapman depicted the boat, gleaming in its drydock, either during its construction or its refurbishment (fig. 8). The artist may have intended for this painting to be a visual record of the navy's modernization and improved maintenance, but it also functions as a portrait of U.S. naval power, with the modern ship as its stationary subject.

As the navy continued focusing on modernization, a major diplomatic incident strained relations between the United States and Spain. On February 9, 1898, William Randolph Hearst published a letter in his *New York*

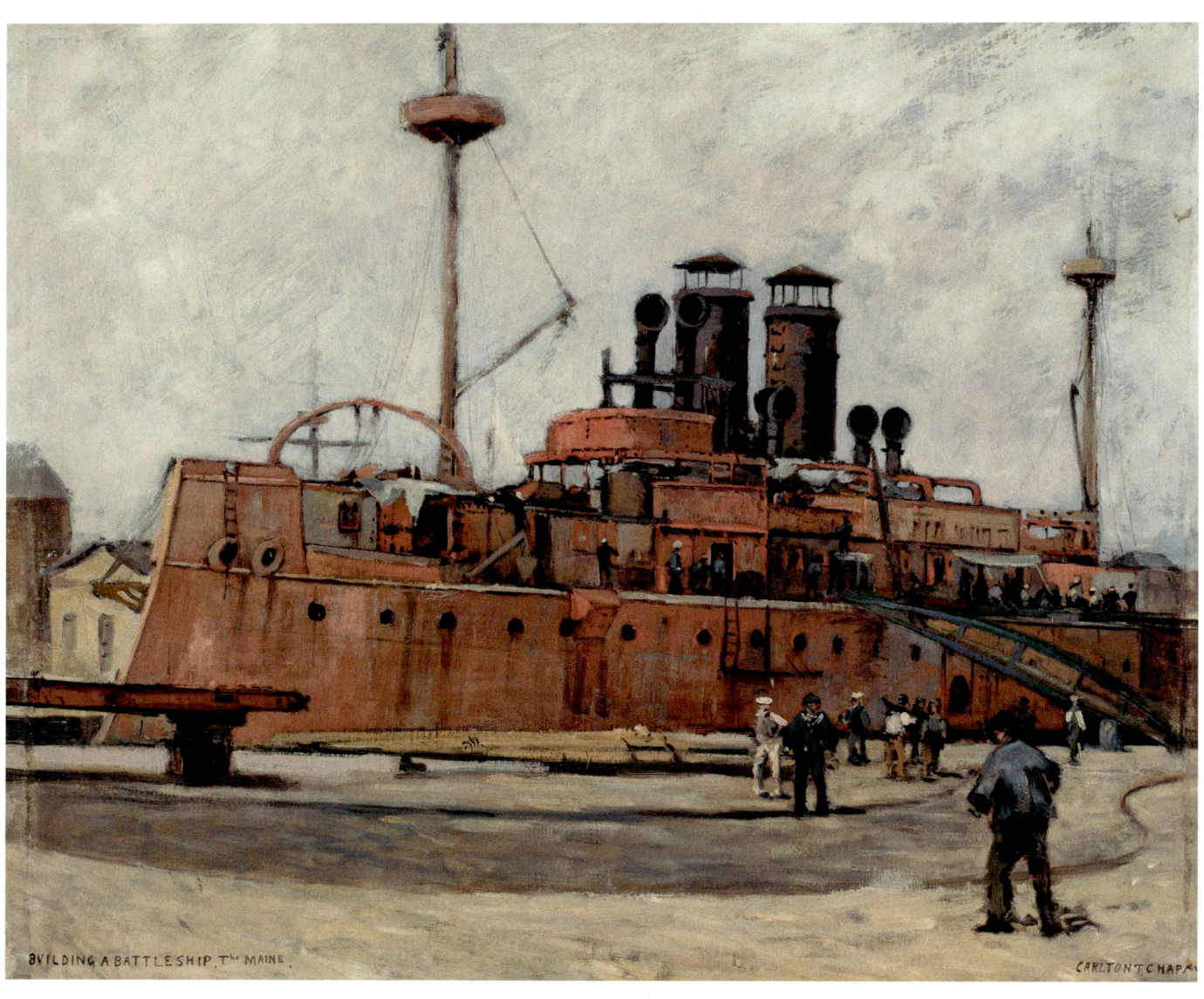

Fig. 8 *Building a Battleship, The Maine*, Carlton T. Chapman (1860–1925), 1888–1895. Oil on canvas; 52.1 × 64.8 cm (20½ × 25½ in.). New-York Historical Society; gift of Mrs. Carlton T. Chapman

Journal from Don Enrique Dupuy de Lôme (1851–1904), the Spanish Ambassador to the United States, to José Canalejas, editor of Spain's *Heraldo de Madrid*. It disparaged McKinley, calling him "weak and a bidder for the admiration of the crowd."[53] Sent to Canalejas while he was in Havana, the letter was intercepted by Cuban rebels, who gave it to Hearst.[54] Subsequently, the brittle relations between the United States and Spain all but shattered.

The *Maine* arrived in Havana on January 25, 1898, and it took to buoy until its mysterious explosion and sinking on February 15, 1898, six days after the de Lôme letter was published.[55] Over 260 U.S. sailors died in an accident likely caused by erupting furnaces.[56] Nevertheless, accusations against the Spanish quickly escalated, and yellow journalism soon capitalized on the crisis. Hearst offered a $50,000 reward "for the conviction of the criminals who sent 258 American sailors to their death."[57] Sensational, exaggerated headlines, such as "Appalling Nature of the *Maine* Disaster Gives Ground for Suspicion of Treachery," "Remember the *Maine*! To Hell with Spain!" and "*Maine* is Annihilated," created a frenzy of newspaper readership.[58] After the explosion of the *Maine*, jingoist members of Congress argued that the United States had to defend its national honor.[59] War hawks grew impatient, and Theodore Roosevelt sent a series of cables to commanders of U.S. naval ships to prepare their charges for fighting. But because Roosevelt had not first sought the permission of his superior, John Davis Long, those cables were quickly recalled.[60]

Between March 20 and 28, McKinley attempted to reach an agreement with Spain on the crisis in Cuba.[61] He asked the Spanish to pay indemnity for the *Maine*, to halt the policy of reconcentration camps, to declare a truce, and to negotiate Cuban self-government through a U.S. mediation of terms.[62] The Spanish eventually agreed to all but the final demand, which was inconceivable for a colonial empire—even a crumbling one. McKinley finally turned to war on April 11, 1898, asking Congress to authorize the use of military forces in Cuba to end the conflict there, on the grounds that the ongoing struggle threatened lives, U.S. property, and tranquility in the United States.[63] On April 20, 1898, McKinley signed the joint resolution calling for the recognition of the independence of the people of Cuba, demanding that the Spanish government relinquish its authority and government in the island, and withdraw its land and naval forces from there. Failure to comply would result in the use by the U.S. land

and naval forces to carry these resolutions into effect.[64] The resolution also included the Teller Amendment, proposed by Senator Henry Teller (1830–1914) of Colorado, which specified that the United States would not annex Cuba.[65] On April 23, Spain declared war on the United States.[66] Two days later, President McKinley announced a blockade of the north coast of Cuba.[67] On April 25, 1898, the United States declared war on Spain.[68]

The U.S. Economy and Sea Power

Without a superior naval force, the United States never would have entered the war. It was clear that control of the sea was critical for the success of its ambitious expansion of economy and empire. Achieving this control, however, was easier said than done. During the Civil War, the Union Navy spent about $5.2 million on ships and other vessels, which is about $108 million in 2021.[69] Yet after the Civil War, congressional funding for the U.S. Navy diminished, and it struggled to keep up with the rapid progression in naval technology. One man in particular helped galvanize Congress to focus on sea power: Alfred Thayer Mahan (see p. 15). A career naval officer, Mahan spearheaded the concept of sea power in 1886 and 1887.[70] Building on these ideas, he proposed revitalizing the navy in his influential 1890 treatise, *The Influence of Sea Power Upon History, 1660–1783*. The popular publication skillfully synthesized military history extending as far back as the ancient Greek historian Xenophon, who observed that control of the sea played a critical role in the winning of land wars. Following this historical survey, Mahan argued that the United States possessed all of the elements required to become a global sea power. He assumed that surplus U.S. production would require overseas markets, and that for economic and imperial expansion, a modern navy was crucial. The power of the sea could be harnessed, he declared, but only by creating a steam and steel navy that operated in large, fleet-sized units. Mahan's aspirations for the U.S. Navy were driven by capitalist desires for economic expansion, which he argued made it necessary to carry out offensive naval tactics against foreign nations. When it came to U.S. foreign policy, he famously called for "manly resolve" rather than "weakly sentiment."[71]

Translated into twelve languages, Mahan's bestseller was often cited by men like Senator Henry Cabot Lodge and Roosevelt to bolster imperialist agendas, especially following the Panic of 1893. Farmers and manufacturers

Fig. 9 *Henry Cabot Lodge* (1850–1924), John Singer
Sargent (1856–1925), 1890. Oil on canvas; 127 × 84.5 cm
(50 × 33¼ in.). National Portrait Gallery, Smithsonian
Institution; gift of the Honorable Henry Cabot Lodge

eager for export markets felt that the U.S. commercial empire was more important than ever, which in turn helped to create great demands on sea power and the navy. Mahan's treatise provided politicians with a persuasive argument to build a stronger U.S. Navy. Lodge admired the potential of his ideas "to make the experience of the past influence the opinions and shape the policy of the future."[72] For his part, Roosevelt predicted that Mahan's book "would soon become a classic" and urged readers to support the construction of a navy complete with battleships.[73] Unsurprisingly, Roosevelt and Lodge advocated the buildup of the navy. Until about 1897, the United States had little capacity to wage an overseas war against a major imperial power.[74] Over half of its navy was composed of old vessels, not the modern steel ships of the 1890s.[75] But, in 1897 alone, under Roosevelt's supervision as assistant secretary of the navy, twenty-six new steel ships were built.[76] By the end of the 1890s, the U.S. Navy possessed more than 120 warships, ranging from new battleships and fast torpedo boats to antiquated ironclads and wooden cruisers.[77]

In his 1945 portrait by Alexander Robertson James (1890–1946), Mahan dominates the stormy seascape in the background, as if nature and man posed no challenge to him. The portrait was painted posthumously, which perhaps explains the 1906 rear admiral's uniform, which he never wore, as well as the Spanish Campaign medal, displayed on his chest to the viewer's right, which was awarded to all who served in the 1898 conflicts after 1920, six years after Mahan's death.[78] The medal to the left is the U.S. Civil War campaign medal, a conflict during which Mahan had active service and achieved the rank of captain (his preferred salutation).[79] This portrait also attests to Mahan's significant influence on naval theory well into the mid-century. Through one-dollar gifts to the Naval War College in 1940, 1,400 alumni helped pay for it.[80]

After Mahan's theories of naval sea power caught the attention of powerful politicians, Congress and the executive branch followed an aggressive shipbuilding policy. Coaling stations for the expanded reach of the U.S. Navy became a priority as well. Lodge, whose Cabot ancestry reached far back to the first English settlements

of colonial America, believed that British-descended Americans like his family were superior to others. His arrogance was captured by famed society portraitist John Singer Sargent in this 1890 portrait (fig. 9).[81] Dressed in a dark three-piece suit with a blue striped silk tie, Lodge holds the chain of his pocket watch in his right hand. His hand resting on his hip, he looks to his left, lost in thought. The viewpoint from slightly below and elbow not quite akimbo—a conventional pose for portraying the European aristocracy—reinforces this sense of distance and superiority.

A nationalist and imperialist who supported an aggressive form of the Monroe Doctrine, Lodge was enormously influential in Congress. Elected to the U.S. Senate for the state of Massachusetts in 1893, Lodge immediately began to call for the annexation of the Hawaiian Islands to defend the United States' West Coast and to secure commercial interests in the Pacific from international competitors.[82] Lodge believed that if the United States did not take Hawai'i, Great Britain or Japan would. Japanese immigration to Hawai'i had increased drastically, tallying 25,000, or about one-quarter of the population, and creating fear among the U.S. businessmen in Hawai'i about Japanese influence in the archipelago. Japanese imperialism was surging. In 1895, Japan triumphed over China during the Sino-Japanese War and claimed control of Korea. In early 1897, the Japanese sent two warships to Hawai'i. Convinced by Lodge, Mahan, and Roosevelt, President McKinley subsequently sent a treaty to Congress proposing to annex Hawai'i in June 1897, but it was voted down in the Senate. Those with business ties especially feared competition from Hawaiian sugar imports.[83] Additionally, Native Hawaiians organized petitions with more than 38,000 signatures that objected to the treaty, and submitted part of these petitions to Congress.[84] Their resistance to annexation, as chapter two explains, was fierce.

The economic and political influence of Anglo-Americans took root with the arrival of missionaries from New England to Hawai'i in 1820, and grew over the following decades. But Great Britain and France also vied for "the crossroads of the Pacific." Seeking to assert its dominance among all these powers, President John Tyler (1790–1862)

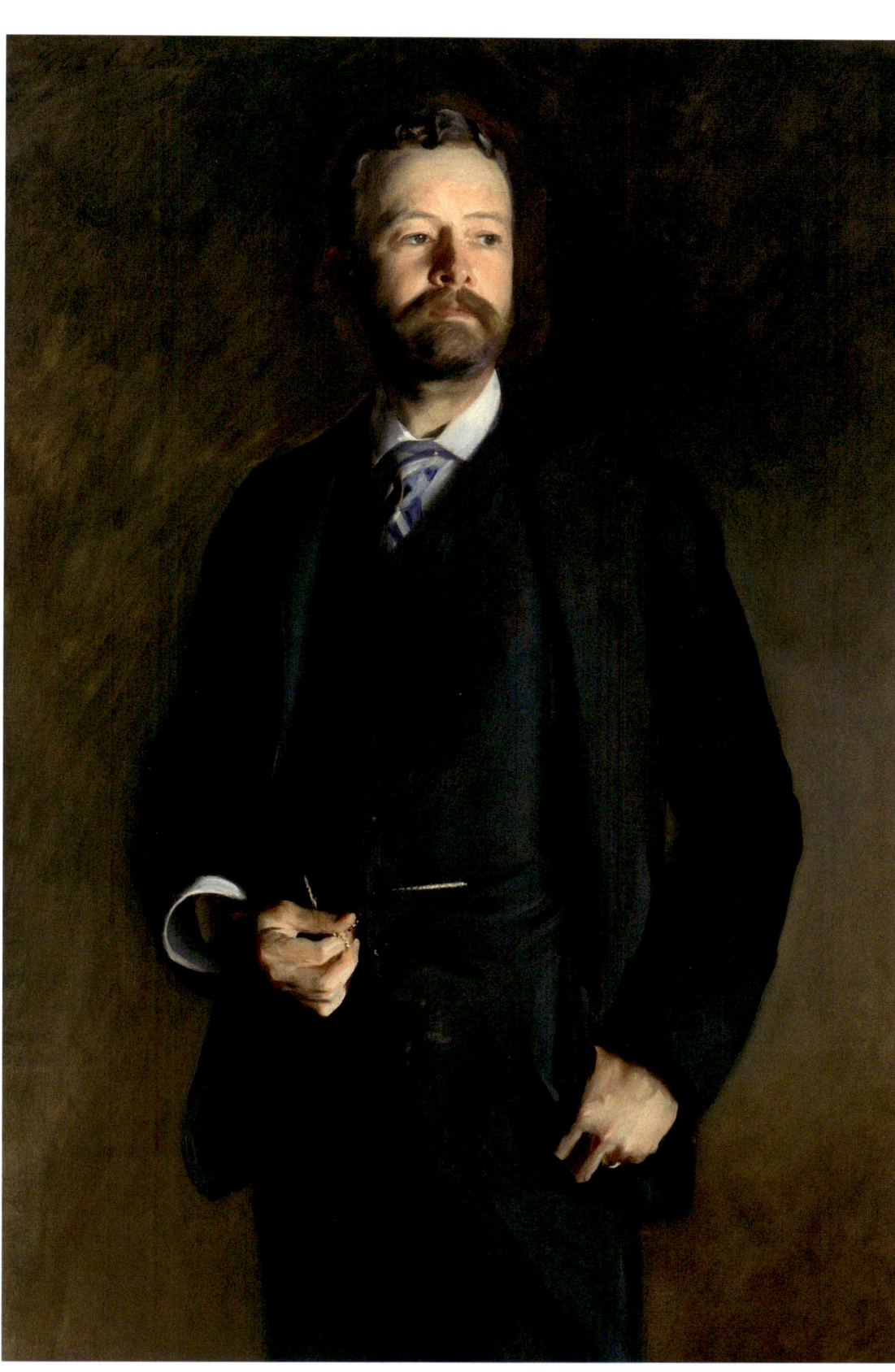

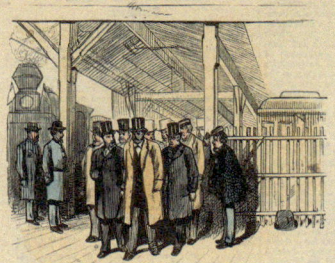

THE ARRIVAL AT THE WASHINGTON STATION.

OUR ROYAL GUEST.

PRINCE DAVID KALAKAUA, who was chosen, February 12th, 1874, almost unanimously by the Legislative Assembly to be the King of the Hawaiian Islands, was born at Honolulu on the 16th of November, 1836, and is therefore in his thirty-ninth year. He is the son of the late Hon. C. Kapaakea and the late High Chiefess Keohokalole, who were connected with the various branches of the High Chiefs descended from the ancient sovereigns. He received a good education at the Royal School, and has filled various public positions, which have given him an opportunity to acquire an extensive knowledge of international law, and fit him to act as sovereign of his native

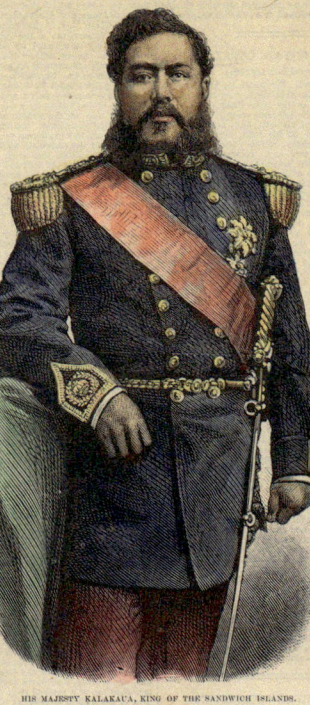

HIS MAJESTY KALAKAUA, KING OF THE SANDWICH ISLANDS.
PHOTOGRAPHED BY BRADLEY & RULOFSON.

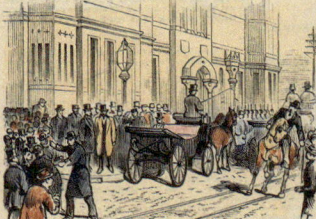

THE ESCORT TO THE CARRIAGE AT THE DEPOT.

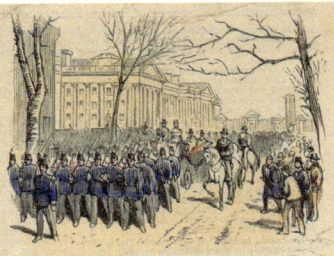

THE RIDE DOWN PENNSYLVANIA AVENUE.

country. In 1863 he married the young Chiefess Kapiolani, daughter of the Hawaiian Chief Keawe, and niece of Keliahonui, a chief of Kauai, and thus consolidated the interests of some of the most influential families of the kingdom.

In his personal appearance the King is a stout, portly gentleman. His complexion is dark, and his side-whiskers and hair are black and curly. He has the easy, self-possessed air of a man of the world. He goes about attired in a suit of black broadcloth of the latest and most fashionable cut. On the lapel of his coat is pinned a small strip of parti-colored ribbon, indicating the royal Order with which

(Continued on page 279.)

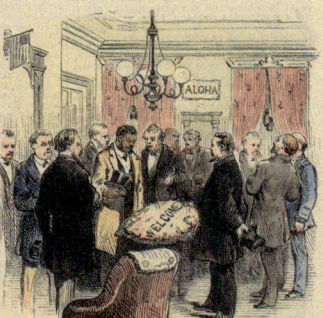

ARRIVAL AT THE PARLOR OF THE KING'S SUITE OF ROOMS IN THE ARLINGTON HOTEL.

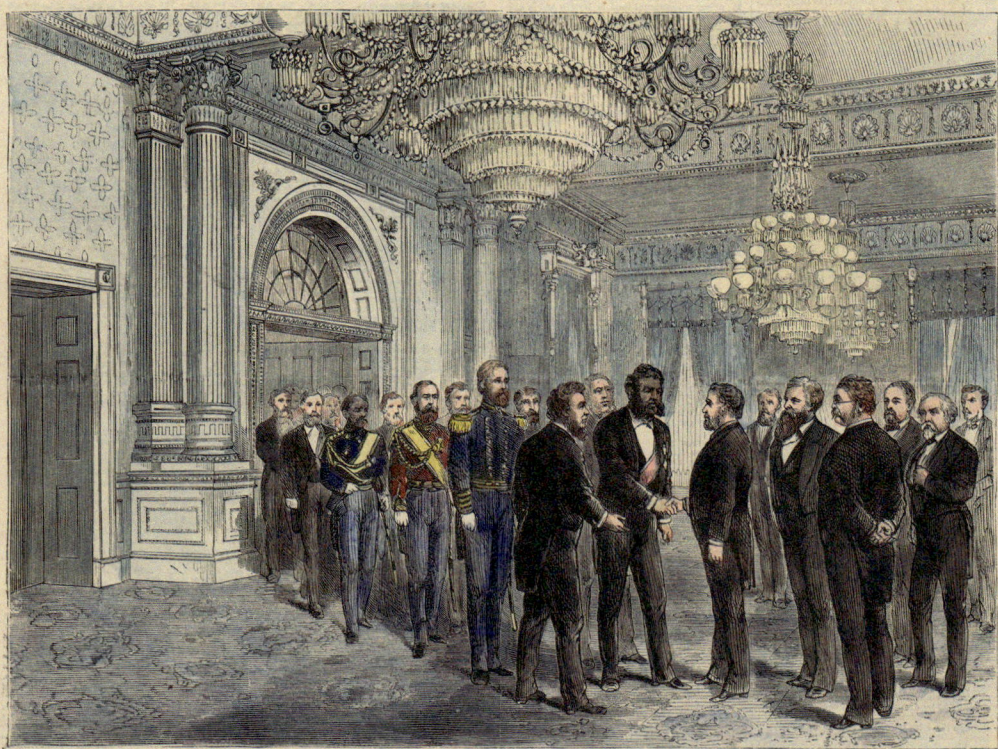

KING KALAKAUA AND SUITE PAYING A FORMAL VISIT TO THE PRESIDENT IN THE BLUE ROOM OF THE WHITE HOUSE.

KING KALAKAUA, OF THE SANDWICH ISLANDS, VISITING WASHINGTON.

extended the Monroe Doctrine to Hawai'i in 1842.[85] Beginning in the 1840s, the idea of annexing the Hawaiian archipelago to the United States gained some traction, particularly among increasingly powerful sugar planters in the islands, who wanted to safeguard their access to the U.S. market. But the proposal did not progress.[86]

Primarily driven by economic interests, relations between Hawai'i and the United States continued to grow closer, as evidenced by this broadside illustrating the visit of King David Kalākaua (1836–1891) to Washington, DC, in December 1874 (fig. 10). Elected to the throne by the Hawaiian Legislature earlier that year, Kalākaua was the first reigning monarch to set foot on U.S. soil.[87] At the center of the page, a three-quarter-length portrait depicts a distinguished man with a mutton-chops beard. Dressed in Western royal attire, he wears a formal blue military coat with a red royal sash over his right shoulder and carries a sword. Vignettes of his arrival into Washington's Union Station, his ride along Pennsylvania Avenue, and his White House meeting with President Ulysses S. Grant communicate the importance of this state visit, during which the king improved trade relations between the two countries and laid the groundwork for a reciprocity treaty that would allow Hawaiian sugar and other products to enter the United States without tariffs.[88] In the treaty negotiations, the United States requested to have Pearl Harbor ceded to it in perpetuity. Although Kalākaua rejected this stipulation, he agreed to lease ports exclusively to the United States during the life of the treaty.[89]

By March 16, 1898, when the Fifty-Fifth Congress was discussing the annexation of Hawai'i, Lodge's rationale for securing markets and military outposts had gained traction in Washington. Trade reports revealed that 75 percent of the sugar plantations were owned by Anglo-Americans and that 75 percent of the business in Hawai'i was controlled by Anglo-Americans.[90] Just as Mahan had predicted, U.S. farms and factories needed every possible outlet for their surplus products. The strengthening of the extant market ties between Hawai'i and the United States as well as the elimination of foreign competition through annexation were key for this interest group.[91]

After the explosion of the USS *Maine*, Lodge realized that U.S. military intervention in Cuba also presented a broader opportunity for territorial expansion in the Pacific. In early 1898, the senator explained that the United States should occupy strategic positions he referred to as the "outworks," which would enable the country to resist Europe's designs in the Western Hemisphere.[92] On April 13, 1898, Lodge delivered his argument for intervention in Cuba to Congress, underscoring the strategic value of Cuba's location in the Caribbean for U.S. trade and commerce. He pointed out, "[Cuba] commands the Gulf, she commands the channel through which all our coastwise traffic between the Gulf and our Northern and Eastern states passes. She lies right athwart the line which leads to the Nicaragua Canal."[93] Although the United States eventually went with a different site—the Isthmus of Panama—it did begin canal construction in 1904, during Theodore Roosevelt's presidency. In Lodge's opinion, the United States needed strategically located coaling stations at locations such as Havana Harbor, Hawai'i, and Guantánamo Bay.[94] Ultimately, Mahan's theory of sea power not only provided an intellectual justification for a war of empire that extended from the Caribbean to the Pacific but also the means to achieve its success.

A Global Empire

When the United States declared war on Spain on April 25, 1898, it sought to vanquish the Spanish empire's naval fleets. Shortly after the beginning of the Cuban blockade, the United States sent naval forces to the Philippines, Guam, and Puerto Rico—the three remaining Spanish colonies in the Pacific and the Caribbean—to accomplish its goal.[95] Commodore George Dewey (1837–1917), commander of the U.S. Asiatic Squadron, found himself in a difficult position. Then concentrated in Hong Kong, he had orders to prepare his squadron for conflict with Spain, but the outbreak of war would prevent him from using any of the major ports in the region so that Britain and other powers could maintain their neutrality.[96] Asked to leave Hong Kong by the British on April 23, Dewey set out to challenge and defeat the Spanish Pacific Squadron.

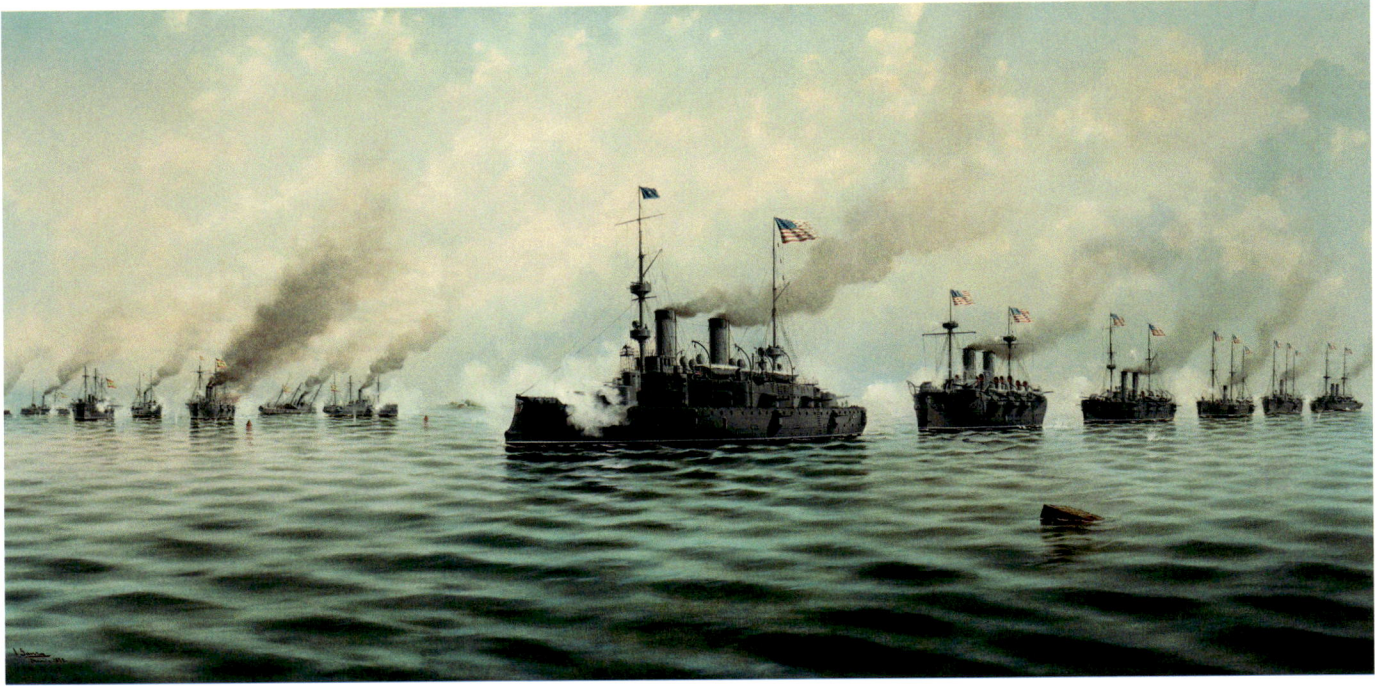

Fig. 11 *Battle of Manila Bay, May 1, 1898* (Batalla en la Bahía de Manila, 1 de mayo del 1898), Ildefonso Sanz y Doménech (1863–1937), 1899

Oil on canvas; 99.1 × 200.7 cm (39 × 79 in.). Courtesy of the Army and Navy Club Library Trust, Washington, DC

On May 1, 1898, Dewey's ships steamed into Manila Bay and destroyed the Spanish flotilla (fig. 11). In this decisive battle, the modern, steel-clad ships of the United States, led by the USS *Olympia*, ruthlessly fired upon the seven unarmored vessels of the Spanish Pacific Squadron. Ildefonso Sanz y Doménech, also known as Alfonso Sanz (1863–1937), a Spanish medical officer on board one of these ships, witnessed and later recorded the naval engagement in this painting.[97] Only nine U.S. sailors were wounded, whereas 161 Spanish sailors and soldiers died, and 210 more were wounded.[98] Meanwhile, although the U.S. Navy had planned for a war of conquest, the U.S. Army had not. Much to his frustration, Dewey did not have the support forces needed to occupy the city of Manila.[99] Although U.S. forces landed in the Philippines in late July, in May, Dewey and his men could not disembark, their morale sinking. Nevertheless, Dewey returned to the United States a war hero.

After the Battle of Manila Bay, Dewey was so beloved in the United States that he was thought to be a credible challenger to McKinley in the presidential race of 1900. Charles Schwab (1862–1939), who succeeded Henry Clay Frick (1849–1919) as the president of Carnegie Company

(which fabricated steel), commissioned the popular French portrait artist Théobald Chartran (1849–1907) to paint the portraits of Dewey and his wife, Mildred Hazen Dewey (figs. 12 and 13).[100] The pendant portraits of these lavishly attired sitters emulate royal portraiture, such as the portrait of Henry VIII by Hans Holbein the Younger. Despite his popularity, Dewey decided not to run against McKinley. But, from 1899 until his death in 1917, he held a plumb leadership position as president of the General Board of the Navy Department, which made naval policy. Schwab's portrait commissions helped Dewey retain his influence on the U.S. Navy—and the millions of dollars spent on steel to transform its fleet into steel warships.[101]

The use of steam-powered warships required hundreds of tons of coal that had to be resupplied regularly. As Henry Cabot Lodge recognized, the United States needed "friendly" ports to store coal as well as offer repair facilities and supplies. And as the country turned its attention to the Philippines, the need to establish a port in Guam, in addition to Hawai'i, increased. On June 20, in command of the USS *Charleston*, Captain Henry Glass (1844–1908) arrived in Guam's Apra Harbor and fired ten shots. The Spanish forces there, unaware of the war

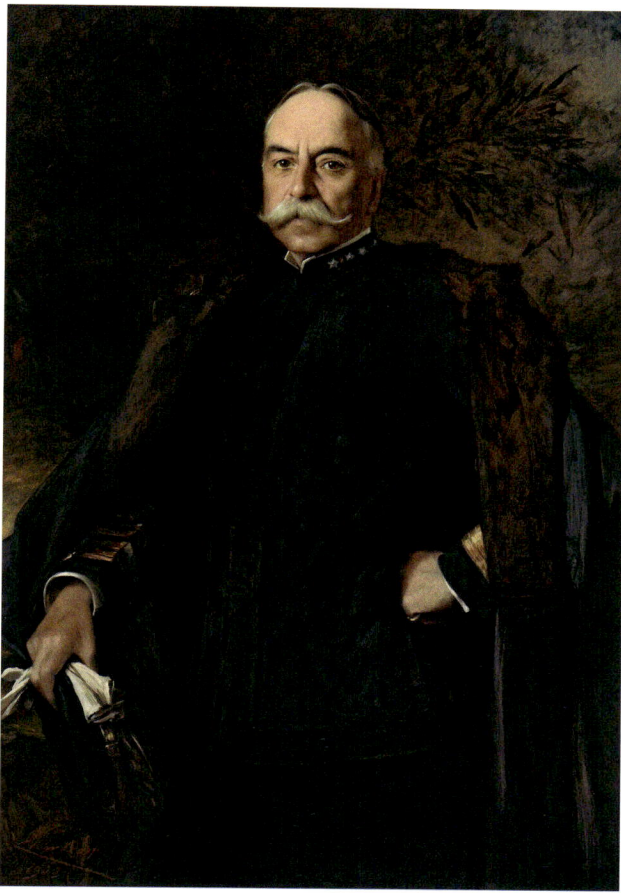

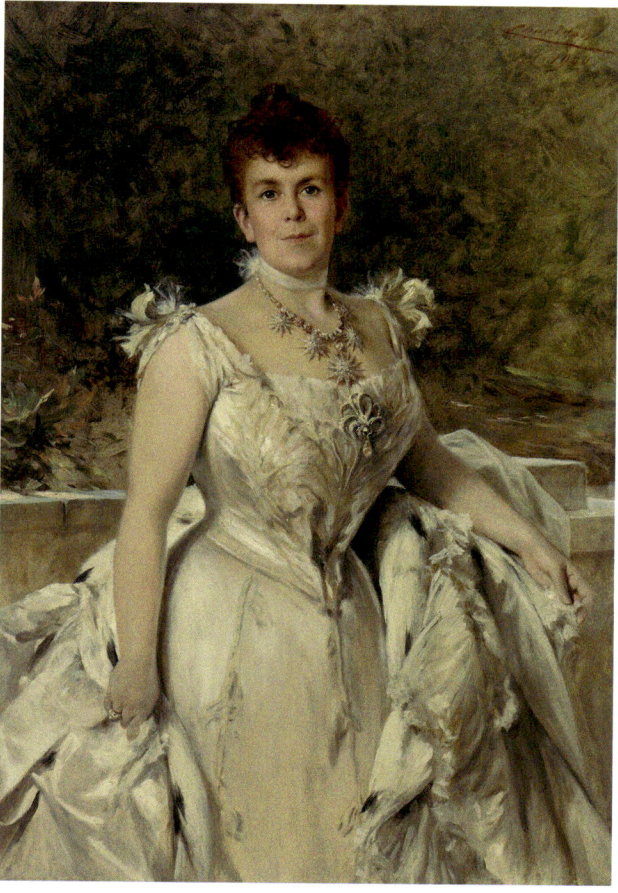

Fig. 12 *Admiral George Dewey* (1837–1917), Théobald Chartran (1849–1907), 1900. Oil on canvas; 125.7 × 87.3 cm (49½ × 34⅜ in.). National Portrait Gallery, Smithsonian Institution; bequest of Frederick McLean Bugher

Fig. 13 *Mildred Hazen Dewey* (1847–1931), Théobald Chartran (1849–1907), 1900. Oil on canvas; 127.3 × 88.9 cm (50⅛ × 35 in.). National Portrait Gallery, Smithsonian Institution; bequest of Frederick McLean Bugher

between the United States and Spain, misunderstood these aggressions as a military salute. Within the next twenty-four hours, Guam's governor surrendered to the United States without combat.[102]

McKinley: The Skilled Politician

In October 1898, the distinguished Puerto Rican artist Francisco Oller y Cestero, capitalized on McKinley's popularity by painting his portrait (fig. 14). Oller had trained in Spain at the Academy of San Fernando and in France with Gustave Courbet (1819–1877) and Thomas Couture (1815–1879), and at the Académie Gleyre. During several prolonged stays in both countries between 1851 and 1896, Oller exhibited his work internationally and became close friends with the Parisian Impressionist circle, including Paul Cézanne (1839–1906) and his fellow

Caribbean painter Camille Pissarro (born in Saint Thomas; 1830–1903). Between travels, Oller returned to Puerto Rico, where he taught and made official portraits of Spanish military figures and colonial administrators. In 1870, he earned the Royal Order of Charles III and two years later, he was appointed Painter to the Royal Chamber to King Amadeo I.[103] More than anything, Oller endeavored to make art about Puerto Rico, portraying its intellectuals, addressing timely issues like the abolition of slavery in 1873, and painting island landscapes, genre scenes, and still lifes of tropical fruit.

As fighting marked the summer months of 1898, Oller contemplated his future commissions. When the United States seized Puerto Rico from Spain during a campaign led by commanding general of the U.S. Army Nelson Miles from July 21 to August 12, 1898, a new political order was

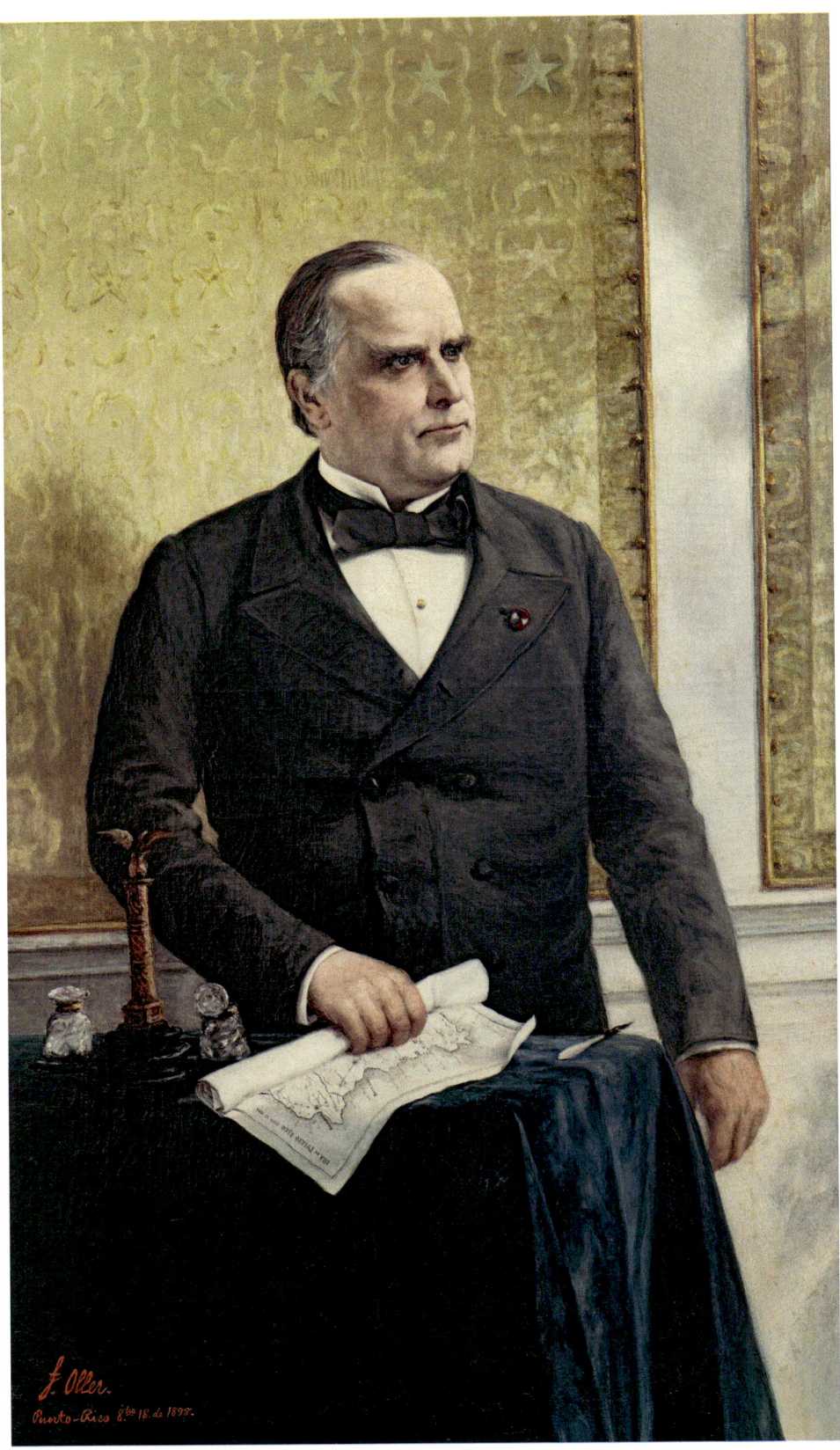

Fig. 14 *President William McKinley* (1843–1901), Francisco Oller y Cestero (1833–1917), 1898. Oil on canvas; 147.3 × 83.8 cm (58 × 33 in.). Collection of Dr. Eduardo Pérez and family

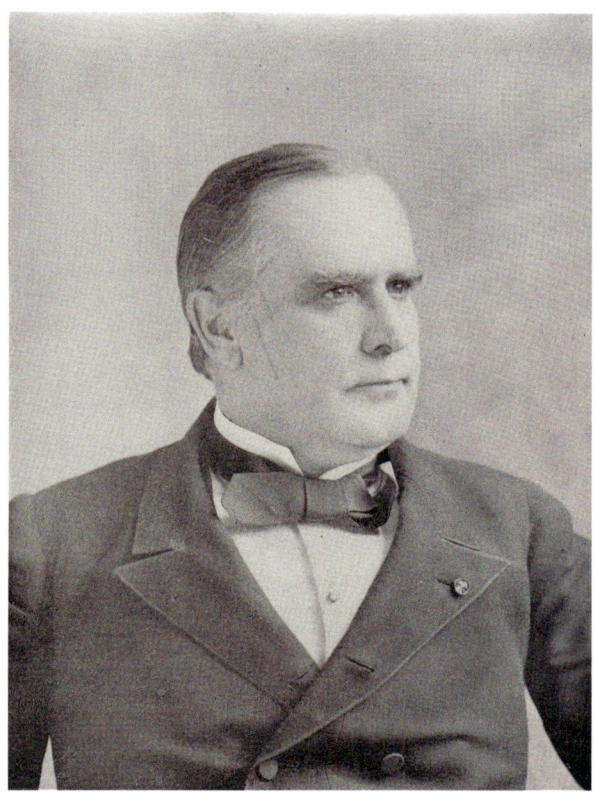

Fig. 15 *President William McKinley (1843–1901)*, Unidentified photographer, c. 1898. Photograph reproduced in *Photographic History of the Spanish-American War: A Pictorial and Descriptive Record of Events on Land and Sea with Portraits and Biographies of Leaders on Both Sides.* New York: Pearson, 1898

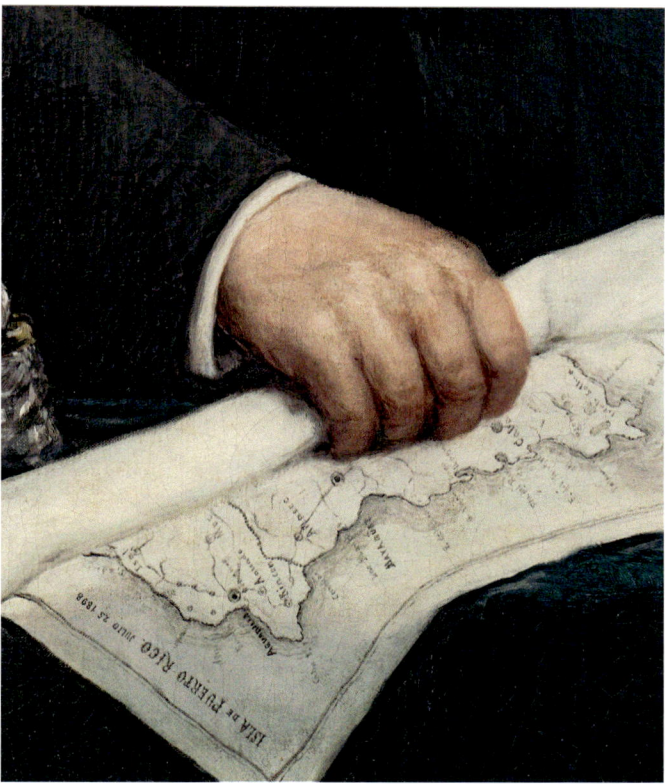

Fig. 16 *President William McKinley (1843–1901)* (detail), Francisco Oller y Cestero (1833–1917), 1898. Oil on canvas; 147.3 × 83.8 cm (58 × 33 in.). Collection of Dr. Eduardo Pérez and family

established.[104] But before it was formalized through the Treaty of Paris that ended the war in December of that year, Oller had begun working on his portrait of McKinley. Oller, who never met McKinley, based the portrait on a well-circulated photograph of the president (fig. 15).[105] The three-quarter portrait represents the president as a bold leader.[106] McKinley wears a black suit adorned with the red, white, and blue rosette lapel pin of the Military Order of the Loyal Legion of the United States, an organization formed in the wake of Abraham Lincoln's assassination to thwart future threats to the nation or its unity. The portrait's elegance reveals Oller's attempt to court the favor of McKinley and the U.S. colonial administration.[107] Yet the painting is more factual than celebratory, and a certain ambiguity remains in McKinley's severe likeness and his grasping of the partly crumpled map, which could be read as a veiled critique of the U.S. occupation of the island (fig. 16).[108] Below Oller's signature on the lower left,

"8.bre 18, 1898" marks the date of the formal transfer of power from Spain to the United States, underscoring the painting's ambivalence.[109] At noon of October 18, 1898, the U.S. flag was raised in every military, insular, municipal, and civil office of Puerto Rico, beginning a period of military governance that would last two years and be followed by the establishment of a civil government.[110]

Under McKinley's guidance, the United States became a globe-spanning imperial power. Although maligned by his critics as weak and apprehensive, McKinley's supporters knew him as a skilled politician.[111] Elihu Root (1845–1937), secretary of war and architect of U.S. territorial policy after the war, even described him as calculating, writing how the president "had a way of handling men so that they thought his ideas were their own. He cared nothing about the credit, but McKinley always had his way."[112] In July 1898, marking a testament to McKinley's skill or the appeal of military adventure, his former enemy—

Fig. 17 *Cuba Libre*, F. W. Guerin (1846–1903), c. 1898. Photograph; 53.3 × 42.9 cm (21 × 16⅞ in.). Library of Congress, Prints and Photographs Division, Washington, DC

the United Confederate Veterans—voted to support him in the imperial war during their meeting in Atlanta.[113] McKinley responded to the resolution by promoting unity between Confederate and white Union veterans in the segregated U.S. Army. His letter, published in the *New York Times* and the *Atlanta Constitution*, reads,

> The present war has certainly served one very useful purpose in completely obliterat[ing] the sectional lines drawn in the last one. The response to the Nation's call to arms has been equally spontaneous and patriotic in all parts of the country. Veterans of the gray, as well as of the blue, are now fighting side by side, winning equal honor and renown. Their brave deeds and the unequaled triumphs of our army and navy have received the gratitude of the people of the United States.[114]

Photographer F. W. Guerin captured this spirit of reconciliation in a photograph staged in St. Louis (fig. 17). He posed two men, one dressed in the gray uniform of the Confederacy on the left, and one dressed in the blue uniform of the Union on the right, clasping hands in a congenial handshake. Between them, a blonde girl representing the Cuban people raises her right hand in triumph, displaying a broken shackle hanging from her wrist. Her left hand bears the other half of the shackle and rests on top of the men's clasping hands.[115] Visualizing the reunion of the former warring factions of the U.S. Civil War helped people rally around McKinley's decision to go to war. Significantly, despite the multiracial character of the final Cuban War of Independence and of the ideal of racial equality that sustained it, in Guérin's tableau photograph the U.S. North and the South can only unite behind the cause of freeing a white Cuba from colonialism.[116] The idea of *Cuba Libre* also contributed to recruiting propaganda so effective that 280,564 U.S. citizens volunteered to fight.

A cult of personality had grown up around McKinley during the four months of combat during the War of 1898. When the cease-fire was declared on August 12, 1898, he had achieved his main goals: a short conflict that gave the United States power over Cuba and control of Puerto Rico, Guam, and the Philippines. Hawai'i was also annexed to the United States. Furthermore, the importance of sea power for the U.S. Navy would never again be questioned.

After McKinley's assassination in 1901, Theodore Roosevelt became president. Roosevelt eagerly wielded the new imperial power of the United States and showed little regard for the people residing in the seized archipelagos or their hard-fought wars for autonomy and self-governance. At the dawn of the new century, the United States joined the ranks of Great Britain, France, Germany, Russia, and Japan as an acknowledged imperial power.

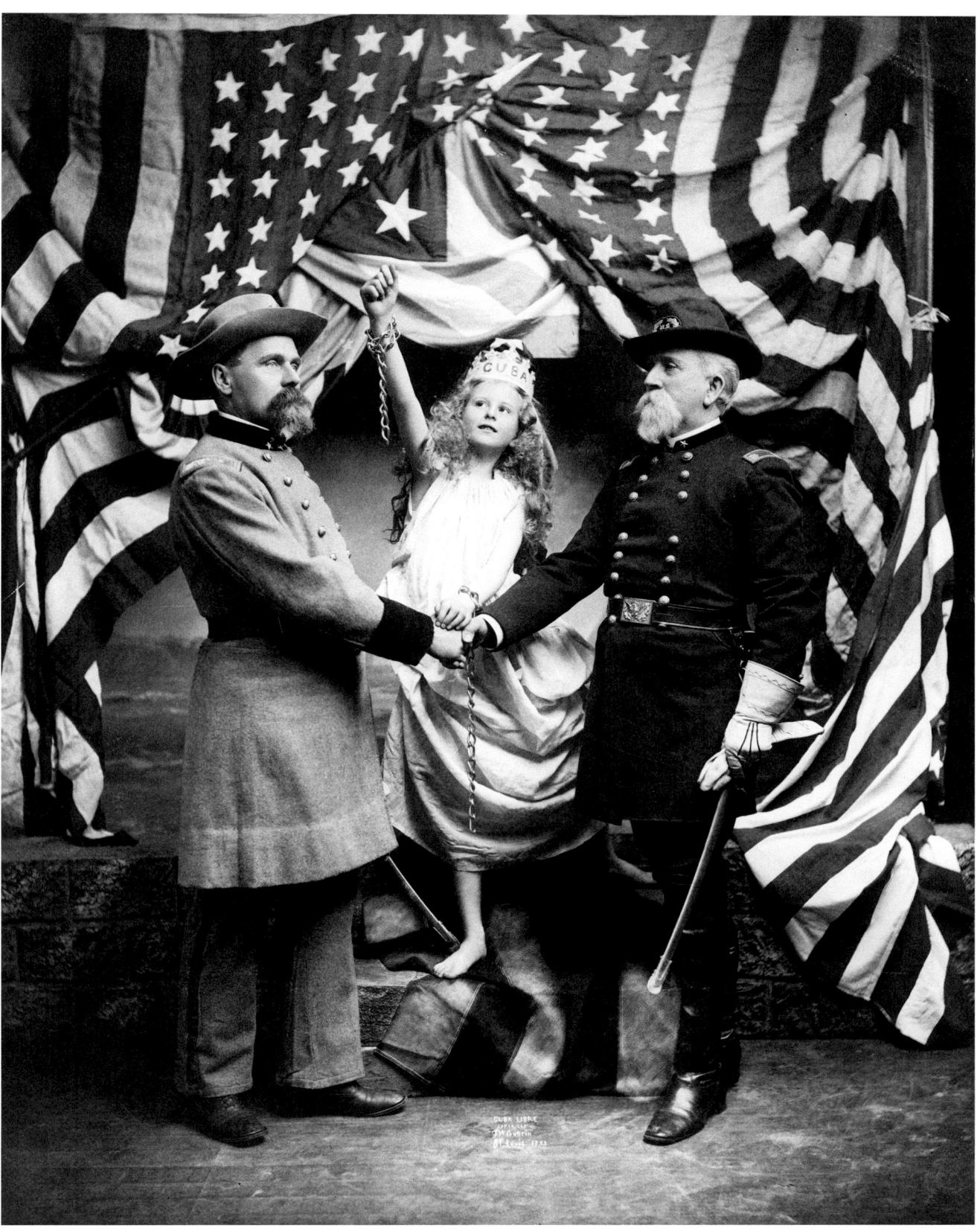

2

"Our Culture Has to Be the Core of Our Resistance"

HEALOHA JOHNSTON

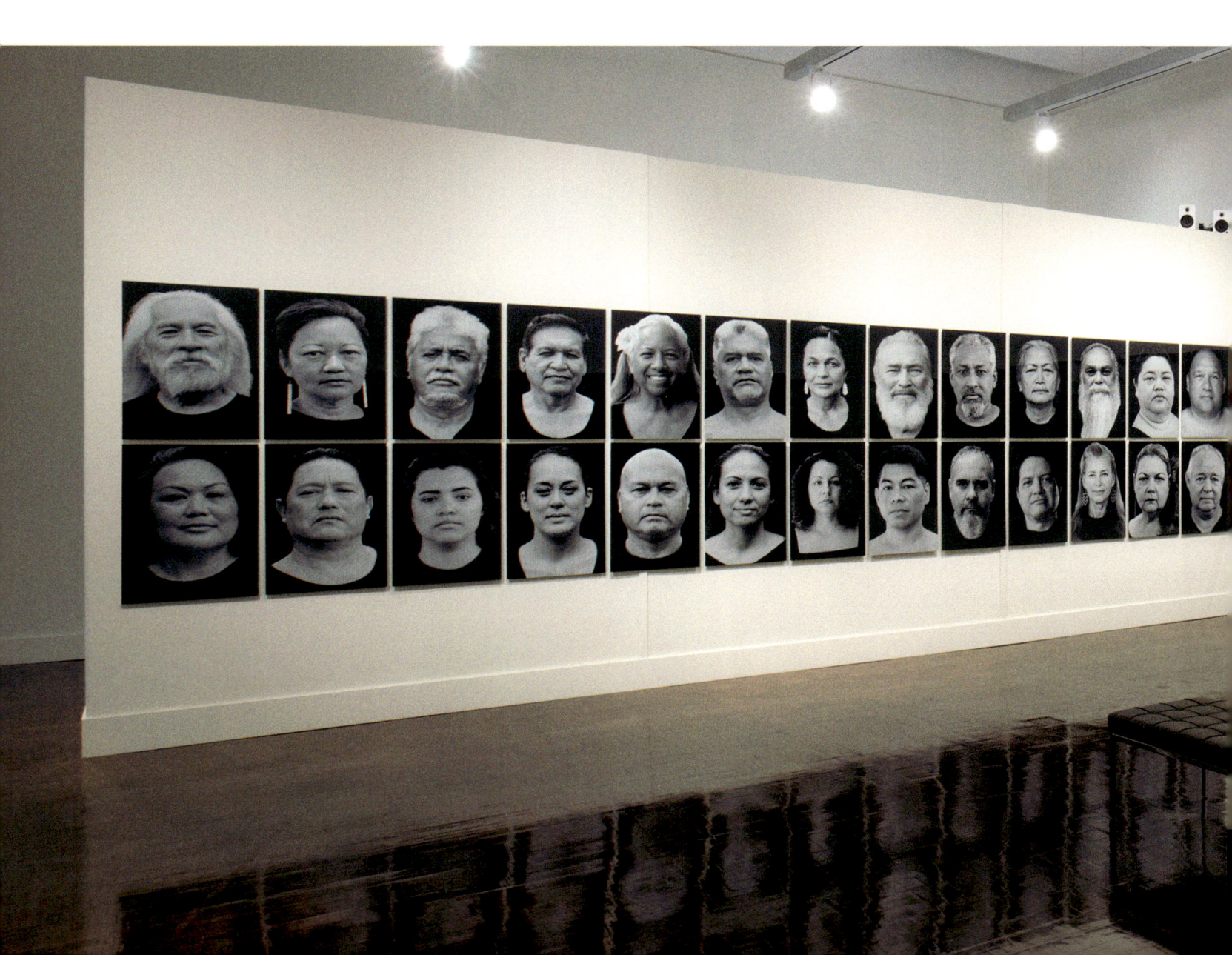

The words of scholar, poet, and political strategist Dr. Haunani-Kay Trask—*Our culture has to be the core of our resistance*—have motivated scholars and artists to situate their work within the political sphere. She spoke these words at a conference titled Hoʻokūʻokoʻa, which was held at Kamehameha Schools in 1985, where she explained that aloha ʻāina (literally meaning love of land/love of country) "has to do with history, it has to do with genealogy, and it has to do with hurt." In her presentation, Trask attributed twentieth-century expressions of aloha ʻāina to George Helm, a political leader during the 1970s Hawaiian Renaissance, who derived his understanding and political contextualization of this philosophy from kūpuna (ancestors, elders, traditions) and nineteenth-century Hawaiian patriots who were loyal to the aliʻi (Hawaiian chiefs, kings, and queens) and to the land in their fight against American imperialism leading up to and following the year 1893.[1]

Trask's articulations of culture as ever-changing yet persistent as a vehicle for Indigenous value systems, and as a source for Hawaiian

Fig. 1 Installation view of the 2019 Honolulu Biennial featuring *ʻAuʻa*, by Kapulani Landgraf (b. 1966). The large-scale installation features portraits of those "whom the artist identified as people who work across disciplines and initiatives to inspire positive change in Hawaiʻi," Johnston writes.

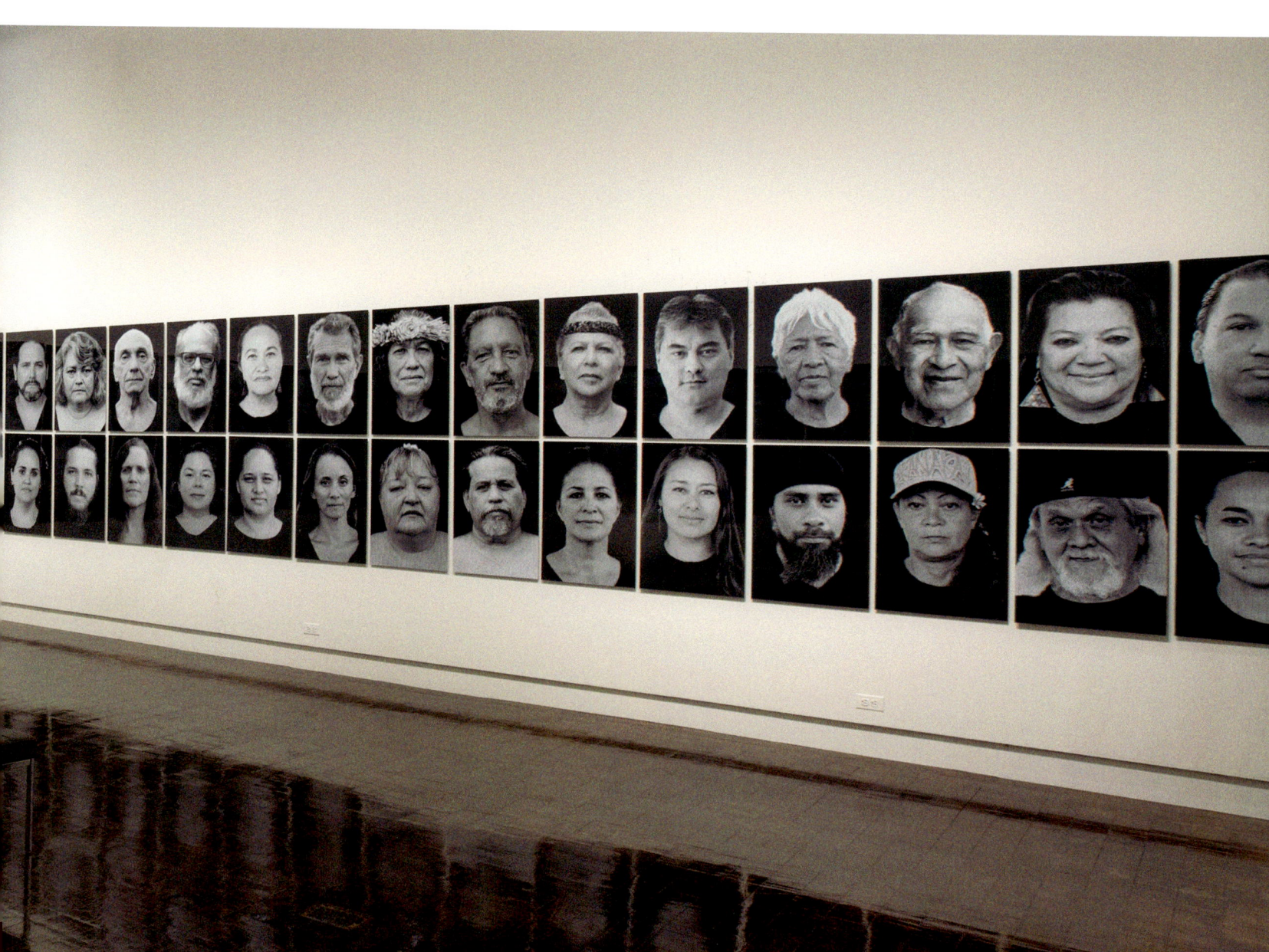

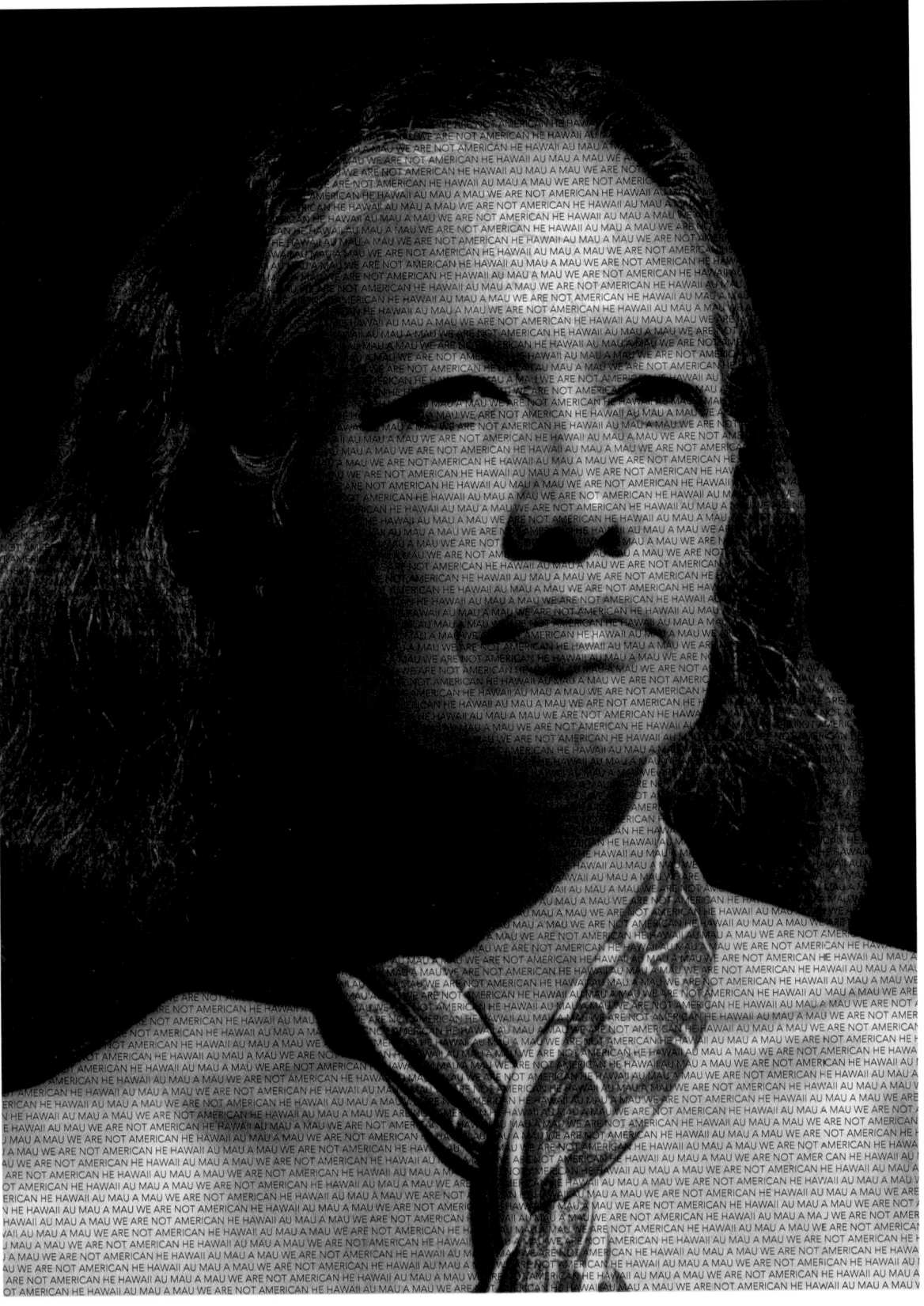

Fig. 2 *Portrait of Haunani-Kay Trask* (1949–2021), Kapulani Landgraf (b. 1966). This is one of 108 digital metal prints that Landgraf featured in her 2019 Honolulu Biennial installation, *'Au'a*. The artist overlaid the portrait of Trask with the words, HE HAWAII AU MAU A MAU WE ARE NOT AMERICAN. "He Hawai'i au mau a mau" translates to "I am Hawaiian for now and for ever."

resistance against U.S. military occupation, emerged out of the Hawaiian Renaissance. She insisted that Kānaka 'Ōiwi (Native Hawaiian people) see themselves in political activism. Trask explained that "cultural people have to become political. It's not just that political people like myself have to become cultural. Our culture can't just be ornamental and recreational. . . . Our culture has to be the core of our resistance. . . . Our philosophy as nationalist Hawaiians should be aloha 'āina. An alternative to tourism and militarism."[2]

Trask's highly visible and unapologetic work at the University of Hawai'i at Mānoa and within grassroots activism brought back into consciousness the continued existence of Hawai'i as an independent country. She therefore described "Hawaiian" as a national identity, rather than an ethnicity within the American national identity. Trask's texts, along with the writings of Dr. Noenoe Silva, describe aloha 'āina as a form of governance that existed in Hawai'i's ali'i system before Hawai'i was recognized as an independent country in 1843, and identify aloha 'āina as the foundation upon which Hawai'i's Native-formed and led constitutional monarchy based its governmental framework.[3] Dr. Kamana Beamer suggests that for those who understand the "pre-European structures, the creation of the Hawaiian Kingdom begins to look less like a European imposition and more like a modification by Hawaiian ali'i, of existing Hawaiian structures."[4]

Trask's speeches, panel discussions, and books continue to serve as a launching pad for artists and scholars who as cultural people answer the call to action to situate their work within the political sphere. Among the most impactful tributes to Trask's intellectual legacy is a recent large-scale installation by photographer Kapulani Landgraf (fig. 1). Landgraf adopted the genre of portraiture for the first time in her multi-decade-long career to render continuity in Hawaiian political consciousness as her contribution to the 2019 Honolulu Biennial (now a triennial event called the Hawai'i Contemporary). Landgraf's series titled *'Au'a* includes 108 photographic portraits featuring

Kānaka 'Ōiwi, all of whom the artist identified as people who work across disciplines and initiatives to inspire positive change in Hawai'i. Unified by a commitment to Hawaiian lifeways, the artist approached individuals of diverse backgrounds—educators, scholars, museum collection managers, kumu hula, ocean navigators, artists, and activists, for example—who are rooted in aloha 'āina (fig. 2).

'Au'a began as the artist's response to a historic speech delivered by Dr. Haunani-Kay Trask at 'Iolani Palace in 1993. An audio accompaniment to the photographs played in the gallery during the Biennial. Museum visitors could hear an oli (Hawaiian chant) combined with an excerpt from Dr. Trask's 1993 speech. "I am not an American. I am not an American. I am not an American . . ." Trask repeated these words fervently to a crowd of ten thousand who gathered at the centennial on 'Iolani Palace grounds in observance of the 1893 American-backed coup d'état that unlawfully deposed Queen Lili'uokalani. Over the course of her speech, Trask modified her opening statements from "I am not an American" to "We are not American! We are not American! We will die as Hawaiians!"[5]

Landgraf's installation evolved to situate this speech within an intergenerational continuum of political protest and aloha 'āina. The text HE HAWAII AU MAU A MAU WE ARE NOT AMERICAN repeats from top to bottom of each portrait, blanketing the faces of each aloha 'āina. He Hawai'i au mau a mau, meaning "I am Hawaiian for now and forever," is a song lyric associated with Hawaiian Renaissance music and 'Ōlelo Hawai'i (Hawaiian language) revitalization. In her artwork, Landgraf asserts a national Hawaiian identity despite prolonged government occupation, and explores the potential to effect change through civic engagement. Landgraf explains: "When put together, it is all about lāhui (people and country). A collective voice, a collective conviction to correct the wrong. Even though there are only 108 people portrayed in *'Au'a*, thousands are represented, including all our ancestors and future generations of ascendents."[6]

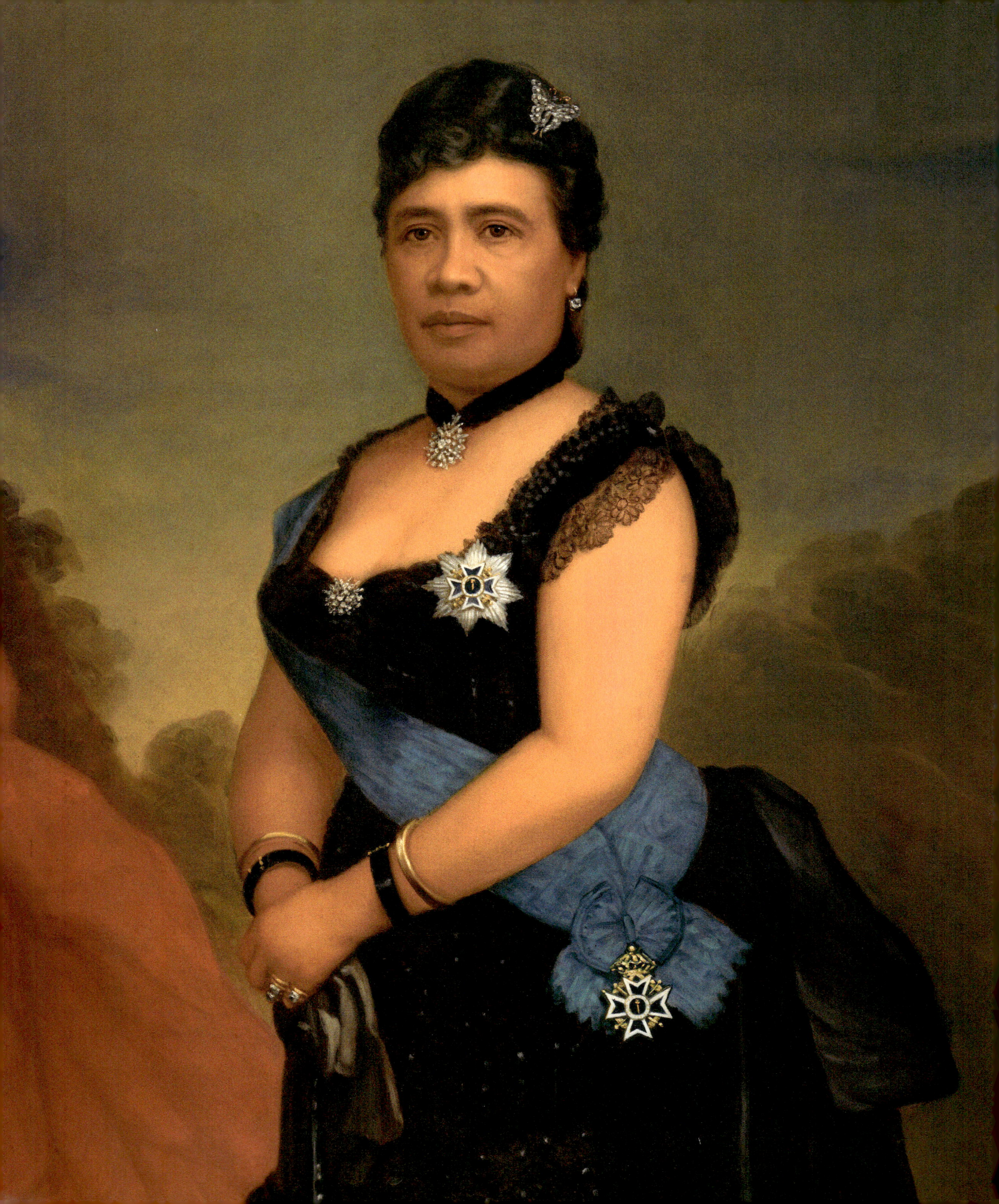

Hawaiian Resistance and U.S. Imperialism

TAÍNA CARAGOL AND KATE CLARKE LEMAY

I, Lili'uokalani, by the Grace of God and under the Constitution of the Hawaiian Kingdom, Queen, do hereby solemnly protest against any and all acts done against myself . . . That I yield to the superior force of the United States of America . . . to avoid any collision of armed forces, and perhaps the loss of life, I do, under this protest and impelled by said forces, yield my authority until such time as the Government of the United States shall . . . reinstate me in the authority which I claim as the constitutional sovereign of the Hawaiian Islands.[1]

—Lili'uokalani to Sanford Dole, January 17, 1893

Queen Lili'uokalani, the Last Reigning Monarch of Hawai'i

On June 15, 1898, the U.S. House of Representatives voted to annex Hawai'i by an overwhelming majority (209–91), ignoring the fact that the legislation through joint resolution was not legal.[2] The claim to annex the island nation marked the culmination of over a century of threats posed by white settlers and explorers—as well as a coup in 1893 by Anglo-Americans. U.S. imperialist ventures in Hawai'i, however, faced many forms of Hawaiian resistance—including the strategic, multivalent efforts of the Hawaiian sovereign, Queen Lili'uokalani (1838–1917).

In 1893, Queen Lili'uokalani faced a daunting choice. Pressure from U.S. and European businessmen who hungered for the dissolution of the Hawaiian monarchy had reached a boiling point. The queen was left to either acquiesce to, or resist, the overthrow of her monarchy. Above all else, she wanted to avoid bloodshed, for the Hawaiian Kingdom, despite having been in place for almost a century, could not hope to match the military power of the United States. On January 16, troops from the USS *Boston* had been stationed outside of Hawai'i's Government Building, located across from and facing the queen's

home, the 'Iolani Palace.[3] As Hawai'i's first queen, she was respected by Kānaka Maoli (Native Hawaiians) and foreign heads of state alike.[4] However, Queen Lili'uokalani had inherited a throne troubled by ever-increasing U.S. power and influence over local Hawaiian affairs. Through a new constitution, she sought to reestablish the primacy of the Hawaiian monarchy. This strategy, however, spurred on her opponents, and with the support of the U.S. military, they enacted a coup, forcing her abdication on January 17, 1893.[5] Undeterred, with support from Kānaka Maoli royalists, Queen Lili'uokalani asserted her right to the throne through cultural as well as political diplomacy.

Early Explorers and U.S. Missionaries in Hawai'i

Even before the tumultuous events of the overthrow, the predecessors of Queen Lili'uokalani, especially Kauikeaouli, or King Kamehameha III (1813–1854), and her brother and direct predecessor King David Kalākaua (1836–1891), encountered European military threats, particularly through incursion on Hawaiian lands.[6] Over many decades, white settlers came to the island kingdom, even before the migration of Protestant missionaries from the

United States in the 1820s. In 1778, British Captain James Cook (1728–1779) and his crew were the first Europeans to reach the Hawaiian archipelago in the Pacific Ocean, which Cook named the Sandwich Islands.

Until recently, most scholars have centered the stories of these explorations through English-language accounts, presenting Hawaiians as passive audiences to the arrival of English captains and crew merchants. Although the outsiders posed significant challenges to Hawaiians, such as the spread of disease, the changes also offered opportunities for them to explore the world on their own terms.[7] Kaʻianaʻahuʻula (1755–1795, generally referred to as Kaʻiana), for example, was an important early Hawaiian explorer who accompanied Captain John Meares (c. 1756–1809) on his travels.[8] While abroad, Kaʻiana made his Hawaiian heritage clear by wearing an ʻahu ʻula (feather cape) and a mahiole (feather helmet); he also bore a spear.[9] The impression he made on non-Hawaiians was so notable that Meares included an engraving of Kaʻiana's portrait in his 1790 book, *Voyages Made in the Years 1788*

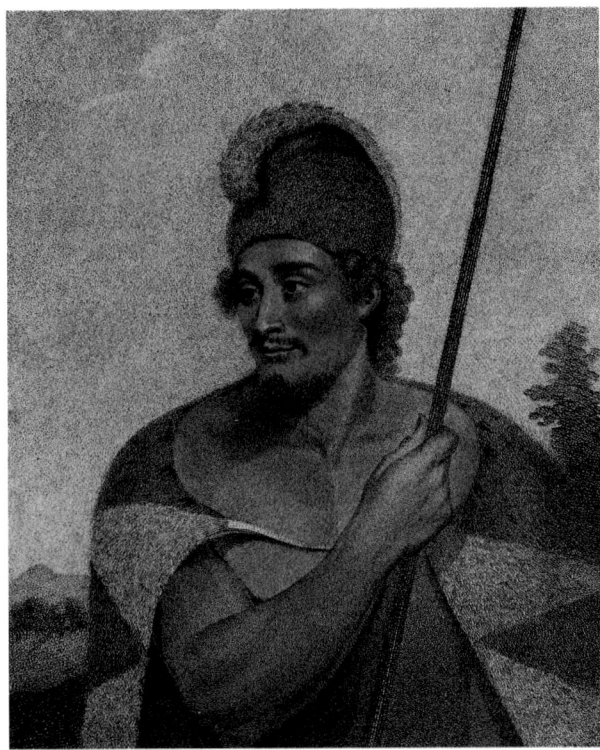

Fig. 1 *Kaʻiana* (c. 1755–1795), by an unidentifed artist, 1790. Reproduced in *Voyages Made in the Years 1788 and 1789, from China to the North West Coast of America* by John Meares. London: Logographic, 1790. University of British Columbia Library, Rare Books and Special Collections

and 1789, from China to the North West Coast of America (fig. 1). The mahiole is depicted with a high crest and sides made of a single color. Regarding the cape, experts believe the pattern of triangles at the edge of the ʻahu ʻula were most likely yellow on a field of red.[10] Between 1787 and 1788, Kaʻiana traveled to China, the Philippines, Palau, and the Pacific Northwest coast of the North American continent.

The arrival of the first U.S. missionaries in Hawaiʻi coincided with a gradual social transition in Hawaiian society, including shifts in religion and land regulation. The first company of missionaries, led by Hiram Bingham (1789–1869) and sponsored by the American Board of Commissioners for Foreign Missions (ABCFM), landed in Hawaiʻi in 1820. King Kamehameha II, known as Liholiho (1797–1824), welcomed the representatives of the mission companies from New England. With his support, the missionaries orchestrated the conversion of Hawaiians to Christianity.[11] The ABCFM was established in 1810 by the General Association of Congregational Churches of Massachusetts, its goal to spread Christianity worldwide.[12] Members introduced literacy, which Hawaiians then spread through their own enthusiastic efforts.[13] Schools such as the Hilo Boarding School were expanded, while others were founded.[14] By the 1830s, the missionaries' influence on the aliʻi, or Hawaiian nobility, was such that businessmen could not lease land without the support of those associated with the ABCFM.[15] The monarchs, several of whom studied with the missionaries, gradually became dependent on members of the mission for financial and political counsel.[16] When the Panic of 1837 diminished the ABCFM's financial support, the missionaries also began to take advantage of Kānaka Maoli labor.[17] The ABCFM continued its mission until 1863, when it handed over its organization to the Hawaiian Evangelical Association (HEA), hoping it would organize churches that were Native-run and led.[18] As time went on, however, it became clear that the members of the HEA felt uncomfortable with Native-led churches, which they believed would undermine the missionaries' power. In fact, Kānaka Maoli balanced their practice of Christianity and their sense of kinship; some native churches, such as Kaumakapili, resisted the overthrow in 1893.[19]

Betsey Stockton and the Stewarts
One early U.S.-born evangelist was Betsey Stockton (fig. 2), a woman whose former enslaver introduced her to the missionaries Charles S. Stewart (1795–1870) and his wife

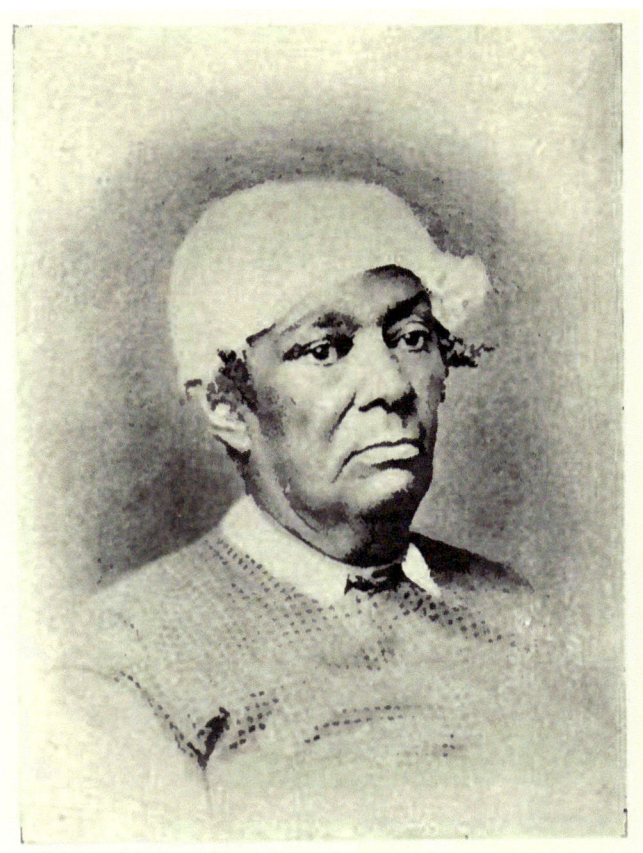

Fig. 2 *Betsey Stockton* (c. 1798–1865), Unidentified photographer, c. 1863. Photograph reproduced in *Portraits of American Protestant Missionaries to Hawaii*. Honolulu: Hawaiian Gazette Co., 1901

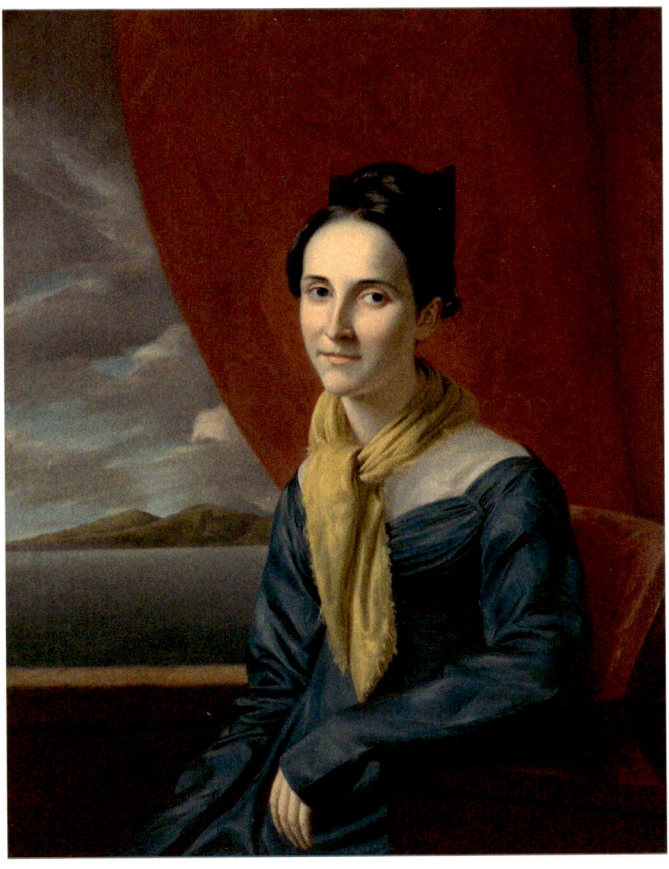

Fig. 3 *Harriet Bradford Tiffany Stewart* (1798–1830), Charles Cromwell Ingham (1796–1863), c. 1822–1823. Oil on canvas; 92.1 × 71.1 cm (36¼ × 28 in.). National Portrait Gallery, Smithsonian Institution; given in honor of Stewart W. Bowers

Harriet Bradford Tiffany Stewart (fig. 3).[20] They arrived with the second company of ABCFM missionaries in 1823, shortly after this portrait of Stewart, by the artist Charles Cromwell Ingham, was made in New York City.[21] Ingham was a neoclassical portraitist who was especially popular among society women. For this painting, the artist portrayed Stewart in front of the hills of Lake Otsego, New York, her beloved adopted hometown.

Stewart was heavily pregnant by the time she boarded the *Thames* to travel to Hawai'i and had secured Stockton to assist her as a companion.[22] Stockton's contract with the ABCFM asked that she "be regarded & treated neither as an equal nor as a servant, but as a humble Christian friend."[23] Charles describes Stockton as "a coloured female, a domestic and assistant Missionary in my own family."[24] Stockton's role as the Stewarts' companion gave

her the opportunity to become a missionary herself. In October 1825, due to Harriet's ill health, the Stewarts departed Hawai'i.

"When you think of me as a stranger in a strange land," Stockton wrote, "think of me still as one who has kind friends, to guide and protect her."[25] Stockton stayed in Hawai'i and continued working there until 1828, teaching in Lāhaina, Maui, at the first school for maka'āinana, or commoners. She later moved to Philadelphia, where she continued teaching but probably did not reunite with the Stewarts before Harriet Stewart's death in 1830.

Stockton lived for another thirty-five years, and this portrait, made after the advent of photography, was taken in Augustus Morand's photography studio in Brooklyn, New York.[26]

The Sugar Trade, the Bayonet Constitution, and the Weakening of the Hawaiian Monarchy

In 1843, through a joint declaration by the British and French governments, the Hawaiian Islands were recognized as an independent state.[27] As early as 1826 and through 1893, the United States had recognized the independence of the Hawaiian Kingdom, entering into treaties of friendship and commercial reciprocity.[28] During this time, King David Kalākaua (1836–1891), whose reign lasted from 1874 to 1891, worked to develop resources to help sustain the Hawaiian economy. However, by the 1870s, economic ties intensified between Hawai'i and the United States, particularly regarding sugar production. On January 30, 1875, Kalākaua signed a Reciprocity Treaty with the United States.[29] The Reciprocity Treaty was a free-trade agreement between the United States and the Hawaiian Kingdom that guaranteed a duty-free market for Hawaiian sugar in exchange for exclusive economic privileges for the United States.[30]

The treaty positioned Kānaka Maoli and U.S. businessmen against one another, fueling bitterness. Organizing among themselves, white businessmen and landowners sought to undermine the monarchy. Those in the Independent Party joined forces with some Kānaka Maoli to criticize Kalākaua's policies.[31] Little by little, they built up their power and eventually formed the Hawaiian League, and sometimes referred to themselves as the Committee of Nine.[32] Founded in early 1887, the Hawaiian League was led by U.S. lawyer and businessman Lorrin Thurston (fig. 4). The grandson of missionaries who had arrived in Hawai'i in 1820, Thurston studied law at Columbia University under John W. Burgess (1844–1931). A leader in Social Darwinist thinking, Burgess emphasized "Teutonic superiority in the art of government."[33] Bolstered by his fervent belief in white supremacy, Thurston masterminded the overthrow of the Hawaiian monarchy. In 1886, he became a member of the Hawaiian legislature as a representative of the islands of Moloka'i and Lāna'i. By 1893, Thurston's influence in Hawai'i had become substantial.

After secretly forming the Hawaiian League, Thurston united it with the Honolulu Rifles, a white male civil militia. Sensing impending violence, King Kalākaua dismissed his cabinet on June 28, 1887. Two days later, a public meeting led by Sanford Ballard Dole, a justice of the Supreme Court of Hawai'i, imposed several resolutions and forced Kalākaua to come to a decision (fig. 5). On July 6, 1887,

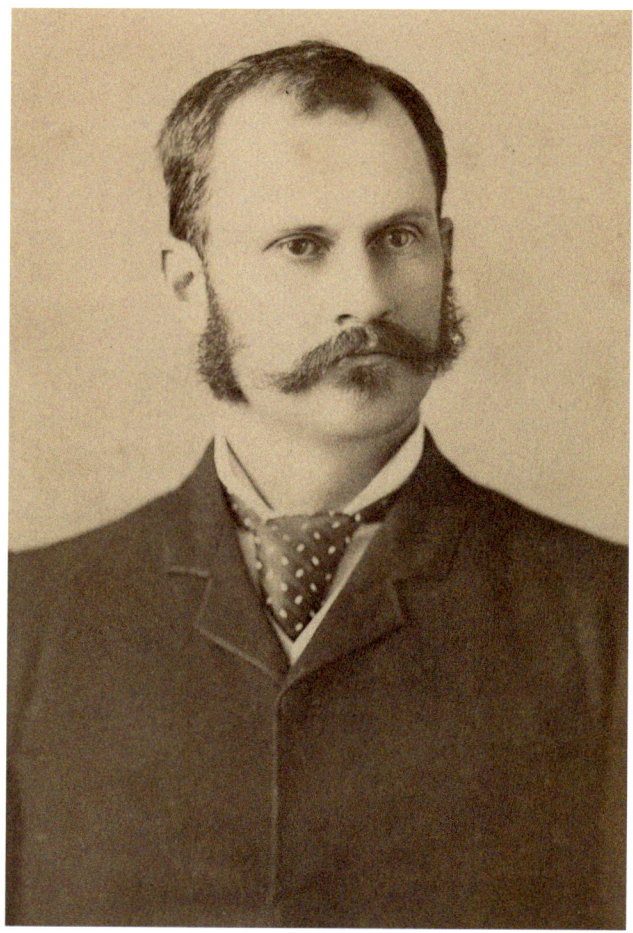

Fig. 4 *Lorrin Thurston* (1858–1931), Unidentified photographer, c. 1895. Albumen silver print; 14 × 8.9 cm (5½ × 3½ in.). National Portrait Gallery, Smithsonian Institution

under threat of U.S. military force, Kalākaua signed an amendment to the 1864 Constitution of Hawai'i and swore to uphold it. This amendment has since been referred to as the "Bayonet Constitution," demonstrating that purposeful language was also part of Hawaiian resistance.

The Bayonet Constitution drastically reduced the power of Kānaka Maoli in government and the authority of the Hawaiian monarch. In fact, the Bayonet Constitution gave the cabinet more power than the king. Thurston was named minister of the interior in the king's new cabinet.[34] Kalākaua could no longer make legislation on his own; his veto could be overridden; and he no longer had control of the military. The Bayonet Constitution also took away land rights from Kānaka Maoli.[35] Further, it expanded the right to vote to all males over twenty who could read English, Hawaiian, or a European language, and who had resided in Hawai'i at least one year—including non-citizens. However, the voters had to meet a financial requirement, which excluded most Kānaka Maoli. Asians could not vote at all.[36] Essentially, the new constitution shifted power from Kānaka Maoli to the U.S., British, and German colonists, who totaled less than five percent of Hawai'i's population.[37] In a devastating blow to the monarchy, Kalākaua was now a mere figurehead.

During this political turmoil, the U.S. Congress had been debating the details of renewal for the 1875 Reciprocity Treaty. With the new cabinet in place following the Bayonet Constitution, a controversial amendment to the treaty, which had been debated since January 1887, was passed: The United States gained exclusive right to enter Pearl Harbor on the island of O'ahu and to establish a coaling and repair station for use by U.S. vessels.[38] With reluctance, King Kalākaua signed the treaty into effect on October 20, 1887. The Reciprocity Treaty of 1887 supported private land ownership and facilitated large-scale sugar production through the plantation system, primarily benefitting settlers of Anglo-American and European descent.[39]

Lili'uokalani, Kalākaua's sister and heir apparent, would later denounce the 1887 constitution. In her 1898 memoir, she wrote, "men of foreign birth . . . forced the king, without any appeal to the suffrages of the people, to sign a constitution of their own preparation, a document which deprived the sovereign of all power, made him a mere tool in their hands, and practically took away the franchise from the Hawaiian race."[40] By contrast, Thurston justified the rebelliousness of the Bayonet Constitution. He wrote, "Unquestionably, the constitution was not in accordance with law; neither was the Declaration of Independence from Great Britain. Both were revolutionary documents, which had to be forcibly effected and forcibly maintained."[41]

By 1889, Hawaiian royalists became increasingly focused on reinstating their sovereignty from the Bayonet Constitution and fending off annexation. The Hui Kālai'āina, an organization dedicated to maintaining Hawaiian control of the nation, developed as a political force. Its members formed an alliance with a mostly white organization, the Mechanics and Workingmen's Political Protective Union. The two groups made up the National Reform Party and gained several

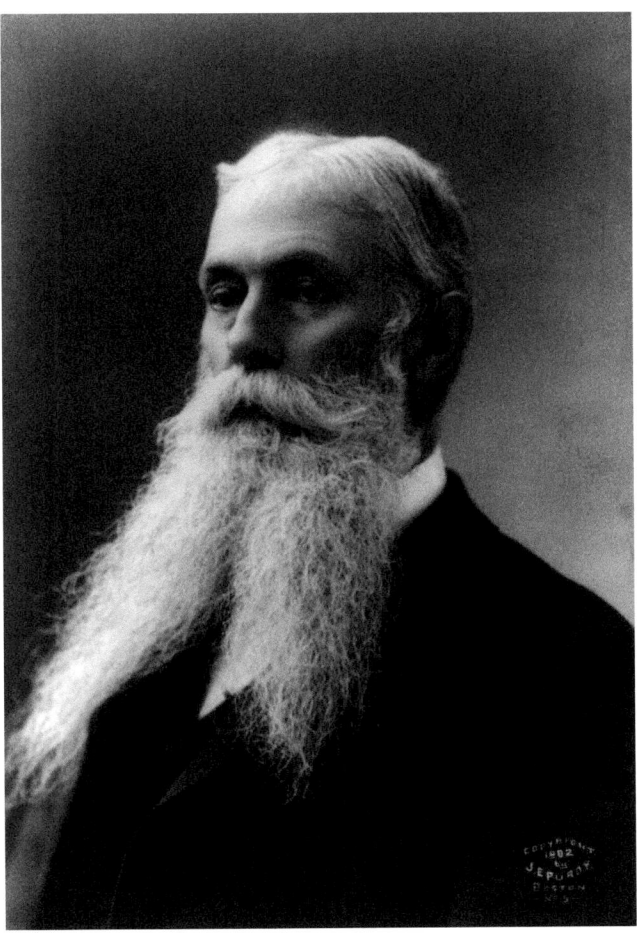

Fig. 5 *Sanford Ballard Dole* (1844–1926), James E. Purdy (1858–1933), 1902. Digitized negative. Library of Congress, Prints and Photographs Division, Washington, DC

Hawaiian-held seats in the government in the election of 1890. They petitioned for a new constitution in 1892, which led to more turmoil when Thurston and Dole formed an even stronger coalition.[42]

Meanwhile, stalwart expansionists in the United States, including Secretary of State James G. Blaine (1830–1893) and John L. Stevens (1820–1895), attempted to negotiate the annexation of Hawai'i.[43] Stevens became the U.S. minister plenipotentiary and envoy extraordinary to Hawai'i in late 1889. As the United States became increasingly interested in annexing Hawai'i, Kalākaua faced enormous pressure. However beneficial the Reciprocity Treaty of 1875 was for the Hawaiian economy, the subsequent McKinley Tariff Act of 1890 ended all profits.[44] Stevens wrote that the tariff "would be the virtual

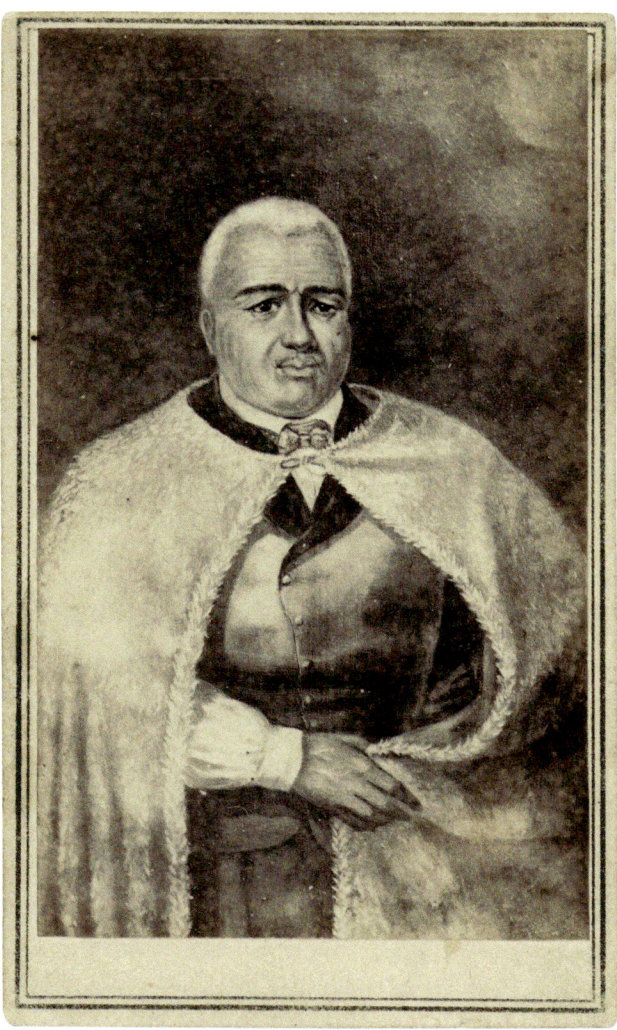

Fig. 6 *King Kamehameha I* (1736–1819), Henry L. Chase (1831–1901), c. 1880. Albumen silver print of portrait by James Gay Sawkins after Louis Choris, 1850, 9.1 × 5.5 cm (3⁹⁄₁₆ × 2³⁄₁₆ in.). National Portrait Gallery, Smithsonian Institution; gift of the Bernice Pauahi Bishop Museum

Kalākaua's Endeavor to Sustain Hawaiian Heritage

During his reign, Kalākaua also sought to embrace and sustain Hawaiian culture and traditions. In 1886, he founded the Hale Nauā Society, an institution whose mission was to collect, study, and revive Hawaiian practices, including featherwork.[47] Hawaiian featherwork, especially garments such as ʻahu ʻula, or cloaks and capes; mahiole, or helmets; lei, or garlands; and kāhili, or feather standards or staffs, were owned and displayed by the aliʻi—including Kaʻiana, as noted above. Kamehameha I wore an ʻahu ʻula in this portrait (fig. 6). For the regalia, the feathers were retrieved from native forest birds, such as the ʻapapane (*Himatione sanguinea*), the ʻiʻiwi (*Vestiaria coccinea*), the mamo (*Drepanis pacifica*), and the kuaiʻi ʻoʻo (*Moho nobilis*, now extinct). Primarily red and yellow with black accents, these garments occasionally featured green as well.[48]

One such object was the ʻahu ʻula (the Kalākaua Cape), which was made by Maria Kealaulaokalani Lane Ena (1862–1924) from the scarlet feathers of the ʻiʻiwi and the lemon-yellow and black feathers of the ʻoʻo in a three-crescent pattern on the back, with one crescent split in half, meant to be connected when tied in the front (fig. 7).[49] The cape is made of olonā (*Touchardia latifolia*) fiber netting connected in straight rows, with pieces joined and cut to form the desired shape. Ena attached the feathers to the netting in small bundles and arranged them in overlapping rows, beginning at the lower edge to create patterns. Scholars think that this cape was the last to be made with traditional materials.[50]

Capes were among the most important symbols of prestige in Hawaiʻi, associated only with individuals of the highest rank.[51] Full cloaks were even rarer, worn exclusively by the highest-ranking chiefs and monarchs on ceremonial occasions.[52] For example, in order to counter claims that he had insufficient genealogical authority, Kalākaua and his advisors included numerous featherwork objects in his coronation ceremony.[53] He may have worn or displayed this feather cloak on the royal throne, as the ʻahu ʻula had become known as the "robe of state" by the mid-nineteenth century.[54] The ʻahu ʻula was made in half and full sizes. The latter is displayed in this portrait of Liliʻuokalani, which may have been taken in 1874 when Kalākaua named her as heir apparent. By posing next to a glorious, full-size ʻahu ʻula draped over the Hawaiian throne, the princess signaled her royalty and status as the

annulment of the reciprocity treaty and the destruction of the prosperity of the islands," and he was right.[45] Attempting a political power play, Blaine used the 1890 tariff to coerce Kalākaua, saying that he would give the same subsidies to sugar planters in Hawaiʻi as in the United States if the king would grant Blaine the right to the following: to speak for Hawaiʻi in foreign affairs, to land troops to quell disturbances, and to veto all treaties between Hawaiʻi and any other country (for example, Britain, France, and Japan). Unhappy, Kalākaua noted in his copy of the treaty draft, "This amounts to a Protectorate."[46]

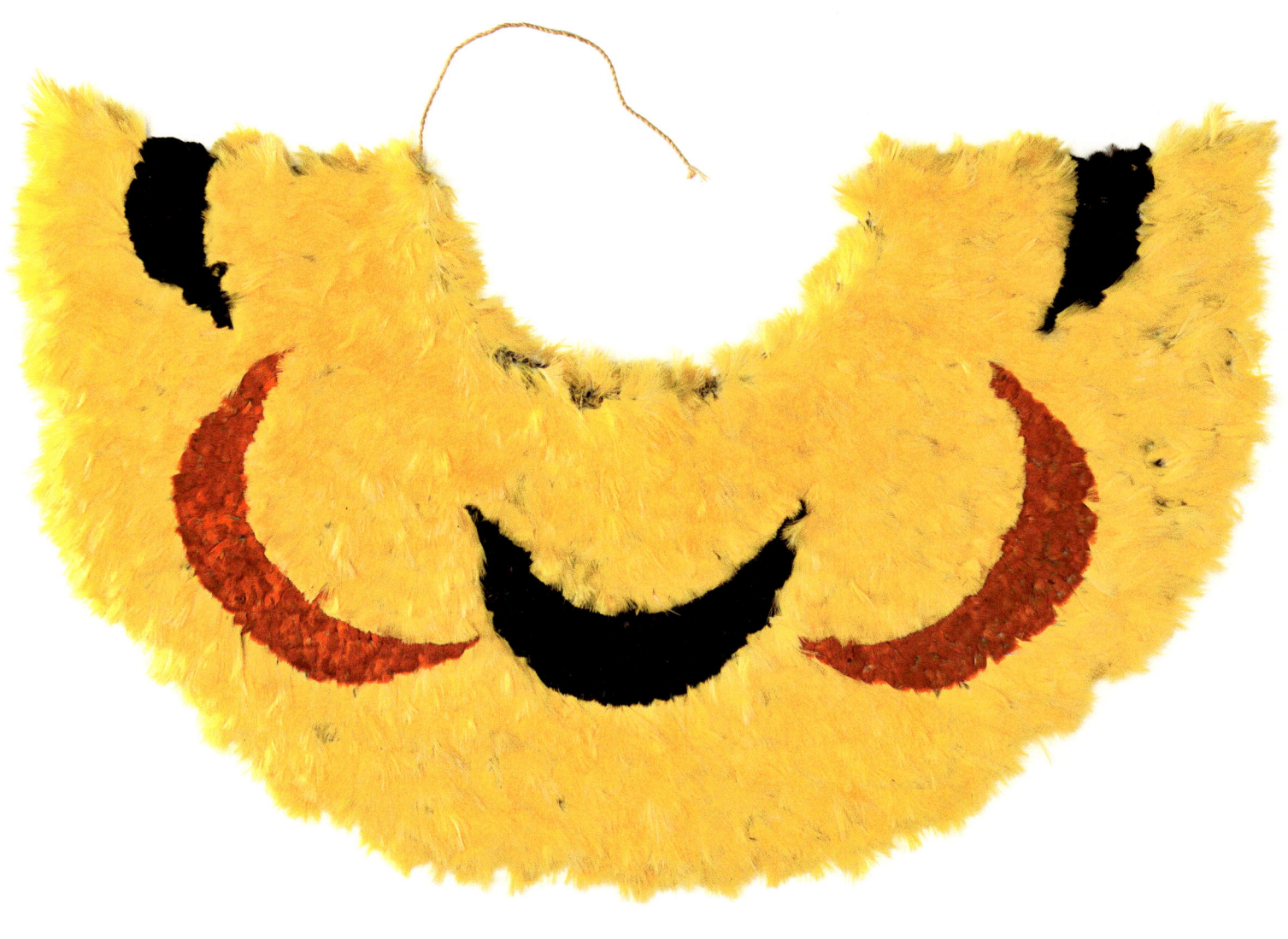

Fig. 7 *'Ahu 'ula* (The Kalākaua Cape), Maria Kealaulaokalani Lane Ena
(1862–1924), Late nineteenth century. Red ʻiʻiwi feathers, yellow and black
ʻōʻō feathers, and olonā fiber; 76.2 × 193 cm (30 × 76 in.). Department of
Anthropology, National Museum of Natural History, Smithsonian Institution

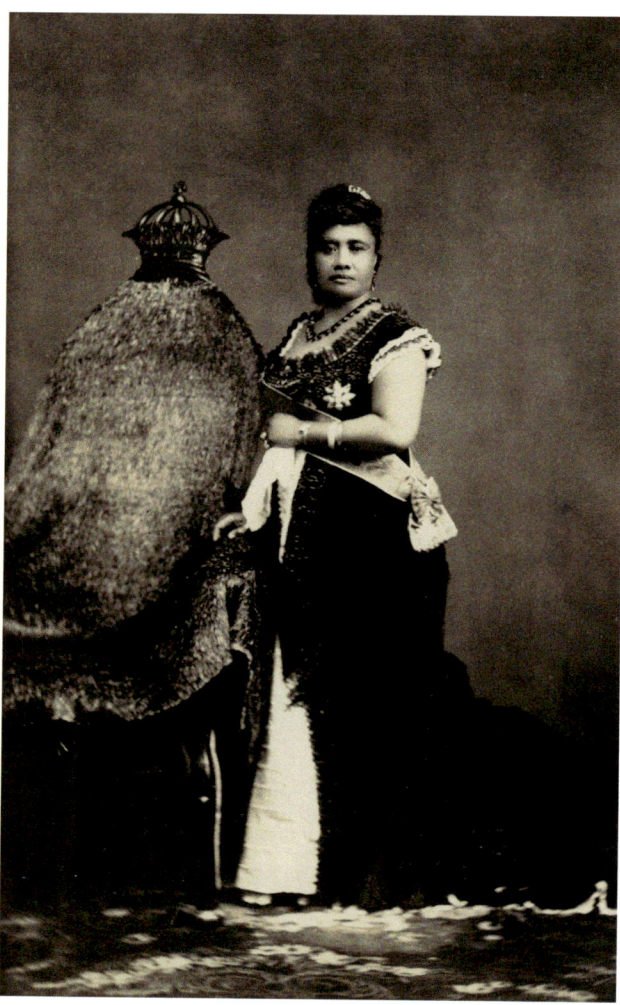

Fig. 8 *Liliʻuokalani, Heir Apparent, Standing next to a Feathered Throne,* Unidentified photographer, pre-1880s. Modern copy of original gelatin silver print; 15.2 × 10.2 cm (6 × 4 in.). Hawaiʻi State Archives

his subsequent world tour. His building of the modern structure, the ʻIolani Palace, was also part of that program of validating his monarchy internationally, for it had electricity before the White House in Washington, DC. Despite his broad use of European markers of power for self-validation, Kalākaua was intent on uplifting Kānaka Maoli culture.[56]

The Queen Reigns

After King Kalākaua's death, Queen Liliʻuokalani ascended to the throne on January 29, 1891, and immediately began organizing a new constitution to restore power to the kingdom and to Kānaka Maoli. Like her brother, she sought ways to reinforce Hawaiian pride through material culture, as well as to validate the monarchy in the eyes of Westerners even as Anglo-Americans undermined her power.[57] One way to assert authority was through photographic portraits.

Displaying a profound understanding of the conventions of European and U.S. grand manner portraiture, the queen acquired a full-length, life-size portrait in 1892. She likely viewed portraiture as a means to assert her right to the throne and legitimacy as head of state (fig. 9).[58] The artist, William Cogswell (1819–1903), a neoclassical painter renowned for an important 1869 White House commission under President Ulysses S. Grant, was working in Hawaiʻi at the time.[59] Born in Sandusky, New York, the self-taught Cogswell nurtured his interest in art by first working in a paint mixing factory in Buffalo.[60] He established a studio in New York City but moved often during his lifetime, living in Wisconsin, Hawaiʻi, and California. In 1879, and from 1890 through 1892, Cogswell established himself in Honolulu, where he painted portraits of the ʻaliʻi and other notable Hawaiians.[61]

By synthesizing conventions of royal portraiture and U.S. presidential portraiture, Cogswell made a decisive statement about the legitimacy of the queen's rule at a time when the fate of monarchy appeared uncertain. As in her photographic portrait, which was likely taken when she was named heir apparent, Liliʻuokalani stands next to the Hawaiian throne, with adornments that speak to her royal status.[62] Attached to her dress is a badge and the breast star of the Order of Kalākaua and the Royal Family Order, which was conferred by the head of a royal family to their female relatives.[63] She also wears a sash in the proper combination for a Knight Grand Cross, the most senior grade of seven British orders of chivalry.[64] Royal orders are

heir apparent (fig. 8). By using ʻahu ʻula in such displays of Hawaiian sovereignty, by the end of the century, featherwork had taken on the mantle of resistance as a powerful symbol of the Hawaiian Kingdom.

As discussed in the first chapter of this volume, during his reign, Kalākaua bridged Kānaka Maoli traditional culture with European and Asian circles of power. Some might consider these realms to be diametrically opposed.[55] Diplomacy, however, was Kalākaua's goal, and he sought legitimizing symbols of his monarchy. To promote Hawaiʻi abroad, he courted international heads of state, presenting himself as a cosmopolitan leader during his visit to the United States, in 1874 and 1875, and

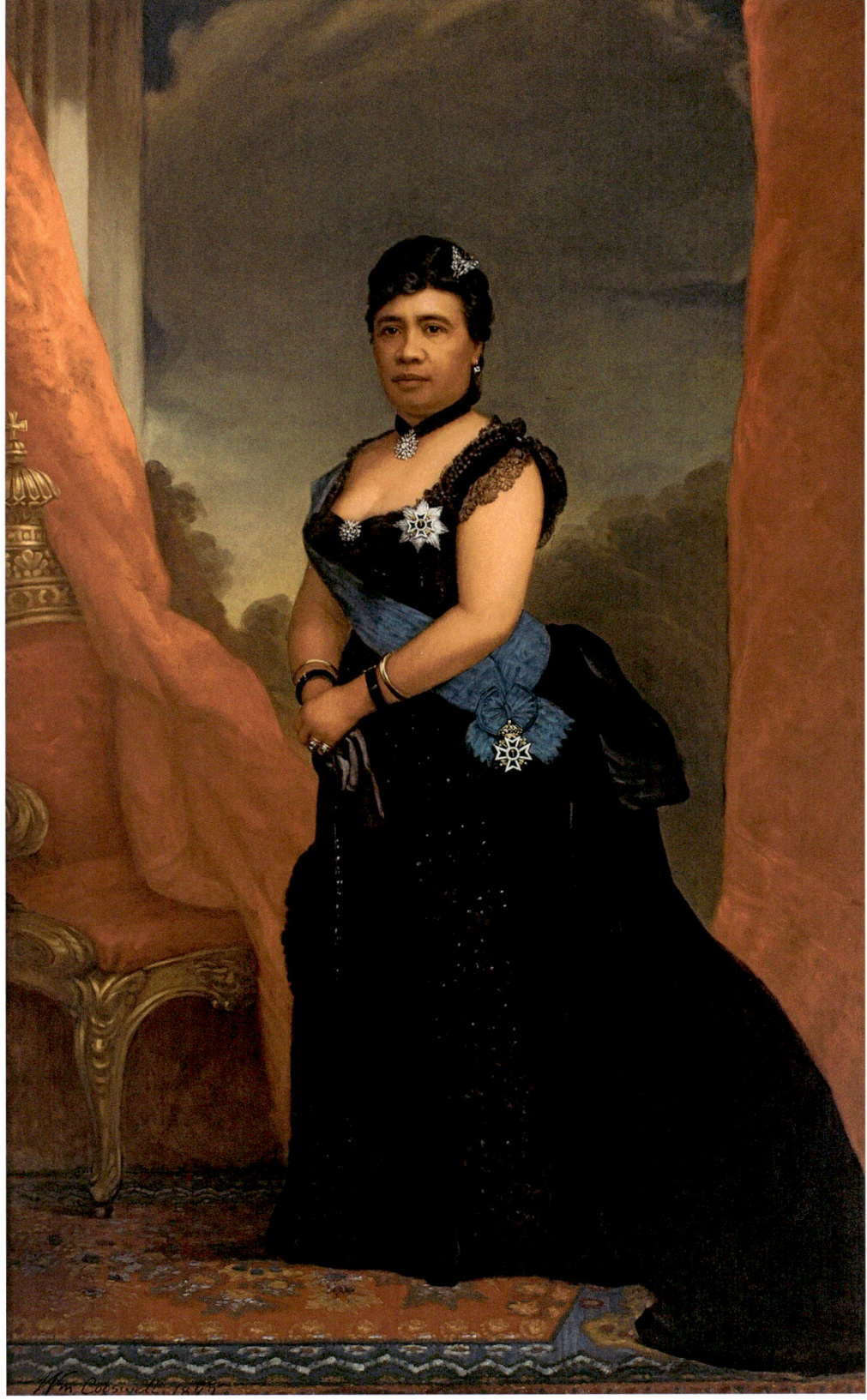

Fig. 9 *Queen Liliʻuokalani* (1838–1917), William F. Cogswell (1819–1903), c. 1891–1892. Oil on canvas; 243.8 × 182.9 cm (96 × 72 in.). Hawaiʻi State Archives

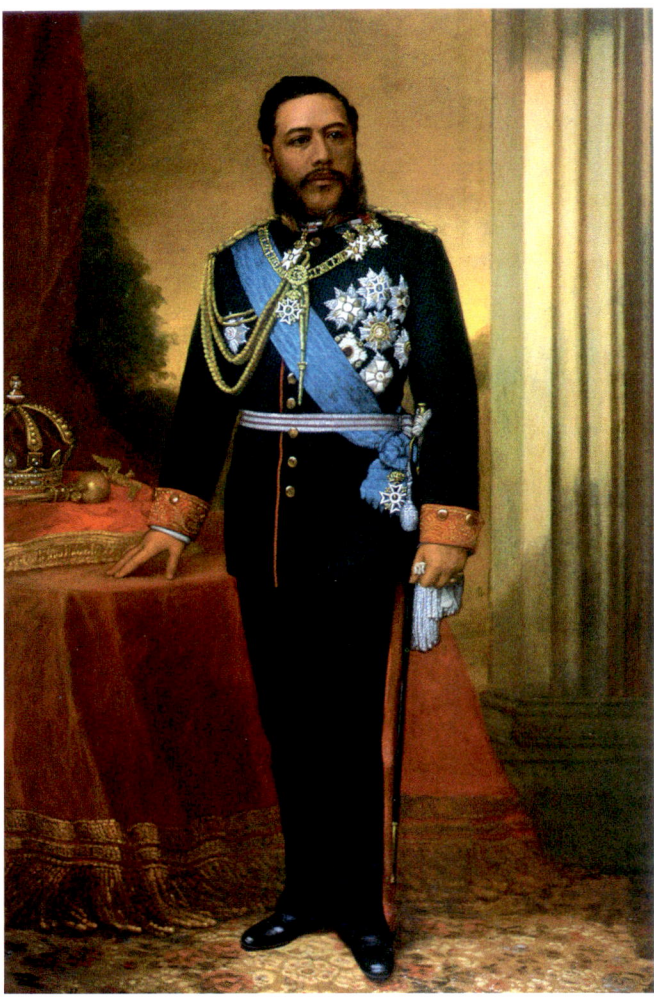

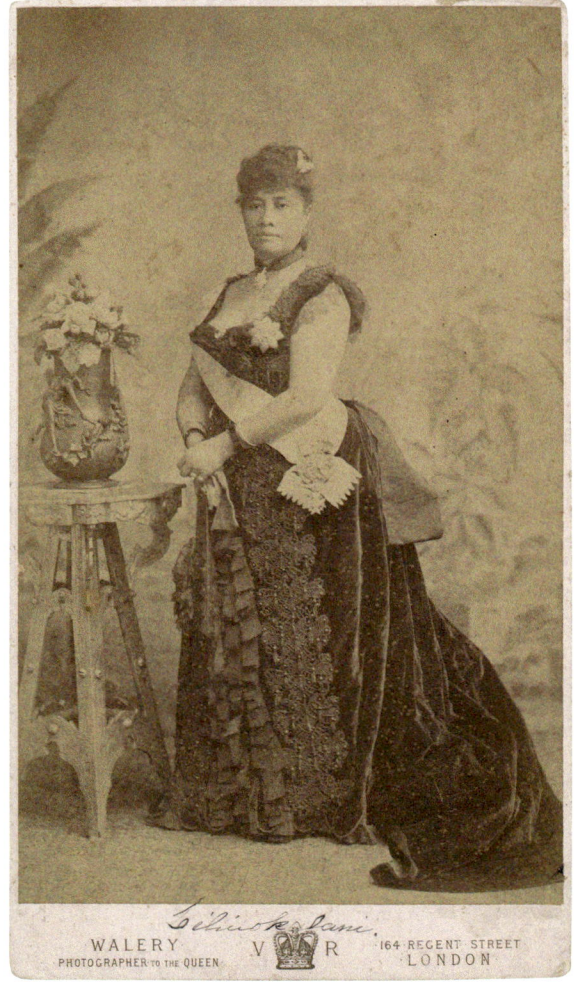

Fig. 10 *King David Kalākaua* (1836–1891), William F. Cogswell (1819–1903), 1891. Oil on canvas; 243.8 × 182.9 cm (96 × 72 in.). Hawai'i State Archives

Fig. 11 *Lili'uokalani at Queen Victoria's Golden Jubilee*, Walery Photographers to the Queen, 1887. Albumen silver print; 33 × 17.8 cm (13 × 7 in.). Hawai'i State Archives

particularly significant, as they acknowledge cultural and political relationships between monarchies, and recognition among leaders. The 1891 posthumous portrait that Cogswell painted of King Kalākaua, for example, features the stars of four Hawaiian orders, as well as several different foreign orders including two from Great Britain, one from Japan, and one from Prussia (fig. 10).[65] Kalākaua rests his right hand on a table upon which the Hawaiian crown and scepter rest—two European signifiers of royalty that Kalākaua had co-opted for the Hawaiian Kingdom.

Although an article in the *Pacific Commercial Advertiser* reported that the queen sat for Cogswell, the artist almost certainly worked from a photograph of the queen in an

exquisite black ribbon dress that was taken in London in 1887, when she was attending Queen Victoria's Golden Jubilee as a fellow royal (fig. 11).[66] The Jubilee, held on June 21, was not only to celebrate the fiftieth anniversary of Queen Victoria's accession but also to provide an occasion for monarchs to meet—and network.[67] Then Princess Lili'uokalani attended with Queen Kapi'olani (1834–1899), the consort of King Kalākaua, and they undoubtedly were on a diplomatic mission, considering the challenging circumstances faced by the Hawaiian monarchy: The king would be forced to sign the Bayonet Constitution in mere weeks, and the 1887 Reciprocity Treaty was under discussion.

Accordingly, during this gathering, Princess Liliʻuokalani and Queen Kapiʻolani chose their attire and jewelry with great care. Liliʻuokalani's velvet gown is trimmed with lace and appliqué, and the back bustle is topped with a wide ribbon surmounting an elaborate train. Modeled after the latest European styles, Liliʻuokalani's attire proves that Hawaiian fashion was equal to that of Europeans.[68] In addition to the royal orders, her jewelry, which includes gemstones at her ears and a ribbon and pendant around her neck, is meaningful. She had bought the diamond butterfly adorning her hair in London in 1887 as well.[69] As queen, Liliʻuokalani must have appreciated that in 1891, Cogswell painted her wearing the same dress and hairpin as she did in 1887 at the British court. This choice, it seems, would have signaled that her monarchy was uncontested in the eyes of other kingdoms. That earlier portrait was popular, too, as two thousand copies of the 1887 photograph were made around early 1892.[70]

The painting may take its cues from the photograph, but the differences between them are telling. While the photograph sets the queen against a decorative backdrop customary of nineteenth-century photography studios, Cogswell's classical column and plush burgundy drapery relates to both Hyacinthe Rigaud's portrait of Louis XIV (fig. 12) and Gilbert Stuart's "Lansdowne" portrait of George Washington (fig. 13). In each of the three paintings, the head of state wears luxurious clothing: Louis XIV is draped in coronation robes of ermine furs and velvet brocade; Washington wears a black velvet gentleman's suit; and the queen is dignified in her velvet haute couture dress. However, their gestures, in particular, demonstrate their unique approaches to power. The king of France assumes an arrogant pose, with his left hand on his hip to

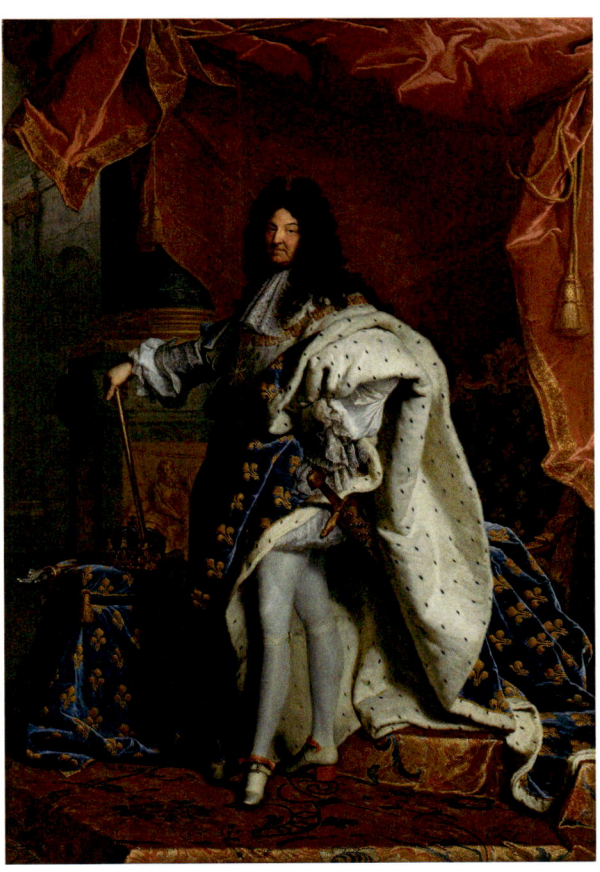

Fig. 12 *Louis XIV* (1638–1715), Hyacinthe Rigaud (1659–1743), 1701. Oil on canvas; 2.8 × 1.9 m (9 ft., 2 in. × 6 ft., 3 in.). Musée du Louvre

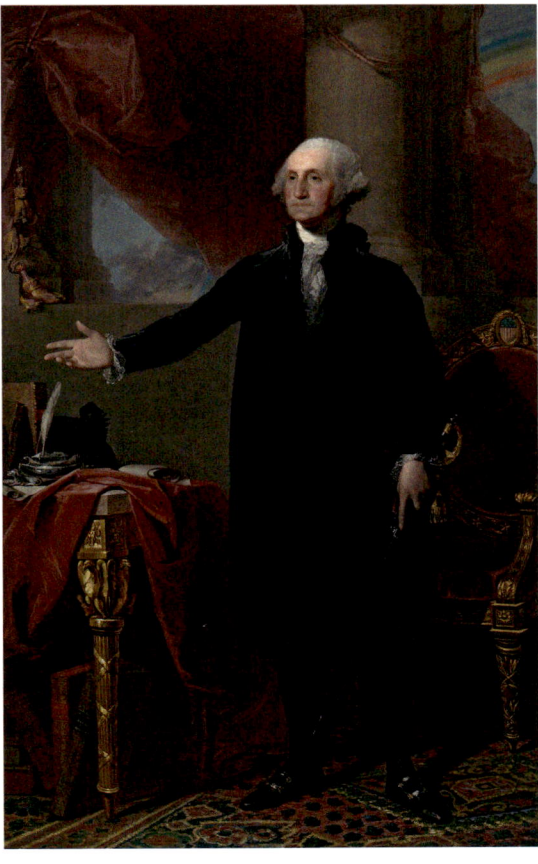

Fig. 13 *George Washington* (Lansdowne Portrait) (1732–1799), Gilbert Stuart (1755–1828), 1796. Oil on canvas; 247.6 × 158.7 cm (97½ × 62½ in.). National Portrait Gallery, Smithsonian Institution; acquired as a gift to the nation through the generosity of the Donald W. Reynolds Foundation

expose his sword. In his right, he bears a scepter that points down to a crown resting on a table, linking two monarchal symbols. The president of the United States outstretches his right hand in a gesture of appeal to the viewer, while his left hand holds a sword emblematic of his role as commander of the American army against the British during the Revolution. Washington's oratorical pose alludes to his address to Congress on December 8, 1795, when he implored his countrymen to support the Jay Treaty (effective February 29, 1796), a negotiation that was much more in Britain's favor, economically, than that of the United States.[71] The treaty had been signed and ratified, but the House of Representatives would not release the funds to carry out its provisions. In effect, Washington argued that unless these funds were released, another war with England would likely ensue. Because the power lay in the hands of the people, however, he is not shown commanding them but, rather, appealing to a desire for peace.[72]

Like Washington, the queen of Hawai'i also wanted to avoid bloodshed and did everything in her power to avoid war. She exhibits both restraint and decorum, demurely holding her gloves before her in a gesture that is more protective than that of Washington but less haughty than that of Louis XIV. Yet her confidence and self-possession are clear in her direct gaze at the viewer. Her assuredness communicates the mana wahine, or "women's power," that was intrinsic to Kānaka Maoli society before European contact.[73] Indeed, women held the rank of chiefs as early as the fourteenth century in Hawai'i, and positions of power were distributed according to rank and prestige, rather than gender.[74] Lili'uokalani's confident composure reveals an inherent power—not one justified by scepter, sword, or crown. A constitutional monarch, she also strikes a different tone than that of an absolute ruler, reflecting the social atmosphere of her kingdom. Hawai'i had long been multiethnic in its citizenry, and the 1852 Ke Kumukānāwai o Ko Hawai'i Pae 'Āina (Hawaiian Constitution) had granted universal suffrage to all men, regardless of race.[75]

Cogswell's full-length portrait of the queen rivals the Rigaud and Stuart portraits in both flourish and dignity. Through the Western genre of state portraiture, commonly reserved for European or Euro-American (most often male) heads of state, the queen's portrait signified her power as a Kānaka Maoli female head of state. In a calculated move, the queen's purchase of this portrait and

its subsequent installation in the 'Iolani Palace with that of her brother, King Kalākaua, symbolizes a long cultural tradition of appropriation and subversion of Western dominant languages by colonial subjects as a deliberately anti-colonial strategy.[76]

The Overthrow of the Queen

Queen Lili'uokalani's resistance to U.S. imperialism extended beyond the soft diplomacy of portraiture and included legislative action. Disappointed after a failed vote on the bill that proposed a new constitution, she made it known that she meant to promulgate a new constitution on January 14, 1893.[77] Consequently, Minister John L. Stevens, Lorrin Thurston, and Sanford Dole conspired with former members of the Hawaiian League to depose the queen and overthrow the monarchy for the purpose of annexation to the United States.[78] On January 16, Stevens authorized forces from the battleship USS Boston to land "to secure the safety of American life and property."[79] In doing so, he violated both his diplomatic authority as well as international law, and was almost immediately removed as the U.S. diplomat. The troops, comprising 162 men equipped with small arms and artillery, disarmed 270 Royal Hawaiian guardsmen (fig. 14). Queen Lili'uokalani sensed disaster and worked to find a non-violent solution, writing in her diary, "For we are without arms, and they are armed to the teeth."[80]

In reaction to Lili'uokalani's promulgation of a new constitution, on January 16, 1893, the U.S. naval forces from the USS Boston brought Gatling guns (the precursor of the machine gun), 14,000 rounds of ammunition, two revolving cannons, and—clearly expecting resistance—a hospital unit. The queen and her ministers, Samuel Parker and William Henry Cornwell, responded by publishing broadsides in Hawaiian and English, declaring, "Authority is given for the assurance that any changes desired in the fundamental law of the land will be sought only by methods provided in the Constitution itself" (figs. 15 and 16). This served only to enrage Stevens and Thurston.

Although Minister Stevens authorized the U.S. Navy to enforce the overthrow, the annexationists were led by Thurston. In January 1893, Thurston secretly contacted the members of the Hawaiian League (the cabinet members forced onto Kalākaua when he signed the Bayonet Constitution of 1887) and organized the "Committee of Safety," or, the Committee of Annexation (fig. 17). A coup d'état displaced Queen Lili'uokalani from her throne on

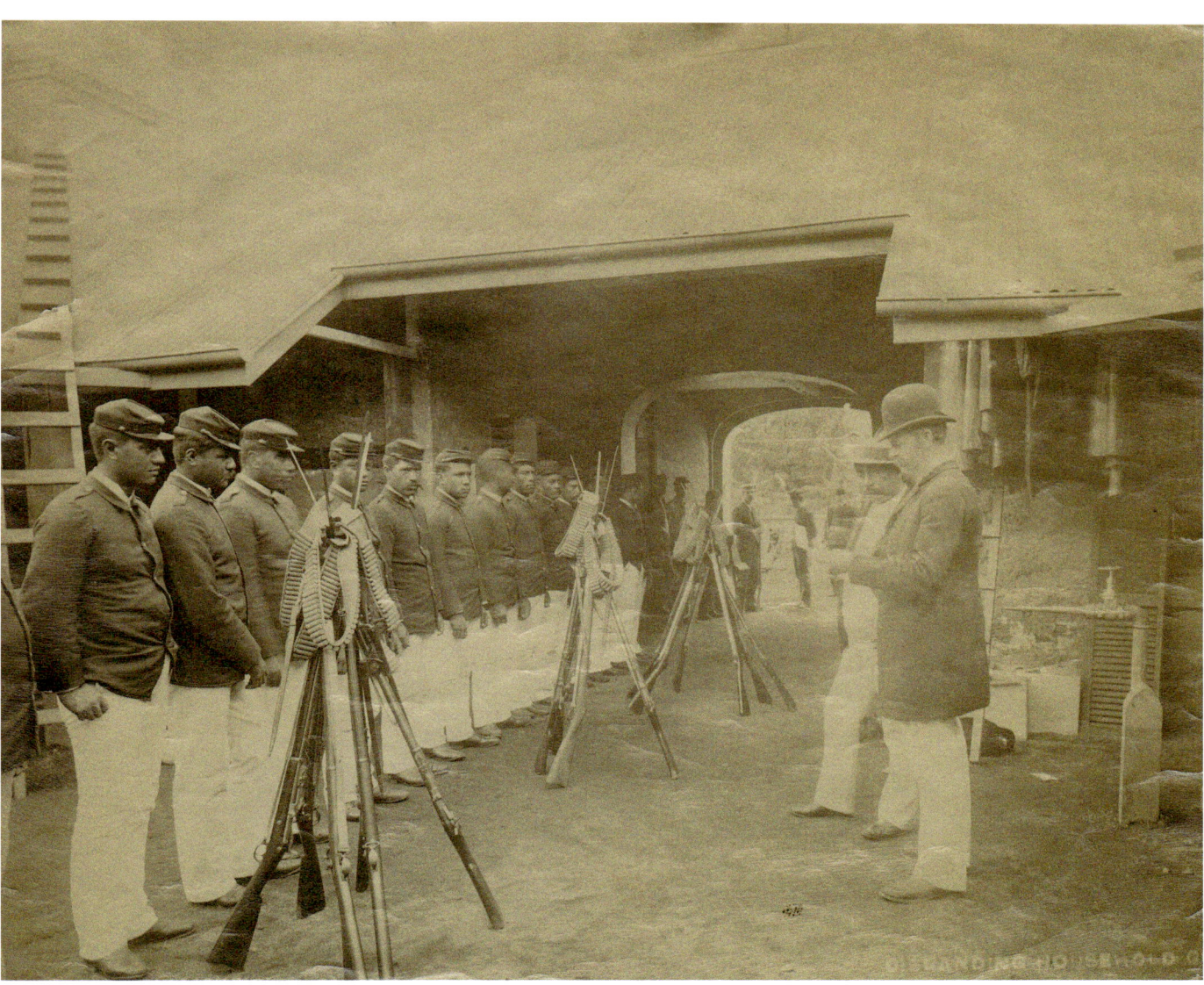

January 17, 1893, and installed the provisional government. Choosing her words carefully, Queen Liliʻuokalani relinquished her power not to the counterfeit "provisional government" led by Thurston but to the "superior force of the United States of America."[81] By positioning the matter as one concerning the United States and international law, the queen stalled the completion of the overthrow.[82] She later wrote, "There was no more for me to do but retire in peace to my private residence, there to await the decision of the United States government. This I did, and cautioned the leaders of my people to avoid riot or resistance, and to await tranquilly, as I was doing, the result of my appeal to the power to whom alone I had yielded my authority."[83]

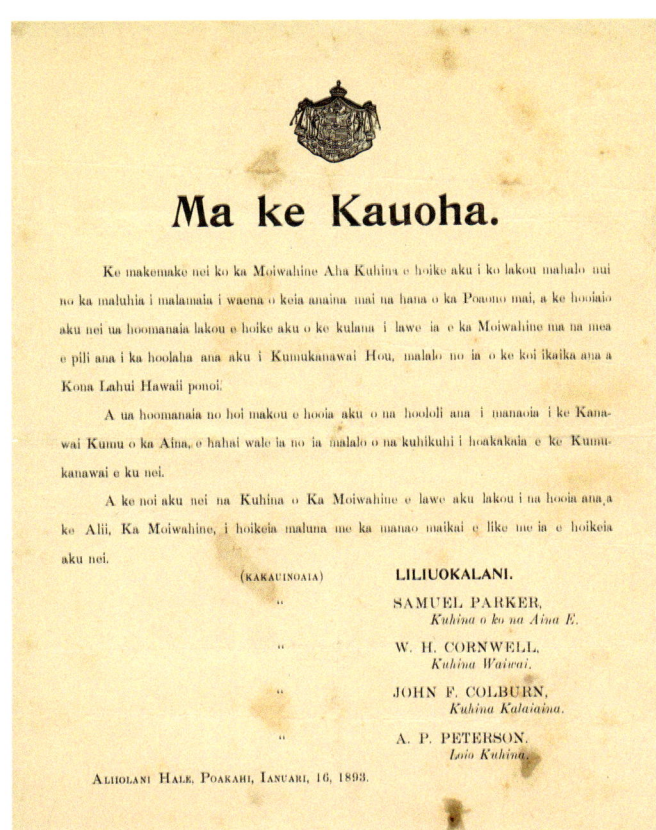

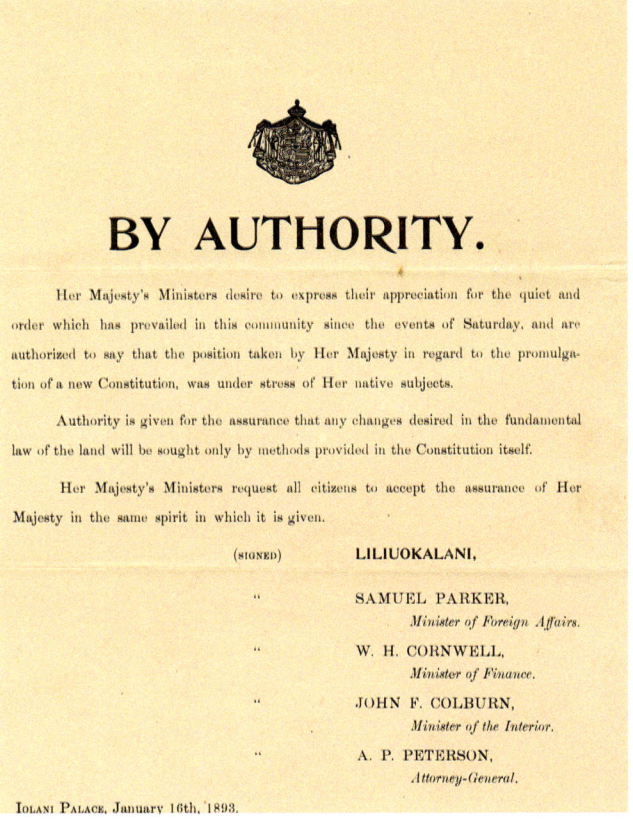

Fig. 15 *Ma ke Kauoha—Statement issued by Queen Liliʻuokalani and her Cabinet regarding the drafting of a new constitution,* January 16, 1893. Printed paper; 25.4 × 20.3 cm (10 × 8 in.). Hawaiian Broadsides Collection. Hawaiian Mission Houses Historic Site and Archives

Fig. 16 *By Authority—Statement issued by Queen Liliʻuokalani and her Cabinet regarding the drafting of a new constitution,* January 16, 1893. Printed paper; 25.4 × 20.3 cm (10 × 8 in.). W. O. Smith Collection. Hawaiian Mission Houses Historic Site and Archives

The queen's diplomacy led President Grover Cleveland (1837–1908) to order an official investigation of the rebellion, to be carried out by Georgia congressman James H. Blount (1837–1903), whom he sent to Hawaiʻi for several months.[84] As Blount's investigation threatened the power of this new, illegal government, its leaders found an ally in John T. Morgan (1824–1907), a U.S. senator from Alabama and a fervent imperialist. Morgan made a separate investigation and essentially wrote a manifesto for the annexation of Hawaiʻi, which came to be known as the Morgan Report.[85] Although he did not convince his fellow lawmakers to annex Hawaiʻi, Congress voted not to intervene on behalf of Queen Liliʻuokalani.[86] The matter of restoring

her sovereignty remained unresolved. Finally, President Cleveland reinstated the queen and her cabinet of ministers, on condition that she would grant amnesty to the insurgents who attempted the coup d'état. On December 18, 1893, they reached an agreement, one that was recognized under international law as a treaty.[87] However, it was not put into place. Liliʻuokalani was forced to retreat to her estate in Waikiki and later to her private residence of Washington Place in Honolulu. She was never allowed to return to the throne to lead the Hawaiian Kingdom as its sovereign. Instead, Dole stepped down from the Hawaiian Supreme Court and replaced Thurston as the head of the provisional government.[88] Symbols of Liliʻuokalani's diminished status include a two-cent stamp with her image altered by the provisional government. This portrait of the queen, elegantly adorned with her diamond butterfly hair comb and necklace, is marred by a red stamp with the words "Provisional Government 1893" (see p. 16). This act of iconoclasm powerfully symbolizes the usurpation of a political structure.[89]

On July 4, 1894, the provisional government announced a new constitution and declared itself the "Republic of

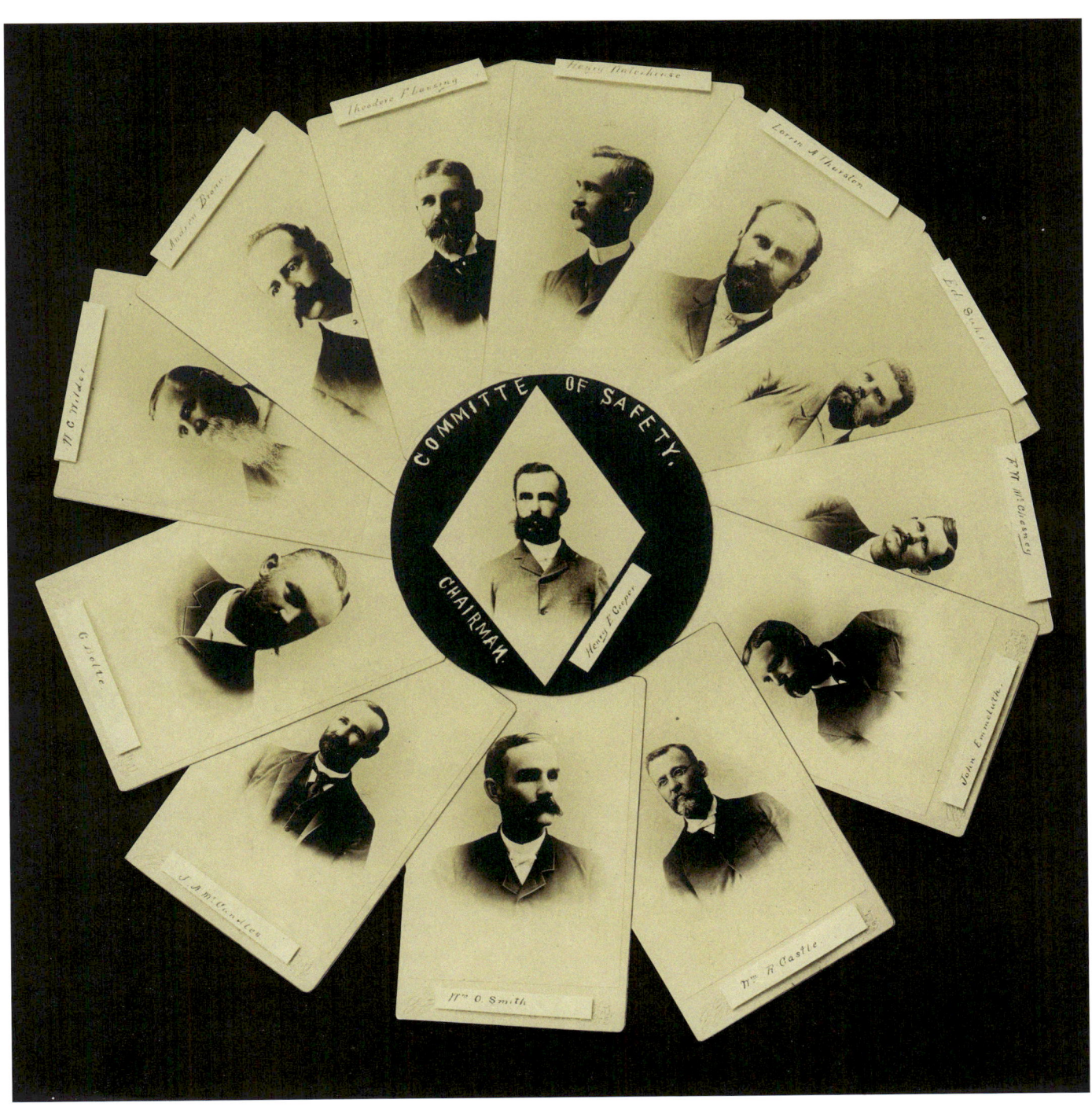

Fig. 17 *Committee of Safety*, Unidentified photographer, 1893. Gelatin silver print; 17.8 × 22.2 cm (7 × 8¾ in.). Hawai'i State Archives

Fig. 18 *Petition against the Annexation of Hawai'i*, Hawaiian Patriotic League, 1897. Ink on paper; 35.6 × 21.4 cm (14 × 8⁷⁄₁₆ in.). National Archives and Records Administration, Center for Legislative Archives, Washington, DC

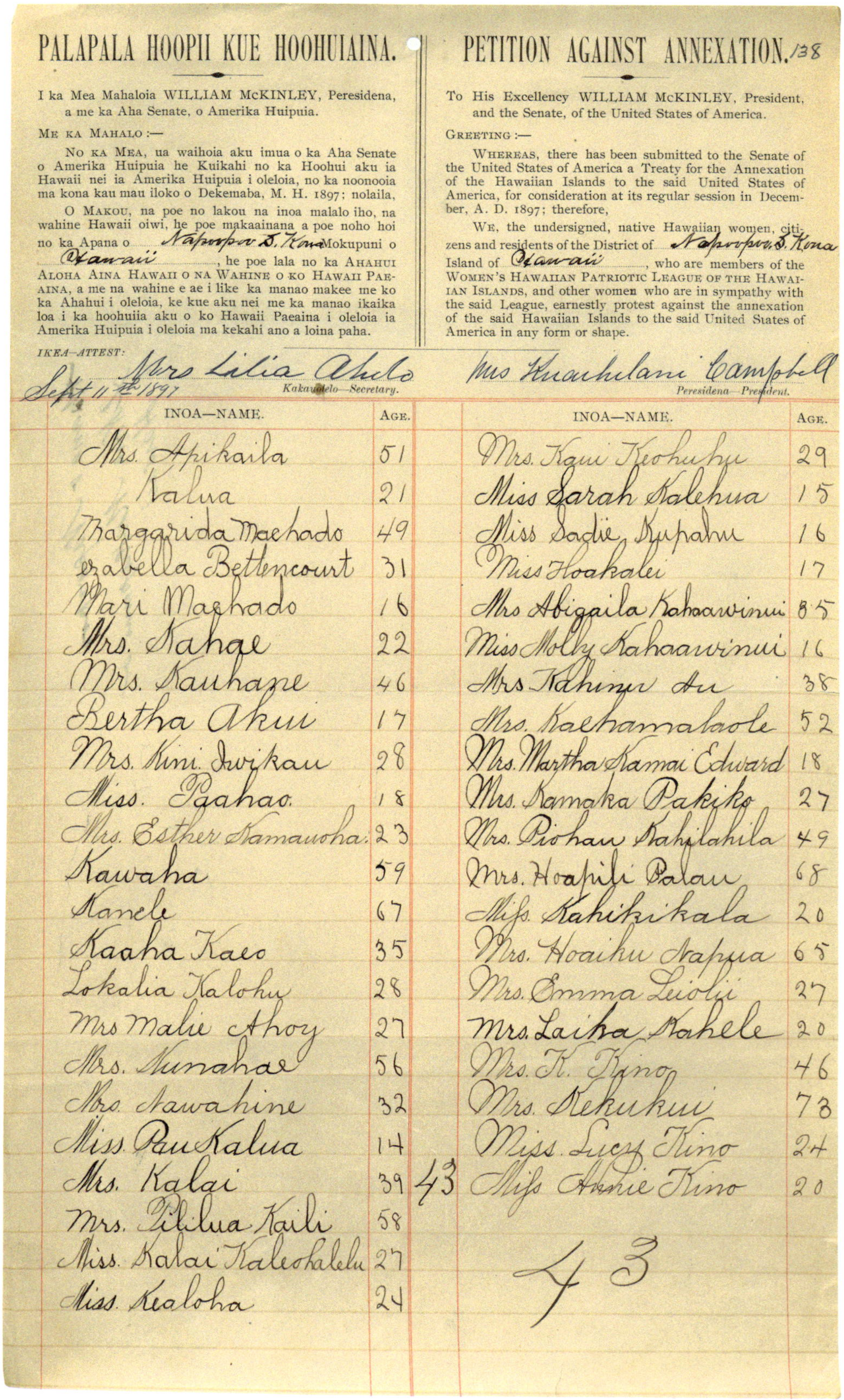

PALAPALA HOOPII KUE HOOHUIAINA.

I ka Mea Mahaloia WILLIAM McKINLEY, Peresidena, a me ka Aha Senate, o Amerika Huipuia.

ME KA MAHALO:—

No KA MEA, ua waihoia aku imua o ka Aha Senate o Amerika Huipuia he Kuikahi no ka Hoohui aku ia Hawaii nei ia Amerika Huipuia i oleloia, no ka noonooia ma kona kau mau iloko o Dekemaba, M. H. 1897; nolaila,

O MAKOU, na poe no lakou na inoa malalo iho, na wahine Hawaii oiwi, he poe makaainana a poe noho hoi no ka Apana o _Napoopoo S. Kona_ Mokupuni o _Hawaii_, he poe lala no ka AHAHUI ALOHA AINA HAWAII O NA WAHINE O KO HAWAII PAE-AINA, a me na wahine e ae i like ka manao makee me ko ka Ahahui i oleloia, ke kue aku nei me ka manao ikaika loa i ka hoohuiia aku o ko Hawaii Paeaina ia Amerika Huipuia i oleloia ma kekahi ano a loina paha.

IKEA—ATTEST:

Mrs Lilia Ahelo
Kakauolelo—Secretary.

Sept 11th 1897

PETITION AGAINST ANNEXATION. *138*

To His Excellency WILLIAM McKINLEY, President, and the Senate, of the United States of America.

GREETING :—

WHEREAS, there has been submitted to the Senate of the United States of America a Treaty for the Annexation of the Hawaiian Islands to the said United States of America, for consideration at its regular session in December, A. D. 1897; therefore,

WE, the undersigned, native Hawaiian women, citizens and residents of the District of _Napoopoo S. Kona_ Island of _Hawaii_, who are members of the WOMEN'S HAWAIIAN PATRIOTIC LEAGUE OF THE HAWAIIAN ISLANDS, and other women who are in sympathy with the said League, earnestly protest against the annexation of the said Hawaiian Islands to the said United States of America in any form or shape.

Mrs Kuaihilani Campbell
Peresidena—President.

INOA—NAME.	AGE.	INOA—NAME.	AGE.
Mrs. Apikaila	51	Mrs. Kani Keohuhu	29
Kalua	21	Miss Sarah Kalehua	15
Margarida Machado	49	Miss Sadie Kupahu	16
Ezabella Bettencourt	31	Miss Hoakalei	17
Mari Machado	16	Mrs Abigaila Kahaawinui	85
Mrs. Kahae	22	Miss Molly Kahaawinui	16
Mrs. Kauhane	46	Mrs Kahinu Au	38
Bertha Akui	17	Mrs. Kaehamalaole	52
Mrs. Kini Iwikau	28	Mrs. Martha Kamai Edward	18
Miss. Paahao	18	Mrs. Kamaka Pakiko	27
Mrs. Esther Kamauoha	23	Mrs. Piohau Kahilahila	49
Kawaha	59	Mrs. Hoapili Palau	68
Kanele	67	Miss. Kahikikala	20
Kaaha Kaeo	35	Mrs. Hoaihu Napua	65
Lokalia Kalohu	28	Mrs. Emma Leiolii	27
Mrs Malu Ahoy	27	Mrs. Laika Kahele	20
Mrs. Nunahae	56	Mrs. K. Kino	46
Mrs. Nawahine	32	Mrs. Kekukui	73
Miss Pau Kalua	14	Miss. Lucy Kino	24
Mrs. Kalai	39	Miss Annie Kino	20
Mrs. Pililua Kaili	58		
Miss. Kalai Kaleohalelu	27		
Miss. Kealoha	24		

43

43

Hawaii." Crowds amassed at 'Iolani Palace to hear the recently appointed President Dole proclaim the new republic. A group representing less than three percent of the total population of the islands was now in control of Hawaiian governance.[90] The United States immediately recognized the Republic of Hawaii, followed by Great Britain, and other nations.[91] Thurston modeled the new constitution after the state of Mississippi's 1890 constitution, which restricted the vote of Black Americans in that state (an infringement on citizenship rights that lasted in Mississippi until the 1960s). Again borrowing from Mississippi's example, Thurston instated a five-dollar poll tax, as well as language restrictions targeting Japanese and Chinese residents.[92] He also purposefully restricted the Kānaka Maoli vote in order to secure the undue influence of white U.S. Americans. The overthrow, however, was not uncontested.

Resistance to the Overthrow

During the events of 1893, those loyal to the queen did not remain idle. One royalist, Joseph Nāwahī (1842–1896), organized a resistance movement. In 1893, Nāwahī founded the grass-roots organization Hui Aloha 'Āina and strategized how to resist annexation.[93] In January 1895, between two hundred and seven hundred armed individuals led by the royalist Robert W. Wilcox participated in an uprising.[94] However, the Republic's guard both outnumbered and outgunned them. Queen Lili'uokalani was among the 355 people who were arrested for treason. After a cache of weapons was linked to her, she was tried and convicted for misprision and treason. "That first night of my imprisonment," the queen wrote, "was the longest night I have ever passed in my life; it seemed as though the dawn of day would never come."[95]

The queen was sentenced to five years' imprisonment and hard labor, and ordered to pay a $5,000 fine; this sentence was subsequently reduced to five years' imprisonment. The queen also suffered the humiliation of having her personal papers taken from her. She recalled, "On the very day I left the house, so I was informed by Mr. Wilson, Mr. A. F. Judd had gone to my private residence without search-warrant; and that all the papers in my desk, or in my safe, my diaries, the petitions I had received from my people, —all things of that nature which could be found were swept into a bag, and carried off by the chief justice in person. My husband's private papers were also included in those taken from me."[96] In a cold move, the only document returned to her was her will. Reflecting on

her experience, she wrote, "I never saw a more unchristian like set as these Missionaries, and so uncharitable as to abuse me in the manner they do from the pulpit."[97]

Lili'uokalani served eight months under house arrest on the second floor of 'Iolani Palace before moving to a second location, Washington Place. She was granted freedom to travel within the island of O'ahu on February 6, 1897. After serving twenty-one months of the five-year sentence, the Republic's executive council granted Lili'uokalani a full pardon.[98] Upon her release, she did not waste any time advocating for the restoration of her sovereignty. In late 1896, Lili'uokalani obtained her passport and left for the United States.[99] The presidents of the Hui Hawai'i Aloha 'Āina, or the Hawaiian Patriotic League; its sister organization for women, the Hui Hawai'i Aloha 'Āina o Nā Wāhine; and the Hui Kālai'āina, were in active communication with the queen, urging her to make one last appeal to President Cleveland before he left office.[100] However, in the spring of 1897, the newly inaugurated President William McKinley (1843–1901) was already meeting with annexationists, including Thurston. By June of that year, he signed and submitted a treaty for Hawaiian annexation to the U.S. Senate for ratification.[101] In response, the three organizations united to protest the treaty, organizing mass meetings and petition drives. Together, the groups collected over 38,000 signatures, a significant number given that the Kānaka Maoli population of the time figured around 40,000.[102] In November 1897, four Kānaka Maoli delegates representing the three Hui traveled to Washington, DC, to present the petitions to McKinley and members of Congress.[103] They arrived on December 6, meeting first with Queen Lili'uoklani to devise a strategy, and decided they would only submit the Hui Aloha 'Āina petitions (comprising 21,269 signatures).[104] They believed that the Hui Kālai'āina petition, which in addition to protesting annexation argued for the restoration of the monarchy, might foster resistance (fig. 18).[105] Each of the 556 pages of the Aloha 'Āina petition included a statement of opposition, in Hawaiian to the top left, and in English to the top right. A space would be left blank to fill in the district and island where the petition came from, including Hawai'i, Molokai, Maui, and Kauai, among others.

On December 9, 1897, when Senator George Hoar (1826–1904) of Massachusetts read the petition to the Senate, fifty-eight of its members were ready to vote to ratify the annexation of Hawai'i.[106] By late February 1898, only forty-six of the sixty senators needed were in favor of voting for annexation. This hesitance succesfully blocked the treaty in Congress. Yet on April 25, 1898, a little over a year after McKinley submitted the treaty, the United States declared war on Spain. The enthusiasm for war helped pave the way for Joint Resolution 259, the "Newlands Resolution," the legislation through which Congress claimed to annex the Hawaiian Islands.[107] Their justification: Hawai'i needed to be possessed as the site for a coaling station, so the United States could properly defend itself.[108] Specifically, as the U.S. Navy defeated the Spanish fleet at Manila Bay, politicians homed in on Hawai'i's Pearl Harbor as a natural coaling station. John Schofield (1831–1906), who had explored Hawaiian geography, deemed that site the best natural harbor in the world, large enough to anchor a fleet of ships and small enough to be defended.[109] The fear that Japan was also interested in claiming the archipelago of Hawai'i also played a role.

Several congressional representatives objected to the annexation of Hawai'i, but to no avail. McKinley inquired whether or not Hawai'i could be annexed through joint resolution, or a total of the votes on the issue from both the House of Representatives and the Senate. This bypassed the normal and legal method of ratification of law, in which the House first votes, and passes a bill, and then the Senate takes a vote.[110] The joint resolution was signed by McKinley on July 7, 1898.[111] Queen Lili'uokalani immediately wrote to the House of Representatives to protest.

Today, some historians point out that a ratified treaty (not a resolution) is required to annex land, and moreover, according to international law, the United States, as an occupying force, should have established a military government to provisionally administer the laws of the occupied state, the Hawaiian Kingdom. However, following the overthrow on January 17, 1893, a puppet government maintained control, and it became the Republic of Hawai'i on July 4, 1894. By statute, the Republic of Hawai'i was renamed the Territory of Hawai'i on April 30, 1900. The Territorial Act granted that "all persons who were citizens of the Republic of Hawaii on August 12th, eighteen hundred and ninety-eight, are hereby declared to be citizens of the United States and citizens of Hawai'i."[112] Much later, on March 18, 1959, Hawai'i became a U.S. state. Both the territorial act and the statehood act, which were authorized by the United States upon Hawai'i, surpassed

the international laws of occupation set forth by the 1899 Hague Convention II that the United States had ratified.[113]

In 1901, the U.S. government received a federal appropriation of $150,000 to establish a naval base at the mouth of Pu'uloa, or Pearl Harbor. It was met with fierce resistance when the owners of the adjacent lands totalling 719 acres to the harbor refused to name a selling price.[114] Meanwhile, the U.S. government vastly undervalued the lands at $16,800. Two trials ensued, during which the lands were valued at $102,523.[115] This cartoon, drawn by Ralph O. Yardley, a California-based cartoonist who spent several years in Hawai'i, comments on the controversy (fig. 19). Between 1900 and 1902, Yardley was the principal cartoonist at the *Honolulu Advertiser*, for which he made about 350 political drawings.[116] Here, a towering Uncle Sam holds a pickaxe and shovel while surveying a Pearl Harbor dotted with "Not for Sale" signs. His scheming expression, however, suggests he has already decided upon his own course of action, and the illustration is captioned, "Waal, by gum! I'd oughter a'got in before them sugar fellers." Published in the *Hawaiian Gazette* on June 7, 1901, the cartoon accompanied an article that predicted, "There is no doubt from the high figures at which the land is held that the Government will have to resort to condemnation proceedings to secure the station desired."[117] Ultimately, the United States acquired the lands by condemnation, a process by which private property is taken for the purpose of public use. U.S. engineers began excavating a channel into what is now known as Pearl Harbor in 1902.[118]

During this period, members of the Hawaiian resistance protested the overthrow, the first annexation treaty, the formation of the Republic, the martial-law trials, the second annexation treaty, its adoption in Hawai'i, the endorsement of the joint resolution in Washington, DC, and the procedure of annexation. The spirit of Hawaiian resistance was strong, and followers of Queen Lili'uokalani made objects of material culture to symbolize their resistance. Foremost among these cultural manifestations were quilts. People who had learned how to make quilts from the missionaries in the 1820s now infused the art with their own traditions. Some Hawaiian quiltmakers, for example, applied their own names to the stitches, the arrangement of the pattern of the square, or the overall design.[119] They also made quilts in response to current events. When the provisional government took over the 'Iolani Palace and declared itself a republic, the Hawaiian

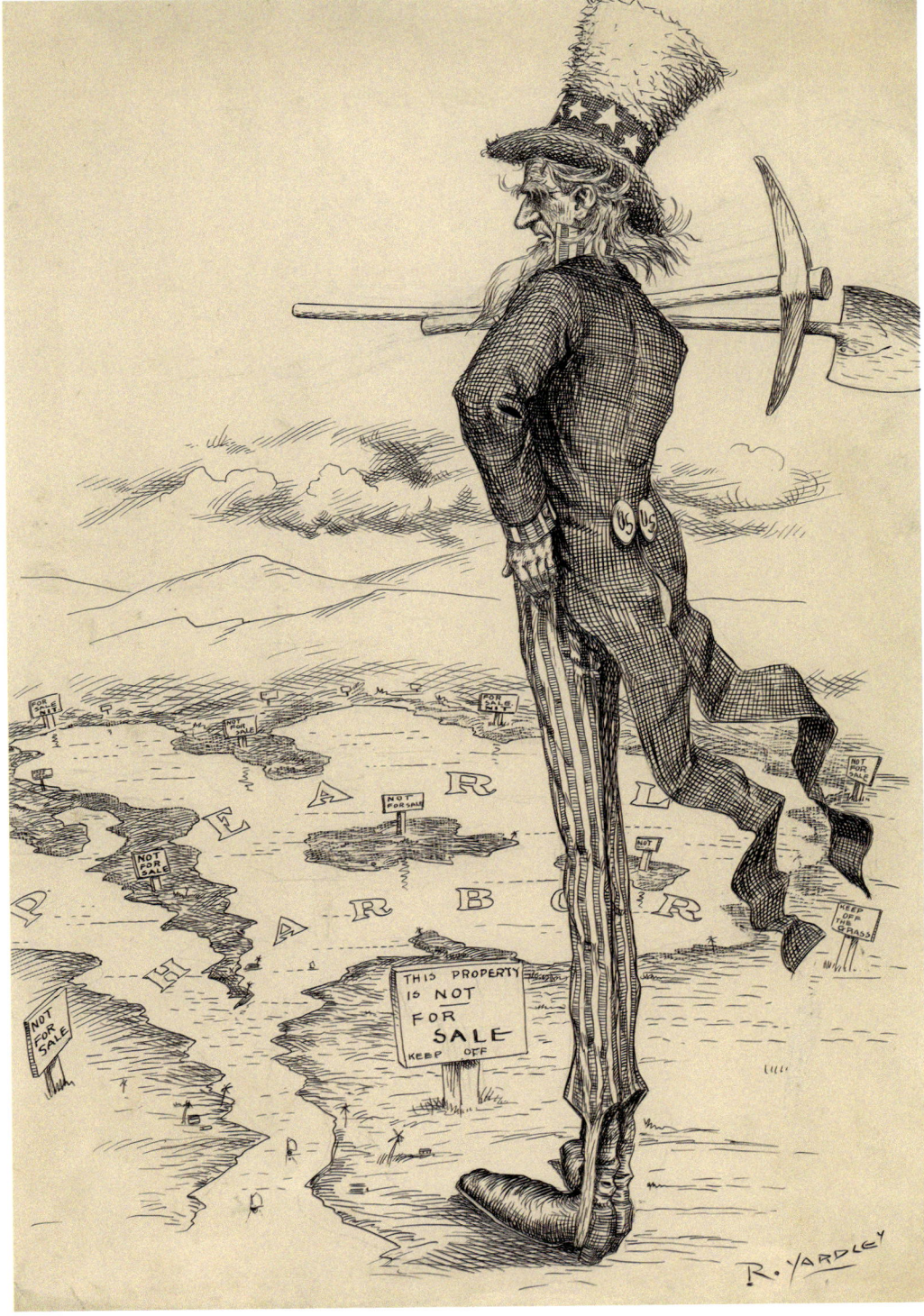

Fig. 19 *Pearl Harbor: This Property Is Not for Sale*, Ralph O. Yardley (1878–1961), 1901. Ink on paper; 48.3 × 38.1 cm (19 × 15 in.). Hawai'i State Archives

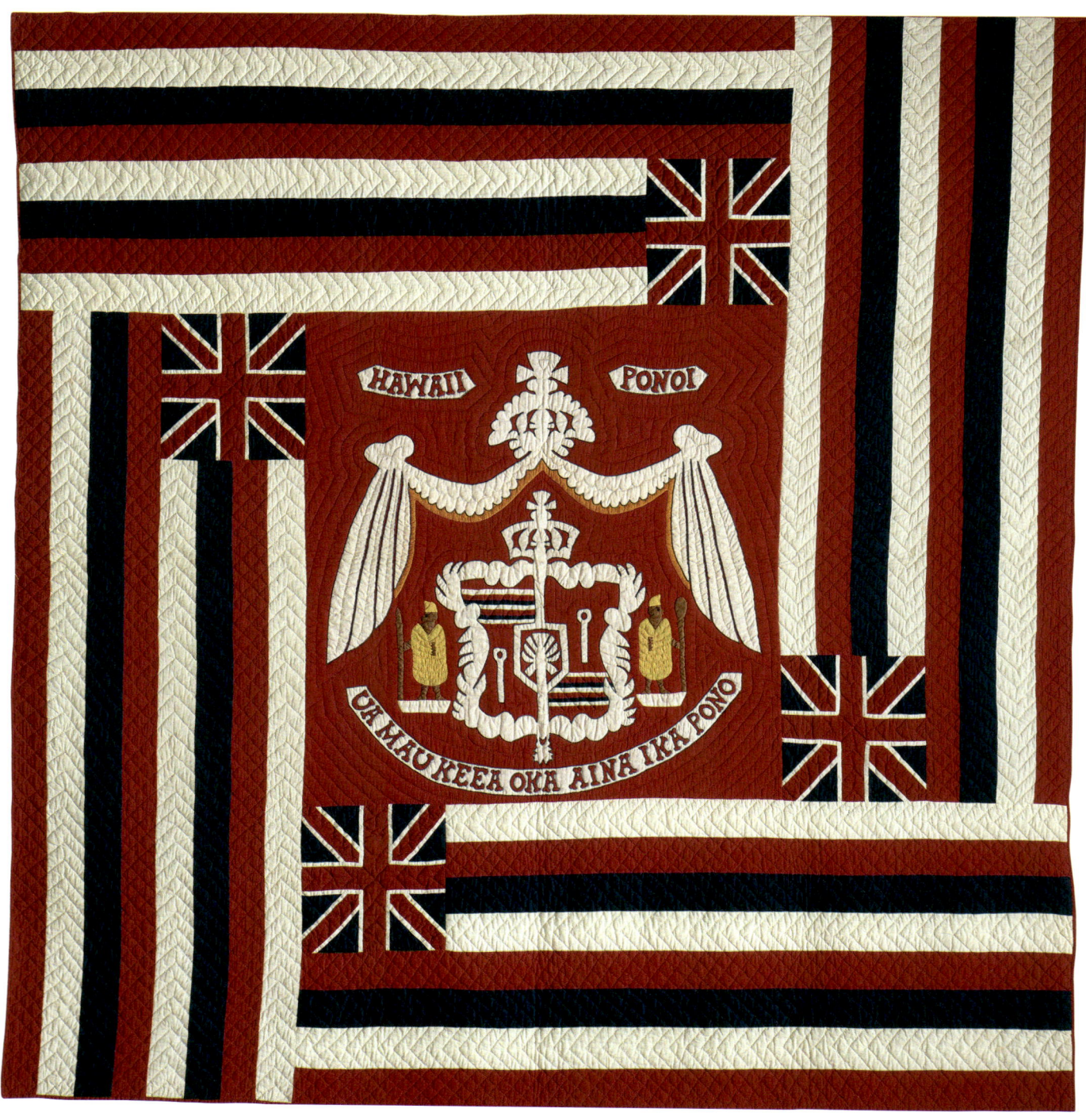

Fig. 20 *Rosina Kalanikauwekiulani Ayers's "Hawaiian Coat-of-Arms" Quilt,* Unidentified artist, 1898. Cotton, silk, and wool; 236.2 × 231.1 cm (93 × 91 in.). National Museum of American History, Smithsonian Institution

flag was lowered.[120] Afterward, it became a symbol of the resistance. Ku'u Hae Hawai'i (My beloved Hawaiian flag) was a popular quilt motif of this era.[121] Typically, a Hawaiian flag quilt displays four Hawaiian flags surrounding a royal Hawaiian coat of arms or crown.[122] The eight stripes of the Hawaiian flag signify the eight major islands of the kingdom. The flags' distinctive quilting is linear, whereas the concentric, wavy forms typical of Hawaiian quilts is reserved for the center.[123] In this way, the quilt accentuates and gives privilege to the flag as a textile object within another textile, creating an "intertextile dialogue" and a visual play of meanings.[124]

One such quilt, the "Hawaiian Coat-of-Arms," was made as a wedding present and given in 1898 to Rosina Kalanikauwekiulani (1877–1966), an ali'i and a descendant of Kamehameha I (fig. 20).[125] Depicting four different flags, it is part of the Ku'u Hae Hawai'i tribute to express loyalty to the Hawaiian Kingdom. However, this quilt has chevron or V-like lines throughout the white stripes of the flags, and diamond-like shapes emerge on the blue and red stripes—instead of straight lines typically used to stitch the stripes. But, like other Hawaiian flag quilts, the four flags also are oriented in such a way that one is always upside down, a traditional signal of nautical distress. One might imagine the impression such quilts made when hung from the posts of loyalists' beds. In essence, their owners flew the flag and declared their allegiance to the queen.

The quilt's design features the royal crown, the Hawaiian coat of arms, and the two outward-facing guardians of King Kamehameha I. Important symbols include the puwalu, or flag of Hawaiian chiefs; puo'ulo'u, or kapu sticks; kāhili, or feather standards; spears, and maile leaves of the lei/garland that is depicted draping the crest.[126] The guardians, often omitted in the designs for these quilted coats of arms, may have been included because Ayers was genealogically linked to Kamehameha I.[127] Such symbols of the crown became particularly important to Hawaiians after the provisional government removed crown motifs following the 1893 overthrow.[128] Additionally, this flag quilt displays an appliqued slogan, Ua Mau ke Ea o ka 'Āina i ka Pono, or "The Life of The Land Is Perpetuated by Righteousness." Scholars point out that this statement is a reference to the restoration of Hawaiian sovereignty in 1843, after Lord George Paulet (1803–1879) claimed the Hawaiian Islands for the British and flew the Union Jack over the

archipelago while ordering all Hawaiian flags to be destroyed.[129] Finally, the quilt features the words Hawai'i Pono'i, or "Hawai'i's own." This was the title of the 1876 version of the state anthem, written by Kalākaua.[130] The song's text stressed loyalty to Hawai'i—and, by extension, to the monarchy:

Hawai'i pono'ī	Hawai'i's own
Nānā i kou Mo'ī	Look to your King
Ka Lani Ali'i	The Royal Chief
Ke Ali'i	The Chief
Makua Lani e	Royal Father
Kamehameha e	Kamehameha
Na kāua e pale	We shall defend
Me ke ihe	With spears
Hawai'i pono'ī	Hawai'i's own
Nāna i na Ali'i	Look to your Chiefs
Nā pua muli kou	The children after you
Nā pōki'i	The young
Hawai'i pono'ī	Hawai'i's own
E ka Lāhui e	O Nation
'O kau hana nui	Your great duty
E u'i e	Strive[131]

With such cultural objects supporting the resistance movement, royalists made their views tangible, including their feelings of loss over their nation. These beliefs were passed down through generations in the form of heirloom quilts, and new quilts preserved these symbols as an acknowledgment of Hawaiian history and heritage. The spirit they have helped carry may be one reason why many supporters of Hawiian soveriegnty remain devoted to their cause to this day.[132]

A Hawaiian Account

Queen Lili'uokalani arrived in Washington, DC, in late 1897 and set up meetings there as well as in New York City. During her trip, she wrote about the events of the overthrow. *Hawaii's Story by Hawaii's Queen*, published in 1898, remains one of the few nineteenth-century accounts of Hawaiian history that was written from the perspective of a Kānaka Maoli and published for an English-speaking audience (fig. 21).[133] Lili'uokalani had read the 1894 Morgan Report, which grossly misrepresented the Hawaiian monarchy and its governance, and she felt the need to respond.[134] Some scholars suspect that she had a close hand in the design of the book because it features two kāhili, or the symbolic staff of the state made from feathers, on the cover. Kāhili are important symbols of Hawaiian royalty, with direct ties to the tradition of featherwork as well as ritual. Here, they mark the book as her textual surrogate.[135] A crowned flower lei encircles "Liliu," the queen's birthname. The volume also features formal portraits of other Hawaiian monarchs, notably a photograph of King Kalākaua.[136]

The book's design was so important because the queen intended it not only as a historical document but also as a political instrument to persuade and garner favor from other heads of state. As she wrote in a letter, "I think it would really be well for you to send to me the books intended for Queen Victoria and President McKinley and also Hon. Grover Cleveland. So they might receive it with my autograph. I think the red binding would be most attractive. Though blue is my favorite color, I think the red would give a better sale for the books, so let it be red."[137]

Despite the queen's many forms of resistance and the efforts of royalist groups who supported her, U.S. expansionists prevailed. Queen Liliʻuokalani returned to Hawaiʻi from her travels on August 1, 1898, but she refused to attend the annexation ceremony, during which the Republic of Hawaiʻi turned over the Hawaiian Islands to the United States on August 12. Although she later traveled back to Washington, DC, several times to request that the Crown Lands of Hawaiʻi seized by the U.S. government be returned to her, her request was always denied.[138] This portrait of the queen was taken in Washington in 1908, during one of these visits (fig. 22). As her resolute expression suggests, she would continue to fight the annexation of Hawaiʻi until her death in 1917.

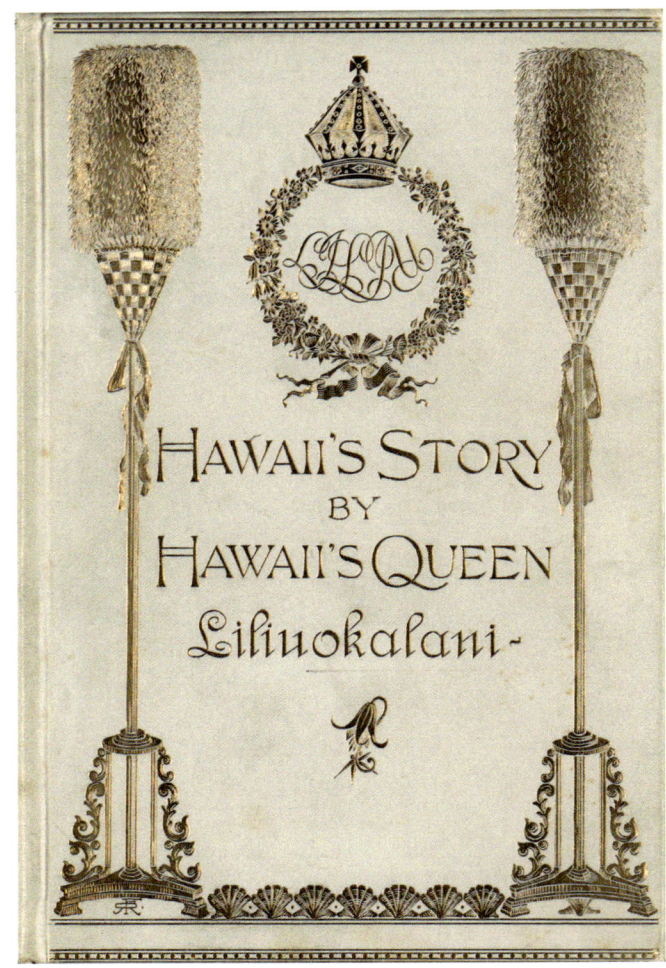

Fig. 21 *Hawaii's Story by Hawaii's Queen*, Queen Liliʻuokalani (1838–1917), Lee and Shepard Publishers, Boston (active 1862–1905), 1898. 20.3 × 14 × 4.4 cm (8 × 5½ × 1¾ in.). Hawaiʻi State Archives, Paul Markham Kahn Collection

Fig. 22 *Queen Liliʻuokalani* (1838–1917), Harris & Ewing Studio (active 1905–1977), 1908. Gelatin silver print; 37.4 × 28.8 cm (14¾ × 11⁵⁄₁₆ in.). National Portrait Gallery, Smithsonian Institution; gift of Aileen Conkey

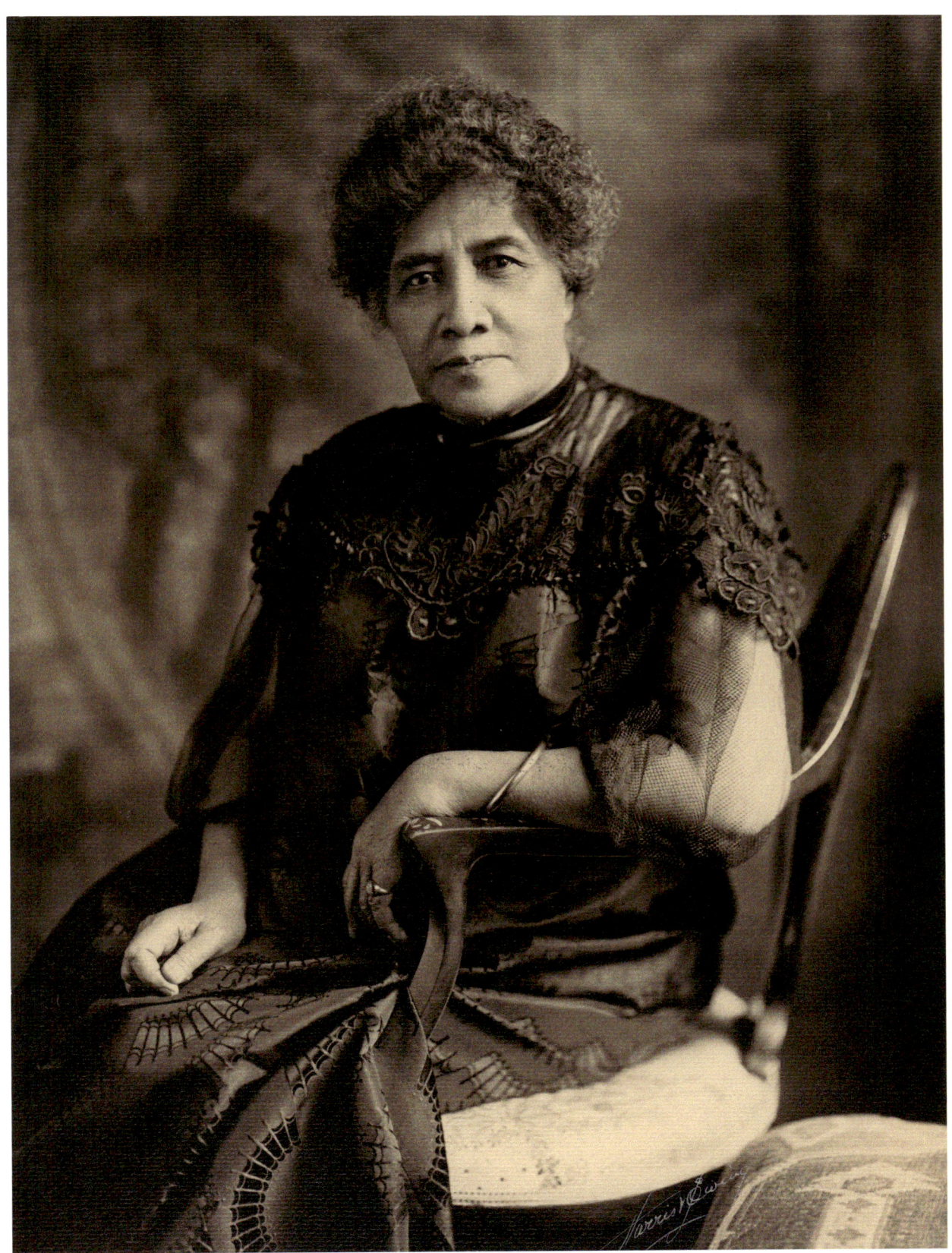

3

"Cuba and Puerto Rico: Two Wings of a Bird?"

JORGE DUANY

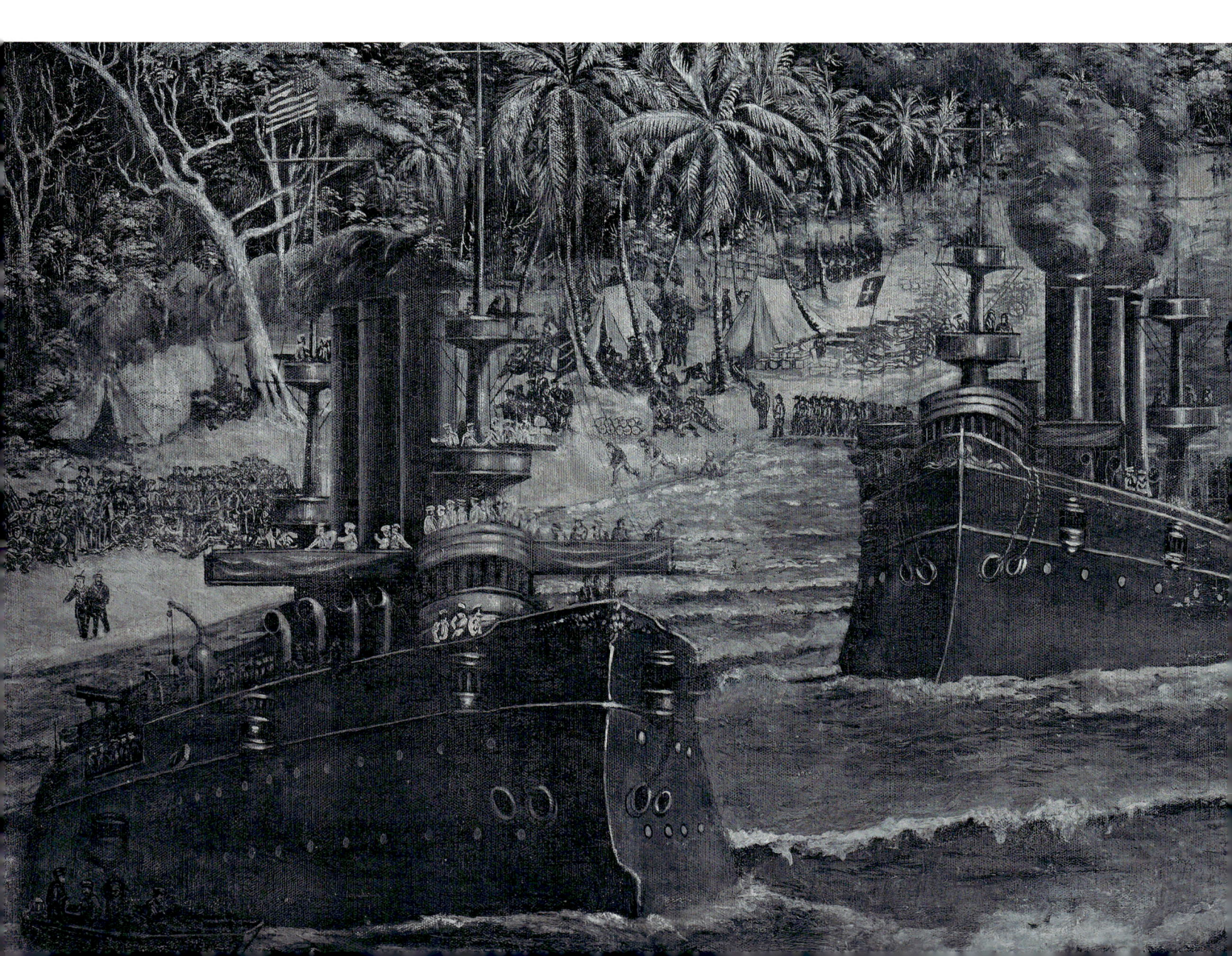

In 1893, Lola Rodríguez de Tió published her famous poem "A Cuba" ("To Cuba"), as part of her collection *Mi libro de Cuba* (My Book of Cuba). When the book was published, the Puerto Rican independence advocate was exiled with her family in Havana, never to return to live in Puerto Rico (see p. 95). In her poem, Rodríguez de Tió wrote: "Cuba y Puerto Rico son / de un pájaro las dos alas / reciben flores o balas / sobre el mismo corazón" ("Cuba and Puerto Rico are / two wings of a bird / they receive flowers or bullets / in the same heart"). She also expressed her longing that the two countries would become a "patria sola" ("single motherland"). Generations of Cubans and Puerto Ricans have recited these verses as an expression of the solidarity between the two peoples, their shared cultural traditions, and the unfinished political project of self-determination.

Nonetheless, the two countries have experienced significant historical differences. Even during the Spanish colonial period, each island played a distinct role within the Spanish empire. After the Spanish conquest and colonization of Mexico and Peru in the early sixteenth century,

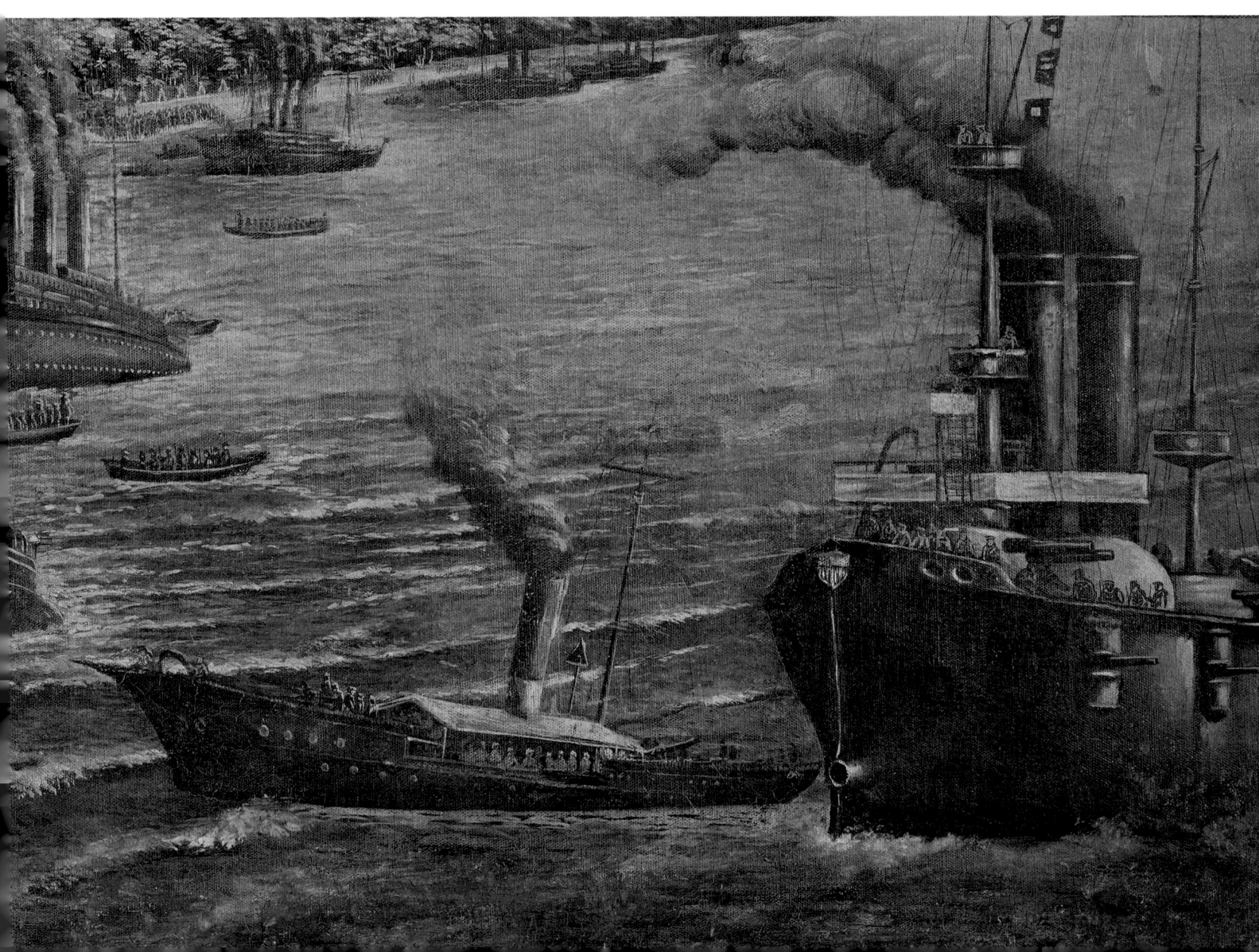

Cuba—and especially Havana—acquired a pivotal position within Spain's Atlantic commercial system, while Puerto Rico languished as a marginal port of call, outside the main sea routes between the Americas and the Iberian peninsula. Furthermore, Cuba developed the largest sugar plantation system in the world during the nineteenth century (after the demise of the plantation economy in neighboring Saint-Domingue, or Haiti, since 1804) (see p. 37). Meanwhile, Puerto Rico remained a frontier settler colony subsisting primarily on a combination of mixed farming, cattle raising, and smuggling at least until 1815. To satisfy the growing demand for labor, Cuba imported nearly one million African slaves during the Spanish colonial period, but Puerto Rico only received about 43,000, according to recent estimates by SlaveVoyages.[1] The free colored population grew rapidly in both countries throughout the nineteenth century, especially in Puerto Rico, where it surpassed 41 percent of the entire population, according to the 1860 census of the island. Finally, Cuba embraced a militant revolutionary tradition, particularly during the insurrections against Spain in the last third of the nineteenth century (1868–1898), while the dominant political movement in Puerto Rico sought to assert autonomy from Spain by peaceful means, which it briefly achieved in 1897. Aside from the 1868 *Grito de Lares* uprising, which was quickly quelched by Spain, armed struggle did not characterize the movement for self-government on the island.

Enter the twentieth century. Although the United States occupied both Cuba and Puerto Rico during the War of 1898, Cuba became an independent nation (at least in name) in 1902, whereas Puerto Rico became an "unincorporated territory" (a colony except in name) of the United States. While the Platt Amendment (1902–1934) to the Cuban Constitution thwarted the sovereignty of the young Cuban republic, it acquired its own constitution, elected president, legislature, armed forces, diplomatic corps, and national symbols such as a flag and anthem. The political and economic hegemony of the United States over Puerto Rico was much more direct and extensive than over Cuba. Moreover, a nationalist ideology was more entrenched in Cuba than in Puerto Rico throughout the first half of the twentieth century. The political trajectories of the two countries bifurcated even more widely after 1959, with the triumph of the revolution led by Fidel

Castro, particularly with his adoption of socialism in 1961, and Puerto Rico's growing integration within the U.S. political and economic orbit under Governor Luis Muñoz Marín (1898–1980), especially after the establishment of the Estado Libre Asociado (translated as Commonwealth in English) in 1952. As Cuba distanced itself from the United States, Puerto Rico grew closer.

During the Cold War, Cuba and Puerto Rico represented two opposite models of political and economic development. Socialist Cuba became a single-party system increasingly reliant on a Soviet-type central planning of the economy, after the nationalization of most of the means of production and the mass media in the 1960s. Puerto Rico adopted a predominantly two-party system (representing autonomist and annexationist forces that alternated in power since 1968) and experienced considerable economic growth under the government-led industrialization strategy between the late 1940s and early 1970s. Critics decried each model's dependence on massive subsidies by one of the two superpowers, the Soviet Union and the United States. Whereas the revolutionary government curtailed civil liberties and human rights in Cuba, the Commonwealth government generally guaranteed them in Puerto Rico—despite constant harassment and persecution of the independence movement by both federal and local authorities. Cuba thus became an anticapitalist paradigm of national sovereignty and social equality, while Puerto Rico was upheld as a "showcase for democracy" and an example of what the free market could do for small developing countries.

In short, 1898 was a momentous year for both Cuba and Puerto Rico, but its long-term effects widened the political and economic gaps between the two countries. During the early twentieth century, Cuba became a "protectorate" of the United States, which many analysts have characterized as a neocolonial relationship. Meanwhile, the United States governed Puerto Rico in a classic colonial fashion during the first half of the century, without significant participation by the governed population (fig. 1). During the second half of the century, each country followed a distinct path—radical separation from the United States in Cuba, further integration in Puerto Rico—which has led many to question the metaphor of "two wings of a bird," despite the longstanding cultural affinities between the islands.

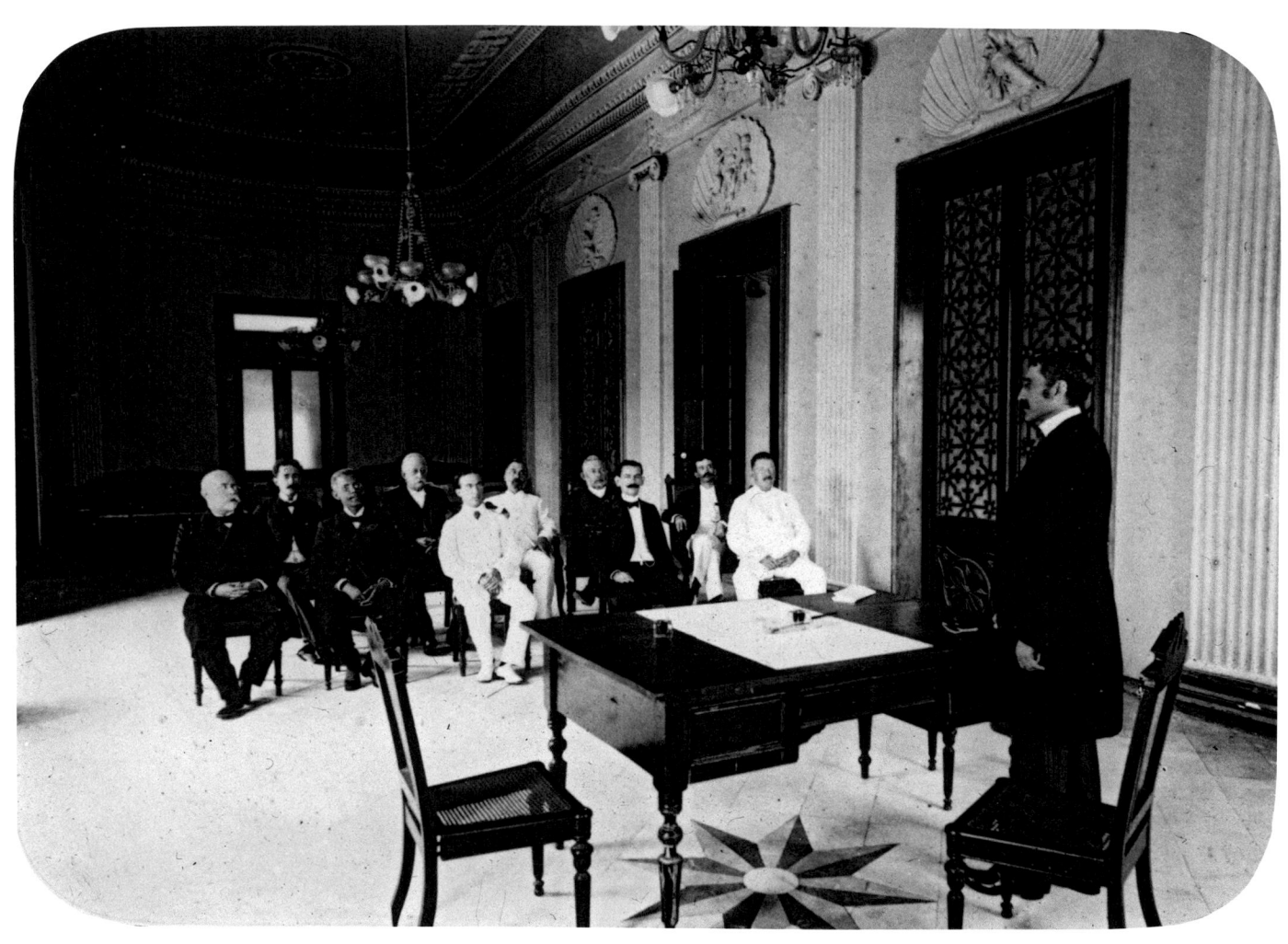

Fig. 1 The Executive Council of Charles H. Allen's Administration, 1900. Glass lantern slide; 8.2 × 10.2 cm (3¼ × 4 in.). National Anthropological Archives, National Museum of Natural History, Smithsonian Institution

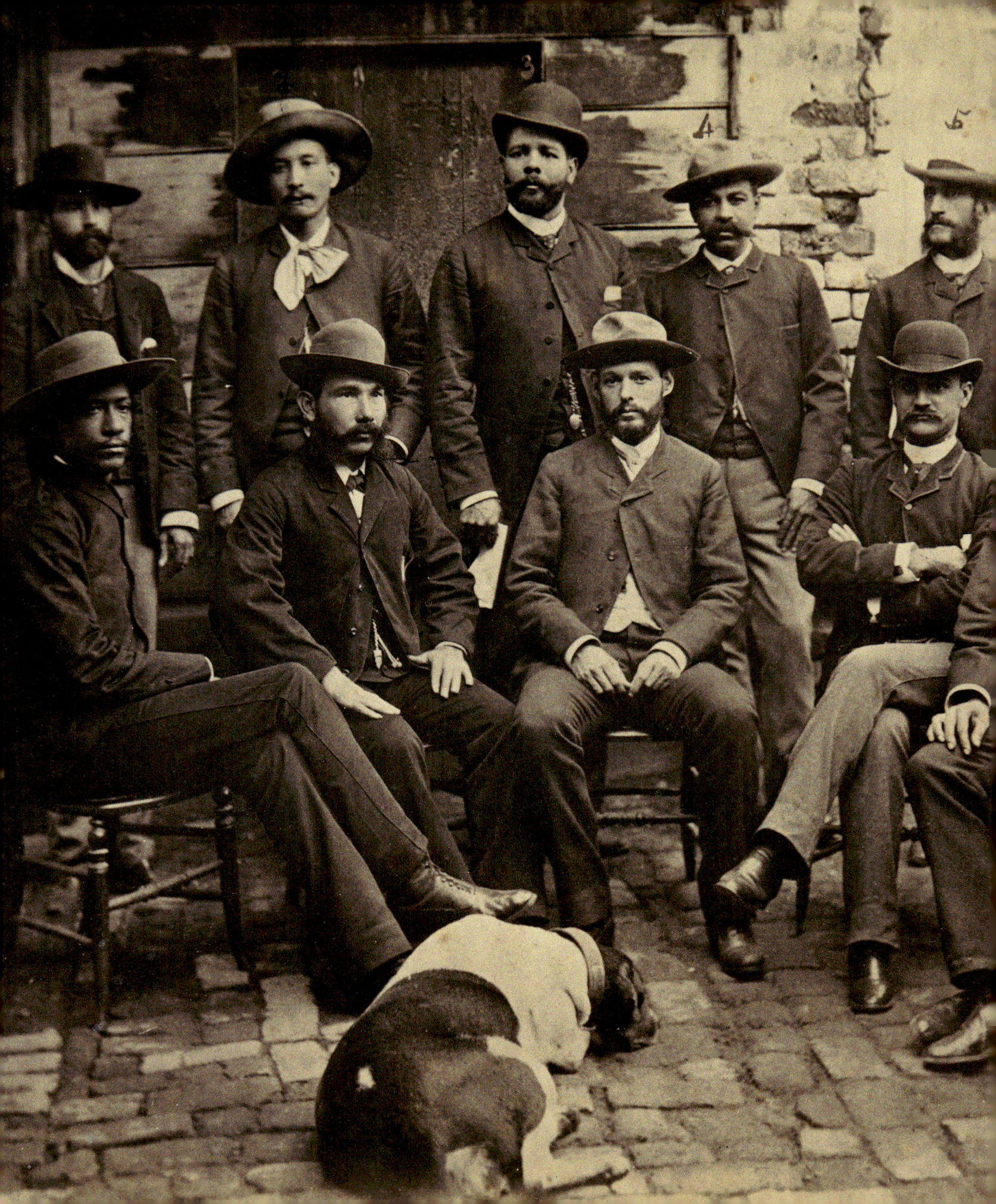

On the Verge of Sovereignty

Cuba and Puerto Rico at the Turn of the Twentieth Century

TAÍNA CARAGOL AND KATE CLARKE LEMAY

"Las Antillas para los hijos de los antillanos"
(The Antilles for the sons of the Antilleans)
—Ramón Emeterio Betances[1]

Cuba and Puerto Rico's Nineteenth-Century Anticolonial Struggles

In 1897, after four hundred years under Spanish colonial rule, Cuba and Puerto Rico were on the verge of change. Sovereignty, a condition that most of the countries of Latin America reached in the first quarter of the nineteenth century, was in sight for both islands.[2] In late November, by royal decree, the Spanish government of the Regent Queen María Cristina (1858–1929) and Prime Minister Práxedes Mateo Sagasta (1825–1903) granted autonomy to the two Antilles.[3] The measure, which gave the islands the right to compose insular parliaments elected by universal suffrage, meant that they could now legislate independently on matters pertaining to the economy, trade, education, agriculture, and public works.[4] Military, legal, and diplomatic affairs, however, remained under Madrid's control.[5] Cubans rejected the decree while Puerto Ricans embraced it jubilantly. Their responses punctuated decades-long anticolonial struggles that had taken divergent paths. Regardless, this moment pointed to the resolution of both islands' colonial relationship with Spain and a redefinition of their political status.[6]

This development was the fruit of Cuban and Puerto Rican collective identities that had been gestating for more than a century, mainly articulated by the *criollo* (Creole) elites, but which also acknowledged other social classes.[7] A sense of belonging and love toward *la patria*, the fatherland, emerged among Cubans and Puerto Ricans, that marked a differentiation from the metropolitan motherland, Spain.[8]

Created a century earlier, in 1797, José Campeche's (1751–1809) *Ex-voto del sitio de San Juan por los ingleses* is emblematic of that sense of burgeoning identity in Puerto Rico. Campeche first learned to paint from his formerly enslaved father, who had purchased his freedom and practiced gilding and painting for local churches (fig. 1).[9] Continuing his training with Spanish Rococo painter Luis Paret y Alcázar (1746–1799), Campeche painted religious scenes and portraits of the island's Spanish colonial rulers and the elite.[10] This ex-voto honors the epic defense mounted by seven thousand *criollo* soldiers and common folk from the bombing of San Juan in an attack by close to six thousand British troops led by Ralph Abercromby (1734–1801) and Henry Harvey (1743–1810) in April 1797.[11] The work not only documents the last attack on Puerto Rico by

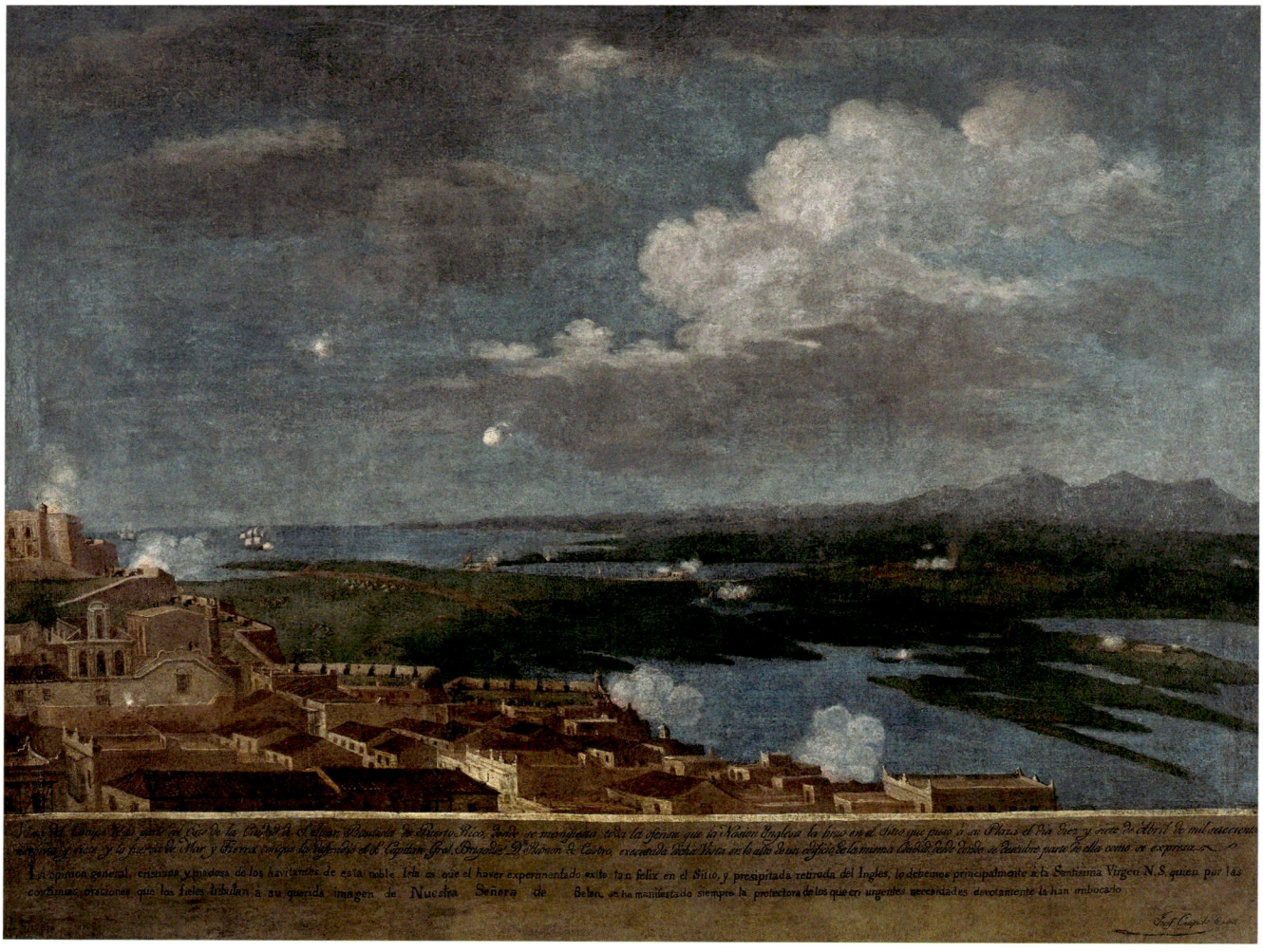

Fig. 1 *Ex-voto del sitio de San Juan por los ingleses* (*Ex-voto painting of the Siege of San Juan by the British*), José Campeche (1751–1809), c. 1797. Oil on canvas; 63.1 × 85 cm (24⅞ × 33½ in.). Archbishopric of San Juan Collection

a European power but also marks a watershed moment in which people from different sectors of society united to defend the island from foreign forces.[12] Remarkably, one hundred years later, in 1898, Puerto Ricans would see foreign forces arrive on its shores again, in a military event that would prove decisive until today.

Cuba, Puerto Rico, and *La Constitución de Cádiz*

A sense of collective identity was also emerging throughout the rest of Spanish America at the turn of the nineteenth century, informing its political processes. Starting in 1809, *criollo* elites, oppressed by the restrictive strictures and tariffs imposed on the colony by the Bourbon dynasty, rose against the Spanish Crown. The insurrections benefitted from the political and social instability provoked by Napoleon's (1769–1821) occupation of Spain

(1808–1814) and the usurpation of King Fernando VII's (1784–1833) throne by Napoleon's brother, Joseph Bonaparte (1768–1844). Many Spaniards organized *Juntas*, or councils, to fight for the restoration of their king. Propelled by the democratic ideals of the Enlightenment, the liberal *Juntas* wanted to modernize Spain's political system. In 1810, the Council Regency—the head of Spain in the absence of its ousted king—invited delegates from the Spanish colonies to attend a special session of the *Cortes*, or parliament.[13]

The constituent assembly debated questions of political representation and equity for the colonies in Spain as well as the abolition of slavery. Cuba's delegates represented the island's *peninsular* planter class. In contrast to their peers from the Americas, they stood firm in their support for the institution of slavery and its trade. Cuban deputy Andrés de Jáuregui (died 1838), even requested that the discussions on slavery be conducted secretly, in order to avoid rumors of emancipation in Cuba.[14] Liberal *criollo* Ramón Power y Giralt (1775–1813), a distinguished navy lieutenant, was Puerto Rico's delegate.[15] Aligned with many of the other deputies from the Americas, Power's message to the *Cortes* expressed Puerto Rico's discontent with unfair taxes, commercial limitations, and the lack of a university. He also expressed the need for the establishment of a peasant workforce that would ensure the sustainability of the sugar economy.[16] Additionally, he requested the establishment of a Diputación Provincial, an official council, which was granted.[17] The resulting Constitución de Cádiz from 1812 demanded an end to absolutism in favor of a constitutional monarchy that recognized the people's sovereignty. It also declared that the Spanish territories in the Americas were no longer colonies; they were *provincias de ultramar*, overseas provinces, with the right to representation in the *Cortes*.[18] Despite these reforms, the countries of Spanish America opted for secession. By 1824, the map of the Americas had changed dramatically, as Spain's viceroyalties were replaced by independent constitutional republics (fig. 2).[19] In the Caribbean, Santo Domingo—the Spanish, eastern half of La Española (Hispaniola)—proclaimed its independence in 1821.[20]

Cuba and Puerto Rico followed a different route (fig. 3). Spain insulated the islands from much of the radical energy that swept through Spanish America during this revolutionary period.[21] From the sixteenth century on, Cuba and Puerto Rico were of military importance for the Spanish Crown as the westernmost and easternmost Greater Antilles. Both protected Spain's colonial possessions from British, French, and Dutch pirates and privateers.[22] Puerto Rico functioned as a powerful garrison for the empire, depending largely on subsidies from New Spain (now Mexico) that primarily served its military build-up. But the rest of its economy and infrastructure remained underdeveloped until the late eighteenth century. Cuba, however, had the geographic advantage of commanding the passage to the Gulf of Mexico. This gave it a central role in the biannual transit of the great Spanish fleet transporting the treasures extracted from the New World back to Spain.[23]

Since their colonization, the socio-economic development of Cuba and Puerto Rico was carried out in relation to Spain's imperial scheme, as opposed to local needs. The Haitian Revolution (1791–1804) was pivotal in launching a new order. When social and political unrest in French Saint-Domingue (present-day Haiti) led to the collapse of the world's largest sugar and coffee economy, Cuba and Puerto Rico began to prosper.[24] The sugar economy, jump-started by European markets and resources, was first to take off in both islands. As Cuba's enslaved population grew exponentially, Spanish authorities used the specter of previous Black uprisings in Haiti to incite racial fear among Cuba's elites, portraying the colonial state as the guarantor of stability.[25]

Despite the economic upturn in Cuba and Puerto Rico, the islands endured political disappointment. Once restored to power in 1814, Fernando VII canceled the Constitución de Cádiz and reinstated monarchic absolutism and traditional colonialism without parliamentary representation. In 1820, liberals in Spain staged another revolution and forced the king to reinstall the constitution.[26] By the year 1837, Spain had expelled the elected Cuban and Puerto Rican representatives from the *Cortes* and announced that the two Caribbean islands and the Philippines would be ruled by *Leyes Especiales*, Special Laws. Conjured by Spanish politicians, the Special Laws were never defined but helped maintain hope for colonial reform over the next twenty years. Instead, the captain generals and civil governors of Cuba and Puerto Rico were endowed with *facultades omnímodas*, or all-encompassing powers that enabled authoritarianism.[27]

Even with these ups and downs, by the 1850s, Cuba and Puerto Rico were on their way to becoming the first and second greatest producers of sugar worldwide,

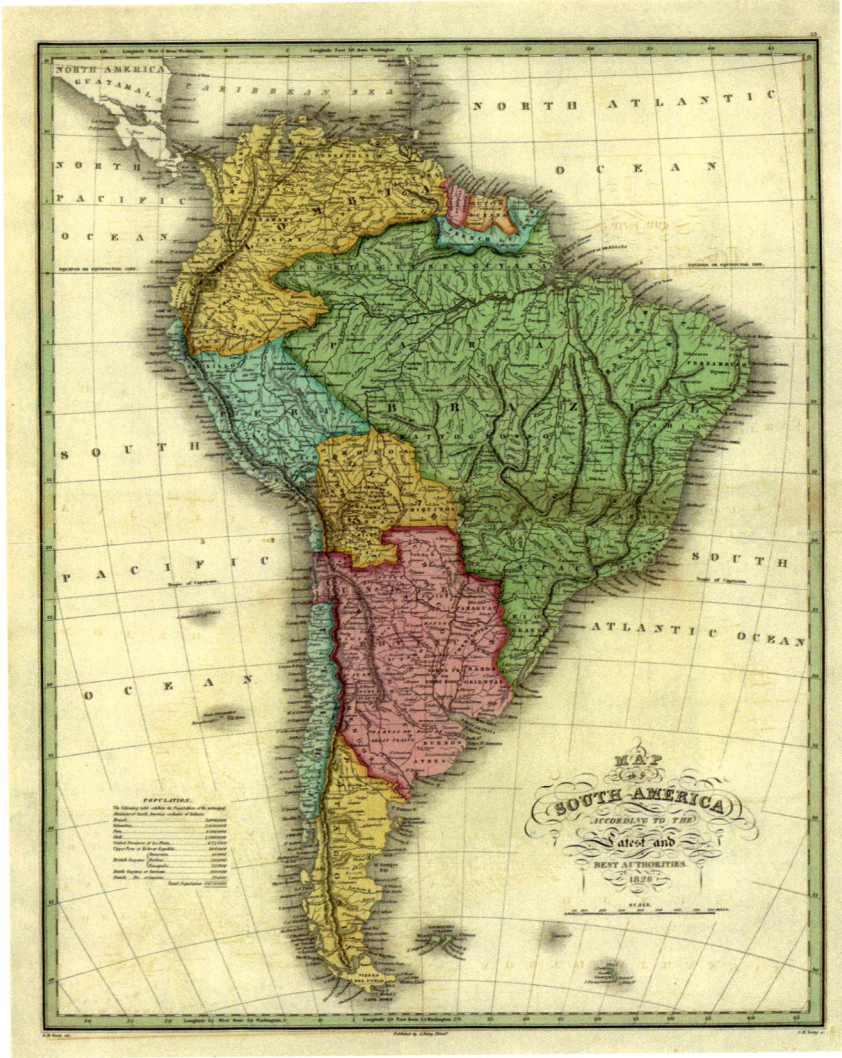

Fig. 2 *Map of South America according to the Latest and Best Authorities*, D. H. Vance del. J. H. Young, Published by A. Finley, Philadelphia, 1826. Hand-colored engraving; 56 × 44 cm (22 × 17⁵⁄₁₆ in.). David Rumsey Collection

Fig. 3 *Colton's West Indies*, Published by J. H. Colton, 1865. Hand-colored engraving; 33 × 40 cm (13 × 15¾ in.). David Rumsey Collection

respectively. Yet their success was dependent on Spain's covert endorsement of slavery and the slave trade, and was buoyed by a competitive new consumer: the United States.[28] The plantation economy also yielded social inequality. The *peninsulares* and *criollo* bourgeoisie were the most powerful classes. In the first decades of the nineteenth century, the immigration of reactionary elements from both classes, including Spanish military and government officials, merchants, and landowners fleeing Latin America's independence wars, strengthened the support for Spanish colonial rule on both Cuba and Puerto Rico. A regime of enslaved people sustained the sugar plantation economy on both islands. In Puerto Rico, *jornaleros*, or day laborers, were also critical to the economy.[29] Submitted to debt peonage, *jornaleros* mainly worked on coffee plantations, which took off in the late 1860s as the sugar economy slowed down.[30] *Peninsulares* and other foreign European creditors kept a tight hold of the Cuban and Puerto Rican economies. Despotic governors secured the social order through censorship and repression.

At the same time, economic prosperity also encouraged a growing desire for modernity on both islands.[31] From the 1820s on, a flourishing press nurtured the spread of liberal ideologies that contested the structures of the colonial government. In 1865, the Spanish government summoned representatives from Cuba and Puerto Rico to a *Junta Informativa de Ultramar*, or Overseas Information Summit, positing the question of reform in areas such as labor, trade, and taxes.[32] Puerto Rican delegates

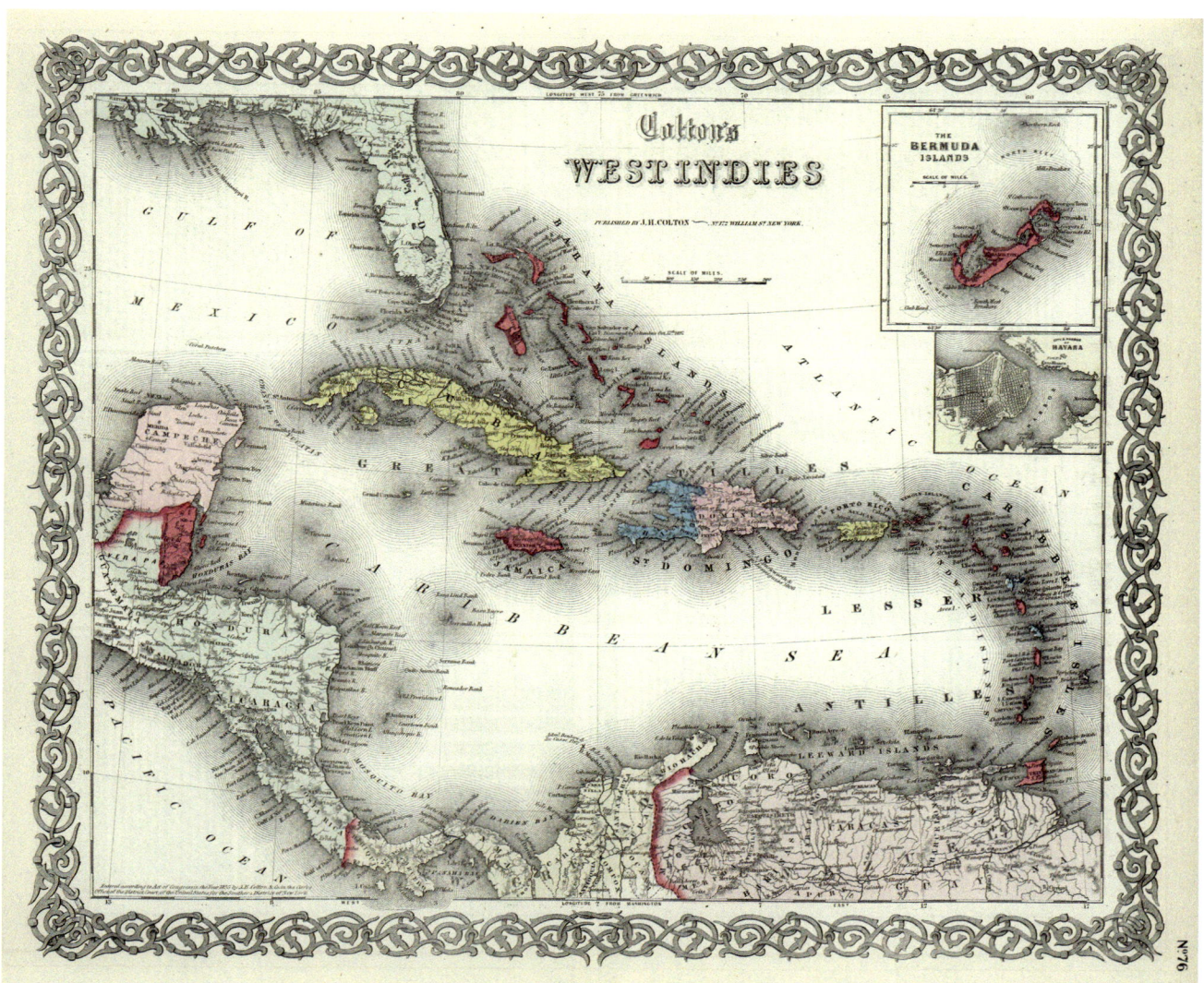

defended a model of modern society that relied on the abolition of slavery.[33] A year later, Spain finally ceased the slave trade permanently.[34] But with a new change of government in Spain, most of the proposed reforms came to nothing, resulting in profound disappointment among reformists in both islands.[35] Toward the late 1860s, the untenable political conditions motivated separatists to take action, linking their independence and abolitionist movements.[36] Cuban and Puerto Rican abolitionists and separatists were often exiled by Spanish authorities. Nevertheless, this kind of punishment strengthened their commitment and collaboration, forging a network from Paris to Caracas, Kingston, Santo Domingo, Saint Thomas, and New York City.

1868: The Final Act of Spanish Domination

Remembered as the beginning of "the final act of the drama of Spanish domination," the year 1868 was a turning point.[37] Cuba and Puerto Rico organized insurrections against the Spanish government that would determine each island's political direction.[38] The year would also become significant for the artistic production of Cuba and Puerto Rico as a landmark in the formation of the islands' national consciousness. Closely tied to a burgeoning sense of nation-building, the leaders of the Cuban and Puerto Rican revolutions of 1868 and advocates for liberal reform would come to anchor the art of portraiture. Photographs, engravings, and oil-on-canvas portraits of the protagonists lent structure to their visual histories and national myths. With a few exceptions, however, the transformation of these figures into icons of Cuban and Puerto Rican history through portraiture is a twentieth-century phenomenon.[39]

Ramón Emeterio Betances (1827–1898) epitomizes the fight for political freedom and the bond between the two islands (fig. 4).[40] This undated, unattributed portrait circulated in 1899, shortly after Betances died.[41] The photograph portrays him at an advanced age, with his characteristic long white beard and curly hair. The stately velvet chair points to his status as a respected intellectual. Considered Puerto Rico's *padre de la patria* (pater patriae), he called himself *El Antillano* (the Antillean), attesting to his Caribbean identity.[42] The son of a merchant father born in La Española (Hispaniola) and a Puerto Rican mother of European ancestry, Betances studied in France and worked there as a surgeon. He returned to Puerto Rico in the late 1850s to lead the abolitionist movement and the fight for Puerto Rican and Cuban independence. Emerging from his activism for decolonization, Betances developed the concept of a Confederación Antillana, or an Antillean confederation, to help Puerto Rico and Cuba achieve independence and protect them, along with the already independent Dominican Republic and Haiti, from foreign intervention.[43]

In 1867, while exiled in Santo Domingo, Betances cofounded the Comité Revolucionario de Puerto Rico and started plotting a revolution.[44] Conscious of the galvanizing power of national symbols, he designed a flag for the future Republic of Puerto Rico that is said to have been embroidered by Mariana Bracetti (1825–1903). The poet and *avant la lettre* feminist Lola Rodríguez de Tió (1843–1924) composed a revolutionary call to arms that she recited at one of the famous salons she organized in her home with her husband, the liberal journalist Bonocio Tió Segarra (1838–1905). In front of the crowd of liberal reformists and political revolutionaries, she reportedly read the militant verses that became the lyrics to the Puerto Rican revolutionary anthem:

Despierta borinqueño que han dado la señal
Despierta de ese sueño que es hora de luchar

"Wake up, borinqueño, they have given the signal. Wake up from your sleep, it's time to fight."[45] The famous lyrics called Puerto Ricans to arise to struggle for their freedom.[46] Rodríguez de Tió's national status as a writer and thinker is evident in her portrait by Fernando Díaz

Mackenna (1873–1931) (fig. 5). Painted in 1918, soon after the artist had moved to Puerto Rico from Spain, this work commissioned by the Ateneo Puertorriqueño, the Puerto Rican Athenaeum, does not show Rodríguez de Tió at seventy-five. Instead, it represents her earlier in life, around the time that she wrote the revolutionary anthem, at the height of her career.[47] Mackenna, who followed in the footsteps of Francisco Oller y Cestero (1833–1917) in portraying historical Puerto Rican figures, captured Rodríguez de Tió's sober style, without earrings and with her hair pulled back. She cultivated this look in opposition to the *criollo* beauty standards of the time.[48]

Betances called for the *Juntas revolucionarias*, or revolutionary committees, in several western towns in Puerto Rico to rise together against Spain.[49] From the Dominican Republic, he and other conspirators would travel to Saint Thomas, to support the revolution that would take place on September 29, 1868. When a Spaniard discovered

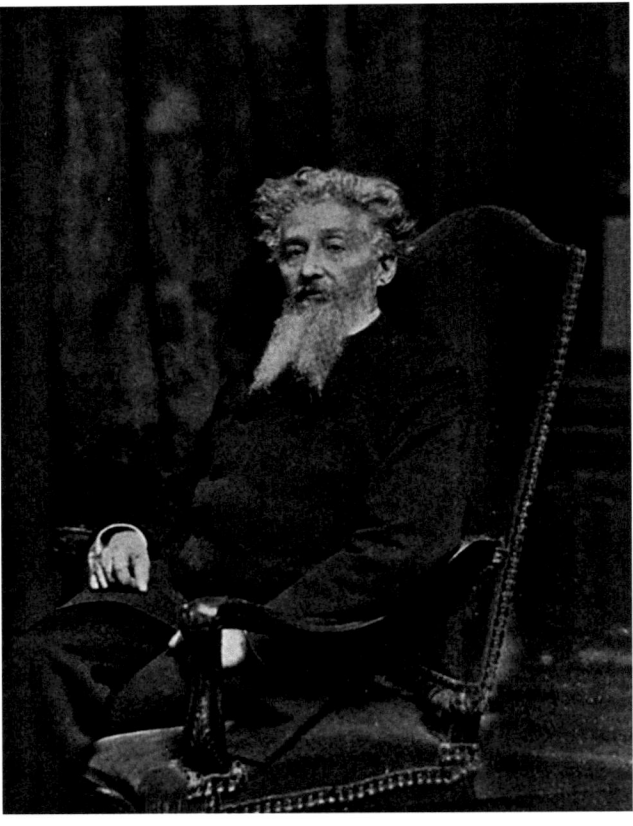

Fig. 4 *Ramón Emeterio Betances* (1827–1898), Unidentified photographer, date unknown. Reproduced in *Ensayos Políticos* by Rafael Serra. New York: A. W. Howes, 1899. Schomburg Center for Research in Black Culture; Manuscripts, Archives and Rare Books Division, The New York Public Library

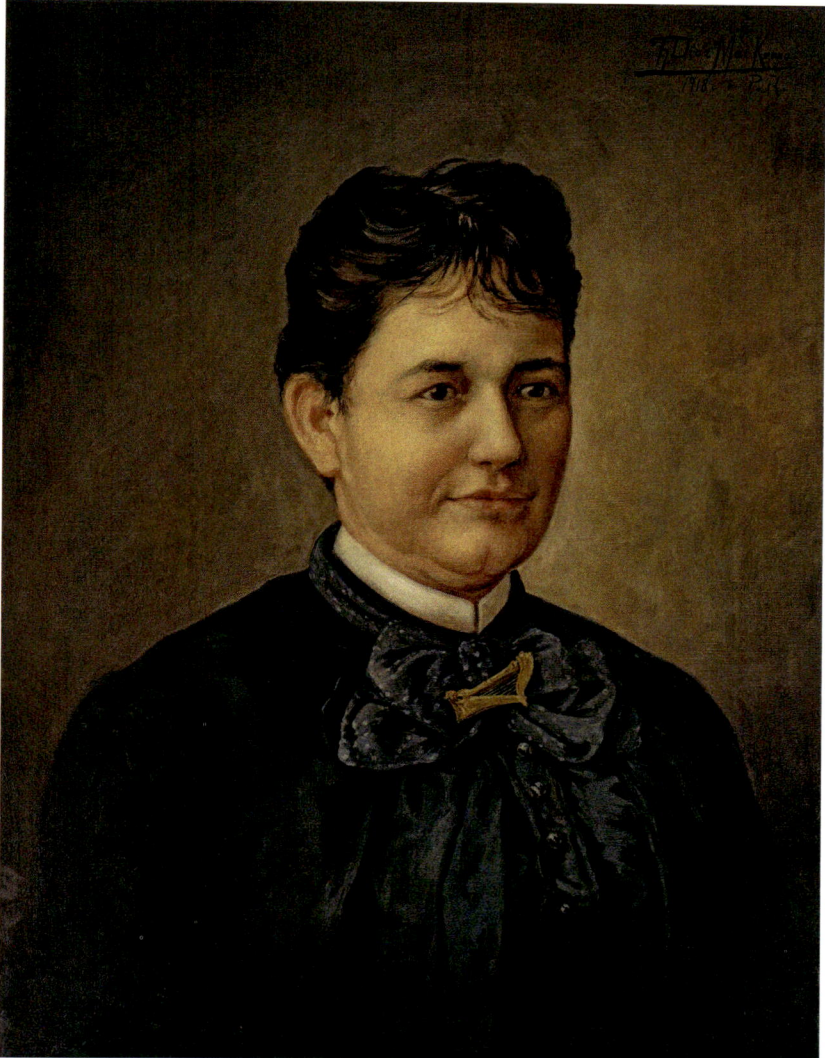

Fig. 5 *Lola Rodríguez de Tió* (1843–1924), Fernando Díaz Mackenna (1873–1931), 1918. Oil on canvas; 70.1 × 53.3 cm (27⅝ × 21 in.). Colección del Ateneo Puertorriqueño

the plan, the uprising was prematurely launched on the night of September 23, at the hacienda of coffee planter Manuel Rojas (1831–1903) in the town of Lares. After listening to a speech by Rojas calling for the end of exorbitant taxes, corrupt colonial officials, and tyrannical rule, the crowd rose to the chant *"¡Viva Puerto Rico Libre!"* (Long live free Puerto Rico).[50] By midnight, they had occupied the municipal seat of government, deposed its leadership, and dispossessed Spanish merchants and clerks of their horses and weapons.[51] They declared Puerto Rico independent, abolished the *jornalero* passbook system, and liberated the enslaved people who joined the call to arms. This revolt became known as *El Grito de Lares*. According to some accounts, the revolutionaries raised the flag that Bracetti had embroidered and sang

Rodríguez de Tió's patriotic "La Borinqueña" before Spanish officials quelled the rebellion (fig. 6).[52] The Spanish authorities arrested more than six hundred people, including workers, enslaved people, merchants, and planters who tried to spread the rebellion to the neighboring town of Pepino, also known as San Sebastián.[53] Betances's vessel was captured in Saint Thomas, and he was forced back into exile. The *Grito de Lares* was one factor that led Spain to grant Puerto Rico the right to organize its first political parties in 1869. Yet, attempts to gain independence for Puerto Rico suffered a decisive blow after the botched revolution.

Simultaneously, in the eastern region of Cuba, representatives of the *criollo* bourgeoisie also plotted a rebellion. In the town of Yara, on October 10—just weeks

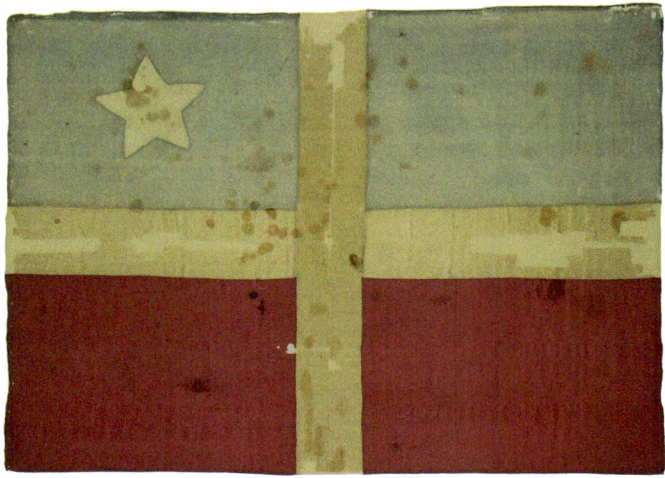

Fig. 6 *Grito de Lares Flag*, Rosalía Márquez (life dates unknown), 1868. Cloth; 83.8 × 119.3 cm (33 × 47 in.). Museo de Historia, Antropología y Arte, Universidad de Puerto Rico, Recinto de Río Piedras

Primary sources describe the waving of a red square flag and a white triangular flag during the insurrection in Lares in 1868. To date, there is no record sustaining that the tricolor flag designed by Ramón Emeterio Betances was unfurled during the uprising. Furthermore, there is debate around the authenticity of the *Grito de Lares* flag said to be sewn by Márquez (after Bracetti) and previously believed to have been unfurled at *Grito de Lares*. Nonetheless, the flag's design, with its white cross, blue and red quadrants, and white star, has been embraced as a symbol of Puerto Rican independence.

after the *Grito de Lares*—sugar planter Carlos Manuel de Céspedes (1819–1874) freed those he had enslaved, enlisting them as soldiers in his insurgent army. Together, they declared Cuba's independence. The event catalyzed the *Grito de Yara*, a revolt that spread quickly across the eastern province of Oriente, eventually giving way to the long struggle that came to be known as the Ten Years' War (1868–1878). The progress of the *mambises*, or guerrilla soldiers, was impeded by the Spanish-built *trocha*, a line of fortifications in the central eastern province of Camagüey built to protect the lucrative sugar regions in the West (see p. 193).[54] There, wealthier *peninsulares* and *criollos*, who benefited from the status quo, stood in support of the Spanish Crown and slavery.[55] The Pact of Zanjón ended the war in 1878, but the *mambises* were not satisfied. Revolutionaries capitulated, having achieved neither independence nor the abolition of slavery. In 1879, the most intractable rebels led the months-long *Guerra Chiquita*, or Little War. Momentum for the cause persisted, and it led to the abolition of slavery in Cuba in 1886.

Cuba and Puerto Rico's Divergent Paths, 1870–1897

The final contours of the islands' struggles for independence took shape from the city of New York, a hub for Cuban and Puerto Rican political exiles. Revolutionary clubs, such as La Liga, Las Dos Antillas, and El Club Borinquen, created community cohesion and organized for the overthrow of Spain. In 1891, the Afro-Puerto Rican typesetter Arturo Schomburg (1874–1938) became the recording secretary of Las Dos Antillas (fig. 7). His early experience there, participating in the formulation of an antiracist and anticolonial political vision for Cuba and Puerto Rico, was the beginning of a lifelong quest to assert Black pride through the documentation of historical achievements of the African diaspora.[56]

The early 1890s were a hotbed of political activism in New York. In 1892, the writer José Martí (1853–1895) founded the Partido Revolucionario Cubano (Cuban Revolutionary Party) (fig. 8). Attesting to Martí's kinship with Betances and Eugenio María de Hostos (1839–1903), and his belief in the Antillean Confederation, he named them general delegates of the party in Paris and Chile, where they each resided. Martí had identified with the ideal of Cuban independence since his teenage years, when he received his first prison sentence for publishing the newspaper *La patria libre* (The free land), in support of the Ten Years' War. From then on, his political activism was accompanied by extensive writing. He was exiled from Cuba twice, in 1871 and in 1879. In between, he led a peripatetic life, spending time in France, Guatemala, Mexico, and Venezuela. In 1880, he established himself in New York, where he lived for the next fifteen years. Martí's time in the city was marked by his admiration for the foundational ideals of freedom and equality of the United States, but also by his strong denunciation of the realities of racism, capitalism, and imperialism that stood against those ideals.[57]

Martí understood the power of visual representation. Along with his writings, which were published in the Americas and Europe, he orchestrated the circulation of his image in the form of photographic portraits that represented him as a thinker and revolutionary.[58] After his death in 1895, during Cuba's third War of Independence, and as the First Republic of Cuba was inaugurated in 1902, Martí's likeness became iconic in Cuban art and central to the teleology of the nation.[59] Miguel Díaz Salinero (1874–1943) was one of the most prolific painters of posthumous portraits of Martí.[60] Between 1920 and 1940, he created

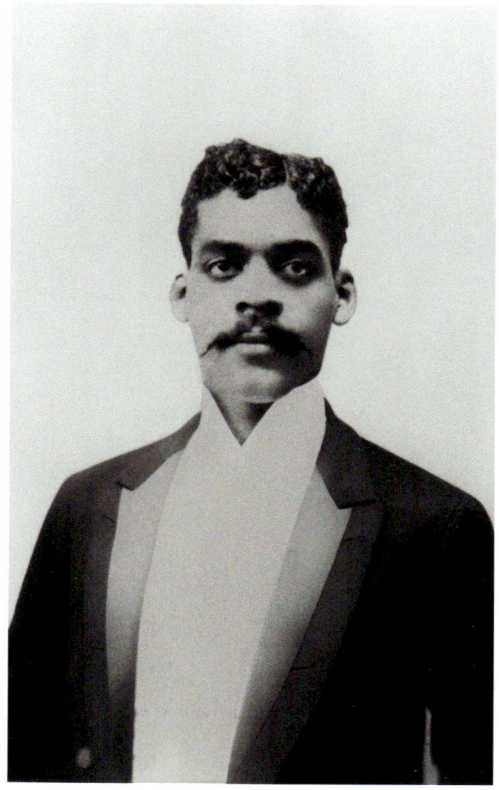

Fig. 7 *Arturo Alfonso Schomburg (Arthur Schomburg)* (1874–1938), Unidentified photographer, 1896. Gelatin silver print; dimensions unknown. Schomburg Center for Research in Black Culture; Photographs and Prints Division, The New York Public Library

Fig. 8 *José Martí* (1853–1895), Miguel Díaz Salinero (1874–1943), c. 1942. Oil on canvas; 130.2 × 84.5 cm (51¼ × 33¼ in.). Collection of Mr. and Mrs. Mike Fernandez

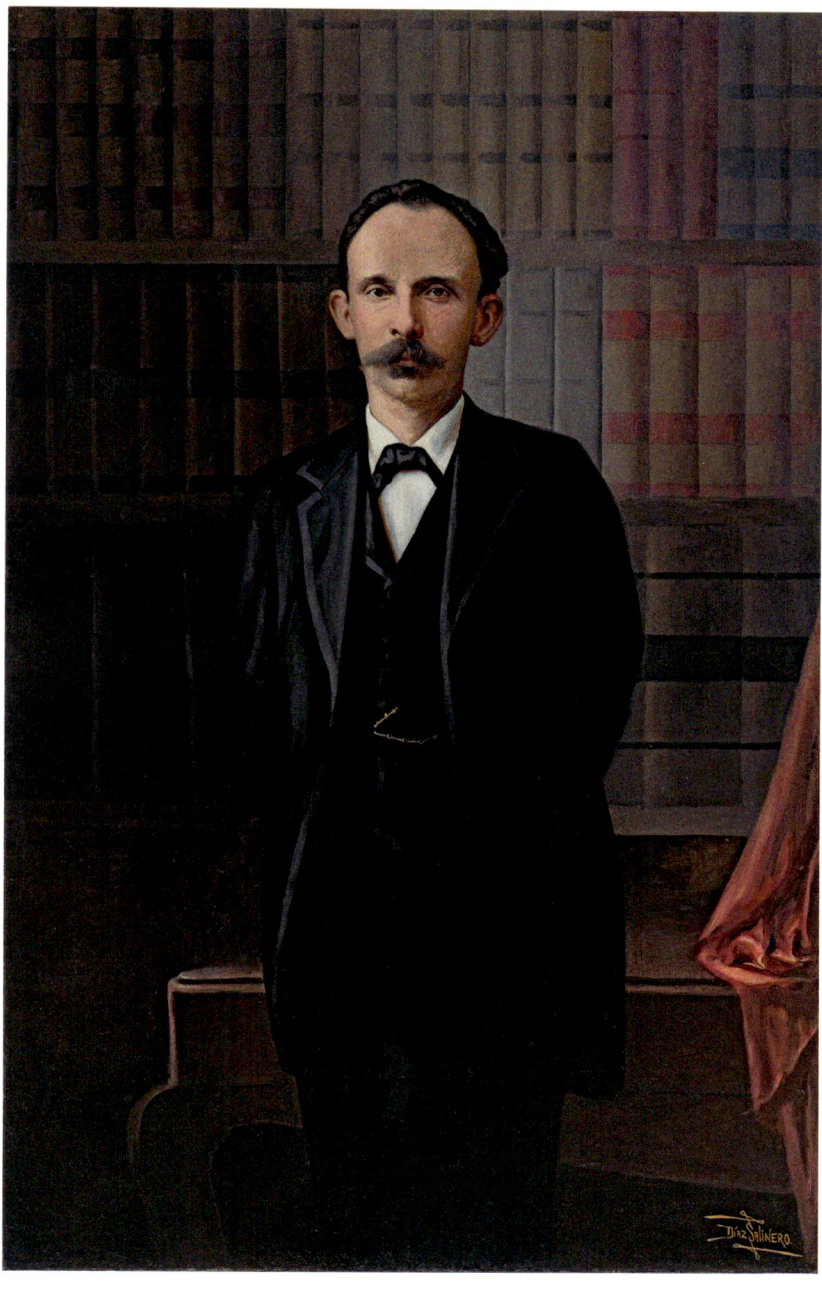

dozens of paintings of "the Apostle of Cuban independence," basing them on historical photographs. This portrait of Martí in formal dress shows him as a man of letters and ideas. Standing in a library, with his forehead subtly lit, Martí's intellect is emphasized.

For Martí, the goal of independence was not only to end Spanish colonialism, but also to establish "a republic for all," a land of interracial equality and harmony.[61] At his invitation, two veteran heroes of the Ten Years' War

accepted the call to lead the third War of Independence: the Dominican-born Máximo Gómez (1836–1905) became the commander in chief of the Liberation Army, and Antonio Maceo (1845–1896) was appointed general lieutenant, or second in command (fig. 9). A man of African ancestry, Maceo had made the abolition of slavery and the end of racial privileges central to the fight for Cuban independence. In 1891, General Antonio Maceo established himself in Costa Rica, where the government contracted him and gave him approximately 24,000 acres to build an agricultural colony that was formed by Cuban veterans and families. The colony of Nicoya, where tobacco was grown, was intended as a safe haven for the exiles, from where revolutionary activities could continue. A portrait taken that year pictures Maceo in the center back row, with other Cuban generals—including the Afro-descendants Flor Crombet (1851–1895), to his left, and Agustín Cebreco (1855–1924), to his right—and Maceo's dog Cuba Libre at the center (fig. 10). Rather than wearing military uniforms, all the generals are wearing formal clothes, presenting themselves as modern men of distinction who are equally at ease in the city. With his chin up and face turned right, Maceo conveys a distinguished air and sense of command over the group.[62] As a Black military leader, he embodied the revolution's promise of racial equality.[63]

After three years of preparation, on February 24, 1895, during the first Sunday of carnival, rebels declared Cuban independence in the eastern town of Baire, and, for the first time, in the western province of Matanzas. This war was different from the previous two in that it was supported by diverse sectors of Cuban society.[64] On May 19, Martí perished in combat in the town of Dos Ríos, consecrating la Guerra Necesaria (1895–1898), "The Necessary War," through his own martyrdom.[65]

A main strategy of the multiracial Cuban Liberation Army in this final war was to extend the conflict beyond Oriente, past the *trocha*, which had never been crossed before. In December 1895, Gómez and Maceo led rebels from the valleys and mountains of eastern Cuba, beyond the province of Camagüey to the island's westernmost point.[66] Supporters joined rebels by the thousands through the operation called "the Invasion."[67] An official Spanish military photograph features the leaders from the Spanish Regiment of Tarragona who participated in the battle of the *Potrero de Saratoga*, the Paddock of Saratoga, between June 9 and 11 of 1896 (fig. 11). The crossing of the *trocha* from the west back to the east by General Máximo Gómez's troops provoked this encounter. The three-day battle, in which Spanish forces surpassed the Cuban insurgent army by three to one was one of the war's bloodiest confrontations. That much, both armies agreed on. However, each also claimed victory.[68] With the Invasion of western Cuba, Gómez's strategy changed from engaging the Spanish in combat to torching the property of the *peninsulares* and *criollos* who collaborated with the Spanish regime.[69]

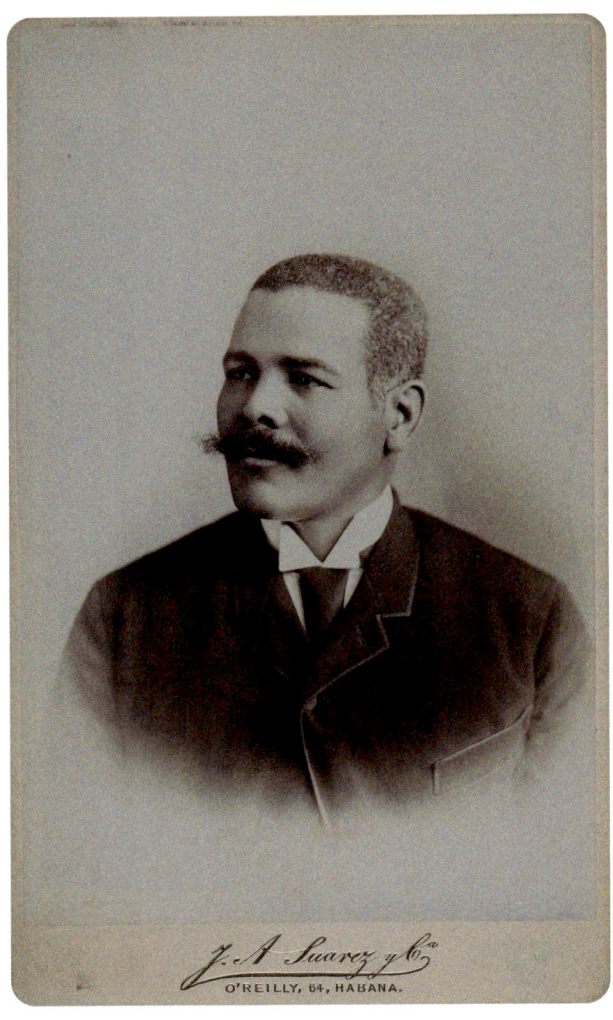

Fig. 9 *Antonio Maceo* (1845–1896), J. A. Suárez y Ca., 1890. Albumen silver print; 19.4 × 12.5 cm (7⅝ × 4¹⁵⁄₁₆ in.). Biblioteca Nacional de España

The Spanish responded to the island-wide conflict by sending the infamous Governor-General Valeriano Weyler (1838–1930) to restore order. Weyler implemented his infamous *reconcentrado* policy by decree, ordering local populations to evacuate the countryside and be moved to fortified towns. By implication, as life in the countryside was criminalized, subsistence agriculture was banned and farmers with livestock had to move their herds to the cities.[70] Reconcentration was aimed at preventing the *pacífico*, or non-fighting population, from supporting insurgents. They had been doing this by gathering intelligence on the movements of the Spanish Army and helping the *mambises* hide weapons. Armando García Menocal (1863–1942) (see p. 314), who served the Cuban Liberation Army

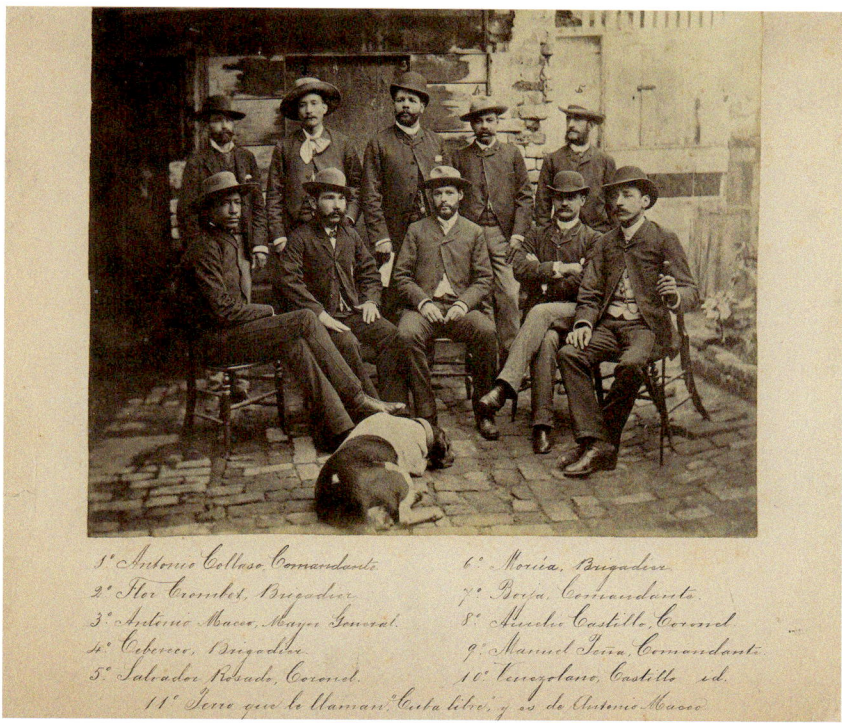

Fig. 10 *Grupo de líderes cubanos* (Group of Cuban leaders), Unidentified photographer, c. 1895–1898. Albumen silver print; 16.9 × 21.3 cm (6⅝ × 8⅜ in.). Biblioteca Nacional de España

Fig. 11 *Guerra de Cuba: Jefes y Oficiales del Regimiento de Tarragona que tomaron parte en el glorioso hecho de armas del potrero Saratoga* (War of Cuba: Chiefs and officials of the Regiment of Tarragona who took part in the glorious armed incident of the Paddock of Saratoga), Unidentified photographer, 1896. Photograph; 15.2 × 22.9 cm (6 × 9 in.). Biblioteca Nacional de España

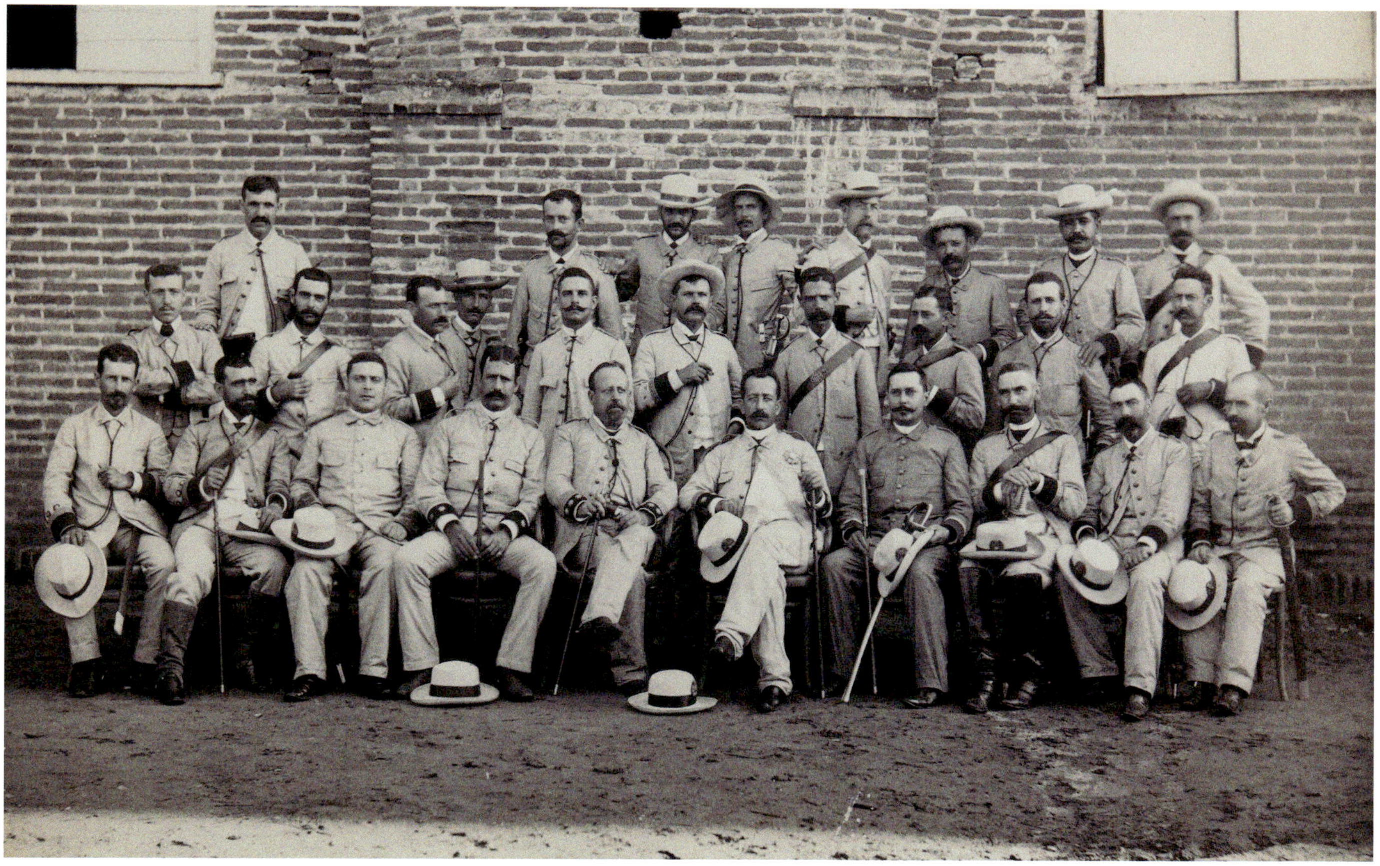

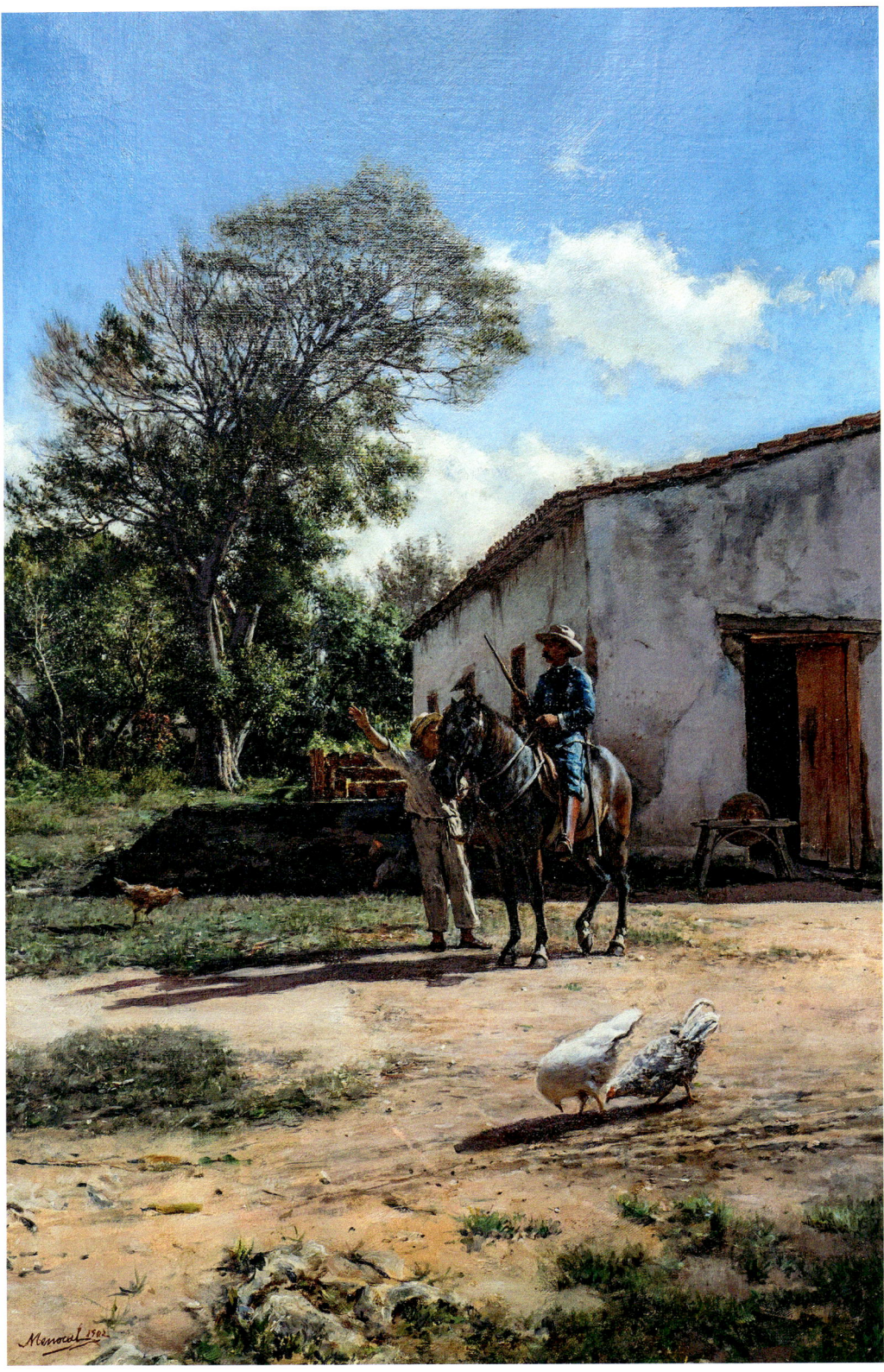

Fig. 12 *Campesino y soldado español* (Peasant and Spanish soldier), Armando García Menocal (1863–1942), 1902. Oil on canvas; 43.2 × 64.8 cm (17 × 25½ in.). Collection of Emilio and Sylvia M. Ortiz

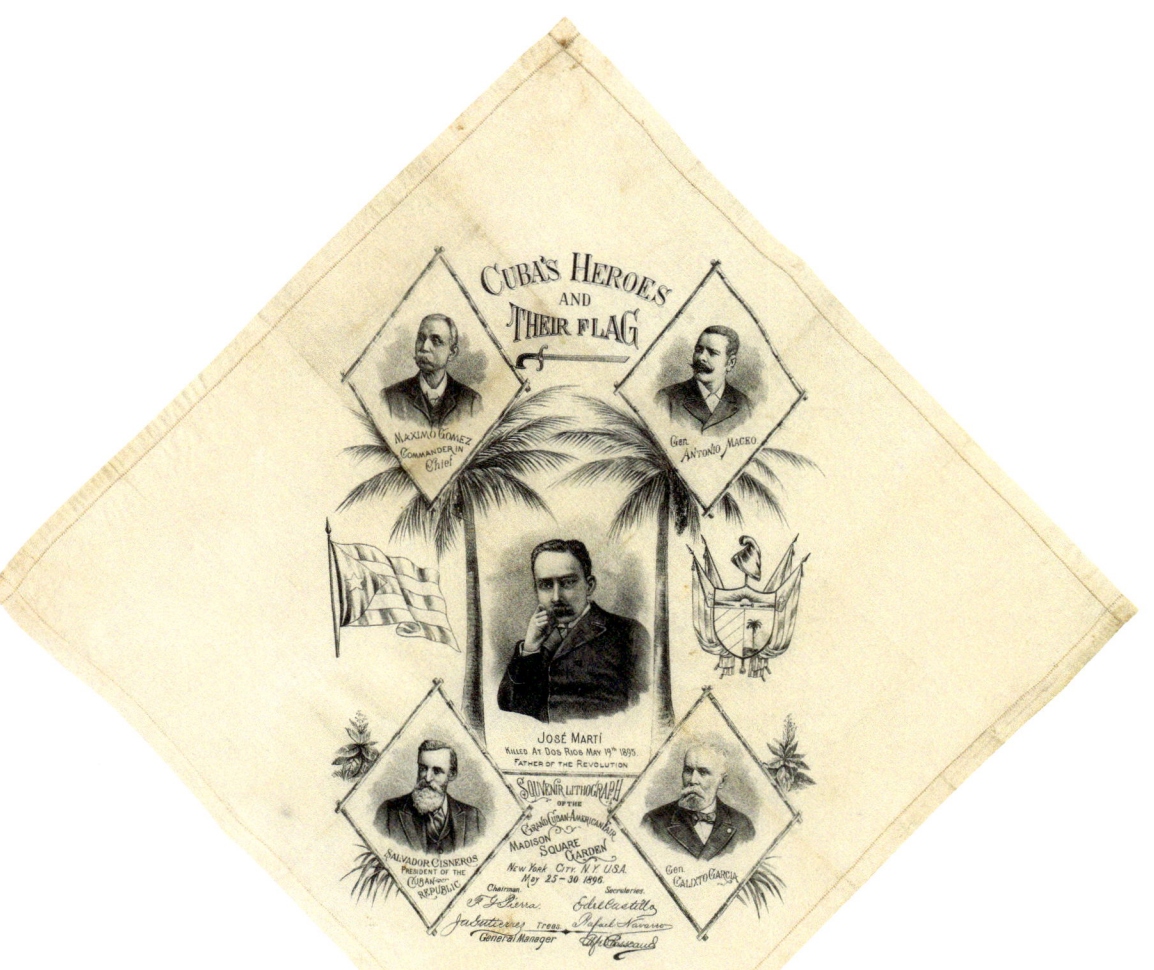

Fig. 13 *Cuba's Heroes and Their Flag*, Unidentified artist, 1896. Lithograph on linen; 45.7 × 45.7 cm (18 × 18 in.), Collection of Emilio Cueto

during the Invasion and reached the rank of major in the 1895–1898 war, painted *Campesino y soldado español* in 1902 (fig. 12). The artwork depicts an interaction between a Spanish soldier on horseback and a Cuban peasant, the latter pointing to the distance.[71] Is the peasant collaborating, or perhaps willingly providing erroneous information to the soldier? The quietude of this scene betrays the tension between these two sectors of Cuban society at a time of war. Weyler also took aim at the autonomist elite, who to that point had repudiated the insurgency but were losing faith that Spain could defeat the rebels. He terrorized them through censorship and imprisonment. With the island plunged deep into war and the economy at the edge of collapse, the Spanish Crown tried to appease the situation by withdrawing Weyler in June 1897 and installing the less severe Ramón Blanco (1833–1906) as governor general.

Throughout the war, supporters of the Cuban cause in New York City continued raising funds for weapons and resources, garnering the favor of U.S. entrepreneurs with investments in Cuba.[72] At a Cuban American fair organized at Madison Square Garden in May 1896, objects such as this silk handkerchief with the title *Cuba's Heroes and Their Flag*, were sold (fig. 13). The textile honored the men who represented Cuba's long fight for independence through engraved portraits, including its ideologue Martí, at the center, as well as Gómez, Maceo, Calixto García (1839–1898), general in command of eastern operations (who also led the Little War), and Salvador Cisneros (1828–1914), president of the Cuban Republic in Arms.

Meanwhile, support for Puerto Rico's independence movement was confined mainly to New York City. Among its leaders was journalist, educator, and sociologist

Eugenio María de Hostos, who after studying in Spain moved to New York in 1869 and became an activist for Puerto Rican and Cuban independence.[73] Hostos was, however, disappointed that most Cubans in New York who opposed Spanish colonialism favored the island's annexation to the United States. Disaffected, he branched out and traveled through South America as an advocate of Puerto Rican independence, launching a revolutionary project of education. In Santo Domingo, he joined the exiled Betances in campaigning for the Antillean Confederation.

Autonomism characterized the political movement of late nineteenth-century Puerto Rico, and after much advocacy it would eventually be at an arm's reach by the end of the century. In the early 1880s, the road to define its terms and strategy lay ahead. Galvanized by the economic crisis of 1886, a number of *criollo* intellectuals formed a movement to demand economic autonomy from Spain. Román Baldorioty de Castro (1822–1889), who had been a Puerto Rican deputy to the Spanish *Cortes* and was a member of the reformist party that sought more civil liberties, proposed an autonomist model based on the government that Great Britain had established in Canada. Rather than being limited to internal administrative affairs, the Canadian model of autonomy operated in the administrative, political, and economic arenas of government.[74] He led the founding of the Partido Autonomista (Autonomist Party) in 1887. Alarmed by the party's popularity, Governor Romualdo Palacio (1827–1908) responded by systematically jailing autonomists and administering physical punishments called *compontes*, meaning rectifications, to "correct" their political persuasion. His repressive measures led people to refer to the year 1887 as *El año terrible*, "The terrible year."[75] Baldorioty de Castro endured a *componte* and was imprisoned in the dungeons of Castillo San Felipe del Morro along with fifteen other autonomists.[76] Upon the sudden destitution of Palacio that same year, Baldorioty was freed.[77] This incident gravely affected his health, and he died two years later in 1889.

Differences in the terms of self-government and how to achieve it divided the autonomists.[78] But in 1892, a young journalist, Luis Muñoz Rivera (1859–1916), rose to prominence with the controversial idea of making an alliance with a Spanish party and supporting their candidates for the *Cortes* in exchange for a promise of governmental autonomy.[79] In 1897, he signed a pact with the Spanish Partido Liberal, presided over by Práxedes Mateo Sagasta, the largest opposition to the conservative party, led by Antonio Cánovas del Castillo (1828–1897), then prime minister of Spain.[80] As fate would have it, Muñoz Rivera's idea prospered after an Italian anarchist murdered Cánovas del Castillo, leading to Sagasta's rise as prime minister of Spain.

Sagasta's declaration of autonomy for Cuba and Puerto Rico on November 25, 1897, was, more than anything, a desperate measure to end the war in Cuba.[81] But after three years of fighting, the Cuban Revolutionary Army refused to depose arms, rejecting anything short of independence. By contrast, Puerto Rican autonomists believed the goal of their activism was within reach.

In the early weeks of 1898, General Máximo Gómez felt certain that the Cuban Revolutionary Army would defeat Spain within the year, and Puerto Ricans constituted a provisional Autonomist Cabinet to begin preparing for an election in March.[82] Yet, the unforseen explosion of the *Maine* on February 15, 1898, triggered a chain of events that ripped both islands' certainty of their political futures. Responding to the jingoist clamoring from a U.S. public convinced by the yellow press that the explosion was caused by Spain, and to pressure from advocates of expansionism in Congress, McKinley declared war on Spain on April 25. To appease skeptics who suspected an imperial conquest of Cuba, Senator Henry Teller (1830–1914) of Colorado proposed an amendment to the war declaration. The Teller Amendment attested that the United States disclaimed "any disposition to exercise sovereignty, jurisdiction, or control over said island except for pacification thereof, and asserts its determination, when that is accomplished, to leave the government and control of the island to its people."[83] In other words, the Teller Amendment ruled out the possibility of annexing Cuba. The war was promoted as a definitive action by the United States to oust Spain from Cuba.

Neither Freedom nor Autonomy for Cuba and Puerto Rico: The Spanish-American War

McKinley called for 125,000 volunteers to conduct the war in the Caribbean and three cavalry regiments were organized by order of Congress. The First Volunteer Cavalry was given to Theodore Roosevelt (1858–1919) to lead after he had resigned as assistant secretary of the navy. Roosevelt turned to his close friend, the more experienced Leonard Wood (1860–1927), to command the regiment as colonel, and assumed the second in-command position of lieutenant colonel. Their regiment became known as the Rough Riders. The name was a misnomer, as thousands of horses had to be left in the U.S. training camps due to transportation difficulties.[84] As Harvard alumni, Roosevelt and Wood proudly recruited volunteers from their alma mater, as well as from other Ivy League universities. However, most of the recruits came from the territories that had recently become the American West, which Roosevelt deemed "the lands that have been most recently won over to white civilization, and in which the conditions of life are nearest those that obtained on the frontier when there still was a frontier."[85]

Charles Dana Gibson's portrait of Roosevelt, published in the January 1899 issue of *Scribner's Magazine*, illustrated the first installment of Roosevelt's memoir of his days as a lieutenant colonel of the Rough Riders, and pictures him in the Brooks Brothers uniform that he had ordered for himself (fig. 14).[86] Capitalizing on his military service as a tool for political advancement, Roosevelt published *The Rough Riders* in book form in 1899. It became a bestseller and, in turn, inspired games and other popular culture collectibles.[87]

The Battle of Santiago Bay

On April 22, 1898, President McKinley ordered a blockade of Cuba's north coast, marking the first step of the naval campaign against Spain. U.S. ships guarded 125 miles of coast, preventing the reinforcement of Spanish troops and commercial exchange between Spain and its colony through August 12, 1898.[88]

The United States also sent a separate blockade to the heavily fortified Bay of Santiago in the island's southeast. Rear Admiral William Sampson (1840–1902) positioned the U.S. fleet in a semicircle around the entrance of the harbor.[89] The Spanish defended the harbor with submarine mines. Beginning on May 19, 1898, the Spanish squadron, led by Admiral Pascual Cervera y Topete (1839–1909), concealed itself in Cuba's Bay of Santiago.[90] In June, the U.S. Army V Corps landed near Santiago, aiming to support the navy and force the city's surrender. A decisive battle took place on July 1, when Major General William Shafter (1835–1906) ordered his forces to attack the Spanish strongholds of El Caney and to capture Kettle Hill and San Juan Hill near Santiago. Roosevelt and the Rough Riders stood fourth in a line to accomplish the mission. After repeatedly requesting a better position, Roosevelt was finally authorized to support the regulars. That is when he

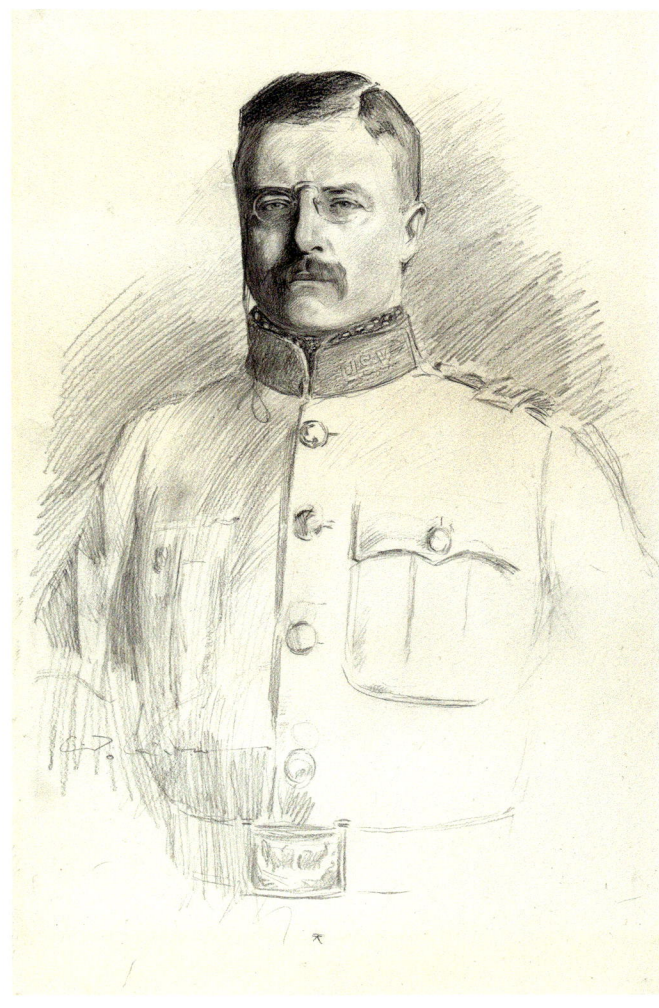

Fig. 14 *Theodore Roosevelt* (1858–1919), Charles Dana Gibson (1867–1944), 1898. Graphite and conté crayon on paper; 44.8 × 30.8 cm (17⅝ × 12⅛ in.). National Portrait Gallery, Smithsonian Institution

rode his horse to the front line and ordered his men to follow on foot.[91] The Rough Riders and the ninth and tenth cavalry regiments of Black soldiers took Kettle Hill and San Juan Hill, gaining the higher ground.

While the U.S. Army was forcing the Spanish out of higher ground, the U.S. Navy was intent on destroying the Spanish fleet in the Bay of Santiago. As the city was about to fall to U.S. hands, Governor General Blanco, concerned that the U.S. military would also seize the Spanish fleet, ordered Admiral Cervera y Topete to break the blockade and exit the bay.[92] On the morning of July 3—which for some scholars sealed the defeat of Spain in this war and earned it the name of *El Desastre*—the Spanish flagship

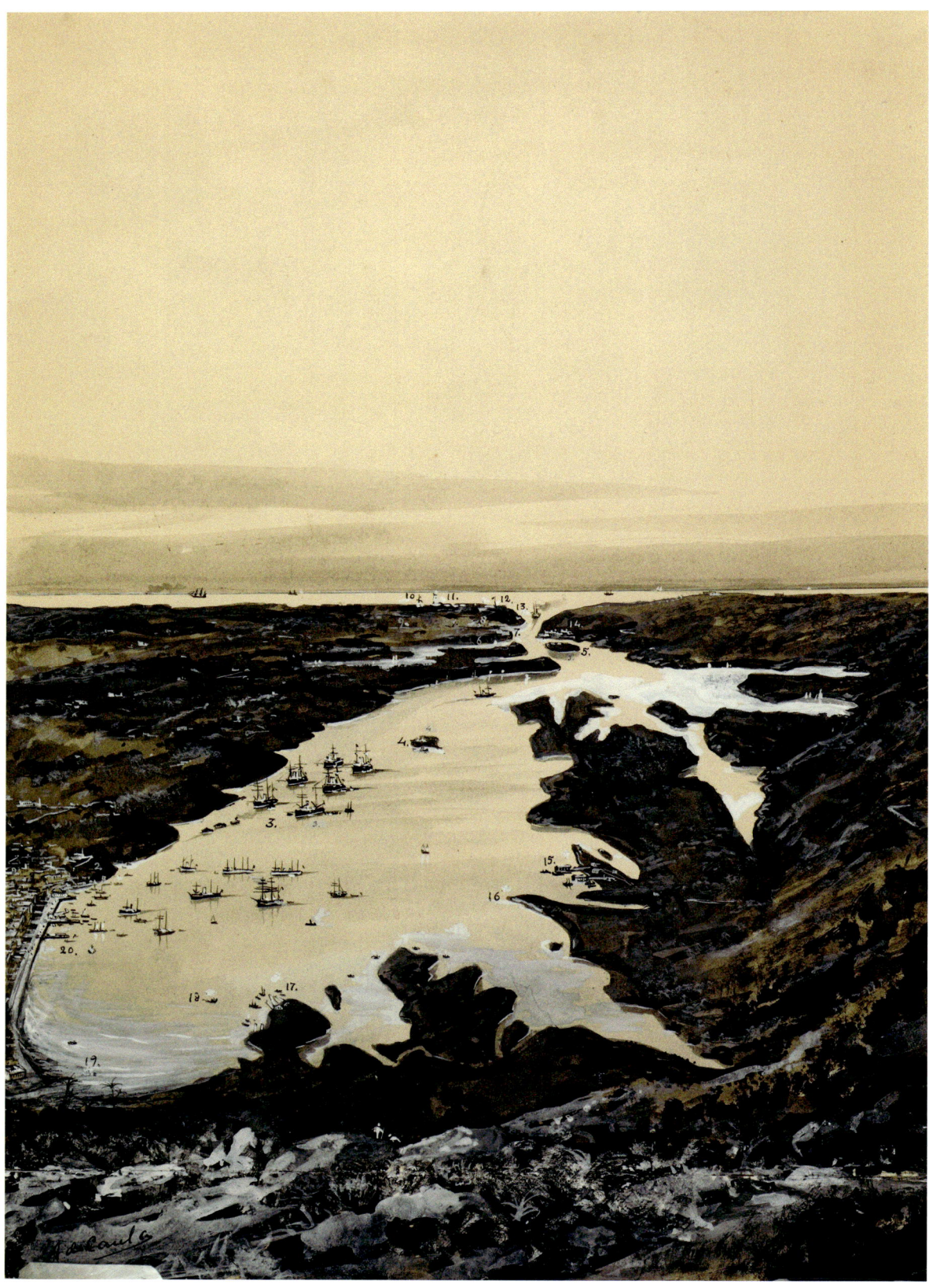

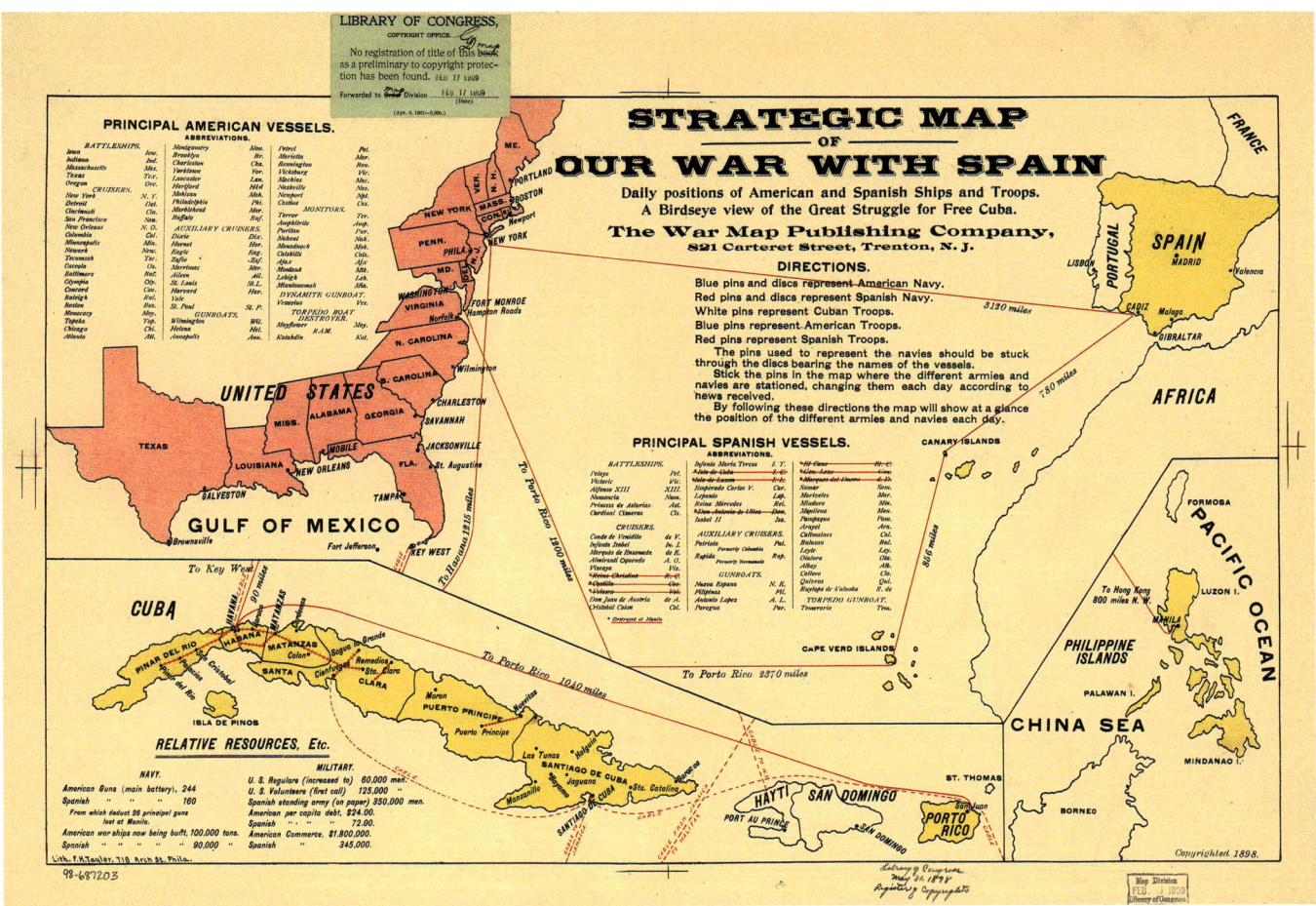

Fig. 15 *La escuadra del almirante Cervera bloqueada en la entrada de la Bahía de Santiago de Cuba* (Admiral Cervera's squadron trapped at the entry of the Bay of Santiago de Cuba), Unidentified artist, 1898. Watercolor on paper; 42 × 30.5 cm (16 ½ × 12 in.). Museo Naval, Madrid

Fig. 16 *Strategic Map of Our War with Spain*, War Map Publishing Company, 1898. Color lithograph; 38.3 × 56.8 cm (15⅟₁₆ × 22⅜ in.). Library of Congress, Geography and Map Division, Washington, DC

Infanta María Teresa headed the procession out of the safety of the bay through its narrow mouth (fig. 15).[93] In decreasing order of scale and artillery capacity, the *Vizcaya*, *Cristobal Colón*, *Almirante Oquendo*, and the destroyers *Furor* and *Plutón* followed. Once outside the bay, the *Brooklyn*, *Indiana*, *Oregon*, and *Iowa* sunk each enemy vessel, giving Spain a second, decisive military blow, after the destruction of its Pacific fleet in Manila on May 1. The city of Santiago surrendered on July 16.[94]

Back in the United States, a commercial industry boomed around the war, making it exciting and accessible to consumers. These objects "brought the war home" to permeate everyday life and functioned as U.S. nationalist propaganda. People could play games in which territory

and coaling stations could be won or follow the military campaigns on maps as news was reported day by day (fig. 16). The U.S. military leaders of the war were heroicized and popularized through their depiction on trading cards and other novelties, such as the Spanish American War Patriotic Fan, which features portraits of U.S. leaders of the Cuban campaign (fig. 17). The fan is made from nine separate paper leaves lined with fabric and attached to wooden sticks. The paper leaves are in the shape of pansy flowers, with embossing that imitates petals. Eight of the pansies also have embossed portraits. The ninth paper leaf is an abstracted flag of the United States on one side, and a similarly abstracted flag of Cuba on the other. The portraits are, from left to right: Theodore Roosevelt Jr.,

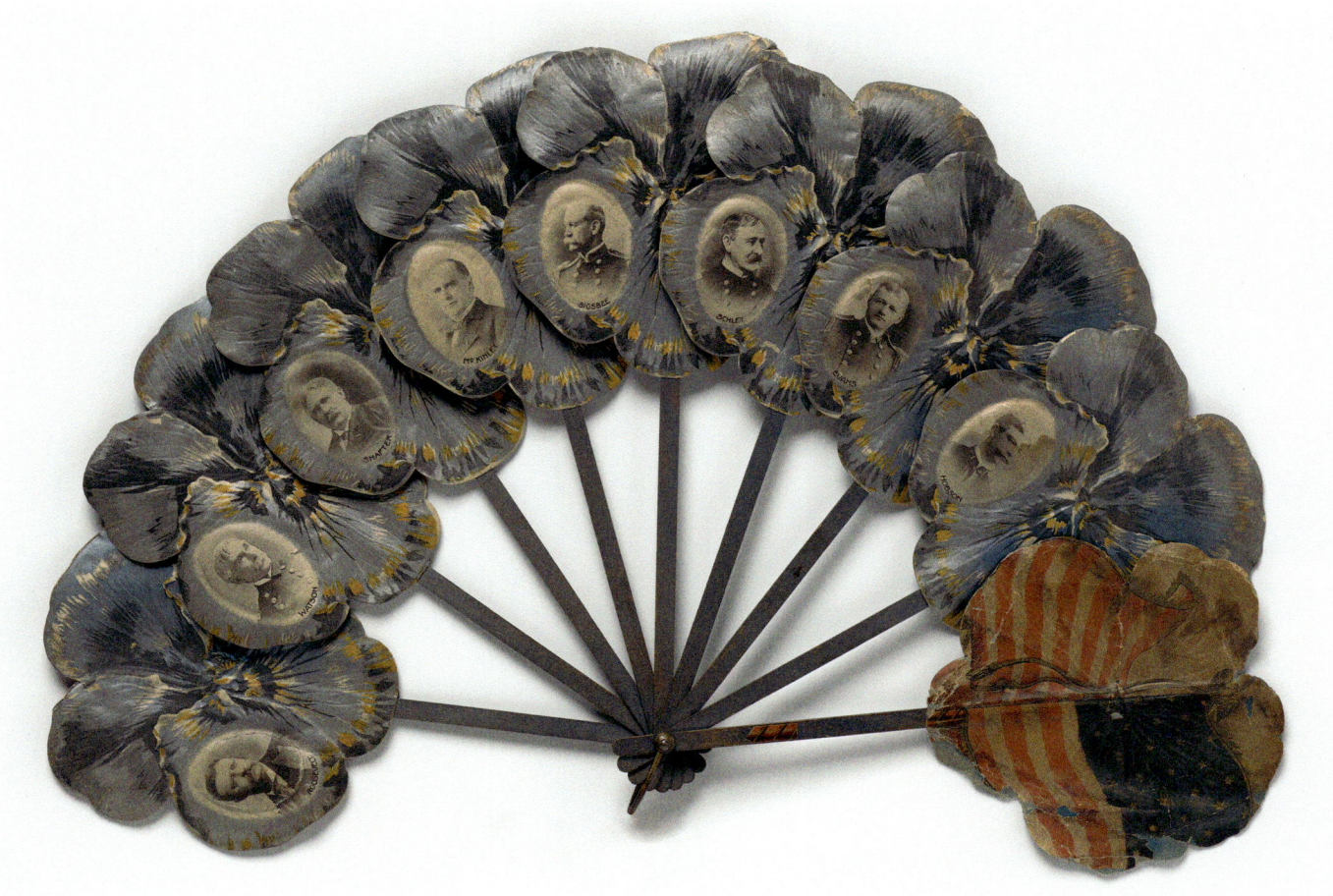

Fig. 17 *Spanish-American War Patriotic Fan*, Unidentified artist, c. 1898. Lithograph, wood, and metal; 17.8 × 35.6 cm (7 × 14 in.), Private collection

Fig. 18 *Raising of the Flag over the Governor's Palace, Santiago*, William Glackens (1870–1938), 1898. Pen, ink, watercolor, and Chinese white on paper; 61 × 42 cm (24 × 16½ in.). Library of Congress, Cabinet of American Illustration, Washington, DC

John C. Watson, William R. Shafter, William McKinley, Charles Dwight Sigsbee, Winfield Schley, Robley Evans, and Richmond P. Hobson. According to the *Oxford Dictionary of English*, in 1899, for a short period, the word "pansy" denoted "a remarkable or outstanding person."[95]

But beyond these objects of U.S. propaganda, what were the implications of the War for Cuba? The Cuban rebels were close to defeating the Spaniards and achieving the island's independence. Although Gómez and García had provided the U.S. military with intelligence crucial for victory, the United States coopted the culmination of the Cubans' thirty-year struggle, renaming the conflict the Spanish-American War. On January 1, 1899, the Spanish flag of El Morro castle in Havana was lowered

and replaced with the stars and stripes (fig. 18). The Cuban generals did not participate in the ceremony.

The War in Puerto Rico

The war also arrived in Puerto Rico. On May 12, 1898, without warning, Admiral Sampson's naval forces bombarded San Juan for three hours to test the island's military readiness. Angel Rivero Méndez (1856–1930), the Puerto Rican captain of artillery in charge of the Spanish troops of the San Cristobal fortress, described the event: "Projectiles rained, shaking like a railway, they flew over our heads in a true tempest of iron."[96] The attack was aimed at the fortress Castillo San Felipe del Morro, but many other structures in Old San Juan were hit. Men and women, children

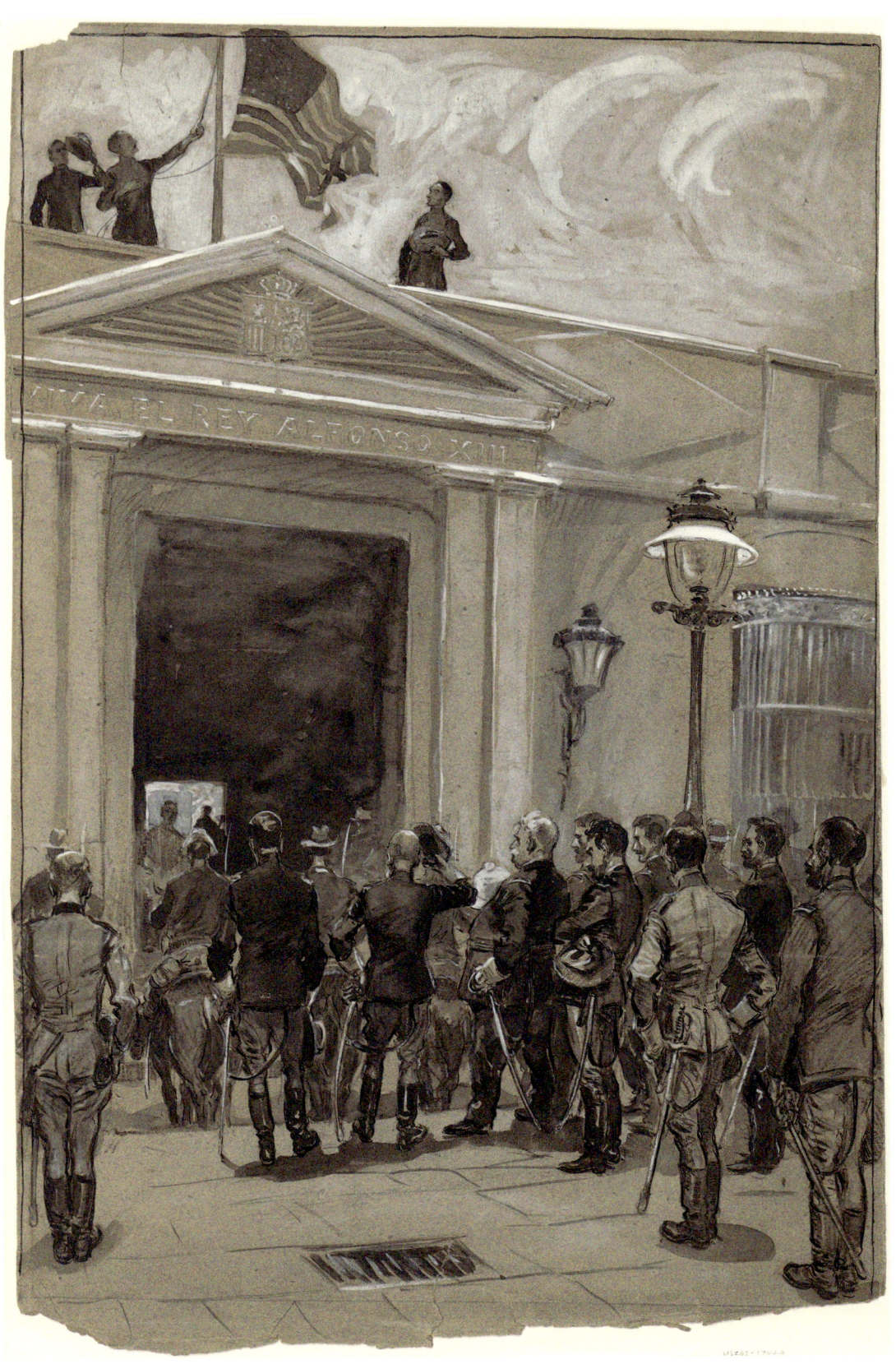

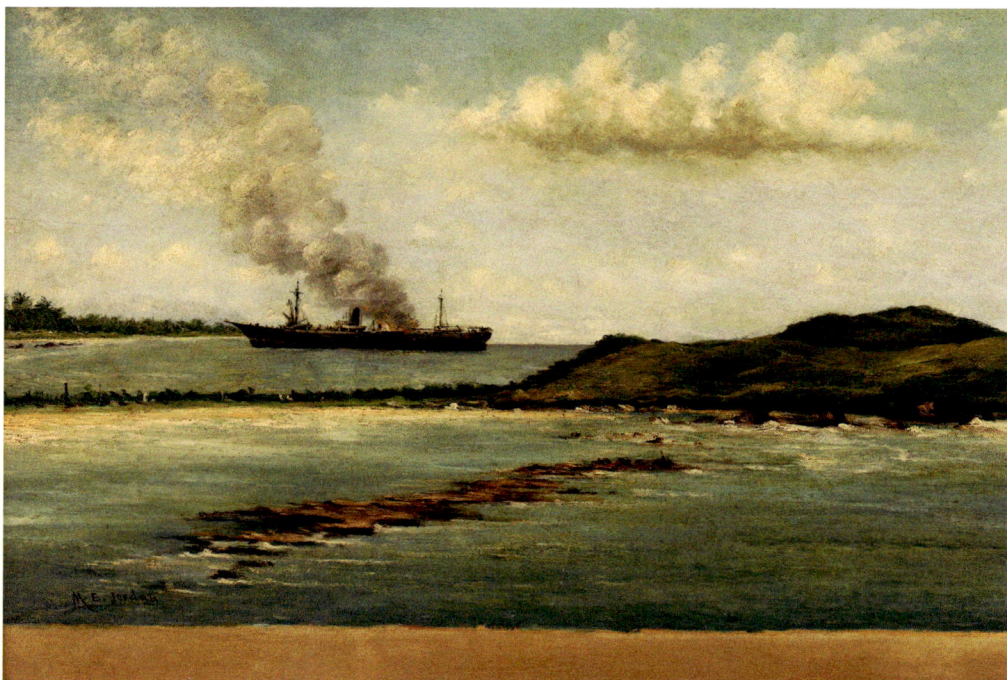

Fig. 19 *Escena de la Guerra Hispanoamericana* (Scene of the Spanish-American War), Manuel E. Jordán (1853–1919), 1898. Oil on wood; 31.8 × 59 cm (12½ × 23¼ in.). Instituto de Cultura Puertorriqueña

Fig. 20 *Spanish Figures of the Spanish-American War, Nelson Miles* (1839–1925), *Queen María Cristina* (1858–1929), *King Alfonso XIII* (1886–1941), *Práxedes Mateo Sagasta* (1825–1903), *Enrique Dupuy de Lôme* (1851–1904), *Valeriano Weyler* (1838–1930), *Basilio Agustín y Dávila* (1840–1910), *Don Carlos, Duke of Madrid* (1848–1909), Franklin Co., c. 1898. Offset lithograph; 36.2 × 27.6 cm (14¼ × 10⅞ in.). Private collection

and elderly people, tried to flee.[97] Among the Spanish forces defending the island, the episode left six dead and fifty wounded. Afterward, Sampson established a month-long blockade of the bay, causing hunger and anxiety.[98]

Manuel Jordán's (1853–1919) seascape *Escena de la Guerra Hispanoamericana* captures the tension between the blockade and the U.S. invasion (fig. 19). As a scene of naval warfare, it reminds us of Campeche's *Ex-voto del sitio de San Juan por los ingleses* from a century earlier. Jordán's painting depicts the shelling of the Spanish transatlantic ship *Antonio López* by the USS *New Orleans* on July 16, 1898. The *Antonio López* had arrived in Puerto Rico from Cádiz on June 28 with weapons and munitions for the Spanish troops. The ship was unsuccessful in running Sampson's blockade facing the USS *Yosemite* in the entrance to the San Juan harbor. Although three Spanish ships prevented the *Antonio López* from being captured by the *Yosemite*, the vessel fatally ran into a reef, where it remained stuck. The incident that Manuel Jordán—a disciple of Francisco Oller—painted is of the final attack on the Spanish boat.[99] The placid waters off the coast of Dorado are shattered on July 16, 1898 by the impact of the shots of the USS *New Orleans* and the sinking *Antonio López*, in the foreground.

Once Santiago de Cuba surrendered, Spain, desperate to keep Puerto Rico, petitioned to McKinley for an armistice on July 22.[100] The United States opted to delay an answer, hoping to occupy as much Spanish territory as possible before laying down arms. By that time, General Nelson Miles (1839–1925), another veteran of the Indian Wars and the commander of the U.S. Army, was aboard the USS *Yale* leading the invasion of Puerto Rico. In this intriguing combinative image (fig. 20), reproduced in an unknown U.S. magazine, Miles's portrait medallion is surrounded by those of the leading political figures of the Spanish empire at the brink of its fall.

Based on outdated intelligence warning of an invasion through Fajardo, the Spanish Army was ready to defend Puerto Rico from the east. On the morning of July 25, the USS *Gloucester* arrived in the southern Bay of Guánica, firing grapeshot over the town. It was followed by four other ships.[101] One bird's eye view of the ships landing in Guánica accentuates the menacing, architectonic lines of these heavily armed steel vessels (fig. 21). Painted in black, white, and gray oil on canvas, the undated *Entry of the U.S. Navy through Guánica Bay* creates a sense of foreboding. Smaller boats surround the larger ones, helping the 3,415 troops disembark. With great precision, the anonymous artist depicts the numerous men setting up camp on the sandy shores of the Barrio Carenero. The ships impose upon the natural setting—its tropical vegetation rendered in great detail—and head toward the viewer in a way that

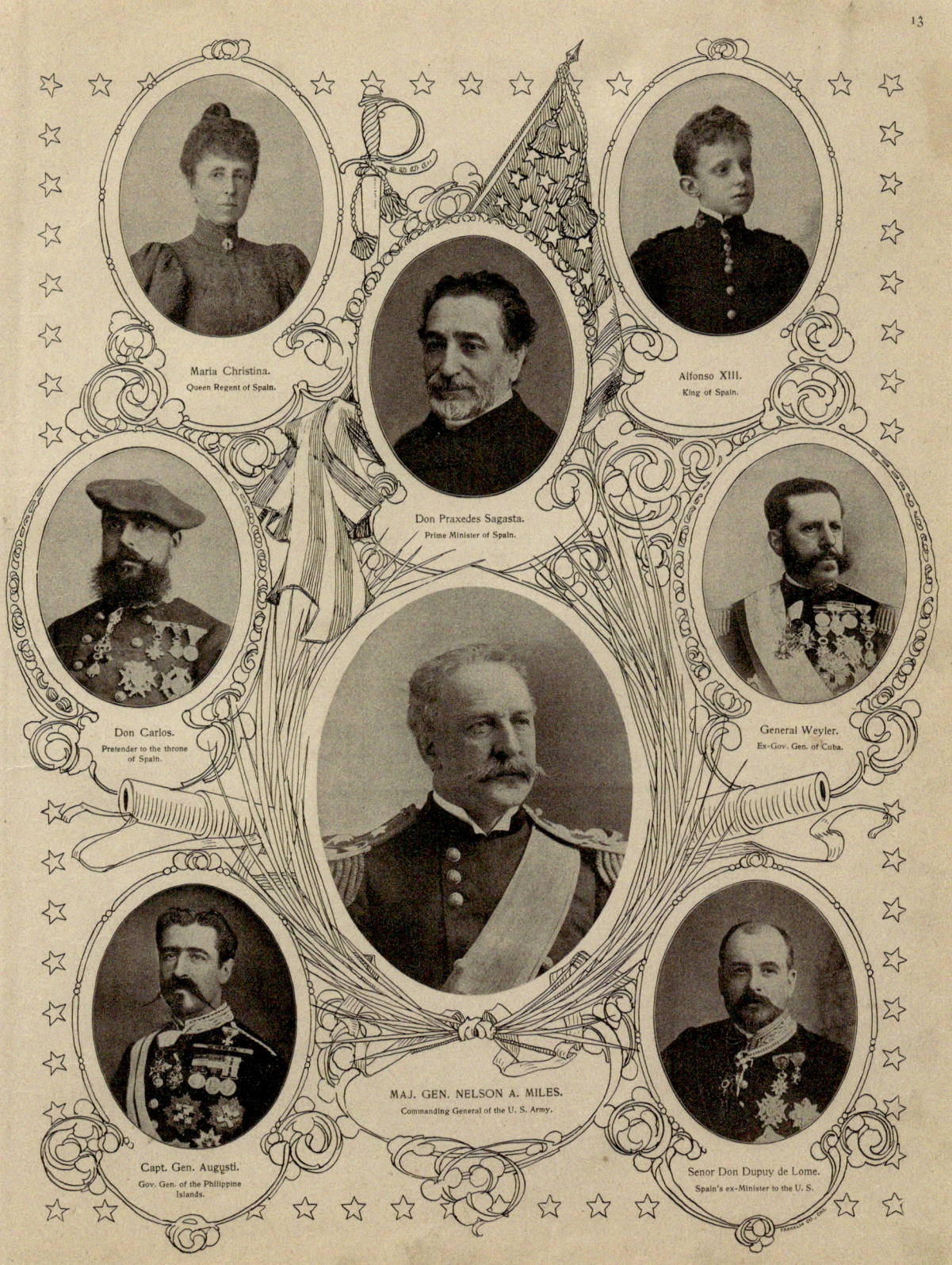

Maria Christina.
Queen Regent of Spain.

Alfonso XIII.
King of Spain.

Don Praxedes Sagasta.
Prime Minister of Spain.

Don Carlos.
Pretender to the throne
of Spain.

General Weyler.
Ex-Gov. Gen. of Cuba.

MAJ. GEN. NELSON A. MILES.
Commanding General of the U. S. Army.

Capt. Gen. Augusti.
Gov. Gen. of the Philippine
Islands.

Senor Don Dupuy de Lome.
Spain's ex-Minister to the U. S.

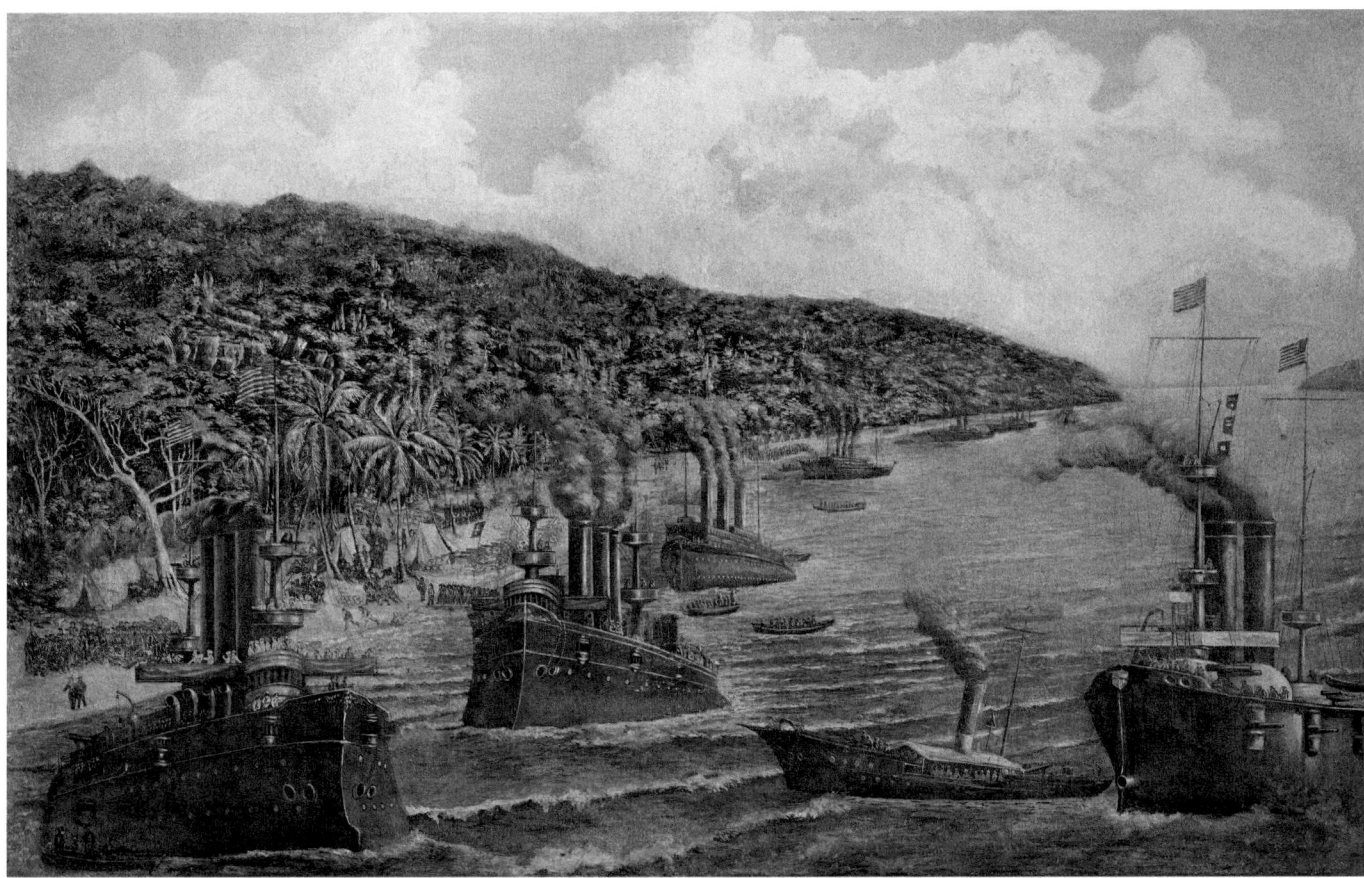

Fig. 21 *Entry of North Americans into Guánica Bay*, Unidentified artist, c. 1898–1950. Watercolor on canvas; 99.1 × 149.9 cm (39 × 59 in.). Collection of Aldarondo and López-Bras, LLC, Attorneys at Law

Fig. 22 *El desembarque de los americanos en Ponce, 27 de julio de 1898* (Americans disembarking in Ponce, July 27, 1898), Manuel Cuyás Agulló (active c. 1850–1900), 1898. Oil on canvas; 59.8 × 99.2 cm (23⁹⁄₁₆ × 39¹⁄₁₆ in.). Museo de Arte de Ponce, The Luis A. Ferré Foundation, Inc.; gift of José and Mary Jane Fernández

conveys the extraordinary nature of the threat. Despite this ominous portrayal, fewer than a dozen Spanish troops met U.S. forces in Guánica. Four of them were killed in a brief skirmish before the United States raised its flag in victory.[91]

Scouts and translators facilitated the progression of U.S. troops to the town of Yauco, which they took on July 27. That same day, a small fleet of three ships, including the USS *Dixie*, USS *Annapolis*, and USS *Wasp*, arrived in the bustling city of Ponce, the island's southern intellectual and economic capital. On July 28, General Nelson Miles read a proclamation from the U.S. government, announcing their arrival as standard bearers of liberty willing to bestow the virtues of democracy on Puerto Ricans.

The painting *El desembarque de los americanos en Ponce, 27 de julio de 1898*, by Manuel Cuyás Agulló (life dates unknown), presents a scene drastically different in mood from the one of the U.S. invasion through Guánica (fig. 22). The work is based on a photograph likely taken by the Puerto Rico-born Frederic Ballell Maymí (1864–1951), an engineer by training. Passionate about photography, he extensively documented the arrival of the United States in Ponce.[102] A painter of maritime scenes in his native Barcelona, Cuyás Agullò was Ballell's brother-in-law.[103] Translating the black-and-white photograph into a painting, Cuyás Agullò presents us with a scene of the island's most dynamic port, as viewed from the neighborhood of La Playa. The painting captures the cautious optimism surrounding the arrival of the United States in the south. Carriages transport merchandise back and

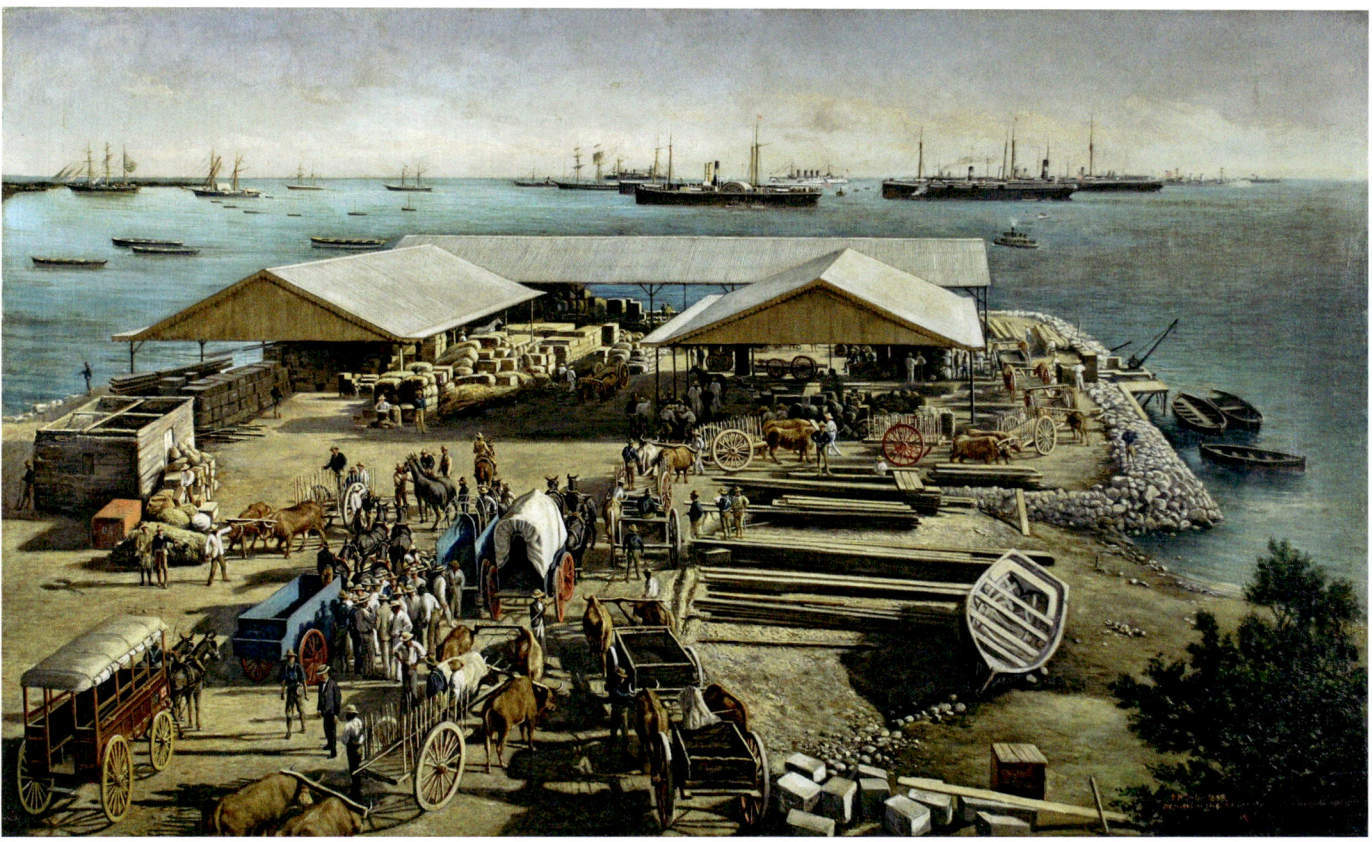

forth to the covered structures of the dock. Amidst piles of straw and crates, uniformed men interact with elegantly dressed ones. The U.S. ships in the calm waters appear as a welcome presence, perhaps even as a protective force against Spanish colonial abuses. From Ponce, the troops continued through the center of the island, facing opposition from the Spanish troops in some towns, notably in Aibonito, and also in the island's west. With minimal losses, the Puerto Rican campaign was characterized by the U.S. as "a picnic," reflecting less on the military prowess of the U.S. and more on the cooperation of disaffected *criollos* and other sectors of Puerto Rican society who expected the United States to bring prosperity, modernity, and freedom.[104]

On August 12, a cease-fire ensued, and on December 10, in the city of Paris, the Treaty of Paris officially ended the War of 1898. Puerto Rico and Cuba, along with the Philippines and Guam, were formally transferred by Spain to the United States. Neither Cuba, which had fought for three decades for its independence, nor Puerto Rico, whose Autonomist Cabinet had been inaugurated eight days before the U.S. invasion, were invited to the negotiations.

As Cuban rebel army General Máximo Gómez later wrote, "it was a pact negotiated by two foreign nations."[105]

Cuba after the War

For more than three years, the United States occupied Cuba. On January 1, 1899, it established a military government led by Major General John R. Brooke (1838–1936), who was replaced by Brigadier General Leonard Wood in December 1899.[106] Racist attitudes of the U.S. military leaders toward the many Cuban rebels of African ancestry prompted conversations about the possibility of a permanent occupation. As a military governor, Wood aimed to empower the country's *peninsulares* and *criollo* upper classes over the "ignorant masses," by ensuring the maximum representation of the former in the first municipal elections in Havana and in the constituent assembly charged with drafting a Cuban constitution.[107] Wood was convinced that eventually these upper classes would clamor for the island's annexation to the United States.[108] As part of his plan, the U.S. government improved Cuba's infrastructure and modernized the island's custom houses as well as its prison and judicial systems.

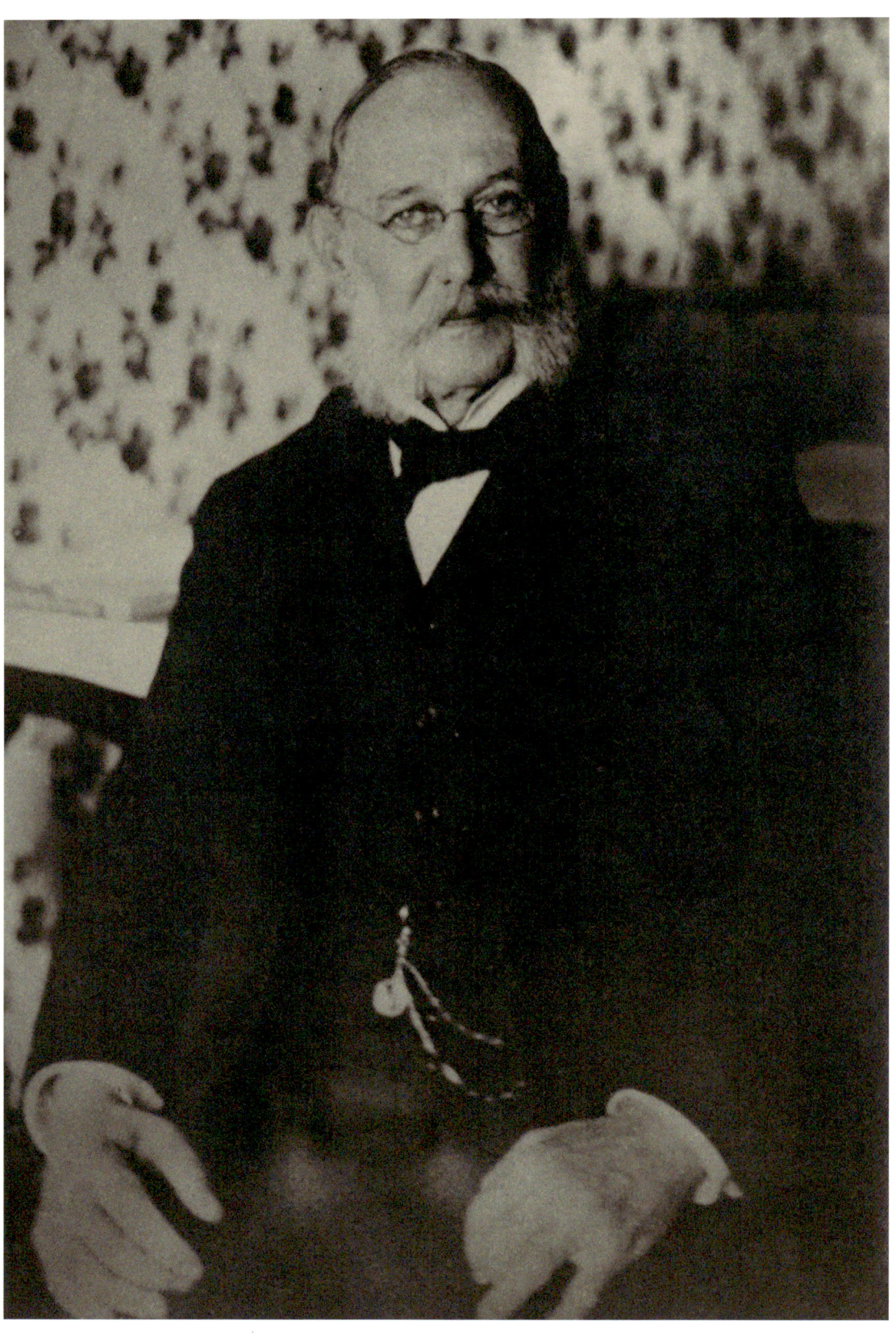

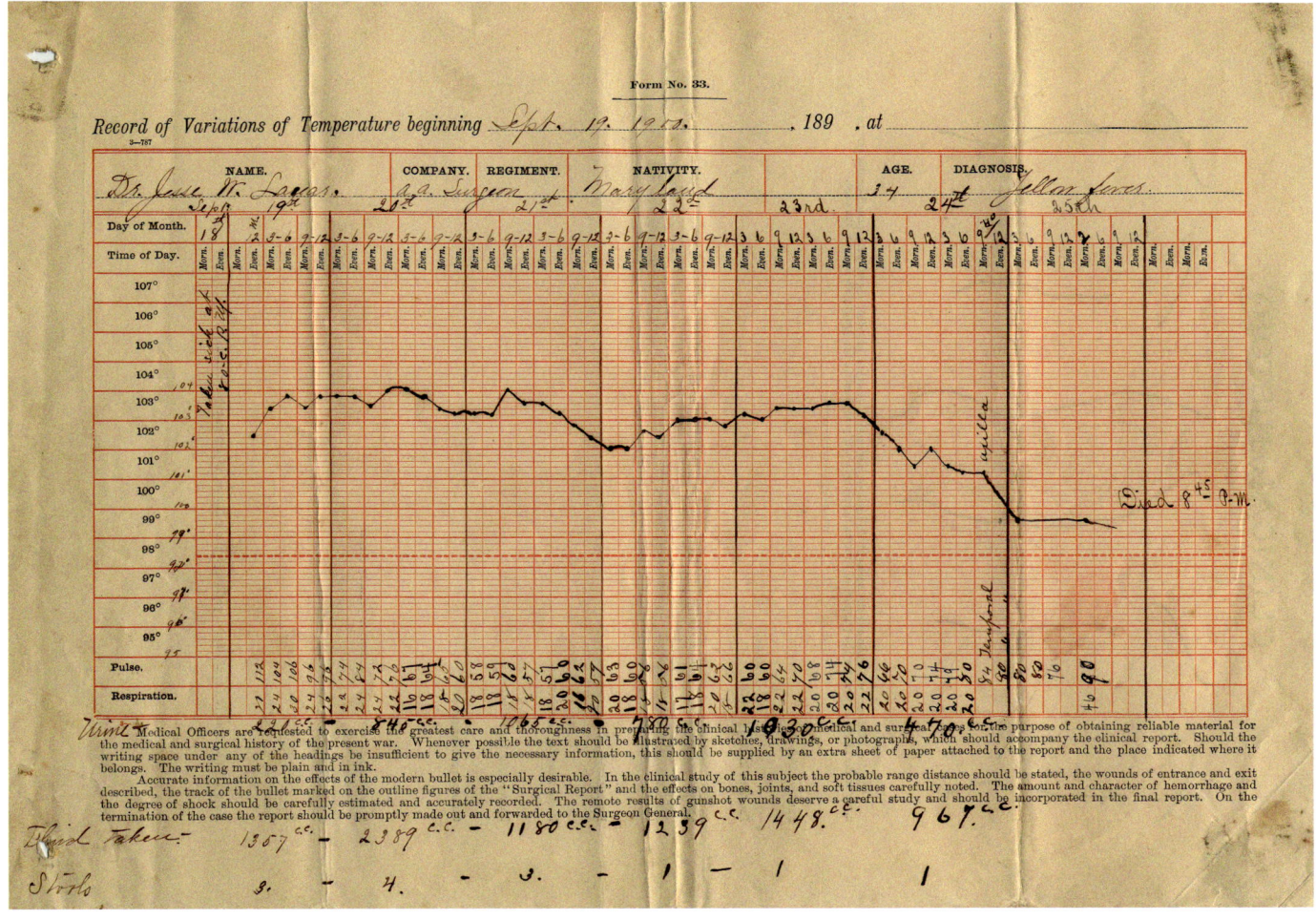

Fig. 23 *Carlos Finlay* (1833–1915), Unidentified photographer, c. 1900. Gelatin silver print; 17 × 12 cm (6⅝ × 4¾ in.). University of Miami Libraries, Cuban Heritage Collection

Fig. 24 Yellow fever chart for Dr. Jesse W. Lazear, 1900. Ink on paper; 26.5 × 40.5 cm (10⁷⁄₁₆ × 15¹⁵⁄₁₆ in.). Claude Moore Health Sciences Library, University of Virginia

Another primary realm of activity for the U.S. military government in Cuba was that of science and health. It was not combat, but rather yellow fever, typhoid fever, and malaria that killed the most U.S. soldiers through all the arenas of the War of 1898. Black troops were thought to be immune against yellow fever, and were, therefore, assigned to care for the afflicted.[109] For years, the American Public Health Organization (APHA) had pleaded for research funds from the United States to study the causes of yellow fever. Once the United States gained control of Cuba, it established the Yellow Fever Commission, led by Major Walter Reed (1851–1902) of the U.S. Army.[110] From 1881 to 1900, the Cuban scientist Dr. Carlos Finlay (1833–1915) had hypothesized that female mosquitos, *Aedes aegypti*, were

the vectors of yellow fever (fig. 23).[111] Reed's experiments involved hatching mosquito eggs from Finlay's collection. After the mosquitos had fed on yellow fever patients from Havana Hospital, he had them bite healthy volunteers. Fever charts such as this one from 1900 were compiled to study the progression of the disease (fig. 24). The chart tracks the symptoms of Jesse Lazear (1866–1900), one of the four surgeon members of the Yellow Fever Commission, and the only one who did not survive the experiment.[112] The experiment validated Finlay's theory and led to the establishment of sanitary methods to control the mosquito population. By 1902, the disease was eradicated.[113] This research proved crucial for the next chapter in the consolidation of the U.S. empire: the construction of

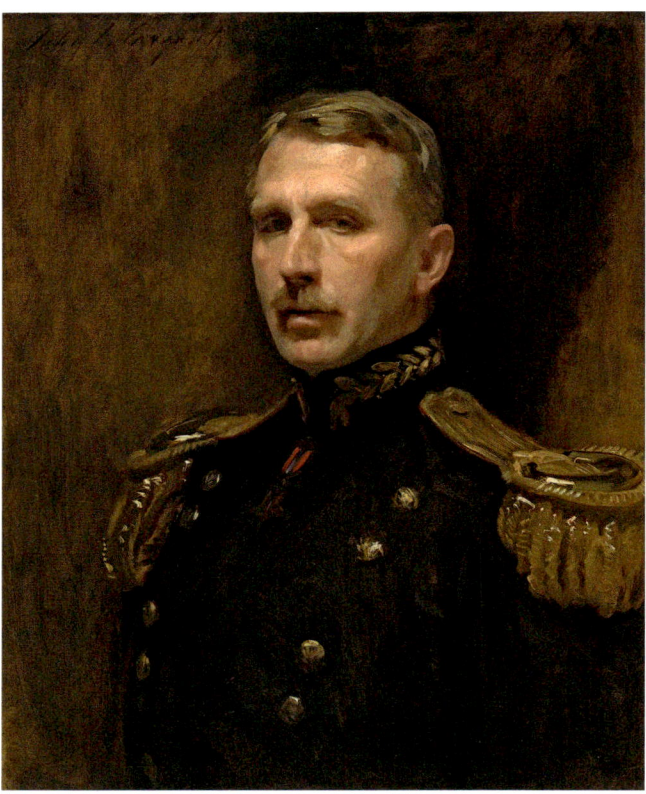

Fig. 25 *Leonard Wood* (1860–1927), John Singer Sargent (1856–1925), 1903. Oil on canvas; 76.5 × 63.8 cm (30⅛ × 25⅛ in.). National Portrait Gallery, Smithsonian Institution

the Panama Canal. The U.S. perception of tropical zones as sites of disease was transformed, and they were henceforth seen as places brimming with economic potential.[114]

Wood considered this medical advancement the most important contribution of the U.S. military government in Cuba.[115] Otherwise, this period was marked by political tension and uncertainty. *Peninsulares* and *criollos* supported the U.S. military and the idea of permanent annexation, but independentist sentiment was stronger. At the same time, U.S. military officials regarded independentists with disdain and were convinced that they were unfit for self-government. Three years into the U.S. occupation, Cuba was a costly burden to keep, but U.S. interests had to be secured before a government transfer.[116] Their solution—the Platt Amendment—maneuvered around the obstacles for U.S. sovereignty over Cuba established in the Teller Amendment by retaining the right of U.S. intervention for the maintenance of a stable government, and the right to hold title to land for naval bases.[117] Protests in Cuba did not deter McKinley from conditioning the transfer of power to Cubans on their acceptance of the amendment.[118] On May 19, 1902, Wood transferred government to the Cubans and their republic was finally inaugurated.

Upon Wood's return to Washington, DC, his government in Cuba was celebrated as a model for U.S. colonial administration.[119] The following year, John Singer Sargent (1856–1925), the leading Anglo-American portraitist of his time, painted his portrait (fig. 25). Sargent depicts Wood in his uniform, in a three-quarter pose against a dark background. The light falls slightly from above, emphasizing the chiseled face that Sargent so admired.[120] His uprightness and stern expression convey authority—one that was recognized by the state, which would send him to be governor of Moro Province at another colonial outpost, the Philippines, in August of the same year.

The War's Aftermath in Puerto Rico

Not everyone was confident that the United States would abide by its values of freedom and democracy. Echoing the fears Martí had expressed for Cuba in 1895, Ramón Emeterio Betances warned Puerto Ricans of imperial control of the island by the United States from his deathbed in France. Upon hearing of McKinley's declaration of war, Eugenio María de Hostos, who in early 1898 was established in Chile, traveled to New York City to mobilize against the invasion of Puerto Rico, but Miles's fleet was already on its way to the island. Hostos then founded the

Liga de Patriotas Puertorriqueños (the Puerto Rican Patriotic League) with José Julio Henna (1848–1924) and Manuel Zeno Gandía (1855–1930) to advocate for the rights of Puerto Ricans, now in the hands of Washington, DC.[121] The fact that the independentist Hostos was making an alliance with Henna, who was president of the Puerto Rican section of the Cuban Revolutionary Party in New York, but favored Puerto Rico's annexation to the United States, reveals the strategic "coalition thinking" of Puerto Rican intellectuals at the time, as they attempted to create leverage for their voices to be heard by the new metropole.[122]

This portrait of Hostos was painted by Puerto Rican Francisco Oller y Cestero, the towering figure of Puerto Rican art in the second half of the nineteenth century (fig. 26). Although the painter did not date it, it is one of numerous portraits of illustrious Puerto Rican figures painted by Oller at the turn of the century.[123] There are no existing records confirming that Oller and Hostos knew each other. The work's provenance is not formally documented, but in his monograph on Oller, art historian and painter Osiris Delgado cites a letter from Felipe Janer, vice-chancellor of the recently established University of Puerto Rico, to the painter from 1912. In the letter, Janer denies Oller's request to ask the student body to raise funds to pay for his three-quarter-length portrait of Román Baldorioty de Castro, which he had sent to the school. He proposes a counteroffer, asking Oller to paint a bust-length portrait of Baldorioty de Castro that would function as a pendant to his portrait of Hostos, which he had previously gifted to the school.[124]

According to Delgado, Oller did not comply. But from this letter, we can deduce that his portrait of Hostos dates from before 1912 and that it was a gift to the University of Puerto Rico. Most likely based on a photograph, it depicts the sociologist in a suit. Placed in Puerto Rico's new institution of higher learning, the portrait also honors his work as an educator. In the context of the early years of U.S. rule in Puerto Rico, Oller's portrait of Hostos marks a counterpoint to the ones he painted of the Anglo-American governors, depicting a Puerto Rican who urged the United States to stay true to its democratic principles and consult Puerto Ricans about their own political future.[125]

But other kinds of activism also took place at this moment, from within the Puerto Rican political class that had emerged in the last years of Spanish rule. Over the first two decades under a U.S. government, Luis Muñoz Rivera tested the limits of the new colonial status. With

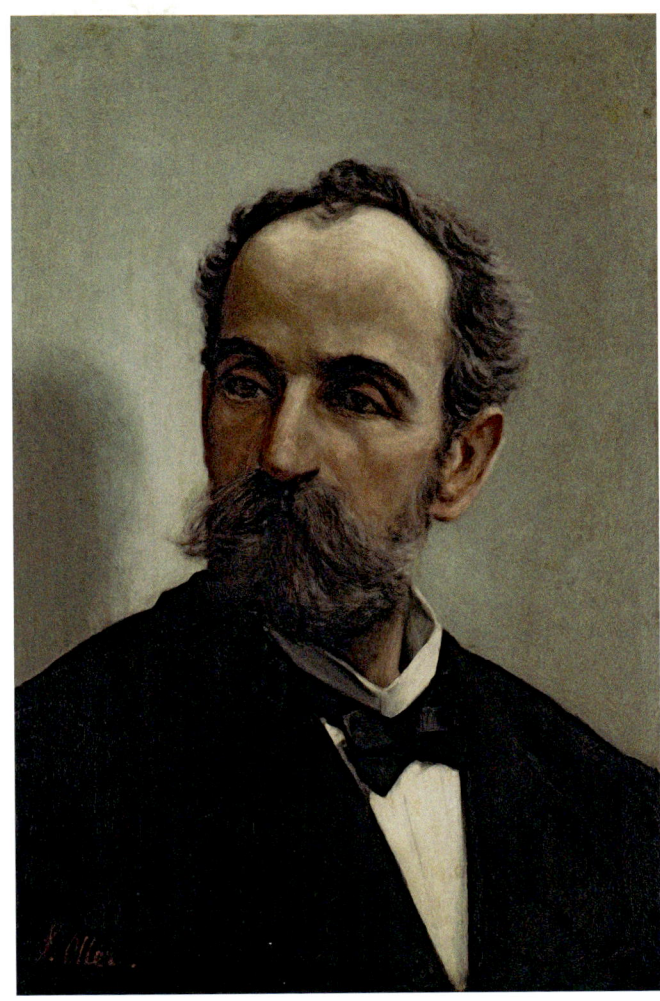

Fig. 26 *Eugenio María de Hostos* (1839–1903), Francisco Oller y Cestero (1833–1917), c. 1903. Oil on wood; 57.8 × 39.1 cm (22¾ × 15⅜ in.). Museo de Historia, Antropología y Arte, Universidad de Puerto Rico

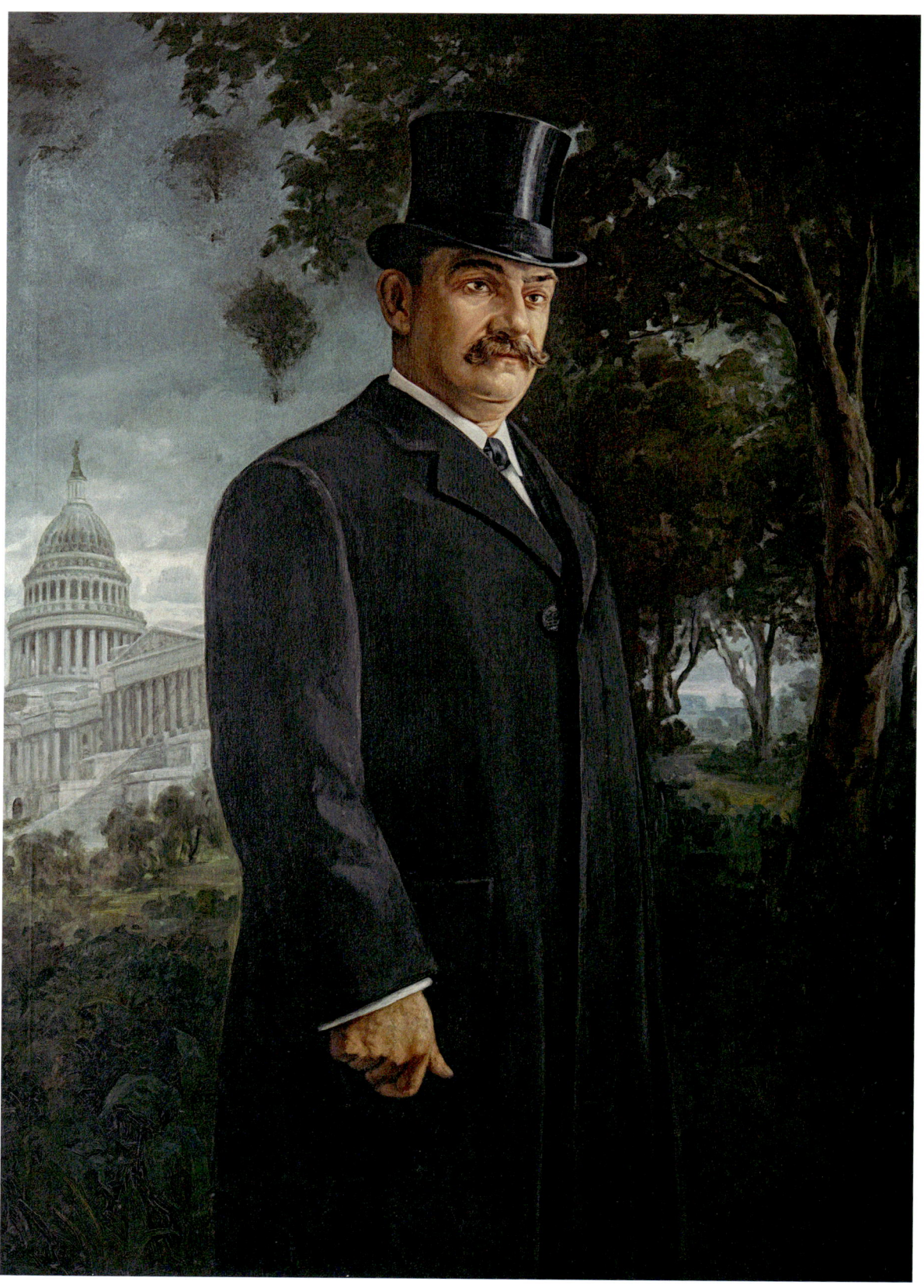

his working knowledge of English and without interpreters, he advocated for reform.[126] Having won the presidency of the Autonomist Cabinet eight days before the U.S. invasion of Puerto Rico, he was among the first local leaders with whom the U.S. military government, active from October 18, 1898, until May 12, 1900, engaged. In short succession, U.S. generals John R. Brooke (1838–1926), Guy Vernon Henry (1839–1899), and George Whitefield Davis (1839–1918) governed the island, implementing a variety of measures for the centralization of government. Brooke changed the spelling of the island's name to Porto Rico and instituted English as its official language.[127] The Autonomist Cabinet initially remained in place, albeit stripped of its powers. Measures were implemented to start the Americanization of the island.

The judicial system was modernized, and certain taxes were eliminated to help the poor, but tariffs imposed on Puerto Rican sugar and coffee hurt the economy. From his cabinet position, Muñoz Rivera organized the Insular Police Corps.[128] At the request of the sugar plantation owners, he traveled to Washington, DC, to lobby authorities for the reduction of trade barriers in agriculture.

A year after the cease-fire, on August 8, 1899, Hurricane San Ciriaco hit the island, causing three thousand deaths and devastation. That same year, the formerly divided Puerto Rican autonomist parties reorganized under new names: the Federal Party led by Muñoz Rivera and the Republican Party, led by José Celso Barbosa (1857–1921). Following the same logic as under Spain, when they sought to be recognized as a province, they both advocated for Puerto Rico's transformation into a state of the Union, with representation in Congress and control of their state government.[129]

Their hopes were crushed in May 1900 after the Foraker Act, which declared Puerto Rico a foreign territorial possession subject to U.S. rule with minimal representation, was enacted.[130] Puerto Ricans were thrown back under a form of colonial government they had fought to escape for more than a century.[131] Muñoz Rivera and the Federal Party criticized the act's colonial politics. He then moved to New York, where he challenged the conditions of the Foraker Act from the pages of his new weekly, the *Puerto Rico Herald*.[132] Of most consequence was his creation of the Partido Unión (Union Party) in 1904 with dissidents from the Partido Republicano (which remained uncritically pro-American) and from the labor movement.[133] He won a seat in the local house of delegates, serving in the Puerto Rican legislature between 1906 and 1909. In 1911, he took the seat of resident commissioner of Puerto Rico, the island's non-voting delegate in Washington, DC. He was reelected to the post in 1914. Until his death in 1916, he remained the dominant figure of Puerto Rican politics during the first sixteen years of U.S. rule. This portrait, by Fernando Díaz Mackenna (1873–1931), was commissioned by the Insular Police Corps, as a funerary homage (fig. 27). Fittingly, it portrays Muñoz Rivera dressed in his suit and top hat, against the backdrop of the U.S. Capitol, in recognition of his struggle on behalf of his compatriots in the new metropolis since 1898.

The War of 1898 marked a turning point for Cuba and Puerto Rico. The positive changes brought by the new U.S. colonial power included the vigorous development of the labor movement, the separation of Church and State, the establishment of the University of Puerto Rico in 1903, increased literacy rates, and an expanded public health system that decreased the mortality rate.[134] Yet, politically, when the United States established its sphere of influence over both islands, it set back anticolonial struggles that predated its arrival. Having a hold on each island's strategic geographic position, the country was one step closer to fulfilling Monroe's doctrine of hemispheric supremacy and Alfred Thayer Mahan's prescription for global ascendency.

4

"Forgetting Empire, Remembering Resistance"

THEODORE S. GONZALVES

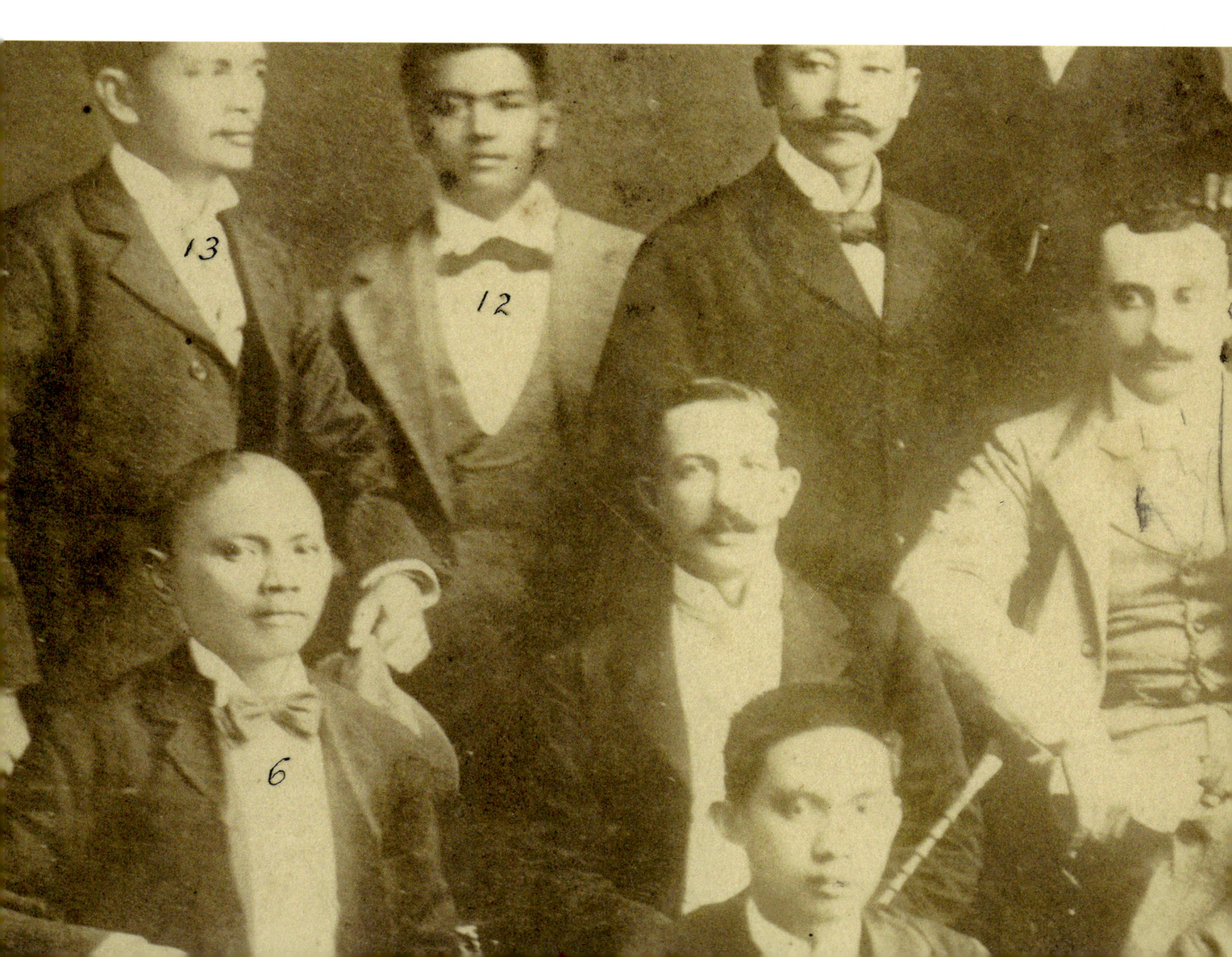

Not all of the hurts of history are healed in the ways we might want or expect, but some of those traumas can be addressed through rigorous scholarship and the relentless pursuit to convey the fullness of what transpired. This exhibition, *1898: U.S. Imperial Visions and Revisions*, affords us an opportunity to both widen and deepen our focus on an obscured time and disparate, seemingly disconnected locales. And while the term "empire" might seem abstracted from our daily lives, we continue to unravel strands of our present-day experiences that keep us anchored to usable pasts.

The next time you're in a bookstore, run your fingers along the spines of the chronologically arranged "U.S. History" section. You'll start at the wars of independence, proceed to the Federalist and Anti-federalist debates, the wars of Indian genocide and removal, the Civil War, Reconstruction, World Wars I and II, the Great Depression, the Jazz Age, the Korean War, postwar suburban bliss, McCarthyism and the Cold War, the (renewed) civil rights struggle, the Reagan era, and—depending on your

Detail of *Filipino Revolutionaries*, Unidentified photographer, 1898. Archivo de Indias, Seville

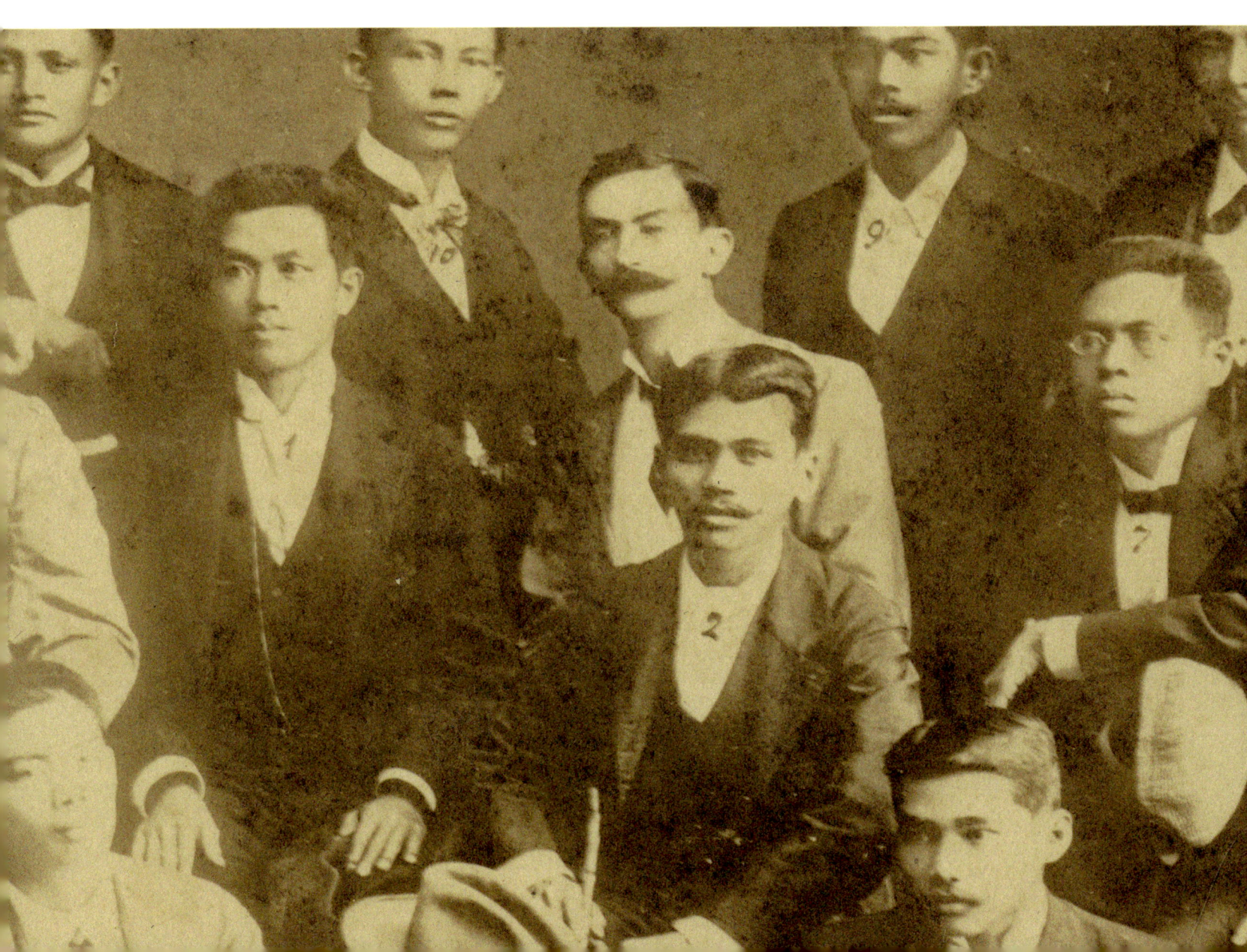

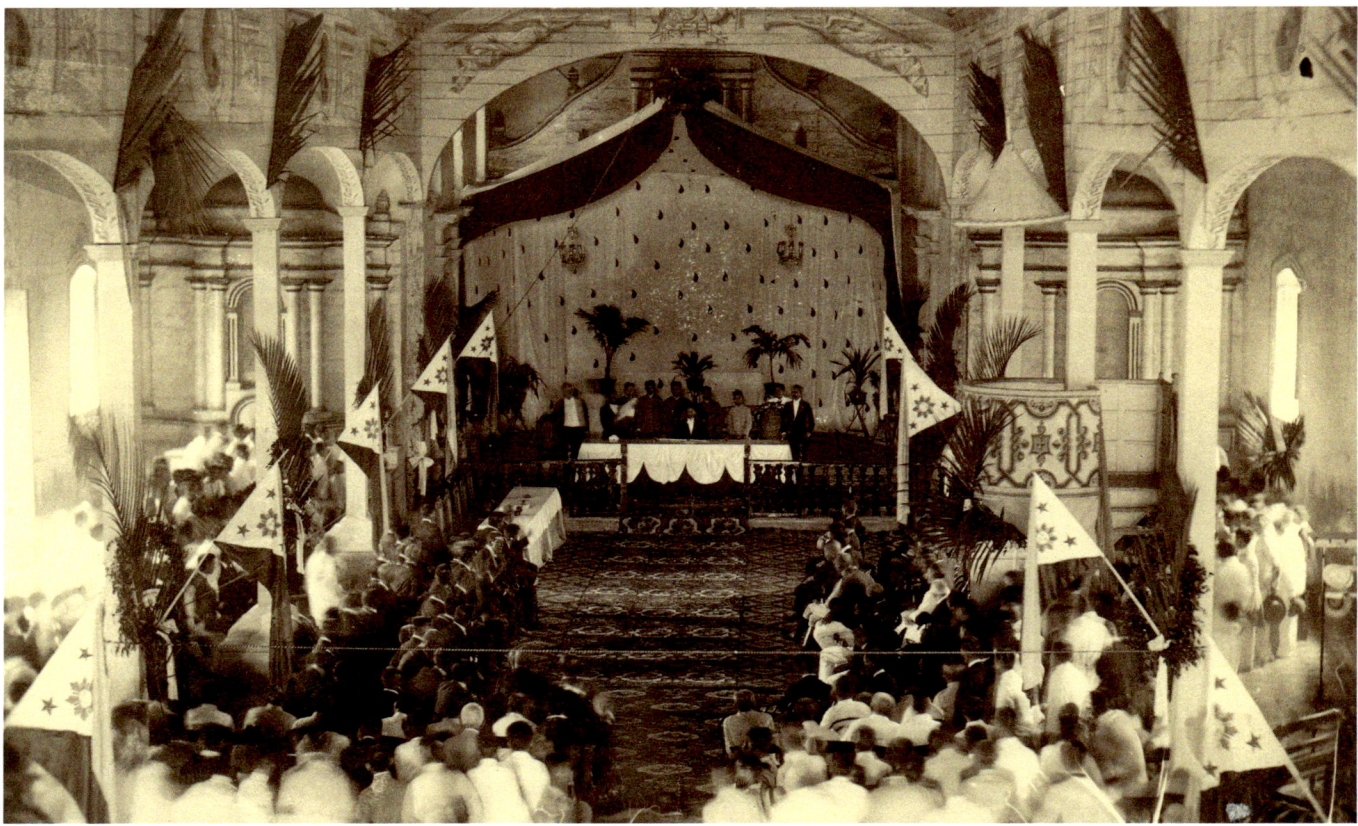

Fig. 1 *Insurgent Congress Hall, Malolos, Bulacan Province, Luzon Island. Aguinaldo in the Chair on the Platform*, Unidentified photographer, 1898. Gelatin silver print; 17.8 × 22.9 cm (9⁹⁄₁₆ × 11¹⁵⁄₁₆ in.). National Museum of American History, Smithsonian Institution

preferred version of neoliberalism—Francis Fukuyama's "end of history" or Barack Obama's so-called post-racial America, and finally encounter texts on the climate crisis, the return of populisms, and pandemics. Go back into the aisle to see if you've missed anything. The absence of American empire in the early years of the twentieth century on those shelves is no accident.

In an 1882 lecture at the Sorbonne, the French historian Ernest Renan asked "*Qu'est-ce qu'une nation?*" ("What is a nation?"). He replied to his own question: "Forgetting, and I would even say historical error, are an essential factor in the formation of a nation."[1] It's no surprise that Americans know so little about their wars with Spain and the Philippines. These spectacles of violence were prettied up with phrases like "splendid little wars" or "savage wars of peace." In the case of the Philippines, it wasn't even supposed to be referred to as a war. Sure, the Filipinos

raised their own flag, composed a national anthem, and declared their independence with Jefferson's document as their template on June 12, 1898 (fig. 1). But U.S. officials knew the precise effect of not sending a delegation to the ceremony. Declarations can only go so far. The other part of the equation is the recognition of sovereignty by others. Imagine the course of the United States' national memory taking a wildly different turn if the nation had extended recognition rather than annexing an archipelago for itself. And what should we do with that Philippine declaration of independence? Forget it ever happened. Instead, deny the combatants their righteous cause by referring to them as bandits (*tulisans*). As Renan said in his 1882 lecture, "Unity is always made brutally."

As the critic Edward Said wrote in *Beginnings*, "to begin is to embark upon something connected to a designated point of departure. Even when it is repressed, the beginning is always a first step from which (except on rare occasions) something follows."[2] How are the beginnings of empire remembered today?

The contemporary Filipino writer Luis Francia revisits an old story with a new protagonist. In his play, *Enrique*

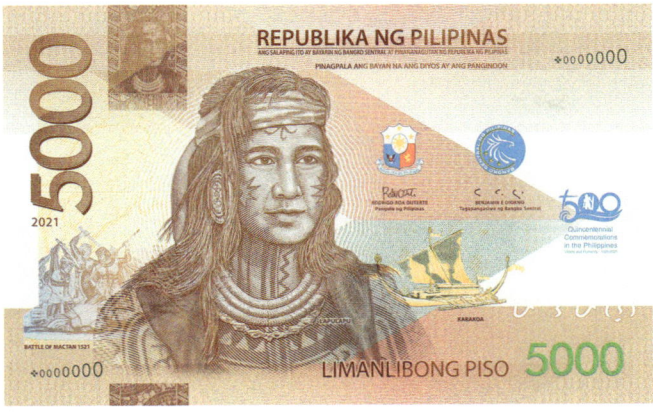

Fig. 2 5,000P Lapu Lapu commemorative banknote issued by the Bangko Sentral NG Pilipinas in 2021

El Negro / Black Henry, the central character is a teen by the name of Enrique who was captured in Malacca (present-day Malaysia) and purchased by Ferdinand Magellan when the Portuguese took that city in 1511.[3] Sailing from Southeast Asia with the commander to Europe and then back out to the Pacific in 1519, it is Enrique who can translate what the locals were saying when Magellan and his crew arrived in the archipelago later known as the Philippines. In 2019, Spain's national naval museum marked the 500th anniversary of the launch of Magellan's voyage with its exhibition *Fuimos los primeros: Magallanes, Elcano, y la Vuelta al mundo* (We Were the First: Magellan, Elcano, and the Journey Around the World). In focusing on the detail of Magellan taking possession of the boy originally in Malacca, Francia offers a new way to assign credit for the title of the world's first circumnavigator: the first to circle the globe was a young enslaved boy from Southeast Asia named Enrique.

While Magellan continues to be celebrated as a hero in Spain, it is Lapu Lapu, the Cebuano chieftain who slayed the Portuguese sailor in the knee-deep waters of Mactan Island, who is feted as "the first Filipino." Statues and murals can be spotted throughout the islands. Lapu Lapu's likeness can be found on local currency as well as on the seal and badge of the Philippine National Police (fig. 2). The PNP understands Lapu Lapu as "the prototype of the best and most noble in Filipino manhood who is the symbol and embodiment of all the genuine attributes of leadership, courage, nationalism, self-reliance and a people-based and people powered community defense."[4]

To mark the 500th year since Magellan arrived in the islands now known as Guam and the Marianas, CHamoru poet and scholar Craig Santos Perez issued a searing meditation on the legacies of empire in his poem, "Mutiny." Here are two excerpts:

> Call this mutiny,
> my retelling of the story
> from our perspective—
> *we discovered you,*
> lost & drifting
> in our already named ocean,
> *we saved you,*
> diseased & starving,
> with food & water,
> yet you mistranslated
> trade as theft, naming us,
> "Islas de Los Ladrones."
> You came ashore,
> burned a village & killed
> seven of my ancestors—
> before you departed.
> *First violence.*
> ...
> I commemorate my people
> rebuilding our canoes,
> resurrecting our religion,
> revitalizing our culture,
> relearning our language,
> reliving our customs,
> resisting colonization,
> protecting our lands,
> and struggling for sovereignty,
> *still standing here.*
> Call this mutiny,
> my commemoration
> of CHamoru resilience,
> which is so vast
> no armada of galleons
> can ever circumnavigate.

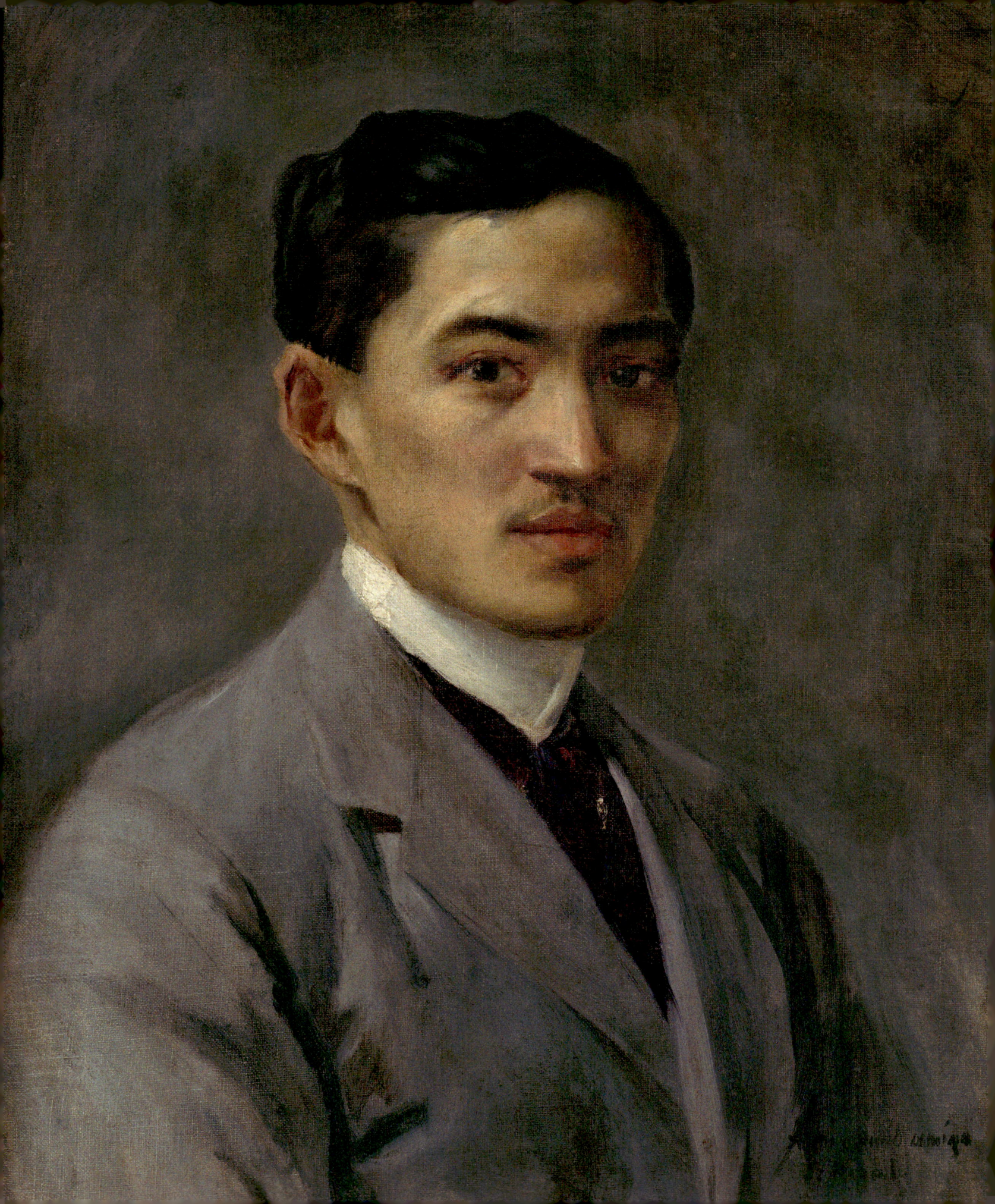

Cutting a Path to Sovereignty

The Complex Political Landscapes of the Philippines and Guam

TAÍNA CARAGOL AND KATE CLARKE LEMAY

If this great country, with its wonderful resources, its great and growing population, and all its elements of strength, 'cannot afford to cultivate the softer virtues,' what nation can?[1]

—Moorfield Storey, 1908,
in response to Theodore Roosevelt

In June 1899, over one hundred thousand readers of *Harper's Weekly* came face-to-face with a violent centerfold image of the Philippine-American War.[2] This picture was reproduced from a painting made by the artist and war correspondent Frederic Remington (1861–1909), *In the Philippines—A Bayonet Rush of United States Troops* (fig. 1). It features U.S. soldiers charging over a hill, firing their rifles as Filipino soldiers fall across the foreground. While the scene erases much of the Filipinos' humanity, it presents the U.S. "Boys in Blue" as heroic warriors.[3] The composition emphasizes some of the racial rhetoric used in the nineteenth century and its supposed hierarchy: At the top, on the hill, white soldiers expertly point and shoot their weapons. At the bottom, we encounter the bodies of Filipinos. Their depiction bears some resemblance to racist caricatures, such as the figure of Emilio Aguinaldo (1869–1964) in the corner of Uncle Sam's "classroom," sullenly wearing a dunce cap (see p. 166). To be fair, Remington was relying on a standard compositional format for combat art, as there are similar pictures of enemies bayonetting each other from the U.S. Civil War, and, later, from the First World War. Yet the painting's composition demonstrates how both combat art and race theory were applied to produce images of empire.

Remington, who had worked as an artist-reporter in Cuba in January 1897 and the summer of 1898, never set foot in the Philippines.[4] Nevertheless, this scene captures a specific and widespread interpretation of the Philippine-American War, one that to this day has marked debates about the degree of brutality it involved.[5] Remington's popular illustrations of military, cowboy, and American Indian themes would have made him the ideal artist to mythologize empire as the new frontier in the Philippines, or "adventure," as it was perceived by some viewers. Even so, the way in which Remington presents Black soldiering as an accepted part of the U.S. professional and cultural tapestry, as opposed to the barefoot and ragged Filipino soldiers, is significant.[6] Remington featured African American "Buffalo Soldiers" in at least fifty of his works of art about soldiers in the West.[7] His article "A Scout with the Buffalo Soldiers" appeared in the April 1889 issue of *Century* magazine.[8] Remington wrote of African American soldiers as uncomplaining, self-reliant, and able—characteristics he conveyed in his art of this period as well. In his oil painting *The Alert*, for example, a mounted Black soldier looks fully in command of his horse, ready to snap his rifle out of its holster (fig. 2). By

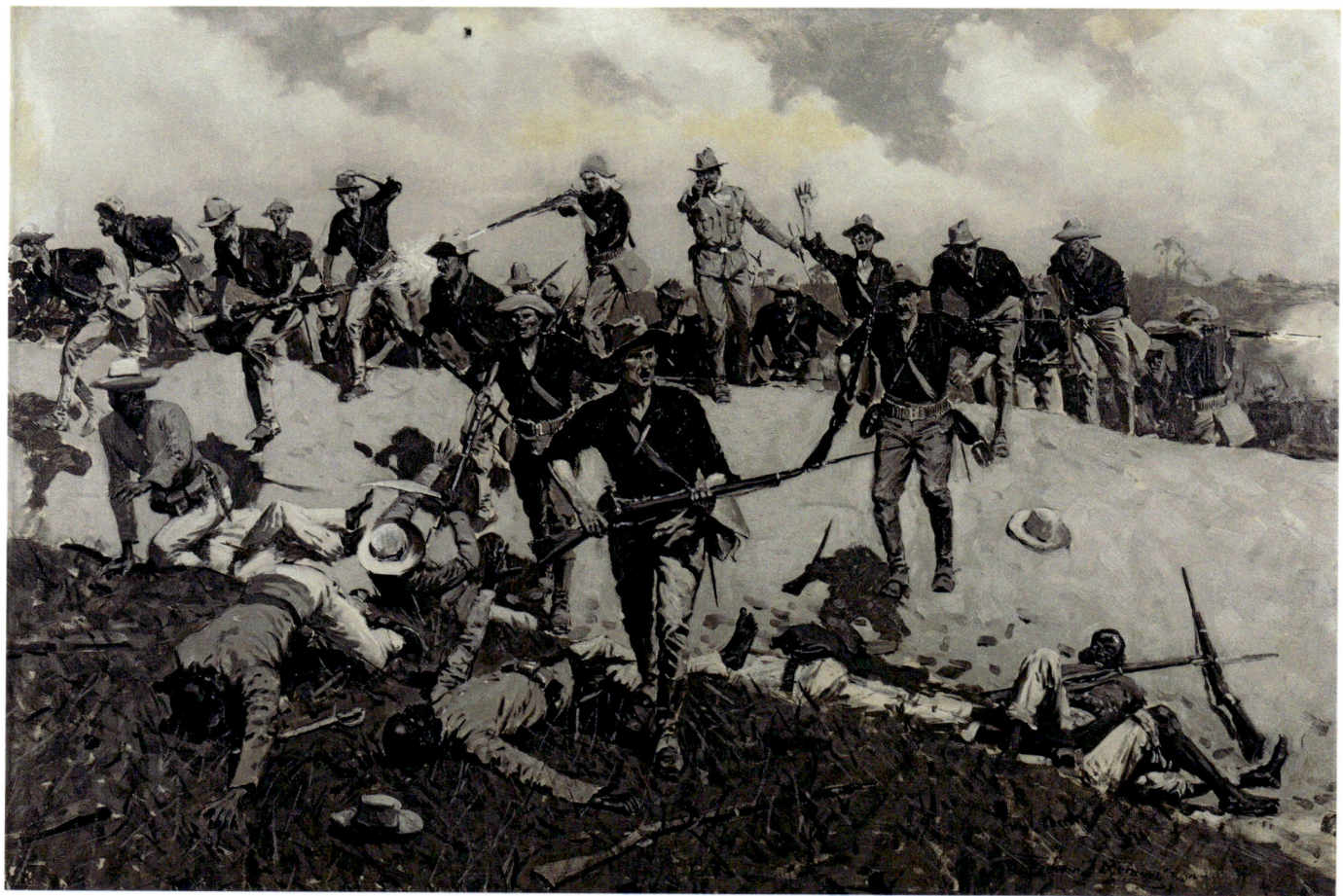

Fig. 1 *In the Philippines—A Bayonet Rush of United States Troops*, Frederic Remington (1861–1909), 1899. Oil on canvas; 81.3 × 114.3 cm (32 × 45 in.). Center of Military History, Museum Division, U.S. Army West Point Museum

comparison, Remington's reductive treatment of the Filipino subject was overtly racist. He was not exceptional in his prejudiced view of the people of the Philippines. Such outlooks influenced the narrative of the War of 1898 and the subsequent Philippine-American War. People such as Senator Albert J. Beveridge (1862–1927), described Filipinos as "savage" and devoid of self-control and chivalrous restraint—reducing a rich culture with customs grounded in deep knowledge to black-and-white terms.[9]

Today, the conflicts of 1898 present a conundrum. As the United States waged a war in the Caribbean in the name of restoring human rights to the Cubans, it simultaneously launched a war in the Philippines in the name of expansion and empire. The Philippine-American War began on February 4, 1899, and ended in 1902, but

smaller military campaigns persisted until 1913, with hostile engagements continuing even after that date.[10] The occupation of the Philippines was a challenge for the U.S. government. In 1898, President William McKinley (1843–1901) and many members of Congress had little knowledge of the Philippines. A vast archipelago, the land of the Philippines comprises approximately 116,000 square miles—a mass slightly larger than the size of the state of Arizona—spread across more than seven thousand islands. There are over forty ethnolinguistic groups to which Indigenous Filipinos belong.[11] The main islands, which stretch from the north to the south are Luzon; the Visayas Islands, which include Cebu, Leyte, Negros, Panay, and Samar; and Mindanao Island (fig. 3).

The first group of U.S. Army Volunteers sent to the Philippines confronted both ethical and practical challenges. As state militia volunteers (the precursor of today's National Guard), they were in federal service but kept their state identity (such as the 1st Colorado Infantry Regiment). These men enlisted in state volunteer groups to fight the Spanish in Cuba, but in addition to the Caribbean campaign, they fought in the Philippines. Many of the U.S. volunteers in the Eighth Army Corps had signed up to fight a war in Cuba, a conflict that they understood as driven by humanitarian needs. These soldiers would have seen newspaper coverage that highlighted the plight of starving children and women in the reconcentration camps. They were surprised, then, to find themselves fighting a war of expansion in the Philippines, especially as they expected a prompt discharge when the campaign in Cuba was over.[12] Yet there was little hope for their immediate relief because the Regular Army of professional soldiers had been devastated by disease in Cuba and would require months to cure its sick and recruit new soldiers. When the volunteer soldiers were sent to the Philippines, they lost morale.[13]

After arriving in the Philippines in July 1898, they found a rebellion against the Spanish already existed in the Manila area that was being led by an influential leader of Cavite Province, Emilio Aguinaldo (1869–1964) (fig. 10). The U.S. Army and Navy forces defeated Spanish troops and occupied Manila on August 13, 1898—a day after the cease-fire with Spain, because word had not yet traveled to Wesley Merritt (1836–1910), the first commander of the U.S. Army in the Philippines.[14] The state militia volunteers then took part in the first battles of the Philippine-American War, driving Aguinaldo into Central Luzon and occupying Negros and Panay before leaving the Philippines in the summer of 1899. However, the Philippine-American War was ongoing, and the United States needed more soldiers. Subsequently, the second group of volunteers was sent to the Philippines. This was a special

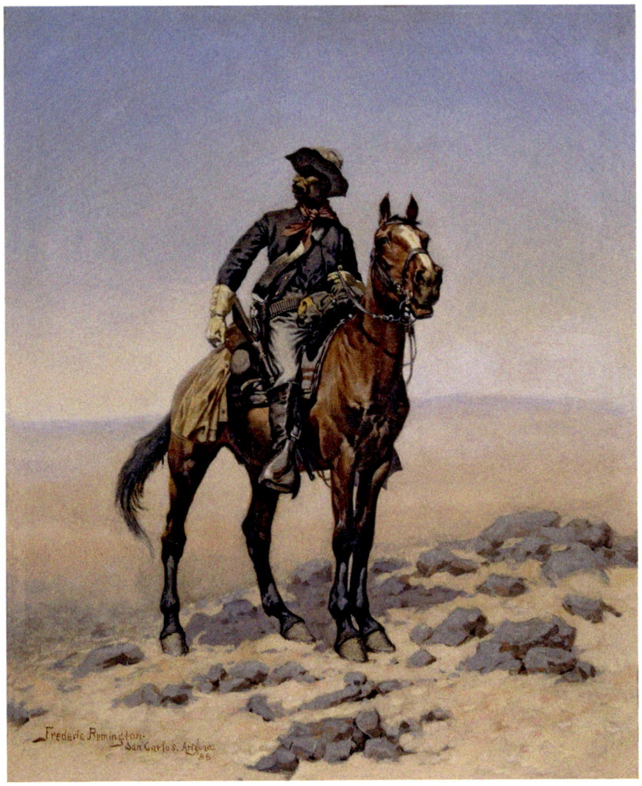

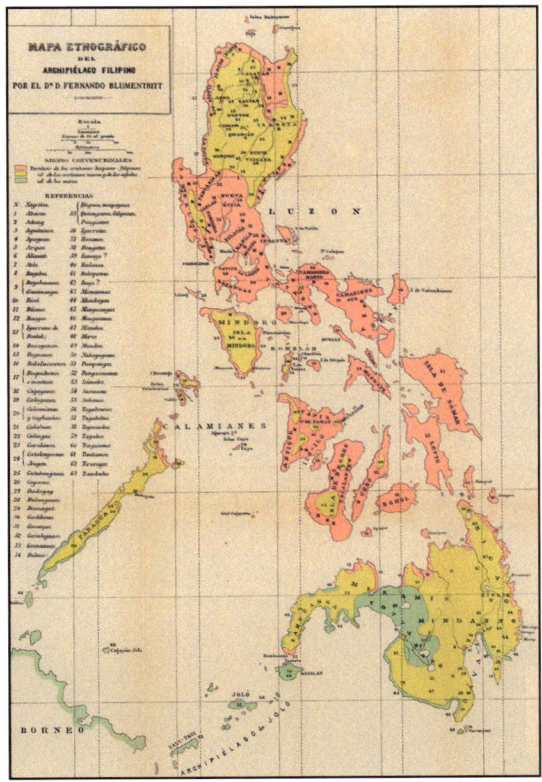

Fig. 2 *The Alert*, Frederic Remington (1861–1909), 1888. Oil on canvas; 55.9 × 49.5 cm (22 × 19½ in.). Private collection

Fig. 3 *Mapa Etnográfico del Archipiélago Filipino* (Ethnographic Map of the Filipino Archipelago), Ferdinand Blumentritt (1853–1913), 1890. 55 × 38 cm (21¹¹⁄₁₆ × 15 in.). Published in the annual report of the Board of Regents of the Smithsonian Institution and by Norris Peters Co. in 1901. Illinois State Library

35,000-strong force organized in the summer and deployed in the fall of 1899. The U.S. Volunteers destroyed Aguinaldo's army, conducted most of the successful regional counterinsurgency operations, and returned to the United States in summer 1901. Thereafter, the rest of the combat (essentially fought in Batangas and Samar) was carried out by the Regular U.S. Army and some U.S. Marines.

According to the standards of the era, sovereignty of the Philippines had passed legitimately from Spain to the United States. Even if the handover occurred according to then-contemporary legal standards, some historians today question the morality and integrity behind it.[15] This is especially important to consider because Aguinaldo and his followers had, in fact, declared the Philippines an independent state. In February 1899, U.S. forces and Aguinaldo's Army of Liberation began fighting around Manila. Initially, this had been a conventional war on the island of Luzon, but after the defeat and demise of the Army of Liberation in late 1899 and the U.S. occupation of the archipelago, there followed a guerrilla war from 1900 to 1902 against a diverse and regional resistance. The final phase of conflict from 1902 to 1913 in the Philippines was a guerrilla war between the U.S. Army against either Muslims on the islands of Mindanao and Jolo, Cavite brigands, small rebellious sects like the Colorums, or fringe religious groups such as the Babylanes or the Dios-Dios (Pulahanes).

The complex history of Filipino society presents a formidable challenge to historians. Because of regional differences within the Philippine archipelago, there is disagreement about the degree to which the seven million Philippine inhabitants of 1898 were a cohesive political body with a unified culture or language.[16] The Philippine nation was still in a nascent form in 1898, and its cultural-linguistic groups did not imagine themselves as a single community. Some Filipinos, like the people of the Negros islands, requested U.S. Army assistance against Aguinaldo's coalition.[17] However, even if the Filipinos were not united at the turn of the century, some historians argue that reducing their resistance to "insurgency," rather than "war," does not recognize their anti-imperialist stance.[18] Within this complex political landscape, a powerful sovereignty movement was gaining momentum.

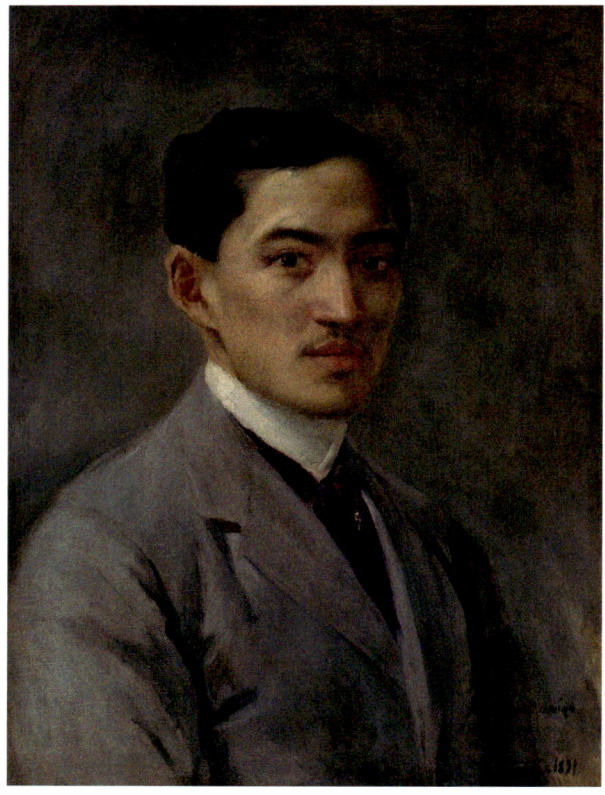

Fig. 4 *José Rizal* (1861–1896), Juan Luna (1857–1899), 1891. Oil on canvas; 65.4 × 49.5 cm (25¾ × 19½ in.). Collection of Luis Antonio and Cecile Gutierrez

The Role of Art in Filipino National Consciousness: Juan Luna and José Rizal

Before the U.S. occupation, many in Spain—as in the United States—believed that Filipinos were "tribally fragmented," incapable of self-government, and racially inferior. Beginning in the 1880s, Filipino intellectuals understood that such characterizations would lead to grave repercussions. The resulting Propaganda Movement, which primarily took place in Spain and lasted from the early 1880s through the early 1890s, proved to be an important line of defense.[19] As a cultural and literary movement of the wealthy bourgeois, its members conceived of a national Filipino community specific to the *principales*, or a class of prosperous Filipinos, such as business owners. The ophthalmologist José Rizal (fig. 4), along with other wealthy, well-traveled intellectuals known as *ilustrados*, served as the group's leader.[20] The *ilustrados* used seventeenth-century texts to better understand pre-Spanish era Filipino history and religion as they set out to demonstrate that Spanish domination had wreaked havoc on Filipino culture and traditions.[21] The Propaganda Movement's pro-Filipino campaign aimed to assimilate the Philippines as a fully recognized, autonomous province of Spain, contributing great culture, art, ideas, and leaders to the Spanish empire.[22] In 1891, as a gesture of admiration, Rizal's friend and fellow *ilustrado*, the eminent painter Juan Luna y Novicio (1857–1899), painted his portrait, most likely after a photographic portrait that Rizal had made in a Madrid studio in 1890, when he was twenty-nine.[23] Luna inscribed it "*A mi querido amigo*" (To my dear friend).[24]

Born in northern Luzon, in Badoc of the Ilocos Norte Province, Luna had trained in Europe, along with other *ilustrados*.[25] In 1884, he won a significant prize at the Exposition of Fine Arts in Madrid for his monumental painting *Spoliarium*, which depicts the bloodied and broken bodies of enslaved gladiators being mourned by their families (fig. 5).[26]

In ancient Rome, a spoliarium was an early version of a crematorium, a building where Romans stripped and burned the bodies of gladiators after they had been killed.

The large-scale painting alludes to class warfare— something that would not have been overlooked by the Filipino *ilustrados*. They saw the Spanish as disparaging the Filipino populations and using them much as the Romans had the gladiators. *Ilustrados* praised Luna's reference to gladiators as a means of portraying Filipinos as worthy, dignified adversaries—and as highly masculine, formidable athletes. By harnessing the story of the Romans, Rizal claimed that Luna had mapped the Filipinos' political struggles into the history of Western civilization. Other *ilustrados* celebrated Luna's tour-de-force painting and its recognition through the prize in Madrid as evidence of their culture's sophistication.[27] In fact, Luna's prize was so significant that it united those in favor of a more aggressive anti-colonial movement with those who argued for a softer approach with the Spanish. During a dinner held in Luna's honor, Rizal raised a glass to the artist's success and described *Spoliarium* as "the spirit of our social, moral, and spiritual life, humanity subjected to trials unredeemed, and reason in open fight with prejudice, fanaticism and injustice."[28]

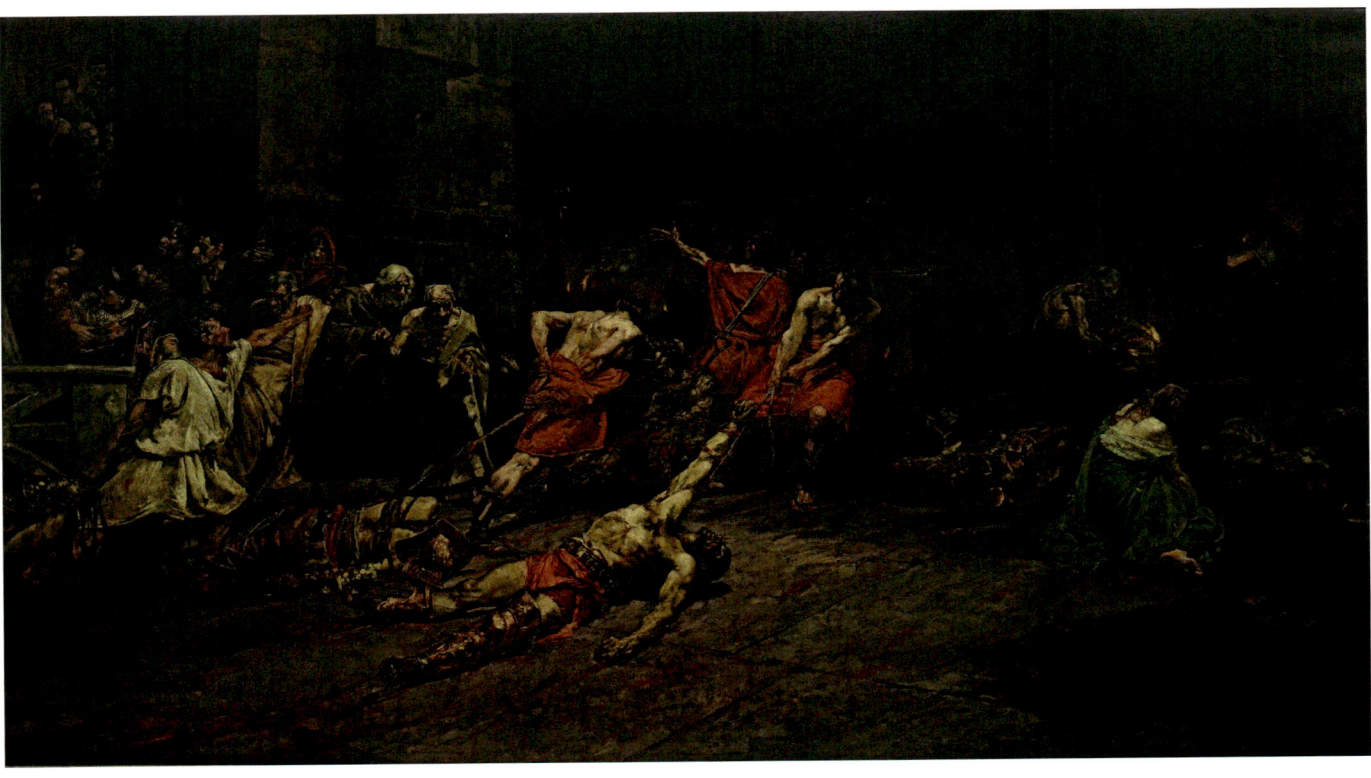

Fig. 5 *Spoliarium*, Juan Luna (1857–1899), 1884. Oil on canvas; 4.2 × 7.7 m (13 ft., 10 in. × 25 ft., 3 in.). National Museum of the Philippines

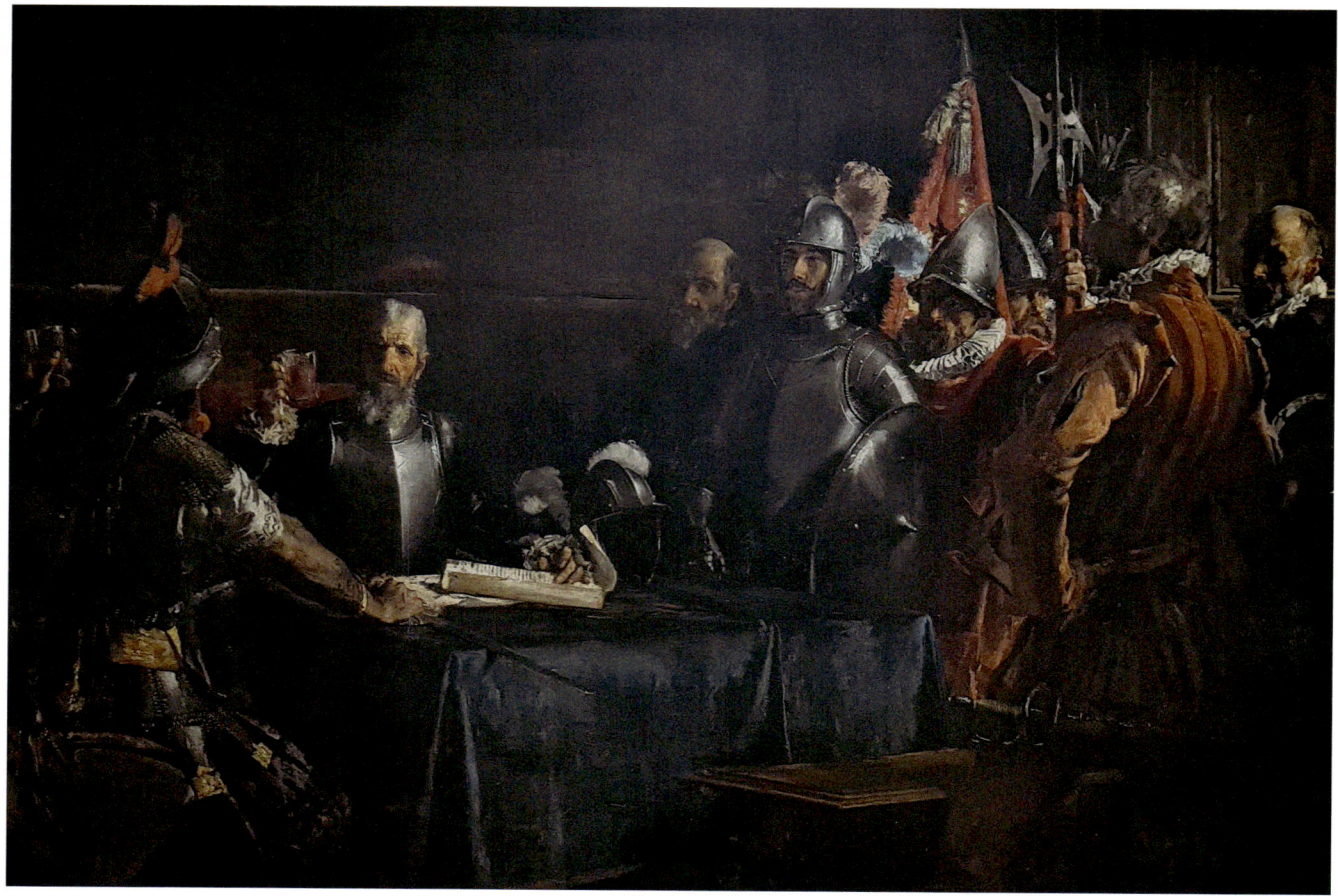

Fig. 6 *El pacto de sangre* (The blood compact), Juan Luna (1857–1899), 1885. Oil on canvas; 2 × 3 m (6 ft., 6 in. × 9 ft., 10 in.). Presidential Museum and Library, Malacañan Palace

Fig. 7 *Coat of Chain Mail Armor*, Unidentified maker, Date unknown. Horn and brass; 78 × 71 cm (30⅝ × 28 in.). Department of Anthropology, National Museum of Natural History, Smithsonian Institution

The toast, made in 1884, was Rizal's first open challenge to Spain.[29] Three years later, Rizal published his most famous work, *Noli me tangere* (Touch me not), a harsh critique of Spain's oppressive rulers, particularly its corrupt religious officials.[30]

In 1885, Rizal and Luna lived together in Paris for six months, and during this time, Luna began painting *El pacto de sangre* (The blood compact), which protests the Spanish colonial regime (fig. 6).[31] In this work, Luna imagines the historic pact of March 16, 1565, made between the Philippines and Spain by Spanish explorer Miguel López de Legazpi (1502–1572), the first governor general of the Philippines, and Datu Sikatuna (born c. 1530), the chieftain of Bohol.[32] The *ilustrado* and Luna's future brother-in-law, Trinidad H. Pardo de Tavera (1857–1925), posed as Legazpi, and Rizal was the model for Sikatuna.[33] The two former

enemies, Sikatuna and Legazpi, share a toast with glasses of wine mixed with drops of their own blood. According to the Philippine custom referred to as *sandugo*, an unbreakable oath was sealed by mixing the blood of leaders.[34] Six Spaniards, dressed in plate armor, bear witness to the scene.[35] Sikatuna, with his back to the viewer, wears armor that is beautifully crafted, if of inferior shielding quality—a breastplate of chain mail linked with plated leather (fig. 7).[36] He also wears a plumed helmet designed after the Spanish silhouette and made of brass or leather with plates of animal horn.[37] He grips his kris, a sword specific to Mindanao Island and the Sulu Archipelago—ready for any sign of betrayal. Since many of the Filipinos of the time were Muslim and/or used the kris, the painting may also be seen as representing a pan-Filipino identity or, perhaps, as addressing religious division.[38]

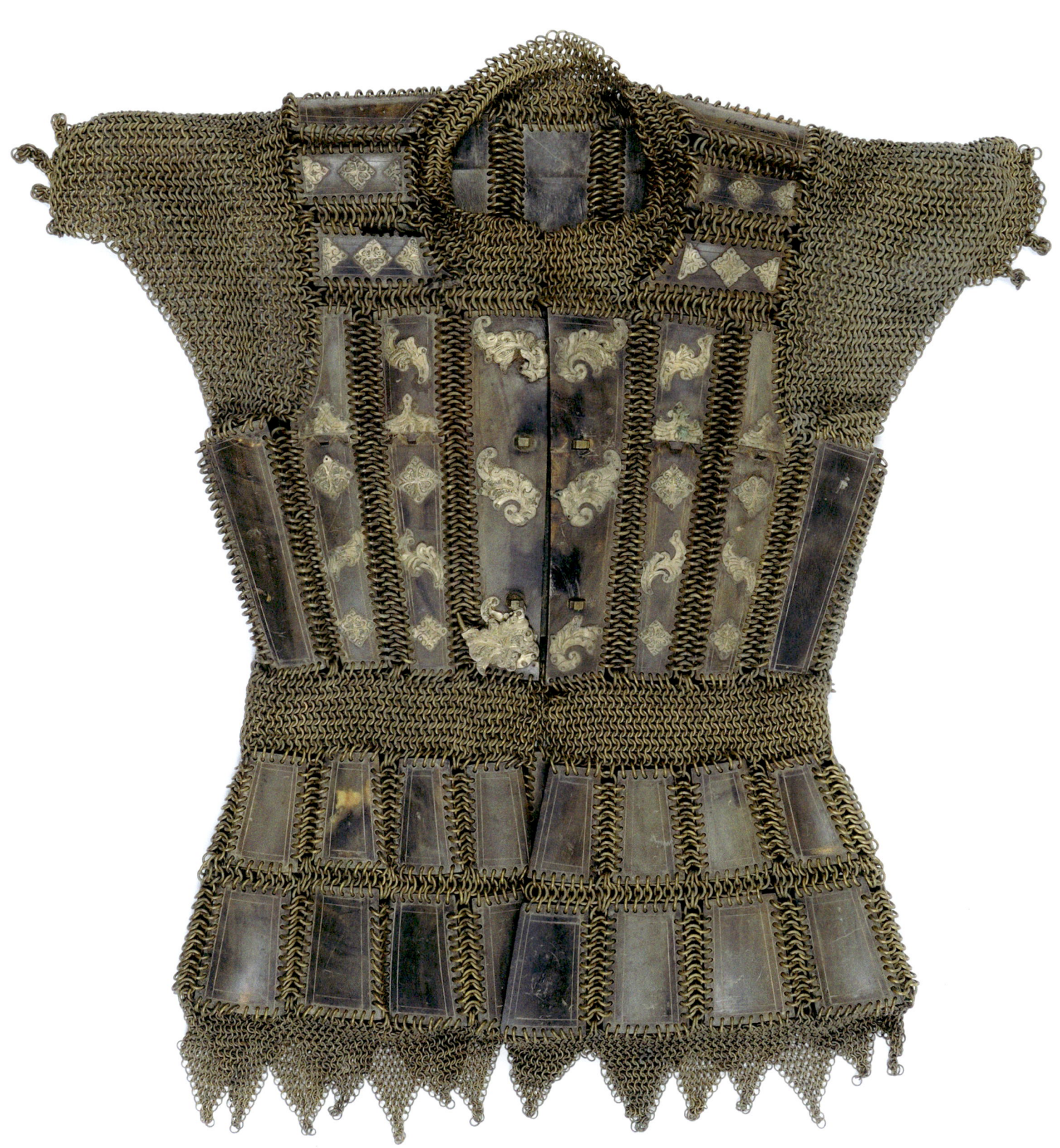

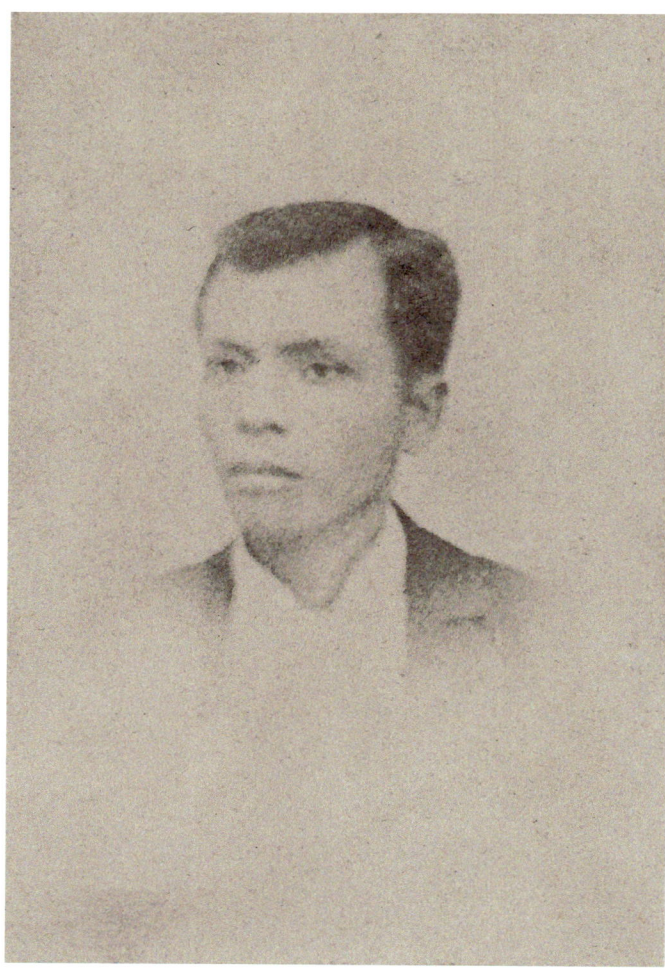

Fig. 8 *Andrés Bonifacio* (1863–1897), Chofré y Ca., 1896. Photograph; 9 × 6.5 cm (3½ × 2½ in.). Archivo General de Indias, Seville

Luna's painting ignited Filipino intellectuals' understanding and imagination of the Spanish-Filipino colonial relationship.[39] The significance of the blood compact was clear for those involved in the Propaganda Movement, as it depicted the equality of Spain and the Philippines as contracting parties, linked by common blood. The premise behind the narrative argued that shared blood between Filipinos and Spaniards should ensure rights for the colonized, and it undermined the racial rhetoric separating Spaniards from Filipinos.[40] In a bold move, Luna gave this painting to the Spanish government.[41] To this day, it hangs in Manila's Malacañang Palace (the Filipino equivalent to the White House), overlooking a grand room in which Filipino government administrators receive state visits.

In 1889, Rizal organized a collective for mutual self-aid, *Los Indios Bravos* (The brave Natives), consisting of himself, Juan Luna, and Valentin Ventura (1860–1935). Their name was a pun that Rizal used after the group saw Buffalo Bill's Wild West Show at the Paris Exposition of 1889.[42] The resignification of the term "indios," which the Spanish had employed in a derogatory sense, also reflected how Rizal and his followers aimed to change the Filipinos' perception of themselves.[43] In the Spanish-colonial Philippines, a "Filipino" was a Spaniard born in the Philippines (or an *insulares*), a term that differentiated them from a Spaniard born in Spain. When *indios* like Rizal called themselves "Filipinos," they presented themselves as *hijos del país* (sons of the country). This was a bold step because they chose to identify with the Philippines—the land of their birth—as opposed to Spain, the mother country.[44] Notably, Rizal, Luna, and Ventura saw Sitting Bull (1831–1890) in this performance (see p. 34).[45] Although the show may have encouraged some in the audience to accept the mistreatment and genocide of the American Indian, the members of *Los Indios* identified with the performers and found their example of anticolonial resistance to be inspiring.[46]

When Rizal returned to the Philippines in June 1892, he began to organize La Liga Filipina, a group focused on promoting an autonomous Philippines.[47] However, he was arrested by the Spanish in early July and deported to Mindanao Island. Beginning in the 1890s, the Propaganda Movement had started to shift its ambition away from self-governance within a colonial regime to focus on total independence from Spain.[48] In 1892, it gave way to the Katipunan, a nationalist revolutionary organization. Andrés Bonifacio (fig. 8) founded the Katipunan in Manila after uniting urban clerks and artisans to the cause of resistance.[49] When the Spanish authorities discovered their conspiracy, momentum built among the people of the lower and lower-middle classes. Notably, at this moment, the *ilustrados* were wary and did not join the first phase of the revolution against Spain led by Bonifacio, but instead participated in the second phase under Aguinaldo. By late August 1896, thousands of men and women were ready to revolt against Spain.[50] When an informer tipped off the Spanish about the Katipunan, the rebellion began.[51] Meanwhile, Rizal had left the village of Dapitan in Mindanao to volunteer his services as a physician to Spanish troops in Cuba. However, with the outbreak of the revolution, the Spanish arrested him in Barcelona, enroute to Cuba, and sent him back to Manila. Tried by courts for sedition, rebellion, and conspiracy, Rizal was

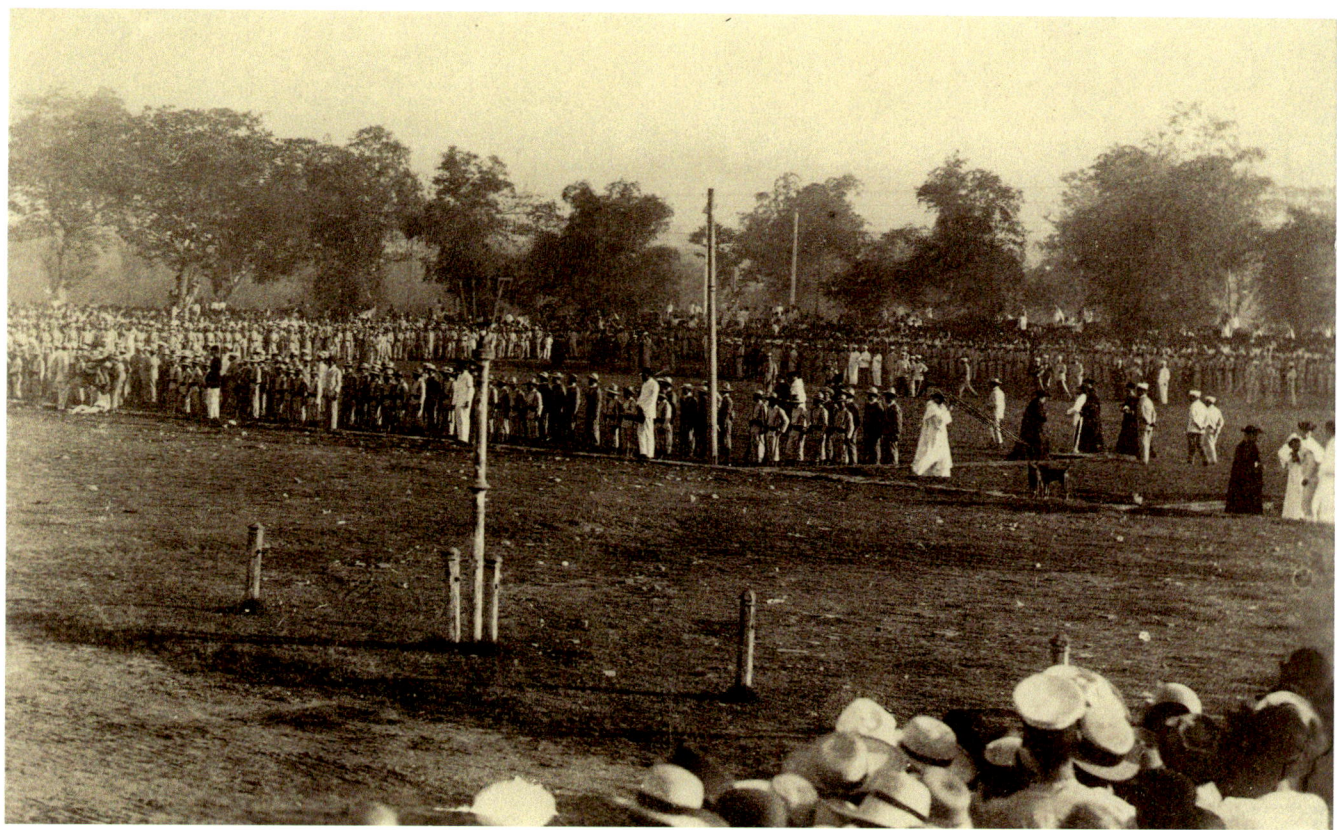

Fig. 9 *Rojas and Companions before Execution on the Luneta*, 1896. Gelatin silver print; 17.8 × 22.9 cm (7 × 9 in.). National Museum of American History, Smithsonian Institution

found guilty on all charges and sentenced to death. He was executed by firing squad on the Luneta in Manila on December 30, 1896 (fig. 9).[52]

The Philippine Revolution against the Spanish

In August 1896, the Philippine Revolution against the Spanish began. Although those fighting under Bonifacio in Manila did not fare well, Filipinos to the south did better.[53] Emilio Aguinaldo's soldiers had seized the town of Kawit, in Cavite Province, south of Manila (fig. 10). The town of Noveleta was also occupied by Filipino forces who had built stockade defenses along a river, and Ramón Blanco Erenas Riera y Polo (1833–1906), then the Spanish governor of the Philippines, was busy organizing the thousands of Spanish soldiers sent to reinforce his ranks, which had numbered fewer than seven thousand men.[54] On November 7, 1896, the Spanish launched a twin attack against both Cavite el Viejo and Noveleta, known as the Battle of

Binakayan-Dalahican. This map, a sketch of the defensive tactics devised by Aguinaldo, shows the river in Cavite Nuevo and Dalahican, in the municipality of Noveleta (fig. 11). Aguinaldo's forces won the first significant victory against 22,000 Spanish soldiers led by Blanco.[55]

The Battle of Binakayan-Dalahican established Aguinaldo as the leader of the rebellion. However, Aguinaldo was a controversial figure, and the Katipunan was falling apart because he and Bonifacio were seen as associated with two rival factions: the Magdalo under Aguinaldo and the Magdiwang under Bonifacio.[56] Aguinaldo unseated Bonifacio on March 22, 1897, in the Tejeros Convention.[57] This convention was meant to settle issues between Magdiwang and Magdalo, and they voted to replace the Katipunan with a revolutionary government. Bonifacio agreed and presided over a quick election, in which Aguinaldo was elected president in absentia. However, Bonifacio was betrayed by the Magdiwang and sentenced to death by a court-martial. Although Aguinaldo attempted to commute his sentence to banishment, he was persuaded by the people of Cavite to have the execution carried out on May 10, 1897.[58]

Recuerdo al sr
Senador, sr.

Prision/Manila/24 Julio 1901.

Emilio Aguinaldo

Fig. 10 *Emilio Aguinaldo* (1869–1964), Unidentified photographer, 1901. Gelatin silver print; 15.2 × 10.2 cm (6 × 4 in.). History Nebraska

Fig. 11 Sketch of the defensive tactics of Noveleta through Cavite Nuevo and Dalajican, constructed by insurgents in the Noveleta Bridge, 1897. Graphite and ink on paper; 11 × 15.8 cm (4³⁄₁₀ × 6⅛ in.). Archivo General de Indias, Seville

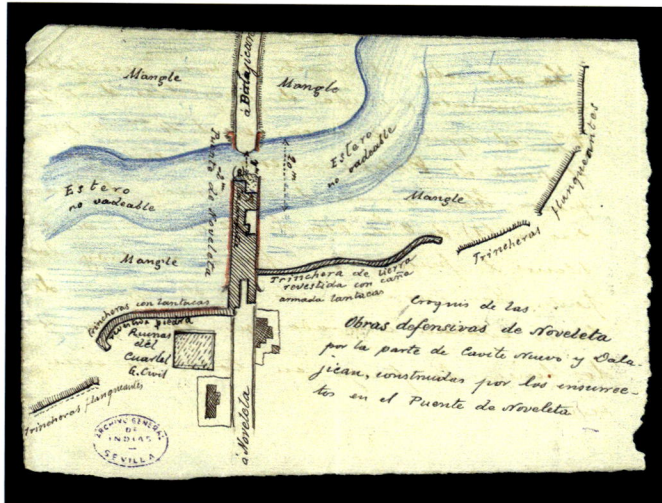

Soon, however, Aguinaldo and his supporters were forced to retreat from Cavite Province to the remote location of Biak-na-Bato in Bulacan Province, where he signed a truce on December 14, 1897.[59] This agreement between Aguinaldo and the Spanish was brokered by the *ilustrado* Pedro Paterno (1857–1911), who later collaborated with the U.S. Army to discuss a surrender in May 1899.[60] Aguinaldo accepted amnesty, as well as 800,000 Spanish pesetas and the promise of Spanish reform.[61] Exiled in Hong Kong, he soon traveled to Singapore and returned to Cavite on May 19, 1898—carried by a U.S. vessel.

George Dewey and Emilio Aguinaldo: A Controversial Partnership

On May 1, 1898, under the command of Commodore George Dewey (1837–1917), the first shots of the Spanish-American War rang out. The U.S. Asiatic Squadron destroyed seven Spanish warships harbored in Manila Bay while suffering few casualties. At that time, the United States did not have a strategy for occupying the Philippines; the Spanish squadron was a target of opportunity as part of the larger war with Spain. However, the demise of the Spanish squadron enormously helped Filipino rebels in Luzon and other islands who now could attack the Spanish forces in their area without worrying about reinforcements.

A window of opportunity opened for Aguinaldo, and he sailed from Singapore to Manila to meet with Dewey.[62] On May 20, 1898, the two men met on Dewey's flagship, the USS *Olympia*, and spoke through a translator until they felt they had reached an agreement. Afterward, they maintained conflicting accounts. Aguinaldo contended that Dewey had promised the United States would not interfere with the independence of the Philippines, whereas Dewey denied having made any such commitment.[63] Some historians believe that the U.S. consul in Singapore, E. Spencer Pratt (1856–1925), led Aguinaldo to believe that the United States would help him win independence for his country.[64] And, Pratt was censured for

overstepping his authority.[65] Others argue that, perhaps, something was lost—or altered—in translation.[66]

On May 24, 1898, McKinley ordered thousands of U.S. Regulars and state militia volunteers sworn into federal service to embark for the Philippines.[67] This was just as Aguinaldo proclaimed himself the dictator of the short-lived provisional government and issued a declaration of Filipino independence on June 12, 1898.[68] Because the proclamation was in Spanish, Dewey simply forwarded the message, unread, to the Navy Department in Washington.[69]

Between June and August 1898, Aguinaldo consolidated his power and built a coalition in Central Luzon, eliminating his rivals or convincing them to join him. He dispersed his forces and some of his top generals to seize control of the rest of Luzon, Panay, and other islands. In concert with Aguinaldo's military maneuvering, the Belgian counsul, Édouard André, brokered an agreement to allow the Spanish to surrender to the United States after a show of resistance, with the understanding that the United States would guarantee the lives and property of the civilians in Manila. On August 13, 1898, in a staged conflict that lasted less than two hours, the United States defeated the Spanish.[70] The Spanish promptly surrendered in a "mock battle," as it is now called, not to the Filipino insurgents, but to the United States.[71] The Spanish commanders cooperated with the United States because they were terrified that Aguinaldo's forces, who had slaughtered Spanish soldiers and civilians—including priests—in other areas, would massacre all Europeans. At the same time, they feared being tried and executed upon their return to Spain if they surrendered without a show of military resistance.

Wesley Merritt (1836–1910) had been appointed as the overall commander of the Philippine expedition, and he had to interpret what the military policy should be, as McKinley never gave him a straight answer about whether to annex all the Philippines or to seize and hold Manila alone.[72] However, Merritt was sickly and requested to be relieved. Consequently, Elwell Stephen Otis (1838–1909) took command on August 20, 1898. Otis had supervised the training, supplying, and disciplining of U.S. soldiers in California, and organized an impressive dispatch of soldiers from San Francisco to the Philippines. He also had chaired the board that selected the Krag-Jorgensen rifle for combat in the Philippines, whose superior smokeless firepower made the weapon the most modern rifle used by the U.S. military in battle (fig. 12).[73] But McKinley gave no direction to Otis about U.S. objectives in the Philippines either, and Otis was left to make policy decisions for months.

Finally, on December 21, 1898, Otis received McKinley's policy for the Philippines. McKinley ordered him to deploy the U.S. Army in the Philippines and "win the confidence, respect, and affection of the inhabitants" by its own good comportment and to show that "the mission of the United States is one of benevolent assimilation, substituting the mild sway of justice and right for arbitrary rule."[74] The so-called benevolent assimilation exemplifies the U.S. colonial mindset that justified its claim to the more than seven thousand islands of the Philippines. It also made the U.S. Army the instrument of enforcing "lawful rule" and protecting Filipino lives, property, and civil rights. The colonialization of the Philippines by the United States was underway.

The Anti-Imperialist Debates Begin

Although initially hesitant to seize the Philippines, McKinley came to believe that its annexation was inevitable. Following a line of thought that the Spanish had mapped out—and that was already prevalent among U.S. military officials in Cuba and Puerto Rico regarding the populations of those islands—McKinley claimed that Filipinos were incapable of self-government.[75] U.S. newspapers began reporting on the "Philippine Insurrection," rather than war. Using the term "war" would imply a conflict between two sovereign entities; an insurrection implies an uprising of subjects against their legitimate ruler.[76] The U.S. raised a force of 35,000, the U.S. Volunteers, to fight the war in the Philippines during the summer of 1899.[77] McKinley was encouraged to annex the Philippines by politicians like Theodore Roosevelt (1858–1919) and Henry Cabot Lodge (1850–1924). Through Alfred Thayer Mahan's (1840–1914) report for the Naval War Board of August 15–20, 1898, McKinley also understood that the Philippine archipelago would be valuable because its location offered a strategic entry point to China.[78] And finally, as a politician, he believed that popular opinion demanded annexation.[79]

McKinley, however, did not have the support of the full U.S. populace. Some prominent U.S. intellectuals, notably W. E. B. Du Bois (1868–1963), objected to the role of the United States in the Philippines (fig. 13). One of the most important intellectuals at the turn of the century, Du Bois studied the question of race in the United States. Reflecting in 1903 on the freedoms that African Americans dreamed might be possible through emigration, Du Bois observed that "nothing has more effectually made this program seem hopeless than the recent course of the United States toward weaker and darker peoples in the West Indies, Hawaii, and the Philippines."[80]

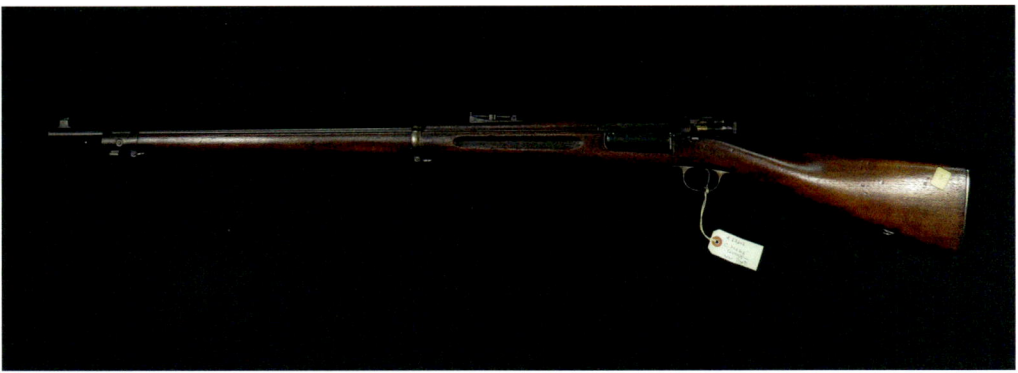

Fig. 12 U.S. Model 1898 Krag-Jorgensen Rifle, Ole H. J. Krag (1837–1916), 1898. 15.9 × 124.8 × 7.9 cm (6¼ × 49⅛ × 3⅛ in.) National Museum of American History, Smithsonian Institution

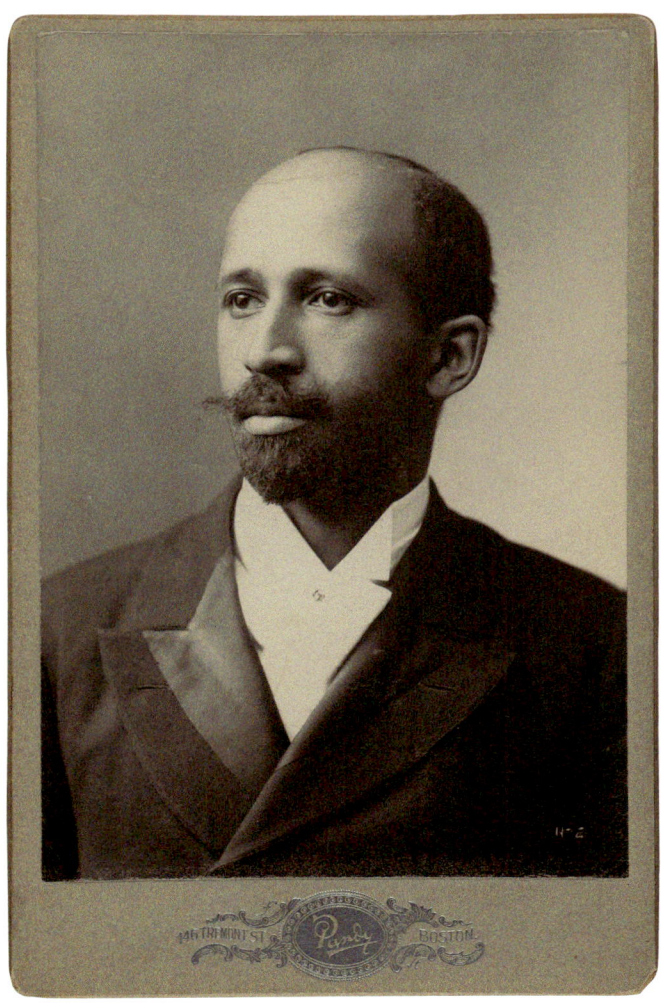

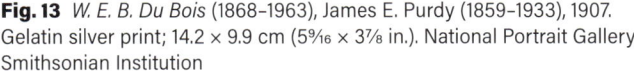

Fig. 13 *W. E. B. Du Bois* (1868–1963), James E. Purdy (1859–1933), 1907. Gelatin silver print; 14.2 × 9.9 cm (5⁹⁄₁₆ × 3⁷⁄₈ in.). National Portrait Gallery, Smithsonian Institution

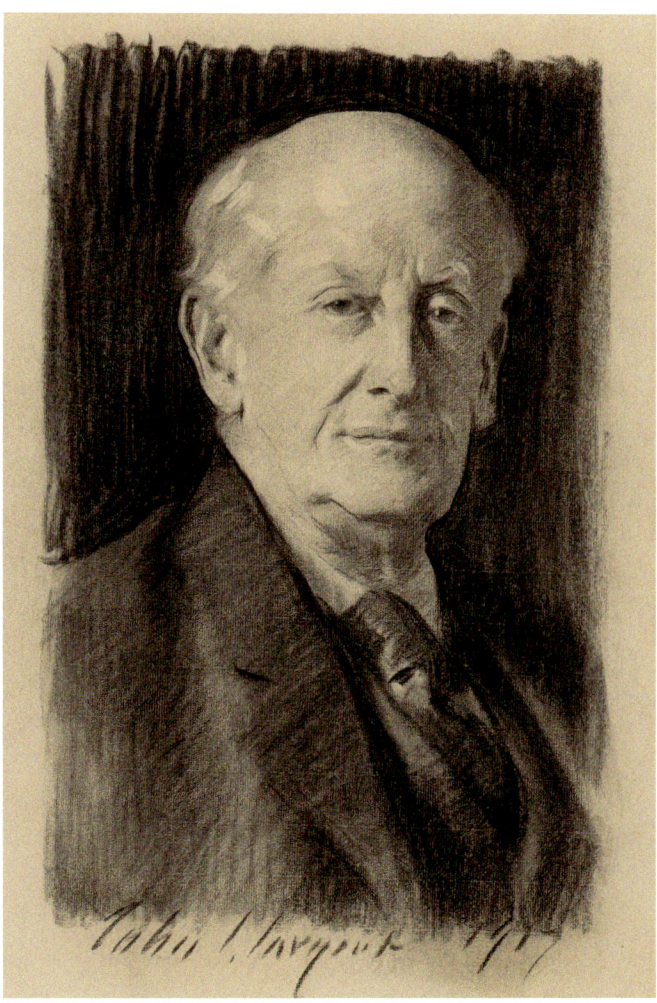

Fig. 14 *Moorfield Storey* (1845–1929). John Singer Sargent (1856–1925), 1917. Charcoal on paper; 63 × 47.8 cm (24¹³⁄₁₆ × 18¹³⁄₁₆ in.). National Portrait Gallery, Smithsonian Institution; partial gift of John Moorfield Storey

Some were so fervently against U.S. imperialism that they began to organize. On June 15, 1898—the same day that the U.S. House of Representatives voted to pass the resolution to annex Hawai'i—detractors of territorial expansion convened in Faneuil Hall in Boston.[81] One speaker, Moorfield Storey (1845–1929), a civil rights attorney and then president of the American Bar Association, proclaimed, "A war begun to win the Cubans the right to govern themselves should not be made an excuse for extending our sway over other alien peoples. The fundamental principles of our government are at stake."[82] John Singer Sargent (1856–1925) made this portrait in 1917, the year that Storey helped found the National Association for

the Advancement of Colored People (NAACP) (fig. 14). Using vigorous strokes in the background to bring forth Storey's dignified features, Sargent added bold highlights accenting his forehead. When he saw this portrait, Storey joked, it should be considered "a fraud on the public, since it represents such an amiable old gentleman instead of a ferocious bruiser."[83]

Others joined Storey in his mission to end U.S. imperialism, and on November 19, 1898, the American Anti-Imperialist League (AIL) was formed.[84] Headquartered in Boston, by 1899 its nationwide membership comprised thirty thousand people, including public figures such as the journalist and reformist Carl Schurz (1829–1906), former

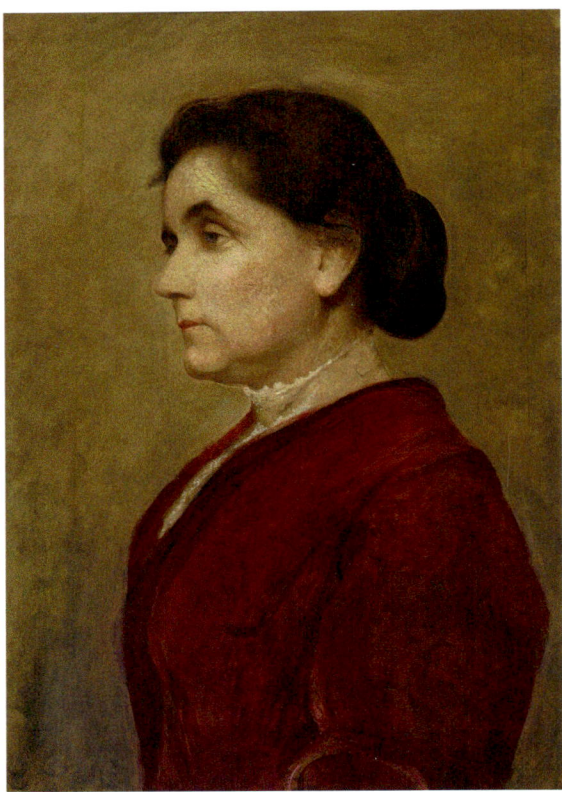

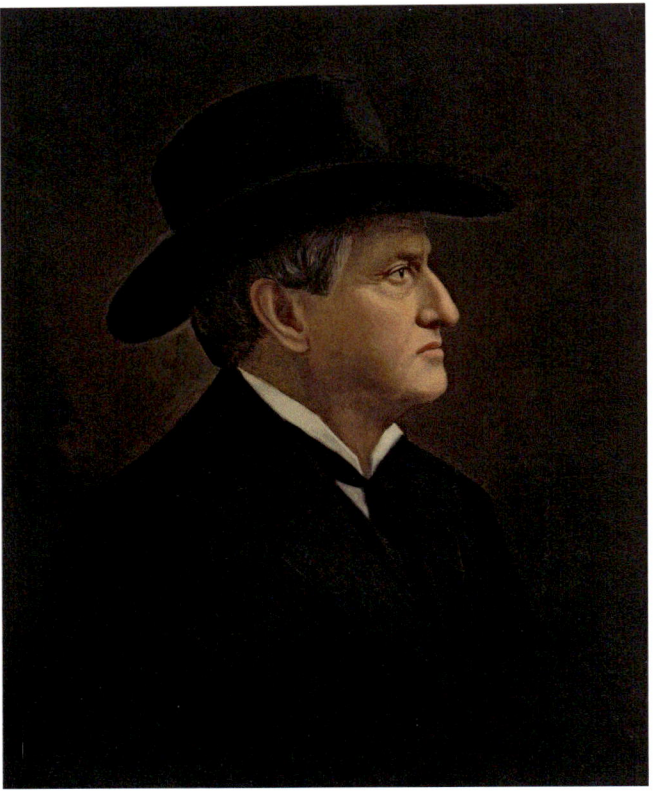

Fig. 15 *Jane Addams* (1860–1935), George de Forest Brush (1855–1941), 1906. Oil on canvas; 62.9 × 45.1 cm (24¾ × 17¾ in.). National Portrait Gallery, Smithsonian Institution; partial gift of Mrs. Nancy Pierce York and Mrs. Grace Pierce Forbes

Fig. 16 *Benjamin Tillman* (1847–1918), Unidentified artist, Date unknown. Oil on canvas, 101.6 × 88.9 cm (40 × 35 in.), framed. National Portrait Gallery, Smithsonian Institution

president Grover Cleveland (1837–1908), industrialist Andrew Carnegie (1835–1919), labor leader Samuel Gompers (1850–1924), and novelist Samuel Clemens, better known as Mark Twain (1835–1910) (see p. 169).[85] The members of the AIL did not necessarily object to continental expansion, but they opposed holding overseas colonies.[86] They also had very different reasons for joining the organization.

Many leaders of the AIL, including Storey and Schurz, were associated with the abolitionist movement and the defense of racial equality. Other anti-imperialists, such as social reformers Jane Addams (fig. 15) and Mary Livermore (1820–1905), came from the suffragist movement, and they related their own political disenfranchisement to U.S. rule over Filipinos.[87] In one public speech against imperialism, delivered in December 1898, Addams pointed out the domino effect such a war would cause, in terms of changing ethics and standards, claiming that

wars of aggression and military occupations would "determine[s] our ideals as much as our ideals determine national events."[88]

This solemn portrait of Addams in profile is by George de Forest Brush (1855–1941), an academic painter known for idealized paintings of Native Americans and mothers and children.[89] Commissioned by her friends, the portrait was made from life, in Dublin, New Hampshire, in 1906.[90] Brush provides psychological insight through his rendering of Addams's dignified, serene manner and her serious, stern expression. Seldom, if ever, satisfied with portraits made of her, Addams detested the work, calling it one of a "long line of dismal failures."[91]

Still others in the AIL leveled racist and anti-immigrant arguments. The group often mixed and matched arguments, and many of those who objected to holding colonies were racist. Samuel Gompers asked, "If these new islands are to become ours, it will be under the form of Territories or States. Can we hope to close the floodgates of immigration from the hordes of Chinese and semi-savage races coming from what will be part of our own country?"[92] Gompers was also likely thinking about limiting the amount of competition for laborers so as to drive up wages. Senator Benjamin Tillman of South Carolina represented a white supremacist faction of the AIL, whose members feared that imperialism would deteriorate the "White Anglo-Saxon race" through mixing with Filipinos (fig. 16). Men like Tillman believed that the annexation of overseas territories would require the United States to extend the rights of the Constitution to their inhabitants, people he felt were not intellectually advanced enough for such rights.[93] Despite all these debates, war began in earnest in the Philippines, especially as the movement for independence gained support across the island of Luzon.

The Philippine-American War, 1899–1913

On June 12, 1898, Aguinaldo issued a declaration of the independence of the Philippines. Intent on establishing his power, he convened the first Filipino parliament, the Malolos Congress, in September 1898 at Barasoain Church in Malolos, Bulacan; known as "the Malolos Church," it was used as Aguinaldo's residence, office, and headquarters (see p. 122).[94] The parliament was made up of members drawn from his supporters in Central Luzon, it was not a representative assembly of the entire archipelago.[95]

Paying Aguinaldo no heed, on October 28, 1898, McKinley directed negotiators to acquire all of the Philippine Islands, rather than just Luzon. The Treaty of Paris was signed on December 10, 1898, and Spain sold the Philippines to the United States for $20 million as part of the settlement. Ignoring the treaty, Aguinaldo focused on consolidating power. The Malolos Constitution, a draft for the constitution of the First Philippine Republic, was signed on January 21, 1899, and Aguinaldo was inaugurated as its president the next day.[96] On January 22, 1899, six weeks after the signing of the Treaty of Paris, the Malolos Congress published a constitution that established the First Philippine Republic. Delegates were sharply divided into three groups: conservatives, who cooperated with the United States; moderates, who sought an in-between route; and hard-liners, who insisted on total independence. Aguinaldo could not follow through his declaration of the Philippine Republic on January 23, 1899, because his government was so divided. Delegates were

landowners, professionals, and merchants who did not prioritize sharing political power or wealth with many of the Filipino population, most of whom were peasants.[97]

Aguinaldo's principal advisor was Apolinario Mabini (fig. 17), a hard-line lawyer who believed that only a strong, centralized national government backed by a robust army could secure independence.[98] Mabini was unwilling to negotiate with the United States. Although he died early on, in the cholera epidemic of 1903, Mabini was nevertheless commemorated as a leader of Filipino nationalism, and his funeral was one of the largest Filipinos had ever seen.[99] This posthumous portrait, made in 1911 by Fabián de la Rosa (1869–1937), was most likely meant to help create a pantheon of Filipino nationalists during the first years of the U.S. colonial era. Portraiture served as an instrumental tool in this effort.[100]

Although Aguinaldo sent Felipe Agoncillo (1859–1941) and Juan Luna as representatives to Paris, they were not recognized because Aguinaldo's government was not regarded as official. A political shape-shifter, the lawyer Agoncillo was one of Aguinaldo's strategists behind the Pact of Biak-na-bato—a role for which Agoncillo earned the designation of "traitor" in the Philippines. But Agoncillo was appointed to represent the Philippines to the United States—a responsibility he took seriously. In January 1899 he traveled to Washington, DC, and submitted his "Memorial to the Senate of the United States," invoking the contradictions between the annexation of the Philippines and the founding democratic principles of the United States.[101]

The prominent Filipino artist Félix Resurrección Hidalgo painted this knee-length portrait of Agoncillo in Paris (fig. 18).[102] Agoncillo models perseverance and restraint in this portrait, standing in formal attire with a relaxed yet resolute expression.

On February 4, 1899, after months of unease, war broke out in Manila between Aguinaldo's forces (numbering between fifteen and forty thousand) and those of the United States (consisting of the 8th Corps, numbering 20,800) (fig. 19). The Battle of Manila of February 5, 1899, was the largest battle of the Philippine-American War.[103] The war began without a plan of action on either side.[104] The Army of Liberation was ill-prepared for battle, although individual Filipino soldiers fought bravely. It was run not as an army but rather as a collection of uncoordinated units. The U.S. soldiers defeated the Army of Liberation outside of Manila, and they soon captured the town of Malolos. On February 14, 1899, on the island of Panay,

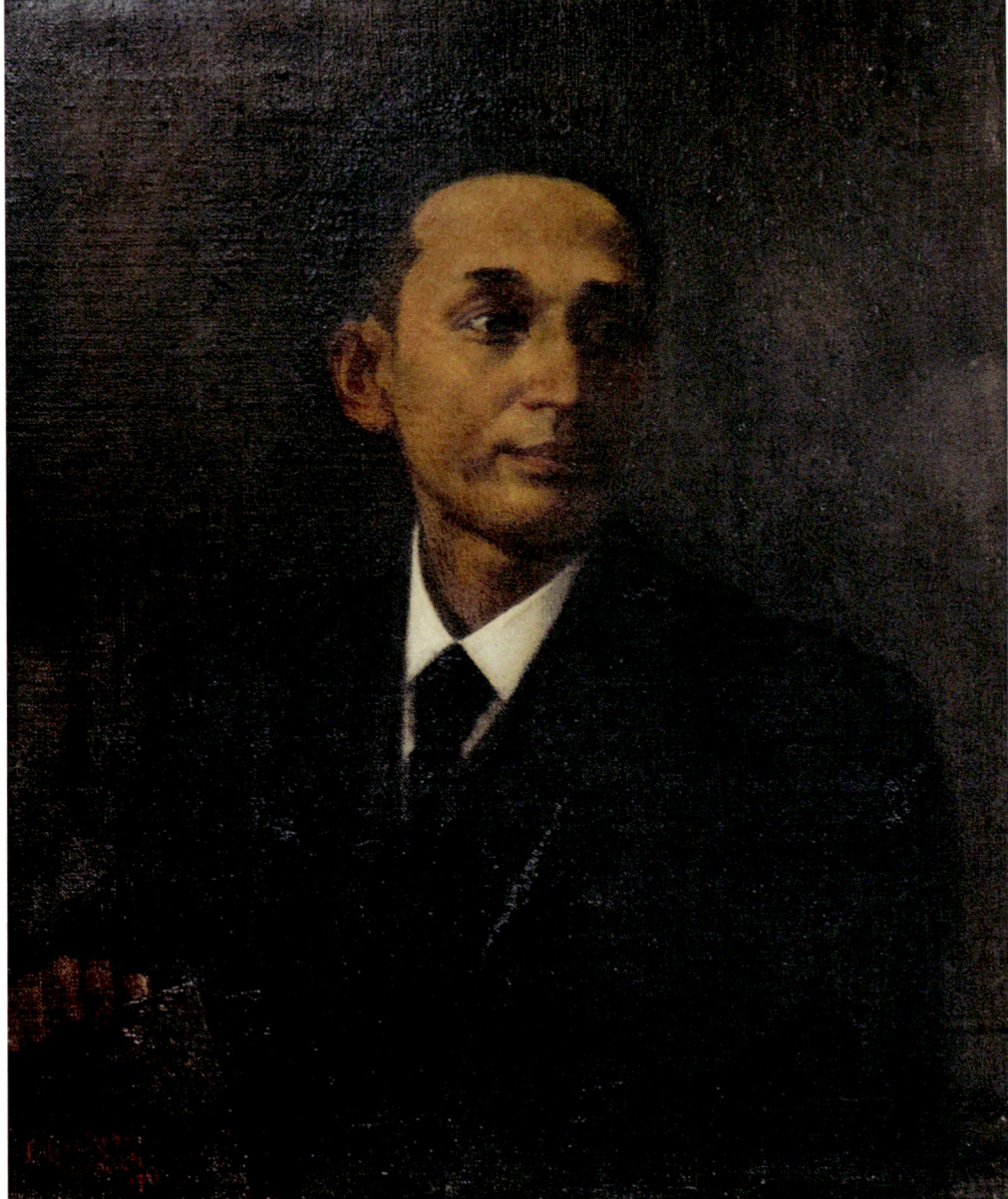

the U.S. captured the main port of Iloilo and landed troops at the request of the government on Negros Island. In Iloilo, Filipinos set fire to the town as they retreated.

Facing the occupation of the vast archipelago of the Philippines, McKinley sent an investigative commission to study the Filipino people. Established on January 20, 1899, this group was chaired by Jacob Schurman (1854–1942), president of Cornell University, and included both Dewey and Otis.[105] The report they issued declared that Filipinos were not prepared for self-government, and they recommended a U.S.-led government be established, as well as schools.

Another commission was then established. The Second Philippine Commission had an administrative role, operating from 1900 to 1916. Known as the Taft Commission, it was directed by William Howard Taft (1857–1930) from March 16, 1900, to July 4, 1901, well before his presidency of 1909 to 1913 (fig. 20). The Commission was granted legislative and executive power over the Philippines.[106] As the archipelago's first "civil governor," Taft had won local support in part by placing Filipinos in

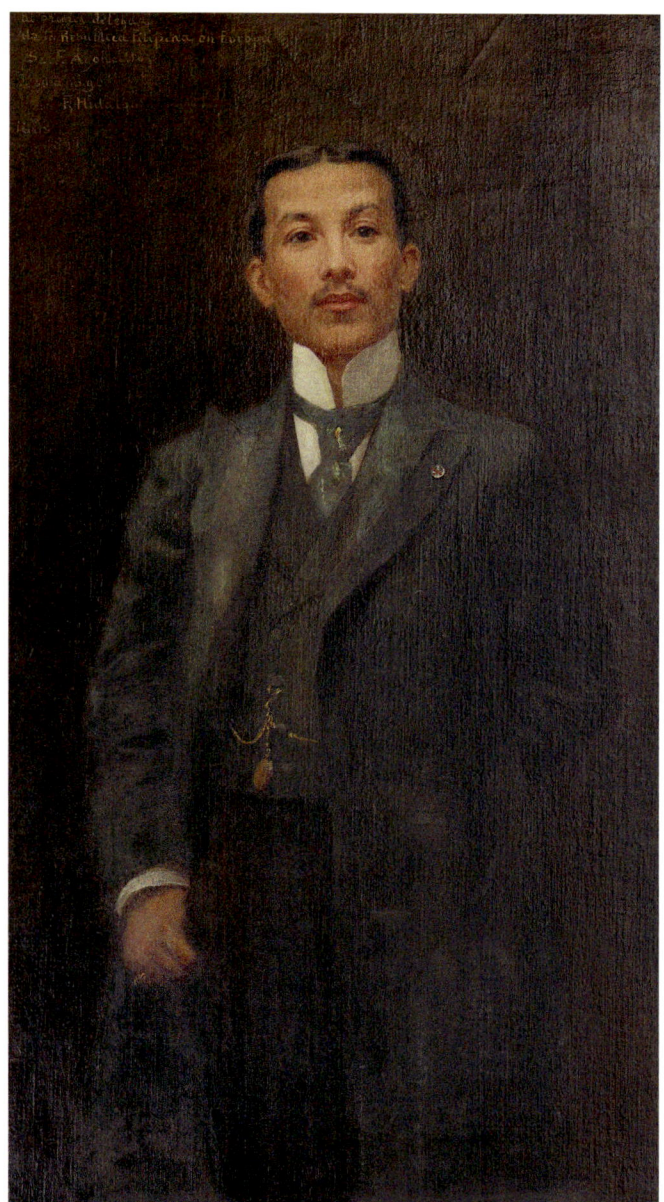

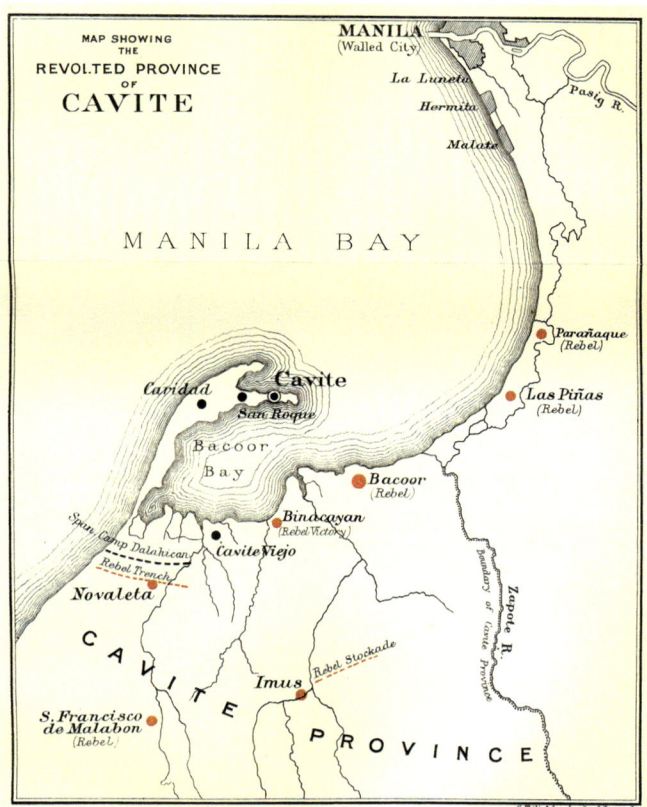

Fig. 18 *Felipe Agoncillo* (1859–1941), Félix Resurrección Hidalgo (1855–1913), 1899. Oil on canvas; 86.4 × 55.9 cm (34 × 22 in.). National Fine Arts Collections of the National Museum of the Philippines

Fig. 19 Map of Cavite Province, John Foreman (life dates unknown), 1899. Reproduced in *The Philippine Islands: A Political, Geographical, Ethnographical, Social, and Commercial History of the Philippines Archipelago, Embracing the Whole Period of Spanish Rule.* London: S. Low, Marston, and Company, 1899

government positions.[107] His favor among Filipinos was such that when President Roosevelt sought to appoint Taft to the U.S. Supreme Court, both Taft and Filipino officials, the local press, and private citizens objected to his removal as civil governor. A telegram of January 7, 1903, signed by Filipino officials read, "The Philippine people have absolute confidence in Taft. At the present moment, departure of Taft would have deplorable effects in the country."[108]

In February 1903, Taft's popularity among Filipinos increased after he declared his intention for the

development of the archipelago as "the Philippines for the Filipinos . . . that every measure, whether in the form of a law or an executive order, before its adoption, should be weighed in the light of this question: Does it make for the welfare of the Filipino people, or does it not?"[109] Filipinos understood his words as a promise of their eventual independence.[110]

The Taft Commission established the Department of Public Instruction in the Philippines on January 21, 1901, initiating a public school system with chaplains and non-commissioned officers of the U.S. Army assigned to teach

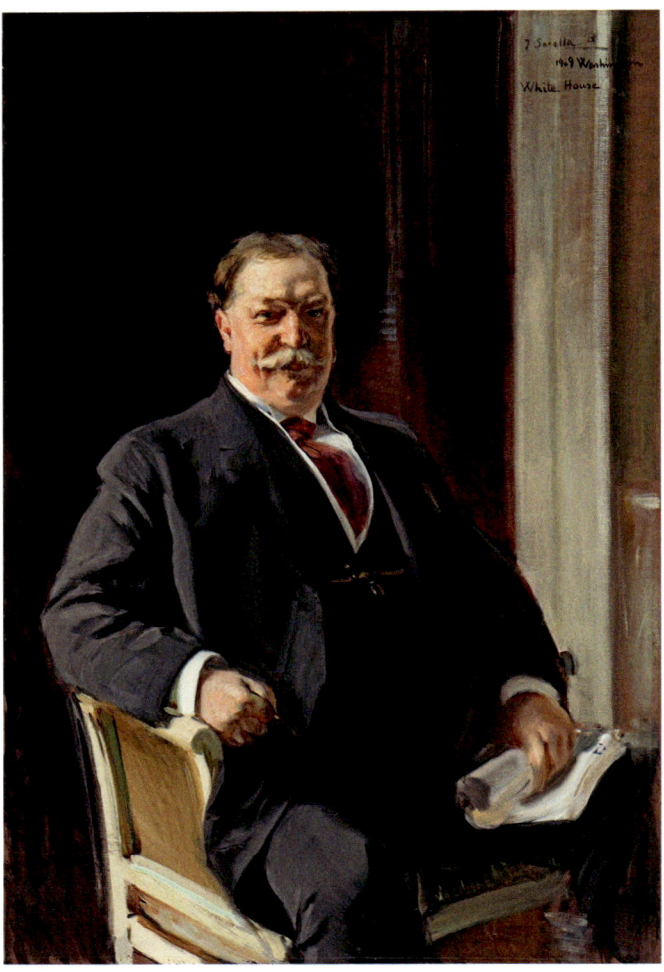

Fig. 20 *William Howard Taft* (1857–1930), Joaquín Sorolla y Bastida (1863–1923), 1909. Oil on canvas; 151.1 × 104.1 cm (59½ × 41 in.). Taft Museum of Art, Cincinnati Ohio; bequest of Charles Phelps Taft and Anna Sinton Taft

English.[111] This aspect of U.S. colonialism would have long-lasting effects on the Filipino education system. English became the most widely spoken language, and English literacy increased from 20 percent in 1901 to 50 percent by 1941.[112] Following the Taft Commission's guidelines, a U.S. chaplain, William D. McKinnon (1858–1902), was charged with establishing a secular public education system in Manila.[113]

Another chaplain, Theophilus Gould Steward (fig. 21), was a prominent educator and clergyman with a storied career. After the Civil War, he organized the first Black school in Marion County, South Carolina, and assisted in the drafting of the 1868 Georgia Republican Party platform. He participated in the labor rights movement and later served as a missionary in Haiti, where he established a church in Port-au-Prince in 1874.[114] From 1886 to 1888, Steward preached at the African Methodist Episcopal Metropolitan Church in Washington, DC, counting Frederick Douglass among his regular congregants. Then in 1891, he was commissioned as chaplain of the 25th Infantry Regiment, a Black regiment, with whom he went to Cuba in 1899.[115]

Steward chronicled his experiences in Cuba in his book *The Colored Regulars in the United States Army*, which was published to commemorate the service of professional Black soldiers, who were referred to as "Black regulars" during the War of 1898. Subsequently, in 1900, he was stationed in the Philippines, where he was appointed superintendent of schools in Luzon. Although many African American soldiers saw commonalities between their own struggle for basic rights and that of Filipinos, Steward saw military service as a way to press for full citizenship.[116]

Some wives of U.S. officers also taught in schools. The redhaired Ida Burr Parker, who was married to John H. Parker, drew attention when she rode on horseback into the jungle to teach Filipino youth (fig. 22).[117] She organized eighteen soldiers to teach at schools in Laguna, and over time she supervised more than two thousand students. Her husband described her as "worth more toward tranquilizing the country than a thousand men, for it [her work] indicated permanence of occupation and friendship for the people."[118] In addition to teaching, women were lauded for their roles in missionary expeditions.

When officers coordinated with local Filipinos through governance, the U.S. Army campaign in the Philippines had greater success. For example, the campaign was

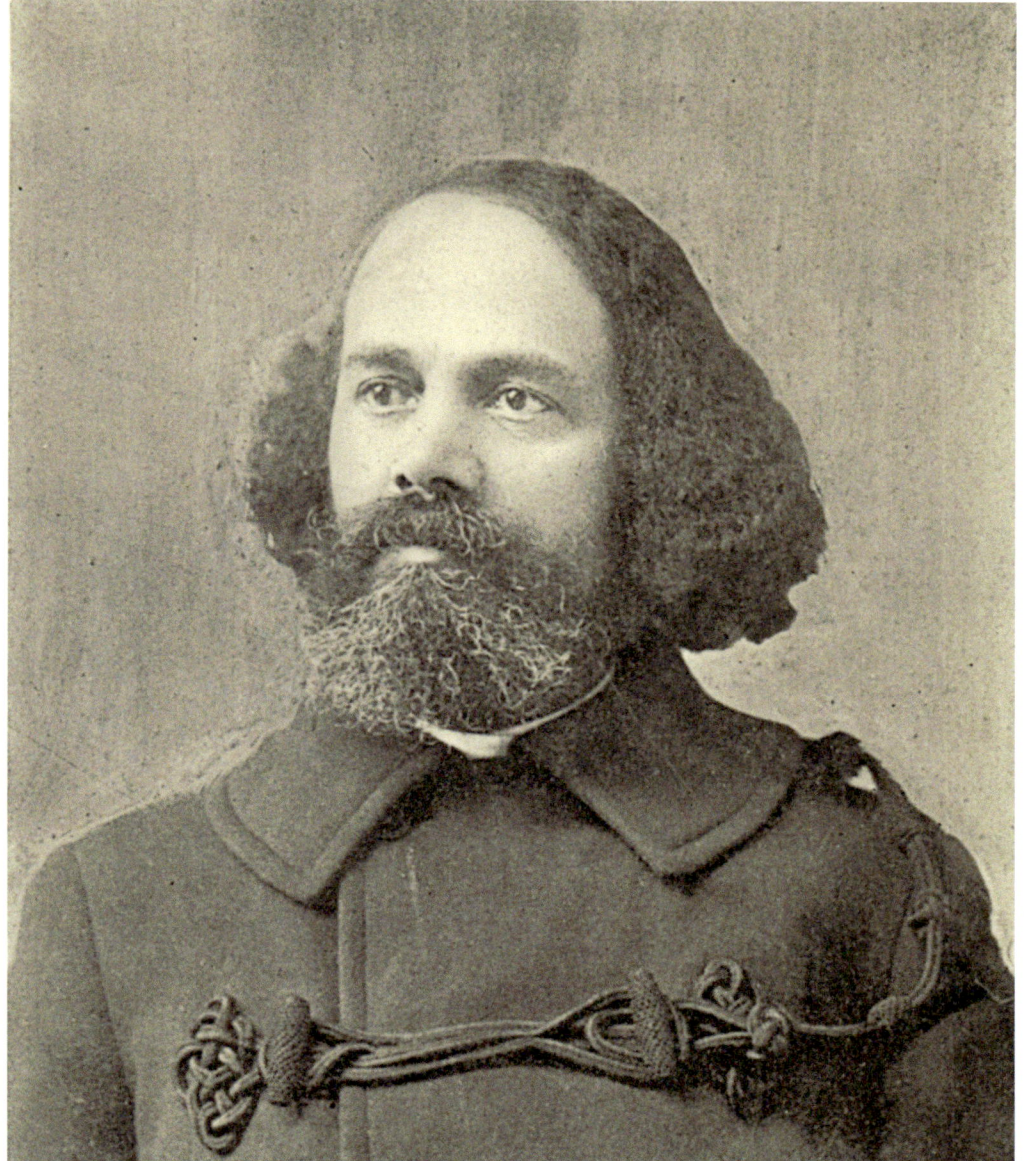

Fig. 21 *Theophilus Gould Steward* (1843–1924), Unidentified photographer, c. 1904. Reproduced in *The Colored Regulars in the United States Army* by Theophilus Gould Steward. Philadelphia: AME Book Concern, 1904. National Portrait Gallery, Smithsonian Institution

effective in Camarines in the Bicol region of Luzon, under the command of Brigadier General James M. Bell (1837–1919) because he recruited local Filipinos to return to the towns by giving them control of the town council and the police force. These groups offered business contracts and leadership in civic groups, including militias and scouts. Bicolanos, in turn, assisted the U.S. soldiers in suppressing the guerrillas. They became instrumental in self-governance and helped establish schools. By March 1901, twelve thousand children were gathering in fifty schoolhouses.[119] That same month, the guerrillas surrendered in Camarines.[120]

As U.S. forces occupied the archipelago, they faced resistance from a variety of opponents who used guerrilla tactics. Some scholars who have studied captured Filipino documents (which were then stored in U.S. archives, such as the Bureau of Insurgent Records) argue that the United States won the war neither through brutality nor through counterinsurgency measures. In their view, the leaders of the resistance made mistakes, which, compounded with the Filipino populace's lack of support, lost them the war.[121] But because acts of extreme brutality occurred during the U.S. Army's campaign in the Philippines, both

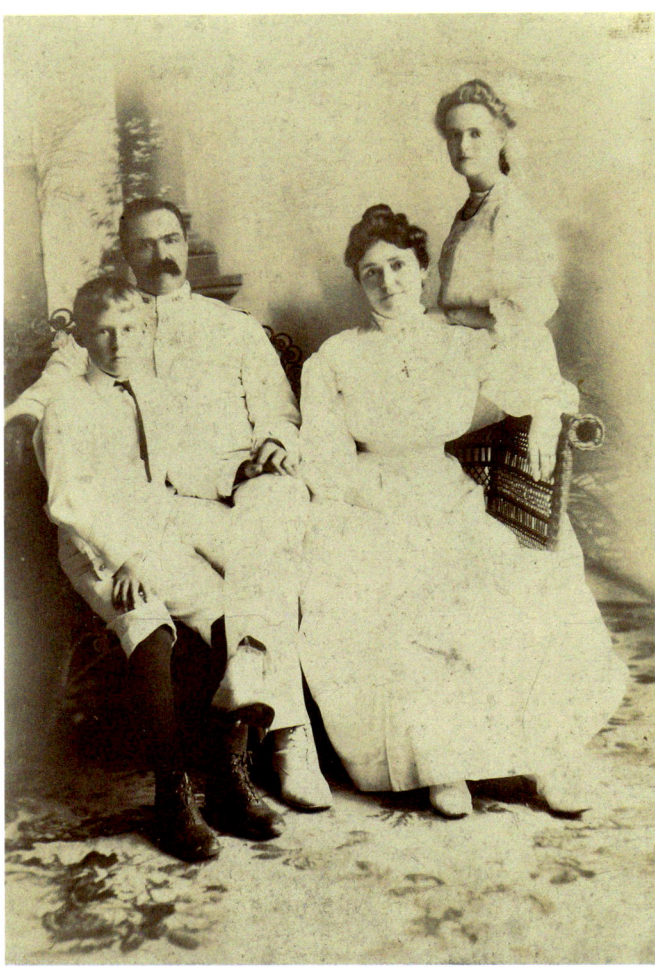

Fig. 22 *John H. Parker* (1866–1942) *and Ida Burr Parker* (c. 1868–1931) *with family*, Unidentified photographer, c. 1907. Photograph; 15.3 × 20.3 cm (8 × 6 in.). Collection of Barbara, Lee, and Jean Parker, granddaughters of Ida and John Henry Parker

the nature of the war and its length have been debated by historians ever since.

In creating a doctrine of war during the nineteenth century, the U.S. Army attempted to balance conciliation and repression. Its aim was to separate noncombatants from combatants, restore order, and prevent further violence through reforms. In the Philippines, implementation of this doctrine included total warfare. As the Filipinos continued to resist, the U.S. Army made the controversial decision to burn crops, destroy homes, and enact imprisonment, expulsion, and death. The U.S. Army used General Orders 100, "Instructions for the Government of Armies of the United States in the Field," to

justify its actions. Issued by President Abraham Lincoln in April 1863 during the U.S. Civil War, this document was in accord with Europe's recognized legal rules of warfare.[122] Although General Orders 100 emphasized the occupier's obligation to restore order and to treat civilians with justice and humanity, it also allowed for the confiscation or destruction of property as well as the imprisonment and execution of any who sustained resistance. In the Philippines, the application of General Orders 100 placed far too much power in the hands of the soldiers of the U.S. Army, however, and some of its provisions are no longer legal under modern humanitarian law.[123] U.S. officers instructed their soldiers to carry out methods of interrogation like the barbaric "water-cure," also known as waterboarding.

The area that offered the strongest resistance to U.S. occupation was south of Manila in the four Tagalog-speaking provinces of Cavite, Batangas, Laguna, and Tayabas. This area included 1.2 million people and, due to geography, is divided into three distinct zones spread across ten thousand miles. The vast department created a challenge for both the Filipino revolutionaries and the U.S. Army.[124] The U.S. command in Southern Luzon failed to create an effective strategy to counter the Filipino insurgents.[125] It took almost two years to develop counterinsurgency tactics, including food deprivation and destruction in some areas, and in other areas, befriending the population.

Mariano Trías (1868–1914), one of Aguinaldo's trusted leaders, was in charge of the Filipino forces in Southern Luzon.[126] Trías issued few directives on matters such as military strategy, policy, taxes, or interactions with civilians.[127] The U.S. Army met its fiercest resistance in the Tagalog districts of Batangas and Laguna, where provincial commanders like Miguel Malvar (1865–1911) and Juan Cailles (1871–1951) operated almost autonomously from Trías and made more deliberate strategic decisions. They each chose guerrilla warfare as their strategy.[128] Filipino soldiers were organized into semipermanent units that knew their areas intimately and could disappear when under attack.[129]

The 1901 Report of the War Department summarized, "the great majority of the people are violently opposed to American rule, and both hate and fear the Americans."[130] By the end of 1900, many Filipinos had concluded that the war must end. Their reluctance to continue may be because their strongest supporters, the wealthy *principales*, were deserting them. Some, like Pedro Paterno (1857–1911), helped form the Federalist Party on December 23, 1900, arguing that the Philippines should aim for statehood in the United States.[131]

Aguinaldo was eventually captured on March 23, 1901, and placed under house arrest at the Malacañang Palace.[132] On April 19, 1901, he issued a proclamation to the Filipinos to accept the United States as the new colonial authority.[133] Nevertheless, the guerrilla forces fighting in Batangas and Laguna under Malvar and Cailles persisted after Aguinaldo surrendered. Cailles was the first to falter, accepting $5,000 on June 24, 1901, to give over his weapons when he and his six hundred men surrendered.[134] Under Malvar, the resistance in Batangas remained strong.

The war in Batangas was especially challenging. Faced with an invisible insurgency, Brigadier General J. Franklin Bell (1856–1919) conducted a counterinsurgency operation that captured guerrillas and made them reveal who else was in their organization. The intelligence that Bell gathered was critical to breaking down Malvar's power. However, Bell also directed his soldiers to implement the tactic of "reconcentration" of the civilian population in parts of Batangas. Soldiers forcibly removed rural inhabitants and placed them in areas separate from guerrillas, establishing "protected" zones.[135] Outside of the zones, U.S. soldiers destroyed much of the food caches. Within the zone, afflicted by disease and starving, about 7,000 residents of Batangas died.[136] Bell was strategic in his application of the reconcentration policy, targeting only the areas that were known to cooperate with Malvar.[137] The U.S. Army's sweeping patrols across the region routed out Filipino revolutionaries in hiding and ended armed resistance. Constantly on the move, Malvar finally surrendered on April 16, 1902.[138] Although reconcentration was successful as a measure against counterinsurgency, U.S. Army officials and the U.S. public alike bitterly debated its morality. Today it is regarded as inhumane.[139]

Other areas in the archipelago endured great violence. The attack on the U.S. garrison in Balangiga, located on the island of Samar of the Eastern Visayas, for example, has had lasting repercussions in Philippine-American diplomacy. On September 28, 1901, Filipinos armed with bolos and led by Lieutenant Colonel Eugenio Daza (1870–1954) attacked seventy-four U.S. soldiers while they were eating breakfast. Forty-eight U.S. soldiers died, and the Filipinos captured one hundred rifles and twenty-five thousand rounds of ammunition, as well as food, medicine, and other equipment.[140] Only four U.S. soldiers escaped unharmed in what was the worst defeat of the U.S. military since the Battle of Little Bighorn in 1876 (see p. 35). Since the skillful attack was coordinated by the ringing of church bells, the U.S. Army took three as war trophies. Their return to the Philippines in 2018 was meant to ease over one hundred years of tension.[141]

Retribution was organized in Samar by Brigadier General Jacob H. Smith (1840–1918). An inept officer, Smith did not coordinate with the U.S. Navy and had been court-martialed twice for insubordination.[142] U.S. Navy gunboats intercepted all commerce and trade and prevented guerrillas from escaping via water routes. Between October 10 and December 31, 1901, soldiers and sailors killed or captured 759 *insurrectos*, 587 carabao (water buffalo), and destroyed tons of rice, 1,662 houses, and 226 boats.[143] The U.S. soldiers were reluctant to let the population suffer, but their commanding officer, Smith, did nothing to help them alleviate the humanitarian crisis. Matters grew worse when Major Littleton W. T. Waller (1856–1926) decided on his own to march U.S. Marines across Samar to find a route for a telegraph line. Waller got lost and deserted his command to look for assistance. When the army rescued the marines, they found Filipino porters carrying their equipment. Nevertheless, eleven marines had died from exposure and disease. In violation of the laws of war, Waller ordered that eleven of the porters be executed, without investigation or trial. Both Waller and Smith were court-martialed, and the U.S. Senate convened hearings to examine events in the Philippines as politicians reflected their constituents' concerns over the brutality reported in the news.[144] With the 1902 midterm elections approaching, President Theodore Roosevelt needed to find a solution, and fast.

On July 4, 1902, Roosevelt proclaimed the "Philippine Insurrection" over.[145] However, sectarian-tribal rebellions in the southernmost provinces continued. There was fighting in Leyte and Samar from 1905 to 1907, and fighting against the Moros went on until 1913.[146] Muslim populations were especially affected when, in 1903, the U.S. administration created Moro Province. In 1904, Roosevelt abrogated the Bates Agreement of 1899, which had promised that the United States would respect the authority of the sultans and datus, or rulers.[147]

In 1906, Leonard Wood (1860–1927) was appointed governor of Moro Province, where he stayed until 1908.[148]

From March 5 to 8, 1906, nearly eight hundred U.S. soldiers and Philippine Constabulary forces fought the rebels in an extinct volcano, Bud Dajo, in Sulu.[149] There, Tausug Muslims had retreated to a defensive position, armed with weapons like kris swords, bolos, firearms, and artillery. During that time, U.S. soldiers were responsible for the deaths of approximately one thousand Tausugs, including women, children, and those who died by suicide. Almost one hundred U.S. soldiers were casualties. An infamous photograph of U.S. soldiers with the Filipino dead was taken at the site and was reprinted in American newspapers (see p. 29). Although Filipinos suffered ten times more dead than the U.S. soldiers, Wood faced no repercussions. Instead, Roosevelt sent him a telegram congratulating him "upon the brave feat of arms wherein you and they so well upheld the honor of the American flag."[150] Anti-imperialists were set aflame, however. "Brutality has been rewarded, humanity has been punished," cried Moorfield Storey.[151]

Spoils of war abounded. Many soldiers took the wave-like kris swords, as did George C. Shaw (1866–1960), a first lieutenant who fought with John J. Pershing (1860–1948) in Mindanao from 1899 to 1903.[152] The kris, which was pictured as Sikatuna's weapon in Luna's painting *El pacto de sangre*, was only used in Mindanao and Sulu (fig. 23).[153] With its wave-like pattern of alternating crests, the blade is characterized by a serpentine outline. The double-edged blade was used as a badge of leadership in the field or as a political marker of significance to its owner.[154] A lethal weapon, its curving blade was made to shred a person's interior organs as it was wielded. After Captain John J. Pershing was appointed commander of Moro Province in 1909, he hoped to disarm the Moros and impose rule of law (fig. 24).[155] Yet when one thousand Moro Filipinos fled to the mountaintop of Bud Bagsak on the island of Jolo, Philippine Scouts suppressed their resistance between June 11 and June 15, 1913. Organized by Matthew Batson (1866–1917), the Philippine Scouts came from Macabebe, fifty miles north of Manila. They consisted of two companies of Filipino soldiers, who were paid by the U.S. Army.[156] Pershing formed two companies of Moro Scouts, the Fifty-First and the Fifty-Second. The first was made up of Maguindanaos from Cotabato, and the latter was comprised of Maranaos from Lanao. He sent the Moro Scouts as well as Philippine Scouts to fight the Tausug warriors, of whom five hundred died in battle.[157] Pershing left the Philippines six months later.

Between 1899 and 1913, it is estimated that approximately 4,200 U.S. soldiers were killed. Around 18,000 Filipino soldiers lost their lives, and at least 100,000 Filipino civilians died from disease, famine, and other war-related causes.[158] Filipino forces employed guerrilla warfare to great effect and almost defeated both Spain and the United States. By seizing the Philippines, the United States established an important foothold in the far east of the Pacific Ocean.[159] Yet politicians like William Atkinson Jones (1849–1918), who chaired the U.S. House Insular Affairs Committee, supported gradual Philippine independence.[160] Jones built support during the first years of World War I, and President Woodrow Wilson (1856–1925) signed the Jones Act on August 29, 1916, promising Filipinos independence "as soon as a stable government can be established therein."[161] This nebulous, ill-defined solution remained the framework for the U.S. administration of the Philippines until 1934, when Congress passed the Tydings–McDuffie Act. This legislature established the Commonwealth of the Philippines and a ten-year countdown to Philippine independence, albeit with some limitations, following the Cuban precedent. The Japanese military invasion of the Philippines during World War II subjected the Philippines to its third colonial ruler in less than fifty years, but after a hard-fought struggle to oust the Japanese occupiers, the United States recognized the Republic of the Philippines as an independent nation in July 1946.[162] In summary, from 1935 to 1946 (excepting the period of exile when Japan occupied the country during World War II from April 9, 1942, to September 2, 1945), the commonwealth government was meant to be a transitional administration to prepare the Philippines for its independence, although the United States

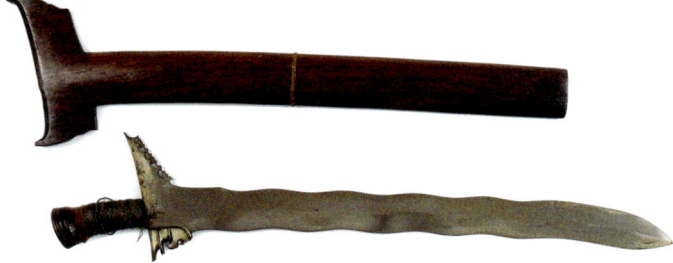

Fig. 23 Kris with wooden scabbard, c. 1903. Iron alloy, wood, twined cellulose fiber; Kris: 16 × 72.5 × 3.5 cm (6⁵⁄₁₆ × 28½ × 1⅜ in.) George Shaw Collection, Department of Anthropology, National Museum of Natural History

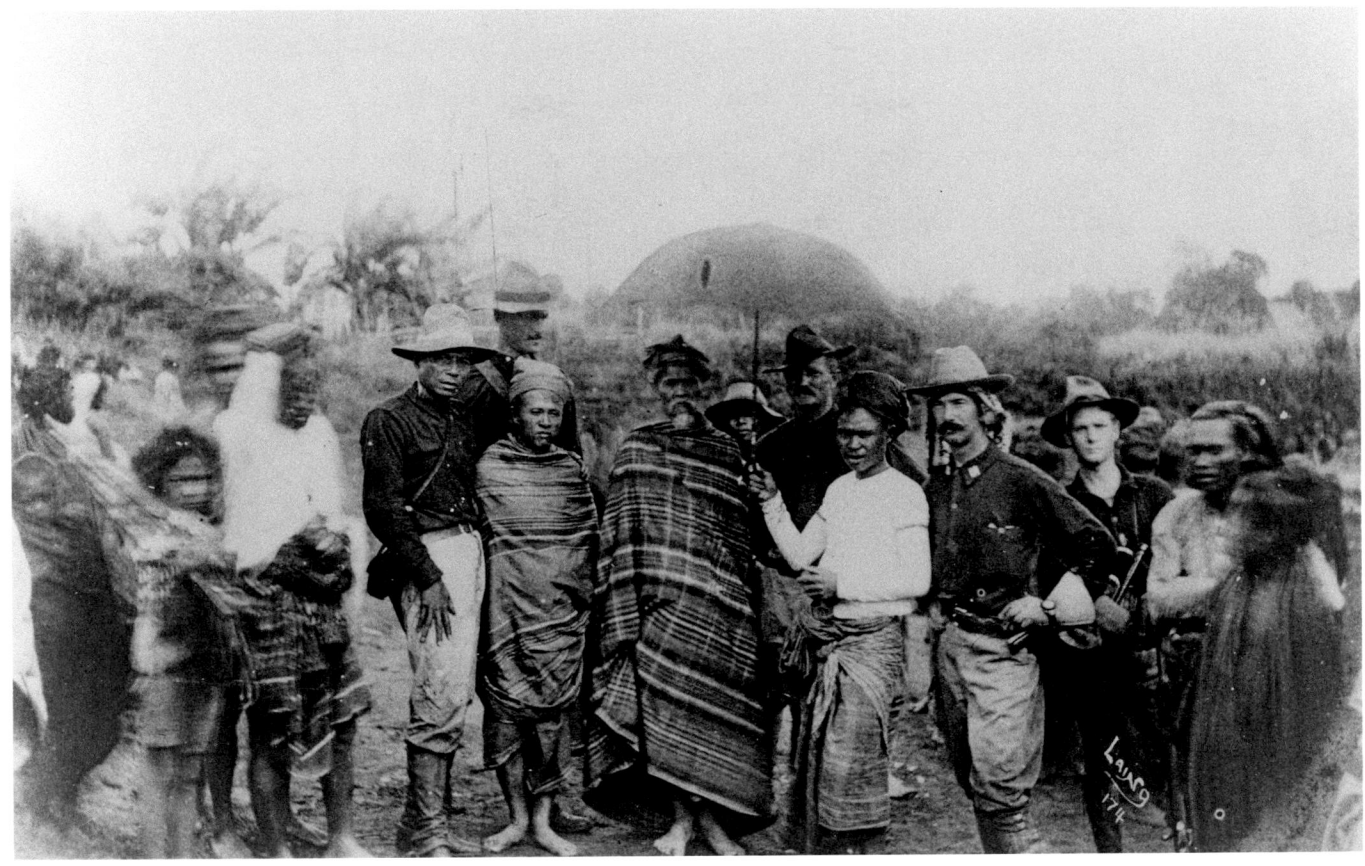

Fig. 24 Under the umbrella, which signifies rank, John J. Pershing stands to the right of the Rajamunda of Marahui, whom he met during his visit to the northern Lake Lanao region in 1903. Photograph reproduced in John J. Pershing, *My Life Before the World War 1860–1917*. Lexington: University of Kentucky Press, 2013

retained naval bases in the Philippines until 1992. The Philippine-American War ultimately linked the militaries and policies of the two nations for over one hundred years.

Guam as a Key to U.S. Imperialism

Following Commodore George Dewey's naval defeat of the Spanish Armada in Manila Bay on May 1, 1898, the United States seized Guam on June 20, 1898. The largest island in the southernmost chain of islands in Micronesia, named the Marianas by Spain in 1668, Guam is located on the seven-thousand-mile route between San Francisco and Manila (fig. 25). It possesses Apra Harbor, a natural deep-water port that made it critical as a coaling station for steam-powered vessels in 1898. Guam was annexed for different reasons than the Philippines, whose vast lands offered the possibility of cash crop production like rice or hemp. U.S. imperialists saw Guam as an important strategic tool to make naval power possible.

From 1668 to 1898, Guam had been a possession of Spain's colonial empire.[163] Yet the island had been inhabited by the seafaring CHamoru, the Indigenous people of Guam and the Marianas, for more than four thousand years. CHamoru society was organized into family clans, with high-ranking clans controlling the most productive land. The earliest CHamoru were matrilineal, and the highest-ranking women, *manmaga'haga* (leading daughters), shared chiefly status alongside their male counterparts, the *manmaga'lahi* (leading sons).[164] These women made the major decisions for their clans as matrilineal conventions pass ownership of land, titles, and other valuables according to the lineage of one's mother.[165] For two centuries, both the CHamoru as well as the creoles, known as Guamanians, were subjects of the Spanish colonial regime.

PLATE LXX.

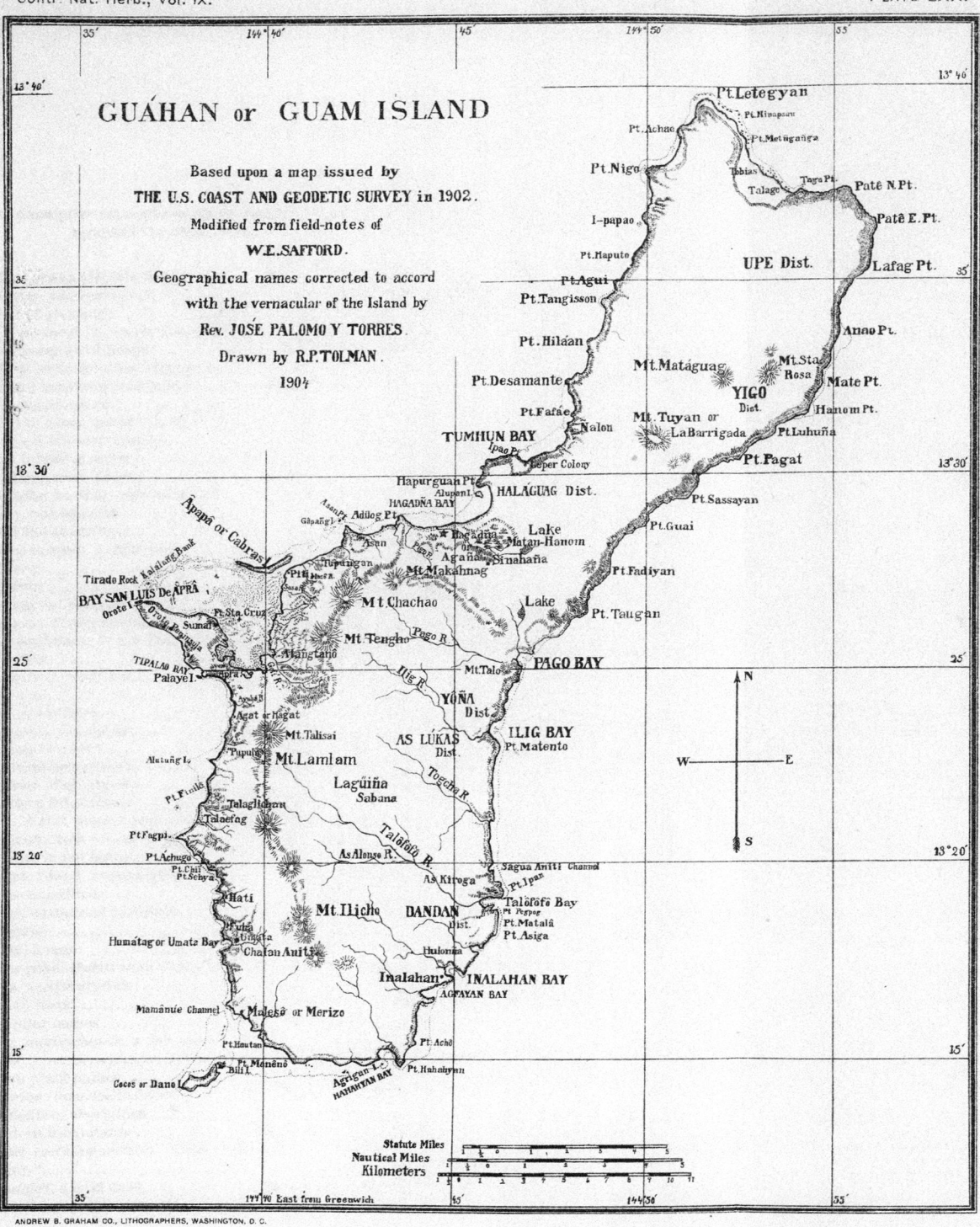

GUÁHAN or GUAM ISLAND

Based upon a map issued by
THE U.S. COAST AND GEODETIC SURVEY in 1902.
Modified from field-notes of
W.E.SAFFORD.
Geographical names corrected to accord
with the vernacular of the Island by
Rev. JOSÉ PALOMO Y TORRES.
Drawn by R.P.TOLMAN.
1904

MAP OF THE ISLAND OF GUAM.

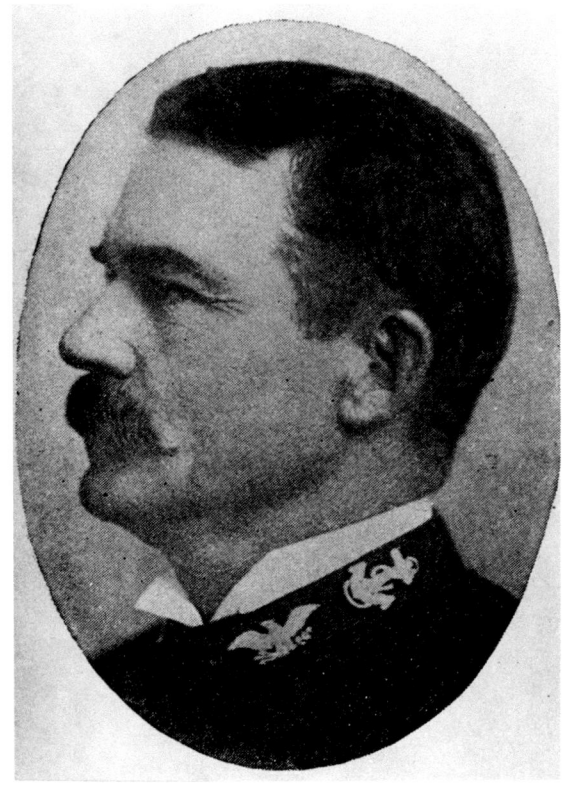

The peace was disrupted on June 20, 1898, when the United States seized Guam as its possession.[166] Captain Henry Glass (1844–1908) of the USS *Charleston* was under orders from Secretary of the Navy John Davis Long (1838–1915) to capture the island of Guam and make prisoners of its Spanish officials (fig. 26).[167] While en route to the Philippines, Glass stopped in Guam and ordered his men to fire upon the Spanish citadel, Fort Santa Cruz. Two Spanish officers then informed Glass and his men that there was no response to the U.S. "salute" because their arsenal had no more gunpowder. The officers were so isolated that they were surprised to learn that the United States and Spain were at war. The Spanish governor, Juan Marina (1846–1909), surrendered Guam to Glass on June 21.[168] Glass subsequently imprisoned fifty-six Spanish soldiers and departed for Manila.[169] Ironically, although it lacked coal, Guam was now a coaling station for the United States.[170] It has been an unincorporated territory—or a portion of the United States that is not a state—ever since.

Meanwhile, Germany secretly negotiated with Spain and agreed to purchase the Marshall and Caroline Islands, including Palau, and all of the Marianas except for Guam. Both countries agreed that the islands would remain under Spanish control until Spain concluded negotiations with the United States.[171] After World War I, Japan took over the German Micronesian colonies through a League of Nations Mandate. This splitting of the Mariana Islands into two separate political entities created problems that extend to this day, but most significantly, during World War II, CHamoru were pitted against one another because while Guamanians remained under U.S. rule, their northern cousins were under Japanese rule. Lingering wartime animosities have since thwarted attempts to reunify the Mariana Islands.

No representatives of Guam were consulted during the Treaty of Paris negotiations between October 1 and December 10, 1898. Unlike the Philippines, Puerto Rico, and Cuba, Guam did not send its own envoy of commissioners to be included in the negotiations. However, because there was no occupying force in Guam, many there thought they might resist U.S. imperialism. In late December 1898, José Sisto (life dates unknown), a civilian administrator of the former Spanish treasury, declared himself governor. He gathered a group of pro-Spanish priests and CHamoru militiamen, hoping to rely on their support. But during his rule, law and order ran amok, and Guamanians and CHamorus removed Sisto from office and arrested him for misusing public funds.[172] Meanwhile, Padre José Torres Palomo (fig. 27) and other prominent CHamoru formed a pro-American group in Guam.[173]

Born in Guam, Padre Palomo was educated at the San Carlos Seminary in Cebu, the Philippines, and ordained into the Catholic priesthood in 1859. An important representative of CHamoru and Guamanian people, he was the first CHamoru Roman Catholic priest.[174] He witnessed Guam change hands from Spain to the United States and led his fellow islanders to ensure a fair rule. Fluent in CHamoru, Spanish, Carolinian, Latin, English, and French, he functioned as a diplomat for Guam during its transition of colonial authority.[175]

For almost eight months, governance of Guam alternated between the CHamorus and Guamanians who were

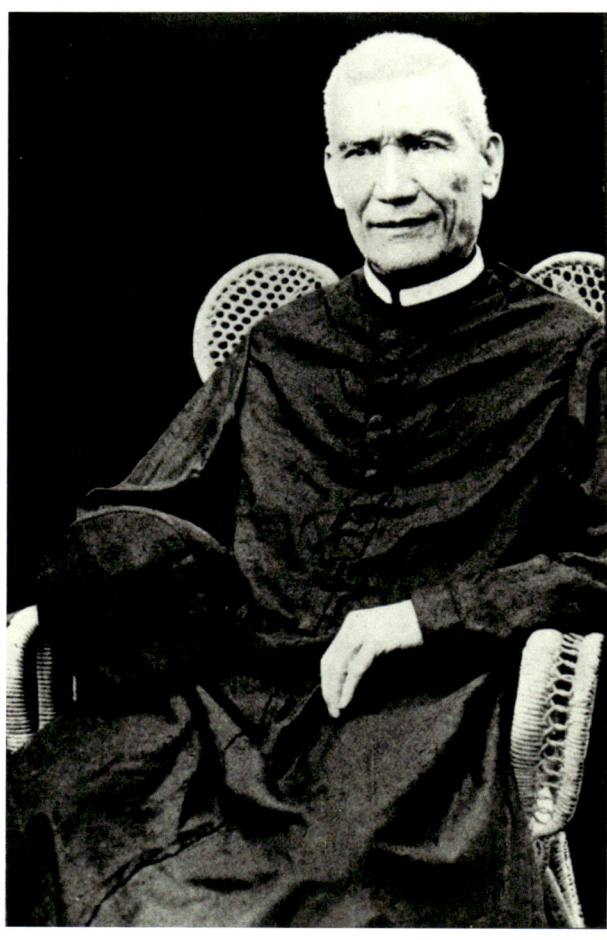

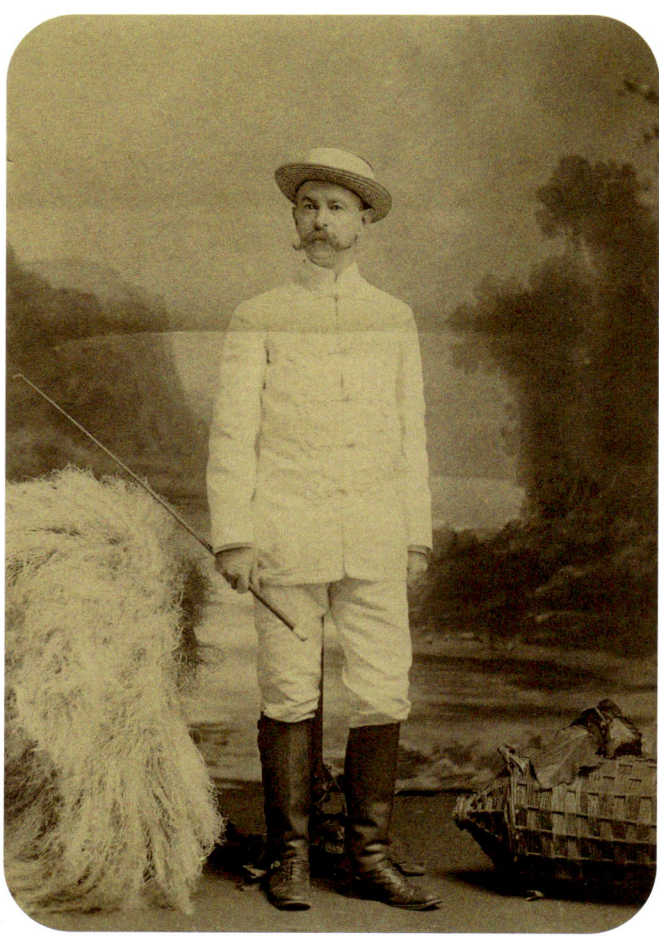

Fig. 27 *Padre José Torres Palomo* (1836–1919), Unidentified photographer, Date unknown. Photograph; 11.5 × 7.3 cm (4½ × 2⅞ in.). The Richard F. Taitano Micronesian Area Research Center

Fig. 28 *Captain Richard P. Leary* (1842–1901), Unidentified photographer, c. 1890. Photograph; 14.3 × 10.3 cm (5⅝ × 4 in.). Special Collections and Archives Department, Nimitz Library, U.S. Naval Academy

loyal to Spain, and those who worked with a rotating roster of visiting U.S. naval captains on their way to the Philippines. When Captain Richard Leary (fig. 28) of the USS *Yosemite* arrived on August 7, 1899, he became the first official naval governor of Guam. Leary graduated in 1864 from the United States Naval Academy, ranking in the bottom 20 percent of the class of fifty.[176] As governor, he stressed the separation of church and state, as well as submission to the U.S. authority (fig. 29). Leary was convinced that the people of Guam were unfit to govern themselves, and he imposed an oppressive rule, issuing twenty-one strict military orders.

For example, Leary issued General Order 4 on August 25, 1899. This prohibited any celebration outside of the church walls on Catholic feast days such as the

Patron Saints of villages. Under the guise of maintaining the "peace," Leary also halted the customary daily tolling of bells. In a controversial move, he expelled all the remaining Spanish priests, who condoned concubinage and had themselves fathered children.[177] When U.S. Catholics learned of the situation, they were infuriated. The Archbishop of New Orleans, Placide Louis Chapelle (fig. 30), whom the Vatican named the apostolic delegate for Cuba, Puerto Rico, and the Philippines, requested permission to visit Guam. Initially, Leary agreed, but he revoked his permission after he received a second letter from Chappelle, who asked that all general orders related to religious liberties be canceled.[178] Although Chapelle sailed to Guam, Leary refused to let him disembark.[179]

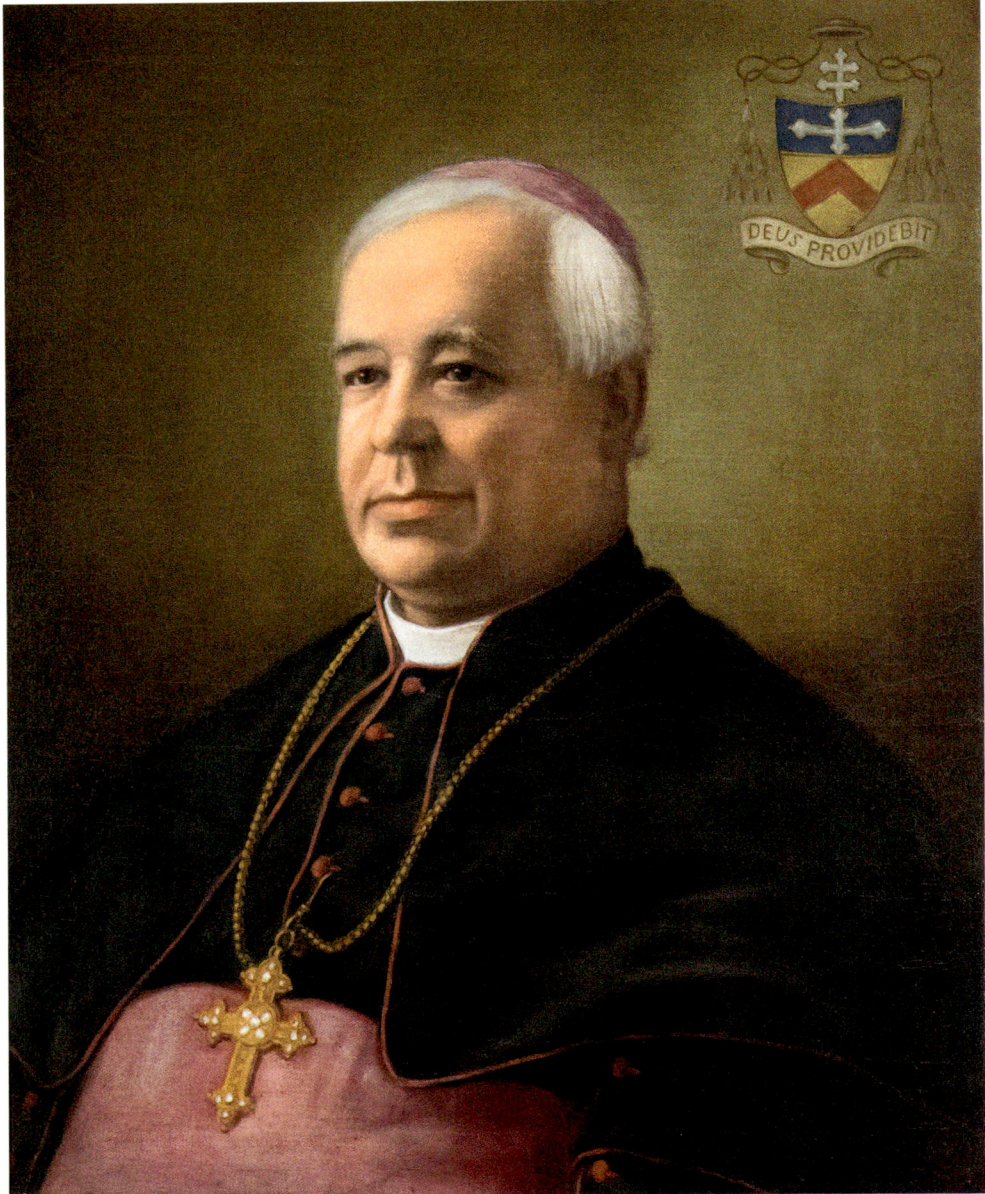

Fig. 30 *Archbishop Placide Louis Chapelle* (1842–1905), Unidentified artist, Date unknown. Oil on canvas; 88.9 × 76.2 cm (35 × 30 in.). Office of Archives and Records, Archdiocese of New Orleans

Although Leary ostensibly abolished peonage, he established that the Hagåtña elite would negotiate debts through labor, sometimes for long periods of time.[180] Of the executive orders issued by Leary, five addressed the problems of discipline among the sailors and marines stationed in Guam, including public drunkenness, assaults on civilians, vandalism, and the abandonment of the duty station without authorization.[181] Despite these orders, the problem of lawlessness in the military persisted, causing resentment among many of the island's civilian inhabitants.[182]

The CHamoru found an advocate in Leary's aide and second-in-command, Lieutenant Governor William Edwin Safford (fig. 31). Padre Palomo introduced Safford to the manak'kilo, the upper-class *mestizos* of Hagåtña. A naturalist who appreciated the island's native flora and fauna, Safford wrote *The Useful Plants of the Island of Guam* (fig. 32), now recognized as one of the best studies of CHamoru culture and history, although some historians also consider it as an example of bioprospecting.[183] Safford, assisted by Palomo, also compiled the first CHamoru dictionary.[184]

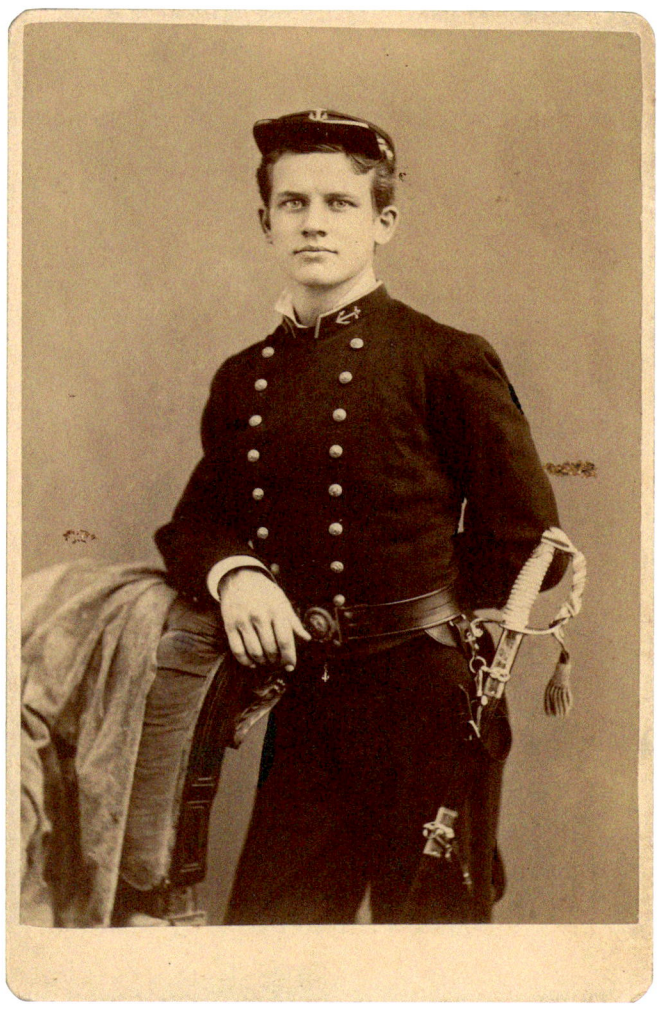

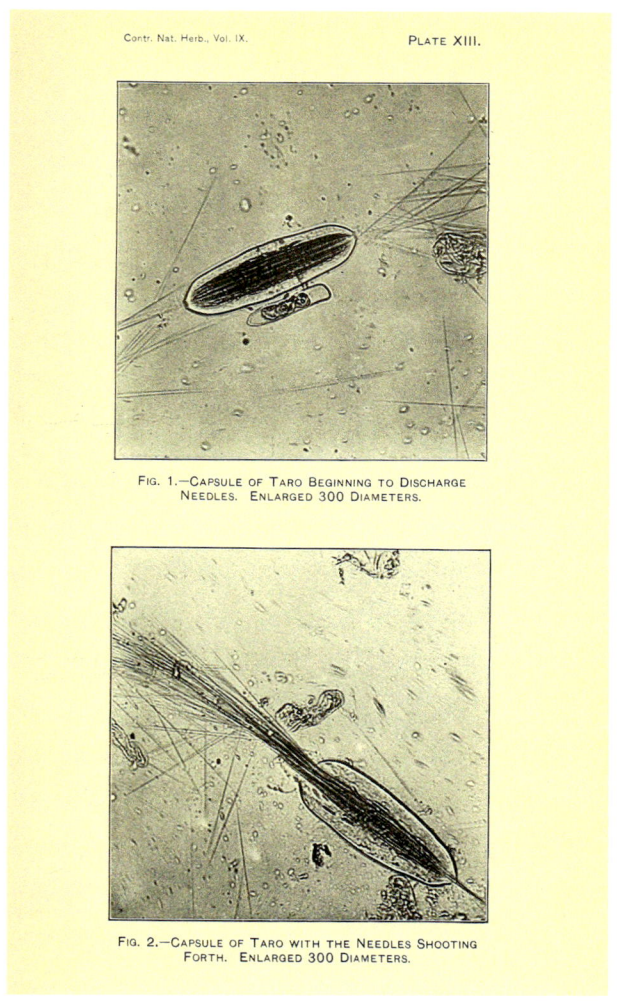

Contr. Nat. Herb., Vol. IX.   PLATE XIII.

FIG. 1.—CAPSULE OF TARO BEGINNING TO DISCHARGE
NEEDLES. ENLARGED 300 DIAMETERS.

FIG. 2.—CAPSULE OF TARO WITH THE NEEDLES SHOOTING
FORTH. ENLARGED 300 DIAMETERS.

Fig. 31 *William Edwin Safford* (1859–1926), 1880. Photograph; 16 × 10.7 cm (6¼ × 4³⁄₁₆ in.). The Richard F. Taitano Micronesian Area Research Center

Fig. 32 Illustrations in *The Useful Plants of the Island of Guam*, by William Edwin Safford. Washington, DC: Government Printing Office, 1905. Smithsonian Libraries and Archives

Leary's harsh edicts resulted in an investigation by his superior officers. General Elwell Otis, then in charge of the campaign in the Philippines, sent Major General Joseph Wheeler (1836–1906) to investigate Leary's rule and the conditions of Guam. During Wheeler's visit, Palomo organized a petition to have Safford instated as governor.[185] Instead, in July, Commander Seaton Schroeder (1849–1922) replaced Leary.[186] He immediately eased some of the harsh orders, including allowing public celebrations of Catholic feast days. However, many of his policies were disliked. In 1900, for example, Schroeder established an order for all CHamoru midwives to take a course in modern hygiene and to obtain licenses.[187] CHamoru women resisted this and other navy orders for years because they went against long-standing traditional customs.[188]

Before 1898, the Mariana Islands were inhabited freely by CHamorus who were able to easily travel between them. However, with the introduction of U.S. and German colonial forces at the turn of the century, the islands became separate. Guamanians and CHamorus did not give up their fight to determine their political futures, however. In 1901, thirty-two CHamorus, including Atanasio Taitano Perez (1874–1950), proposed self-governance and U.S. citizenship (fig. 33). To that end, Perez presented a petition to the U.S. Navy and Congress to study the conditions in Guam. Schroeder endorsed the petition, but the Navy Department disapproved, and the matter died

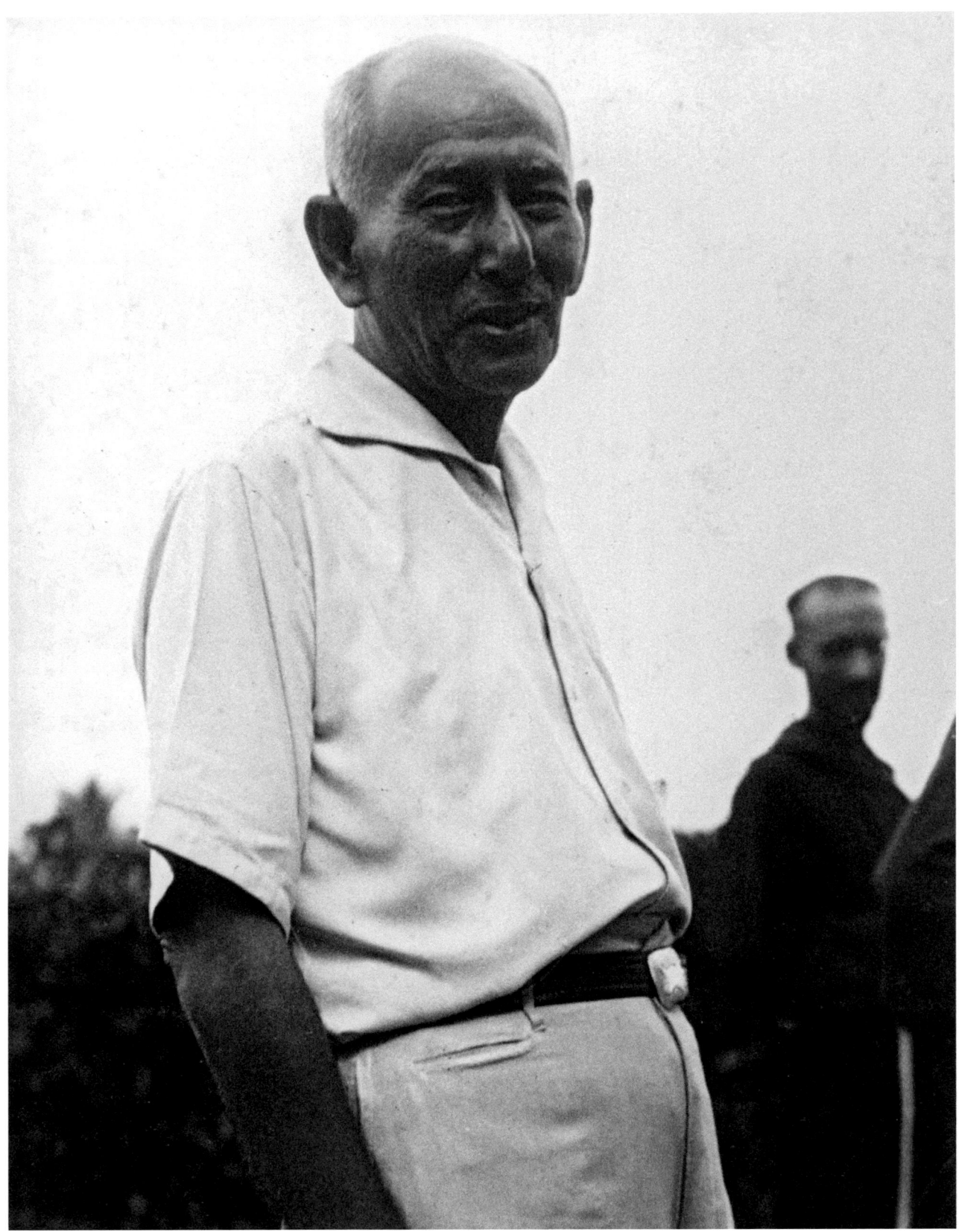

on the floor of the House of Representatives. The 1901 petition declared CHamoru loyalty to the United States yet described how the island enjoyed more freedoms under Spanish rule. CHamorus objected to the military government, stating that "at best [it] is distasteful and highly repugnant to the fundamental principles of civilized government."[189] At least seven other petitions were organized over the years in protest of the U.S. naval government.[190] In 1925, Perez drew attention to the lack of citizenship rights in Guam: "The CHamorus are neither citizens nor aliens—they are truly without a country. When the United States acquired sovereignty over the Virgin Islands [1917], citizenship was immediately conferred on the inhabitants, but Guam, for 26 years a U.S. possession, has not yet been granted that privilege."[191] In 1950, the people of Guam became U.S. citizens.[192]

Guam was under the control of the U.S. Navy from 1898 until 1941, when the Japanese invaded and brutally occupied the island. On July 21, 1944, the U.S. Armed Forces recaptured Guam and soon began confiscating large swaths of Native farmlands for military use. In 1946, CHamorus owned a third of the land in Guam; by the next year, 1,350 CHamoru families lost their land and homes.[193] The U.S. naval government of Guam remained in place until 1950, when the Organic Act of Guam was enacted by Congress. The Organic Act was catalyzed in part by the 1949 Guam Congress Walkout, a protest against the ongoing American military rule.[194]

After World War II, the Northern Marianas became the Commonwealth of the Mariana Islands, under the control of the United States, and Guam's government transitioned from the navy to a civilian government. However, today, as Guam is an unincorporated territory of the United States, not all parts of the U.S. Constitution apply to its citizens. In 1950, after years of agitation by both Guam residents and U.S. activists, President Harry Truman (1884–1972) signed the Organic Act into law, which created a domestic legislature. Although Guam is self-governing as of 2022, it is still subject to the plenary power of the U.S. Congress, and the U.S. military still maintains six military installations and about 15,000 military personnel and their dependents there. Approximately one-third of the island is inaccessible to its Native population because of these military installations, a cause of controversy within Guamanian politics today.[195] CHamoru lawyer, activist, and author Julian Aguon writes, "The military buildup now underway is happening over the objections of thousands of the island's residents. Many of these protesters, including myself, are indigenous Chamorros whose ancestors endured five centuries of colonization and who see this latest wave of unilateral action by the United States simply as the latest course in a long steady diet of dispossession."[196]

5

"America Has a Colonies Problem"

NEIL WEARE

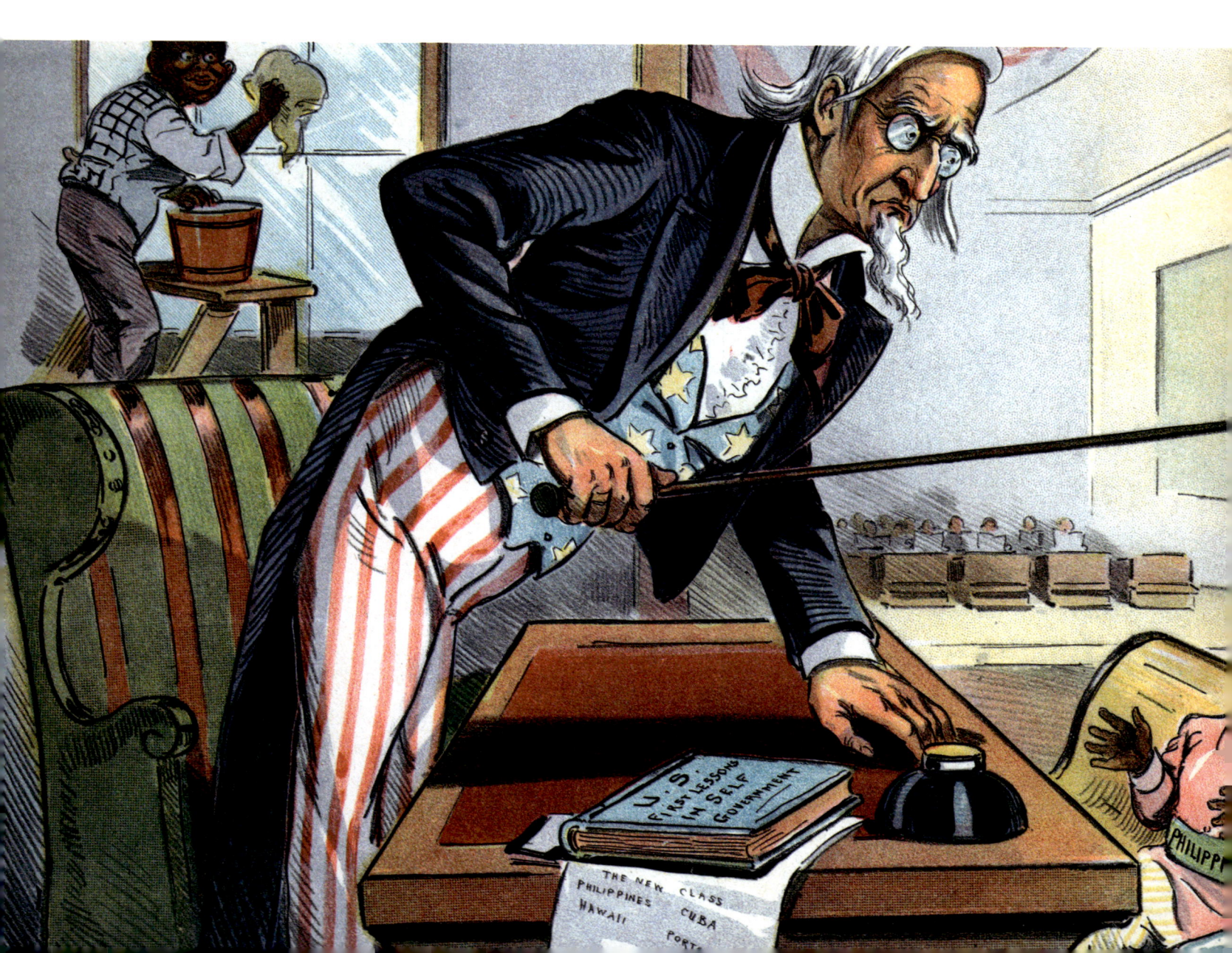

Every child is taught in school about the Thirteen Colonies and how the American Revolution was waged to reject British colonial rule. Many schoolchildren memorize the founding ideals that "all men are created equal" and that governments "deriv[e] their just powers from the consent of the governed."[1] Not usually taught, however, is that the United States *itself* today holds five overseas colonies: Puerto Rico, Guam, the U.S. Virgin Islands, the Northern Mariana Islands, and American Samoa. Few Americans realize that the population of these five U.S. territories— 3.6 million, 98 percent of whom are people of color—equals that of the five smallest states combined. These modern-day colonial subjects are denied the right to vote for president and voting representation in Congress. At the same time, Congress nonetheless holds complete authority over them, denying them equality in a broad range of federal benefits programs while taxing them billions of dollars a year. In short, America has a colonies problem.

Detail of *School Begins*, Louis Dalrymple (1866–1905) for *Puck* magazine, January 25, 1899. Chromolithograph, Library of Congress, Washington, DC (see p. 312)

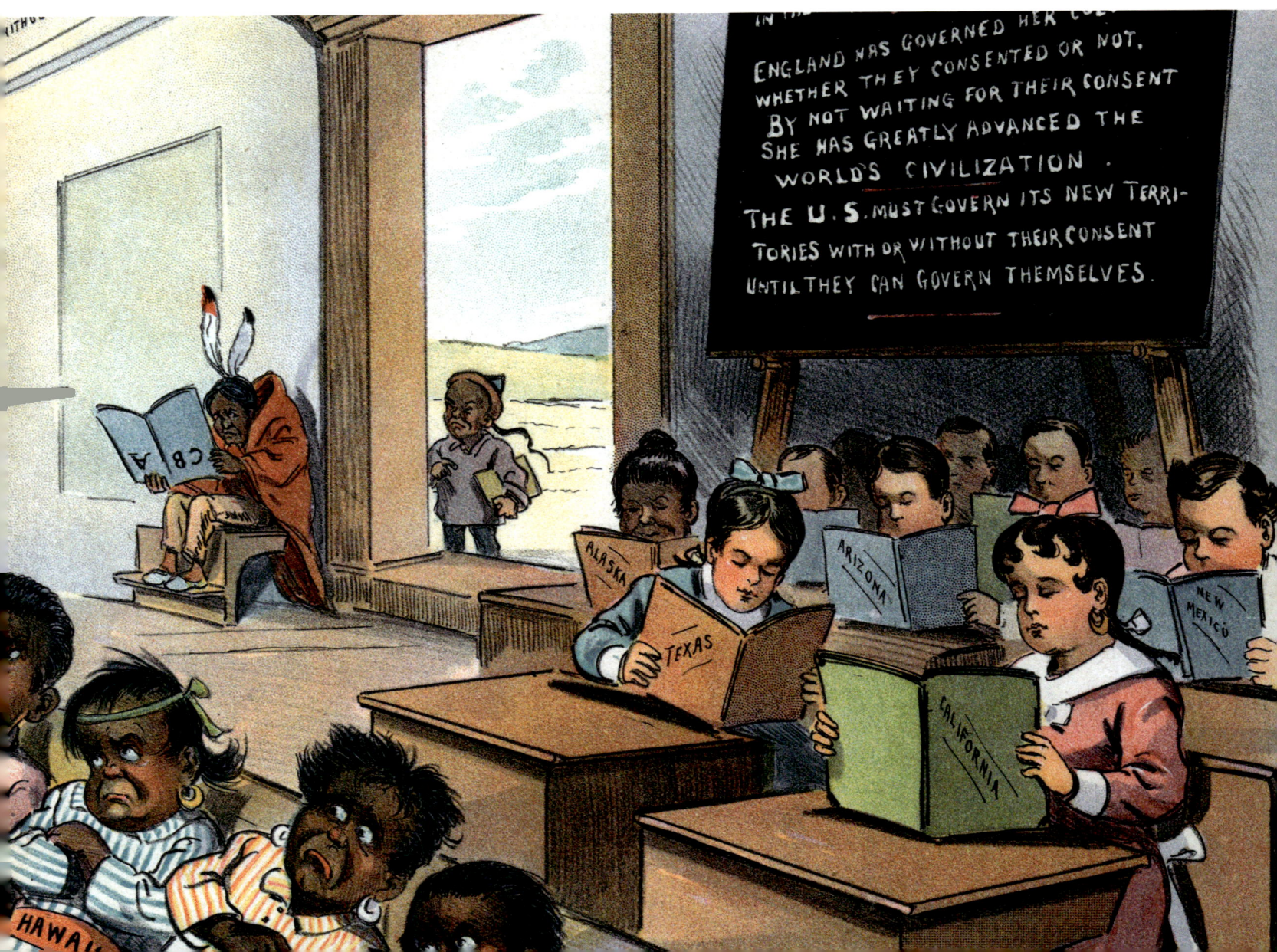

The year 1898 marks a bright line between a United States that rejected colonial empire and one that embraced it. While the U.S. has always had territories, territorial status was originally understood as temporary, with those living in territories constitutionally guaranteed full U.S. citizenship and eventual political participation through statehood.[2] But as America's ambition for empire surged following the 1898 Spanish-American War, this constitutional understanding was tested. Suddenly in possession of new lands and new (non-white) people, the United States faced what historian Daniel Immerwahr called a trilemma: "Republicanism, white supremacy, and overseas expansion—the country could have at most two."[3]

This trilemma came to head in the *Insular Cases*, with a deeply divided Supreme Court sacrificing fidelity to the Constitution and America's founding ideals to the altar of empire and white supremacy.[4] Characterizing the people of these newly acquired territories as "alien races,"[5] "savage tribes,"[6] and "uncivilized race[s],"[7] the Court drew a new racialized distinction between so-called "incorporated" and "unincorporated" territories. Territories acquired pre-1898 (that were majority white) were labeled "incorporated," and nothing changed. Territories acquired in 1898 and after (that were overwhelmingly non-white) were labeled "unincorporated," meaning the Constitution would apply "only in part" and they would no longer be "destined for statehood."[8] In a stark break from all precedent, colonialism became constitutional.

The *Insular Cases*' turn from America's founding ideals was highly controversial from the start, with Justice John Marshall Harlan the chief critic.[9] More recently, that mantle has been held by the Honorable Juan Torruella, who served as a federal judge in Puerto Rico from 1982 until his passing in 2020 (fig. 1). Declaring that "the *Insular Cases* represent classic *Plessy v. Ferguson* legal doctrine and thought that should be eradicated from present-day constitutional reasoning,"[10] he long criticized the Supreme Court for countenancing a "doctrine of separate and unequal"[11] and a "regime of political apartheid."[12]

Legal challenges to the *Insular Cases*' colonial framework now span more than a century. One early fighter was Isabel González, a Puerto Rican woman who was detained at Ellis Island in 1902 after arriving in New York from Puerto Rico (fig. 2). Excluded as an undesirable "alien" because she was a pregnant and single mother, González argued that she became a U.S. citizen when the United States annexed Puerto Rico in 1898. Her goal was not just

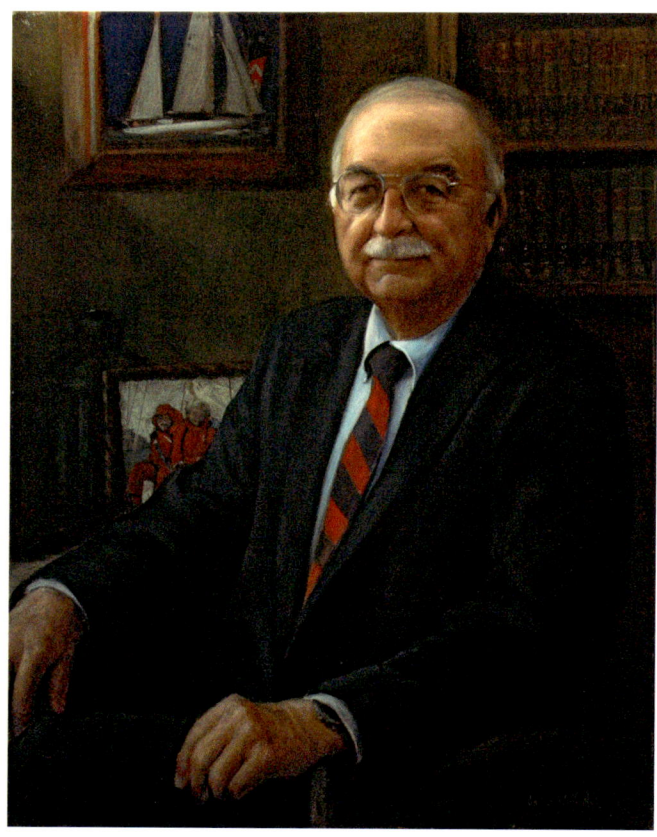

Fig. 1 *Juan Torruella* (1933–2020), David Wells Roth (born 1957), 2007. Oil on canvas. Commissioned in 2007 by the United States District Court of the District of Puerto Rico

to gain entry to New York, but to secure recognition of citizenship for all Puerto Ricans. Ultimately, the Court concluded she was not an "alien," but it refused to say if U.S. citizenship followed the flag to Puerto Rico and other territories.[13]

Continuing Isabel González's fight today is John Fitisemanu, who argued the Citizenship Clause of the Fourteenth Amendment makes him a U.S. citizen based on his birth in American Samoa, a U.S. territory since 1900 (fig. 3). While Congress now recognizes people born in most territories as "statutory" U.S. citizens, it still labels people born in American Samoa as so-called "non-citizen U.S. Nationals." As a result, Fitisemanu—a passport-holding, tax-paying resident of Utah—cannot vote, serve on a jury, or hold certain state and federal jobs. For Fitisemanu, this is not just unfair, it is unconstitutional. Unfortunately, just as the Supreme Court passed on answering whether Isabel González was a citizen in

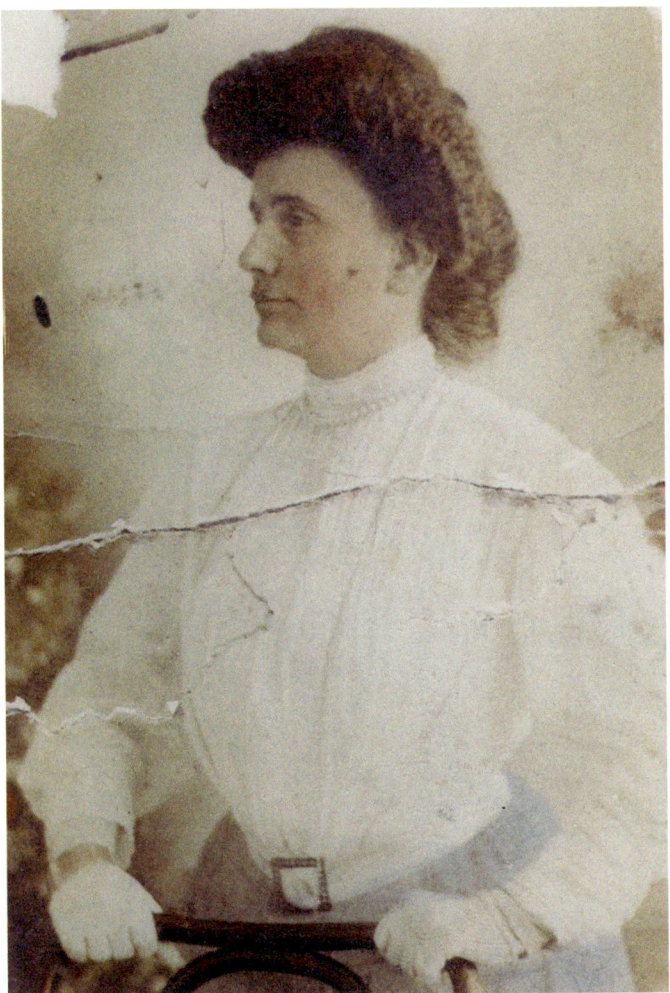

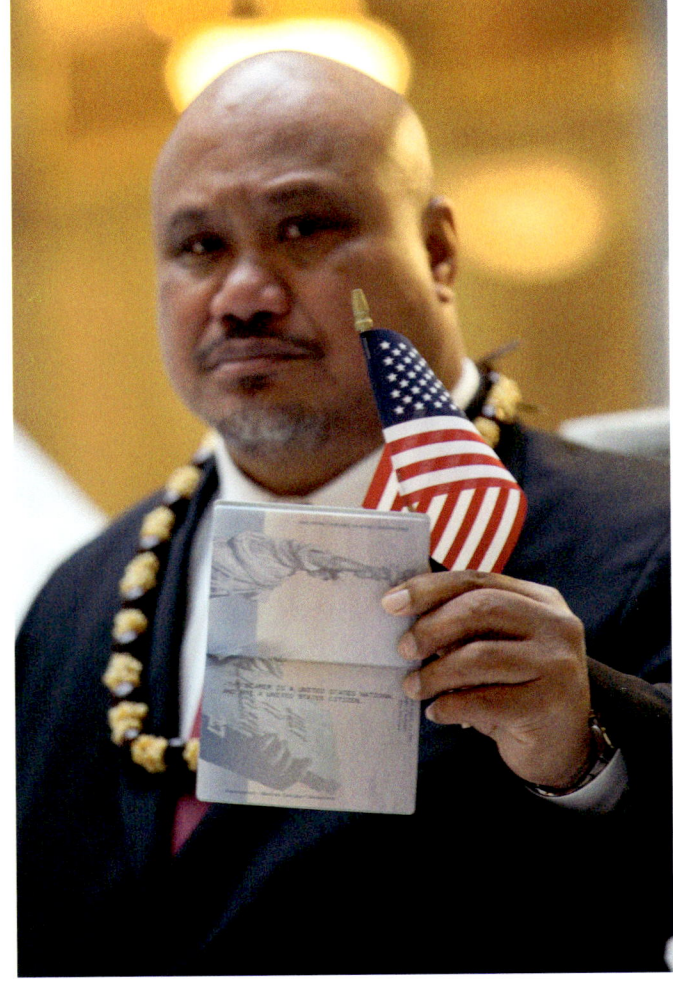

Fig. 2 Isabel González in the early 1900s. Copy of torn photograph (now lost). Courtesy of Belinda Torres-Mary, great grand-daughter of Isabel González It is possible that González's attorneys produced this portrait to show their client in a sympathetic light. González was accused of possessing questionable morals and would become a ward of the state.

Fig. 3 John Fitisemanu, who was born in American Samoa, holds up his passport. The disclaimer reads, "THE BEARER IS A UNITED STATES NATIONAL AND NOT A UNITED STATES CITIZEN." Photograph by Keil Creations

1904, the Supreme Court recently passed on answering whether John Fitisemanu is a citizen, leaving in place a lower court ruling that relied on the *Insular Cases* to deny birthright citizenship in so-called unincorporated territories.[14] As a result, despite recent calls by Justices Neil Gorsuch and Sonia Sotomayor for the Court to overrule the *Insular Cases*, these racist decisions stubbornly remain on the books.[15]

America has from the beginning often struggled to live up to its founding ideals. The first step in America doing better has always been America recognizing it has a problem. On the 125th anniversary of 1898, it is time to recognize America has a colonies problem—and to do something about it.

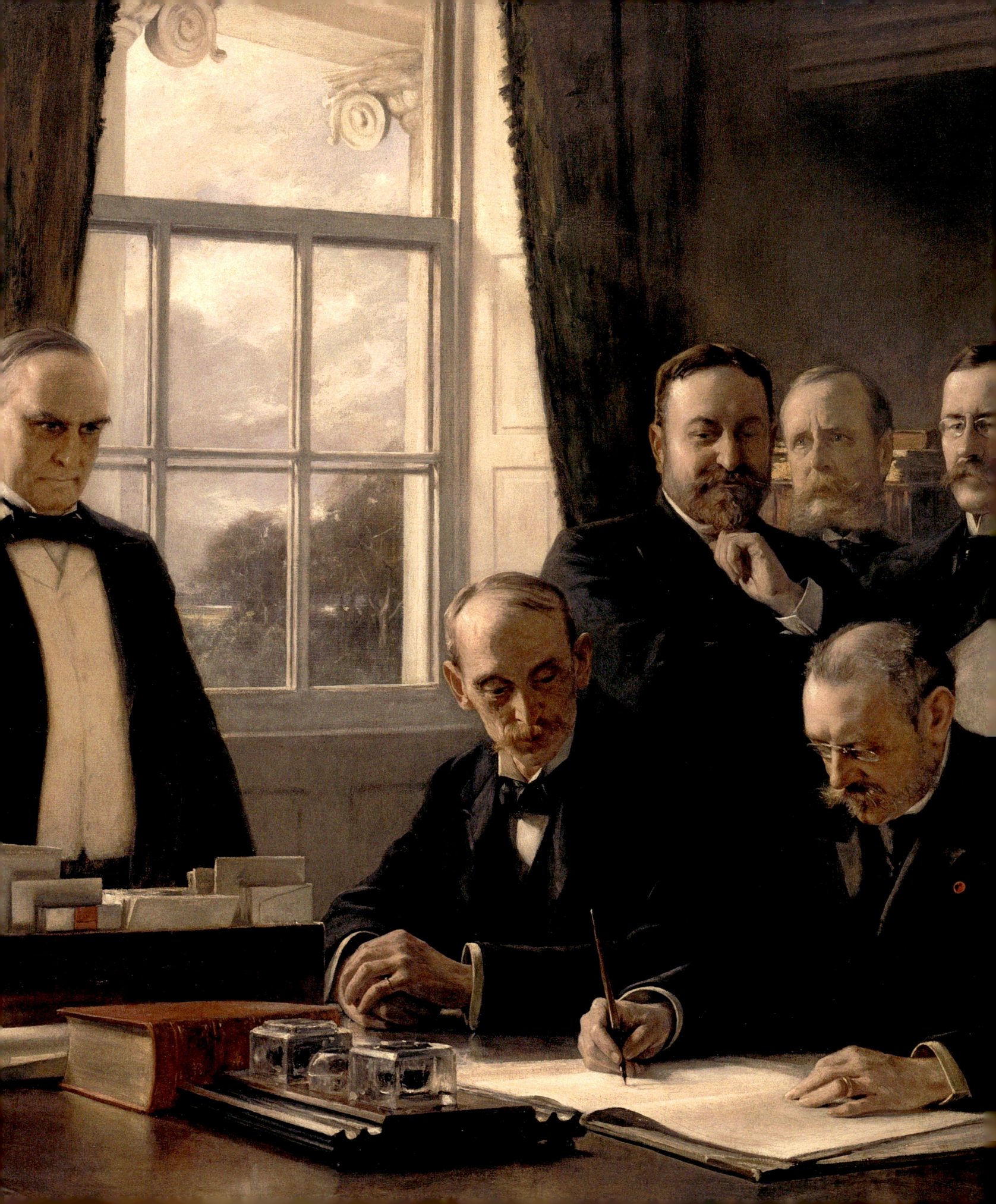

1898

A Contest in Memory

TAÍNA CARAGOL AND KATE CLARKE LEMAY

Republic or empire? That is the question, the only question of any importance before the country.[1]
—George S. Boutwell,
on the presidential election of 1900

On July 26, 1898, after U.S. forces had achieved decisive military victories against the Spanish in multiple campaigns, the United States and Spain began discussing a cease-fire. Representatives of the two nations signed a peace protocol a few weeks later, on August 12, where they outlined their requirements. After almost five months of treaty negotiations, the War of 1898 officially ended with the signing of a permanent peace contract on December 10, 1898. Authorized in the French capital, the Treaty of Paris specified that Spain would relinquish claims to Cuba and cede Guam, the Philippine Islands, and Puerto Rico to the United States. For the Philippines, the United States paid $20 million in compensation to Spain.[2]

Through its actions in all four former Spanish colonies, the United States had positioned this war as one of liberation from colonial oppression.[3] Yet as the United States seized overseas lands, calling them "new possessions" or "territories," members of its government chose to rule them as a new colonial authority. Article 9 of the treaty states, "The civil rights and political status of the native inhabitants of the territories hereby ceded to the United States shall be determined by the Congress."[4]

This article represented a substantial departure from previous land acquisition treaties, where the U.S. government included language for eventual incorporation of the territories and their inhabitants into the Union.[5] Article 9 instead asserted the power of Congress over the new possessions and territorial subjects without making promises for their inclusion into the national community, foreshadowing long legal debates as to the terms of governance of the lands and their people.

Visual culture embraced the new moment of U.S. empire. After President William McKinley (1843–1901) was elected to a second term in 1900, *Harper's Weekly* published a commemorative issue with articles on the inauguration ceremonies and celebrations (fig. 1).[6] The magazine's cover features a stylized bald eagle, whose wings encircle the dome of the U.S. Capitol at the center.[7] Appearing triumphant, the bird holds four red arrows in its talons, each arrow symbolizing a major territory under the U.S. sphere of influence. Interspersed in the corners of the design are heraldic shields representing the Philippines, Cuba, "Porto Rico," and "Hawaii"; Guam is missing from this picture of U.S. empire. All of the shields bear an image of a fortress flying the U.S. flag.

HARPER'S WEEKLY

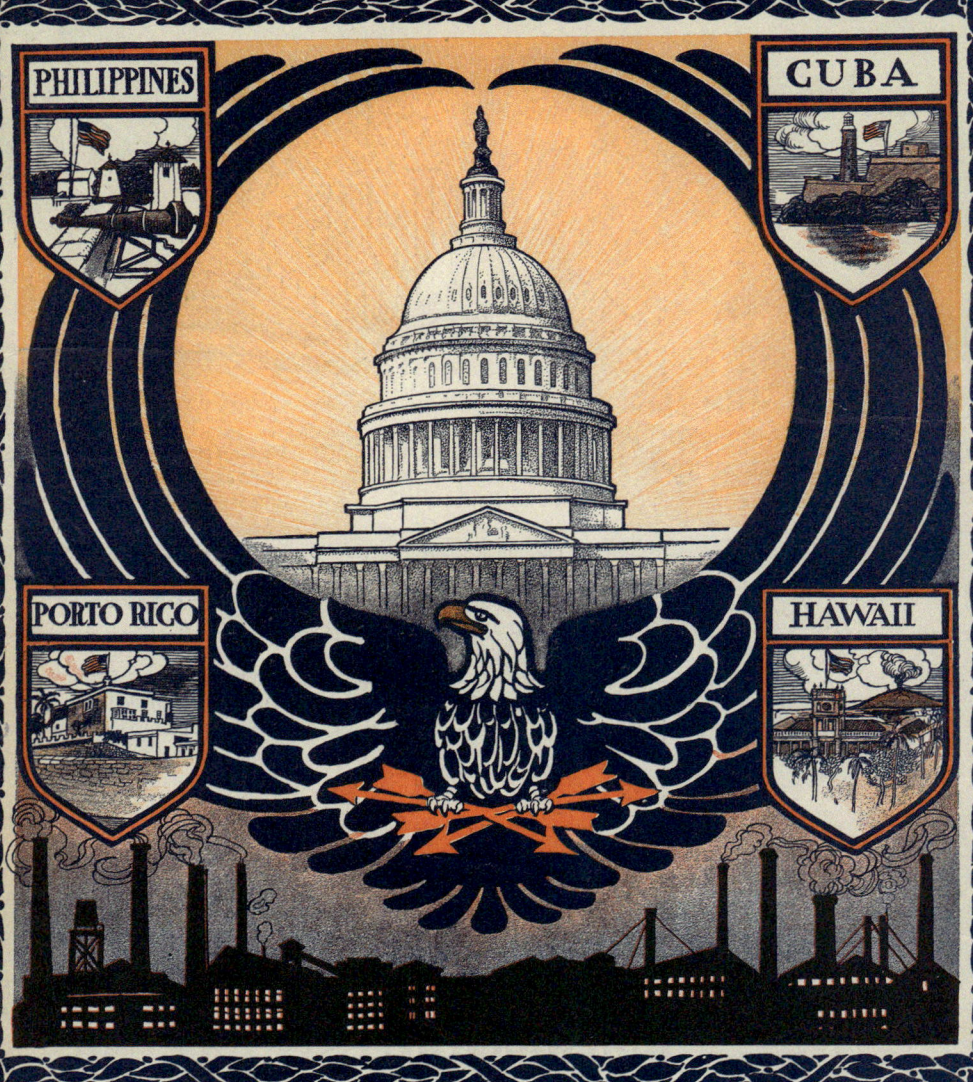

PHILIPPINES

CUBA

PORTO RICO

HAWAII

INAUGURATION NUMBER

This cover design also demonstrates how concerns that dominated McKinley's first presidential term—foreign policy and industrial development—heralded his second. Silhouettes of factories and smoking chimneys decorate the bottom of the cover, conveying U.S. industrial might. The Capitol is backlit by a blazing, symbolic halo consecrating Washington's central role in national and international affairs. Such a celebratory imperial vision focused on the economic value that the new territories would offer the United States. Yet other visions of empire revealed the racial anxieties that undergirded the public discussion about how the inhabitants of the insular possessions would be included in the U.S. national community.

1898: Race and the Empire

At the conclusion of the war, there was uncertainty and debate as to how the lands and people of Puerto Rico, the Philippines, and Guam were to be incorporated in the U.S. polity. Similarly, in concert with this moment of expansion, debates about Hawai'i continued. Cuba did not present the same questions, as the Teller Amendment barred the United States from annexing the island. While many U.S. public officials were eager to establish transoceanic trade routes through the new territories, they feared the consequences of incorporating peoples of various races, languages, religions, cultures, and legal systems. Their mindset reflected the heightened nativist sentiment that was prevalent in the late-nineteenth-century United States. Such attitudes were expressed in policies such as the Chinese Exclusion Act, in effect since 1882, and the legalization of racial segregation through *Plessy v. Ferguson*, the 1896 Supreme Court decision that upheld the racist laws of the Jim Crow era (approximately 1877–1964).

The racial tension was brought forward in popular publications, such as *Harper's Weekly*.[8] For its issue of August 27, 1898, just after the peace protocol was signed, the magazine's cover featured personifications of the federal government of the United States and the new territories in a classroom setting. Against the backdrop map of the United States and its "Neighboring Countries," with tiny U.S. flags pinned to the new territories, "Uncle Sam," in the role of the teacher, strikes two unruly students

seated before him with a stick (fig. 2).[9] With dark complexions and disheveled hair and clothes, students labeled "Cuban Ex-Patriot" and "Guerilla," fight each other, breaking a slate chalk board and crumpling books. To their left, Máximo Gómez (1836–1905) reads a "Rule Book." Behind them, Emilio Aguinaldo (1869–1964) is being punished by having to stand on a stool and wear a dunce cap, his arms crossed in disgruntlement. To the right, children with headdresses labeled "Hawaii" and "Porto Rico" model perfect student behavior.

The racialized biases of the United States toward the "new possessions" are manifested in the imaging of the islands as children and the variations in skin tone, gender, and gesture, which alternately convey obedience, ignorance, or rebellion. The space of the classroom was an apt visual metaphor, especially for imperialists, who argued that the United States had an ethical responsibility to educate the peoples of the new territories according to republican values and democratic traditions. The illustration points to the most debated question about U.S. empire: How to incorporate the people of the newly acquired territories into the U.S. political body? The U.S. perception of racial and cultural differences between the islands informed the country's approaches to their administration.[10] This image and others like it reinforced existing stereotypes, normalized racial prejudices, and helped inform the public discourse and political debates surrounding the "new possessions."

Cuba: Almost Free

The illustration of Uncle Sam with his students sheds some light on the question of what to do with Cuba. Gómez was reading his book, yes—but in essence, the caricature asks, would he follow the "rules"? U.S. relations with the newly independent Cuba were in question. Imperialists coveted Cuba as a U.S. territory, arguing that Cubans were unfit for self-government and independence. For instance, General Leonard Wood (1860–1927), who became the military governor of Cuba in late 1899, feared that the newly elected Cuban government was made up of the "worst agitators and political radicals in Cuba."[11] U.S. Senator Albert J. Beveridge (1862–1927) concurred, asking, "If it is our business to see that the Cubans are not

HARPER'S WEEKLY

A JOURNAL OF CIVILIZATION

Vol. XLII.—No. 2175.
Copyright, 1898, by Harper & Brothers.
All Rights Reserved.

NEW YORK, SATURDAY, AUGUST 27, 1898.

TEN CENTS A COPY.
FOUR DOLLARS A YEAR.

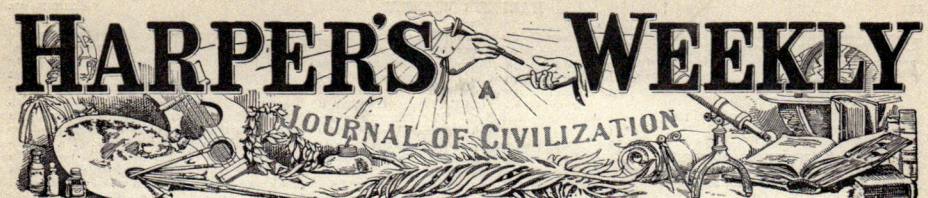

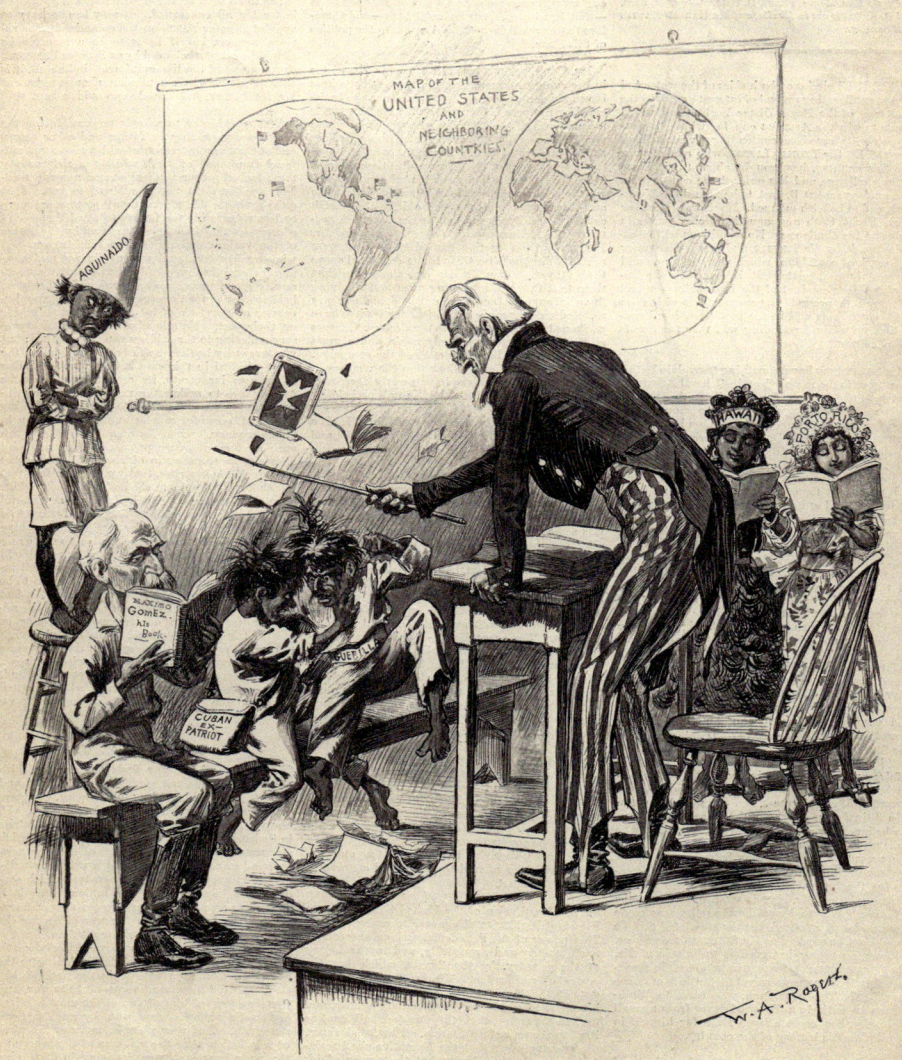

UNCLE SAM'S NEW CLASS IN THE ART OF SELF-GOVERNMENT.

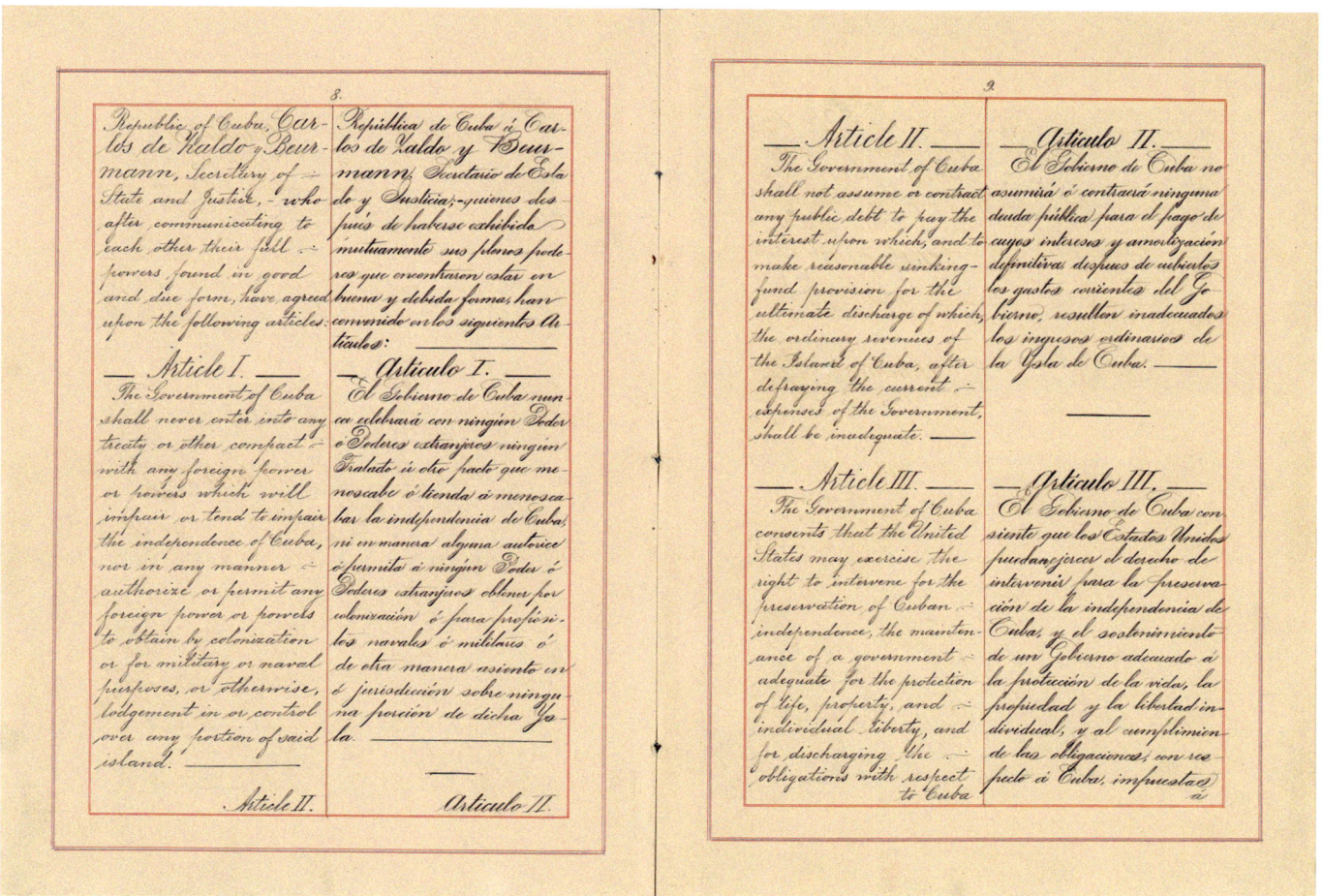

destroyed by any foreign power, is it not our duty to see that they are not destroyed by themselves?"[12]

Annexation, however, was not an option. Not only did the Teller Amendment forbid it, but nationalist sentiment among Cubans would not allow for annexation after three decades of separatist warfare. Consequently, U.S. Secretary of War Elihu Root (1845–1937) devised a plan to circumvent the Teller Amendment and retain influence over Cuban affairs. Root entrusted his plan to U.S. Senator Orville H. Platt (1827–1905) of Connecticut, who introduced in Congress the resolution that became known as the Platt Amendment (fig. 3).[13] Its provisions included the right of the United States to intervene in Cuban affairs to safeguard the island's independence and preserve a stable government, under the premise that Cuba could not achieve this on its own.[14] The amendment also forbade the Cuban government from entering any treaty with a foreign government that could interfere with Cuban sovereignty. In addition, it secured for the U.S. the ability to lease lands in Cuba for coaling and naval stations, also under the pretext of preserving Cuban independence.[15] Once approved by the U.S. Congress, the Platt Amendment was presented to the Cuban constitutional convention as a condition for the end of the U.S. military occupation.[16]

Across the island, Cubans gathered to protest the extensive U.S. powers over Cuban affairs set forth in the Platt proposal.[17] Some traveled to the United States to express their objections, with Root defending the Platt Amendment as a mere update to the Monroe Doctrine.[18] Originally, those present at the Cuban Constitutional Convention in 1901

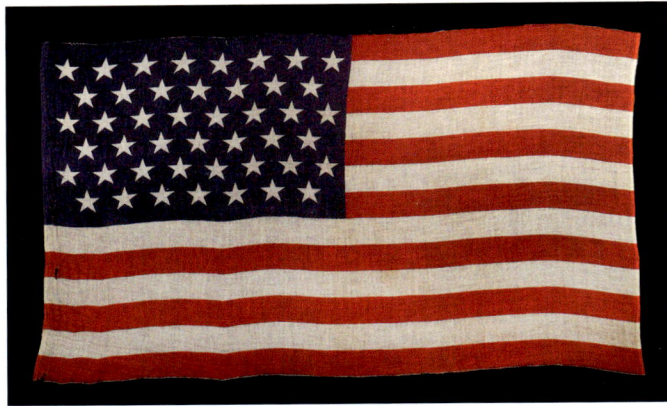

Fig. 4 *United States Flag Hoisted at Las Cabezas de San Juan, Puerto Rico, August 1898*, Unidentified maker, c. 1898. 49.5 × 85.1 cm (19½ × 33½ in.). The Robert von Stolberg de Acosta Foundation

refused to include the amendment, but the U.S. government promised them a trade treaty that would guarantee Cuban sugar exports access to the U.S. market.[19] The Cubans still tried to reject or modify the amendment, but in the end, they reluctantly agreed to incorporate the provisions into the 1901 Cuban Constitution, which turned the Cuban Republic into a U.S. protectorate, giving Cuba its independence but depriving the island of full sovereignty.[20] The Platt Amendment was ratified as a bilateral relation by way of the Permanent Treaty of 1903.[21]

Hoisting the U.S. Flag Overseas

The lowering of the Spanish flag and the hoisting of the U.S. flag was a ritual of ownership, signifying the transition to U.S. sovereignty. Sometimes enthusiastic citizens of the Spanish colonies raised the U.S. flag themselves to welcome the new power.[22] In Hawai'i, too, the annexation ceremony on August 12, 1898—the same day of the War of 1898 cease-fire—involved the playing of "Hawai'i Ponoi," the Hawaiian national anthem, and the hoisting of the U.S. flag, followed by "The Star-Spangled Banner."[23] If the imagined planting of U.S. flags in foreign soil was an aim of some of the board games marketed during the war, its consummation in real space was the clearest symbol of the territorial expansion it yielded. This U.S. flag is a relic of that ritual (fig. 4). In the weeks surrounding the invasion, the flag was raised by the U.S. military at the lighthouse on Puerto Rico's eastern coast keys, known as Las Cabezas de San Juan, in the municipality of Fajardo, at the hacienda of the Becerril family.[24]

The power of the U.S. flag flying overseas was satirized by the writer and figurehead of the Anti-Imperialist League, Samuel Clemens, better known as Mark Twain (fig. 5). In his most famous political essay, "To the Person Sitting in Darkness," published in 1901, Twain subverted the trope of the stars and stripes to decry the contradiction of the U.S. war to liberate the Philippines from Spanish colonialism while refusing to recognize Filipino independence and suppressing revolutionaries. He wrote, "As for the flag for the Philippine Province, it is easily managed. We can have a special one—our States do it: we can have just our usual flag, with white stripes painted black and the stars replaced by skulls and cross-bones."[25]

By the turn of the twentieth century, most of the contiguous United States settled by Euro-Americans was represented on that flag, which bore forty-five stars. Within the continental United States, the "organized territories" of New Mexico, Arizona, and Oklahoma were still in the process of becoming states. They would follow the usual framework, a three-step process to statehood, first outlined in the Northwest Ordinance of 1787.[26] As the stars and stripes flew over the "new possessions," inhabitants both within and outside the continental United States asked: What would it mean for the lands overseas to exist under that flag? Which privileges, protections, and freedoms would the United States bestow upon the inhabitants of these islands? What would the administration of government look like? Considering these questions, from 1898 to 1899, the *Harvard Law Review* and the *Yale Law Journal* published a series of articles debating how the United States should rule them. The issues these articles debated were summarized by the metaphorical question: "Does the Constitution follow the flag?," articulated by anti-expansionist politicians, such as William Jennings Bryan in the 1900 presidential campaign.

Administrating the Insular Territories: The Long Legal War of 1898

White supremacist attitudes that had been normalized through legislation, visual culture, and popular discourse set the stage for the debates that would determine the legal and administrative relationship between the United States and the insular possessions. Some of the debates around the annexation of Hawai'i presaged those concerning Puerto Rico and the Philippines.[27] For example, some congressional representatives were worried about the annexation of non-contiguous territory, and others

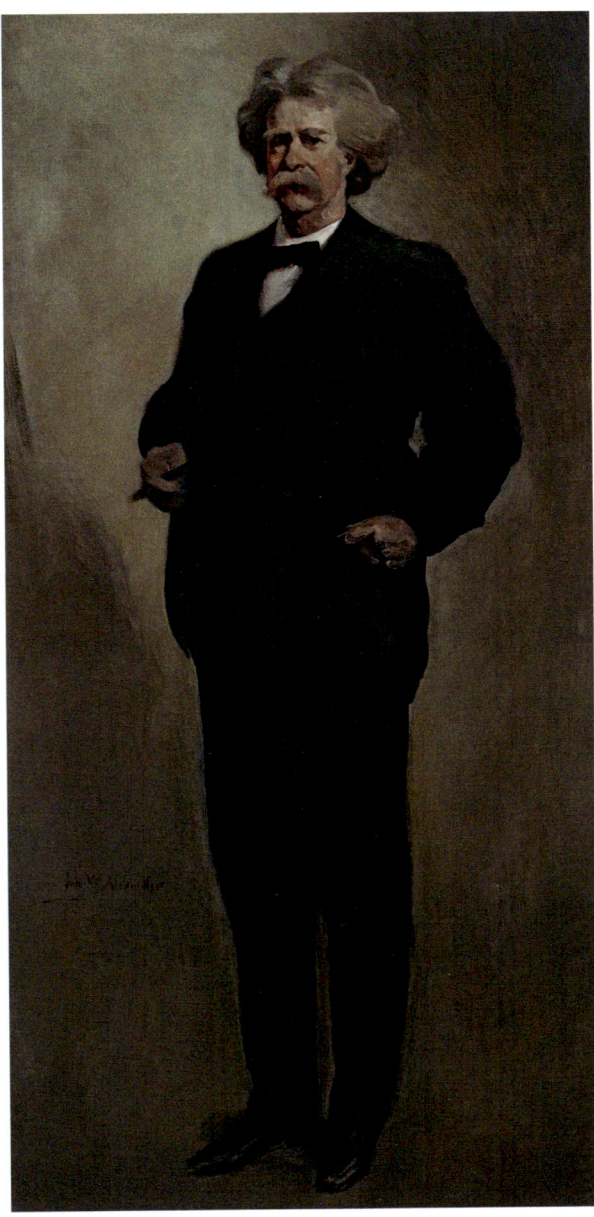

Fig. 5 *Samuel L. Clemens (Mark Twain)* (1835–1910), John White Alexander (1856–1915), 1912–1913. Oil on canvas; 192.4 × 92.1 cm (75¾ × 36¼ in.). National Portrait Gallery, Smithsonian Institution

Chinese immigrants who made up 22 percent and 19 percent, respectively. The latter had arrived in great numbers to fulfill the need for low-cost labor in the sugar industry.[29]

In the end, the decisive factor for annexation was the imminent need for a Pacific coaling station located en route to the Philippines during the War of 1898. But the fact that Hawai'i had undergone a process of settler colonialism for eight decades, during which Euro-Americans gradually asserted hegemonic power, helped establish the governmental framework for the archipelago.[30] In 1900, Congress created the Territory of Hawai'i and appointed Sanford B. Dole (1844–1946) as its governor; he had served as president of the Republic of Hawai'i, the puppet government that had overthrown Queen Lili'uokalani (1838–1917).[31] U.S. citizenship was granted to all former citizens of the Hawaiian Republic, including Euro-Americans and Kānaka Maoli residents. Japanese and Chinese residents were excluded from citizenship. In 1959, Hawai'i became the fiftieth state.

At the turn of the century, with the question of how to administer Hawai'i determined, the United States still needed to establish governments for overseas territories that had not been Americanized through settler colonialism. The discourse on what constitutional rights to extend to Puerto Rico and the Philippines dominated the discussion, while Guam was ignored.[32] Some argued that the Constitution applied to the new insular territories, as in the case of continental territories. Others feared extending constitutional privileges to peoples they deemed uncivilized.[33] An article by Massachusetts lawyer and legal scholar Abbott Lawrence Lowell (1856–1943) provided the basis for the legal theory that prevailed. Asserting that "possessions acquired by conquest or cession do not become part of the United States," Lowell contended that "treaty-making authorities" should define the relationship of the new possessions.[34]

Concurrent with these legal debates, politicians often viewed the question of insular administration through a lens of racial and cultural difference, attributing certain characteristics to one group or the other, and also understanding them in relation to a predominantly white, Anglo-Saxon United States.[35] For example, Puerto Ricans were often described as being primarily European, "of Caucasian race," or *mestizo* (of mixed-race background), neglecting the Afro-descendant component of the island's population.[36] Filipinos, meanwhile, were described as a mix of African and Asiatic races that could never be fully assimilated into U.S. society. Within the framework of

by how to protect the business and industry of the continental United States from the territories. Still more were trepidatious of accepting people of "alien races" into the political body of the United States.[28] These "alien races" included not only Kānaka Maoli, or Native Hawaiians, who according to the Hawaiian Census of 1896 represented 28 percent of the population, but also Japanese and white Anglo-Saxon supremacy in the United States, Filipinos were associated in political discourse with Native Americans, African Americans, and Chinese immigrants, and portrayed as lazy, treacherous, and premodern.[37] For example, Theodore Roosevelt (1858–1919) referred to them as "a jumble of savage tribes," and he countered anti-imperialist arguments with the rationale that if white people were "morally bound to abandon the Philippines, we were also morally bound to abandon Arizona to the Apaches."[38] Similar racist arguments were used to characterize Filipinos as incapable of self-government and in need of help from the United States, but unworthy of U.S. citizenship. Many lawmakers and colonial administrators interpreted this diversity as proof that the concept of a Filipino nation as promoted by the *ilustrados* did not exist.[39]

With its geographic position in the Caribbean, Puerto Rico was seen by many politicians as quasi-contiguous to the United States, strategically important, and therefore, easy to imagine under permanent U.S. sovereignty.[40] By contrast, the distant and numerous Philippine islands were approached as a temporary possession, born of political practicality and designed to train the Filipinos in Anglo-Saxon civilization.[41] The enthusiasm of many Puerto Ricans for the democratic values of the United States was also interpreted as a counterpoint to the rebelliousness of Filipinos, many of whom resisted U.S. rule.

In early 1899, with the aim of studying the conditions at each location and offering recommendations for local governance, McKinley assigned separate commissions to the Philippines and Puerto Rico.[42] Henry K. Carroll (1848–1931) led the commission visit to Puerto Rico. His report maintained that the existing institutions and laws of Puerto Rico did not require drastic reform. Arguing that the people of Puerto Rico had the potential to develop a "high type of citizenship," the Carroll Report recommended that Puerto Rico be given territorial status.[43] In his annual address to Congress in December of 1899, McKinley echoed the report's observations, prompting Senator Joseph B. Foraker (1846–1917) to introduce a bill for Puerto Rican citizenship and the establishment of a civil government. However, Congress feared that recognizing Puerto Ricans as citizens would establish a precedent for eventual decisions regarding the Philippines.[44] As a result, the citizenship provision was taken out of the Foraker bill, and the Foraker Act was approved on April 12, 1900.[45] The Foraker Act established a civil government comprising a presidentially appointed governor, a

supreme court, and a bicameral legislature with an appointed upper house, which also functioned as an "executive committee," and an elected lower house.[46] Furthermore, it established a tax on imported goods to support the expenses for territorial government. This tax would become a point of contention as a marker of otherness in relation to the continental United States.

Jacob Schurman (1854–1942) led the First Philippine Commission, which among its five members also included Admiral George Dewey (1837–1917) and General Elwell Stephen Otis (1838–1909). Their report stated that the archipelago was not ready for self-government because it did not possess "a community of blood, race, and language."[47] In 1900, William Howard Taft (1857–1930) led the Second Philippine Commission, which was granted some executive and legislative powers in the archipelago.

Both Philippine Commissions and U.S. lawmakers used the cultural heterogeneity of the archipelago as a justification to establish a period of political tutelage over the territory. In 1902, at the official end of the Philippine-American War, the U.S. Congress passed the Philippine Organic Act to establish a civil government in the Philippines.[48] Like that of Puerto Rico, it had a presidentially appointed governor and a bicameral legislature, with a minority of elected members in the lower chamber. In Puerto Rico as much as in the Philippines, the U.S. president exerted control through appointments to all branches of government. In the Philippines, colonial administrators classified the different ethnic groups under three main categories: Christian, animist, and Muslim.[49] The latter two were often referred to as "non-Christian" or "uncivilized tribes." The United States established divergent provincial governments adjusted to the perceived cultural and religious differences of each area and their corresponding need of U.S. oversight. Provinces with Christian majorities were given limited municipal self-government with partially elected officials, and the opportunity of representation in the Philippine Assembly. By contrast, the provinces "inhabited by tribal Indians," where local governments were led by "sultans, datos, [*sic*] or chiefs," were barred from representation in the Filipino legislature and placed under the rule of the governor-general and the Philippine Commission.[50]

The U.S. government's privileging of Hispanicized, Christian Filipinos enticed their collaboration, while it provoked tensions and revolts among Indigenous and Muslim Filipinos.[51] The U.S. president exerted control over Puerto Rico and the Philippines through appointments to all branches of government. These governmental structures did not fully eliminate the gray areas in the relationship between the territories and the United States. For instance, the imposition of the Foraker Law tax in Puerto Rico, and the question of whether it was constitutional, triggered the consequential Supreme Court decision in *Downes v. Bidwell* (1901), one of a series of decisions known today as the *Insular Cases*.[52]

Originally comprising nine cases debated in 1901, the *Insular Cases* defined how the U.S. Constitution applied to the new territories. They emerged from controversies around commercial operations.[53] Of the nine cases, seven of them concerned the status of Puerto Rico, while one addressed Hawai'i and the other, the Philippines.[54] *Downes v. Bidwell* (1901) significantly reoriented the future of U.S. territorial policy. In this case, Samuel Downes (life dates unknown), owner of Downes and Company, sued George Bidwell (1848–1958), the customs collector at the port of New York, for charging him import duties on a cargo of oranges from Puerto Rico. Downes appealed to the uniformity tariff clause of the Constitution, according to which "all duties, imports, and excises shall be uniform throughout the United States." In other words, had the oranges come from any state of the Union, they would not have been subject to an import tax. The Supreme Court majority concluded that the tariffs in the Foraker Act were constitutional because Puerto Rico was not "in the United States" for purposes of the clause.[55]

Justice Edgar Douglass White Jr. (1845–1921) issued a concurring opinion that formulated what became known as the "incorporation doctrine." Echoing Abbott Lawrence Lowell's argument, he contended that the treaty of annexation determined whether constitutional provisions applied to the territory or not, and that the incorporation of a territory into the Union was not automatic. White wrote in his opinion, "The result of what has been said is that whilst in an international sense Porto Rico was not a foreign country, since it was subject to the sovereignty of and was owned by the United States, it was foreign to the United States in a domestic sense, because the island has not been incorporated into the United States, but was merely appurtenant thereto as a possession."[56] Puerto Rico was consequently considered a so-called "unincorporated" territory, where according to the Supreme Court's majority opinion, not every provision of the Constitution was necessarily applicable.[57] By extension, the Philippines

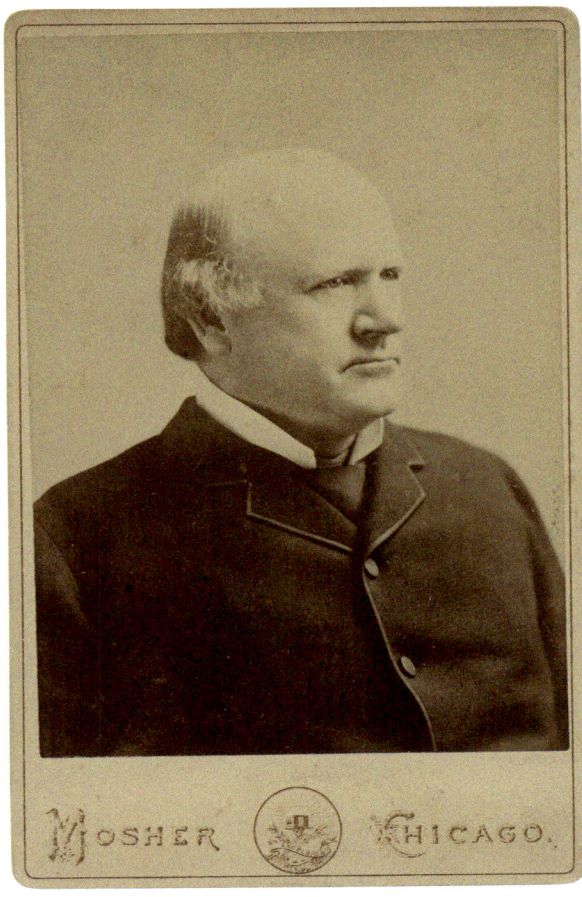

Fig. 6 *John Marshall Harlan* (1833–1911), Charles D. Mosher (1829–1897), c. 1880. Albumen silver print; 13.5 × 9.9 cm (5⁵⁄₁₆ × 3⁷⁄₈ in.). National Portrait Gallery, Smithsonian Institution; gift of Ben Schneiderman

and Guam were also "unincorporated territories." Through the creation of this new territorial category, *Downes v. Bidwell* became the most important precedent on territorial law to this day.[58] Under its logic, the Constitution did not follow the flag in the insular unincorporated territories.[59] Not everyone agreed with this new ruling. Justice John Marshall Harlan (fig. 6) issued a dissent, arguing the Constitution must apply with full force in the newly acquired territories.[60] Appointed to the court in 1877, and known as the "Great Dissenter," Harlan, who was the only dissenter in *Plessy v. Ferguson*, was a champion of civil rights.[61]

While *Downes v. Bidwell* established that Puerto Ricans and Filipinos were not citizens, it did not clarify their administrative legal status.[62] The 1904 Supreme Court case *Gonzales* [sic] *v. Williams* approached the issue but

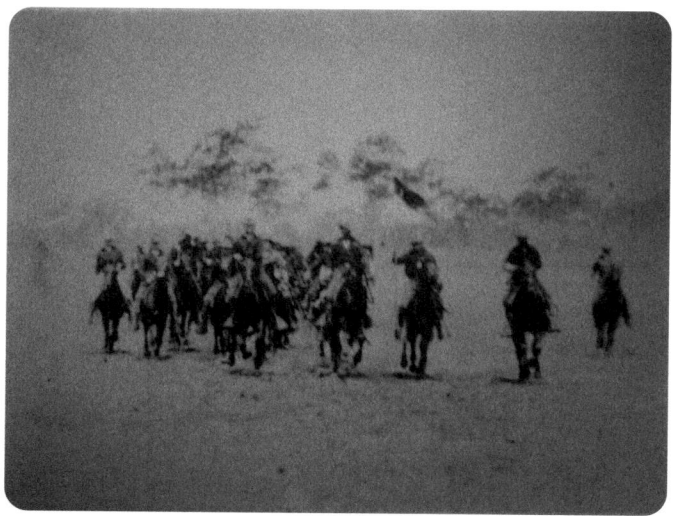

Fig. 7 *Roosevelt's Rough Riders*, American Mutoscope and Biography Company (active 1895–1916), 1898. Black-and-white film, 25 seconds. Library of Congress, Motion Picture, Broadcasting and Recorded Sound Division, Washington, DC

only vaguely. The litigant in this case was Isabel González (1882–1971), a single pregnant mother who was traveling from Puerto Rico to New York. In 1902, González was detained as an alien on Ellis Island by the commissioner of immigration William Williams (1852–1947).[63] A narrow majority determined that González had been unlawfully denied entry into the United States. According to the ruling, Puerto Ricans and Filipinos were not "alien immigrants" because they owed allegiance to the United States. They could therefore enter and exit the continental United States at will.[64] The ruling, however, did not go so far as to state that the residents of unincorporated territories were U.S. citizens. As neither aliens nor U.S. citizens, Puerto Ricans and Filipinos were best described under the anomalous sociopolitical condition of U.S. "nationals."[65]

Years passed as these questions about citizenship were debated. Against the backdrop of the *Insular Cases*, President Woodrow Wilson (1856–1924) signed the Jones Act (or the Philippine Autonomic Act) in 1916 as well as the Jones-Shafroth Act (or the Jones Act, or Jones Law of Puerto Rico) in 1917.[66] The Philippine Autonomic Act promised independence to the Philippines when the U.S. government deemed Filipinos capable of managing a stable government.[67] It also placed larger control of domestic affairs in Filipino hands, and it gave the Philippines the authority to provide Philippine citizenship to natives of the islands and other residents.[68] The measure on Philippine citizenship was a strategic move at a moment of spirited debate over the possibility of extending U.S. citizenship to Puerto Rico, when lawmakers were trying to deter Filipinos from seeking the same right.[69] In 1934, the path toward independence was mapped out by the Philippine Commonwealth and Independence Act (known as the Tydings-McDuffie Act), which established a commonwealth government with a ten-year timeline for a full transfer of power to Filipinos.[70] The United States recognized the independence and sovereignty of the Philippine Islands on July 4, 1946.

By contrast, the Jones-Shafroth Act recognized Puerto Ricans as U.S. citizens, a measure that had a mixed reception among Puerto Rican political leaders from the Partido Unión, who felt that citizenship without the promise of statehood or without substantial self-government perpetuated colonialism.[71] At the same time, the Jones-Shafroth Act expanded Puerto Rican participation in the government through a bicameral legislature (Senate and House of Representatives). Yet the U.S. president continued to appoint the highest political officers of the island and retained the power to veto any law passed by the local legislature.[72]

In 1948, Puerto Ricans elected Luis Muñoz Marín (1898–1980) as their governor in the first open elections allowed by Congress on the island.[73] He is remembered for negotiating with Congress Puerto Rico's right to a separate constitution, among other things. His efforts led to the creation, in 1952, of the Estado Libre Asociado (ELA), translated as the Commonwealth of Puerto Rico. Muñoz Marín presented this political development, a redefinition of Puerto Rico's relationship to the United States, as a compact or a bilateral agreement.[74] However, the ELA retained Congress's plenary powers over the island. Matters of citizenship, military defense, immigration, foreign relations, and maritime commerce remained the exclusive prerogative of the U.S. Congress, and in case of conflict between the island and the United States, federal law would prevail. Puerto Ricans on the island would also continue to be excluded from voting for the U.S. president, and their representative in Congress would continue to be non-voting. These provisions were heavily criticized by some sectors of society that maintained that the ELA was no more than the legalization of Puerto Rico's colonial status.[75] These conditions remain in place today.[76]

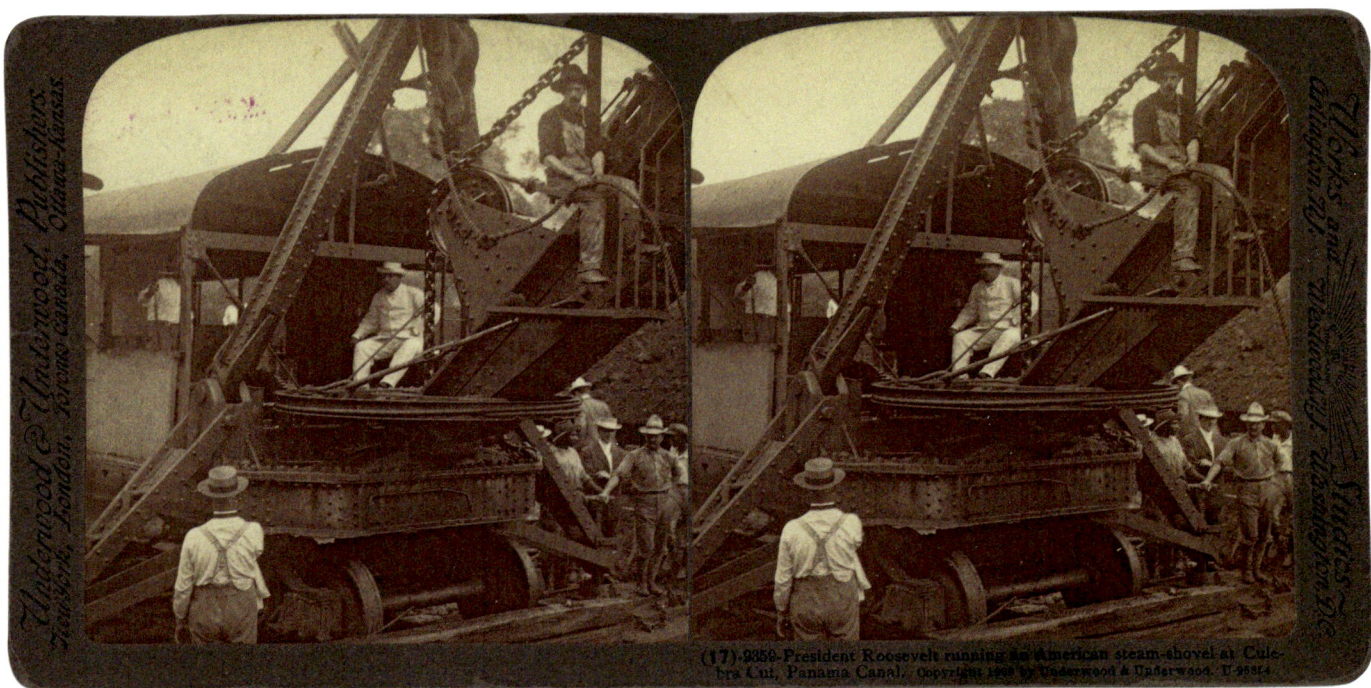

Fig. 8 *President Roosevelt running an American steam-shovel at Culebra Cut, Panama Canal*, Underwood & Underwood (active 1881–1940s), 1906. Gelatin silver prints (stereograph); 7.6 × 17.8 cm (3½ × 7 in.). Library of Congress, Prints and Photographs Division, Washington, DC

As for Guam, the island's rich seafaring culture and strategic location made it an asset to the United States. The United States conceived of the island as a naval base, and accordingly installed a naval government in 1899, cycling through numerous administrators who were unfamiliar with the island. There were thirty-eight U.S.-appointed governors in Guam between its annexation in 1899 and World War II.[77] During the war, the Japanese brutally occupied Guam, and by the time Allied forces reclaimed the island in 1943, combat and bombardments had destroyed four-fifths of the homes on the island and demolished all of the civilian structures of government and culture.[78] The establishment of an Organic Act in Guam took place on August 1, 1950. It recognized the island's residents as citizens of the United States and established a non-military, civil government. In 1968, the U.S. Congress passed an act to allow citizens of Guam to elect their own governor.[79] During the 1990s, as U.S. military bases shrank or were removed from places like the Philippines, the military continued building up its base in Guam, drawing mixed responses from its residents.[80] Lisa Linda Natividad, a professor at the University of Guam, decried the expansion in 1995: "This is old-school colonialism all over again. It boils down to our political status—we are occupied territory."[81] In 1964, the Kumision I Fino' Chamorro, or the Chamorro Language Commission, was established, ushering in a revival of CHamoru, the native language of Guam and the Northern Marianas.[82]

Theodore Roosevelt and the Inter-Ocean Highway

On September 6, 1901, less than seven months into McKinley's second presidential term, he was shot by an anarchist while visiting the 1901 Pan-American Exposition in Buffalo, New York. He died eight days later, and Vice President Theodore Roosevelt swiftly stepped into the role of president.[83] During the War of 1898, Roosevelt had cultivated his image as a military and political leader. For example, with film technology on the rise, he restaged in West Orange, New Jersey, a charge of the Rough Riders for the Edison Films production of sixty-eight motion pictures titled *The Spanish-American War in Motion Pictures* (fig. 7).[84] Roosevelt was so successful in crafting his image that in 1900, McKinley named him as his running mate. As president, Roosevelt pursued his dreams of a pan-isthmian canal to link the Atlantic and Pacific Oceans (fig. 8).[85]

In 1902, the U.S. Congress passed the Spooner Act, approving $40 million for the purchase of assets of the bankrupt French company that had sought to build an interoceanic canal through Panama, then a province of Colombia.[86] When negotiations with the Colombian government reached a deadlock, Roosevelt looked to U.S. investors and independence-seeking Panamanians for backup as he approved a plan to support the armed secession of Panama.[87] The following year, in 1903, the United States negotiated the conditions of a treaty through the offices of Frenchman Philippe Bunau-Varilla (1859–1940), acting foreign minister of newly independent Panama.[88]

The Hay–Bunau-Varilla Treaty outlined the agreement for the Panama Canal Zone.[89] It ceded a land area thirty miles long and five miles wide on each side of the proposed canal, "which the United States would possess and exercise if it were the sovereign of the territory."[90] The Zone created a divide within the Republic of Panama. Only employees of the Panama Canal, the U.S. military, and their families could reside there.[91] Commerce, financial matters, and daily life within the Zone were also fragmented. When construction began in 1904, the canal administration established separate pay systems for U.S. citizens and for West Indian and Native Panamanian workers; U.S. citizens were compensated on the gold payroll, which had twice the value of the silver payroll used to pay non-American citizens. The pay scale difference solidified into a system of segregation comparable to that of the coexisting Jim Crow South.[92] Crews from Barbados, Jamaica, and other nations carved out 150 million cubic meters of rock and soil, a perilous undertaking that, combined with disease, took more than 5,600 lives.[93] The vast engineering project moved enough earth and rubble to create a sixteen-foot-wide tunnel reaching the center of the Earth.[94]

Meanwhile, U.S.-appointed sanitarians ordered the draining of wetlands and created new water systems in port cities to eradicate disease.[95] In 1904, the United States treated the densely populated Panama Canal Zone like an unincorporated territory. Its residents were expelled by the executive order of William Howard Taft in 1912.[96] The canal cost $639 million and was completed in 1913.[97] Although U.S. citizens could move to Panama, those born in the Zone were not automatically entitled to U.S. citizenship. It was not until 1937 that the U.S. Congress declared that children born in the Canal Zone after 1904 with at least one parent who was a U.S. citizen were U.S. citizens by virtue of birth.[98] The Torrijos–Carter Treaties, which had abolished the 1903 Hay–Buneau-Varilla Treaty in 1977, went into effect in 1979. As a consequence, U.S. troops were gradually withdrawn from the Zone, and in 1999, Panama took control over what had been the Zone.[99]

The Conquerors (Culebra Cut, Panama Canal), by the Norwegian-born artist Jonas Lie (1880–1940), visualizes a section of the nine-mile cut made into the Culebra Mountain and reveals the intense human exertion required by the construction (fig. 9). Lie, who had trained at the Art Students League in New York, had been impelled to travel to Panama in 1913, shortly after viewing the early color movie *The Making of the Panama Canal* (1912). He made a series of paintings depicting the canal's construction over the course of his three-month trip. *The Conquerors* features steam-excavating shovels powered by coal, hydraulic rock crushers, and steam-powered locomotives. A seemingly endless line of workers emerges from the depths of the dark and menacing pit.

In addition to physically linking the Atlantic and Pacific Oceans, the Panama Canal ensured U.S. sea power—and therefore, economic influence—in South America. As president, one of Roosevelt's first challenges was a crisis between Venezuela and its European creditors. In 1902, British, German, and Italian vessels blockaded Venezuelan ports, forcing its president to acquiesce to foreign demands. Roosevelt grew uneasy that this incident would set a precedent for European intervention in the Americas and would jeopardize U.S. interests in the region.[100] In 1903, a bankrupt Dominican Republic (then called Santo Domingo) was similarly being threatened with intervention by European creditors who wanted to seize customs as payment for delinquent debts.[101] As a result, in a December 1904 message to Congress, Roosevelt declared the right of the United States to intervene in the countries of the Caribbean and Central and South America to ensure that they paid their debts to international creditors, lest they compromise the stability of the entire hemisphere.

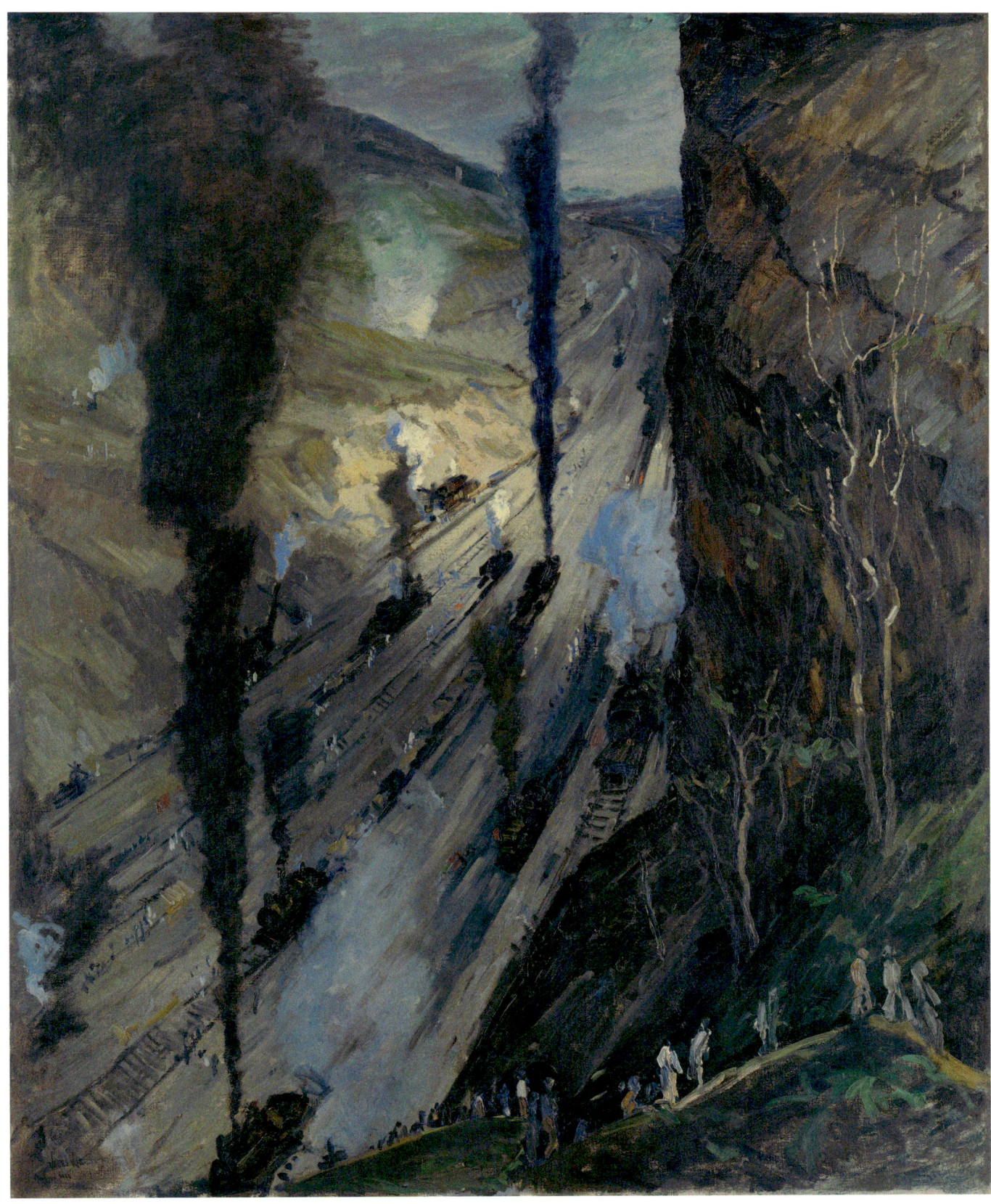

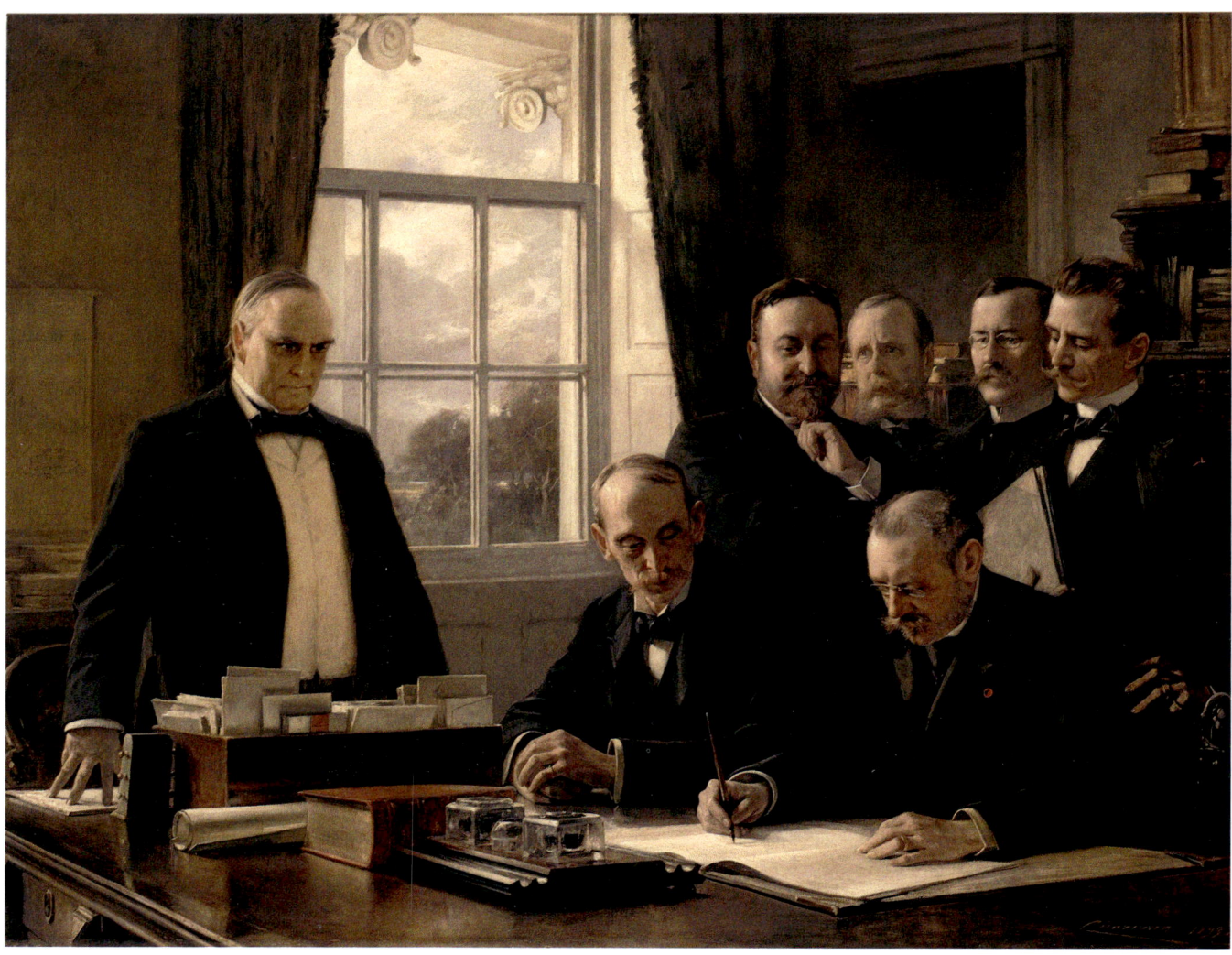

Fig. 10 *Signing of the Peace Protocol between Spain and the United States, August 12, 1898*, Théobald Chartran (1849–1907), 1899. Oil on canvas; 157.8 × 208.4 cm (62⅛ × 82¹⁄₁₆ in.). White House Historical Association (White House Collection)

Fig. 11 *Declaration of Independence*, John Trumbull (1756–1843), 1826. Oil on canvas; 3.7 × 5.5 m (12 × 18 ft.). United States Capitol, Washington, DC

In Roosevelt's words:

Chronic wrongdoing, or an impotence which results in a general loosening of the ties of civilized society, may in America, as elsewhere, ultimately require intervention by some civilized nation, and in the Western Hemisphere the adherence of the United States to the Monroe Doctrine may force the United States, however reluctantly, in flagrant cases of such wrongdoing or impotence, to the exercise of an international police power.[102]

This plenipotentiary proclamation, known as the "Roosevelt Corollary to the Monroe Doctrine," revised the passive language of President James Monroe (1758–1831), whose 1823 policy had also sought to claim the Western Hemisphere for the United States but had done so without specifying a strategy to achieve that aim. The Roosevelt Corollary instead asserted the right to *active* intervention. Thereafter, and throughout the first decades of the twentieth century, the Roosevelt Corollary justified the use of U.S. military force in Cuba, the Dominican Republic, Haiti, Nicaragua, Panama, and other countries to restore internal

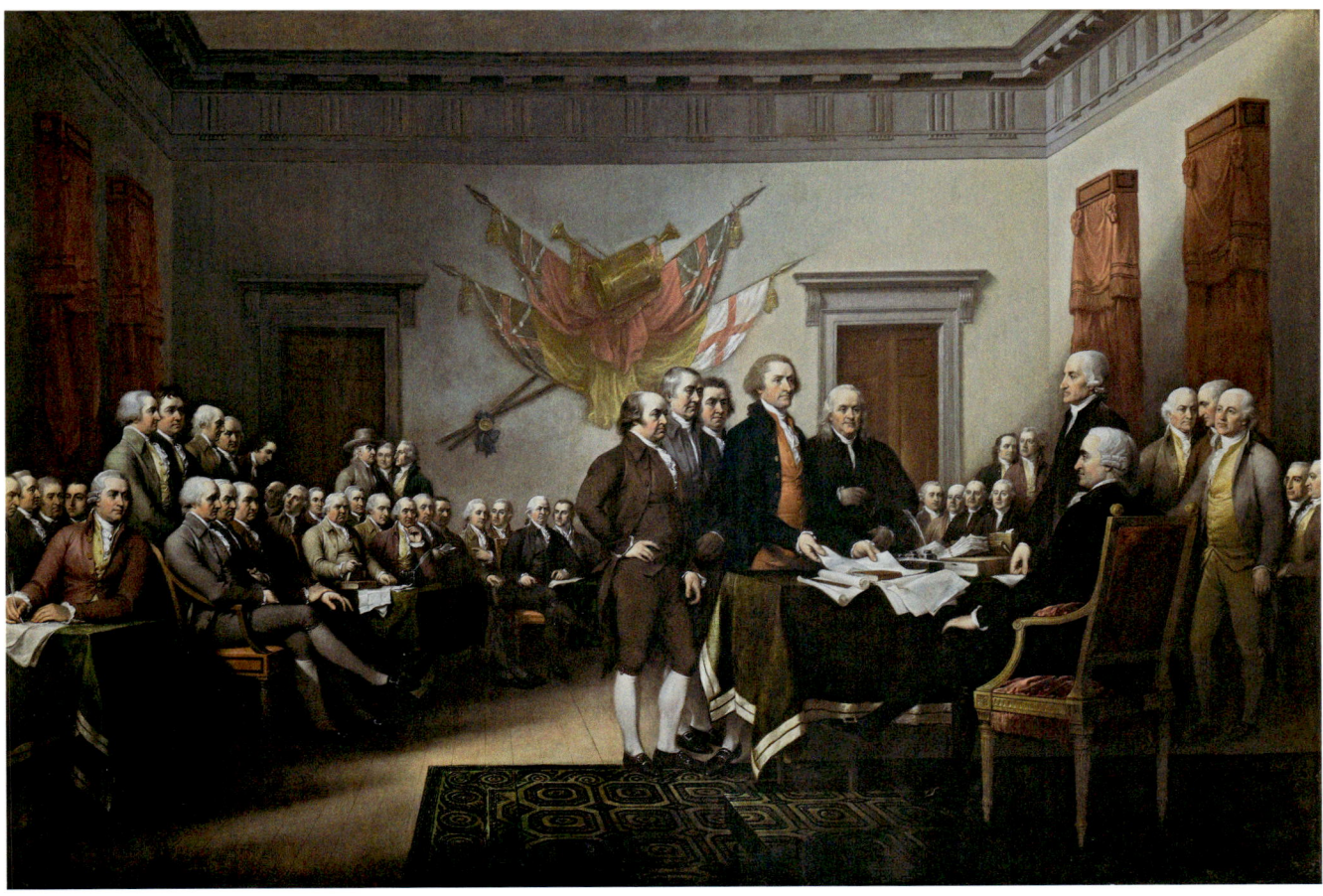

stability, to secure an ideological alignment with their governments, and to safeguard their economic interests.[103]

1898: A Contest in Memory

When all is said and done, and living memory has passed, portraiture and other forms of art and visual culture reinforce the impact of momentous events within collective memory. French artist Théobald Chartran's (1849–1907) large-scale group portrait *Signing of the Peace Protocol between Spain and the United States, August 12, 1898* (1899) commemorates this pivotal moment of the War of 1898 (fig. 10). Based on a photograph by Frances Benjamin Johnston (1864–1952), Chartran's composition is reorganized to include the window in the background (see p. 311).[104] More than a mere document of an event, this painting reveals the new power structure established through the war, as the French ambassador to the United States Jules Cambon (1845–1935) signs the protocol on behalf of Spain with U.S. Secretary of State William R. Day (1849–1923). In the background, three U.S. assistant secretaries and the secretary of the French embassy look on.[105] McKinley towers over the gathering, his feverish eyes locked on the document.

Like the *Declaration of Independence* (1826) by John Trumbull (1756–1843) (fig. 11), *Signing of the Peace Protocol* is both a group portrait and a history painting. Trumbull's painting is displayed in the U.S. Capitol Rotunda, and Chartran's canvas hangs in the White House's Treaty Room—two highly symbolic locations of U.S. governance. Building upon Trumbull's precedent, Chartran depicted the seemingly minor act of a pen stroke. The signing of the document, however, was a power move with significant global ramifications.

The visual culture of imperialism bridges the 125-year distance between the present and this historical chapter, while simultaneously revealing how U.S. official portraiture both relied on and cemented colonial thinking and systems. Other forms of visual culture, such as history paintings, newspaper illustrations, games and tokens of consumer culture, and books also participate in the colonial scheme. Explorations of the archive, however, reveal deeper complexities within these pictures of power, including their financing by industrial giants and patrons of presidents.

As an important archival record and primary source for historical research, portraiture reveals as much about the surrounding society and culture as it does about individual likeness, biography, and personality. Chartran's painting, for example, does not include representatives from the former colonies of Spain, who were left out of these negotiations. With its emphasis on the United States as the victor, the painting sidesteps Cuba's hard-fought third War of Independence (1895–1898), as well as Puerto Rico's 1897 Autonomic Charter, and the ongoing fighting in the Philippines (1899–1913). These histories simply were not a matter of concern for Chartran or for the man who commissioned the painting, Henry Clay Frick (1849–1919). Instead, the group portrait seals McKinley's legacy and reflects a powerful relationship between its theme—U.S. imperialism—and Frick, a business tycoon from Pittsburgh who made millions from the coal, coke, and steel industry.[106] Frick paid Chartran $20,000 (about $671,812 by 2022 standards) to make the painting, a huge sum that demonstrates the painting's significance as a memorial to this moment and its grand gesture of homage to McKinley, his presidency, and his lasting influence on world affairs.[107] And perhaps more importantly, the painting also reveals that U.S. industrialists expected McKinley's ongoing favor.[108]

Frick had long offered McKinley financial support, at both the personal and national levels. The succession of bank failures in 1893 severely affected the national economy and brought on the worst depression in its history to date. When McKinley lost much of his personal wealth, Frick loaned him money.[109] At the national level, U.S. gold reserves were catastrophically depleted. Financier J. P. Morgan (1837–1913), who owned the company Frick directed, among others, bailed out the government by buying up foreign gold and lending it to the U.S. Treasury. In the presidential campaign of 1895–1896, William Jennings Bryan (1860–1925) proposed dropping the gold standard and endorsing the free coinage of silver, effectively turning financial elites like Henry Clay Frick against him.[110] Frick subsequently wielded the gold standard as a weapon to manipulate the value of soft currencies and wanted it to remain. During the presidential election of 1896, Frick did all he could to ensure that McKinley

would prevail, donating $250,000 to his campaign.[111] With Chartran's large-scale painting as a visual endorsement of McKinley, Frick hoped to ensure his reelection in 1900.

An altogether different kind of group portrait completes the limited account presented by Chartran's painting and testifies to the events following the signing of the peace protocol from the perspective of those who had been denied the right to govern themselves. After the cease-fire, the protocol, signed in August, stated that Spain and the United States would appoint their own commissioners to negotiate the conditions of the peace treaty.[112] Representatives from the lands whose futures the treaty would decide were excluded from these negotiations. However, between the beginning of negotiations in late August, and the ratification of the Treaty of Paris on February 6, 1899, commissioners from the islands of Cuba, the Philippines, and Puerto Rico attempted to present petitions and letters to McKinley and Congress in which they demanded representation in the negotiations.[113] Newspapers documented these events. Significantly, a group portrait of some of these commissioners serves as archival proof of their presence in Washington, DC (fig. 12). Pictured in the photograph, seated from left to right, are Ramón Villalón Sánchez (1864–1938) from Cuba; Felipe Agoncillo (1859–1941) from the Philippines (see p. 141); and Eugenio María de Hostos (1839–1903) and José Julio Henna (1848–1924), both from Puerto Rico.[114] Standing in back, third from right, is the Filipino artist Juan Luna (1857–1899) (see p. 128).[115]

The Puerto Rican Commission wrote a series of letters addressed to President McKinley, protesting the U.S. military government established in Puerto Rico after the cease-fire, reiterating that the U.S. needed to consult with the Puerto Rican people to determine the type of government to be established on their island.[116] In an interview with the *Washington Post*, Hostos, the president of the Puerto Rican Commission, said, "I hope history will not say that Porto Rico [*sic*] was treated like a dog by America. Such treatment would be contrary to your history and your institutions.".[117] Agoncillo, a member of the Filipino commissioners, also published letters in the press. He wrote:

I claim, in the name of the Filipino nation . . . the fulfillment of the solemn declaration made by the illustrious William McKinley . . . that, on going

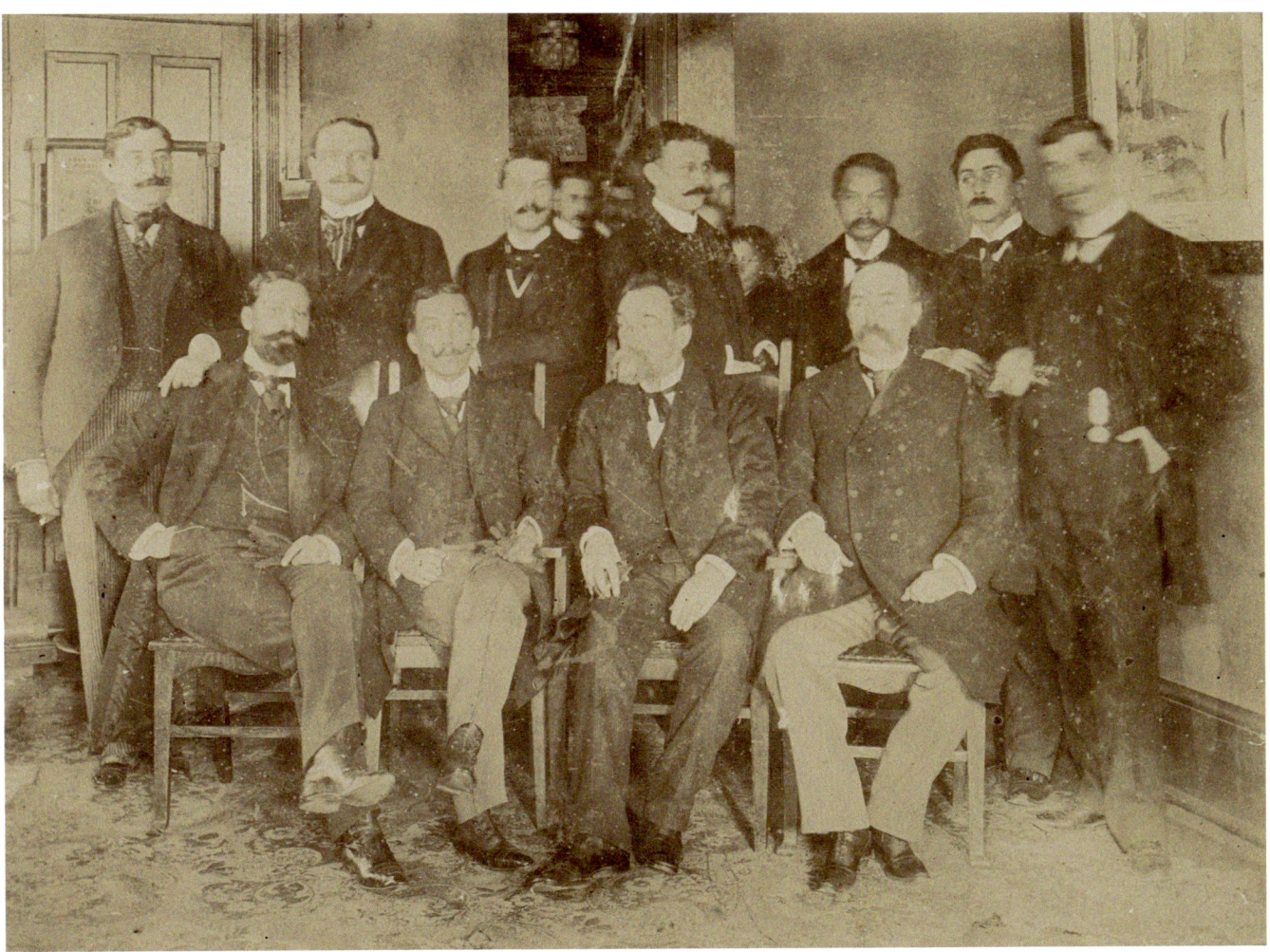

Fig. 12 *Commissioners from Cuba, the Philippines, and Puerto Rico in Washington, DC*, Unidentified photographer, 1899. Photograph; 12.7 × 17.8 cm (5 × 7 in.). Eugenio María de Hostos and Eugenio Carlos de Hostos Papers, Manuscript Division. Library of Congress, Cabinet of American Illustration, Washington, DC

to war, he was not guided by any intention of aggrandizement and extension of National territory, but only in respect to the principles of humanity, the duty of liberating tyrannized peoples, and the desire to proclaim the unalienable rights, with their sovereignty, of the countries released from the yoke of Spain.[118]

Although McKinley met with some groups himself and had his representatives meet with others, the president ultimately ignored their statements and requests.

If Chartran's painting alone were to represent this moment in U.S. history, the commissioners from the former Spanish colonies who attempted to negotiate their new political status would be destined to oblivion. Although the photograph of the commissioners augments this biased account, its quality and graininess remain a poor record of their visit. People pile into the back of the room, some of their faces blurred. While the seated individuals have been identified, the names of the others have been lost to time. These two historical records, Chartran's painting and the weathered photograph of the commissioners, clearly attest to the power dynamics during the signing of the peace treaty. The monumental scale of Chartran's painting—with its brilliant execution, elegant composition, and pristine condition, as well as its prestigious repository—stands against the small blurry photograph. Now a fragile print, pasted onto board, the image of the commissioners has, for the most part, been obscured within Eugenio María de Hostos's undigitized papers in the Library of Congress. These conditions establish a hierarchy between both group portraits that serves and validates the victor's memory of the war. The formidable painting testifies to U.S. power at the turn of the century and the enduring, triumphant narrative surrounding it. The record of McKinley's silencing of those who objected to his policies takes a more ephemeral form—and, for over a century, has only been accessible to those who know where to look.[119]

There are many ways to approach the history of war, imperialism, and nation-building. Exploring the conflicts of 1898 through portraiture helps concretize the role of people in these conflicts, thus making historical events seem less inevitable. As a collective fabric, portraits put faces on the agents of history, but they also carry ideologies. Depending on the artists, sitters, those who commissioned them, and the repositories that hold them, portraits might embody statements of political power and military might over others—or serve as a rebuttal to such power. Through this exhibition and catalogue, we more deeply understand the visual rhetoric of empire through works such as Charles Dana Gibson's homage to Theodore Roosevelt in his Rough Rider uniform and John Singer Sargent's commanding likenesses of Henry Cabot Lodge and Leonard Wood. At the same time, thoughtful

and meditative portraits of figures such as Jane Addams by George de Forest Brush and Samuel Clemens by John Alexander White reflect the U.S. voices who opposed territorial expansion and colonization.

Conversely, the artworks created in Cuba, Hawai'i, the Philippines, and Puerto Rico presented in this exhibition and catalogue signal the launching of new visual discourses of self-representation articulating distinct national identities and efforts for political agency. Queen Lili'uokalani's display of her portrait by William Cogswell was a statement of Hawaiian national and cultural sovereignty. Juan Luna's portrait of José Rizal embodied the kinship between sitter and artist who together, as Filipino cultural and political activists, worked in tandem to empower their country. On the other hand, with his portrait of William McKinley, Francisco Oller attempted to record the island's transition from Spanish to U.S. hands, and to carve a space of artistic agency for himself, and Armando García Menocal made a powerful tribute to the icon of Cuban independence, Antonio Maceo Grajales. These varied uses of portraiture demonstrated the importance of the genre as a vehicle for empowerment.

This catalogue and the accompanying exhibition, *1898: U.S. Imperial Visions and Revisions*, seek to reinscribe stories that have been subsumed under narratives of U.S. ennoblement. From the points of view of many Cubans, CHamorus, Guamanians, Filipinos, Kānaka Maoli, and Puerto Ricans, the U.S. narrative of benevolent conquest does not articulate the historic experience of colonialism or limited self-governance. Furthermore, U.S. control since 1898 resulted in profound legal, economic, and cultural changes that continue to pose challenges on the civic and political liberties of ordinary people in these lands. By tending to these histories and thinking critically about how the past has been framed, we can begin to shift awareness toward a more empathetic understanding of the past and, most importantly, of one another.

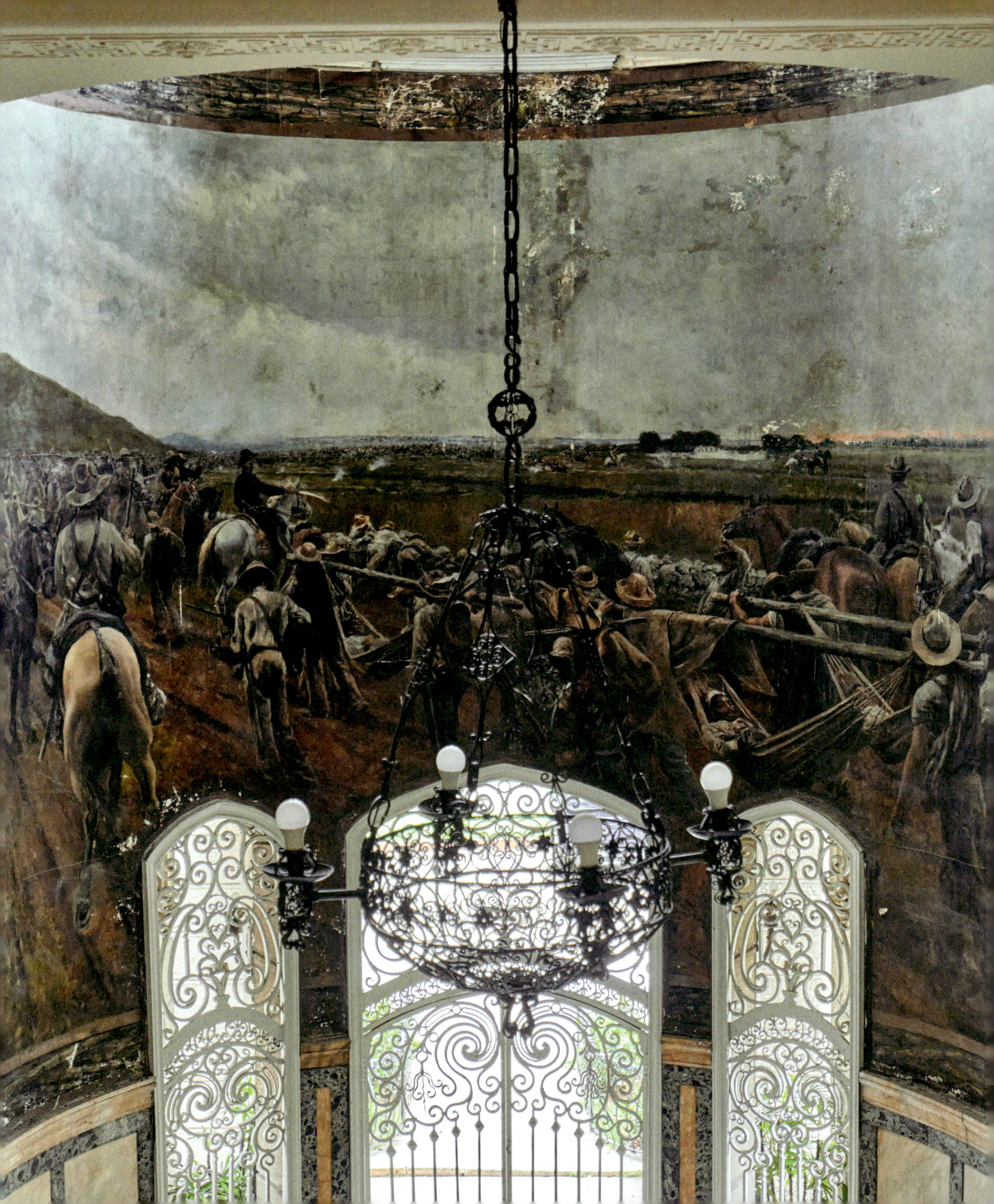

Forces at Play

War and Empire in the Art of Winslow Homer and Armando García Menocal

KATE CLARKE LEMAY

The famously reticent Winslow Homer (1836–1910) never directly commented on the War of 1898.[1] From 1899 to 1902, however, he made *Searchlight on Harbor Entrance, Santiago de Cuba*, a major painting about the battle between the U.S. Navy's North Atlantic Fleet and the Spanish Squadron, when the latter was trapped in Santiago Bay from May 27 to July 3, 1898 (fig. 1).[2] This work may be interpreted as Homer's endorsement of U.S. imperial expansion. In making it, Homer synthesized his most political act, his pledge of loyalty to the Union during the U.S. Civil War—a conflict that he had witnessed as an artist correspondent—with his imagining of a place of a battle whose outcome guaranteed the U.S. transformation into a colonial empire. *Searchlight on Harbor Entrance, Santiago de Cuba* reflects the moment in which power shifted in three nations: the crumbling of Spanish dominion, the emergence of the U.S. empire, and the birth of the Cuban nation.

The last point is especially important for this essay. When *Searchlight on Harbor Entrance, Santiago de Cuba* is paired with two works, *Batalla de Coliseo* (Battle of Coliseo) (1903–1905), and *La muerte de Maceo* (The death of Maceo) (c. 1908), by the preeminent Cuban artist Armando García

Menocal (1863–1942), a more complete history emerges (figs. 2–3).[3] At the turn of the century, Menocal painted these works to honor and commemorate the *mambises*, the Cuban insurgents who fought against Spanish colonial rule. A *mambí* himself, Menocal fought during the entire third War of Independence (1895–1898), sustaining at least one wound.[4] His soldiering gave him material and cause for mythmaking, and his artistic training and talent made him the foremost pro-Cuban propagator of public memory. The visual language he established in *Batalla de Coliseo* and *La muerte de Maceo* facilitated the emergence of a unifying historical narrative for the new Cuban nation. The first painting memorializes his personal experience of chaotic combat, while the second honors and mythologizes an important war hero, Antonio Maceo Grajales (1845–1896). When considered together, the works by Homer and Menocal offer first-hand, in-depth accounts of the period when U.S. imperialism and Cuban nationalism emerged on the world stage, and their two points of view help us understand the struggle and strain between these two nations.

Each artist was present in the Caribbean when the other was not, and the complementary Homer-Menocal

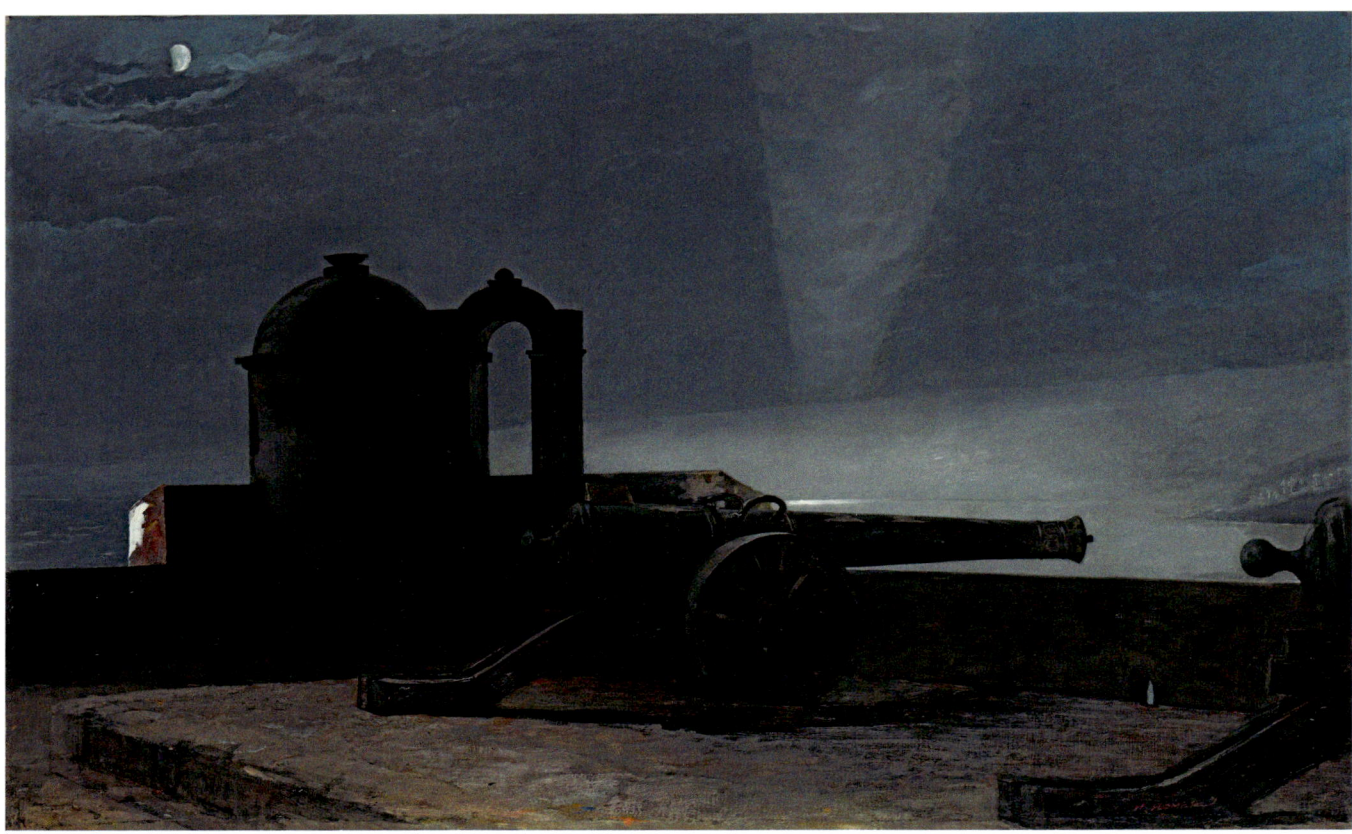

Fig. 1 *Searchlight on Harbor Entrance, Santiago de Cuba*, Winslow Homer (1836–1910), 1902. Oil on canvas; 77.5 × 128.3 cm (30½ × 50½ in.). The Metropolitan Museum of Art; gift of George A. Hearn, 1906

timeline provides a window into the Cuban struggle for independence. Homer, who was a generation older than Menocal, was briefly in Santiago, Cuba, from December 1884 to February 1885. At that time, Menocal was in Spain, studying at the Academy of San Fernando with the virtuoso history painter Francisco Jover y Casanova (1836–1890).[5] Later, from December 1898 through February 1899, while Menocal was adjusting to a U.S. neocolonial rule in Cuba immediately after the conclusion of the War of 1898, Homer was again in the Caribbean, visiting Nassau, the Bahamas.

Homer and Menocal were both battle-hardened, albeit in distinct ways. Their specific experiences of war led them to understand combat tactics, technology, and strategy. However, they responded to wartime violence differently in their art, and this key point helps us understand the different prerogatives and priorities of Cuba versus the United States through their respective works. Menocal

embraced history painting, whereas Homer spurned it. Homer featured war's most modern technology in his art, while Menocal avoided depicting technological advantages employed by Cuban soldiers, and instead focused on machete warfare to emphasize courage and bravery. Their varying approaches reflect their roles as citizens of nations with distinctive stakes in the War of 1898. Together, the perspectives set forth in *Searchlight on Harbor Entrance, Santiago de Cuba*; *Batalla de Coliseo*; and *La muerte de Maceo* reflect the forces at play in empire ending and nation-building. They picture a more complete story about the ascent to national (Cuba) and international (United States) power, narrating key figures, political ideologies, modern warfare's technologies, and pivotal strategic locations.

Homer, Menocal, and History Painting

Homer was a "special" (freelance) artist-correspondent for *Harper's Weekly* during the U.S. Civil War (1861–1865). He made three trips to the front and witnessed several battles, including the violent Siege of Yorktown in 1862 and the bloody Battle of Spotsylvania Courthouse in 1864.[6]

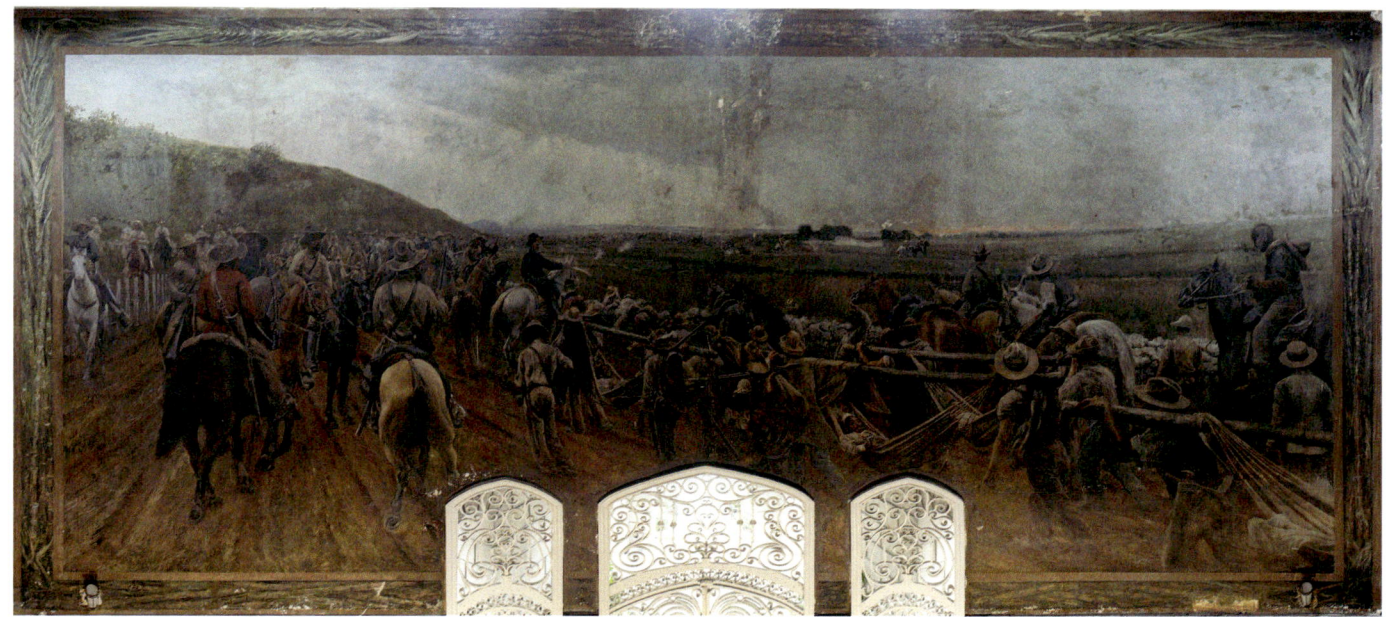

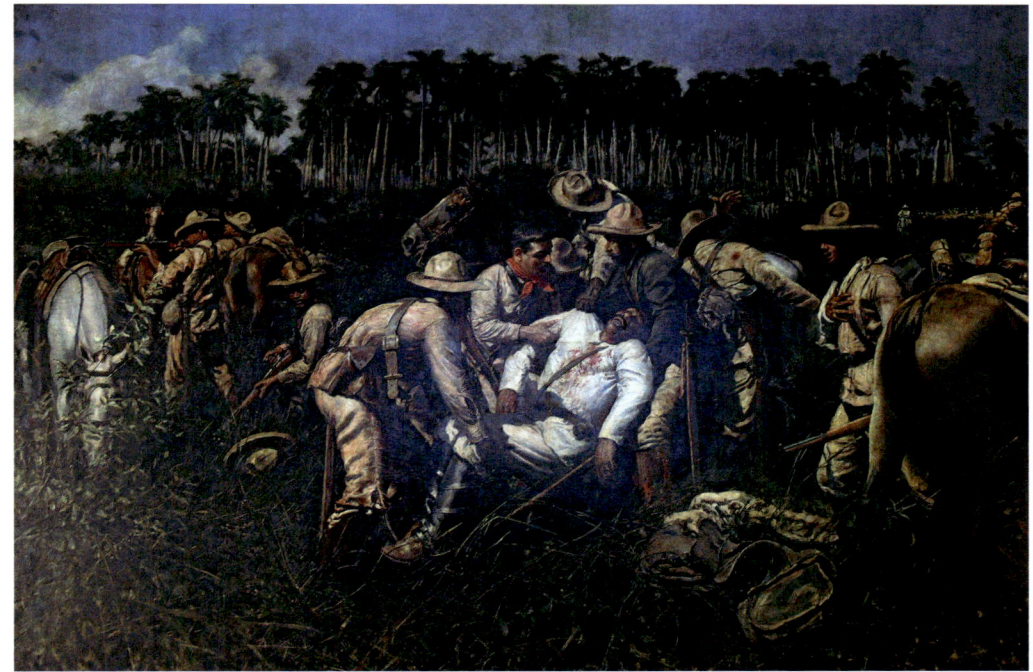

Fig. 2 *Batalla de Coliseo* (Battle of Coliseo), Armando García Menocal (1863–1942), 1903–1905. Marouflage (painted canvas mural), approx. 9.1 × 4.6 m (30 × 15 ft.). Casaquinta Las Delicias del Palatino, Havana

Fig. 3 *La muerte de Maceo* (The death of Maceo), Armando García Menocal (1863–1942), c. 1908. Oil on canvas; 1.1 × 1.6 m (3¾ × 5¼ ft.). Palacio de la Presidencia, República de Cuba

The latter especially was characterized by grit, determination, and sacrifice. One Union officer observed, "The [battle] was a boiling, bubbling, and hissing cauldron of death. Clubbed muskets and bayonets were the modes of fighting for those who had used up their cartridges, and frenzy seemed to possess the yelling, demonic hordes on either side."[7] After witnessing such traumatic scenes, Homer did not attempt to convey war's brutal realities through a traditional history painting, like *La muerte de Maceo* by Menocal. Such lofty and theatrical celebrations of war heroes did not align with the slaughter he witnessed. This is partly because the visual tradition was radically changed when photographers such as Alexander Gardner and Mathew Brady revealed the sordid truths of the Civil War's carnage. Instead, Homer developed a non-conventional, realist approach that eschewed heroicizing and idealism. Grappling with painting war in this new world of visual culture characterized by such unvarnished realism, Homer depicted antiheroes like the figure in *Trooper Meditating beside a Grave* (fig. 4). This work depicts an anonymous soldier in an unbuttoned jacket that reveals only darkness at the center where his heart would be. Immediately after the Civil War, in works like *Prisoners from the Front*, Homer painted a classical frieze of figures—but he placed a defeated Confederate soldier in the middle of the composition, a position normally reserved for the hero (fig. 5). *Prisoners from the Front* illustrates a deadpan faceoff between the unruly Confederate officer and the elegant Union soldier (modeled after Homer's friend, General Francis Channing Barlow). Critics loved the deliberate contrast of types, in part because its unconventional embrace of realism subverted history painting.[8]

Homer continued to pursue anti-heroism in his paintings about war and conflict. Two decades later, when he made his watercolors in Cuba, from December 1884 through February 1885, Homer opted for scenes without figures.[9] Nevertheless, Homer struggled with this decision. For *Searchlight on Santiago de Cuba*, x-ray technology reveals that he carefully considered including a figure. The conservator of paintings at the Metropolitan Museum of Art recently discovered the figure of a Spanish soldier to the left of the guard tower—one that Homer later painted out. Choosing to create a battlescape, but one void of any figure, with unseen ships from the vantage point of the fortress overlooking the mouth of the harbor, Homer narrowed the painting's focus to the searchlight.

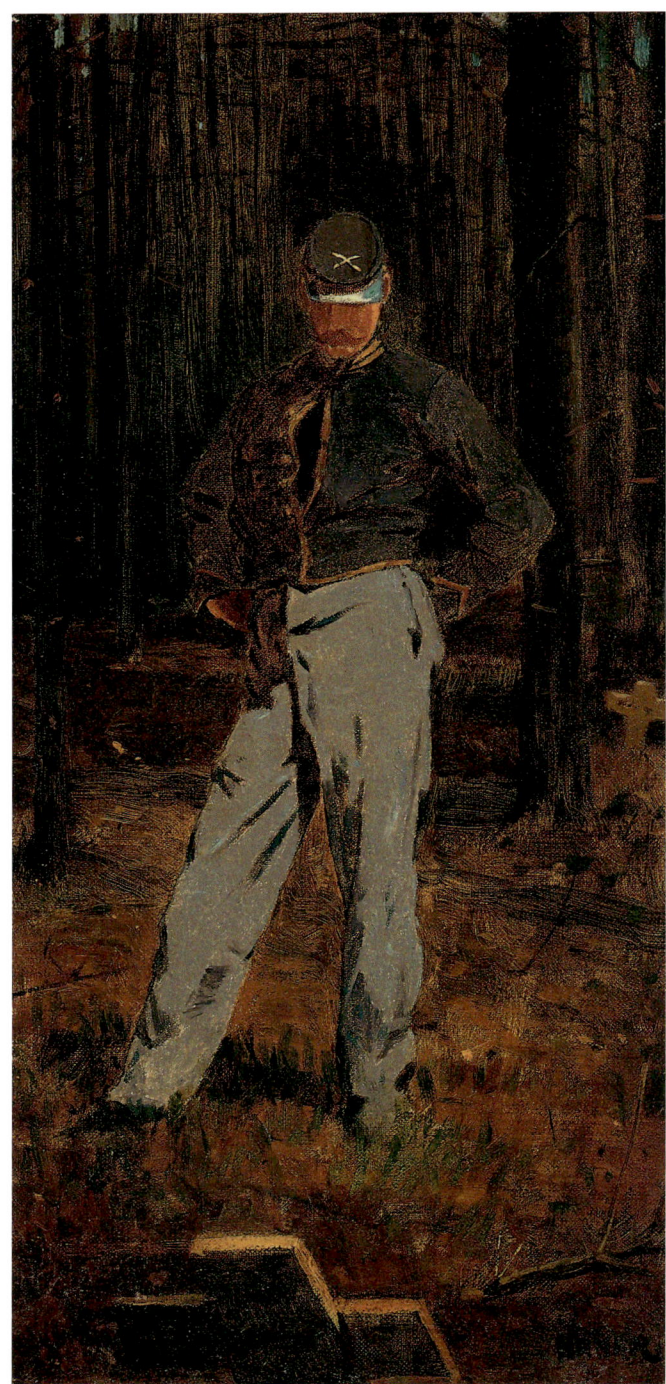

Fig. 4 *Trooper Meditating beside a Grave*, Winslow Homer (1836–1910), c. 1865. Oil on canvas; 40.6 × 20.3 cm (16 × 8 in.). Joslyn Art Museum, Omaha; gift of Dr. Harold Gifford and Ann Gifford Forbes

The presence of the U.S. Navy is suggested by the illumination of the night sky by the beams of two searchlights cast from the U.S. ships that formed the naval blockade of Cuba.[10] Homer's decision to remove the figure may be interpreted as following his work about the Civil War—the figure was too close to the tradition of history painting that he had rejected.

Depicting key figures, however, was critical for Menocal, whose primary goal was to envision Cuba as a triumphant new nation. Menocal made a case for academic training and for following the intellectual tradition of history painting.[11] In 1902, he was quoted in the Cuban newspaper *El Figaro*, arguing that a canon of Cuban art needed to be established. He stated, "We need to incorporate scenarios and elements severely lacking and impossible to improvise such as models, traditions, and history. . . . In countries such as ours, art forms exclusively inspired by the soul and intuitive understandings, such as poetry, can be fruitfully cultivated, but not those that require the mastery of a technique that cannot be intuitively learned . . . without museums, without teachers, what is art in Cuba if not a timid albeit revered exercise."[12] From 1906 through 1908, Menocal created the large-scale *La muerte de Maceo* after accepting an invitation from the *Ayuntamiento*, Havana's city council, to commemorate the ten-year anniversary of Maceo's death.[13] In his imagining of the death of Maceo, who is at the center, Menocal depicts the soldiers on the left continuing to fight, taking aim at someone outside of the frame. Positioned around Maceo are Cuban leaders of the Army of Liberation, including José Miró Argenter (1851–1925) on the right, and Alberto Nodarse Bacallao (1867–1924) on the left. With his back to the viewer, Juan Manuel Sánchez, a Black soldier, holds Maceo's knees. Maceo wears white clothes stained by blood from a second posthumous wound on his chest. His mouth slack, Maceo's head falls back into the arms of Miró Argenter (fig. 6).

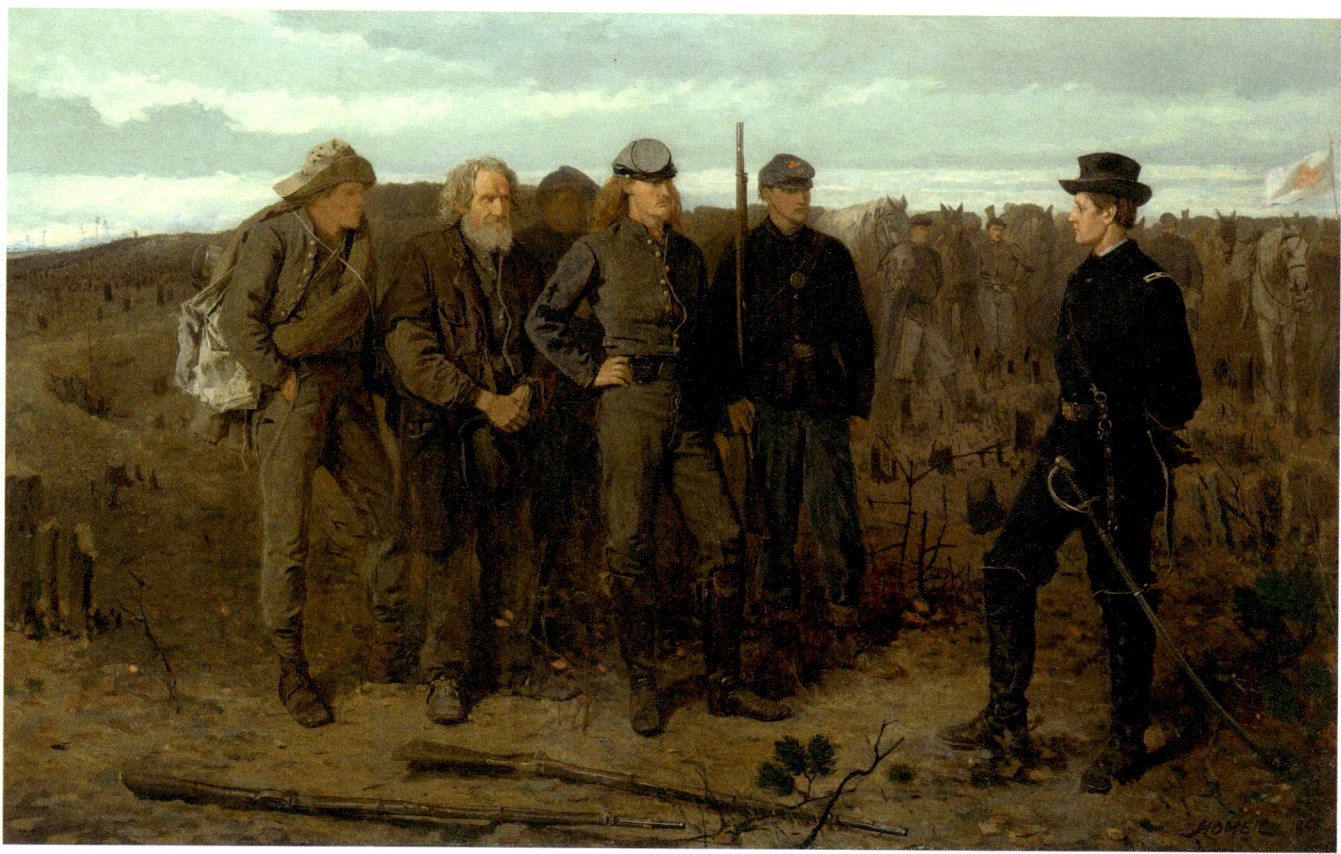

Fig. 5 *Prisoners from the Front*, Winslow Homer (1836–1910), 1866. Oil on canvas; 61 × 96.5 cm (24 × 38 in.). The Metropolitan Museum of Art; gift of Mrs. Frank B. Porter

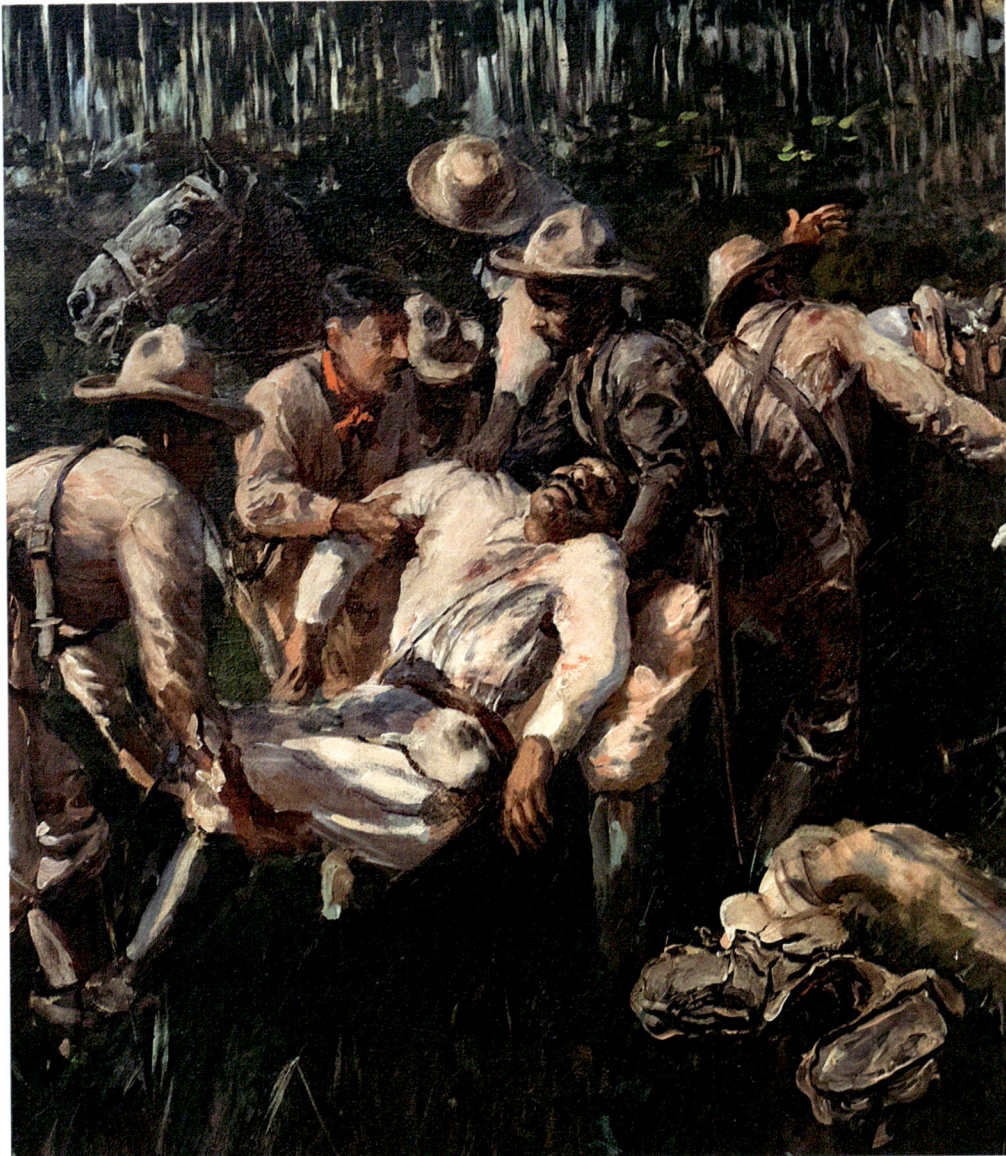

Fig. 6 Detail of *Boceto de La muerte de Maceo* (Study for *The death of Maceo*), Armando García Menocal (1863–1942), c. 1908. Oil on canvas; 1.1 × 1.6 m (3¾ × 5¼ ft.). Museo de la Ciudad, Havana

Although conservative in composition, *La muerte de Maceo* cloaked a radical endeavor: the promise of an independent Cuba. By commemorating Maceo's death, Menocal sought to establish a lasting iconography symbolizing an independent Cuba through the premise of the martyr—Maceo—who died for the cause of Cuban freedom. *La muerte de Maceo* was especially significant, as Cuban independence was only a quasi-reality from 1909 through 1933. During this period, the United States formally embedded itself in Cuban power structures, owning companies responsible for the nation's modern infrastructure, like the power company—and exerting undue political influence.[14] Even before this era, U.S. businessmen had major investments in Cuba, which they sought to protect in 1901 by amending the proposed Cuban Constitution to include what would later be known as the Platt Amendment.[15] Among other restrictive measures against Cuban sovereignty, the Platt Amendment guaranteed the United States access to land in Cuba for coaling and naval stations.[16] While painting a key narrative of martyrdom for the Cuban nation, Menocal was also navigating the political hierarchies of the neocolonial U.S. government.[17] In the process, it was crucial for him to remain in the good graces of those in power. For example, Menocal owed his

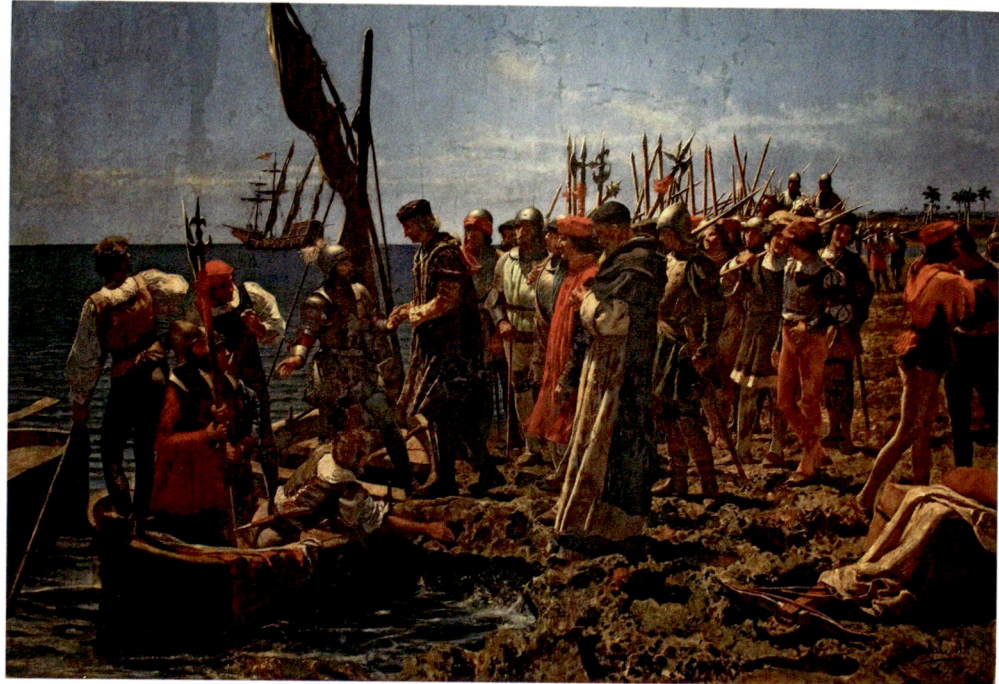

Fig. 7 *Embarque de Cristóbal Colón por Bobadilla* (Embarkation of Christopher Columbus by Order of Bobadilla), Armando García Menocal (1863–1942), 1893. Oil on canvas; 3 × 4.6 m (9⅞ × 15 ft.). Museo Nacional de Bellas Artes de Cuba, Havana

continued appointment as chair of landscape at the Academy of San Alejandro in 1900 to U.S. colonial administrator Adna R. Chaffee.[18]

Despite the precarious political situation in Cuba, Menocal's dramatic figurative paintings always worked to subvert the colonial power in favor of an independent Cuba. For example, in 1893—while the Spanish were commemorating the 401-year anniversary of colonization of the Americas—he painted *Embarque de Cristóbal Colón por Bobadilla* (Embarkation of Christopher Columbus by Order of Bobadilla), a work that was explicitly opposed to the Spanish Crown's colonial endeavors (fig. 7). Although Columbus was a symbol of Spanish glory, Menocal presents him during his political arrest in 1500 in Santo Domingo, Hispaniola, by then-governor Francisco Bobadilla (c. 1448–1502). Wearing chains around his ankles, Columbus is being banished from the Indies for charges of abuse of power. By selecting this moment, Menocal alludes to how Cubans saw the enchained Columbus as "a thief with a persistent and greedy soul"— and they relished this painting because of its allusions to how Spain kept the colony of Cuba enchained.[19] When the painting was to be exhibited in the 1893 World's Columbian Exposition in Chicago in the Spanish empire's section, the Spanish ambassador to the United States, Enrique Dupuy de Lôme, asked Menocal to paint over the chains. Although he would eventually comply, Menocal first exhibited the unchanged painting at the Teatro Tacón in Havana, cementing his reputation as a pro-Cuban painter. *Embarque de Cristóbal Colón por Bobadilla* did not receive an award in Chicago.[20] After the painting returned to Cuba, Menocal repainted Columbus's chains.[21]

Loyalty to a Nation: Political Ideology of Homer

Menocal's political ideology may be read quite easily through his artwork. By contrast, for Homer, it is necessary to consider the ways his experiences in the Civil War informed his political ideology, and how this in turn shaped his view of the War of 1898. In 1862, Homer spent six to eight weeks on the front lines, embedded with the 61st New York Volunteer Infantry as part of the II Corps of the Army of the Potomac.[22] In order to gain admittance to the front lines, Homer signed a loyalty oath to the Union printed on the back of his pass on April 1, 1862 (fig. 8). By signing the oath, Homer pledged not "to give aid, comfort, or information to the enemies of the U.S. Government in any way whatsoever." With this pass, Homer declared his loyalty to the United States.

A fierce sense of allegiance to the United States often characterized the political ideology of Civil War veterans. For example, as president, William McKinley displayed

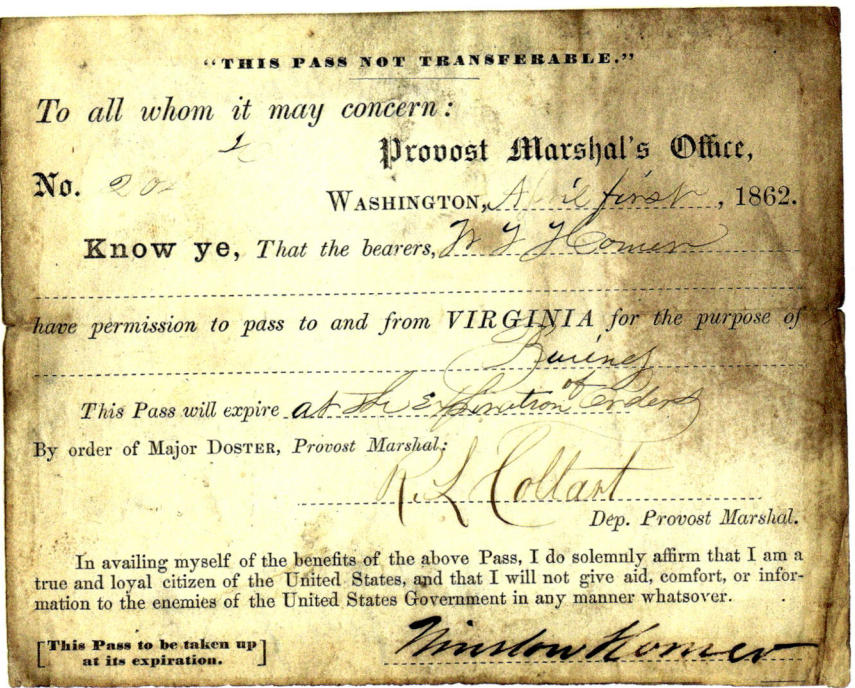

Fig. 8 *Civil War Pass: signed by Winslow Homer*, April 1, 1862. Ink on paper; 11.1 × 14 cm (4⅜ × 5½ in.). Bowdoin College Museum of Art, Brunswick, Maine; gift of the Homer Family, 1964.69.152

his loyalty to the United States by wearing a red, white, and blue rosette pin when he sat for a formal photographic portrait (see p. 49). The pin symbolizes the Military Order of the Loyal Legion of the United States, an organization formed in the wake of Abraham Lincoln's assassination to thwart future threats to the federal government. McKinley was a heavily decorated military veteran, and his choice to wear this simple rosette is highly representative of the political values of the time. Homer kept his pass with his sworn oath and later pasted it into his 1835 copy of Jared Sparks's book *The Life and Treason of Benedict Arnold*.[23] By pasting it into a traitor's biography, it is evident that Homer felt his pledge to remain true to the United States was important. Although he never overtly declared any political beliefs, in this case, his placement of his pass into the biography of a traitor highlights his staunch Republican views.

Why would Homer feel so devoted to the nation, when normally he refused to comment on anything political? He was undoubtedly marked by his reporting as an artist during the Civil War and his newfound understanding of the ramifications of the technology of modern warfare. Beginning April 16, 1862, Homer saw and sketched events and scenes that took place during the Siege of Yorktown (April 5–May 4, 1862).[24] There, he observed sharpshooter technology as it was used for the first time in U.S. combat.

Homer drew the first two sharpshooter regiments that were raised by the U.S. Army, the Berdan Sharpshooters, as they fought in the Peach Orchard during the Battle of Yorktown.[25] Often they were armed by the Union Army with .52 caliber Sharps rifles. But many brought their own private rifles, like the match rifle that Homer depicts in his first painting, *The Sharpshooter* (fig. 9).[26]

Homer began *The Sharpshooter* in 1862, after returning from the front, and finished it in 1863.[27] This work depicts a Union soldier, with a red mark on his army forage cap (presumably the clover leaf insignia of the 61st), precariously balancing on a tree branch. Steadying the rifle against a smaller branch, the sharpshooter gazes down a telescopic sight on the rifle's barrel. The improved rifling and telescopic sight, which used the latest available lenses, made it possible to shoot a person from three to five hundred yards away.[28] An officer later reported that Berdan's sharpshooters "did good service in picking off the enemy's skirmishers and artillerists whenever they should show themselves."[29] Only experienced sharpshooters, such as those who brought their own match rifles, like the man Homer depicts, knew how to take advantage of such technology.[30] Homer accurately drew a match rifle, made distinctive by its heavy, octagonal barrel and a single set trigger. Notably, this represented the latest in rifle technology. Homer was fixated on the professional

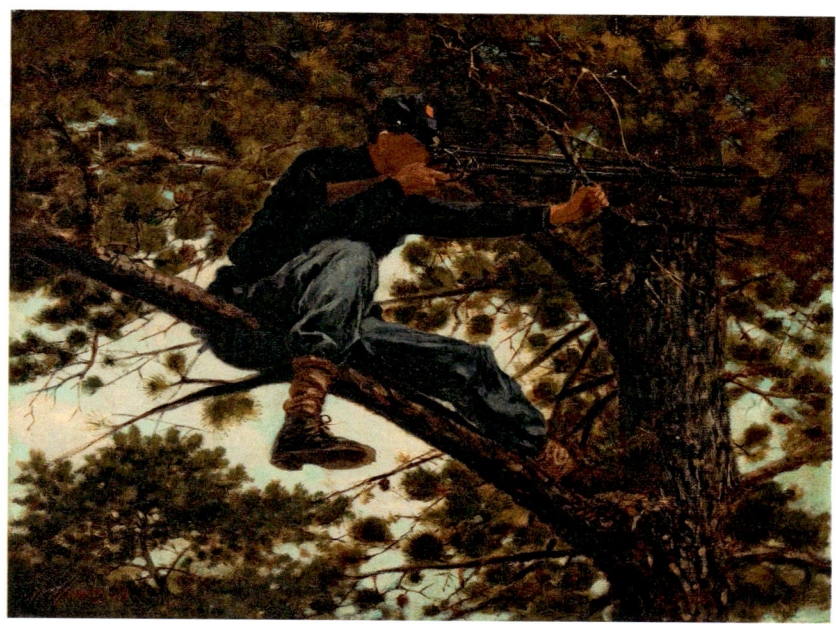

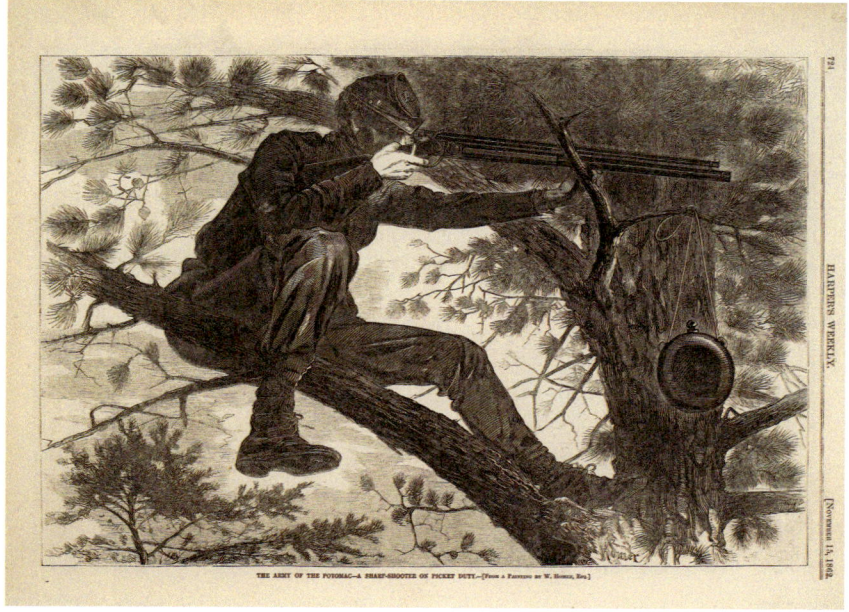

Fig. 9 *The Sharpshooter*, Winslow Homer (1836–1910), 1863. Oil on canvas; 31.1 × 41.9 cm (12¼ × 16½ in.). Portland Museum of Art, Maine; gift of Barbro and Bernard Osher

Fig. 10 *Army of the Potomac—A Sharp-Shooter on Picket Duty, Harper's Weekly,* November 15, 1862, Winslow Homer (1836–1910). Wood engraving; 23.2 × 35.1 cm (9⅛ × 13¾ in.). Davis Museum at Wellesley College

marksmen and made several works about the subject, including an engraving based on *The Sharpshooter* for *Harper's Weekly*, published on November 15, 1862 (fig. 10).

In both painting and engraving, the soldier is about to pull the trigger, but the cold focus of his gaze stands out more in the finely detailed print. Here, as he would later do in *Searchlight on Harbor Entrance, Santiago de Cuba*, Homer focused on the high drama of the hunt. Although Homer was clearly fascinated by the weapon's technology,

he was simultaneously repulsed by war's degradation of humanity. In an 1895 letter that features a sketch of a man within the crosshairs of a telescopic sight, he described the sharpshooter as a cold-blooded killer (fig. 11). He wrote, "I looked through one of their [Berdan Sharpshooters's] rifles once when they were in a peach orchard in front of Yorktown in April 1862—this is what I saw—I was not a soldier—but a camp follower & artist, the above impression struck me as being as near murder as anything I

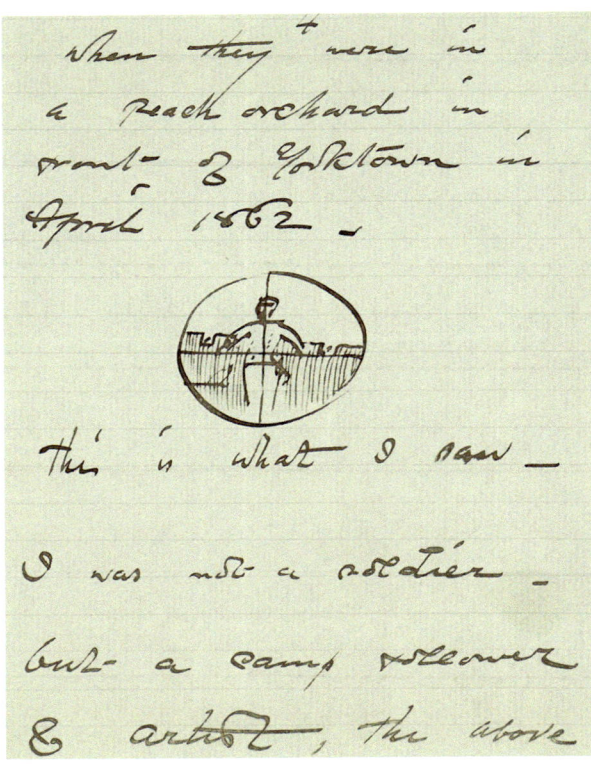

When they were in a peach orchard in front of Yorktown in April 1862 —

This is what I saw —

I was not a soldier — but a camp follower & artist, the above

Fig. 11 Letter from Winslow Homer to George G. Briggs, February 19, 1896. Winslow Homer Collection, 1877–1945, Archives of American Art, Smithsonian Institution

could think of in connection with the army & I always had a horror of that branch of the service."[31] *The Sharpshooter* works by Homer connect the war technology of telescopic sight to its deadly intent, a theme he would later revisit with respect to the War of 1898.[32]

The Civil War changed Homer. Francis Channing Barlow reported on April 23, 1862, "[Homer] says he shall go home after the battle . . . His head is shaven & he looks like Hell."[33] After he returned, Homer's mother, Henrietta, observed in a letter, "He suffered much, was without food 3 days at a time & all in camp either died or were carried away with typhoid fever—plug tobacco & coffee were the Staple . . . He came home so changed that his best friends did not know him."[34] From this moment on, Homer endeavored to use his art as a tool to expose ambiguities in the terms of life, casting events of the late nineteenth century, like the War of 1898, with such nuances that the viewer is forced to confront unglorified and even ugly realities.

Menocal and an Independent Cuba: The Will to Win

Like Homer, Menocal was affected by war, but his political ideology was always clear because he had fought for an independent Cuba. The third Cuban War of Independence began on February 24, 1895, when revolutionaries in eastern Cuba proclaimed independence from Spain. Menocal enlisted in the V Corps on June 5, 1895, along with five of his cousins.[35] His early date of enlistment is significant, as a good number of the forty thousand Cuban revolutionaries joined the fight only after the Spanish declared a unilateral cease-fire in April 1898.[36] As an aide to the commander of the Cuban Liberation Army, Máximo Gómez (1836–1905), Menocal helped carry out "the Invasion," which refers to the campaign from Baraguá in the east to El Mariel in the west. Soldiers of the Cuban Liberation Army fought without rest from October 22, 1895 through January 22, 1896.[37] The Invasion consisted of seventy-eight marches that covered over 1,696 kilometers.[38] A major breakthrough in the thirty years' struggle against Spain, the Invasion achieved a psychological as well as a military victory: for the first time, physical war was taken to the economic and political centers of the island, located in the west (fig. 12).[39] Menocal fought in most, if not all, of the battles incurred during the Invasion.[40]

One such fight was the Battle of Mal Tiempo (December 15, 1895), during which Menocal witnessed the use of Cuban machete warfare.[41] This was a turning point in the war, for it sealed the defeat of the Spanish and opened the road out of Oriente (eastern) Province and into the western part of Cuba. The Cuban light cavalry, at the time the best in the world, numbered three thousand as it moved west toward Matanzas.[42] While near a sugar mill and plantation named Santa Teresa, scouts spotted a force of 1,500 Spanish infantrymen—three hundred of whom were marching directly toward the Cuban revolutionaries.[43] Immediately Gómez and Maceo planned to set a trap, hoping to use the element of surprise. However, when Cuban scouts began shooting, they alerted the Spanish to their presence, and the light infantry had no choice but to charge directly into the Spanish.[44] The Cubans, who had superior numbers but few rifles, fought back using hand-to-hand combat with their machetes. The Spanish cowered, "most of them flattened against the ground, under the terrible impression of panic like pigeons in sight of the goshawk."[45] With nothing to lose, the Cuban Liberation Army demonstrated an extraordinary will to win,

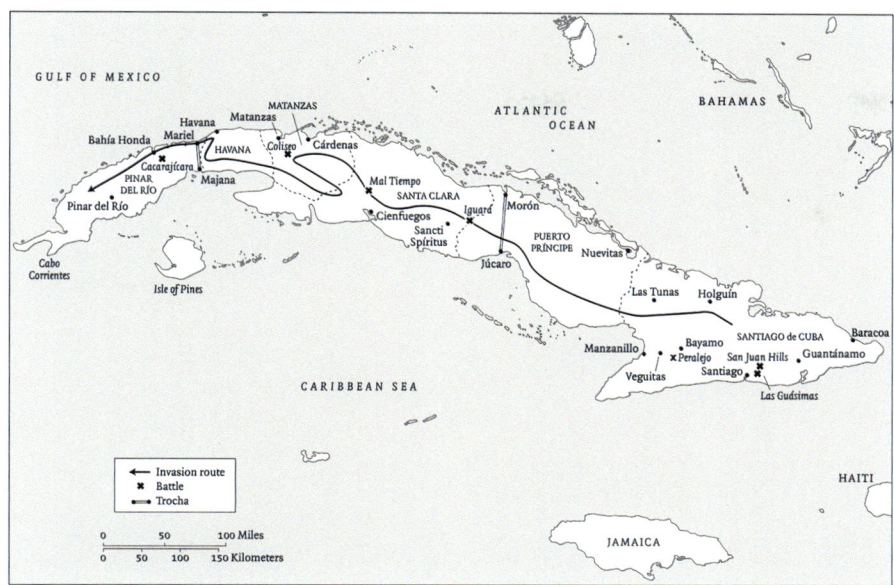

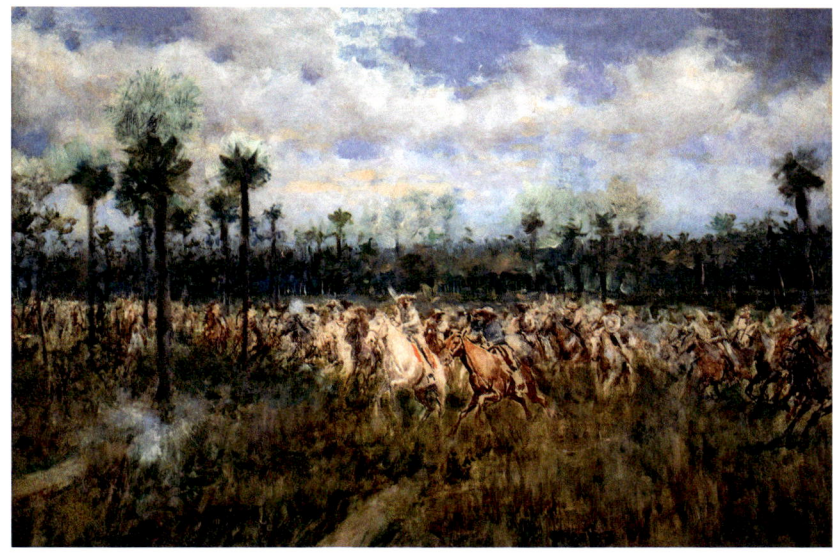

Fig. 12 Map of Cuba outlining the invasion and the *trocha*. Reproduced in John Lawrence Tone, *War and Genocide in Cuba*. Chapel Hill: University of North Carolina Press, 2006

Fig. 13 *Carga al Machete* (Charge with machetes), Armando García Menocal (1863–1942), c. 1895. Oil on canvas; 40.5 × 61 cm (15¹⁵⁄₁₆ × 24 in.). Museo Nacional de Bellas Artes de Cuba, Havana

destroying six companies of Spanish infantry in fifteen minutes. They captured rifles and ten thousand rounds of ammunition and suffered only six battle fatalities and forty-six wounded. By contrast, the Spanish lost sixty-five men, and forty were wounded.[46]

Machete warfare, of course, did not usually win battles against the Spanish. Cubans fought more often with captured Spanish Mauser rifles, exploding bullets, dynamite, and captured Spanish artillery. However, Menocal devoted a pen-and-ink sketch and an oil sketch to the use of the

machete in battle (fig. 13).[47] An archaic battle weapon, the machete was essentially a short broadsword. By focusing on it, Menocal redirected the narrative emphasis to the Cuban courage and will to win. And, in an era before machine guns, such élan did help to win wars—some scholars argue that the French based their entire battle strategy on élan during World War I.[48] Only after the Gatling gun, the first machine gun, was used in Cuba by the United States to fight the Spanish in 1898, was élan no longer enough.[49] In the end, superior technology

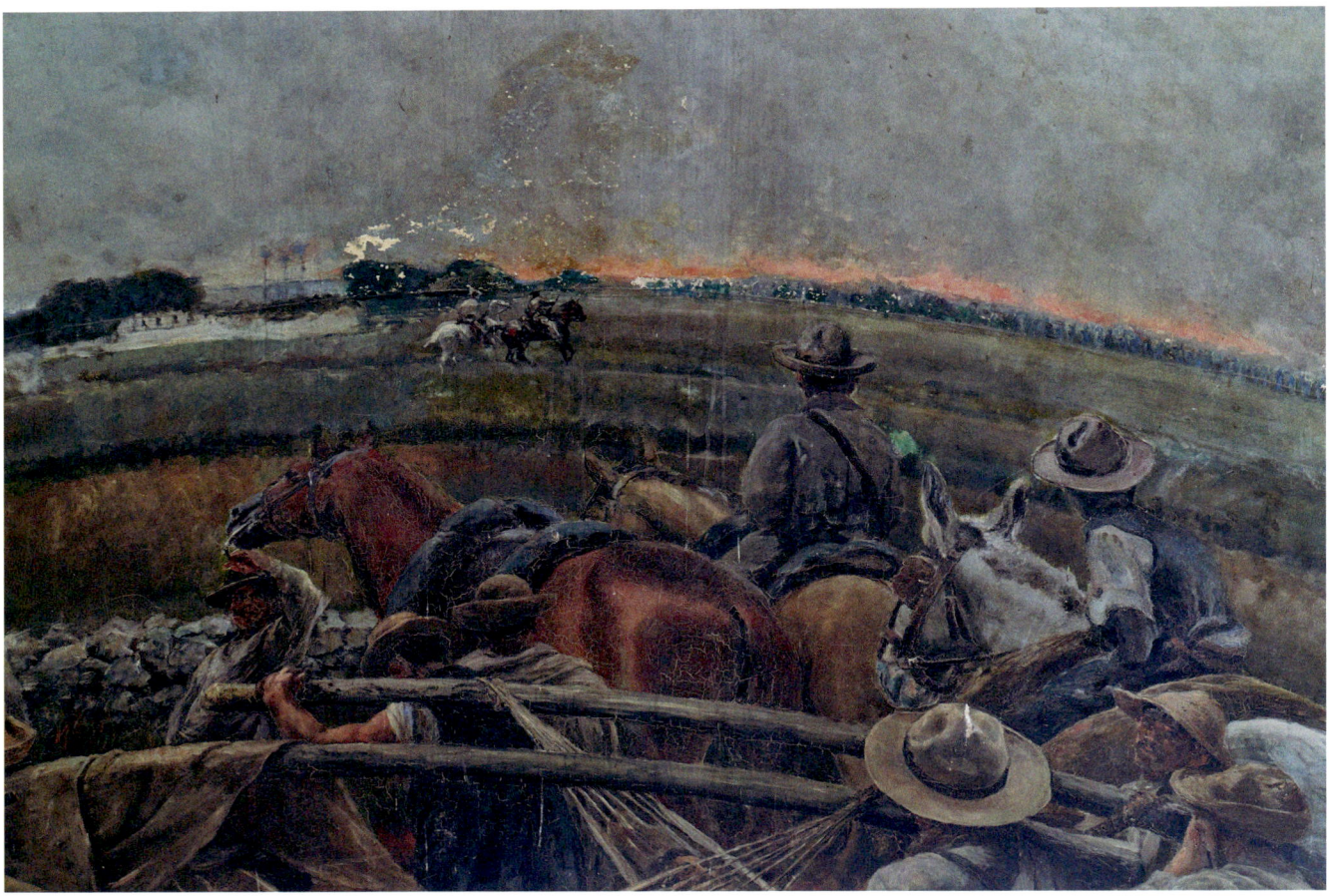

Fig. 14 Detail of Audaz Sugar Factory burning from Armando García Menocal's *Batalla de Coliseo* (Battle of Coliseo) (see fig. 2)

Fig. 15 Detail of wounded man gazing from Armando García Menocal's *Batalla de Coliseo* (Battle of Coliseo) (see fig. 2)

triumphed—but to visualize an independent Cuba, Menocal dedicated himself to the myth of the machete.

Between 1903 and 1905, Menocal created a series of highly regarded murals for *Las Delicias* (also known as *La Finca de los Monos*, or the Monkey Farm), the home of sugar plantation owner and philanthropist Rosalía Abreu (1862–1930).[50] For this commission, Menocal featured the Battle of Coliseo (December 23, 1895) in a large, curved mural for the Abreu home's entry foyer (fig. 2). During this fight, two columns of Cubans, led by Gómez and Maceo, met the Spanish, led by Arsenio Martínez Campos y Antón (1831–1900). Cuban insurgents outsmarted the Spanish, who thought they had stopped the revolutionaries' advances. When the Spanish transported their army by water, hoping to block their path, the Cubans doubled back.[51] The Cubans outmaneuvered the Spanish, and then continued the famous trek westward.[52]

The Abreu commission brought Menocal important acclaim and cemented his reputation as *el pintor mambí* (painter of the *mambises*). The panoramic mural features several scenes of Cuban revolutionaries in a composite rendering of the battle, including the burning of the Audaz sugar factory, in the background on the right (fig. 14). Radically foreshortened, Gómez—identifiable by his white moustache and machete—and his men gather behind a stone wall at the left and in the middle ground. In the middle and in the distance, the Cuban cavalry charges directly into Spanish infantry formations, horses tumbling.[53] On the right, Cubans behind the wall carry the wounded, one of whom looks directly at the viewer (fig. 15). Others look toward the burning of the sugar factory—and the Spanish soldiers in formation to the right, in the far distance.

Menocal's use of radical foreshortening and composite scenes capture both the confusion of the moment and

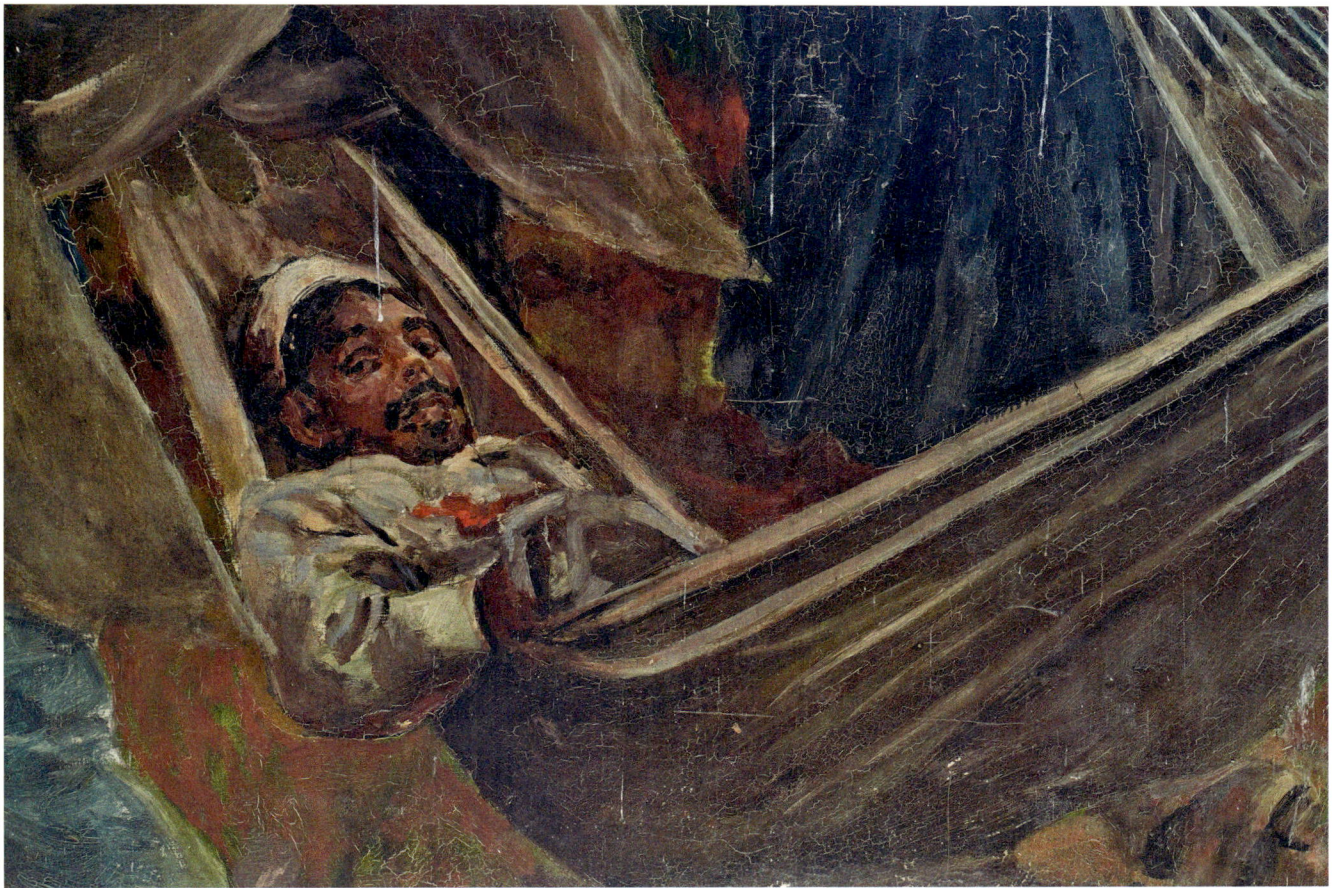

the disordered images of a memory flashback. The stare of a wounded *mambí*, the horses falling in the distance, and the burning of the sugar plantation work together to capture a surreal window into the war. The panoramic mural is situated in a circular foyer and hallway with a second-level landing that allows visitors another, elevated viewpoint. Due to its height, and the multiple viewpoints, the grand painting offers a panopticon-like view into the battle. As the last thing a person views before exiting Abreu's home, it also serves as a threshold of both memory and commemoration. In this way, the mural functions as a memorial to sacrifices made by Cubans in their struggle for independence.

Homer and Imperialism

Unlike Menocal, Homer did not value Cuban independence; in fact, *Searchlight on Harbor Entrance, Santiago de Cuba* points to his support of the U.S. neocolonial project in Cuba. Throughout the 1890s, Homer distanced himself from almost all political landscapes, which is one reason

why *Searchlight on Harbor Entrance, Santiago de Cuba* is so interesting, as it represents a key battle location in a controversial war. While in Cuba in 1884 and 1885, Homer generally painted elemental themes and cityscapes, but most were without human actors. By removing figures from his Cuban scenes, Homer skirted political issues that would have been impossible to avoid at the time. As seen through Homer's eyes, Santiago lacked a local constituency—a viewpoint that completely disregards its largely Black population.

In 1902, Homer described the strategic location of *Searchlight on Harbor Entrance, Santiago de Cuba*, which features the promontory upon which the Castillo de San Pedro de la Roca (Morro Castle) sits, overlooking Santiago Bay and the Caribbean Sea. He wrote in a letter to Charles Knoedler how he imagined the view from the Morro Castle during the "stirring sights of June & July 1898."[54] By "sights," Homer meant the Battle of Santiago (May 28 to July 3, 1898). His letter includes a sketch of the Bay of Santiago and refers to the U.S. North Atlantic Fleet's round-

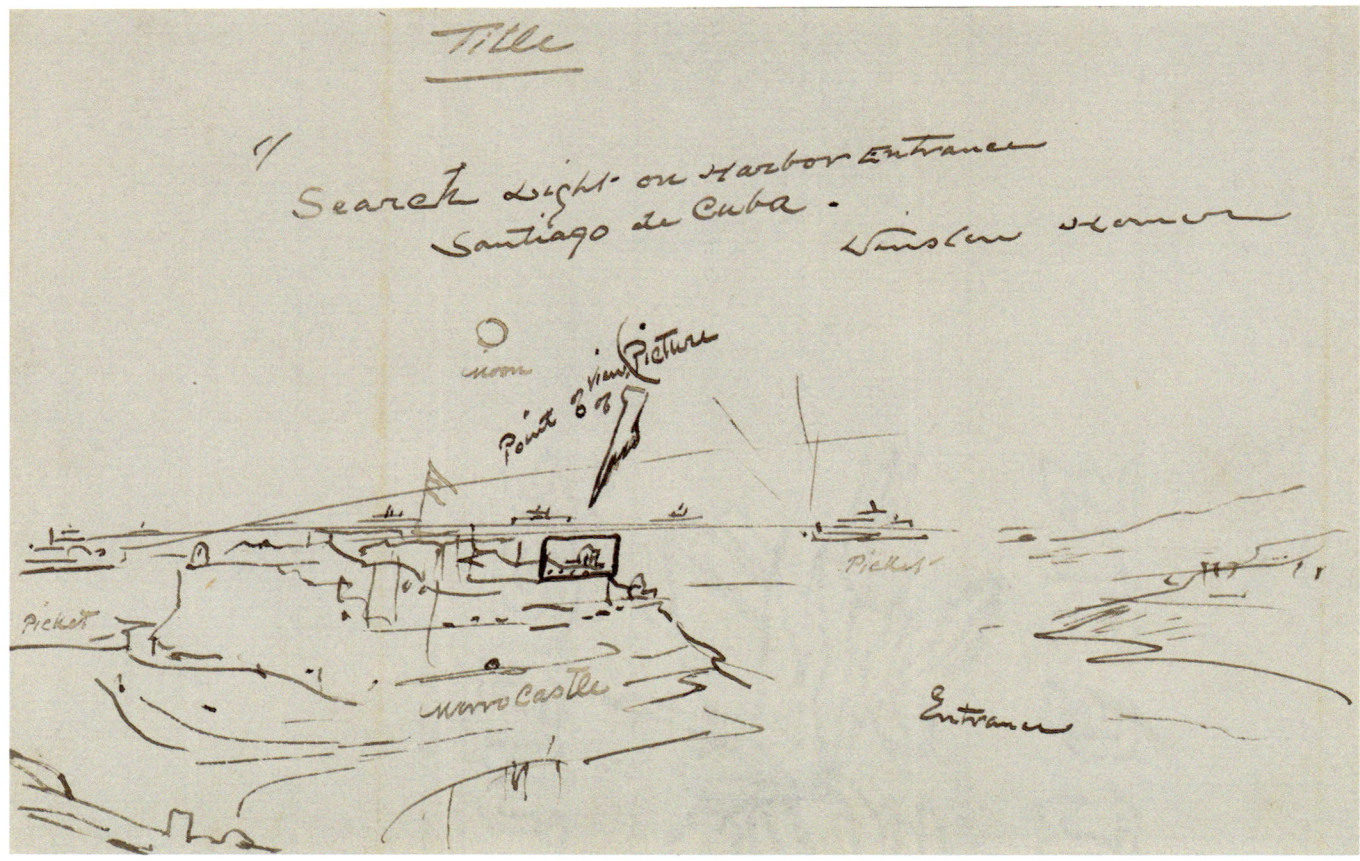

Fig. 16 Sketch of *Searchlight on Harbor Entrance, Santiago de Cuba*, Winslow Homer (1836–1910), December 30, 1901. Graphite on paper; 12.5 × 20 cm (6 × 8 in.). Winslow Homer Collection, Archives of American Art, Smithsonian Institution

the-clock blockade of the harbor that was in place by June 1, 1898 (fig. 16). On July 3, the Spanish squadron, following orders by the captain general of Cuba, Ramón Blanco (1833–1906), tried to break through the blockade. Led by Admiral Pascual Cervera y Topete (1839–1909), the Spanish ships attempted a daring escape at first light. The narrow channel of the bay was not in their favor, however, and the ships were forced to exit one by one. Outgunned, the Spanish met a dismal fate when the U.S. ships picked them off, ultimately sinking every vessel in the squadron (fig. 17).[55]

The painting represents the Santísima Trinidad platform of the Morro Castle, the highest level of the main structure, with a viewpoint overlooking the sea. It encompasses the sentry lookout and a crenelated wall and two cannons. These components are the same as those in Homer's 1885 drawings, but with the addition of a second

cannon. In the painting, the quiet, blue, nocturnal sky is lit by a partially shadowed moon at the upper left, and a searchlight's beam sweeps upward in the distance. The precise origin of the searchlight, aboard a U.S. vessel somewhere in the water, is obscured by a band of fog. The searchlight was one of the U.S. Navy's most advanced forms of technology in 1898. A glaring, white highlight appears on the crenelated wall to the left, a reflection of a second searchlight's beam that lights up the harbor's coastline. Homer painted the slice of visible land with tiny brushstrokes, depicting palm trees cast silver-gray in the night.

The searchlight was invented in 1893, and it was showcased in the World's Columbian Exposition in Chicago, where Homer may have seen it on display.[56] Acting Rear Admiral William T. Sampson (1840–1902) issued an order on June 8, 1898, to use searchlights on the harbor entrance from the U.S. American ships in the water.[57] The searchlight swept from one side of the harbor to the other, hunting for escaping Spanish vessels, but it also swung up to the sky and back around. Sampson described how

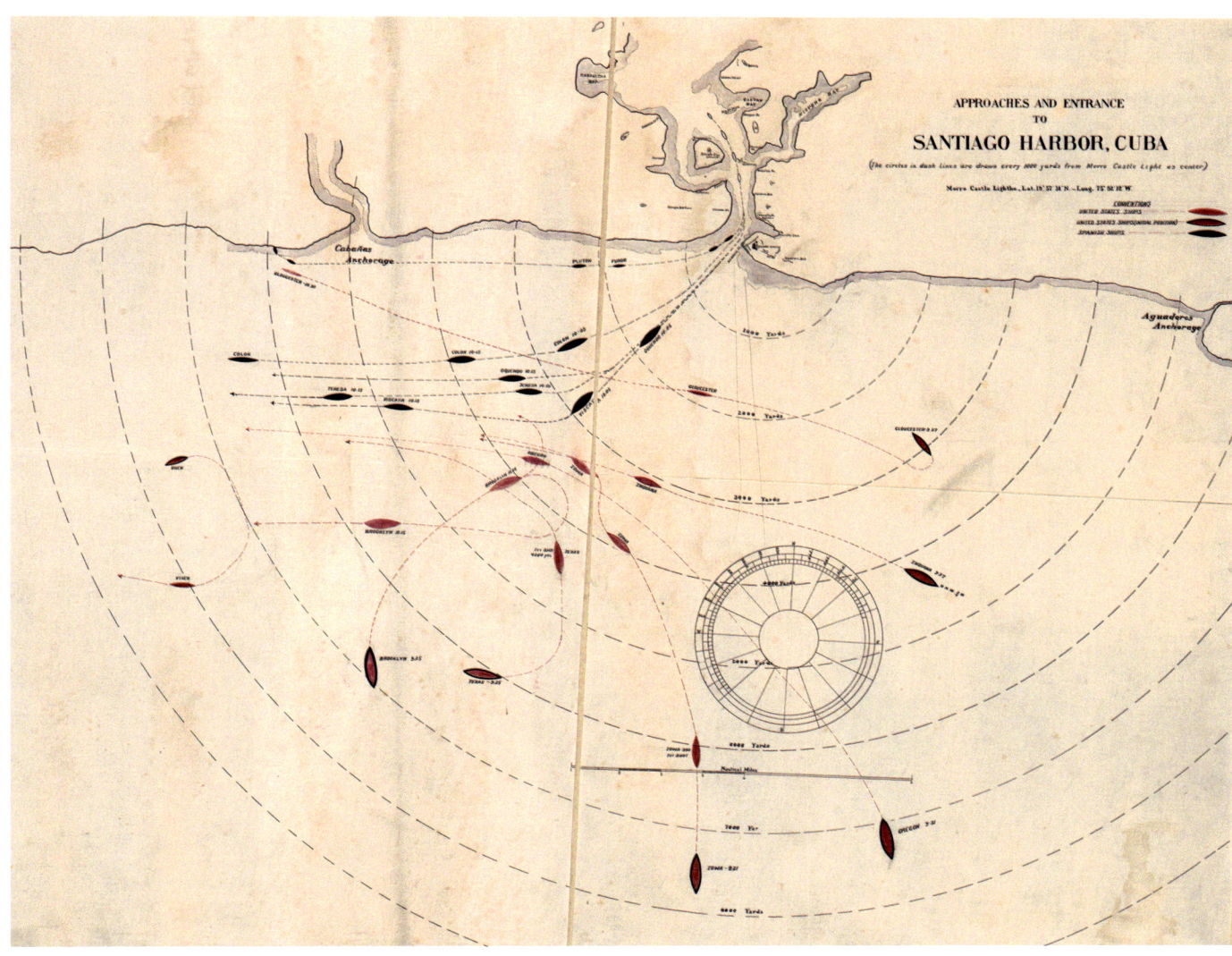

Fig. 17 *Approaches and Entrance to Santiago Harbor, Cuba*, United States Hydrographic Office, July 1898. Pen-and-ink map on tracing linen; 108.6 × 158.4 cm (42¾ × 62⅜ in.). Library of Congress, Geography and Map Division, Washington, DC

This map represents the U.S. vessels in red and the Spanish vessels in black. It traces how, during the battle, the USS *Brooklyn* tried to maneuver into position to pursue Spanish vessels, and in doing so, almost collided with the USS *Texas*. This incident was discussed during a Naval Board of Inquiry in 1901, and this map of the battle was likely submitted as evidence.

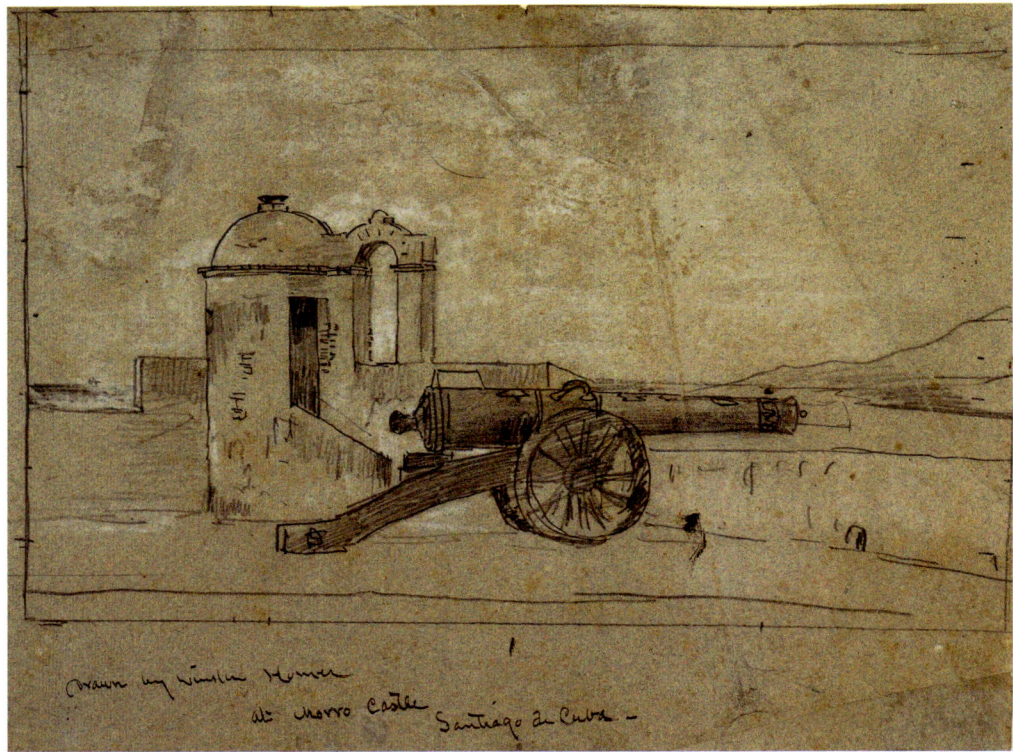

Fig. 18 Drawing, Study for *Searchlight Harbor Entrance, Santiago de Cuba*, Winslow Homer (1836–1910), c. 1901. Graphite and white chalk on gray paper; 12.4 × 20 cm (4⅞ × 7⅞ in.). Cooper Hewitt, Smithsonian Institution; gift of Charles Savage Homer Jr.

Fig. 19 *View of Santiago de Cuba,* Winslow Homer (1836–1910), 1885. Watercolor, pen, and black ink over graphite on wove paper; 27.3 × 50.5 cm (10¾ × 19⅞ in.). National Gallery of Art, Washington; bequest of Julia B. Engel

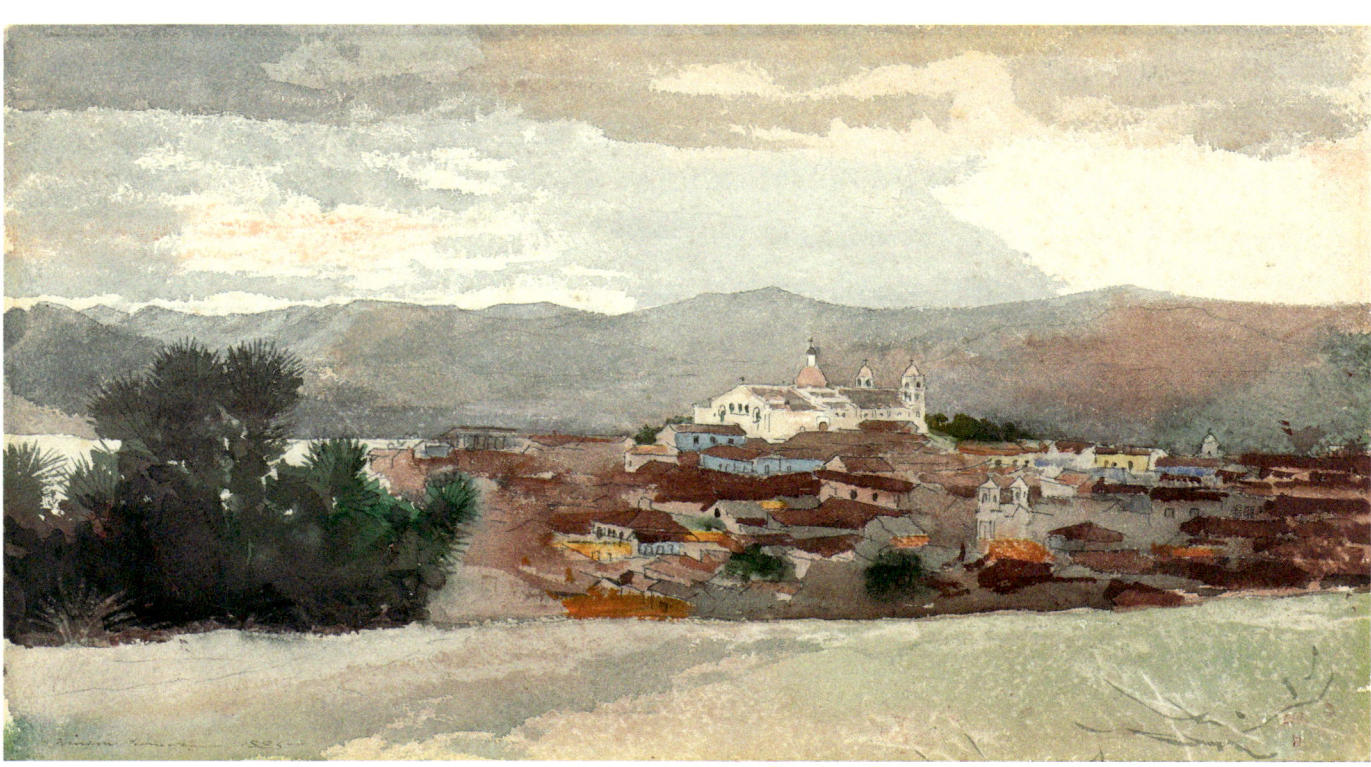

sailors learned to use it most efficiently in an 1899 article about the searchlight in the *Century Magazine,* a publication which Homer avidly read. Because it demonstrates a process of strategy involved in the use of the light, it is worth quoting at length:

> The search-light, as will be seen, was a very important factor of the blockade. At first everybody felt that it was desirable to explore the coast on each side of the harbor, and every ship acted for herself, and began in the same way, moving the search-light up and down the coast. But we found, after one or two trials, that where the beam of one light was intersected by the beam of the next we could see nothing. Moreover, the slightest movement of the pivot of the light made the beam change so rapidly that little could be made out. We therefore restricted the service to a single light at any one time, keeping it stationary and pointed exactly up the harbor, which it illuminated perfectly. . . . The scene on a moderately dark night was a very impressive one, the path of the searchlight having a certain massiveness, and the slopes and crown of the Morrow (*sic*) cliff being lighted up with the brilliancy of silver.[58]

Sampson's words must have made an impression on Homer, for he painted one beam of the searchlight turned to the sky, perhaps in mid-scan, and another casting from left to right, highlighting a silvery sliver of the Cuban coastline. Working with an earlier 1885 sketch of Santiago and Morro Castle, Homer may have folded the paper to experiment with lines casting upward to depict the beam searching the sky.[59] In doing so, Homer rendered a site he had visited as a tourist as a war scene (fig. 18). In the sketch, he folded the paper so that the lines from the top of the page open gradually toward the bottom, crossing the shaft of the left cannon. For the painting, however, he would reverse the lines, making them extend upward, shining from across the harbor. Writing about *Searchlight on Harbor Entrance, Santiago de Cuba* in early December 1901, Homer reported to Knoedler, that he was "in a most happy state of mind as I am hard at work on a *fine subject* that I can paint without any trouble right here in my studio."[60]

During his 1884–1885 visit to Santiago, Homer sought out the picturesque views, making watercolors of the city

from El Tivolí, with views of the Loma de Santa Ana, the highest point of the city (fig. 19). Although Santiago was populated by many Black Cubans, Homer avoided depicting any person in his watercolors—an omission made more obvious when comparing the studies to his watercolor scenes painted a month prior, in Nassau, the British colony in the Bahamas.[61]

Unlike the Bahamas, where there was comparatively little resistance to colonialism, Cuba was rife with political activity at the end of 1884. Cuban revolutionaries had failed to win their independence during the Ten Years' War (1868–1878), but in Santiago especially, they were still coordinating efforts to reinvigorate the revolutionary movement. At least three separate filibustering enterprises were organized, but none achieved a revolution.[62] Homer visited at a boiling point, the year before the Spanish abolished slavery in 1886. In a letter, the artist reflected upon the extreme tension between the Spanish and Cuban revolutionaries: "This is a red hot place full of soldiers. They have just condemned six men to be shot for landing with arms, & from all accounts they deserve it. The first day sketching I was ordered to move on until the crowds dispersed. Now I have a pass from the mayor 'forbidding all agents to interfere with me when following my profession.'"[63] Homer noted the presence of the Spanish soldiers in a watercolor of the Customs House, picturing innumerable troops and bayonet-tipped guns silhouetted through the architecture's arcade.

The men to whom Homer refers were a group organized by the Cuban insurgent Ramón Leocadio Bonachea (1845–1885). Bonachea was attempting to start a new revolt against the Spanish. During the Ten Years' War, he had reportedly fought in one hundred battles, turning to independent guerrilla fighting after peace was declared in 1878.[64] In 1883, he published a manifesto and spent time in New York City and Philadelphia, drumming up support for a revolution from Cuban Americans. While on the East Coast, U.S. newspapers heavily criticized him for making his proclamations from safe harbors, as well as for revealing his strategy to the Spanish, thereby endangering his compatriots.[65] Essentially, Bonachea was perceived to be squandering energy better put to supporting men like Gómez and Maceo, who were looking to fund their own expedition in 1884.[66] Homer's choice of phrase, "from all accounts," is telling, perhaps hinting at how supporters of Maceo and Gómez believed that Bonachea and his followers were wasting time and money. Bonachea's expedition met a dismal end when he and his fellow compatriots were imprisoned on January 13, 1885, in Morro Castle, and shot on March 7, 1885.[67] Notably, the failure of the insurrection marked the end of the use of political mobilization in the eastern region of Cuba until 1895.[68]

While in Cuba, Homer made watercolors reflecting the sun-bleached architecture and vibrant colors, including a mortar cannon, angled high as if to shoot its shell, next to the crenelated wall of Morro Castle (fig. 20).[69] The date "166x" is discernible in the rounded wall of the sentry lookout, next to the cannon.[70] Perhaps Homer added the date to remind himself that he was sketching on the Santísima Trinidad platform, which was built in the 1660s. But more notable is that Homer made this watercolor and one sketch of Morro Castle knowing that Bonachea and his men had been imprisoned in the castle, and were shot there.[71] And yet, the painting is devoid of any Cuban or Spanish presence.

In contrast to Homer, Menocal sought to mythologize and create a hero for the emerging nation of Cuba. Unlike Homer's depopulated Cuba, Menocal actively employed the figure, especially the Black figure of Antonio Maceo Grajales, and placed him at the heart of his imagined independent Cuba. Menocal sought to destabilize the era's accepted assumptions about race through loose interpretations of historical events, employing his paintings to create legends.

Menocal and Cuba, the "Raceless Nation"

Maceo became one of the most important Cuban icons of freedom and independence—thanks in part to Menocal. Unlike Homer, who painted the suspenseful moment before an event in *Searchlight on Harbor Entrance, Santiago de Cuba,* Menocal chose the height of the drama in *La muerte de Maceo.* This work demonstrates the power that art has in nation-building, especially as it was in service to the idea of Cuba as a "raceless nation."[72] A Black soldier from Oriente, Maceo had fewer opportunities for advancement than white or creole Cubans. Nevertheless, he rose to leadership, ultimately serving as second in command of the Cuban Liberation Army after Gómez. Wounded more than thirty times during his soldiering, Maceo became legendary, with a reputation for being invincible.[73] He also was cold-blooded, "uniting" the east by insisting that men

join with him—or die.[74] But on December 7, 1896, his forces were ambushed in Punta Brava, and Maceo, known by then as the "Bronze Titan," was killed.[75] Falling from his horse, he died quickly while his soldiers gathered around him in shock.

Menocal's mythical gathering of men was critical to the creation of the fabled status of Maceo as the savior of Cuba. Maceo's body is displayed in a pose reminiscent of the dead Christ in a lamentation, as in Tintoretto's *Descent from the Cross* (fig. 21). As in other history paintings depicting recent events, Menocal harnessed Christian iconography to convey a political message.[76] Appealing to the mostly Catholic population of Cuba, Menocal drew sympathy and reverence for this version of Maceo. But more importantly, he portrayed a figure whose élan helped inspire the *mambises* in this manner.

Menocal broke radically from convention when he pictured Maceo, a Black man, as a Christ-like figure. There are virtually no precedents. In doing so, Menocal provides an early visualization of the idea of the raceless nation. Promoting Cuba as a nation that came into being through a Black man's sacrifice, Menocal's painting reflects a movement that arose during the third War of Independence, in which Black soldiers and officers used the cause of freedom to reveal and object to what they perceived as racism within the nationalist movement.[77] By painting the hero of the Cuban revolution as a martyr and symbol of Cuban independence, Menocal employed his art in a two-pronged manner, emphasizing a Christ-like martyr and the birth of a new nation in one fell swoop.

From the 1890s on, elites worked to counter the powerful, albeit false, claim that the island's Black population and its recent history of slavery undermined its capacity for nationhood.[78] The Cuban independence movement took off when wealthy, white elites realized that revolution, encompassing equality for all races, was the only way to modernize the country and create a promising path forward. As in the Philippines, to successfully enact a revolution, Cuban leaders had to counter longstanding arguments against independence.[79] Radical intellectuals worked to revise the relationship between race and nation, as colonialist constructs had disregarded and oppressed people of color.

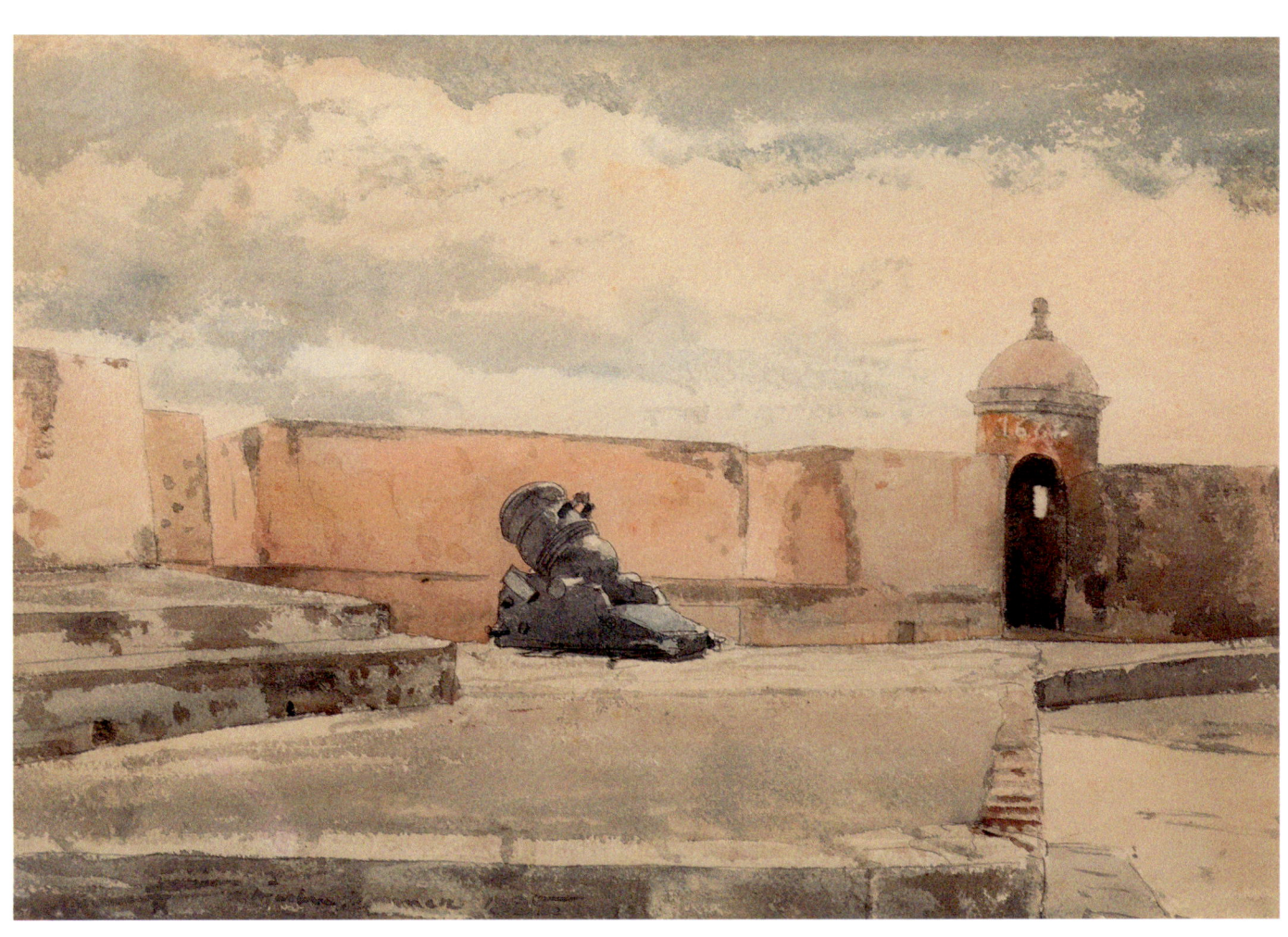

Three of the thirteen visible soldiers in *La muerte de Maceo* are clearly shown as Black. Although Menocal's contemporaries vehemently criticized him for failing to represent more Black soldiers, as many were on the scene, those who are pictured take active, intelligent soldiering roles.[80] In the composition's left middle ground, we see one man kneeling as he reloads his gun and glances over his shoulder at Maceo. Meanwhile, another man is seated on a horse behind Maceo, reaching down and grasping his shirt. Despite these representations, critics of the painting launched an investigation into the authenticity of its narrative. A jury from the Academy of San Alejandro ruled that the work was of sound technique and composition.[81] José Miró Argenter and Alberto Nodarse Bacallao concluded that the painting's account was legitimate, although asking them to judge the painting's accuracy was highly problematic because they were so clearly—and favorably—represented in the composition. Nevertheless, Menocal's commission was approved, and the work was accepted by the *Ayuntamiento*.[82] He was paid what the contract stipulated, $5,000 (or, almost $162,000 in 2022 dollars) in 1908. In 1915, Menocal sent the painting to the Pan-American Exposition in San Francisco, where it received the Silver Medal.[83]

At the time of Menocal's commission in 1906, the *Ayuntamiento* was led by Eugenio Léopoldo Aspiarzo.[84] The commission may have been influenced by the fact that Menocal's cousin, Mario García Menocal, was rising in politics.[85] Menocal most likely was charged by Aspiarzo to create a vision of an independent Cuba associated with Maceo, in time for the tenth anniversary of Maceo's death.[86] Significantly, this commission was on the heels of the U.S. intervention in Cuba. The occupation of the island, which lasted from 1906 through 1909, was overseen by military governor Charles Edward Magoon (1861–1920). During this time, there was no Cuban president, and after a contentious election, all Cuban government officials within Magoon's administration pledged their loyalty to the government of the United States.[87] Within the contexts of the U.S. occupation of Cuba in 1909, Menocal was also marking a watershed moment, when U.S. imperialism mingled with competing concepts of Cuban nationhood.[88]

Art and Subversion: Forging A New Visual World Order

For both Homer and Menocal, life, death, and violence were important themes throughout their careers. Homer

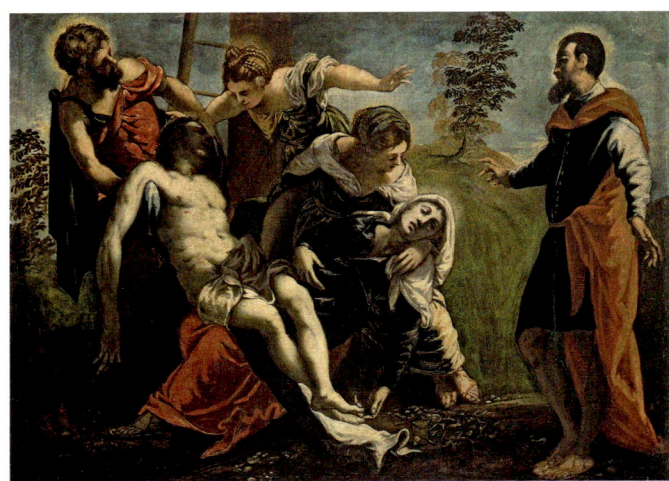

Fig. 21 *Descent from the Cross*, Tintoretto (1518–1594), c. 1547–1549. Oil on canvas; 91 × 122 cm (35¹³⁄₁₆ × 48 in.). Kunsthistorisches Museum, Vienna

deeply ruminated on the War of 1898, and his interest was in large part driven by experiences of witnessing Civil War battles. Although he was not a sentimentalist, and usually divested himself from politics, it is almost certain that Homer considered the signing of the oath of allegiance to the United States as both a political and a moral declaration. Similarly, Menocal, a combat veteran, deployed his battle experiences in the service of a raceless new nation. Through an homage to the courage of the *mambí*, as well as to key figures and locations, Menocal laid the pictorial foundations for the next stage of Cuban nationalism—one that would endure a neocolonial United States.

Together, Homer's and Menocal's art presents a more complete narrative of the U.S. and Cuban conflicts. Yet the two artists had different objectives: Homer supported U.S. empire-building, whereas Menocal devoted himself to the emergence of the Cuban nation. Both remained loyal to their chosen cause: Homer to the United States and its imperial project, and Menocal to the transformation of Cuba into an independent nation. Homer supported the expansion of the U.S. territory beyond the bounds of the continent, and Menocal sought to undermine both the Spanish colonial regime and the subsequent neocolonial U.S. government. To achieve their divergent goals, the two artists' compositional strategies could not be more different. Homer presented a moment before the decisive action. Menocal focused on the resolution, and preferred history painting to strengthen the visualization of Cuban nationalism. Menocal also focused on the legendary, if antiquated, technology of machete warfare, whereas Homer was drawn to forms of superior sight, like the telescopic lens and the searchlight.

Both Menocal and Homer depicted scenes of war that help us comprehend the significance of harnessing powerful icons to create national myths and legends, how empires and nations depend on military technology, and the role that race played in the wars of 1898. *La muerte de Maceo* proposes a national iconography and a visual language for a national consciousness. Menocal helped invert the position of the colonized when he created an icon of independence, whereas Homer's rendering of the chilling violence of naval warfare undermined the glory of the era's normally triumphant narrative of U.S. imperialism. In Cuba, Homer elided race completely, creating a marked absence that reveals his discomfort with Black colonial subjects organizing what would eventually be a massive resistance in the Cuban Army of Liberation. Conversely, Menocal elevated the Black soldier to create an emblem of martyrdom—one in service to the nation of Cuba. War shaped the careers of both Menocal and Homer. In turn, both artists created work that responded to imperialism's harsh realities but also alludes to the forces involved in nationalism and empire-building that were much greater than themselves.

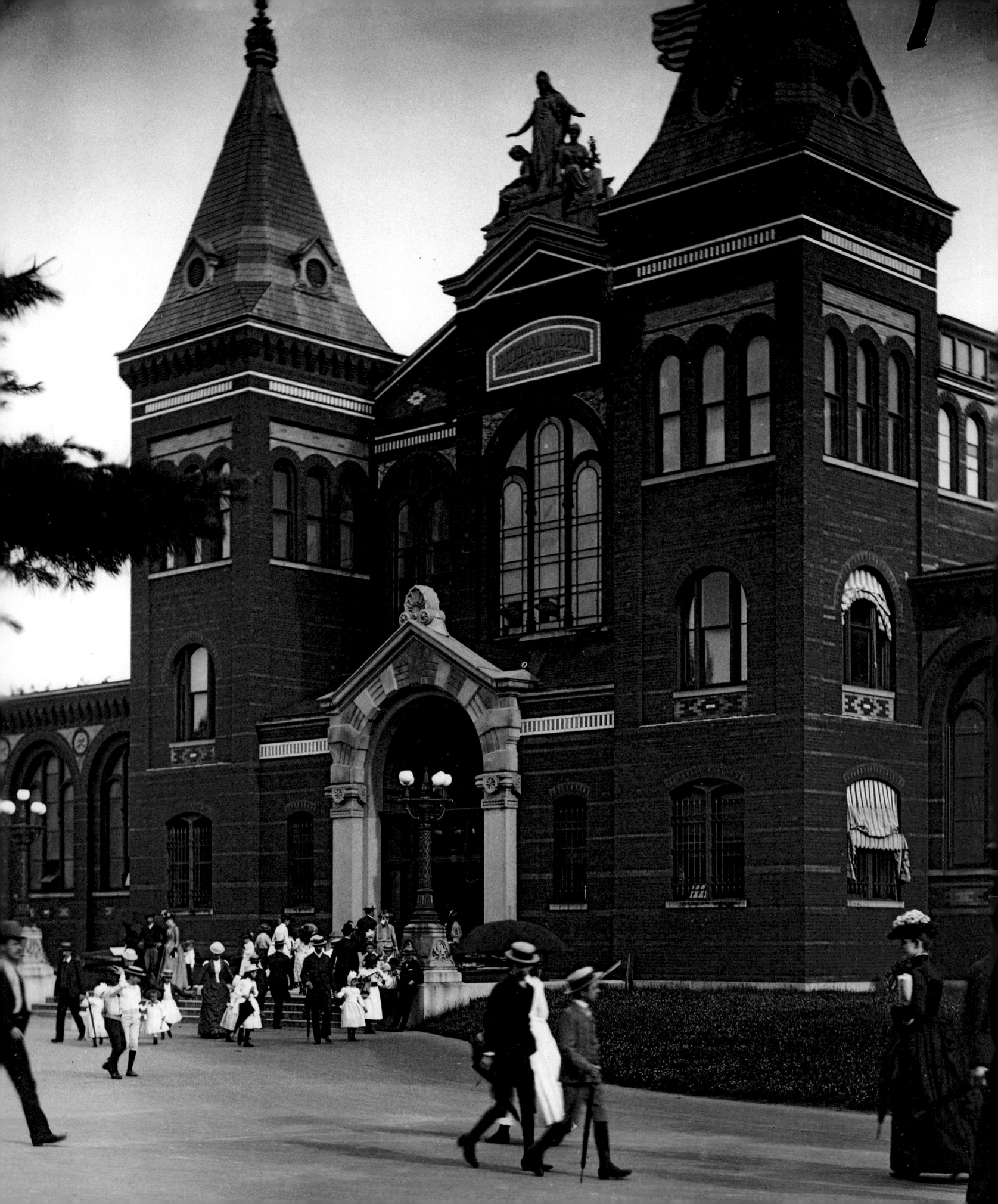

New Possessions

Colonial Curios, Trophies, Weapons, and Museum Collections from the Philippine-American War

PAUL A. KRAMER

From a certain angle, the vast collection of Philippine armaments that anthropologist Herbert W. Krieger meticulously gathered for his 1926 publication, *The Collection of Primitive Weapons and Armor of the Philippine Islands in the United States National Museum* (1926), was a kind of treasure trove (fig. 1). The 120-page book was published as part of the Smithsonian Institution's *Bulletin* series, which provided ample room for the curator of ethnology to document the National Museum's extensive collection of weapons from the largest overseas U.S. colony.[1] Krieger crafted a scholarly description and analysis for each object. He also created a comprehensive reference guide for staff working with "the many excellent Philippine weapons collections throughout the United States" so that they might classify and identify their own holdings.[2] His interest was also likely shaped by his own earlier work with the U.S. colonial education system in the Philippines, as an instructor of economics and commercial geography at the Bureau of Education's School of Commerce in Manila in the early 1910s.

Krieger systematically registered the individuals who had donated items.[3] For instance, the crossbow entry reads: "Collected by Gen. Jacob Kline, United States Army. Cat. 313947, U.S.N.M."[4] The majority of these donors were active or former U.S. military personnel who had served in the Philippines. But the guide provided almost no other background information about how the weapons collections had come to exist. Krieger noted that most of the museum's Philippine weapons were "recent accessions," suggesting that the donors had kept the objects until their retirements or deaths.[5] He also registered a correlation between the collections and the colonial-imperial wars of 1898–1902. Remarkably, he depicted these linkages in the passive voice, refusing to acknowledge any individual agency or intent behind their acquisition. "Under the stimulus aroused by the Spanish-American War and the native insurrection in the Philippines," he wrote, "additional accessions of Philippine weapons and armor began to arrive at the National museum."[6]

Amid dense descriptions of ornamental knives and metalcraft, there were passing references to a "punitive expedition" and the "invasion and occupation of the Philippine Islands by the United States troops."[7] Overall, the

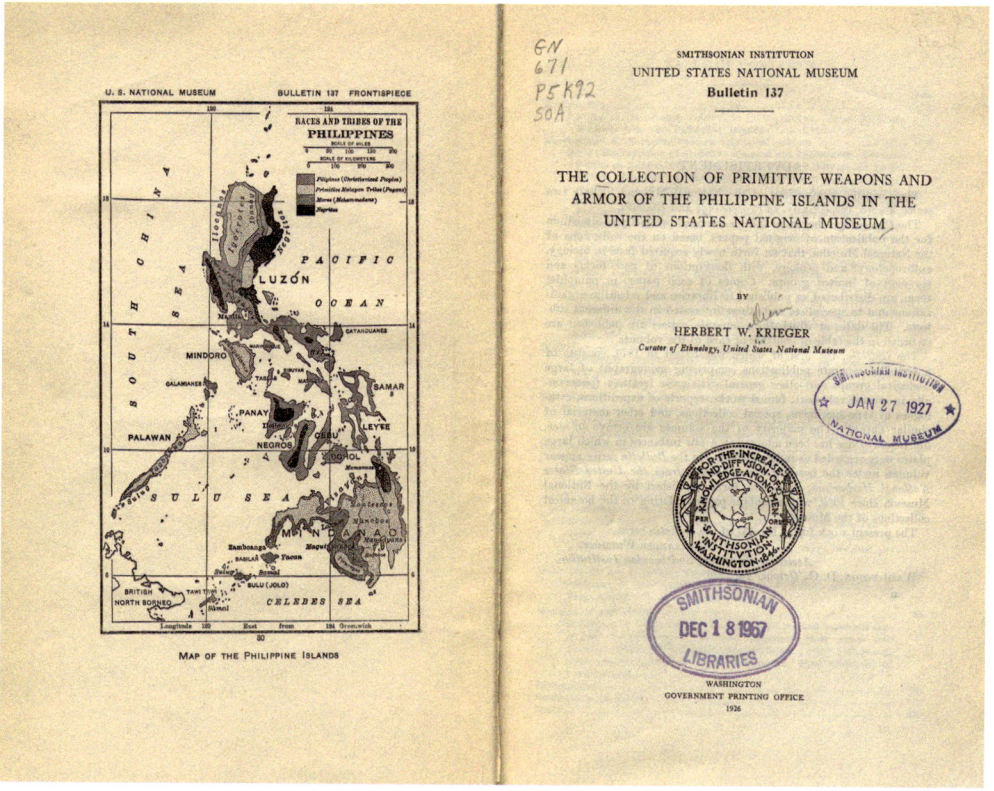

Fig. 1 Frontispiece and title page for Herbert W. Krieger, *The Collection of Primitive Weapons and Armor of the Philippine Islands in the United States National Museum.* Washington, DC: Government Printing Office, 1926. Smithsonian Libraries and Archives

colonial-imperial origins of the collection did not seem to have interested Krieger, apart from the sheer geographic reach of the U.S. military that had made the museum's wide-ranging collection possible. "As the field of operations of the Army was widespread throughout the islands of the Philippine Archipelago," Krieger wrote, "it was possible to include in the collections weapons from those sections where the natives were especially adept in the metal crafts." It had been the "interest and cooperation" of U.S. Army officers that gave the museum's weapons collection its "comprehensive and representative nature."[8]

How was it that the Smithsonian Institution, and other museums in the metropolitan United States, came to possess large-scale collections from the Philippines in the first place? Answering this question requires reconstructing the ways U.S. military personnel, but also travelers, tourists, and museum collectors gathered materials from the Philippines, how they used them, and how they invested them with meaning. Museums, including the Smithsonian's United States National Museum, sent out dedicated expeditions with the goal of collecting Philippine artifacts, displaying them, making them available for scholarly studies like Krieger's, and celebrating the newly

expansive power of the United States. They also acquired materials from individual collectors directly tied to a violent and exploitative colonial project. That Krieger felt so little need to provide background on the military and colonial dimensions of the artifacts' origins suggests the triumph of a certain kind of imperial sublimation: brutal, racialized conquest successfully refined into erudite, social-scientific knowledge.

Probing deeper than Krieger's account of the collection's origins, this essay responds and hopes to add to recent and ongoing efforts to "decolonize" museums with respect to their collection objects, their interpretive frameworks, and their evolving relationships to shifting national and transnational publics.[9] These questions have involved reckoning with museums' national and imperial histories: uncovering and reflecting critically on the ways that museums were (and, perhaps, remain) directly linked to originating projects of racialized, colonial violence and exploitation, especially during the era of "high imperialism" from the late nineteenth to the mid-twentieth century. At the same time, this essay contributes to scholarship on the material culture of U.S. colonialism in the Philippines and on scholarship on the U.S.-facing cultural histories of the Philippine-American War.[10] And it hopes to provide an early twentieth-century case study of the intersections of U.S. military-imperial power and tourist economies and cultures, studies of which have focused so far on the mid-to-late twentieth century.[11] This preliminary study draws from newspaper accounts and the archives of the Smithsonian Institution and hopes to facilitate future studies that might draw, for example, on sources such as U.S. military and museum archives. Many more histories remain to be told of Filipino producers, artisans, vendors, collectors, and intellectuals, and their relationships to colonial collecting. Through such work, historians stand to learn more about how exactly such materials "began to arrive" in the United States.

The Hunt for Curios: U.S. Military Personnel in the Philippines

Throughout their campaigns in the Philippines, U.S. military personnel voraciously pursued what were called "curios." Their hunger for these items was detailed by a reporter in Manila in late February 1899, just weeks into the start of the Philippine-American War: "If everyone carries back to America the quantities of native embroidery, silver-work and antique arms that they hope to find," the writer observed, "the town and country will be stripped of its treasures." It spoke to this demand that U.S. soldiers had been stationed at Manila's Intramuros district to keep their compatriots from seizing valuable artifacts. "It requires the constant presence of soldiering," the reporter continued, "to hold back the eager throng of venturesome Americans who would, each and all, like to put the old walled city and all its treasures in their pockets, if such a feat were possible."[12] Policymakers encouraged such collecting and made it easier for soldiers to ship their acquisitions home, by allowing them to use the military's mail system and not charging them import tariffs on goods reported for personal use.[13]

Americans in the Philippines were apparently most enthralled with the prospects of acquiring valuable antiques from the Spanish colonial era, especially weapons. One reporter noted that it would take resourcefulness and determination to find these objects, often held in churches, and to convince clergy to part with them. There was only one place in Manila where "the finest specimens of native arms extant" were stacked away: the dark, moldy interior of the arsenal of Fort Santiago. The arms were "begrimed and rusting, and their wooden and leather

seats are warped and musty and falling apart," but they "could not be bought for all the American Eagles in Manila." Still, he prophesied, it was only a matter of time before the United States took possession of them. "They are the prizes Uncle Sam claims for his share of the Manila campaign, and someday the eyes of the connoisseur may feast upon them, properly arranged and historically tabulated, in the Smithsonian Institution in Washington."[14]

The unloading of soldiers' accumulated goods featured prominently in press coverage of their returns to the United States. A San Francisco reporter detailed the possessions of the returning California infantry in 1899. "In addition to the eight-inch shell from the *Olympia* that tore a hole through a big church at Cavite and the quaint little red painted Filipino gun carriage and the weather and service-stained regimental colors," there were "great solid wood circular shields curiously carved by hand and some long narrow ones wondrously hewn from single pieces of hardwood for protection against spears and knives." There were "bows and arrows and machetes and bolos old rifles and spears and a fine old cannon and odds and ends of other things not yet unpacked."[15]

When the USS *Raleigh* landed in New York in April 1899 and entertained an estimated 2,500 guests onboard, the sailors "turned to showing the visitors their collections of curios, which consisted of almost everything from a blunderbuss to a bird's nest," according to the *New York Times*. At one point, Seaman John Gunnison, identified as the "comedian of the crew," called those assembled to order, mounted a cracker box, and read out a poem entitled "The Curio Fiends" that accurately described and gently mocked U.S. soldiers' and sailors' rapacious collecting habits in the Philippines.[16] The poem begins:

> They've got flags and scraps of iron,
> Tomahawks and bay'nets, too,
> Soldiers' pants without the linin',
> 'Nother's got a woman's shoe.[17]

The first stanza suggests that the hunger for weapons and "curios" devolved into indiscriminate plundering. Yet when carefully selected objects from the Philippines were displayed back home, they often carried far more serious messages. The playful, comedic, and highly public character of this poem—first, as gleeful performance, and second as recounted in a newspaper story—made clear that, far from their being regarded as anything surprising or inappropriate about U. S. soldiers' capture of "curios," it was seen as a fully expected and unserious feature of colonial warfare in the islands, and the occasion for metropolitan celebration.

Making Sense of Philippine Curios and Trophies

Soldiers and others used and assigned meanings to these items in several ways. These objects were meant to reflect and physically embody soldiers' records of service, reminding community members and policymakers of society's obligations to veterans. Displaying Filipino weapons, for example, conveyed both the fearsomeness of the enemy as well as the magnitude of the U.S. soldiers' sacrifices. They were also meant to help create and anchor the veteran community. Upon the return of one unit, a reporter observed that "[r]egime curios and trophies of war are not lacking to form an interesting collection of relics for future reunions."[18] Veterans' organizations did indeed exhibit "Philippine curios" at their reunions; in February 1903, the California chapter of the Army of the Philippines initiated an exhibition of curios "for the purpose of raising funds to place the society on a firm foundation."[19] In such contexts, the distinction between "curios" and "trophies," usually blurred, could become meaningful. Whereas the former—acquired by any means—connoted beautiful or unusual objects gathered to satisfy one's curiosity and draw attention, the latter evoked military, masculine prowess and triumph; the term referred to things that had been taken by legitimate and valorous force. Trophies included symbols of captured Filipino power: weapons or flags taken from Filipino soldiers, for example, or, in one case, "a small ebony cane with a fanciful head, a mark of office carried by the insurgent president of the town of Libertad on the island of Samar."[20]

Acquiring objects from the Philippines often meant literal disarmament and symbolic disempowerment, especially when these items were weapons. Whether arrayed on tables in community lecture halls or enclosed in museum glass, the display of captured weapons forcefully conveyed the neutralization of Filipinos' capacities to resist U.S. conquest and colonization (fig. 2). Indeed, Krieger's descriptions of the ways people from various Filipino cultures used the weapons, which emphasized cruelty and ferocity, contributed to this larger discourse, even as he skirted how they were acquired.[21] This message may have been especially pertinent given Filipino forces'

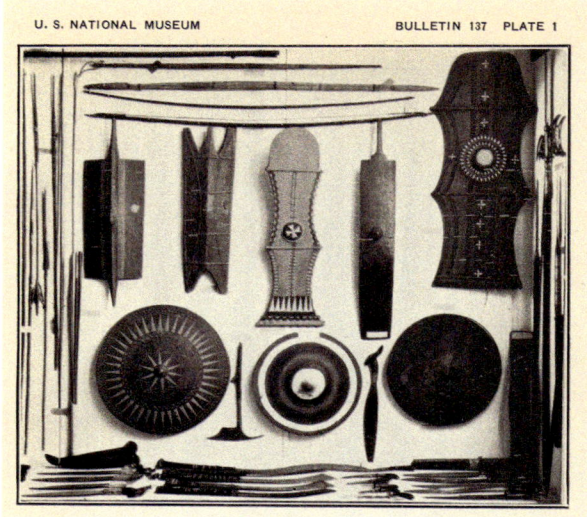

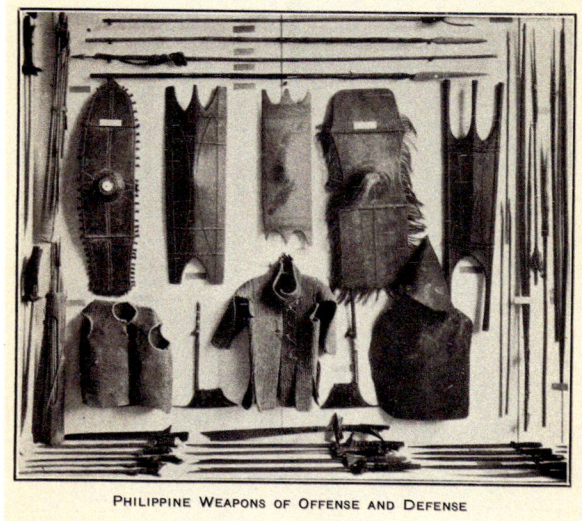

Fig. 2 Plate 1 in Herbert W. Krieger, *The Collection of Primitive Weapons and Armor of the Philippine Islands in the United States National Museum.* Washington, DC: Government Printing Office, 1926. Smithsonian Libraries and Archives

This plate represents what Krieger called "Philippine weapons of offense and defense." Displayed in museum cases, however, they no longer represent a threat. At the top left, there is a blowgun, created by the Moro peoples of Jolo or Suolu, that Frank Hilder acquired in the Philippines. It was on view at the Pan-American Exposition in Buffalo, New York, in 1901.

successful use of guerrilla tactics, and the difficulties U.S. commanders and public officials faced in making good on their repeated assurances that victory was imminent. The transmutation of a weapon into a curio or "war relic" was frequently accompanied by descriptions of its

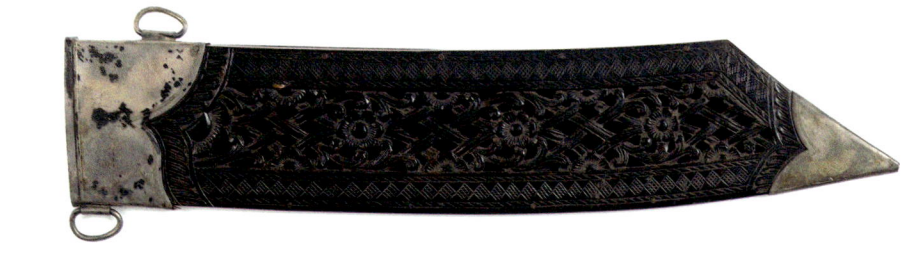

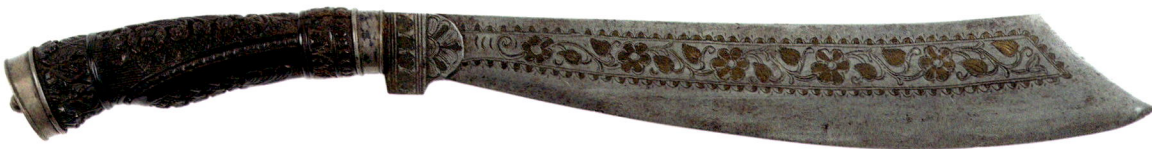

Fig. 3 *Borong Bolo Type and Sheath.* Steel blade with horn handle and sheath; Scabbard: 6.5 × 32.8 × 1.5 cm (2½ × 13 × ½ in.). Blade with handle: 5 × 45.5 × 3 cm (2 × 18 × 1 in.) Collected by Frank Hilder and displayed at the Pan-American Exposition in Buffalo, New York, in 1901. National Museum of Natural History, Smithsonian Institution

previous threat. For instance, the collection of Prof. George Becker of the U.S. Geological Survey was said to contain "an unusually fine lot of krises, campilans, larongs, and terciadas," as well as extremely sharp wooden bolos; according to the *Washington Post*, "hundreds of American soldiers who served in the Philippines can testify to the murderous character of these wooden swords."[22] Becker's wife later donated a Moro kris and sheath with a "three-wave blade" and "deeply carved base" to the U.S. National Museum (fig. 3).[23]

Such bladed weapons were abundant in U.S. private collections. The *Detroit Free Press* claimed that "[n]early every American officer or soldier who has stationed there has secured at least one or two specimens of native weapons."[24] Lieutenant Claude N. Feamster of the 4th U.S. Infantry was said to have the most extensive trove, including some seventy weapons, "nearly every one of which is of a different pattern"; practically every weapon in his collection had apparently been "captured in battle in some part of the Philippines."[25] Another extensive collection of "various types of cutting, slashing, and decapitating weapons" was gathered by one Beckwith Hawkins, interestingly identified by the *Chicago Daily Tribune* not as a soldier who happened to be collecting, but "a young Georgian collector at present serving with the army in the Philippines."[26] Lieutenant J. H. Allen, executive officer of the Presidio General Hospital, stressed that, rather than purchasing his "remarkably complete collection of knives" in the Philippines, he had "personally gathered most of the implements, finding many on or near battlefields on which he had fought, taking others from the bodies of dead savages."[27]

Bladed weapons were discussed in highly anthropological terms. Collectors, along with newspaper and magazine articles that publicized their holdings, arrayed various blades with detailed, often admiring descriptions of their shape and ornamentation, uses, manufacture, and social meanings, particularly in terms of gradations of status and rank. "Through all ages the implements of war of the people faithfully reflected their characteristics and habits," noted one paper. "Historians find in ancient weapons which have withstood the ravages of time the means of gaining knowledge available from no other source."[28] Soldiers' weapons collections became the basis for major museum collections. Hawkins sold his collection to the U.S. National Museum; he and Paul E. Beckwith, then curator of historical collections, had "for months applied themselves to the study of the extensive lore of these weapons." Beckwith then presented the "correct classifications of these weapons" for "the first time in history" to the American Anthropological Association.[29] The curator himself donated items from the Philippines to the museum, including a bamboo mouth harp, acquired at the 1904 Louisiana Purchase Exhibition in St. Louis, and a ceramic earring.[30]

Curios from the Philippines also functioned as tokens that granted their U.S. holders the power to speak authoritatively on the Philippines and Filipinos, especially when it came to the all-important question of their "civilization" and prospects for "self-government."[31] When U.S. soldiers, tourists, and lecturers decoded the objects for family members, newspaper editors, and public audiences, embedded in narratives of travel, war, and adventure, the items played a talismanic role in conveying the authenticity of their experiences and the legitimacy of their knowledge, across domains that stretched far beyond the objects themselves. Take, for example, a lecture series on the "Incidents of the Campaign in the Philippines," given by Captain John Bordman Jr., previously of the 26th U.S. Volunteers, in his hometown of Concord Junction, Massachusetts, in September 1901. Bordman, who appeared in an officer's uniform, seems to have focused on his rise through the ranks, capture by insurgents, and supervision of an execution; the talk was "listened to very attentively," according to the Boston newspaper that covered it. That night, Association Hall had been decorated with a "large and varied collection of guns, lances, bolos, krises, daggers, relics and curios," and the "doors were open early to give all an opportunity to examine the war implements of the Filipinos."[32]

But interpreting objects from the Philippines was not always this straightforward. Accounts of the processes used to create daggers, swords, and shields; their uses and histories; and the meanings assigned to them by their Filipino makers implied other, non-U.S. authorities. Admitting that one's knowledge had come from Filipino interlocutors perhaps diminished the power of one's own direct, unmediated perception and experiences, and revealed an unsettling dependence on "native" ways of knowing, the disparaging of which was central to arguments for U.S. colonial empire. Such citations complicated the possessor-speakers' efforts to impose themselves as the sole intermediaries between metropole and colony, ones anchored within metropolitan interests and viewpoints.

And it was, of course, possible to acquire and possess objects without understanding them. Not for nothing were curios often identified as strange, or "queer." One headline ran, "Queer Things Among Them," and went on to describe "an interesting collection of curios" held by a Detroit woman. Her collection—it was not clear how she had obtained it—included a bamboo mouth harp "unlike anything ordinarily seen."[33] Similarly, one reporter found himself fascinated and bewildered by the cargo of a ship newly docked at the New York pier that had just returned from the islands. "Philippine bamboos, beautiful screens of closely woven basket work folding together in many leaves, hammocks, screens for water jars, native fishing and pleasure boats and all sorts of queer things are stowed on board," he wrote.[34] Where Americans used the

term "picturesque" to frame colonial realities, it conveyed a confident, self-satisfied sense that their existing perceptual categories stood fast even in environments they registered as different; potentially strange and threatening worlds obligingly conformed to pre-existing templates. "Queer" did the opposite, flagging the uneasy places where one's power to possess was unmatched by one's power to know, places where easy, familiar categories broke down, and new and elusive ones—"native" ones—might be needed.

Looting and Anti-Colonialist Politics

Soon after hostilities between U.S. and Filipino forces began, American soldiers wrote home to their families and hometown newspapers, describing abuses and atrocities that quickly found their way into the anti-colonialist press and sparked broader, public debates about the conduct and morality of the war. Looting by U.S. forces featured prominently in many of these letters. One of them, written by Guy R. Osbourne of the Navy to his father and published in the Oregon Statesman in April 1900, told of a landing party from the gunboat USS Paragua at Nueva Caceres that had looted the town; Osbourne detailed the loot that had been taken. When the Navy Department received an outraged letter with the clipping, it forwarded Osborne's letter to the commander of the Paragua, who denied the charge; upon their return to the ship, he said, the landing party had been inspected and "found to have with them only an old Winchester shotgun and a few war bolos." Osborne, speaking before witnesses, now claimed "he had endeavored to make a good story rather than tell the plain truth and the facts."[35]

The most charged controversies erupted over word that U.S. soldiers had looted Catholic churches in the Philippines of sacred items, especially vestments and vessels, as part and parcel of a broader mistreatment and desacralization of church property. This exploded with the publication, on the cover of Collier's Weekly in September 1899, of a photograph of U.S. soldiers setting up telegraph lines inside a captured church in Caloocan, which they were using as their headquarters (fig. 4). Captioned "Respectfully Referred to the Secretary of War," the photograph's accompanying description specified that telegraph wires had been attached to the tabernacle and that a captain present at the scene carried a cigarette.[36]

During protest and investigation by organized Catholic groups in several cities, evidence surfaced that suggested U.S. soldiers had looted churches in the Philippines.[37] Activists cited one letter by Robert H. Knight, Company D, 12th U.S. Infantry in Manila, which described U.S. soldiers rummaging through church vaults in search of treasure. "The worst of all is in the ruins of the Guadalupe Church," Knight's letter read, "in the vaults where the dead are buried. The volunteers broke them open, pulled out the bodies, broke open the coffins, and robbed the dead. You can see the skull where the feet ought to be, and the ribs all mixed up. One body lies there half pulled out of the vault, and just where the hands crossed on the breast was all poked over looking for gold rings and crosses."[38]

The Metropolitan Truth Society, an organization dedicated to countering anti-Catholic prejudice and abuse, claimed in September 1899 that it possessed substantial evidence along these lines; the Society had been

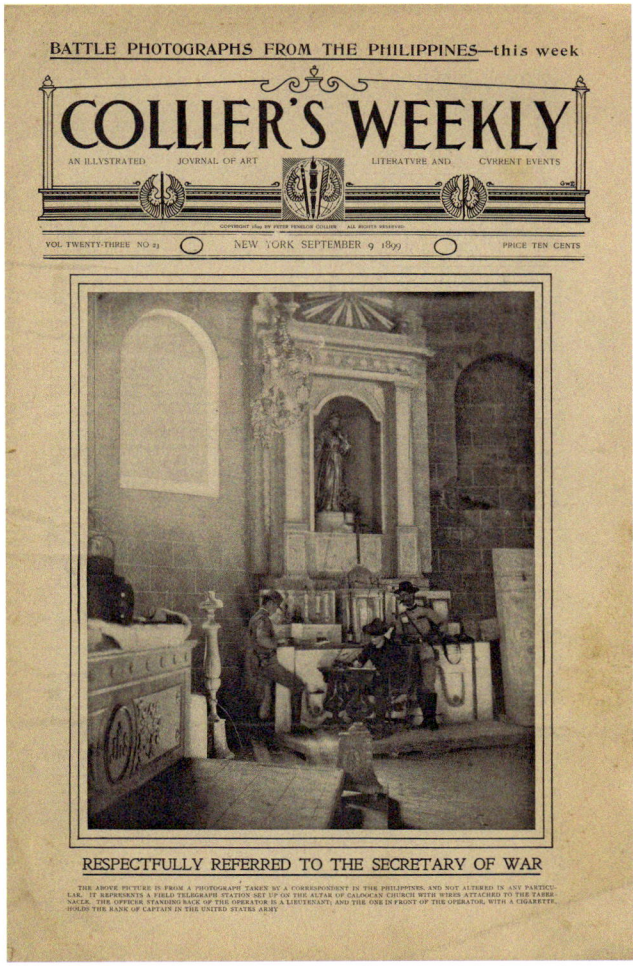

Fig. 4 Cover of *Collier's Weekly*, September 9, 1899. Private collection

"diligently gathering and classifying all the evidence concerning alleged desecrations and outrages upon churches in the Philippines and the thefts of the priestly vestments and sacred vessels, and their use insulting and indecent ways," and had "a great mass of data carefully arranged and fully authenticated."[39] While not necessarily tied to questions of looting, investigators claimed that sacred church items from the Philippines had been "publicly exhibited" in inappropriate ways in New York, Chicago, San Francisco, St. Paul, Minneapolis, and Omaha.[40]

It is difficult to pinpoint the scope of U.S. soldiers' possession of church property. Indeed, some returning U.S. soldiers had Catholic religious objects in their possession or had sent such items home to their families through the mail. According to the *Cincinnati Enquirer*, in September 1900, a young man in Elkhart, Indiana, received from a brother serving in the Philippines a "valuable package of curios which, from the sacredness in which they are held by the Roman Catholic Church, rarely get without the precincts of the order." It included "two richly gold embroidered vestments used by the priesthood, a silver figure about six inches long, which seems to have been taken from a crucifix, a rosary, a large iron key of distinctly foreign make, probably for the outer or the tabernacle door of the church where the other articles were secured." The newspaper claimed the items' authenticity was assured by the fact that the package carrying them bore "the approval of a commanding officer."[41]

The soldiers' defenders claimed they had not stolen such goods from churches themselves; they had purchased them from vendors, who had acquired them, presumably, from actual looters. The original theft was commonly blamed on Filipino revolutionaries or Chinese workers, and not U.S. soldiers.[42] Market transactions, apparently, had ethically purifying power when it came to the status of previously stolen goods changing hands. The scandal over the alleged looting of churches died down after November 1899, when numerous prominent Catholic leaders in the United States spoke out publicly to defend U.S. forces and deny charges of looting as the work of bragging soldiers and treasonous war critics, even as they insisted that looting churches was standard Filipino troop conduct.[43]

Perhaps the most striking element of this brief, sharp, ultimately fleeting debate was what was mostly not at stake. Public debates about whether individual U.S. soldiers were looting Philippine churches or homes, and whether the army disciplined them, occasionally spilled over into broader questions about what the United States was doing in the Philippines. But much more frequently, they remained tightly bounded to specific charges and the military's institutional response to them.

And as much as this controversy kept public criticism of U.S. colonial violence alive, this narrowing arguably represented a victory for the advocates of U.S. colonial empire to the extent that issues of military means supplanted that of imperial ends. After all, some anti-colonialists in the Philippines, and in the United States, saw the violent taking of the Philippines by the United States itself as an act of looting, on a geopolitical scale.[44] Colonialists replied that, to the contrary, there had been a diplomatic settlement with Spain, a deal had been struck, and the United States had paid $20 million for Philippine sovereignty, fair and square.[45]

Objects in Motion: From the Philippines to International Expositions and Museum Galleries

In addition to the walls of homes, offices, and veterans' halls, soldiers and their families saw museums as possible repositories for their trophies and curios, as did many enterprising museum officials. For donors, this represented a way to contribute to hometown institutions and, perhaps, to garner public acclaim. For curators, it was a way to expand their holdings, attract visitors drawn especially to novel and newsworthy acquisitions, and enhance the prestige of their institutions as geographically expansive and diverse, educationally enriching, and contributing positively to the national and imperial interest.

That the Smithsonian Institution found itself vying for a position as a hub of colonial-imperial research was not surprising. It had, after all, been closely tied to the United States' imperial, settler-colonial dispossession of Native peoples, especially through the capture and study of their material culture, and sponsorship of evolutionary theories that rationalized imperial violence against them in the name of inevitable historical progress.[46] Acting chief of the Bureau of American Ethnology W. J. McGee (1853–1912) was frustrated in his efforts to get the phrase "and other aborigines of American territory" added to his institution's mandate, along with an additional appropriation.[47] But by mid-1899, the resourceful, well-connected McGee had found a backdoor to Smithsonian collecting in the Philippines. Under the auspices of the U.S.

Government Exhibit for the upcoming Pan-American Exposition in Buffalo, New York, he would have collectors assemble a Philippine collection which, after the event was over, would pass into the hands of the U.S. National Museum (fig. 5).[48] McGee tasked Colonel Frank Hilder (1836–1901), the bureau's clerk and "ethnologic translator," then in his early sixties, for the role.[49]

Hilder, a former British Army officer, journeyed to the Philippines in early 1900, hired an assistant named Penoyer Sherman, and began extensive travel, negotiating and haggling for items. But even with promises of support from the U.S. military, he met innumerable obstacles. Transportation, especially to remote areas, was limited and costly; Hilder found himself more dependent on urban markets in Manila than he'd hoped. The war had devastated production of the very agricultural and industrial goods Hilder had hoped to display before potential American investors, importers, and consumers. And it was dangerous to collect out in the countryside, where the conflict was raging. Regarding herbs that Hilder hoped to acquire, storekeepers told him that "the natives had refused to collect them, on account of the great danger of being shot." During their travels, more than one of the Filipinos that Hilder and Sherman bought from were captured or killed. But Hilder's greatest obstacle may have been the U.S. military itself. The U.S. Army and Navy had directed their officers to collect for the War Department. And beyond that, there were what Sherman called the "curio crazy volunteers." Ordinary soldiers' frenzy of curio-buying was driving up prices, but so too were hundreds of army officers' wives who, Sherman said, were "collecting without rhyme or reason."[50] The officers of the U.S. military police, responsible for confiscating insurgent goods, were each "running his own collection, and so there is nothing on hand!"[51]

Nevertheless, Hilder's and Sherman's efforts bore fruit, and the result was what one newspaper called "a representative exhibit of the manufactures, trades, arts, tools, domestic utensils, costumes, weapons, woods and industries of the islands" that consisted of roughly fifteen thousand items. It contained models of Filipinos' houses and boats, agricultural and fishing implements, "photographs showing native manners and costumes," and an array of musical instruments "from the very crudest made of bamboo, to the finest product of the workshops of Manila."[52]

Hilder also gathered much-desired materials related to the war itself, especially captured weapons taken from

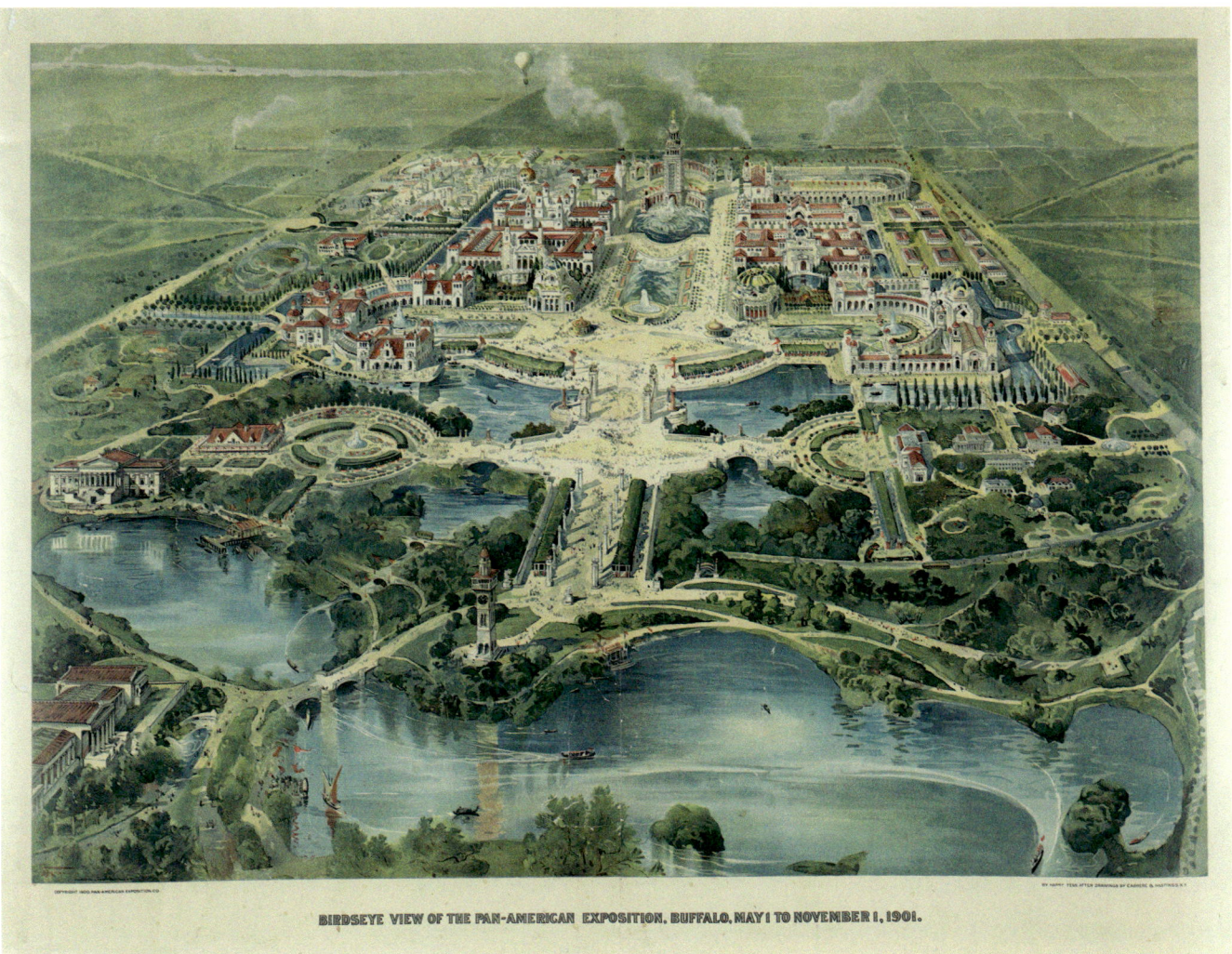

BIRDSEYE VIEW OF THE PAN-AMERICAN EXPOSITION, BUFFALO, MAY 1 TO NOVEMBER 1, 1901.

Fig. 5 *Birdseye View of the Pan-American Exposition, Buffalo, May 1 to November 1, 1901.* Pan-American Exposition Company. Photo-offset print, c. 1901. Library of Congress, Prints and Photographs Division, Washington, DC

The Pan-American Exposition in Buffalo, New York, was a destination that drew President William McKinley, who was assassinated there. Expositions and world's fairs helped justify imperialism, showcasing modern Western technology and culture in contrast to the ostensibly backwards ways of life in colonized lands. In 1901, objects from Frank Hilder's expedition were displayed in the Philippine Village and the Ethnological Building before their dispersal to the Smithsonian and other institutions.

Filipino insurgents; Krieger would come to include photographs of three weapons from Hilder's expedition in his publication (fig. 6). Hilder continued to pressure Otis and, "after several late interviews with him I succeeded in obtaining permission to visit the arsenal and make a selection," one that included an insurgent bamboo cannon wrapped in telegraph wire and "the garrote with which the Spanish executed captured insurgents and criminals."[53] Hilder and Sherman also sought to collect human bones. By April, Sherman had already contracted with a Captain Parker to provision the museum with skulls.[54] After Hilder's return to Washington, DC, Sherman continued to collect, reporting "I have eight skulls to go to you, and with request that you let me know if more are desired." It had not been easy to obtain them, he observed. "As you know none were to be had in Manila or suburbs, and it was only by sending way out for them that we got any at all."[55] Frustrated at his failure to obtain the skeleton of an Igorot or Negrito—the "non-Christian tribes" most discussed by Americans—for lack of transportation, Sherman suggested a grisly, illuminating

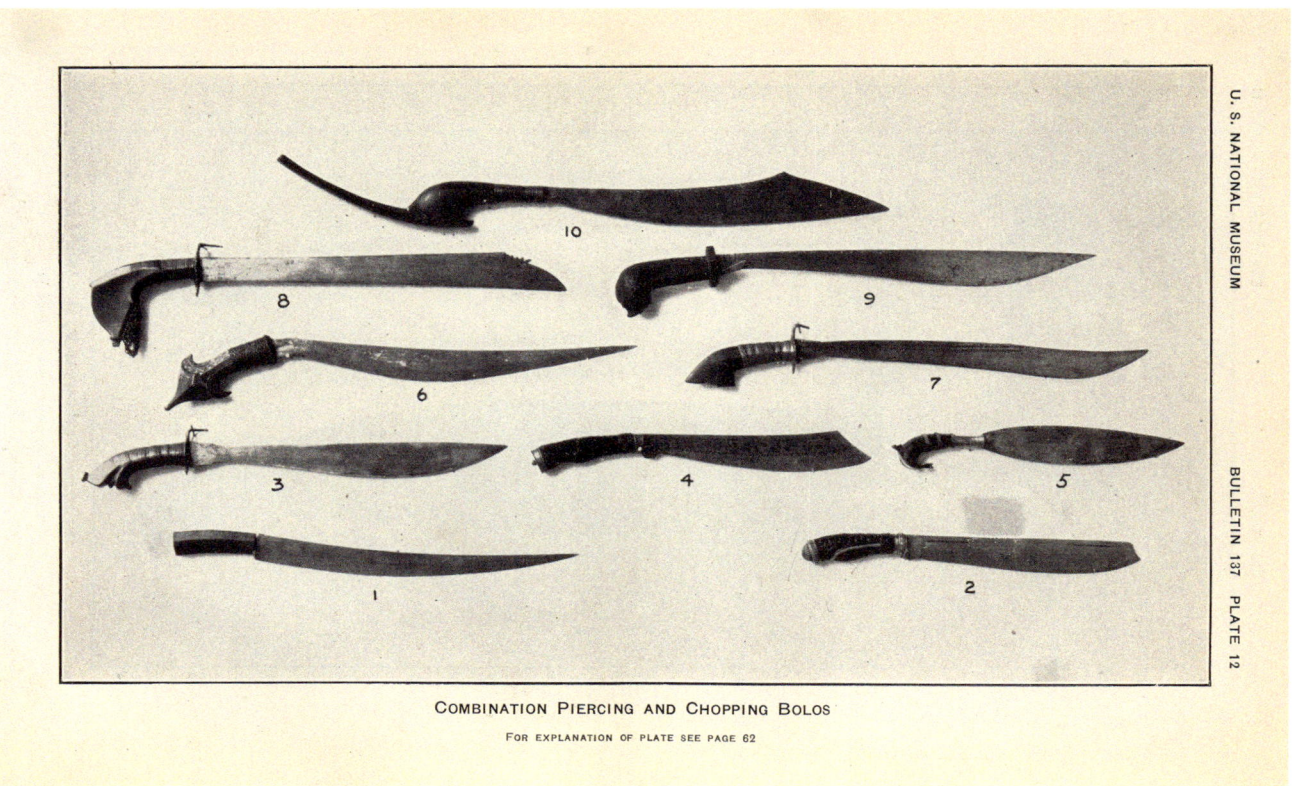

U. S. NATIONAL MUSEUM   BULLETIN 137   PLATE 12

COMBINATION PIERCING AND CHOPPING BOLOS

FOR EXPLANATION OF PLATE SEE PAGE 62

Fig. 6 Plate 12 in Herbert W. Krieger, *The Collection of Primitive Weapons and Armor of the Philippine Islands in the United States National Museum.* Washington, DC: Government Printing Office, 1926. Smithsonian Libraries and Archives

Hilder collected the bolo (no. 4) in the Philippines, and the weapon was on display in 1901 at the Pan-American Exposition in Buffalo, New York. Fig. 3 pictures the same object.

dovetail between military and scientific purposes. "What ought to be done," he wrote to Hilder:

> is for the Natl. Museum or the Smithsonian to get an order on the Military authorities here notifying some one here every time an igorrote or negrito was to be hanged so that the agent would have time to make arrangements to secure the brain, skull or whatever else was wanted. Some fine material could be secured in that way.[56]

Hilder's career as colonial expert was cut short when he died suddenly of pneumonia shortly after installing the exhibit at Buffalo.[57] But his work in securing the Smithsonian a foothold in Philippine collecting had succeeded.

When the Buffalo exhibits were shipped to Washington, DC, after the closing of the exposition, they formed the foundation of the National Museum's Philippine collections, as McGee and others had hoped. Other objects include four canoes like the ones pictured here at the 1904 Louisiana Purchase Exposition in St. Louis (fig. 7). In the lead-up to the St. Louis event, the U.S. colonial government in the Philippines decided to sponsor and organize a massive display of power and uplift, one that might counter lingering charges of wartime barbarity, convey the stability and success of nascent colonial government, and promote U.S. investment in Philippine industries (fig. 8). Immense collections were necessary, and U.S. officials and contractors in the islands found themselves at a loss in securing many desired items. To do so, they discovered, required the cooperation of well-to-do Filipinos who possessed these items and might be willing to loan them to the exposition on a temporary basis. But, as the main organizer canvassed for donors, recounted one history of the exhibit, "he met with many rebuffs; there was a lack of appreciation that was most discouraging."[58] Many Filipinos were hesitant to part with valuable property that would be shipped across the Pacific Ocean by steamship and then halfway across the United States by rail. And some had bitter memories of the display of "non-Christians" at expositions in Spain and the United States, in ways that many believed had deliberately misrepresented the islands' population.[59]

To win over Filipino elites, U.S. planners promised donors, lenders, and other participants several potential benefits. An "honorable commission" of select leaders would travel to St. Louis and participate in ceremonial functions. The exposition board also spoke of a prestigious, if hypothetical, scientific society to which Filipino participants in the exposition might belong. Any submissions of materials for the expositions "must be formulated as a request for membership" in this organization, which would perhaps be called the "Philippine Academy of sciences, arts, commerce, and industries or the Philippine Society of geography, exact and social sciences, or Philippine National Museum of commerce, industry, natural history, ethnography, arts, and sciences."[60] The incentives appear to have succeeded. "Many a prized relic has been turned over to the board," recorded one contemporary account of the making of the exhibit, "many an hour of time has been graciously given that some particular

article or design might be secured in time to show the people of the United States."[61] By August 1903, a first shipment of five hundred tons of material was on its way to St. Louis.

The complex story of how the exhibit took shape, what Filipinos and U.S. visitors made of it, and its political fallout, has been told elsewhere.[62] But what became of the collected objects afterward? In an abrupt change of plans, the exposition organizers decided not to return anything to the islands. U.S. museums would compete for overall control of the collection, and other Philippine artifacts would be sold off locally in St. Louis to the highest bidders. The sell-off, it was hoped, might make up for what had ultimately been financial disappointment. When final ticket receipts were tallied, the costly Philippine Exposition had a net loss of $600,000. Clarence Edwards of the Bureau of Insular Affairs was quoted as saying that the exhibition's success in "acquainting the American people with Philippine conditions was worth the price."[63] But that did not prevent government officials from trying to make back their losses, selling articles ranging from "pictures and statuary" to "fine samples of wood carving from Bilibid prison in Manila."[64]

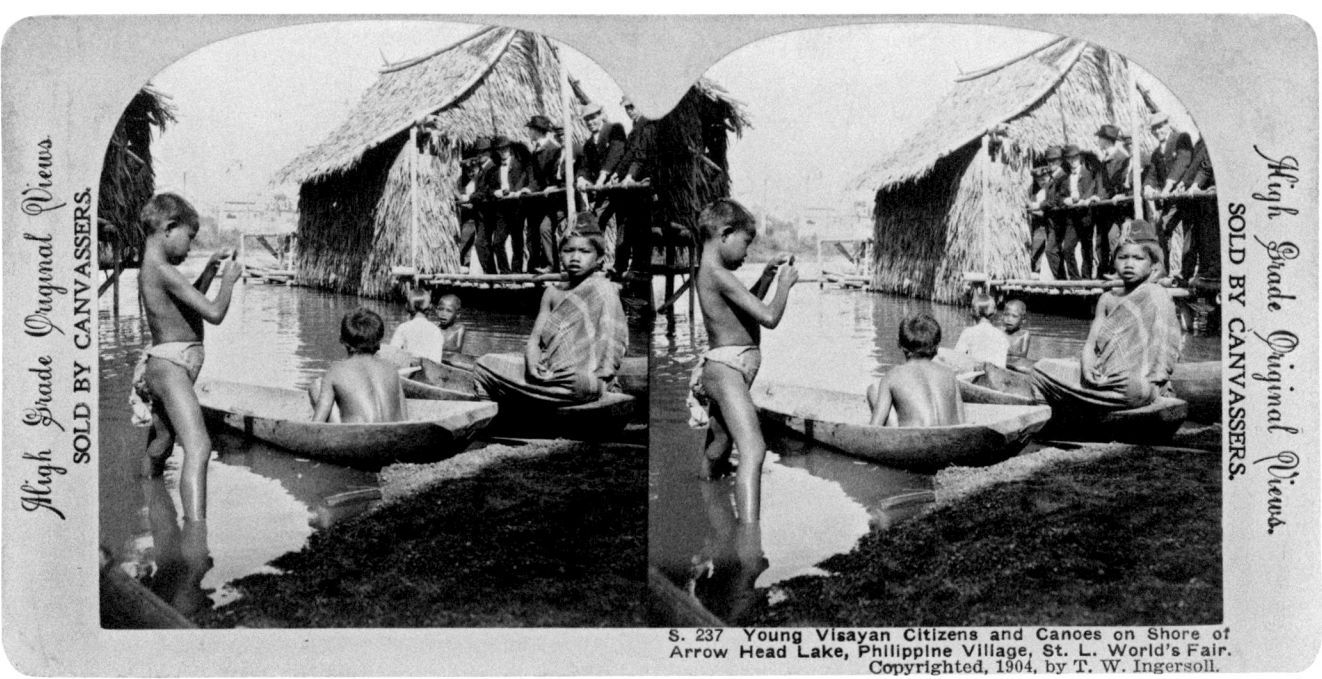

S. 237 Young Visayan Citizens and Canoes on Shore of Arrow Head Lake, Philippine Village, St. L. World's Fair. Copyrighted, 1904, by T. W. Ingersoll.

Fig. 7 *Young Visayan citizens and canoes on shore of Arrow Head Lake, Philippine Village, St. L. World's Fair*, T. W. Ingersoll, 1904. Photographic print on stereocard. Library of Congress, Washington, DC

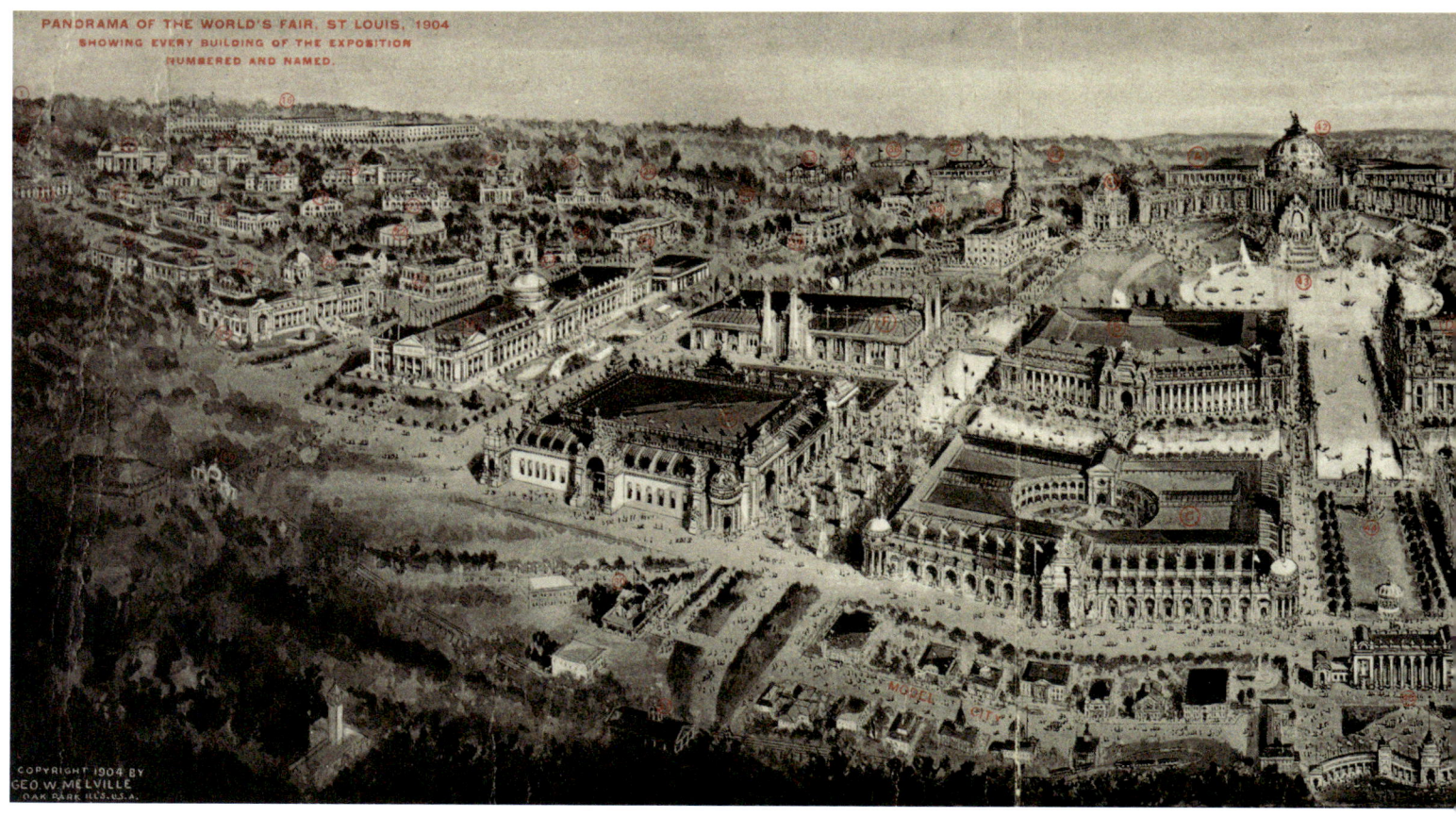

Fig. 8 *Panorama of the World's Fair, St. Louis, 1904*, George W. Melville (1856–1928), 1904. Photomechanical print; 12.7 × 47 cm (5 × 18½ in.). Library of Congress, Department of Prints and Drawings, Washington, DC

Competing U.S. museums wrangled for ownership of the remaining collection, which was extensive. The challenge, according to the *New York Times*, was that "the Filipino exhibit was too vast for any one museum."[65] The objects were, therefore, shipped to the American Museum of Natural History in New York, which would select the items it wanted to retain and send the rest on to the Smithsonian, the Philadelphia Commercial Museum, and the Field Museum in Chicago. As of February 1905, fourteen carloads of Philippine exhibits were already in New York or in transit from St. Louis. The *Times* reported that the shipment contained "enough samples of American colonial curios to stock a five-story addition to New York's Museum," and that museum officials were already contemplating "applying to the city to have it built."[66] In celebrating the acquisition, director

Hermon C. Bumpus expressed the museum's hope to "take up seriously the exploration and exploitation of natural history in the American colonial possessions in its broadest sense." Hundreds of students would soon "come sit among the fossils and the Filipino things and learn geography."[67]

Promises of an enormous new museum tied to an elite society for exposition collectors seem to have been abandoned. Of the exhibits that did find their way back to the islands, "a good many" were "without numbers or labels of any kind," according to a government anthropologist, which "materially lessened their value."[68] In fact, as private exhibitors began to file claims for the return of their items—items that were now in the hands of metropolitan museums or purchasers—colonial officials who oversaw the existing Insular Museum of Ethnology, Natural History and Commerce in Manila discussed giving away its holdings "to make good these losses."[69] McGee's arrangement for the Pan-American Exposition had sponsored a single expedition; the settlement at the end of the St. Louis Exposition had expropriated far more extensive,

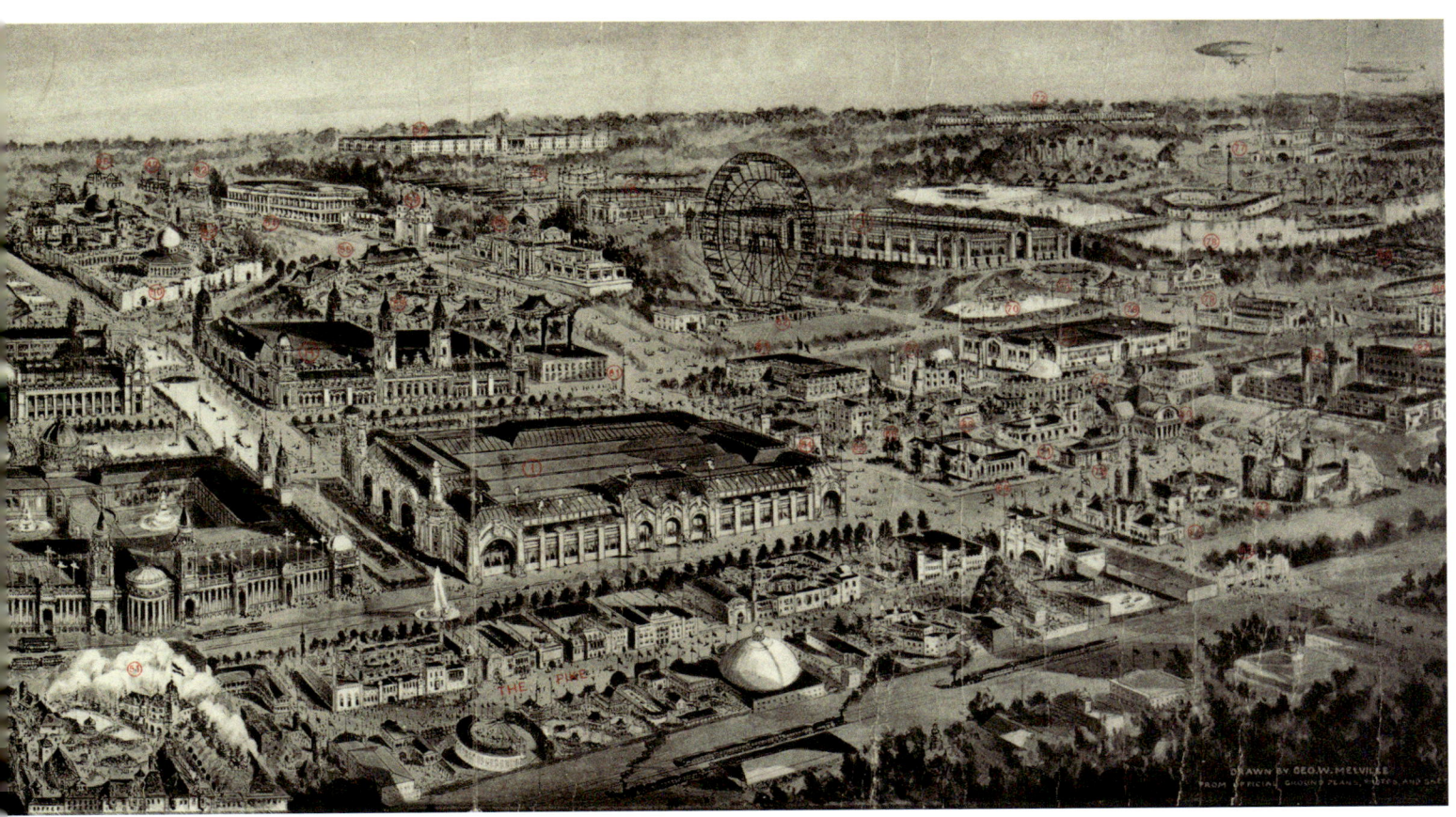

valuable holdings through what had amounted to a policy of collection by trans-Pacific bait-and-switch.

At the turn of the twentieth century, Americans coined a peculiar new phrase to refer to the newly conquered and occupied overseas colonies of the United States: "our new possessions."[70] The "our" did a great deal of work here, conjuring from a fractious U.S. society a single, unified, national possessor, and providing assurances that the islands were, in fact, possessed. Many of the people who lived there had very different ideas.

But "possessions" was also semantically loaded. The word was partly a euphemism that circumvented the charged language of colonialism and empire. It also embodied and expressed racialized political, legal, and cultural ambivalence and anxiety about the status of the territories and their populations with respect to the metropolitan United States. "Possessions" were neither outside (subject to other sovereignties) nor fully inside. Owned and held, they occupied a liminal space between inside and outside, at empire's threshold.[71]

"Possession" also rendered colonialism in something like the passive voice, making questions of process somewhat beside the point. How had these artifacts and archipelagos come to be "possessed"? Who had they previously belonged to? How had they come to change hands? In the case of transported curios, trophies, and weapons, who had taken them so far from their points of origin?

Krieger's disinterest in the particular relationship between the "stimulus" of war and the acquisition of the Smithsonian's Philippine collections—conveyed in his bland statement that weapons and armor "began to arrive" after the turn of the twentieth century—was emblematic of the ways that U.S. overseas colonialism, and the broader imperial projects which it anchored, could become naturalized and backgrounded, something that Americans did not need to explain to themselves or others. Perhaps it seemed advantageous if the objects' war stories went untold. But there was no reason why Krieger needed to have the last word.

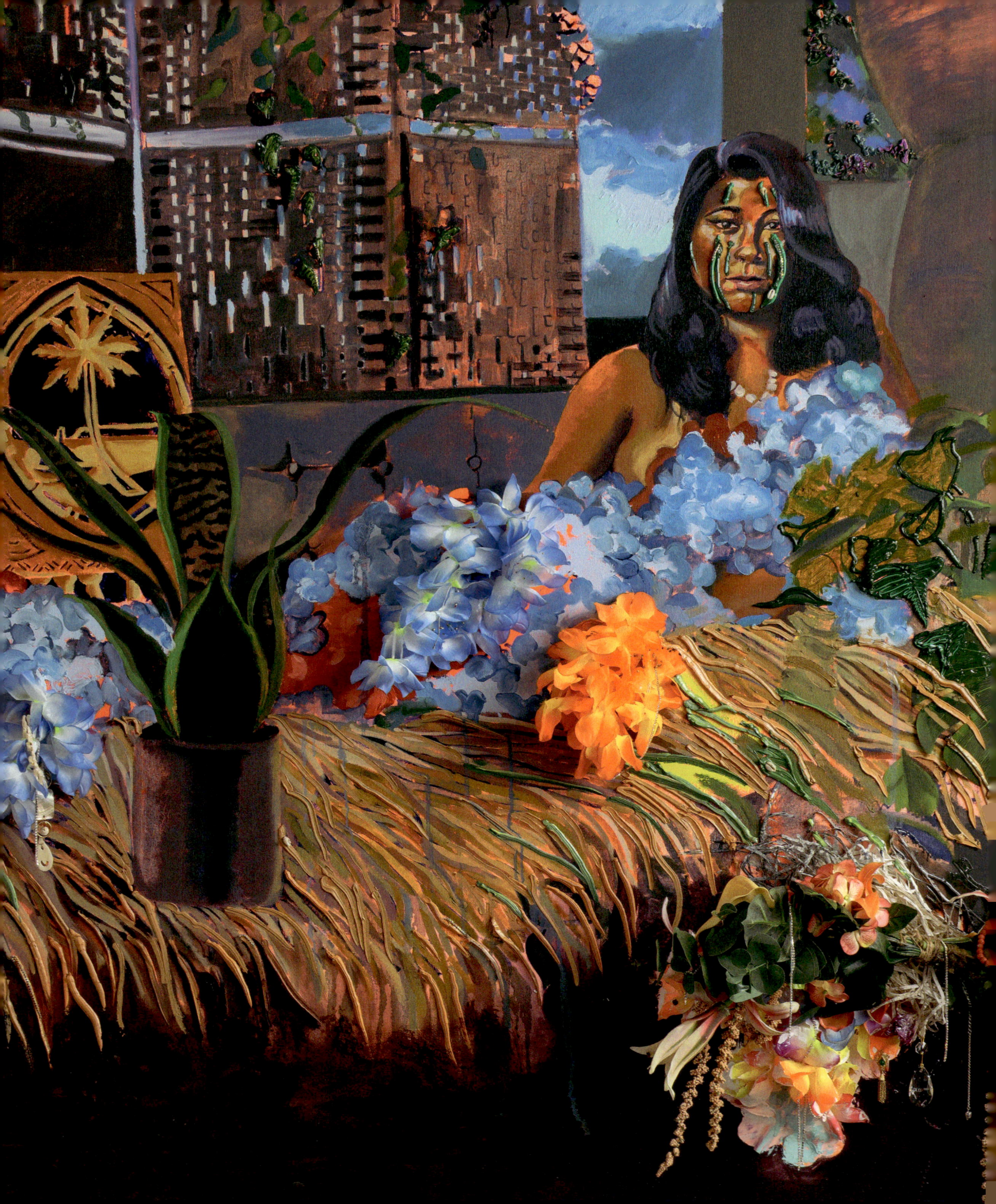

The 1898 Diasporas

Contemporary Artists Redefining Portraiture

TAÍNA CARAGOL

Throughout history, wars have remapped the world. But border shifts are easier to detect on continental land than on wide seas dotted by islands. Often considered "uncharted territory," islands can seem negligible in geographic and geopolitical imaginaries. Their names, locations, and political status remain fuzzy in the minds of many, only noticeable in times of political, climatic, or financial crisis.[1]

Irrespective of the differing terms under which Puerto Rico, Guam, and the Philippines came under the U.S. sphere of influence in 1898 and its aftermath, they all entered into a new kind of relationship with the United States. Through a series of judicial decisions known as the *Insular Cases*, the Supreme Court of the United States defined Puerto Rico as "foreign in a domestic sense."[2] It *belonged* to the United States, without being *a part* of it. The Supreme Court created a territorial distinction, classifying the territories of the continental United States as incorporated while labeling Puerto Rico and all the overseas possessions resulting from the War of 1898 as "unincorporated territories." In unincorporated territories, the rights and duties granted by the U.S. Constitution were to be applied only selectively. This ambiguous status established a condition of subalternity among the islands that the United States now ruled.[3] Subalternity entailed not only a position of social disempowerment but also one of subjection in the national narrative. If not a space of racial and ethnic degradation, it was at least one of silence.[4]

For decades, and through a variety of strategies, art has been a primary arena of contestation of colonialism and subalternity in the lands the United States established as its "imperial archipelago."[5] Today, one hundred and twenty-five years after 1898, Filipinx American artists Stephanie Syjuco (b. 1974) and Maia Cruz Palileo (b. 1979), CHamoru artist Gisela McDaniel (b. 1995), and Puerto Rican artist Miguel Luciano (b. 1972) challenge the silencing of the colonized through their practice. In such a broad artistic field, it might seem arbitrary to focus this essay on the aforementioned artists. However, as a curator working in a museum of national history and portraiture, I am interested in how they offer a rebuttal of traditional racialized "regimes of representation" generated by colonialism to define the people of the Philippines, Guam, and other Pacific Islands, as well as Puerto Rico.[6] These four diasporic artists, who all live in the United States, contend with the portrayal of their communities as "others" in the Euro-American imaginary, dismantling its visual hierarchies and seeking historical recognition. I will discuss distinct bodies of work by Syjuco, Palileo, McDaniel, and Luciano, in which they reimagine the genre of portraiture to interrogate and challenge the representation of Filipinos, CHamorus, and Puerto Ricans as powerless colonial subjects and to assert their presence in the U.S. historical narrative. The position of these artists as members of the diasporas is central, and background on the migrations that came about in the wake of 1898 is crucial to understanding their subversive work.[7]

Of the four artists in this essay, Syjuco and Luciano were born in the Philippines and Puerto Rico, respectively, and Palileo and McDaniel in the continental United States. Their individual histories may depart from the overarching narrative of migration of their ethnic communities. Yet, they recognize themselves as diasporic subjects and exist in relation to their ethnic and cultural communities in that transnational diasporic space of fluidity, where the homeland and the host land are sometimes interchangeable. It is key to provide this context to approach an understanding of the ramifications of 1898 for their work—and for the present moment.

The Migrations of 1898

The year 1898 generated new circuits of migration, from the United States to the island territories it claimed, between the territories themselves, and from the territories to the continental United States.[8] The U.S. occupation of Puerto Rico accelerated a foreign-controlled capitalist agrarian system, where the sugar plantation economy protected by the United States drowned out the smaller sectors of coffee, tobacco, and food staples.[9] Quickly, emigration presented itself as an escape valve for populations that were viewed by U.S. government officials as excess and, therefore, fodder for relocation as a cheap source of labor.[10] The earliest movements of Puerto Rican workers were not a "continental emigration" but were directed to other islands, such as Hawai'i, Cuba, the U.S. Virgin Islands, and the Dominican Republic.[11]

In the 1920s, Puerto Ricans also started settling in the continental United States, on the East Coast and in the Midwest, but most substantially in New York City, with emigration climaxing between the mid-1940s and 1970.[12] As Puerto Rico transitioned from an agrarian to an industrial economy, displacing agricultural workers from the island, Puerto Ricans migrated north and took on factory jobs or seasonal work in the United States. Since the

island entered an economic recession in 2006, and declared bankruptcy in 2015, Puerto Ricans have been moving to the continental United States in numbers not seen in more than fifty years. For more than a decade Puerto Rico has been experiencing a net population loss.[13]

As members from a seafaring culture, CHamorus from Guam started arriving in the continental United States in the early 1900s as whalers, or *balloneros*. Migration increased as CHamorus were introduced into military service in the 1930s. The reconstruction period after World War II and the drafts for the wars in Korea and Vietnam led many to relocate from Guam to the continent for military service. They not only served in the U.S. Navy, but also served in the U.S. Army and Air Force.[14] A large number of Chamorus established themselves in the vicinity of bases in California.

Currently there are more Puerto Ricans and CHamorus living in the continental United States than on the islands of Puerto Rico and Guam.[15] In 2019, the population of stateside Puerto Ricans amounted to 5.8 million, while the island's population in 2020 amounted to 3.2 million.[16] According to the most recent census figures, 160,773 Guamanians and CHamorus live in the continental United States, while the island has a population of 153,836.[17]

Within the imperial archipelago, Filipinos were those the United States considered most racially different from Anglo-Saxons. They were not welcomed in the continental United States. However, bound by an international convention that allowed the entry of imperial subjects back to "the motherland," the United States had no choice but to accept their entry.[18] They first came to work on the sugar plantations of Hawai'i. Others settled in California as field laborers.[19] This migration fueled an intense U.S. nativist backlash against Filipino American laborers. The signing of the 1934 Tydings-McDuffie Act, which put the Philippines on a path toward complete independence (to be achieved in 1946, after a decade-long transitional period of Commonwealth government), included a provision that imposed a cap of fifty Filipino immigrants per year. This new law, combined with the economic effects of the Great Depression, brought immigration from the Philippines to a trickle.[20] World War II reopened immigration channels through Filipino military recruits, soldiers from the mainland United States stationed in the Philippines who came back to the continent married, and Filipinos who came to pursue health-care training in the continental United States and stayed. The removal of national-origin

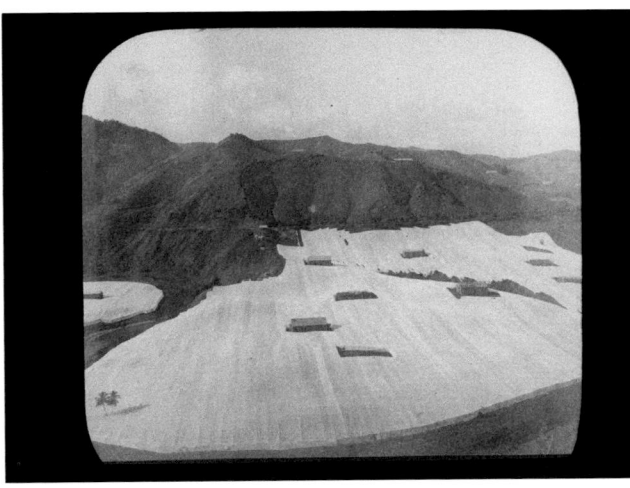

Fig. 1 *Tobacco Fields under Cheese Cloth*, Helen Hamilton Gardner (1853–1925), 1902. Glass lantern slide; 8.25 × 10.6 cm (3¼ × 4 in.). Helen Hamilton Gardener Photograph Collection, National Anthropological Archives, National Museum of Natural History, Smithsonian Institution

immigration quotas in 1965 led to a new increase in immigration.[21] According to the 2019 American Community Survey, 2.9 million people who identify as Filipino live in the United States.[22]

Although historically related, these three diasporas are rarely discussed together or acknowledged in U.S. history as an outcome of the country's imperial thrust at the turn of the twentieth century. Colonial diasporic populations like the ones to which the artists Syjuco, Palileo, McDaniel, and Luciano belong, often live in a kind of limbo, not fully accounted for in the country where they reside or the one from where they or their ancestors hail. Within the condition of subalternity that colonialism produces, the added feeling of being between places, of not belonging fully, can generate an acute sense of self-awareness, as much as an ability to negotiate one's identity situationally. The artists find in that outsider status, vis-à-vis the United States, the impetus to create their work. They transform their situation of "in-betweenness" into what postcolonial critic Homi Bhabha calls "the beyond," a space of intervention to elaborate new forms of individual and communal selfhood and empowered forms of representation.[23] In turn, these new forms of representation expand our understanding of what constitutes "the nation."[24]

As diasporic artists, Syjuco, Palileo, McDaniel, and Luciano not only have to contend with the omission of

their communities from the national historical narrative but also with the history of representation of U.S. colonial subalterns. Against the practice of formal, dignified, ceremonial portraiture, the publishing industry at the turn of the nineteenth century exploded with images representing the people and lands of the "new possessions" acquired by the United States. The visual representation of the colonial subjects as weak, poor, backward, and inferior justified the United States's imperial rule as part of a messianic civilizing project.[25] Cartoons in popular magazines and weeklies, such as *Puck* and *Harper's*, represented Puerto Ricans, Filipinos, and Hawaiians as "primitive"—dark-skinned children in need of Uncle Sam's paternal care (see pp. 166 and 312). New photographic technologies, from the stereographic images to halftone lithography and the lantern slide, were also employed to represent the new peoples. Additionally, commercial photography studios produced landscape images that portrayed the islands as expansive, fertile, and prime for U.S. industrial development (fig. 1).

Books, such as the oversize two-volume *Our Islands and Their People as Seen with the Camera and Pencil*, used realistic photography, textual narration, and social statistics to map out the new empire for the "patriotic and public spirited American" (fig. 2).[26] Like other books of this type, the aim of *Our Islands and Their People*, a widely popular publication that sold an estimated four hundred thousand copies, was to acquaint U.S. readers with the lands it seized.[27] Pairing photographs of landscapes and people from far away with accessible prose that blended data and first-hand U.S. military observations, it portrayed colonial subjects as "others" in need of political tutelage from the United States. The book sought to validate the U.S. imperial project as unequivocally beneficial.[28]

Contemporary sensibilities recognize the overt racism of such images, and their circulation has, for the most part, ceased. Yet the problem of visualizing the people of the colonies and understanding how they relate to the political and cultural body of the United States persists. It is revealing that until this exhibition, the National Portrait Gallery—one of the primary cultural institutions to articulate national discourse in the United States—presented a history of 1898 in alignment with the triumphant narratives that prevailed immediately after the War of 1898. The marginality or absence of the stories from the imperial archipelago within the space of the Portrait Gallery is a symptom of that problem of visualization. Revealing and

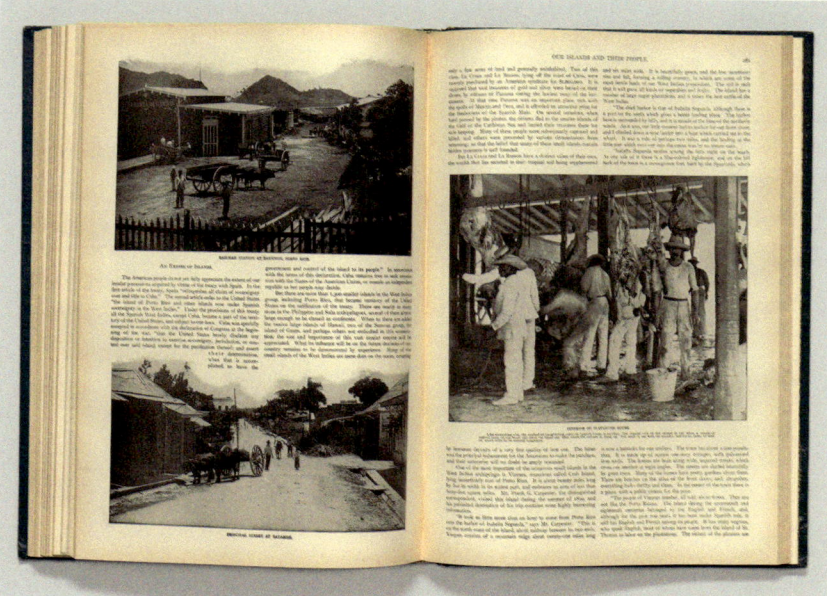

Fig. 2 *Our Islands and Their People as Seen with the Camera and Pencil*, José de Olivares, N. D. Thompson Publishing Co., 1899. 41 × 29 cm (16⅛ × 11⁷⁄₁₆ in.). Collection of Dr. Laura Katzman

Fig. 3 *Pileup (Eastman)*, Stephanie Syjuco (b. 1974), 2021. Hand-assembled pigmented inkjet prints on Hahnemuhle Baryta. Edition of 3 + 2AP; edition 2/3; 121.9 × 91.4 cm (48 × 36 in.). Courtesy of the artist, Catharine Clark Gallery, San Francisco, and RYAN LEE, New York

dismantling the colonial bias of a national museum and its collection or archive requires a strategic intervention. Sometimes such interventions are embedded in exhibition practice and curation. At other times, it is the artists themselves who have taken on the decolonial task.

Stephanie Syjuco: Turning One's Back on the Colonial Gaze

In Stephanie Syjuco's expansive artistic practice, histories of empire have been a topic of research for close to a decade, with the year 2016 bringing a renewed sense of urgency.[29] For her, the strident nativist and racist discourse that emerged around the presidential election called into question the American promise of an equitable future.[30] But it also seemed to be a symptom of historical amnesia, a collective forgetfulness of how the United States had engendered its own diverse demography through expansion and colonialism, pushing its geographic boundaries within the continent and overseas, displacing and colonizing people. This realization drove her to focus more closely on the topic, thinking about herself as a member of the Filipino diaspora and researching its traces through the broader narrative of U.S. history.

In 2020, Syjuco was awarded a Smithsonian Artist Residence Fellowship (SARF), which gave her the opportunity to access Smithsonian collections and build upon her research-based work. Her project's aim was to "search for evidence of the Philippines" in the national museums and their archives.[31] During the residency, Syjuco spent most of her time at the National Museum of American History, but she also investigated the collections of the National Museum of Asian Art and the National Museum of Natural History, which includes the National Anthropological Archives. Throughout those collections, evidence of the Philippines was vast. Yet the bountiful materials were limited in scope: ethnographic photographs, weapons captured by U.S. soldiers during the Philippine-American War, musical instruments, and mineral samples collected on survey expeditions. That evidence pointed to the colonial relationship between the United States and the Philippines between 1898 and 1946.[32] The sum of the materials pointed to an outsider's gaze surveying a foreign land and its people.[33] The evidence of Filipino presence was that of their position as "others" in the national historical narrative. From the experience of absorbing and processing the contents of those archives, both intellectually and emotionally, Syjuco created several bodies of work, one of which she titled *Pileups* (figs. 3–5).

Each of the three *Pileups* is an amalgamation that the artist likens to a "portrait of the Philippines, through the archives of the empire."[34] *Pileup (Eastman)*, whose title references the Eastman portable camera in the center of the composition, features images that Syjuco gathered from the National Museum of American History. Popular among both professional and amateur photographers from the 1880s until the beginning of the century, the

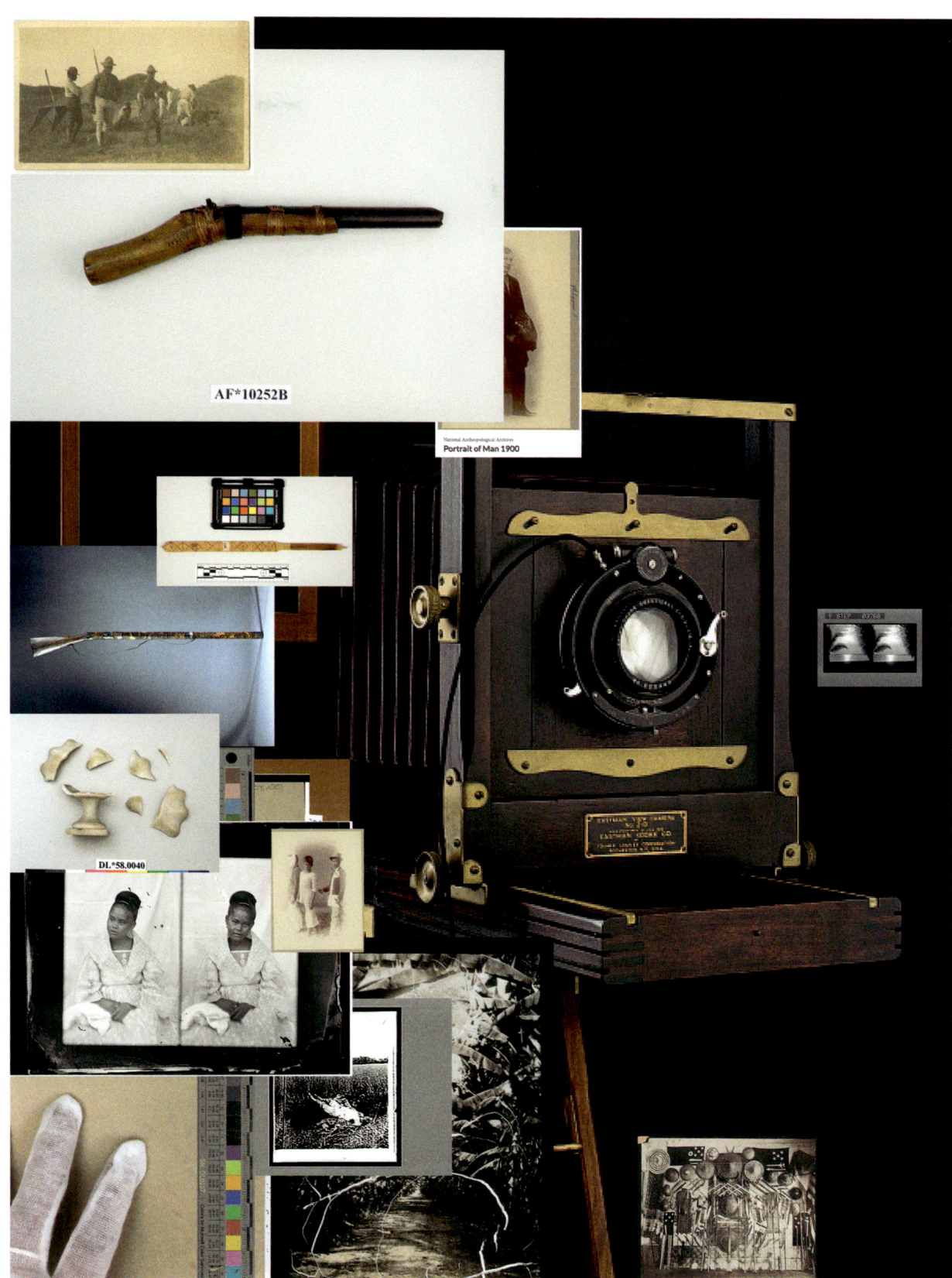

AF*10252B

National Anthropological Archives
Portrait of Man 1900

DL*58.0040

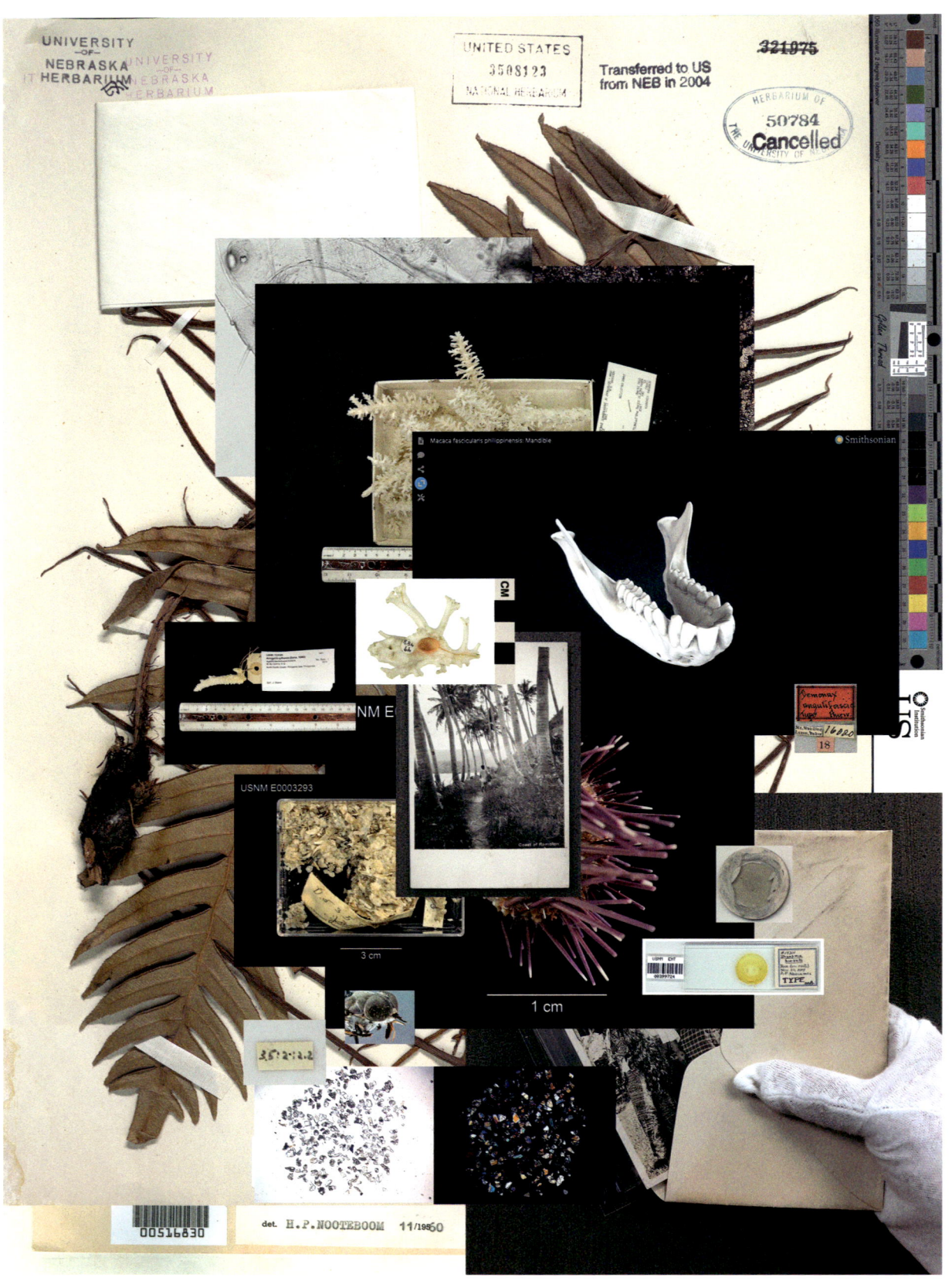

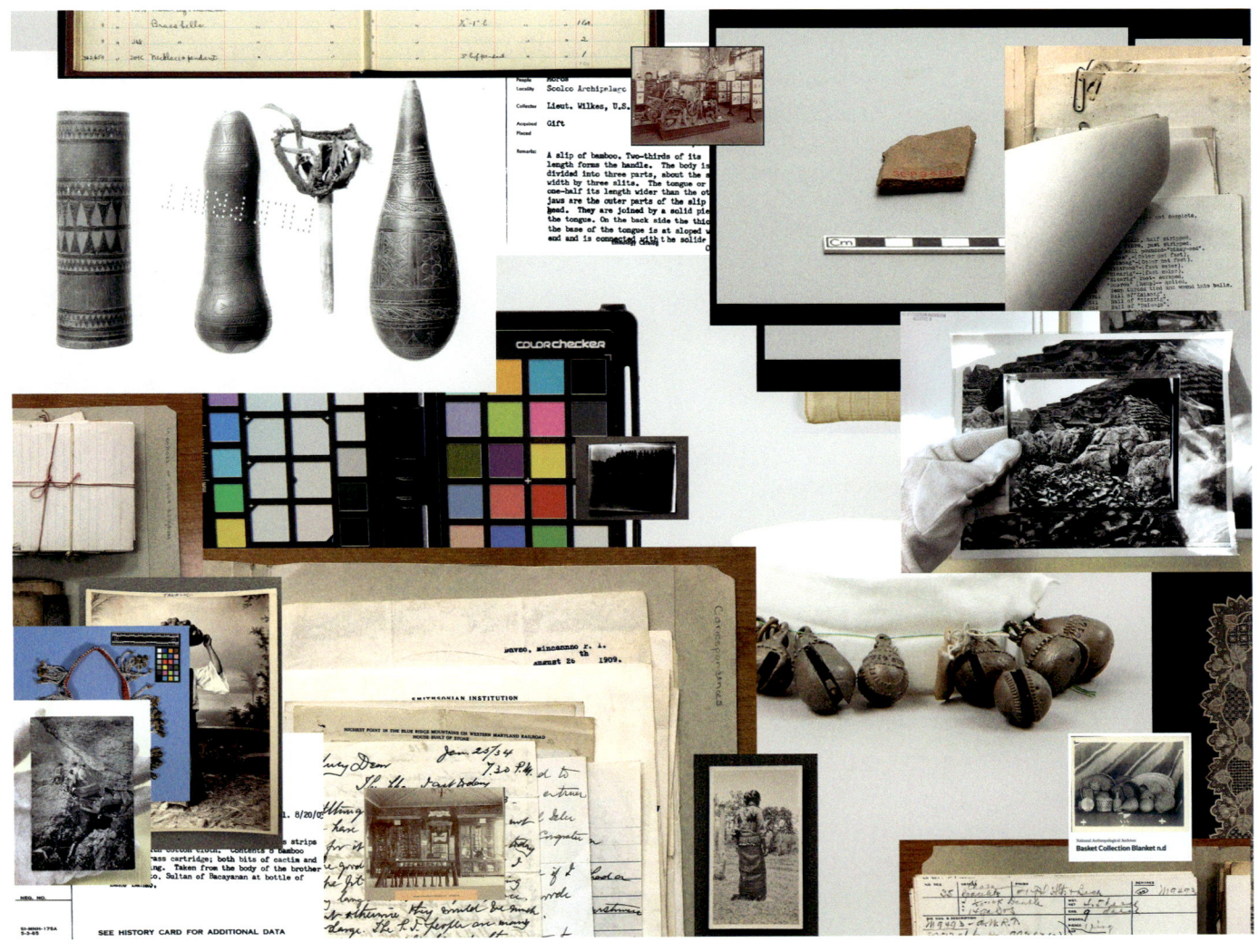

Fig. 4 *Pileup (Herbaria)*, Stephanie Syjuco (b. 1974), 2021. Hand-assembled pigmented inkjet prints on Hahnemuhle Baryta. Edition of 3 + 2AP; edition 2/3; 121.9 × 91.4 cm (48 × 36 in.). Courtesy of the artist, Catharine Clark Gallery, San Francisco, and RYAN LEE, New York

Fig. 5 *Pileup (Brass Bells)*, Stephanie Syjuco (b. 1974), 2021. Hand-assembled pigmented inkjet prints on Hahnemuhle Baryta. Edition of 3 + 2AP; edition 2/3; 91.4 × 121.9 cm (36 × 48 in.). Courtesy of the artist, Catharine Clark Gallery, San Francisco, and RYAN LEE, New York camera served to make U.S. territorial expansion widely visible, almost tangible, in the continental United States. The composition is layered with images of handmade guns that were made by Filipino insurgents during the Philippine-American War; a picture of a broken footed bowl made from alabaster; a double portrait of an elegantly dressed mestizo young woman who gazes alternately at the camera and away from it with a certain defiance; and a pixelated image of a lifeless body lying in a trench.[35] Behind the guns, a likeness of José Rizal with the caption "Portrait of a Man" is partly visible. The man in question was, of course, a founding figure of Filipino nationalism, but in the National Anthropological Archives, he remains nameless.

Pileup (Herbaria) combines imagery from the National Museum of Natural History's collection of biological, mineral, and animal specimens with images of ethnographic material from the National Anthropological Archives. The large-scale photograph of a botanical specimen serving as a natural backdrop for the rest of the arrangement can be interpreted as a metaphor for nature's exuberance. Images of the natural world are piled up on top of it: minute, iridescent rocks; a purple sea urchin; dead coral specimens from the Philippine Sea; 3D scans of animal jaws. Blue, black, and purple rubber stamps on the white support read, "University of Nebraska Herbarium," "Herbarium of the university – CANCELLED," and "Transferred to the US from NEB in 2004," pointing to a cycle of information gathering, discarding, and transferring that also reinforces the unstable values of what has been collected.

Pileup (Brass Bells) superimposes images of objects that the National Museum of Natural History and the National Museum of Asian Art have classified under the rubrics of ethnography and culture. These objects include elaborately carved gourds, brass bells strung using varied techniques, baskets, a photograph of exhumed graves with Westerners holding human skulls, and catalogue cards with fragments of text that read, "ing. Taken from the body of the brother" and "to, Sultan of Bacayanan at bottle of."

In all three *Pileups*, the image overlays convey the intense experience of conducting research in an archive. As the eye and the mind engage in the act of absorbing and making sense out of the fragmentary information that objects and records yield, we are made aware of the archives' organizing principles. Color bars on pictures of museum objects remind us of the limits of the camera, while reinforcing the human manipulation that is present in a photograph. In other words, the archive bears evidence of a fact, but it is also a mediated repository, where knowledge is organized according to power structures that are firmly rooted in imperialism.

Describing her experience of processing the archive intellectually, psychologically, and emotionally, Syjuco has said:

> There's something about sitting with these massive amounts of documents and archives, only to find yourself confronted by images of peoples who are not unlike you being positioned as subjects in a story that they had no part in shaping. . . . The white gaze was everywhere and seeped into everything I looked at. To be an object and not the interlocutor felt palpable, and it also felt like there was an incredibly thin barrier between the brown people I was viewing and where my own body—physically sitting there—was located.[36]

Syjuco intends for each work to be aesthetically beautiful and also disturbing in its ability to quantify, record, and encapsulate its subject into a totalizing collection. Syjuco's characterization of the *Pileups* as "portraits of the Philippines through the archives of the empire" visually articulates the difference between those who comprise the nation and those who belong to it through their status as colonial subjects and objects of study. Rejecting that representational logic, she turns the tables on it through a variety of strategies that give agency to individuals photographed. The partial occlusion of the photograph of José Rizal behind a gun in *Pileup (Eastman)* suggests a furtive and insurrectionary presence. In *Pileup (Brass Bells)*, Syjuco blocks from our view a Tagalog woman carrying a basket of fruit on her head. While in that same composition, and in *Pileup (Herbarium)*, she deliberately represents subjects with their backs turned toward the camera. Syjuco refuses to embrace or let her ancestral community accept the role of "a silent object of study." Instead, they collectively turn their backs on the imperialist archive's ethnographic, colonial gaze.

Maia Cruz Palileo: Reordering the Past and Letting the Imagination and Memory Fill in the Blanks

An ordinary white wall comes alive as it is transmuted into a delicate world through an ethereal installation by Maia Cruz Palileo (they/theirs). Articulating a vision of their ancestral land using graphite and paper, the work presents a man with a staff, a stream, peasants, a dog, two women in sarongs walking together, banana trees, clouds, Western men in military uniforms sitting and talking, a heron standing quietly, men playing flutes, birds flying (fig. 6). Conjured with images that stand between reality and memory, the installation stirs the senses. A subtle breeze, the sound of birds, and the smell of plants envelop the viewer.

This work emerged shortly after Palileo conducted research at the Newberry Library in Chicago in 2017, under the auspices of a Jerome Foundation Travel and Study Grant. There, in one of the largest world collections of Filipiniana, Palileo encountered the art of Damián Domingo (c. 1796–1834), the first director of the Art Academy of the Philippines, along with the photographic archives of zoologist Dean Conant Worcester (1866–1924).[37] Details on Domingo's life are sparse, but he was a sought-after portraitist in his time, and Palileo was impressed by his colorful and highly detailed gouache illustrations in

Colección de Trajes de Manila, an album of traditional Filipino country types and costumes from around the 1820s (figs. 7 and 8). Worcester, whose life is well known, was a zoologist from Michigan who made his first two trips to the Philippines in 1887 and 1889 on expeditions to document and collect specimens for the Universities of Michigan and Minnesota, respectively.[38] Upon his return to the United States, he authored several books on the Philippines, including the popular *The Philippine Islands and Their People*, published in September 1898, only a month after Admiral George Dewey (1837–1917) led the U.S. Navy's occupation of Manila.[39] As the United States seized the archipelago, President William McKinley (1843–1901) appointed Worcester to the Schurman Commission to assess the material resources of the archipelago, its inhabitants, and its commercial possibilities in order to determine its geopolitical usefulness to the United States and to recommend government policies to rule it.[40] Worcester was then appointed secretary of the interior of the commissioned government and put in charge of several government bureaus, including Health, Agriculture, Government Laboratories, and Non-Christian Tribes. A fierce detractor of Philippine independence, Worcester produced thousands of ethnographic photographs and wrote books and articles for *National Geographic* that

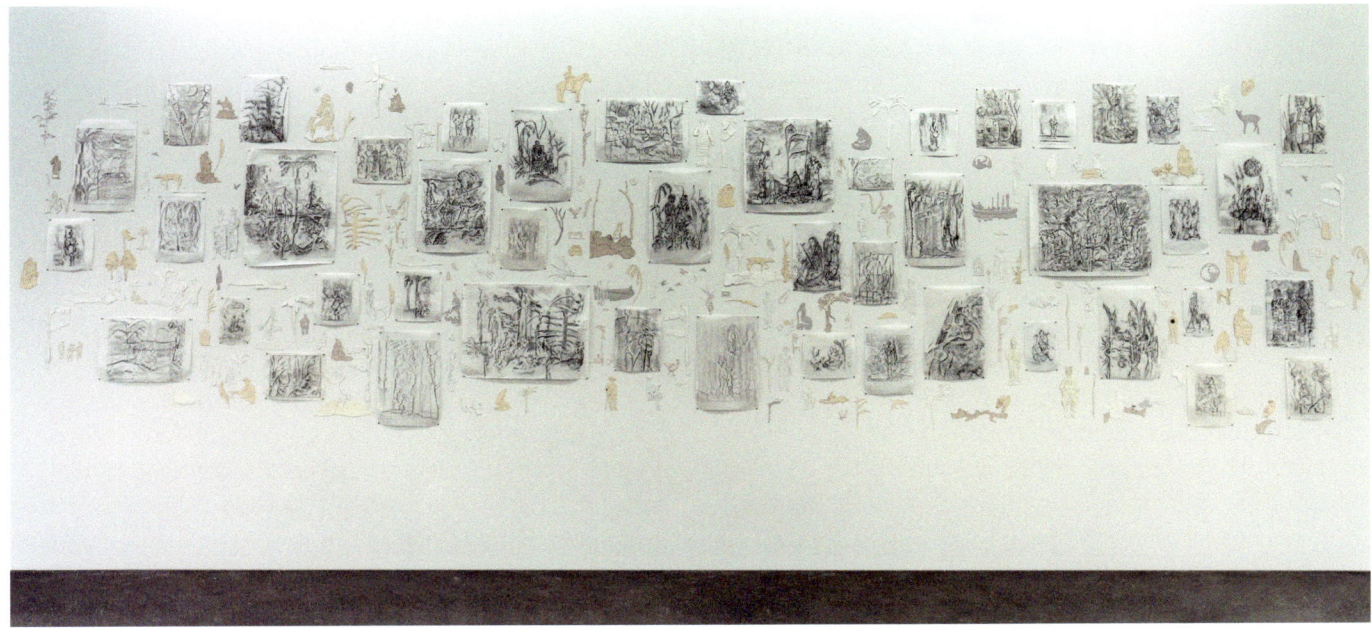

Fig. 6 Installation of graphite rubbings and cardstock cutouts, Maia Cruz Palileo (b. 1979), 2019. Courtesy of the artist

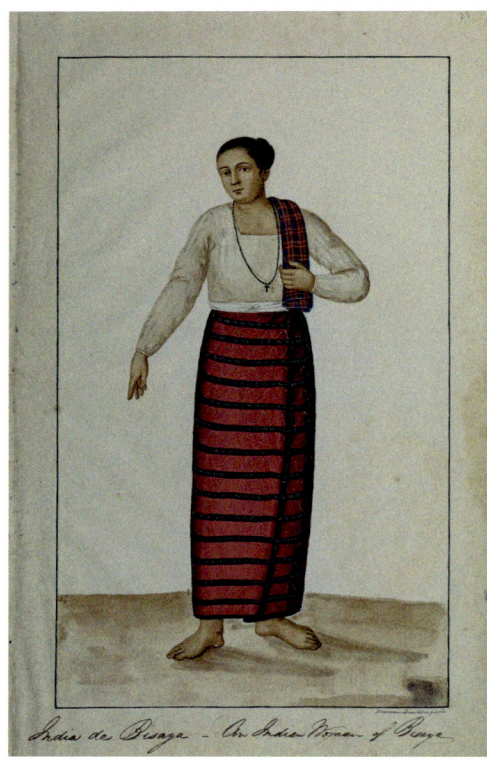

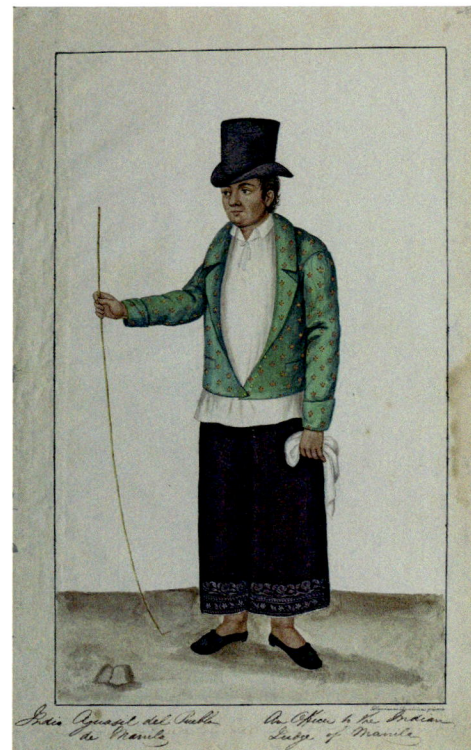

Fig. 7 *India de Bisaya – An Indian Woman of Bisaya,* illustrated in *Colección de trages de Manila tanto antiguos como modernos, de toda clase de yndias,* Damián Domingo y Gabor (1796–1834), c. 1827–1832. Watercolor on paper; 42 × 27 cm (16½ × 10⅝ in.). Edward E. Ayer Digital Collection, Newberry Library

Fig. 8 *Indio Aguacil del Pueblo de Manila – An Officer to the Indian Judge of Manila,* illustrated in *Colección de trages de Manila tanto antiguos como modernos, de toda clase de yndias,* Damián Domingo y Gabor (1796–1834), c. 1827–1832. Watercolor on paper; 42 × 27 cm (16½ × 10⅝ in.). Edward E. Ayer Digital Collection, Newberry Library

emphasized the plurality of tribes of the Philippines as an obstacle to national cohesion, and in his view, the evolutionary backwardness of the non-Christian ones.[41] He claimed, for example that the Negritos were incapable of civilization, the Ilongots were unable to count to ten, and the Moros were "treacherous and unreliable to the last degree."[42] For him, the United States had the moral duty to protect the archipelago and bring civilization to its inhabitants.

Reminiscing about the research, Palileo states:

It was definitely a difficult process to look at the archive. All of the ideas around that time, in the middle of the American empire moving west. Racism was just the thing. In a lot of these photographs, people had numbers. It was really dehumanizing. And then the writing about it, the captions. There were very thick volumes for every group of fifty photographs. So there's a big narrative arc going on if you look at the captions for each image. When I was looking at the images, I was drawn to figures who looked defiant or had self-possession, and had agency. Because they

did. This archive tried to squash that out, but it wasn't successful at that.[43]

The difference in approaches to representing Filipinos between Domingo's album and Worcester's photographs is stark. The grace of the figures in the album, the care for representing their social and cultural specificity through dress, contrasts deeply with the objectifying lens of Worcester's photographs (fig. 9). This contrast had a profound impact on Palileo, as a Filipinx American trying to understand the motherland.[44]

The artist was motivated to undo the subjugating effect of Worcester's photographs, to break apart the visual system that presented Filipinos as "other than human."[45] To that end, Palileo started isolating elements that stood out to them by drawing on cardstock: figures, animals, plants. Then, they cut out the drawings and added movement to the figures' clothes, volume to their hair, dynamism to a dog's pose, density to the clouds. Like an archaeologist recording a petroglyph or a descendant remembering a relative by creating a rubbing of their tombstone, Palileo made rubbings of these cutouts, imprinting the historical record of their re-envisioned reality. Then, the artist interspersed the paper figurines

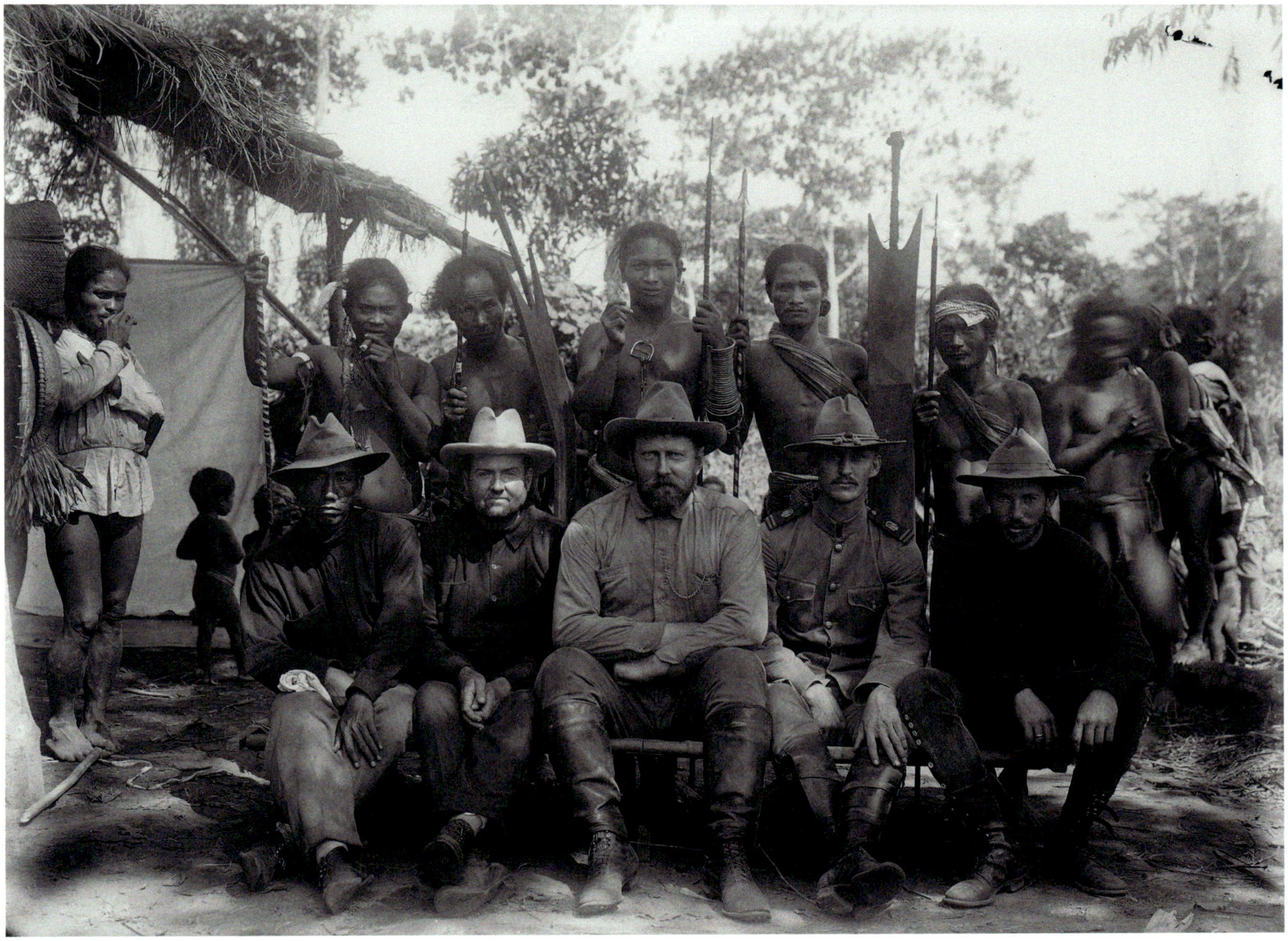

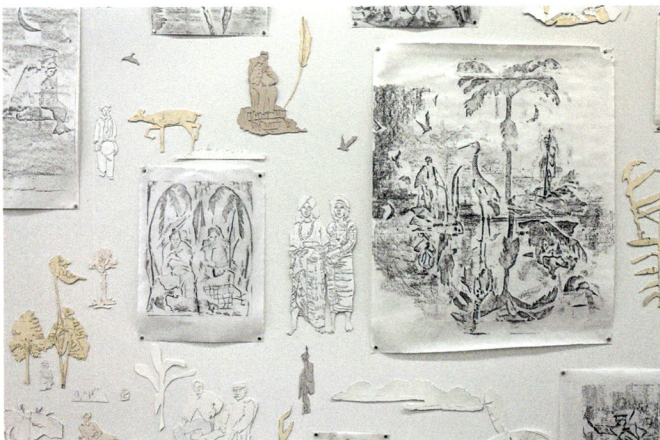

Fig. 9 *Our Party and a Group of Ilongote Chiefs*, 1900. Digitized negative; 5 × 7 in. format. The Dean C. Worcester Photographic Collection, University of Michigan

Fig. 10 Detail of fig. 6 showing graphite rubbings and cardstock cutouts, Maia Cruz Palileo (b. 1979), 2019. Courtesy of the artist

and the rubbings on the wall, taking up space, rearticulating the past (fig. 10). In their version, the figures in Worcester's photographs have been freed from the fixating spell of ethnographic and imperial photography. No longer depicted at odds with contemporary life or with the Western world, or on the losing side of a military conflict that would lead to almost half a century of colonialism, the Indigenous figures here are acknowledged and recontextualized in a story where they own the space they inhabit. They are not predestined to disappear or be acculturated. Colonial administrators and militaries are still there, but their arrogance is tempered by the self-possession of the islanders.

In some ways, the monochrome, ghostly presence of this paper installation forms the skeletal support for Palileo's contemporaneous paintings. In the paintings, however, the representations gain solidity and dimension through the artist's expressive colors and brushstrokes.

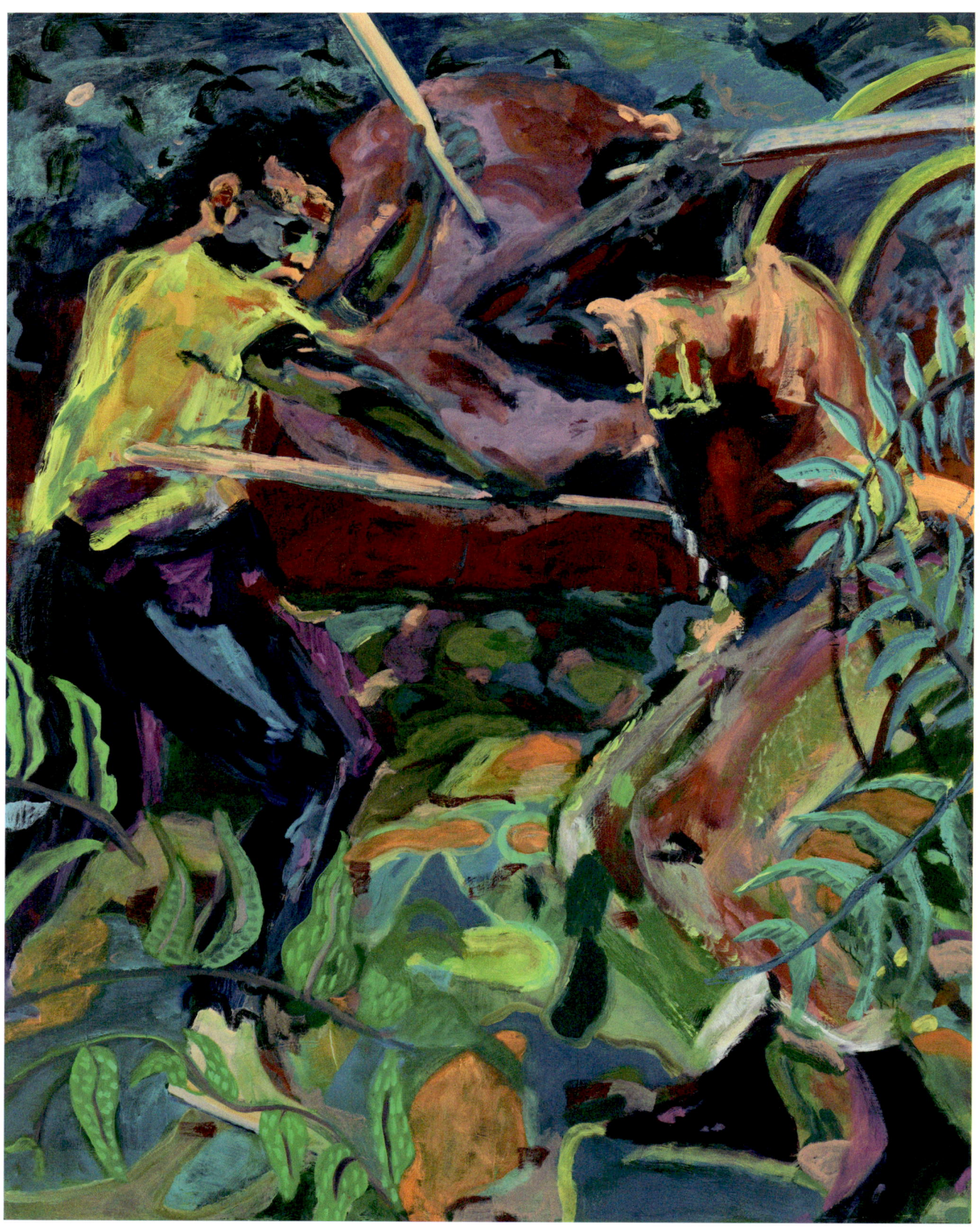

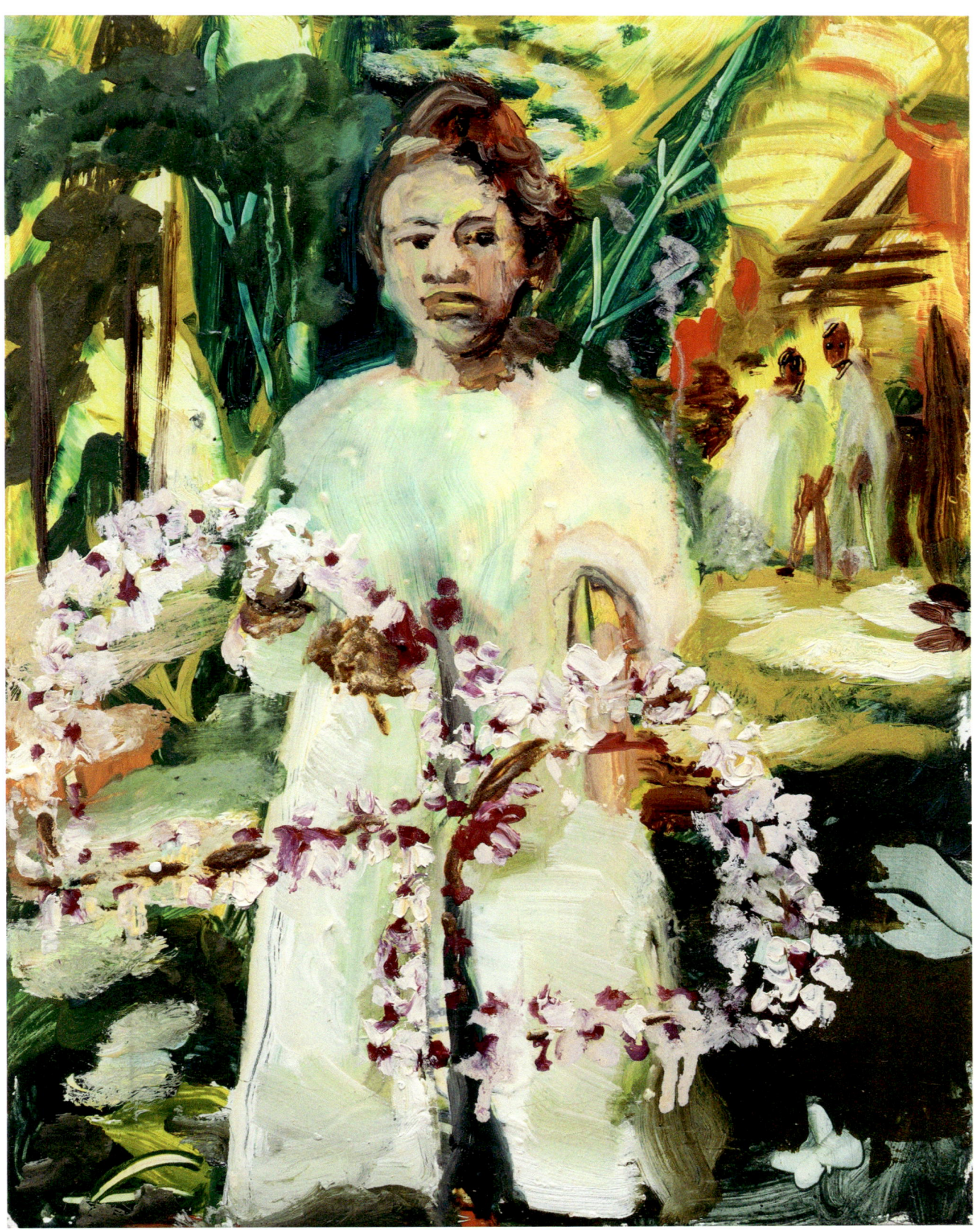

Fig. 11 *Sayaw (Dance)*, Maia Cruz Palileo (b. 1979), 2020. Oil on canvas; 162.6 × 137.2 cm (64 × 54 in.). Courtesy of the artist

Fig. 12 *Sampaguitas*, Maia Cruz Palileo (b. 1979), 2019. Oil on canvas over panel; 25.4 × 20.3 cm (10 × 8 in.). Courtesy of the artist

Sayaw (Dance) (fig. 11) and *Sampaguitas* (fig. 12), in a sense, emancipate figures from Worcester's archive. These portrayals, which join others from Palileo's family archives and those birthed by the artist's imagination, come alive. Filling in the gaps of official historical narratives, these paintings provide insight into the individuals' experiences and occupations as well as their joys, worries, and desires. "I want to give the subjects I paint a sense of agency and interiority," Palileo remarked.[46] Across pre- and postcolonial temporalities and the oceans that blur the lines of home and host land, the artist observes that "there are some things that cannot be erased, a deeper kind of memory that cannot be eliminated."[47]

Gisela McDaniel: Portraits with a Voice

Similar to Syjuco's gesture of setting obstacles to the colonial archive's totalizing logic and Palileo's rearrangement of the figures in Worcester's photographs to recognize these individuals' power, Gisela McDaniel also works against an established representational mode, that of primitivist painting featuring Pacific Islanders.[48] The originator of this genre is French artist Paul Gauguin who, starting in 1891 with his first prolonged stays in French Polynesia, created a body of work that projected onto the islands a Western fantasy of an uncorrupted Eden inhabited by people who upheld the attributes of the "noble savage" archetype developed by Enlightenment philosopher Jean-Jacques Rousseau.[49] Paintings such as *Three Tahitians* (1899) present a romanticized vision of island life, where locals exist half-dressed, living a carefree life, in a timeless space, almost like allegories. This arcadian vision that Gauguin was depicting was one invented, as he found himself disappointed with the effects of French colonization in Tahiti, particularly its modernity and cultural heterogeneity.[50] More controversially, Gauguin's paintings from Polynesia eroticize Tahitian girls and young women, veiling the artist's fixation through an interest in local spiritual traditions, as in *Manaò tupapaú* (Spirit of the dead watching) (fig. 13), and sexual mores that differed from those in Europe.[51] Gauguin's work epitomizes many Euro-American colonialist views, and its impact in art history has been monumental, securing its place in the

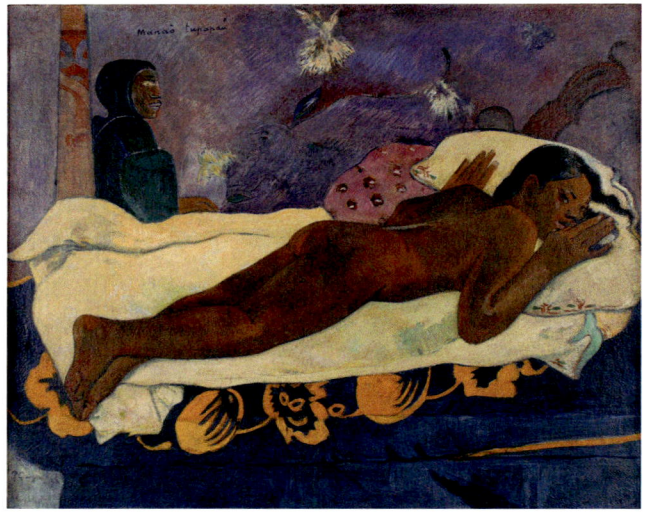

Fig. 13 *Manaò tupapaú* (Spirit of the dead watching), Paul Gauguin (1848–1903), 1892. Oil on jute mounted on canvas; 116.1 × 134.6 cm (45.68 × 53 in.). Albright-Knox Art Gallery

Fig. 14 *Paloa'an Míhinilat*, Gisela McDaniel (b. 1995), 2021. Oil on canvas, found objects, jewelry from subject-collaborator, resin, and sound; 165.1 × 152.4 × 40.6 cm (65 × 60 × 16 in.). Courtesy of the artist and Pilar Corrias, London

canon and shaping a sexualized and racialized image of Oceanian Indigenous women. Furthermore, these interpretations have contributed to a flattened view of the region as a tourist's paradise.[52] This view, in turn, has facilitated a general ignorance about contemporary Native Pacific Islander cultures and the issues they face.

McDaniel disrupts the tradition of primitivist painting of Pacific Islanders. In *Paloa'an Míhinilat*, for example, her subject gazes at us (fig. 14). She rests on a bed of straw, and although fragments of her torso appear naked, most of her body is covered with straw and blue flowers. She is in a space that is both open and enclosed. A straw-weave screen filters the light and suddenly opens up to the ocean and sky behind her head. In the foreground, a potted *dravaena trifasciata*, or snake plant, with its vigorous verticality echoes the inner strength that the subject's eyes convey. Behind it, the seal of Guam points to the sitter's heritage.[53] The overall composition exceeds the canvas as some of the natural elements become three-dimensional, outgrowing the painting, bursting into the viewer's space.

Måmes portrays a sitter in an exterior space (fig. 15). The painting is a likeness of Dan Taulapapa McMullin (b. 1957), an artist and poet from American Samoa who

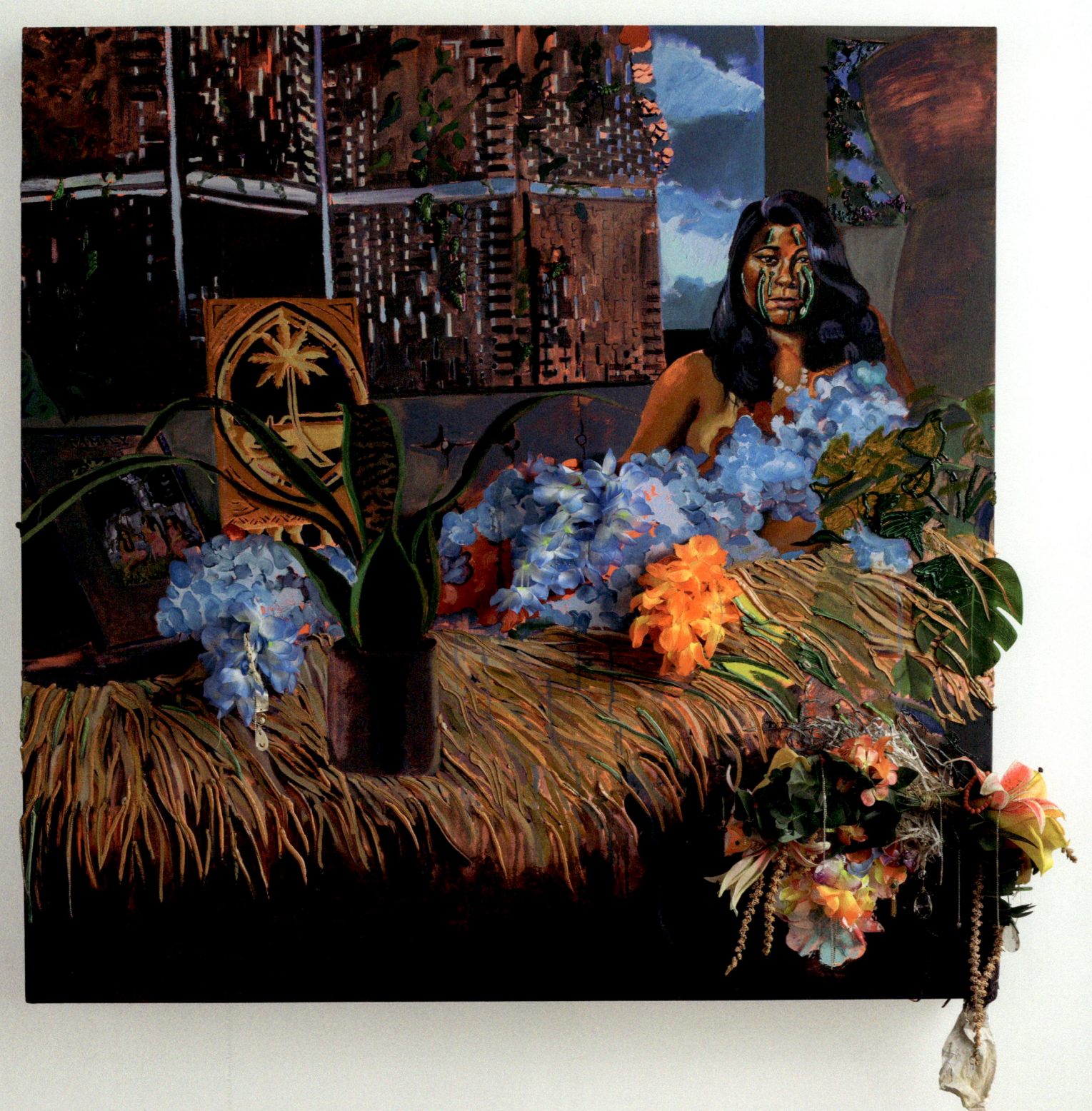

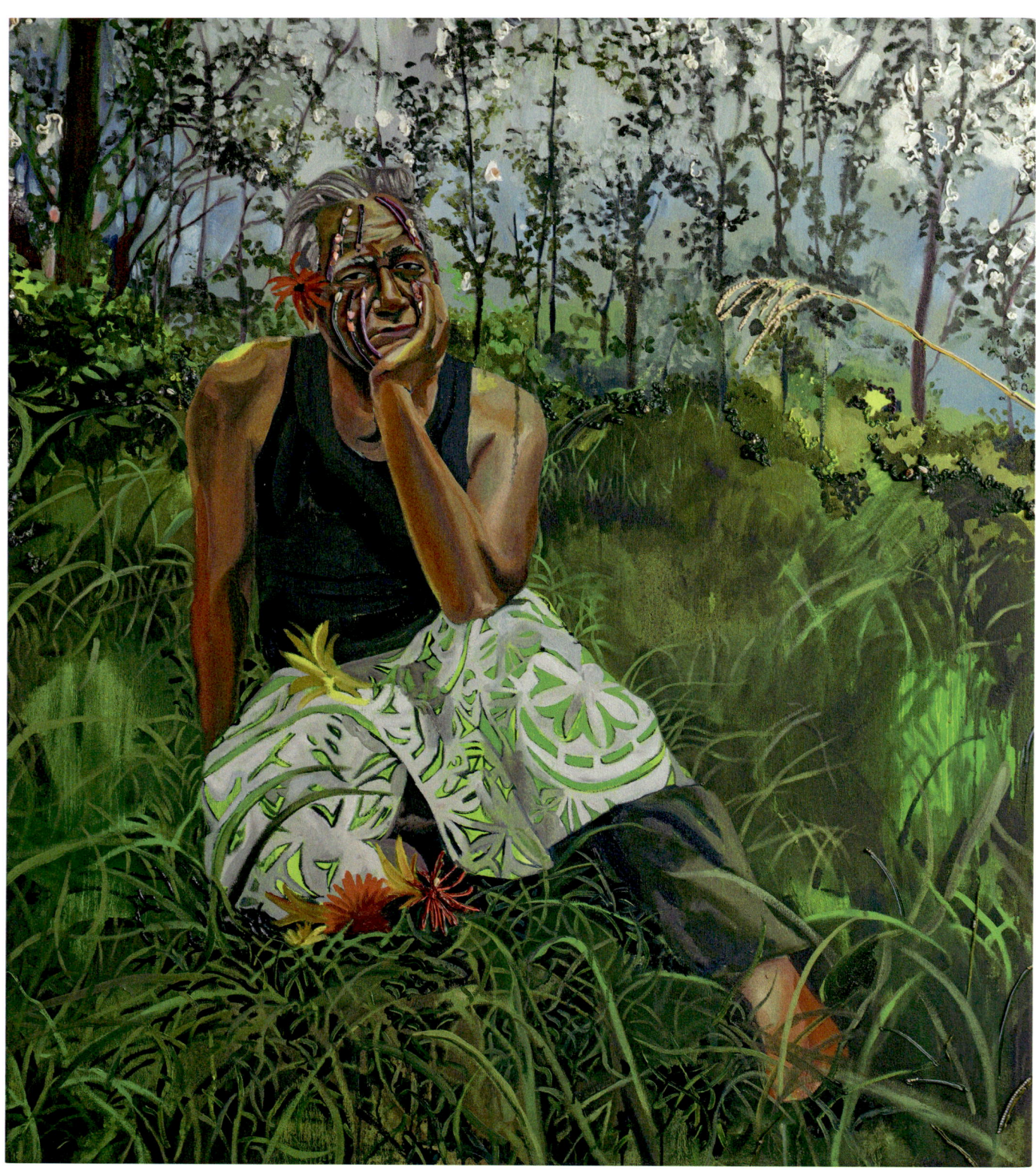

Fig. 15 *Mâmes*, Gisela McDaniel (b. 1995), 2021. Oil on canvas, found objects, shells from subject-collaborator, and sound; 114.3 × 129.5 × 14 cm (45 × 51 × 5½ in.). Courtesy of the artist and Pilar Corrias, London

identifies as *fa'afafine*, a person of third gender in traditional Samoan culture. McMullin is known for their poetry on themes of colonialism, exoticism, and the body. In this painting, McDaniel portrays them in a relaxed pose, dressed in a black tank top and a white-and-green pareo. With one hand supporting their chin, McMullin returns our gaze with a blasé expression.

Paloa'an Míhinilat and *Mâmes*, both multimedia works, embody McDaniel's emphasis on making present CHamorus—the Indigenous people of Guam and the Mariana Islands—in art and history. McDaniel's experience growing up in Ohio as a CHamoru is key in this pursuit. As the granddaughter in a CHamoru military family who emigrated from Guam and settled in the continental United States in San Diego, the artist's Indigenous identity took root while attending family gatherings as a child. During those events, her older relatives shared stories of the homeland with her in CHamoru and emphasized traditional values and the importance of respecting one's elders. Yet, reflecting on her early life outside the home, McDaniel said:

> It hurt that nobody knew where Guam was. Still today, on the rare occasions you hear about the island, it's in relation to nuclear threats. As Indigenous people, CHamorus, from the island and the diaspora, are not spoken for. With my painting, I want to assist the motion of their voices, to preserve them in art and history through portraiture in a way that is not exotified. I title my paintings in CHamoru, to prioritize my people and their disappearing language.[54]

Rather than conveying the dreamy or placid introspection of Gauguin's sitters, McDaniel's sitters Paloa'an Míhinilat and Mâmes look back at the viewer with unabashed seriousness or skepticism. Such active stares prompt the question of who is looking at whom. Conceiving the practice of portraiture as reliant on the trust and reciprocity between artist and sitter, the artwork emerges from the exchange between the two. With the aim of gifting the sitter an image of pride, the artist takes direction from them as to the pose and place for the portrait, their

clothing, and the objects they would like to have depicted or embedded in the portraits. On all of her sitters, McDaniel paints textured lines that function as "make-up masks," which she views as a protective device, a shield against bad intentions.

These works are part of a recent body of multimedia work in which the artist pushes the boundaries of sensorial engagement for visual art.[55] These paintings demand not just to be seen but also to be heard. McDaniel invites the sitters to share personal stories and thoughts that she then records and blends into collective overlaid soundscapes. The paintings have motion sensors and become activated when the viewer is six feet away from them. Through a cacophony that is only sometimes intelligible, we hear testimonials and streams of consciousness from different voices:

> I was going all the way back to that moment . . . when Magellan . . . In some ways that violence was more importantly connected to genocide. It was a way of killing us in the same ways that the threat to our waters has led to children being born with birth defects. [. . .] Our oceans, our islands being used as bombing sites. Institutions have been part and parcel of how people have been displaced from their lands. [. . .] There are things I never told you about. [. . .] I was embarrassed of my accent. It's all very hard. [. . .] Always weighing through trauma.[56]

The soundscape stresses of the relentless acts of violence that have been the product of colonization since the 1521 arrival of Ferdinand Magellan in Guam and continue through Spanish colonization in 1565, the transfer of power in 1898 to the United States 333 years later, and until the present.[57] These have resulted in the rapid decline of the CHamoru population in the twentieth century, particularly after World War II, as a result of U.S. military buildup and an imported workforce coming from the continental United States.[58] The United States' use of the land as a bombing practice range and the testing of chemical weapons, such as Agent Orange, which have polluted the waterways and caused public health damage,

Fig. 16 *Porto Rican Cotton Picker*, Miguel Luciano (b. 1972), 2011. 1971 Schwinn Cotton Picker, restored and customized. Background: Felícita Méndez (c. 1950), *Arizona Labor Journal* (October 2, 1926). Courtesy of the artist

are also referenced.[59] The end of the narrative poignantly signals the psychological effect of colonization: the inferiority complex it causes in the colonized, as analyzed by psychiatrist and pioneer of postcolonial theory Frantz Fanon.[60]

There are no quiet subjects in the work of Gisela McDaniel, no placid souls living in paradise. There are only assertive Indigenous people. They bring their cultural identities to the forefront as they powerfully articulate the challenges they have faced as a result of colonization.

Miguel Luciano: A Portrait of Migration and Racial Solidarity

Miguel Luciano's work revolves around the themes of history, social justice, and popular culture. He has devoted much of his oeuvre to exploring the entanglements between colonialism, economics, and migration in Puerto Rico. Luciano's multimedia works combine Puerto Rican historical references with commercial objects—which allude to the place that Puerto Ricans have occupied in the U.S. economy as colonial subjects—and symbols of negotiation that reveal a resistance to U.S. political oppression and cultural assimilation.

Born in Puerto Rico in 1972 and raised between the island and the United States, Luciano came of age at a time of heightened awareness around the topic of colonialism. "The year 1998 was a major turning point in my artistic life, a major time of growth," he said.[61] On July 25 of that year, he attended the large-scale demonstration at the site of the U.S. invasion that had occurred one hundred years earlier in the Puerto Rican town of Guánica, where the experience of meeting and listening to nationalist leader Lolita Lebrón had a great impact on him.[62] Less than a year later, in April 1999, U.S. Navy ground control officer David Sanes was accidentally killed during a bombing practice that was being held in the Puerto Rican island municipality of Vieques. The tragedy brought into sharp relief the militarization of the archipelago as a result of its territorial status and refueling a sixty-year-old movement demanding that the U.S. Navy leave Vieques. All sectors of Puerto Rican society came together, giving decisive momentum to that cause.[63] In 2003, after four years of intense protests and civil disobedience, President

George W. Bush (b. 1946) ordered the cessation of all military exercises in Vieques. A victory of colonial resistance, the cessation of military activity in Vieques is one of the most significant historic landmarks of the turn of the twenty-first century in Puerto Rican history. Luciano's work highlights instances of resistance and "speaking truth" to colonial power. Vieques was perhaps the most significant example of resisting colonial authority in Puerto Rico as he was coming of age as an artist.

Among his expansive multimedia oeuvre, Luciano's installation *Porto Rican Cotton Picker* and *Freedom Rider Vest (Homage to Felícita Méndez)* centers on the infamously named "Cotton Picker" Schwinn model made in 1971 (figs. 16 and 17). The 1970s witnessed the rise of Schwinn bike clubs as important circles for community building, cultural affirmation, and urban enjoyment among Puerto Rican diasporic communities, most notably in New York and Chicago.[64]

By pairing the bicycle, whose racialized name alludes to the Black and Brown field workers who picked cotton, and the leather vest, a symbol of anti-conformism in bike culture, Luciano created a perfect metaphor to embody the struggle of Felícita Méndez.[65] Born in Juncos, Puerto Rico, in 1916, Felícita Méndez (b. Gómez Martínez) moved to Arizona in 1926.[66] Her family was among the 1,500 Puerto Ricans recruited by the Arizona Cotton Growers Association to make up for labor shortages in the Southwest of the United States.[67] Before leaving Puerto Rico, the workers were promised free transportation from the island to Arizona, as well as decent wages and living conditions. But they were disappointed when reality set in: the growers' association charged them for transportation and meals while in transit, put them in barracks without electricity, and lowered their salary from the promised $2.00 a day to $1.37.[68] The press of the time documented how Puerto Rican cotton pickers, whom they interchangeably referred to as "Porto Ricans" and "negroes," staged one of the most important labor protests in Arizona history.[69] Armed with their U.S. citizenship, which granted them the possibility of looking for other opportunities, more than fifty percent of the workers—including Felícita's parents—deserted their jobs.[70] This was the earliest of various experiences of racialization that

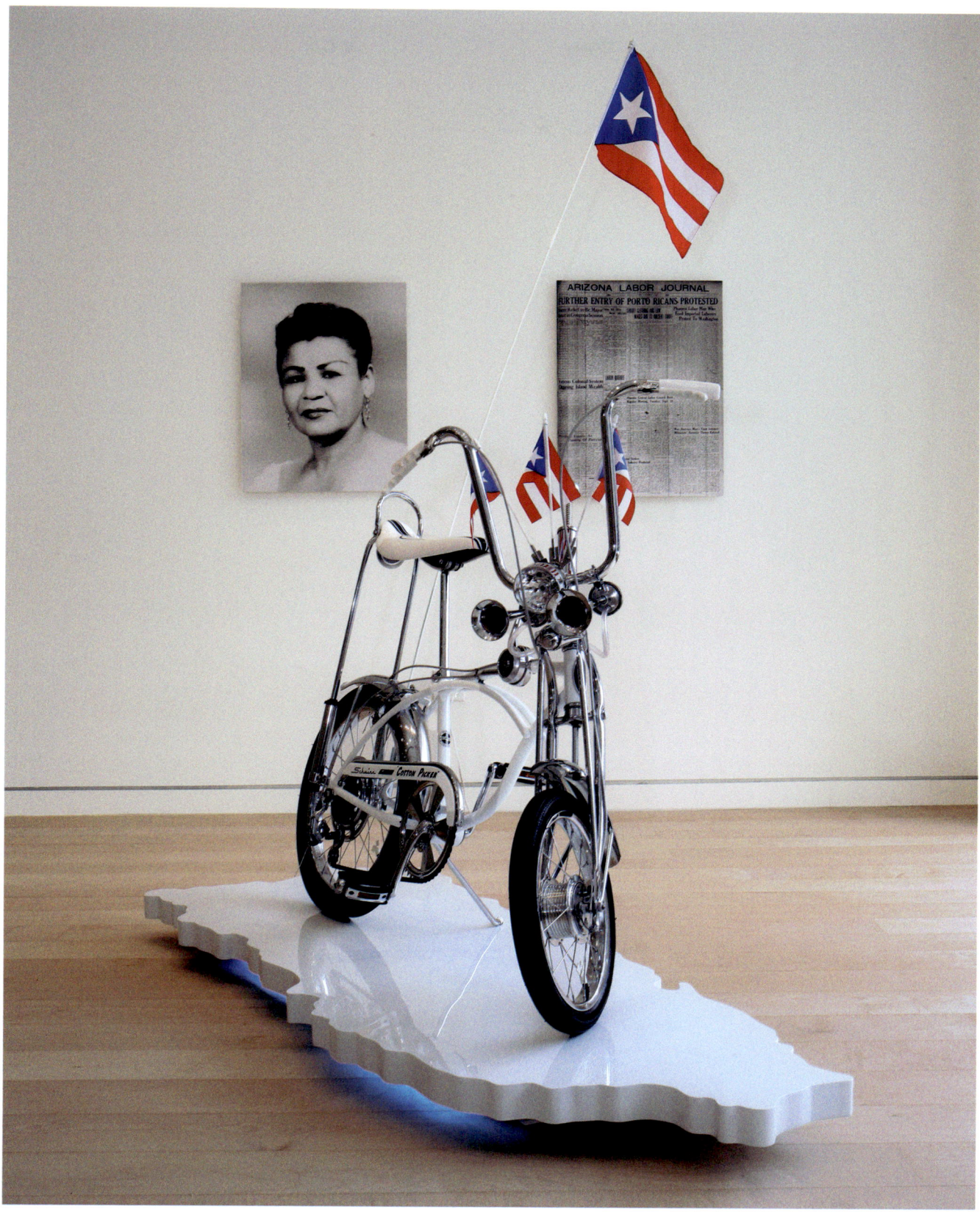

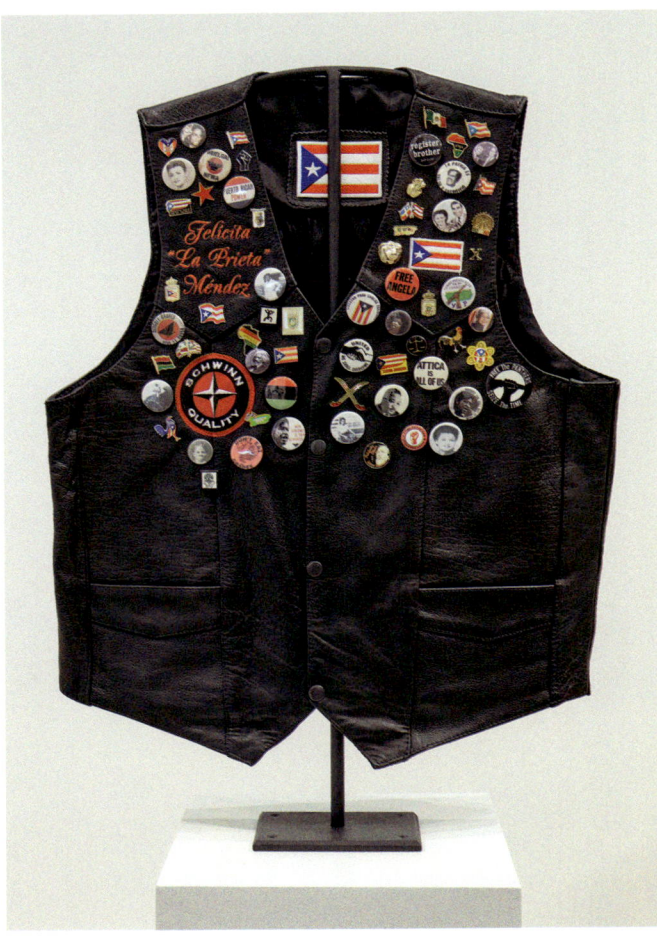

Fig. 17 *Freedom Rider Vest (Homage to Felícita Méndez)*, Miguel Luciano (b. 1972), 2011. Embroidered leather vest and vintage buttons. Courtesy of the artist

Felícita endured through her life, which underscored how U.S. racial hierarchies undermined citizenship.[71]

Felícita's family moved to California as migrant farm workers, eventually settling in Orange County. As an adult, she married Gonzálo Méndez (c. 1913–1964), a Mexican-born naturalized U.S. citizen. In 1943, their children were not admitted to a local school, but their nieces and nephews, who had lighter skin and whose family name was not recognizable as Latino, were admitted. Working with the League of United Latin American Citizens (LULAC) and other community members, Méndez sued four California districts for discrimination in 1944. Although her husband was the one named as the plaintiff in *Méndez v. Westminster*, Felícita also testified in court, participated in parent meetings, met with school officials, organized supporters of the case, and successfully ran the farm that paid for most of the legal costs they incurred.[72] The landmark civil rights ruling in 1946 established that "a paramount requisite in the American system of public education is social equality. It must be open to all children by unified school association regardless of lineage."[73] The decision inspired the Anderson Bill in 1947, which ended legal segregation in California schools before the landmark U.S. Supreme Court ruling in *Brown v. Board of Education* in 1954.

As an admirer of the old-school Schwinn bike clubs of the Puerto Rican diaspora, Luciano was inspired to create *Porto Rican Cotton Picker* and *Freedom Rider Vest* when he found and purchased a vintage "Cotton Picker" Schwinn on the market. "I wanted the bike to tell the story."[74] Politically incorrect, even in the 1970s, Schwinn discontinued this bike after just one year, which has made it a real rarity in the market. Luciano restored the bicycle in the tradition of the bike clubs, adorning it with multiple Puerto Rican flags and placing it on a customized platform in the shape of the island. This sculptural object is accompanied by a leather biker's vest that points to the identity of the bicycle's imaginary rider. The garment, titled *Freedom Rider Vest*, carves out a place for Felícita Méndez in the genealogy of individuals who have fought for racial justice, by evoking through its title the Black and white Freedom Riders of 1961 who risked their lives by traveling together in interstate trains and buses, successfully forcing their desegregation. Reinforcing that genealogy, the vest is adorned with vintage pins that commemorate Black and Brown social struggles, including buttons with the portraits of Frederick Douglass (1818–1895), Martin

Luther King Jr. (1929–1968), César Chávez (1927–1993), Puerto Rican Nationalist Pedro Albizu Campos (1891–1965), and Felícita herself, as well as flags of Puerto Rico and Mexico, a "Free Angela" button, maps of Africa, Taíno icons, a Young Lords Party button stating "*Tengo Puerto Rico en mi corazón*" (I have Puerto Rico in my heart), and a "Free the Panthers, Seize the Time" pin, among others.[75] Amidst all these messages of liberation and cultural and racial affirmation, Felícita *"La Prieta"* Méndez is emblazoned on the top left. Méndez proudly went by the nickname *La Prieta*, meaning "the Black woman." The scale of justice and the words "Méndez vs. Westminster" adorn the back of the *Freedom Rider Vest*. Additional elements of the installation that are selectively shown by the artist, depending on the exhibition venue, include blow-ups of a photographic portrait of Méndez and a clipping from *Arizona Labor Journal* documenting the historic strike led by Puerto Rican cotton pickers.

As a conceptual portrait, this installation honors Méndez and refers to the larger arc of her life and the various experiences of disenfranchisement that she and her family endured—and challenged—as people of color. *Porto Rican Cotton Picker* appropriates a bicycle model with a racist name and repurposes it as a vehicle of cultural affirmation for the commemoration of struggles for racial justice, all the while positioning Méndez as a key figure in those efforts.

Conclusion

It sometimes takes an outsider, someone who does not fully belong to the nation, to perceive the blind spots of the master narrative and hear its muffled voices. National galleries are auxiliary institutions for nation and identity building. As museums created under the aegis of the state, they exist to express the nation's values, its identity, and its political journey.[76] Within this category, national portrait galleries have a mission to shed light on a country's history using the genre of portraiture to explore the lives of individuals who have shaped the nation.[77] But the tradition of portraiture is selective. Singularity is what makes an individual deserving of a portrait, and social, economic, and political power have preconditioned that singularity through the centuries.

Prior to this exhibition, the National Portrait Gallery's emphasis on McKinley, Theodore Roosevelt (1867–1944), Leonard Wood (1856–1925), and Dewey, as well as the themes of military heroism and U.S. global power in the way it told the story of 1898, upheld an imperialistic perspective set forth in traditional scholarship since the end of these wars. The museum's national narrative assumed the silence of the colonized—or did not bother to ask for comment. This historical narrative has been constructed on the shoulders of a suppressed other. Very often, the trait of national discourses is that they are all-encompassing and pervasive.

As individuals who embody the diasporas of 1898, artists Stephanie Syjuco, Maia Cruz Palileo, Gisela McDaniel, and Miguel Luciano recover the presence and voices of their communities through their work. In subverting the racialized regimes of representation that have been constructed to reinforce the subaltern status of the U.S. imperial archipelago, their artmaking is an act of decolonization, a clear refusal of the objectifying and racializing imperial gaze, and a reformulation of what portraiture can be.

Notes

INTRODUCTION: 1898: U.S. IMPERIAL VISIONS AND REVISIONS

1. As the southernmost point in the United States, only ninety miles from Cuba, Key West played an important role during the War of 1898. It was from Key West that the USS *Maine* was dispatched on January 24, 1898, for the Bay of Havana and that the U.S. Navy left on April 21 to impose a blockade on Cuba.

2. See the instructions accompanying the game *Uncle Sam at War with Spain* (1898), produced by the Rhode Island Game Company in Gardner, Rhode Island, and designed by Robert L. Birtwistle.

3. After 1898, Spain maintained colonies in Africa, including Ceuta, Melilla, Equatorial Guinea, and Morocco.

4. French diplomat and political philosopher Alexis de Tocqueville coined the idea of "American exceptionalism" in his 1830 book *Democracy in America*, which considered the United States as qualitatively different from countries in Europe for succeeding in its establishment of a stable democracy. Historically the ideology of American exceptionalism has posited that the United States is an outlier, as the first colony in history that became a nation, with a creed that encompasses liberty, egalitarianism, individualism, populism, and laissez-faire economics. See Seymour Martin Lipset, *American Exceptionalism: A Double-edged Sword* (New York: W. W. Norton, 1997), 17–28.

5. Shortly after the War of 1898, the United States annexed a portion of the Samoan archipelago in 1899 and the U.S. Navy took the uninhabited Wake Island. The chain of possessions in the Pacific facilitated the extension of U.S. economic and political influence to China. This burst of imperial activity culminated with the United States connecting its Atlantic and Pacific holdings through the construction of the Panama Canal (1904–1914). Although publisher Henry Luce proclaimed the "American Century" as a phenomenon of cultural and political influence in the pages of *Life* magazine in 1941, some authors situate the beginning of the "American Century" in the victory over Spain in 1898. See Warren Zimmermann, *First Great Triumph: How Five Americans Made Their Country a World Power* (New York: Farrar, Straus, and Giroux, 2002), 7–8. See also César Ayala and Rafael Bernabe, *Puerto Rico in the American Century: A History since 1898* (Chapel Hill: University of North Carolina Press, 2007), 1.

6. See John M. Gates, "War-Related Deaths in the Philippines, 1898–1902," *Pacific Historical Review* 53, no. 3 (August 1984): 370; 374–76. The reported number of U.S. military casualties from the War of 1898 (April 21, 1898, to December 10, 1898) in all three arenas (Cuba, the Philippines, and Puerto Rico) was 1,668. See Clerk of the Joint Committee on Printing, *The Abridgement: Message from the President of the United States to the Two Houses of Congress*, vol. 1 (Washington, DC:

Government Printing Office, 1899), 19. Of these, about 900 Spanish troops and 385 from the United States died in combat. See Michael Clodfelter, *Warfare and Armed Conflicts: A Statistical Encyclopedia of Casualty and Other Figures, 1492–2015* (Jefferson, NC: McFarland, 2017), 244–45. It is unclear how many Spanish casualties from the war with the United States there were in Cuba, where the Spanish had fought local insurrection wars since 1895. 200,000 Spanish troops fought in the final War of Independence in Cuba, of which 38,137 died, according to the Spanish Ministry of War. Yellow fever caused almost 20,000 of those deaths, while less than 4,000 were due to combat. According to John Lawrence Tone, 40,000 soldiers fought in the Cuban Liberation Army. Approximately 5,180 were killed in combat or died of wounds. See Clodfelter, *Warfare and Armed Conflicts,* 308. About 170,000 Cuban civilians died during the final Cuban War of Independence in reconcentration camps after 1896. See Silvia Sánchez Abadía, "Olvidos de una guerra: el coste humano y económico de la independencia (Cuba-España, 1895–1898)," *Revista de Indias* 41, no. 121 (2001): 113–40; John Lawrence Tone, *War and Genocide in Cuba* (Chapel Hill: University of North Carolina Press, 2006), 223; Christopher Schmidt-Nowara, "Imperio y crisis colonial," in *Más se perdió en Cuba: España, 1898 y la crisis de fin de siglo* (Madrid: Alianza Editorial, 1999), 31–89. In the Philippines, of 50,000 Spanish troops fighting the 1896 independentist insurrection led by Emilio Aguinaldo, around 200 men died in combat and 3,000 of disease. The number of deaths among the Filipino insurgents is unknown. See Fernando Puel de la Villa, "Guerra en Cuba y Filipinas: Combates Terrestres," *Revista Universitaria de Historia Militar* 3, no. 2 (2013): 34–57. The Philippine-American War (1899–1902) resulted in the deaths of over 4,000 U.S. troops and approximately 50,000 Filipino troops. See Paul A. Kramer, *The Blood of Government* (Chapel Hill: University of North Carolina Press, 2006), 157. There was not a conflict in Puerto Rico preceding the War of 1898. The U.S. military campaign there resulted in three dead and forty wounded among the 15,000 U.S. troops and 88 wounded and 324 prisoners among the 18,000 Spanish troops. See Héctor Andrés Negroni, *Historia militar de Puerto Rico* (Madrid, Spain: Ediciones Siruela, 1992), 340.

7. The labels accompanying each portrait at the National Portrait Gallery aim to provide the visitor (onsite and online) with an overview of the sitter's biography and their impact on U.S. history, as well as some insight into the artwork. Because they run between 140 and 150 words, they are—by their very nature—limited. Since 2020, the staff of the Portrait Gallery has been invested in a process of label revision in order to present a multifaceted view of history that takes account of the result of violent historical processes and institutions such as slavery, colonialism, and the displacement and genocide of Native Americans. The aforementioned label on Theodore Roosevelt accompanied his portrait in *America's Presidents* between 2018 and 2022, while the label on

George Dewey accompanied his portrait in the exhibition *American Origins* between 2006 and 2021.

8. More information on the protests against the Platt Amendment can be found on pages 167–68 in this volume. See also Louis A. Pérez, *Cuba: Between Reform and Revolution* (Oxford: Oxford University Press, 2015), 149.

9. The Smithsonian Institution sent anthropologists, archaeologists, zoologists, and other experts to survey the "new possessions" and generate knowledge that could be disseminated through publications and exhibitions at its own museum and in large-scale expositions. This knowledge often served the purpose of justifying the U.S. imperial project and the need for political tutelage in the territories. The Smithsonian also became the repository of objects and collections donated by military officials who participated in the War of 1898 or the colonial administration of the territories. See Jorge Duany, *The Puerto Rican Nation on the Move: Identities on the Island and in the United States* (Chapel Hill: University of North Carolina Press, 2004), 39–121; Paul A. Kramer, *The Blood of Government*, 233–36; Miguel A. Bretos, "Imaging Cuba Under the American Flag: Charles Edward Doty in Havana," in *Journal of Decorative and Propaganda Arts* 22 (1996): 82–103. See also Paul A. Kramer's essay "New Possessions: Colonial Curios, Trophies, Weapons, and Museum Collections from the Philippine-American War," in this volume, pp. 205–17, and Taína Caragol, "The 1898 Diasporas: Contemporary Artists Redefining Portraiture," pp. 219–39.

10. In 1945, Cuban historian and journalist Emilio Roig de Leuchsenring called on all Cuban historians of his generation to use and popularize "the Spanish-Cuban-American War" for the conflict. See Emilio Roig de Leuchsenring, "La guerra hispano-cubano-americana," in *13 conclusiones fundamentales sobre la guerra libertadora cubana de 1895* (Mexico City: Colegio de México, 1985), 39.

11. It should also be understood that approximately 60,000 loyalist Cubans fought with the Spanish army, and approximately 8,000 Filipinos fought with the Spanish from 1896 to 1898. See John Lawrence Tone, *War and Genocide in Cuba, 1895–1898* (Chapel Hill: University of North Carolina Press, 2006), 9; and for Filipinos fighting with Spanish soldiers, see Carlos Quirino, "The Spanish Colonial Army," *Philippine Studies* 36, no. 3 (Third Quarter 1988): 385. Regarding a name that includes all arenas of war, historian Daniel Immerwahr argues that the name "Spanish-American-Cuban-Puerto Rican-Philippine War" would be appropriate. See Daniel Immerwahr, *How to Hide an Empire: A History of the Greater United States* (New York: Farrar, Straus, and Giroux, 2019), 70.

12. Immerwahr makes a similar point without including Guam, which saw no theater of war and became part of the United States through the Treaty of Paris. See Immerwahr, *How to Hide an Empire*, 70.

13. Todd Shepard, *Voices of Decolonization: A Brief History with Documents* (Boston: Bedford / St. Martin's, 2015), 16–17.

14. The population of the Philippines at the time of the war was around ten million. President McKinley's speech to the Notification Committee on July 12, 1900, is cited in *The Republican Campaign Text-Book* (Philadelphia: Republican National Committee, 1900), 49.

15. In accordance to this nomenclature, books on the "new possessions" claimed by the U.S. in 1898 became widely popular at the turn of the century. See Lanny Thompson, *Imperial Archipelago: Representation and Rule in the Insular Territories under U.S. Dominion after 1898* (Honolulu: Hawai'i University Press, 2010), 1.

16. Clause IX of the Treaty of Paris, stating that "the civil rights and political status of the native inhabitants of the territories hereby ceded to the United States shall be determined by the Congress," which still applies to Puerto Rico and Guam, stands as the irrefutable proof of this status.

17. We are grateful to Lanny Thompson for underscoring this distinction in regard to the discursive use of "self-government" in the United States in the aftermath of 1898.

18. We are grateful to historians Silvia Álvarez Curbelo and Emanuel Bravo for their insight into the use of the term "self-government" in Autonomist circles of the late nineteenth century in Puerto Rico and Cuba. For specific uses of the word in texts of the time, see Antonio Angulo Heredia, "Estudios sobre los Estados Unidos" in *Revista Hispano-Americana*, no. 4. (January 27, 1865): 6, 9–10.

19. Guam also endured Japanese occupation during WWII, as "Cutting a Path to Sovereignty: The Complex Political Landscapes of the Philippines and Guam" in this volume explains.

20. See essays dedicated to Puerto Rico, Guam, Hawai'i, and American Samoa in Frances Negrón-Muntaner, ed. *Sovereign Acts: Contesting Colonialism across Indigenous Nations and Latinx America* (Tucson: University of Arizona Press, 2017), 37–125.

21. See David Keanu Sai, "American Occupation of the Hawaiian State: A Century Unchecked," *Hawaiian Journal of Law & Politics* 1 (Summer 2004): 46–82.

22. Dánica Coto, "Puerto Ricans Speak Out on US Territory's Political Status," *Washington Post*, June 4, 2022, https://www.washingtonpost.com/world /puerto-ricans-speak-out-on-us-territorys-political -status/2022/06/04/c6183138-e458-11ec-ae64 -6b23e5155b62_story.html.

23. Jon Letman, "Guam: Where the U.S. Military is Revered and Reviled," *The Diplomat*, August 29, 2016, https://thediplomat.com/2016/08/guam-where-the -us-military-is-revered-and-reviled/.

24. The words "CHamoru," "Chamoru," and "Chamorro" refer to the Indigenous people of the Mariana Islands and their language. Throughout our exhibition and catalogue, we use the spelling CHamoru, abiding by the orthographic standards established by the Commission on CHamoru Language and the Teaching of the History and Culture of the Indigenous People of Guam, re-established in 2020. See Jerick Sablan, "Language Commission Launches Latest CHamoru Orthography," *Pacific Daily News*, January 21, 2021, https://www.guampdn.com/news/local/language -commission-launches-latest-chamoru-orthography /article_c900f6fc-6655–54b6-acad-4e761b11e347.html. For Palomo, see Anne Perez Hattori, "Colonialism, Capitalism and Nationalism in the U.S. Navy's Expulsion of Guam's Spanish Catholic Priests, 1898–1900," *Journal of Pacific History* 44, no. 3 (December 2009): 285. For Perez, see https://www.guampedia.com/atanasio -taitano-perez/ and "Who's Who in Guam: Mr. Atanasio Taitano Perez," *The Guam Recorder* 13, no. 11 (February 1937): 4.

25. See D. J. Walker, *Spanish Women and the Colonial Wars of the 1890s* (Baton Rouge: Louisiana State University Press, 2008).

26. Territorial expansion and the implied displacement of Native Americans in the continental United States predates the Declaration of Independence. As the United States became independent and took responsibility for its own actions, however, it continued this trajectory of expansion and displacement. We are thankful to Kristin Hoganson for her insight into this shift of responsibility.

27. Thomas Jefferson to Archibald Stuart, January 25, 1786, in *Founders Online*, National Archives, https:// founders.archives.gov/documents/Jefferson /01–09–02–0192.

28. This address was shaped by Secretary of State John Quincy Adams, but it was adopted by President James Monroe in 1823. It became known as the Monroe Doctrine after 1844. See Walter LaFeber, *The American Age: U.S. Foreign Policy at Home and Abroad, 1750 to the Present* (New York: W. W. Norton, 1994), 83–88.

29. See Davianna Pōmaika'I McGregor, "Recognizing Native Hawaiians: Reality Bites," in *Sovereign Acts: Contesting Colonialism Across Indigenous Nations and Latinx America*, ed. Frances Negrón-Muntaner (Tucson: University of Arizona Press, 2017), 125–50.

"THE PORTRAITS IN THE GALLERY HAVE NEVER BEEN ONLY NATIONAL"

1. On land areas: "What is a federal Indian reservation?" Frequently Asked Questions, U.S. Department of Interior, Indian Affairs, https://www.bia.gov/faqs /what-federal-indian-reservation.

2. Pablo Navarro-Rivera, "The Imperial Enterprise and Educational Policies in Colonial Puerto Rico," in *Colonial Crucible: Empire in the Making of the Modern American State*, ed. Alfred W. McCoy and Francisco A. Scarano (Madison: University of Wisconsin Press, 2009), 163–74.

3. Brandon Mills, *The World that Colonization Made: The Racial Geography of Early American Empire* (Philadelphia: University of Pennsylvania Press, 2020).

4. Navarro-Rivera, "The Imperial Enterprise," 163–74.

5. Julie Greene, *The Canal Builders: Making America's Empire at the Panama Canal* (New York: Penguin Press, 2009).

6. Ibid.

7. Paul Kramer, "Making Concessions: Race and Empire Revisited at the Philippine Exposition, St. Louis, 1901–1905," *Radical History Review* 73 (Winter 1999): 74–114; Laura Wexler, *Tender Violence: Domestic Visions in an Age of U.S. Imperialism* (Chapel Hill: University of North Carolina Press, 2000); Rebecca Tinio McKenna, *American Imperial Pastoral: The Architecture of U.S. Colonialism in the Philippines* (Chicago: University of Chicago Press, 2017).

8. Shana Klein, *The Fruits of Empire: Art, Food, and the Politics of Race in the Age of American Expansion* (Oakland: University of California Press, 2020), 137–39.

9. Ibid.

10. Tommy R. Thompson, "John D. Brady, the Philippine-American War, and the Martial Spirit in Late 19th Century America," *Nebraska History* 84 (2003): 142–53.

11. Ibid.

PRELUDE TO EMPIRE: INDIAN WARS AND SEA POWER

1. Alfred Thayer Mahan, *Retrospect and Prospect: Studies in International Relations, Naval and Political* (Boston: Little, Brown, and Company, 1902), 111.

2. According to Benedict Anderson, the concept of "nationalism" emerged at the end of the eighteenth century, becoming operative as a historical force in the nineteenth century. Benedict Anderson, *Imagined Communities: Reflections on the Spread of Nationalism,* rev. ed. (New York: Verso, 2006), 4. See also Caterina Bassetti, "States, Nations, and Regionalisms in the Perspective of the European Integration Process," in *Empires and Nations from the Eighteenth to the Twentieth Centuries*, ed. Antonello Biagini and Giovanna Motta, vol. 1 (Newcastle, UK: Cambridge Scholars Publishing, 2014), 407.

3. In Europe, ethno-linguistic communities informed by the Enlightenment principles of freedom and equality, and the rise of capitalism, among other factors, came together to fight against dynastic systems where power was hereditary and divinely ordained, rather than stemming from the people. See Anderson, *Imagined Communities*, 85. The first quarter of the nineteenth century also saw most of the colonies of Spain in Latin America fight for their independence. Eventually, many of these new nations engaged in warfare among themselves as they settled the borders of their nations.

4. Spanish conquistador Juan Ponce de León colonized Puerto Rico in 1508, establishing its first settlement in Caparra, south of the San Juan Bay.

5. In North America, the displacement and dispossession of Native American communities by Europeans and Euro-Americans began in 1513, when Spanish explorer Juan Ponce de León arrived in present-day southwest Florida.

6. See Piero Gleijeses, *America's Road to Empire: Foreign Policy from Independence to World War One* (London: Bloomsbury Academic, 2021), 62–63.

7. See Thomas Jefferson to Archibald Stuart, January 25, 1786, in *Founders Online,* National Archives, https://founders.archives.gov/documents/Jefferson/01-09-02-0192.

8. See Jay Sexton, *The Monroe Doctrine: Empire and Nation in Nineteenth-Century America* (New York: Hill and Wang, 2011). Since its declaration, however, the Monroe Doctrine was applied unevenly. For example, the United States did not intervene when Britain occupied the Falkland Islands in 1833, or in 1861, when Spain reasserted colonial rule in the Dominican Republic, or when Napoleon III instated his cousin Maximilian I to be the puppet ruler of Mexico in 1864. This hands-off interpretation of the Monroe Doctrine was replaced by a policy of intervention in the late nineteenth century. See Warren Zimmerman, *First Great Triumph: How Five Americans Made Their Country a World Power* (New York: Farrar, Straus, and Giroux, 2002), 19.

9. Cherokee resistance took their case to the United States Supreme Court, and in the 1831 decision, Chief Justice John Marshall ruled that an Indian tribe was "a distinct political society," and that they held the status of "domestic dependent nations." In 1832, the Court ruled that federal law—not state law—directed relations with Native tribes. See Walter LaFeber, *The American Age: U.S. Foreign Policy at Home and Abroad, 1750 to the Present* (New York: W. W. Norton, 1994), 99. Roosevelt was reluctant to embark on additional wars and annex more territory, as seen in his "porcupine statement" on the Dominican Republic. See Theodore Roosevelt to Joseph Bucklin Bishop, February 23, 1904, Theodore Roosevelt Center at Dickinson State University, https://www.theodorerooseveltcenter.org/Research/Digital-Library/Record?libID=o281261.

10. A joint resolution required only a majority of the House and Senate, rather than two-thirds Senate vote—a precedent that laid the foundation for the United States to annex Hawai'i in 1898.

11. See Tom Coffman, *Nation Within: The History of the Occupation of Hawai'i* (Durham, NC: Duke University Press, 2016), 56.

12. Christopher Conway, ed., *The U.S.-Mexican War: A Binational Reader*, trans. Gustavo Pellón (Indianapolis: Hackett Publishing, 2010), 127.

13. Theodore Roosevelt, *American Statesman: Thomas Hart Benton* (Boston: Houghton, Mifflin, 1889), 40.

14. Many U.S. generals, like Nelson Miles, climbed the ranks of the professional army during the Indian Wars and later applied their knowledge in various arenas of the War of 1898 and in the subsequent Philippine-American War from 1899 to 1902. See Katherine Bjork, *Prairie Imperialists: The Indian Country Origins of American Empire* (Philadelphia: University of Pennsylvania Press, 2019).

15. The Sioux were not one tribe, rather groups of related tribes. The Sioux originally consisted of seven autonomous, yet related, groups, divided between eastern tribes, Dakota, and western tribes, Lakota. Lakotas are comprised of seven tribes, including "Hunkpapa," which roughly translates to "Campers at the Opening of the Circle." The Lakota lived in the High Plains between the Missouri River and the Bighorn Mountains, ranging from Canada to the Platte and Republican Rivers. See Robert J. Utley, *Sitting Bull: The Life and Times of an American Patriot* (New York: Henry Holt, 1993), 3–4.

16. Sitting Bull's place of birth is debated and may never be known. For the account by Sitting Bull's great-grandson, see Jess Blumber, "Sitting Bull's Legacy," *Smithsonian Magazine*, October 30, 2007. https://www.smithsonianmag.com/history /sitting-bulls-legacy-175332903/. Robert J. Utley suspects that Sitting Bull was born on the Grand River at Many Caches. See Utley, *Sitting Bull*, 3.

17. In 1868, the Sioux, led by Red Cloud, signed the Second Treaty of Fort Laramie, which recognized territory in what is now southwestern South Dakota as their sovereign territory. When the U.S. Army invaded the Black Hills, it was in clear and flagrant violation of the treaty. This invasion, along with the U.S. Army's attempt to force Lakotas not already living on the reservation back onto the reservation, ignited warfare.

18. Gregory J. W. Urwin, "Battle of Little Bighorn," *Britannica Academic*, https://www.britannica.com /event/Battle-of-the-Little-Bighorn.

19. Utley, *Sitting Bull*, 2.

20. Thank you to Ann McMullen for her consultation on this portrait.

21. Frank Goodyear III, "Wanted: Sitting Bull and His Photographic Portrait," *South Dakota History* 40, no. 2 (Summer 2010): 136–62; Sarah A. Hanson-Pareek, "An Extremely Rare and Perhaps Significant Photograph of Tatanka Iyotake (Sitting Bull)," *Archives and Special Collections Blog* (blog), University Library, University of South Dakota, September 16, 2020, https://archives andspecialcollections.wordpress.com/2020/09/16 /an-extremely-rare-and-perhaps-significant -photograph-of-tatanka-iyotake-sitting-bull/.

22. Some Filipinos saw Sitting Bull perform and were inspired by him. See p. 132 in this volume.

23. *Britannica Academic*, "Sitting Bull"; see also Utley, *Sitting Bull*.

24. For more information, see Candace Greene, "Significance of the Ledger Drawings," in *A Pictographic History of the Oglala Sioux: Drawings by Amos Bad Heart Bull*, 50th Anniversary Edition, ed. Emily Levine and Candace Greene (Lincoln: University of Nebraska Press, 2017), xxvii–xxxix. Thank you to

Candace Greene for sharing her research and for consulting with us about the muslin painting by Amos Bad Heart Bull.

25. Greene, "Significance of the Ledger Drawings," 7–9.

26. Bad Heart Bull's ledger drawings include a series entitled *Battle of the Little Bighorn*, nos. 126 to 185, in the collection of the University of Nebraska library archives. The objects were photographed, and the original negatives are in the National Anthropological Archives. For online access to the National Anthropological Archives, see http://siris-archives.si.edu. Images from the negatives are also available through the Plains Indian Ledger Art project, online at PlainsLedgerArt.org.

27. Greene, "Significance of the Ledger Drawings," 3, 7.

28. Greene, "Significance of the Ledger Drawings," 3.

29. J. P. Morgan bailed out the U.S. Treasury in 1893, and McKinley himself had to be bailed out by political donors. As president, McKinley led the country by tightly controlling the State Department and Congress. He maintained this vigilant oversight in part through daily use of the telephone and typewriter; he was the first U.S. president to do so. See LaFeber, *The American Age*, 196.

30. In 1890, while representing Ohio (1877–1891) in Congress, McKinley was chairman of the Ways and Means Committee. In this position, he framed the 1890 Tariff Act. As a result of the passing of the 1890 Tariff Act, the United States entered into reciprocity trade agreements with the Dominican Republic (1891), Spain for Cuba and Puerto Rico (1891), El Salvador (1891), Guatemala (1891), Nicaragua (1892), Honduras (1892), Great Britain for the West Indies (1892), the German Empire (1892), and Austria-Hungary (1892). U.S. Tariff Commission, *Reciprocity and Commercial Treaties* (Washington, DC: Government Printing Office, 1919), 150. The 1890 McKinley Tariff had disadvantageous effects for the Hawaiian sugar trade, which had benefited from its own reciprocity treaty with the United States since 1875. See César J. Ayala, *American Sugar Kingdom: The Plantation Economy of the Spanish Caribbean, 1898–1934* (Chapel Hill: University of North Carolina Press, 1999), 51–62.

31. The 1895 tariffs ended a particularly profitable boom in Cuban sugar trade with the United States from 1890 to 1894. By 1894, $98 million of Cuba's total $116 million exports went to the United States. See Louis Pérez, *Cuba: Between Reform and Revolution*, 3rd ed. (New York: Oxford University Press, 2006), 113.

32. To preserve its financial interests, the firm became involved in the Ten Years' War for Cuban Independence (1868–1878). See Richard Salvato, "Guide to the Moses Taylor Papers," New York Public Library, https://www .nypl.org/sites/default/files/archivalcollections/pdf /taylor.pdf. Thank you to Marysol Nieves for sharing her provenance research on this painting.

33. Although the U.S. newspapers reported on the Spanish as the perpetrators of punitive policies toward citizens, such as the reconcentration camps, the

Cuban Liberation Army was also partly responsible for this episode. Its strategy of total warfare displaced people from their villages and towns, causing a refugee crisis. See Lawrence Tone, *War and Genocide in Cuba, 1895–1898* (Chapel Hill: University of North Carolina Press, 2006), 195–207.

34. Pérez, *Cuba Between Empires*, 127. By Tone's count, 295,357 Cubans were forced into reconcentration camps. This number does not include La Habana province, which did not record any data in its census. See Tone, *War and Genocide in Cuba*, 223.

35. Vermont senator Redfield Proctor visited Cuba, witnessed the reconcentration camps, and publicly changed his antiwar stance on March 17, 1898. See LaFeber, *The American Age*, 201.

36. William H. Gerdts lists twelve that were published. See Gerdts, *William Glackens, Life and Work* (New York: Abbeville Press; Museum of Art, Fort Lauderdale, Florida, 1996), 265. Heather Coyle Campbell lists only six as having been published. See "The Character and Rhythm of Modern Life," in *William Glackens*, ed. Avis Berman (New York: Skira Rizzoli; Philadelphia: Barnes Foundation, 2014), 47. For recent scholarship on Glackens, see Ramey Mize, "Battle Grounds: Painting, War and Witness in the Americas, 1861–1902," PhD diss., University of Pennsylvania, 2023.

37. Tone, *War and Genocide in Cuba*, 217.

38. Glackens also published his work in *Munsey's*, but *McClure's* commissioned his work.

39. Tone, *War and Genocide in Cuba*, 210.

40. The gift was apparently beyond his personal means. See Nick Kapur, "William McKinley's Values and the Origins of the Spanish-American War: A Reinterpretation," *Presidential Studies Quarterly* 41, no. 1 (March 2011): 26–27.

41. LaFeber, *The American Age*, 197. See also Pérez, *Cuba*, 10. Pérez outlines how U.S. investments increased from $50 million in the late nineteenth century to $1.3 billion by the 1920s.

42. McKinley was speaking to his physician, Leonard Wood—another Civil War veteran and, later, a key combatant in the War of 1898, who rose to the rank of general. See Lewis Gould, *The Presidency of William McKinley* (Lawrence: Regents Press of Kansas, 1980), 78. During the Civil War, McKinley fought in the Battle of Antietam, the single bloodiest day of the Civil War. Twice cited for valor, he earned a battlefield promotion to major and was referred to as such for the rest of his life.

43. In 1858, President Buchanan urged Congress to appropriate money to buy Cuba. However, the slave controversy, aggravated in 1857 with the Supreme Court's ruling on the Dred Scott case that slavery could be taken into U.S. territories, divided Republicans. Free-Soilers, a rapidly growing wing of the Republican Party, led by William H. Seward, jettisoned any hope Buchanan had to annex Cuba. See LaFeber, *The American Age*, 143–45. After the U.S. Civil War, many Confederates moved to Cuba or visited frequently, feeling a kinship with planters and slaveholders there. See Ferrer, *Cuba*, 119–25.

44. The issue of the balance of slave states long plagued U.S.–Cuban relations. During the antebellum period, Presidents Polk and Pierce had offered Spain $100 million and $150 million, respectively, although annexing Cuba would have upset the balance of slave and free states in the United States. Following the Emancipation Proclamation of 1863, Cubans hoping to preserve the institution of slavery no longer considered annexation to the United States as a solution. In 1880, Spain enacted a law of abolition, allowing a period of eight years as a transition to full emancipation. During the transition, *patrocinados,* or the formerly enslaved, assumed the social standing of "apprentices" and their former enslavers had to pay them monthly wages. In 1885, two years before the scheduled end of gradual abolition, a royal decree brought slavery to an end. By then, fewer than thirty thousand enslaved Cubans remained. See Pérez, *Cuba: Between Reform and Revolution*, 81–83, 94–96.

45. Walter LaFeber argues that McKinley did not annex Cuba because he felt "it would bring too many unpredictable races into the Union." Instead, McKinley believed that Cuba, with its proximity to the United States, could be easily controlled through legislative means like the Platt Amendment. See LaFeber, *The American Age*, 209–10. The 1887 Cuban Census numbers the total Black population in Cuba at one third, 32.4 percent. In 1899, the Black population numbered 32.1 percent. U.S. Bureau of the Census Library, *Cuba: Population History and Resources* (Washington, DC: U.S. Bureau of the Census, 1909), n.p. https://www.census.gov/library/publications/1907/dec/cuba-1907.html.

46. Cubans were divided on the issue of annexation; they also funded $1 million in payment to lobbyists and possibly to congressmen supporting the Teller Amendment. See LaFeber, *The American Age*, 203.

47. William McKinley, First Inaugural Address, March 4, 1897, *University of Virginia Miller Center*, https://millercenter.org/the-presidency/presidential-speeches/march-4-1897-first-inaugural-address.

48. This was the last of three liberation wars that Cuba fought against Spain, the other two being the Ten Years' War (1868–1878) and the Little War (1879–1880). For more information see "On the Verge of Sovereignty: Cuba and Puerto Rico at the Turn fo the Twentieth Century." in this volume, pp. 89–117.

49. John D. Long described the circumstances to McKinley. See Ivan Musicant, *Empire by Default: The Spanish-American War and the Dawn of the American Century* (New York: Henry Holt, 1998), 114.

50. The navy, led by Benjamin Franklin Tracy (1830–1915) from 1889 to 1893, had poured its resources into new ships. It built its first steel warship in 1885 and built at least five warships a year from 1893 to 1896. See Timothy S. Wolters, "Recapitalizing the Fleet: A Material Analysis of Late-Nineteenth-Century U.S. Naval Power," *Technology and Culture* 52, no. 1 (January 2011): 115.

51. The USS *Maine* was modeled after the British-built Brazilian battleship *Riachuelo*, which was the most powerful warship in the Western Hemisphere. See Musicant, *Empire by Default*, 116–17.

52. The ship was commissioned in September 1895 and built in the New York Navy Yard. See "USS *Maine* (1895–1898), originally designated as Armored Cruiser #1," Naval History and Heritage Command, https://www.history.navy.mil/our-collections/photography/us-navy-ships/battleships/maine.html. Sailors chipped away at the paint and accomplished the work in about a month. See Musicant, *Empire by Default*, 114–15.

53. The letter was written in mid-December 1897. See LaFeber, *The American Age*, 199.

54. Musicant, *Empire by Default*, 132–33.

55. Some historians describe the *Maine* as patrolling, but this is inaccurate. Most likely, it was tied to a buoy until its explosion. See "Report of the Naval Court of Inquiry Upon the Destruction of the United States Battleship Maine in Havana Harbor, February 15, 1898," Naval History and Heritage Command, https://www.history.navy.mil/research/publications/documentary-histories/united-states-navy-s/destruction-of-the-m/report-of-the-naval-0.html.

56. Of those 260 sailors, 252 were dead or missing and 8 would die later. See Jerry Keenan, *Encyclopedia of the Spanish-American & Philippine-American Wars* (Santa Barbara, CA: ABC CLIO Press, 2001), 219. In 1976, Admiral Hyman Rickover published a thorough investigation that determined that the vessel most likely had been destroyed by an internal explosion. See Hyman Rickover, *How the Battleship* Maine *Was Destroyed* (Annapolis, MD: Naval Institute Press, 1994).

57. Musicant, *Empire by Default*, 144; citing Wisan, *The Cuban Crisis as Reflected in the New York Press* (New York: Octagon, 1965), 390–91.

58. See "Appalling Nature of the Maine Disaster Gives Ground for Suspicion of Treachery," *The Tennessean*, February 17, 1898; "The Whole Country Thrills with War Fever: Remember the Maine! To Hell With Spain!" February 18, 1898, *New York Journal;* and "Maine Is Annihilated," *Dixon Evening Telegraph*, February 16, 1898.

59. See Kristin Hoganson, *Fighting for American Manhood: How Gender Politics Provoked the Spanish-American and Philippine-American Wars* (New Haven, CT: Yale University Press, 1998), 68–87.

60. McKinley recalled the orders, except the one for George Dewey and his Asiatic Fleet. See LaFeber, *The American Age*, 200.

61. As early as September 1897, the newly appointed U.S. ambassador to Spain, Steward L. Woodford, communicated to the Spanish government that if hostilities with Cuba were not resolved by November of that year, the United States would be obliged to intervene. See Nick Kapur, "William McKinley's Values and the Origins of the Spanish-American War," 28; and LaFeber, *The American Age*, 201–2.

62. In November 1897, after much hesitation, Spain had offered Cubans an autonomic charter with the aim of enticing the Cuban Liberation Army to depose arms, but they rejected the offer. It is, therefore, interesting that McKinley's ultimatum to Spain before declaring war did not define exactly what it meant by "self-government." On March 26, 1898, McKinley wired his request to the U.S. minister to Spain, Stewart L. Woodford. See Nick Kapur, "William McKinley's Values and the Origins of the Spanish-American War," 28; LaFeber, *The American Age*, 201–2; José Manuel Allendesalazar, *El 98 de los americanos* (Madrid: Ministerio de Asuntos Exteriores, 1997), 67.

63. McKinley wrote, "to authorize and empower the President to take measure to secure a full and final termination of hostilities between the Government of Spain and the people of Cuba, and to secure in the island the establishment of a stable government, capable of maintaining order and observing its international obligations, insuring peace and tranquility and the security of its citizens as well as our own, and to use the military and naval forces of the United States as may be necessary for these purposes." See William McKinley, "April 11, 1898: Message Regarding Cuban Civil War," Miller Center, University of Virginia, https://millercenter.org/the-presidency/presidential-speeches/april-11-1898-message-regarding-cuban-civil-war. McKinley, however, refused to recognize the Cuban revolutionaries or sign the Turpie-Foraker Amendment, which would have recognized Cuban independence. He also adopted the $400,000,000 bond that Spain had set to pay for its military expenditures, and which was to be repaid through Cuban revenues. See Paul S. Holbo, "Presidential Leadership in Foreign Affairs: William McKinley and the Turpie-Foraker Amendment," *The American Historical Review* 72, no. 4 (July 1967): 1321–35.

64. William McKinley, "Call for volunteers–Spain," April 25, 1898, Department of State, Office of the Historian, https://history.state.gov/historicaldocuments/frus1898/d637.

65. The Teller Amendment's text specifies that the United States "hereby disclaims any disposition of intention to exercise sovereignty, jurisdiction, or control over said island except for pacification thereof, and asserts its determination, when that is accomplished, to leave the government and control of the island to its people." See "The Teller Amendment," Investigating U.S. History, City University of New York, https://investigatinghistory.ashp.cuny.edu/files/1898TellerAmendment.pdf. Teller, a Republican, was attempting to protect the sugar beet industry of Colorado, whose economy would have tanked if Cuban sugar came to the fore. See LaFeber, *The American Age*, 203.

66. Keenan, *Encyclopedia of the Spanish-American & Philippine-American Wars*, xxvii.

67. On the Cuban blockade, see "Spanish-American War," Naval History and Heritage Command, https://www.history.navy.mil/research/publications/documentary-histories/united-states-navy-s/blockade-of-northern.html. McKinley issued a call for 125,000 volunteer men on April 22, 1898, to be ready in a month's time. See Musicant, *Empire by Default*, 189. The regular army was unable to draw the 36,000 men it needed for a wartime capacity because the War Department's recruitment for volunteers was much more appealing than becoming a professional soldier. In the volunteers, enlistees had easier discipline, and a chance to serve alongside friends and neighbors. See Musicant, *Empire by Default*, 247; 259.

68. McKinley admitted that he took sleeping potions so that he could rest during this stressful week of negotiations about the war. See LaFeber, *The American Age*, 202.

69. See Robert Gudmestad, "Elusive Victory: The Union Navy's War along the Western Waters," *Civil War History* 62, no. 2 (June 2021): 97.

70. Born in New York's Hudson Valley, Alfred Thayer Mahan grew up at West Point, where his father was a professor at the United States Military Academy. After graduating in 1859 from the United States Naval Academy in Annapolis, he fought in the Civil War with the Union Navy. In 1885, Stephen Luce asked Mahan to help found the Naval War College in Rhode Island, where he later lectured. For Mahan's biography, see Suzanne Geissler, *God and Sea Power: The Influence of Religion on Alfred Thayer Mahan* (Annapolis, MD: Naval Institute Press 2015).

71. Kristin Hoganson expands on the idea of gender and manliness during the age of empire. See Hoganson, *Fighting for American Manhood*.

72. Cited in Robert Seager II, *Alfred Thayer Mahan: The Man and His Letters* (Annapolis, MD: Naval Institute Press, 1977), 209.

73. Theodore Roosevelt, "The Influence of Sea Power Upon History," *Atlantic Monthly* (October 1890): 563–67; also cited in Seager, *Alfred Thayer Mahan*, 210.

74. Had Germany fought the United States over Samoa in 1888–89, for example, victory would have been a struggle for the United States. See Timothy S. Wolters, "Recapitalizing the Fleet," 105–6.

75. When war with Spain commenced in 1898, the old navy still accounted for about half of all ships in the navy's inventory. See Wolters, "Recapitalizing the Fleet," 118–19. The older ships were used in combatant roles, like the ten monitors used for the "mosquito flotilla," or the coastal defense of the Atlantic seaboard. See Wolters, "Recapitalizing the Fleet," 120–21.

76. See "U.S. Navy Ship Force Levels, 1892–1897; 1898–1903," Naval History and Heritage Command, https://www.history.navy.mil/research/histories/ship-histories/us-ship-force-levels.html#1892. For Theodore Roosevelt, see John B. Hattendorf and William P. Leeman, eds., *Forging the Trident: Theodore Roosevelt and the United States Navy* (Annapolis, MD: Naval Institute Press, 2021), especially Leeman, "From

Knowledge, Sea Power: Theodore Roosevelt, Naval Education, and the New Navy," 82–103.

77. From 1869 to 1899, the U.S. Navy owned 246 major warships. See Wolters, "Recapitalizing the Fleet," 115, 126.

78. Since his service in the Wars of 1898 was on the Naval War Board in Washington, DC, he did not qualify for the medal during his lifetime. In 1898, Mahan was called into service as an advisor to the Navy and returned from Europe. See Musicant, *Empire by Default*, 335–37.

79. Thank you to John Hattendorf of the Naval War College for this information. Email with the author, December 24, 2021.

80. See John Hattendorf, *Faces of the Naval War College* (Newport, RI: Naval War College Press, 2009), 3.

81. Sargent, whom Lodge met in Nahant, a summer colony just north of Boston, held similar aristocratic beliefs. See Charles Merrill Mount, "The Rabbit and the Boa Constrictor: John Singer Sargent at the White House," *Records of the Columbia Historical Society, Washington, DC* 71/72 (1971 and 1972): 620, 630.

82. Alfred Thayer Mahan was one of the experts cited in the pro-annexation arguments. Mahan, commenting on Hawai'i's strategic location in the Pacific, described it as "having no rival" as a naval base of operations to protect the Pacific coast. See "Fifty-fifth Congress, March 16, 1898, Annexation of Hawaii," in *Compilation of Reports of Committee on Foreign Relations of the United States Senate, 1789–1901, First Congress, First Session, to Fifty-Sixth Congress, Second Session: Diplomatic Relations with Foreign Nations—Affairs in Cuba* (Washington, DC: Government Printing Office, 1901), 226, https://hdl.handle.net/2027/uc1.b3989748.

83. See LaFeber, *The American Age*, 203.

84. See Ronald C. Williams Jr., "'Aole Hoohui Ia Hawaii': U.S. Collegiate Teams Debate Annexation of Hawai'i and Independence Prevails, 1893 to 1897," *Hawaiian Journal of Historiography* 43 (2009): 169.

85. On December 30, 1842, President John Tyler sent a message to Congress recognizing the independence of the government of Hawai'i and the primacy of the United States as a trading partner with the archipelago, and opposing any attempt by another power to take control of the archipelago, to colonize it, or "subvert its Native government." See Edward P. Caprol, *John Tyler: The Accidental President* (Chapel Hill: University of North Carolina Press, 2012), 158, 172. A transcript of Tyler's message to Congress can be found here: https://loveman.sdsu.edu/docs/1842TylerDoctrine.pdf.

86. President Franklin Pierce made a proposal for annexing the archipelago in 1854, but he dropped it when King Kamehameha III set as a condition that the multiracial population of Hawai'i be recognized as citizens with full rights. In 1897, another attempt at annexing Hawai'i was countered by more than 30,000

Native Hawaiians, who were loyal to the Kingdom of Hawaiʻi and who signed the Kūʻē Petitions that they delivered to Washington, DC.

87. Douglas V. Askman, "Our Royal Guest: American Press Coverage of King Kalākaua's Visit to the United States, 1874–1875," *Hawaiian Journal of History* 54 (2020): 131–62.

88. The Reciprocity Treaty was approved in 1875, leading to a surge in Hawaiʻi's sugar industry. After the opening of the first plantation in 1835, it took forty years for sugar production to reach twelve thousand tons; it doubled in four years. It then doubled three more times by the end of the century. This growth required the massive importation of low-cost laborers, brought from China and Japan, to work in the fields. As a result, Native Hawaiians became a minority in their own land. See Tom Coffman, *Nation Within: The History of the Occupation of Hawaiʻi* (Durham, NC: Duke University Press, 2016), 62–68.

89. Ibid., 62. However, when the treaty was renegotiated in 1887, he was forced to cede the use of Pearl Harbor to the United States. See Van Dyke, *Who Owns the Crown Lands of Hawaiʻi?*, 126.

90. The trade report was compiled by a group named American Commerce for Greater America that represented U.S. business and industrial interests. See "Annexation of Hawaii, Appendix 6," in *Compilation of Reports of Committee on Foreign Relations, United States Senate 1789–1901,* 300–3, https://hdl.handle.net/2027/uc1.b3989748.

91. Ibid.

92. William C. Widenor, *Henry Cabot Lodge and the Search for an American Foreign Policy* (Berkeley: University of California Press, 1980), 110. Lodge also proposed the annexation of Greenland in 1905. See Fromkin, "Rival Internationalisms," 77. Lodge knew that the Caribbean was a sensitive region, especially as it had drawn the eye of Kaiser Wilhelm II, Germany's ruling monarch—who had gone so far to draw up plans for war—but did not have enough ships. See David Healy, *U.S. Expansionism: The Imperialist Urge in the 1890s* (Madison: University of Wisconsin Press: 1970), 112–13. See also LaFeber, *The American Age*, 246. Later, in 1905, when Roosevelt was president, he was aware of the Kaiser's designs. In a letter to British envoy Cecil Spring-Rice he wrote, "I think I succeeded in impressing on the Kaiser . . . that the violation of the Monroe Doctrine by territorial aggrandizement on his part around the Caribbean meant war, not ultimately, but immediately and without delay." See "Roosevelt Warning to Kaiser Revealed," *New York Times*, November 8, 1929, 14.

93. "Intervention in Cuba: Speech of Hon. Henry Cabot Lodge, of Massachusetts, in the Senate of the United States, April 13, 1898," Record, 54 Cong., 1 Sess., pp. 1971–72, https://www.mtholyoke.edu/acad/intrel/lodge1.htm.

94. To this day, the United States possesses Guantánamo Bay as a naval base. The Cuban-American Treaty of Relations of 1903 and the 1934 Treaty of Relations stipulate the terms of the lease, which Cuba contests. For terms, see "Agreement Between the United States and Cuba for the Lease of Lands for Coaling and Naval Stations; February 23, 1903," https://avalon.law.yale.edu/20th_century/dip_cuba002.asp.

95. The Philippines had been a Spanish colony since Ferdinand Magellan claimed the archipelago for the Spanish in 1521. Ruy López de Villalobos christened the island of Leyte as Filipina, in honor of Felipe II, in 1542. Colonization efforts began in earnest in 1565 with Miguel López de Legazpi, who established the colony of Cebú. Patrick Williams, "Phillip II, the Philippines, and the Hispanic World," in *Reshaping the World: Philip II of Spain and His Time*, ed. Dámaso de Lario Ramírez (Manila: Ateneo de Manila University Press, 2008), 14.

96. See Derek B. Granger, "Dewey at Manila Bay—Lessons in Operational Art and Operational Leadership from America's First Fleet Admiral," *Naval War College Review* 64, no. 4 (Fall 2011): Article 10, https://digital-commons.usnwc.edu/cgi/viewcontent.cgi?article=1557&context=nwc-review.

97. Object label, "Battle of Manila Bay, May 1, 1898," The Army and Navy Club, https://collections.armynavyclub.org/objects/battle-of-manila-bay/.

98. Brian McAllister Linn, *The Philippine War 1899–1902* (Lawrence: University Press of Kansas, 2000), 8.

99. Instead, he had to request a dispatch of a garrison to occupy Manila, which he did on May 13, 1898. See Musicant, *Empire by Default*, 260.

100. The gift cost Schwab around $5,000 per portrait—roughly $330,000 in 2021 dollars. See "Portraits of the Deweys: Gift of C. M. Schwab to the Couple—M. Chartran the Artist," *New York Times*, April 19, 1900.

101. See Sue Morris, "The Art of Politics and the Politics of Art: Part Two," The Frick Pittsburgh, December 10, 2020, https://www.thefrickpittsburgh.org/Story-The-Art-of-Politics-and-the-Politics-of-Art-Part-Two.

102. Colonel Jerry M. River, *Guam USA: America's Forward Fortress in Asia Pacific* (New York: Verdun Press, 2014).

103. See entry for *General Baldrich*, by Marimar Benítez, and entries for *Conuco, Trapiche meladero,* and *Hacienda Aurora*, by Haydée Venegas, in the exhibition catalogue *Francisco Oller: un realista del impresionismo* (Ponce, Puerto Rico: Museo de Arte de Ponce, 1983), 162, and Edward J. Sullivan, *From San Juan to Paris and Back: Francisco Oller and Caribbean Art in the Era of Impressionism* (New Haven, CT: Yale University Press, 2014), 65.

104. See "On the Verge of Sovereignty: Cuba and Puerto Rico at the Turn of the Twentieth Century" in this volume, pp. 89–117.

105. This photograph circulated in the publication *Photographic History of the Spanish-American War: A Pictorial and Descriptive Record of Events on Land Sea with Portraits and Biographies of Leaders on Both Sides* (New York: Pearson Publishing Company, 1898).

106. Edward J. Sullivan aptly describes Oller's portrait of McKinley as suggesting boldness and methodical leadership. See Sullivan, *From San Juan to Paris and Back*, 159.

107. Shortly after Oller finished the portrait of McKinley, he sent the painting as a gift to the president's office in Washington, DC. This was the first of several portraits of U.S. historical figures and officials that Oller painted as Puerto Rico changed hands from an overseas province of Spain to a territory of the United States. See Sullivan, *From San Juan to Paris and Back*, 159. Between 1898 and 1907, Oller also created portraits of each succeeding U.S.-appointed governor of Puerto Rico, including George Whitefield Davis (1839–1918), William Henry Hunt (1857–1949), and Beekam Winthrop (1874–1940), along with other portraits of U.S. or colonial officials and historical figures. In addition, in 1902, Oller made a portrait of George Washington (now lost) that was based on Gilbert Stuart's *Lansdowne* portrait. See Natalia Ángeles Vieyra, "Fragmentary Impressions: Camille Pissarro and Francisco Oller in the Americas: 1848–1898," PhD diss. (Temple University, 2021), 27, 151, and chapter 4. See also "Problem Portraits: Francisco Oller in the Age of U.S. Imperialism," *Panorama: Journal of the Association of Historians of American Art* 7, no. 2 (Fall 2021), https://doi.org/10.24926/24716839.12642.

108. Sullivan contrasts the imposing physicality of McKinley to the partly crumpled map, held in his right hand—the hand of power in depictions of authority starting with Hebraic-biblical tradition—as an iconography that suggests domination. He elaborates on the ambivalence of the painting as pointing perhaps to an ideological alignment between Oller and the many Puerto Ricans who were receptive to the change in colonial government from Spain to the United States because it promised the island's modernization and a more democratic society. See Sullivan, *From San Juan to Paris and Back*, 159; 162–66.

109. Sullivan notes the peculiarity of Oller's abbreviation of "October" as *8.bre,* which would read as "8.ber" in English. He stresses that it is interesting that Oller painted this portrait before the signing of the Treaty of Paris on December 10, 1898, at a moment when the international community had not yet recognized the U.S. triumph in the War of 1898. Sullivan does not mention the connection between the transfer of power effective on October 18, 1898. See Sullivan, *From San Juan to Paris and Back*, 160.

110. Enrique Vivoni Farage, "San Juan de Puerto Rico: de plaza fuerte a ciudad bella," in *Los arcos de la memoria: el '98 de los pueblos puertorriqueños*, ed. Silvia Álvarez Curbelo, Mary Frances Gallart, and Carmen I. Raffucci (San Juan: Universidad de Puerto Rico, 1998), 19–38.

111. McKinley left no papers beyond his political speeches, and few letters. Theodore Roosevelt reportedly described McKinley as having "no more backbone than a chocolate éclair." See LaFeber, *The American Age*, 202. About McKinley's political skills, Nick Kapur writes: "Congress moved so rapidly to make war on Spain, but only after it had secured McKinley's stamp of approval, and after acceding to all of his stated wishes, illustrates that McKinley maintained a strong personal control over not just his administration, but the entire U.S. government during that time." See Kapur, "William McKinley's Values and the Origins of the Spanish-American War: A Reinterpretation," 23.

112. Evan Thomas, "The First Modern President," *New York Times*, November 17, 2017. McKinley read, and often extensively revised, all important diplomatic correspondence emanating from the State Department to foreign nations that were signed by his secretaries of state. See Kapur, "William McKinley's Values and the Origins of the Spanish-American War: A Reinterpretation," 24.

113. Ralph Lowell Eckert, "John Brown Gordon: Soldier, Southerner, American. (Volumes I and II) (Georgia)." (1983), Louisiana State University Historical Dissertations and Theses, 3881, p. 409.

114. William McKinley, "President to Gen. Gordon: Letter of Thanks in Response to Resolutions Adopted by Confederate Veterans' Association at Atlanta," *New York Times*, July 24, 1898, 1.

115. The visual rhetoric of reconciliation may have been effective war diplomacy, but the North and the South would continue to harbor resentments well into the twentieth century, and some would argue, even to the contemporary moment. On reconciliation versus reunion, see Caroline E. Janney, *Remembering the Civil War: Reunion and the Limits of Reconciliation* (Chapel Hill: University of North Carolina Press, 2013).

116. See "On the Verge of Sovereignty: Cuba and Puerto Rico at the Turn of the Twentieth Century" in this volume, pp. 89–117.

"OUR CULTURE HAS TO BE THE CORE OF OUR RESISTANCE"

1. ʻŌiwi o Hawaiʻi and Maka o ka ʻĀina, *Hoʻokūʻokoʻa '85: conference on Hawaiian sovereignty 1985* (Nāʻālehu, Hawaiʻi: Nā Maka o ka ʻĀina, 2006), DVD.

2. Ibid.

3. See books such as Haunani-Kay Trask, *From a Native Daughter: Colonialism and Sovereignty in Hawaii,* rev. ed. (Honolulu: University of Hawaiʻi Press, 2021), 37, 127–28. Noenoe K. Silva and Ngũgĩ wa Thiongʻo, *The Power of the Steel-Tipped Pen: Reconstructing Native Hawaiian Intellectual History* (Durham, NC: Duke University Press, 2017). https://doi.org/10.1215/9780822373131. Nālani Minton, Jonathan Kay Kamakawiwoʻole Osorio, Jamaica Heolimeleikalani Osorio, and Noenoe K. Silva, *Kūʻē petitions: a mau loa aku nō* (Honolulu: Kaiao Press in partnership with Friends of the Judiciary History Center, 2020).

4. Kamanamaikalani Beamer, *No Mākou ka Mana: Liberating the Nation* (Honolulu: Kamehameha Publishing, 2014), 48

5. Puhipau, Joan Lander, Haunani-Kay Trask, Lilikalā Kameʻeleihiwa, Richard K. Blaisdell, Charles Ewart, Jon Kamakawiwoʻole Osorio, et al., *Act of War: The Overthrow of the Hawaiian Nation* (Nāʻālehu, Hawaiʻi: Nā Maka o ka ʻĀina, 1993), DVD.

6. Kapulani Landgraf, personal communication, February 2019.

HAWAIIAN RESISTANCE AND U.S. IMPERIALISM

We extend our gratitude to David Aiona Chang for his thoughtful feedback on this essay.

1. Liliʻuokalani to Sanford Dole, January 17, 1893. See "Excerpt from Blount Report," https://libweb.hawaii .edu/digicoll/annexation/protest/liliu2.php. See also Liliʻuokalani, *Hawaii's Story by Hawaii's Queen* (Boston: Lee and Shepard, 1898), 387–88.

2. On May 4, 1898, Congressman Francis Newlands submitted to the U.S. House of Representatives a joint resolution for the annexation of the Hawaiian Islands. David Keanu Sai argues, "the Hawaiian Kingdom was never extinguished and continues to exist as an independent and sovereign state, and it has been under the longest belligerent occupation in the history of international relations." See David Keanu Sai, "Hawaiian Neutrality: From the Crimean Conflict through the Spanish-American War." (Paper presented at the Sovereignty and Imperialism: Non-European Powers in the Age of Empire conference, held at University of Cambridge, UK, Centre for Research in the Arts, Social Sciences and Humanities, September 10–12, 2015), 31; 39 https://www2.hawaii.edu/~anu/pdf /Cambridge_Paper_Hawaiian_Neutrality.pdf.

3. See "Apology Resolution," or Public Law No 103–150, Senate Reports: No. 103–126 (Comm. on Indian Affairs), Congressional Record 139 (1993), https://www.govinfo .gov/content/pkg/STATUTE-107/pdf/STATUTE-107 -Pg1510.pdf.

4. Until 1893, Hawaiʻi was one of only forty-four independent and sovereign states (there are 197 today). Hawaiʻi was recognized as a state in 1843 by Belgium, the United States, Great Britain, and France. Hawaiʻi's status in the 1850s as a recognized independent state was unique in the Asia-Pacific region, and Hawaiians considered all of Oceania to be under their sphere of influence. See Lorenz Gonschor, *A Power in the World: The Hawaiian Kingdom in Oceania* (Honolulu: University of Hawaiʻi Press, 2019), 27–28; 32–35; and David Keanu Sai, "American Occupation of the Hawaiian State: A Century Unchecked," *Hawaiian Journal of Law and Politics* 1 (Summer 2004): 47–82.

5. The Hawaiian monarchy began in the late eighteenth century. In 1795, King Kamehameha I (1782–1819) defeated his opponents, including ten thousand soldiers comprising the army of Maui. Kamehameha I unified Hawaiʻi, a chain of eight major islands and 124 islets, in 1810, following the Battle of Nuʻuanu. See Tom Coffman, *Nation Within: The History of the American Occupation of Hawaiʻi* (Durham, NC: Duke University Press, 2016), 176. The sons of Kamehameha I succeeded him: Liholiho (Kamehameha II, 1796–1824) in 1819, and Kauikeaouli (Kamehameha III, 1813–1854) in 1825; grandsons Alexander Liholiho (Kamehameha IV, 1834–1863) in 1854; and Lota Kapuāiwa (Kamehameha V, 1830–1872) in 1863. When Lota died without naming an heir, a grandson to Kamehameha's half-brother, William Charles Lunalilo, was elected to the throne in 1873. Upon his death, there was no successor, and David Kalākaua was elected in 1874. Kalākaua's sister, Queen Liliʻuokalani, succeeded him after his death in 1891. See Stacy L. Kamehiro, *The Arts of Kingship: Hawaiian Art and National Culture of the Kalākaua Era* (Honolulu: University of Hawaiʻi Press, 2009), 80–105.

6. For example, Kauikeaouli ceded sovereignty to Great Britain for five months in 1843 under duress. See Jon M. Van Dyke, *Who Owns the Crown Lands of Hawaiʻi?* (Honolulu: University of Hawaiʻi Press, 2008), 4.

7. Unfortunately, in addition to setting the stage for far-reaching Hawaiian exploration, these captains and merchants also introduced typhoid fever, dysentery, and cholera to the archipelago. Later, missionaries brought tuberculosis and other diseases. By the late 1850s, the population of Kānaka Maoli had fallen 75 percent or more from its pre-contact level. Seth Archer writes, "Recent studies of tuberculosis (TB) and American migration (or medical tourism) have tended to focus on the period after 1850 and have failed to consider Hawaiʻi. While Kānaka Maoli (Native Hawaiians) may well have been exposed to TB before 1820, the disease undoubtedly arrived with missionaries in the 1820s." Archer also writes, "The figure is based upon the lowest credible estimate for pre-contact population (Robert C. Schmitt's 250,000)—Stannard argued vehemently for 800,000 or more—relative to official census data from 1860, which put the Kānaka Maoli population at 66,984 (including 1,337 part-Hawaiians). Debates over pre-contact population and the rate of Kānaka Maoli depopulation to 1820 are contentious and unresolved." See Archer, "Remedial Agents: Missionary Physicians and the Depopulation of Hawaiʻi," *Pacific Historical Review* 79, no. 4 (November 2010): 515n5 and 515n9.

8. David A. Chang, *The World and All the Things upon It: Native Hawaiian Geographies of Exploration* (Minneapolis: University of Minnesota Press, 2016), 25–28; 39; 43–45.

9. Chang, *The World and All the Things upon It*, 48–49.

10. See Christina Hellmich, "Hawaiian Featherwork Abroad," in *Royal Hawaiian Featherwork: Nā Hulu Aliʻi*, ed. Leah Calderia, et al. (Honolulu: University of Hawaiʻi Press, 2015), 111.

11. Kapu, which can mean "taboo" or "sacred," essentially is "a marker of what is restricted because it is special." Gradually, Hawaiians saw changes in religion, including kapu. See Chang, *The World and All the Things upon It*, 199–201.

12. Jennifer Fish Kashay, "Agents of Imperialism: Missionaries and Merchants in Early-Nineteenth-

Century Hawaii," *New England Quarterly* 80, no. 2 (June 2007): 280.

13. Kashay, "Agents of Imperialism," 284.

14. Hilo Boarding School was founded in 1836. See Chang, *The World and All the Things upon It*, 111.

15. Kashay, "Agents of Imperialism," 290–93.

16. Kamehameha IV was the first Hawaiian monarch to attend the school established by the missionaries. Thank you to David A. Chang for this note.

17. One founding missionary, Artemas Bishop, used Kānaka Maoli labor to build a sugar mill on Oʻahu. See Kashay, "Agents of Imperialism," 294–95. By 1840, another founding missionary, Hiram Bingham, owned extensive fields of sugar cane. See Archer, "Remedial Agents," 535n65.

18. See Ronald C. Williams Jr., "To Raise a Voice in Praise: The Revivalist Mission of John Henry Wise, 1889–1896," *Hawaiian Journal of History* 46 (2012): 3.

19. For kinship, see Chang, *The World and All the Things upon It*, 195–225. For Kuamakapili, see Williams, "To Raise a Voice in Praise," 20–22.

20. Betsey Stockton was born into slavery and lived in the household of Robert Stockton, until he gave her to his daughter, Elizabeth Stockton Green. In 1817, Stockton joined the First Presbyterian Church in Princeton. Subsequently, she was freed by Ashbel Green, Elizabeth Stockton Green's husband. After her emancipation, Stockton worked for wages. Ashbel Green connected her with Charles and Harriet Stewart. See John A. Andrew, "Betsey Stockton: Stranger in a Strange Land," *Journal of Presbyterian History* 52, no. 2 (Summer 1974): 157–66.

21. They set sail in November 1822 and arrived in Honolulu, Hawaiʻi, on April 27, 1823. See Hawaiian Mission Children's Society, *Portraits of American Protestant Missionaries* (Honolulu: Hawaiian Gazette, 1901).

22. The Stewarts were married on June 6, 1822. See "Married," *Hampshire Gazette*, June 6, 1822. For their arrival date, see "Missionary Life in Hawaii (1800s)," Titus Coan Memorial Library, June 22, 2017, https://www.tc-lib.org/Missionaries/Profiles/StewartCS.html.

23. Stockton kept a journal of her time with the missionaries, among whom she was the only unmarried woman and the only woman of color. Her contract is in the archives of the Hawaiian Mission Children's Society (HMCS) in Honolulu. Cited in John A. Andrew, "Betsey Stockton," 159.

24. Charles Stewart and William Ellis, *Journal of a residence in the Sandwich Islands, during the years 1823, 1824, and 1825: including descriptions of the natural scenery, and remarks on the manners and customs of the inhabitants; an account of Lord Byron's visit in the British frigate Blonde, and of an excursion to the great volcano of Kirauea in Hawaii,* 2nd ed. (New York: J. P. Haven, 1828), 28.

25. Cited in Andrew, "Betsey Stockton," 161. Andrew notes that some of her letters and excerpts from her journal were printed by Ashbel Green in the *Advocate* between 1823 and 1825.

26. Some scholars have incorrectly identified Stockton's headdress as influenced by Kānaka Maoli ones. Rather, the style may have been influenced by Creole culture in the Louisiana area.

27. Sai, "American Occupation of the Hawaiian State," 12.

28. The treaties were: Treaty with Hawaii on Commerce, December 23, 1826; Treaty with Hawaii on Friendship, Commerce, and Navigation, December 20, 1849; Treaty with Hawaii on Commercial Reciprocity, January 30, 1875; Treaty with Hawaii on Commercial Reciprocity, November 9, 1887. See Van Dyke, *Who Owns the Crown Lands of Hawaiʻi?,* 153–54. David Keanu Sai notes that Hawaiʻi was recognized as an independent state in 1843 and was then introduced into the family of nations. See Sai, "Hawaiian Neutrality," 53.

29. Van Dyke, *Who Owns the Crown Lands of Hawaiʻi?,* 120.

30. The Reciprocity Treaty of 1875 entered into force on September 9, 1876. President John Tyler also recognized Hawaiʻi as independent in 1842 and declared that the Monroe Doctrine would include the Hawaiian archipelago, stating that the United States would not stand for "the adoption of an opposite policy by any other power." See Van Dyke, *Who Owns the Crown Lands of Hawaiʻi?,* 118–20; 154.

31. The Independent Party was formed in 1883.

32. Jon Osorio, *Dismembering Lāhui: A History of the Hawaiian Nation to 1887* (Honolulu: University of Hawaiʻi Press, 2002), 210–24.

33. Coffman, *Nation Within*, 89–90.

34. Van Dyke, *Who Owns the Crown Lands of Hawaiʻi?,* 120–23.

35. Van Dyke, *Who Owns the Crown Lands of Hawaiʻi?,* 120.

36. Alice Kim, "Bayonet Constitution," *Hawaiʻi Digital Newspaper Project.* https://sites.google.com/a/hawaii.edu/ndnp-hawaii/Home/historical-feature-articles/bayonet-constitution.

37. Lydia Kualapai, "The Queen Writes Back: Liliʻuokalani's Hawaii's Story by Hawaii's Queen," *Studies in American Indian Literatures* 17, no. 2 (Summer 2005): 33.

38. Van Dyke, *Who Owns the Crown Lands of Hawaiʻi?,* 124.

39. See Carol A. MacLennan, *Sovereign Sugar: Industry and Environment in Hawaiʻi* (Honolulu: University of Hawaiʻi Press, 2014), 237; and Coffman, *Nation Within*, 91–92. The 1887 Reciprocity Treaty, which included the Pearl Harbor amendment, was signed on October 27, 1887. See Van Dyke, *Who Owns the Crown Lands of Hawaiʻi?,* 126.

40. See Liliʻuokalani, *Hawaii's Story by Hawaii's Queen* (Boston: Lee and Shepard, 1898), 180–81.

41. Coffman, *Nation Within*, 87–88.

42. Coffman, *Nation Within*, 103; 119–20.

43. See "Blaine's Alleged Treaty Ill-Treated: Hawaiians Excited and Indignant at The Secretary's Proposals," *Chicago Daily Tribune*, October 11, 1889, and "Treaty with Hawaii: Proposals for Closer Relations with The United States: An Interview with Minister Carter—The Four Propositions He Will Present to Secretary of State Blaine—Hawaii to Make No Treaty Without the Knowledge of The United States," *St. Louis Post-Dispatch*, November 13, 1889.

44. The U.S. economy was producing too many agricultural and industrial products, so the Republican Party looked to expand foreign markets and simultaneously salvage the domestic one. In 1890, the new tariffs were imposed, increasing average duties across all imports from 38 percent to 49.5 percent. See Joanne Reitano, *The Tariff Question in the Gilded Age: The Great Debate of 1888* (University Park: Pennsylvania State University, 1994), 129.

45. Cited by Coffman, *Nation Within*, 102.

46. Ibid.

47. About 120 Hale Nauā feather capes were made using nontraditional materials of dyed feathers stitched onto a cloth base. Twenty of these have been identified; some of the Hale Nauā revival capes are now in the collection of the Smithsonian Institution. See Stacy L. Kamehiro, "Featherwork in the Hawaiian Monarchy Period," in *Royal Hawaiian Featherwork: Nā Hulu Aliʻi*, ed. Leah Caldeira, et al. (Honolulu: University of Hawaiʻi Press, 2015), 89.

48. Kamehiro, "Featherwork in the Hawaiian Monarchy Period," 80–81.

49. Maria K. Lane Ena was married to John Ena Jr., a "prominent and active member of the Hale Nau-a." See "The Life of Late John Ena," *Hawaiian Star*, December 29, 1906. Very little is known about Maria Ena, who may have belonged to the Hale Nauā Society. See object record for catalog entry E384231-0, Collections of the National Museum of Natural History's Ethnology Division, https://collections.si .edu/search/detail/edanmdm:nmnhanthropology _8419351?q=kalakaua+cape&record=2&hlterm =kalakaua%2Bcape. Adrienne Kaeppler surmises that women did not make featherwork because such garments were made by priests, who were exclusively male during the pre-Christian era. The fishnet knotting styles are associated with men in Hawaiʻi and throughout Polynesia. See Adrienne Kaeppler, "Hawaiian Featherwork in the Age of Exploration," in *Royal Hawaiian Featherwork,* 46. The tradition of feather craft is now taught in Hawaiian cultural programs. See Betty Lou Kam, "The Aloha of Sharing a Hawaiian Art," in *Royal Hawaiian Featherwork*, 124–31. The most brilliant colors of Hawaiian featherwork come from five species in two families. See Marques Hanalei Marzan and Samuel M. ʻOhukaniʻōhiʻa Gon III, "The Aesthetics, Materials, and Construction of Hawaiian Featherwork," in *Royal Hawaiian Featherwork*, 28–29.

50. Kamehiro, "Featherwork in the Hawaiian Monarchy Period," 89.

51. Marzan and Gon, "The Aesthetics, Materials, and Constructions of Hawaiian Featherwork," 30.

52. Kaeppler, "Hawaiian Treasures at the Smithsonian Institution," in *Royal Hawaiian Featherwork*, 10.

53. Kamehiro, "Featherwork in the Hawaiian Monarchy Period," 93.

54. Kamehiro, "Featherwork in the Hawaiian Monarchy Period," 86.

55. For Kalākaua in Asia, see Masaji Marumoto, "Vignette of Early Hawaii-Japan Relations: Highlights of King Kalakaua's Sojourn in Japan on His Trip Around the World as Recorded in His Personal Diary," *Hawaiian Journal of History* 10 (1976): 52.

56. See Kamehiro, *The Arts of Kingship*, 89–93.

57. King Kalākaua had commissioned portraits of the royal family made according to Western traditions, and he had them displayed throughout his reign. See Leah Caldeira, "Visualizing Hoʻoulu Lāhui," in *Hoʻoulu Hawaiʻi: The King Kalākaua Era*, ed. Healoha Johnston (Honolulu: Honolulu Museum of Art, 2018), 32.

58. The *Honolulu Advertiser* reported Cogswell as "making an oil painting" on August 3, 1891. According to an article in the *Pacific Commercial Advertiser* from October 21, 1891, Cogswell painted the queen's portrait from life. On October 27, 1891, the *Hawaiian Gazette* reported that the "Queen expressed herself as being well-pleased with the artist's work." Cogswell also painted a posthumous portrait of King Kalākaua; for both paintings, the queen paid "near his price of $4,000." See Junior League Files, record for *Bulletin*, October 20, 1892, IV, no. 553, p. 3, Column 2. https:// cdm17266.contentdm.oclc.org/digital/collection /p17266coll1/id/3185/rec/5. After its sale to the queen in 1892, Cogswell signed it with that date.

59. Cogswell made his name in 1869, when President Ulysses S. Grant chose him over the renowned portraitist George Peter Alexander Healy to paint a portrait of President Abraham Lincoln for the White House. This portrait is the official White House portrait of Abraham Lincoln and remains in the White House Collection. Cogswell earned $3,000 for this commission. See "William F. Cogswell," Wisconsin Art, https:// wisconsinart.org/archives/artist/william-f-cogswell /profile-811.aspx. See also: George C. Groce and David H. Wallace, *The New-York Historical Society's Dictionary of Artists in America, 1564–1860* (New Haven, CT: Yale University Press, 1957), 136. The collection of the ʻIolani Palace also holds the receipt that Cogswell made for the payment of the painting.

60. Groce and Wallace, *Dictionary of Artists in America*, 136.

61. A friend of King Kalākaua living in San Francisco commissioned a portrait of the king by Cogswell. Upon arriving in Hawaiʻi by April of 1879 to work on the portrait, Cogswell set up a studio in the Museum Room of the Government Building. See *Hawaiian Gazette*, April 2, 1879; and *Ko Hawaii Pae Aina*, April 19, 1879, 2.

Cogswell was a resident of Hawai'i in 1890. He had his studio at 9 Spreckles Block. See *1890: Directory and Handbook of the Kingdom of Hawaii* (Honolulu: George Bowser & Co.), 155.

62. The throne is not the one that the queen would have used in the 'Iolani Palace, but rather, the former one, associated with the Kamehameha line. See Duccio Kaumualii Marignoli and Marzi Ratti, *Matteo Sandonà and Hawai'i: A Capital Ambition* (Philadelphia: Trans-Atlantic Publications, 2007), 17.

63. Per email correspondence between Kate Clarke Lemay, Zita Cup Choy, and Douglas Askman, June 4, 2021.

64. See Stacy Kamehiro, "Worlding the Kingdom of Hawai'i," in *Ho'oulu Hawai'i: The King Kalākaua Era*, ed. Healoha Johnston (Honolulu: Honolulu Museum of Art, 2018), 93–96.

65. The king wears the Royal Order of Kalākaua; the Royal Order of Kamehameha I; the Royal Order of Kapi'olani, and the Royal Order of the Crown of Hawai'i. He also wears the Order of St. Michael and St. George (Britain); the Order of Leopold (Belgium); the Order of the Red Eagle (Prussia) and the Order of the Chrysanthemum (Japan). See Rhoda E. A. Hackler, "Royal Portraits of Hawai'i," *Iolani Palace: Portraits* (Honolulu: Friends of 'Iolani Palace, 1982), 33. The Royal Order of Kamehameha I was established by Kamehameha V to recognize the exemplary service of Hawaiian subjects or of foreigners to the Hawaiian Kingdom. It was first established in April 1865. The Royal Order of Kapi'olani, founded in August 1880 by Kalākaua, was rarer, as it was given for "services in the cause of humanity, science, art and services rendered to the state or sovereign." The Japanese Order of the Chrysanthemum was not only notable but also extremely valuable, worth $4,000 in the 1880s. See Kamehiro, "Worlding the Kingdom of Hawai'i," 95.

66. Queen Victoria also had a portrait made at this studio to celebrate her Golden Jubilee in 1887, as did a number of other aristocrats and royals that year. See: "Walery," National Portrait Gallery, London, https://www.npg.org.uk/collections/search/person /mp14017/walery.

67. Queen Victoria gave a vanity box encrusted with sapphires to Queen Kapi'olani, for example, during the Jubilee celebrations. See Alice Christophe, "Imperial Jewels," in *Ho'oulu Hawai'i: The King Kalākaua Era*, ed. Healoha Johnston (Honolulu: Honolulu Museum of Art, 2018), 178–81.

68. It is possible the dress was from the French fashion house, the House of Worth. For fashion and political power, see Kristin L. Hoganson, *Consumers' Imperium: The Global Production of American Domesticity, 1865–1920* (Chapel Hill: University of North Carolina Press, 2007), 58–102.

69. See Teresa Williams Valencia, "Feathers, Diamonds, and Gowns," in *Ho'oulu Hawai'i: The King Kalākaua Era*, ed. Healoha Johnston (Honolulu: Honolulu Museum of Art, 2018), 183.

70. *Evening Bulletin*, August 1, 1891, 4, no. 189, 3. The "Walen" (Walery) portrait was exhibited in McInerny's Store in Honolulu, and two thousand copies were made for distribution. See *Hawaiian Gazette*, January 12, 1892, 27, no. 2, 3. See also Junior League Files, https:// cdm17266.contentdm.oclc.org/digital/collection /p17266coll1/id/3906/rec/3.

71. Amanda C. Demmer, "Trick or Constitutional Treaty?: The Jay Treaty and the Quarrel over the Diplomatic Separation of Powers," *Journal of the Early Republic* 35, no. 4 (2015): 579–98.

72. Pennsylvania Senator William Bingham was a leader in the Senate and largely responsible for their ratification of the treaty, and while the House was debating, Bingham commissioned Gilbert Stuart to make this work. After the portrait was completed, Bingham sent it to British statesman William Petty, the Marquis of Lansdowne, who like Bingham wanted to preserve commercial relations between England and the United States. See Ellen Miles, "Gilbert Stuart Paints George Washington," *Face to Face: A Blog from the National Portrait Gallery*, National Portrait Gallery, February 19, 2016, https://npg.si.edu/blog/gilbert -stuart-paints-george-washington.

73. See Lisa Kahaleole Hall, "Strategies of Erasure: U.S. Colonialism and Native Hawaiian Feminism," *American Quarterly* 60, no. 2 (June 2008): 273–80; and J. Kēhaulani Kauanui, "Native Hawaiian Decolonization and the Politics of Gender," *American Quarterly* 60, no. 2 (June 2008): 281–97.

74. Hall, "Strategies of Erasure," 277–78; and Lilikala Kame'elehiwa, *Na Wahine Kapu* (Honolulu: Ai Pohaku Press, 1999).

75. Ronald C. Williams Jr., "Ke Ko'o o Hawai'i," in *Ho'oulu Hawai'i: The King Kalākaua Era*, ed. Healoha Johnston (Honolulu: Honolulu Museum of Art, 2018), 51.

76. Postcolonial literary theorist Edward Said called this strategy "the voyage" in "a conscious effort from the peripheral world to enter in the discourse of the West and make it acknowledge suppressed histories." See Edward Said, *Culture and Imperialism* (New York: Vintage Books, 1994), 216. The queen purchased the portraits of herself and her brother for $1,500 each. See receipt from William Cogswell to Queen Lili'uokalani, October 19, 1892, collection of the 'Iolani Palace. It reads, "Her Majesty Liliuokalani to Wm. Cogswell / full length portrait of his late Majesty Kalakaua including frame 1500 / full length portrait of herself with frame 1500/ $3000/ Received payment." The bottom of the receipt includes a note from Cogswell, dated October 20, where he sends his regards to the queen for taking interest in the portraits and expresses regret over the sales price. "Had I taken a second thought," he writes "I certainly would not have sold them for less than 3,500." He concludes that he is satisfied and hopes the queen is too. Archives of the 'Iolani Palace. Thank you to Zita Cup Choy for sharing this primary source.

77. "Liliuokalani, 1893 to James H. Blount excerpt from Blount Report," https://libweb.hawaii.edu/digicoll /annexation/protest/liliu1.php.

78. In referring to themselves as the Committee of Safety, the group alluded to the American Revolution, when a network of committees authorized by the Continental Congress governed until state governments were formally established.

79. Cited in Kualapai, "The Queen Writes Back," 34.

80. Cited in Coffman, *Nation Within*, 177.

81. Cited in Kualapai, "The Queen Writes Back," 34.

82. Lili'uokalani asked President Cleveland to reinstate her, and he rejected the treaty of annexation sent to Congress by his predecessor, President Benjamin Harrison.

83. Lili'uokalani, *Hawaii's Story by Hawaii's Queen*, 243.

84. Blount was in Hawai'i from March to August 1893. See Senate Report 1275 quoted in Kualapai, "The Queen Writes Back," 35–36. Kualapi writes that Blount was authorized to investigate three points of U.S. interest: "the causes of the revolution by which the queen's Government was overthrown, the sentiment of the people toward existing authority, and, in general, all that can fully enlighten the President." See Senate Report 1275, quoted in Kualapai, "The Queen Writes Back," 35–36.

85. The Morgan Report was presented to Congress on February 26, 1894, as the Senate Report 227 of the 53rd Congress.

86. On May 31, 1894, the Senate voted unanimously to pass the Turpie Resolution, deciding against supporting further attempts to restore the queen or to move toward annexation. See Kualapai, "The Queen Writes Back," 41.

87. See Sai, "Hawaiian Neutrality," 25.

88. Coffman, *Nation Within*, 125–27.

89. For further examples of U.S. iconoclasm, see Wendy Bellion, *Iconoclasm in New York: Revolution to Reenactment* (University Park: Pennsylvania State University Press, 2019).

90. The provisional government consisted of nineteen appointed members and eighteen elected members. See Coffman, *Nation Within*, 158. For further statistics, see Kualapai, "The Queen Writes Back," 41.

91. President Cleveland had increasingly turned to U.S. expansionism as one way to resolve the financial crisis of 1893 and saw Hawai'i as key to opening foreign markets. See Coffman, *Nation Within*, 164–65.

92. Coffman, *Nation Within*, 156.

93. In 1895, he started the *Ke Aloha 'Āina*, a Hawaiian language newspaper, that was the mouthpiece for the Hui Hawai'i Aloha 'Āina (Hawaiian Patriotic League of the Hawaiian Islands).

94. Wilcox had also organized a rebellion in 1889. See Van Dyke, *Who Owns the Crown Lands of Hawai'i?*, 128–29.

95. Lili'uokalani, *Hawaii's Story by Hawaii's Queen*, chapter 43.

96. Lili'uokalani, *Hawaii's Story by Hawaii's Queen*, chapter 43.

97. Diary of Queen Lili'uokalani, Lili'uokalani Manuscript Collection, Bernice Pauahi Bishop Museum Archives, Honolulu. Cited in Williams, "To Raise a Voice in Praise," 27.

98. Kualapai, "The Queen Writes Back," 41–42.

99. Coffman, *Nation Within*, 263.

100. The Hui Kālai'āina was formed to protest the Bayonet Constitution of 1887 and to restore the presence of Kānaka Maoli in government. The Hui Hawai'i Aloha 'Āina organizations were formed in response to the 1893 overthrow with the aim of restoring the monarchy and thwarting impeding annexation. Noenoe Silva notes that the English translation "Hawaiian Patriotic League" is imperfect. Aloha 'āina means "love of the land," which is directly tied to Kānaka Maoli cosmology, and, therefore, differs from the gendered "patriotic" and its ties to the West. See Noenoe Silva, *Aloha Betrayed: Native Hawaiian Resistance to American Colonialism* (Durham, NC: Duke University Press, 2004), 130; and Noenoe Silva "The 1897 Petitions Protesting Annexation," University of Hawai'i at Mānoa Library, 1998, http://libweb.hawaii.edu/digicoll/annexation/petition/pet-intro.php.

101. Silva, *Aloha Betrayed*, 145–46.

102. While there is speculation that some people may have signed both petitions, the signature total is significant given the 1890 and 1896 census reports. See Silva, *Aloha Betrayed*, 151; and Coffman, *Nation Within*, 281.

103. They met with Senators Richard Pettigrew and George Hoar. The latter agreed to present their petition to the Senate and to the Senate Foreign Relations Committee. See Sai, "Hawaiian Neutrality," 28.

104. See Ronald C. Williams Jr., "'Aole Hoohui ia Hawai'i': U.S. Collegiate Teams Debate Annexation of Hawai'i and Independence Prevails, 1893 to 1897," *Hawaiian Journal of History* 43 (2009): 169.

105. Sai, "Hawaiian Neutrality," 28.

106. Sai, "Hawaiian Neutrality," 30.

107. "The 1897 Petition Against the Annexation of Hawaii," https://www.archives.gov/education/lessons/hawaii-petition#background. For explanation of the claim of annexation, see Williamson Chang, "'A Rope of Sand:' A Documentary History of the Failure of the United States to Annex the Hawaiian Islands," SYS Law 530-006. https://kipdf.com/a-rope-of-sand-a-documentary-history-of-the-failure-of-the-united-states-to-anne_5ac71fe61723dd349641765c.html. Also see Williamson B. C. Chang, "Hawai'i's Ceded Lands: The Ongoing Quest for Justice in Hawai'i," William S. Richardson School of Law, University of Hawai'i at Manoa, Faculty Lecture Series, October 1, 2014. https://www.academia.edu/62576921/Hawaii_s_Ceded_Lands_and_the_Ongoing_Quest_for_Justice_in_Hawai_i.

108. House Committee on Foreign Affairs Report, also cited by Sai, "Hawaiian Neutrality," 32.

109. Coffman, *Nation Within*, 304.

110. The annexation of Hawai'i involved many logistical meetings. See Coffman, *Nation Within*, 303–5; 308–11.

111. Those who objected included Thomas H. Ball and Augustus Bacon. See Sai, "Hawaiian Neutrality," 32.

112. "Fifty-Sixth Congress, Session I, 1900," https://www.doi.gov/sites/doi.gov/files/uploads/31_stat_141_hawaiian_organic_act_1900.pdf. Cited by Sai, "Hawaiian Neutrality," 34.

113. Sai, "Hawaiian Neutrality," 35.

114. For a list of the landowners, see *United States v. Estate of Bishop*, 1 D. Haw. 257 (1902), https://cite.case.law/d-haw/1/257/. For number of acres, see Van Dyke, *Who Owns The Crown Lands of Hawai'i?*, 221.

115. See *United States v. Estate of Bishop*.

116. See D. Tanabe and D. Skeem, "Finding Aid to Ralph O. Yardley Political Cartoon Collection," *Hawaii State Archives*, https://ags.hawaii.gov/wp-content/uploads/2020/03/hsa_manuscript-Y_fa.pdf.

117. See "Pearl Harbor: Board Reconvenes at Washington, Admiral Barkley Presiding," *Hawaiian Gazette*, June 7, 1901, https://chroniclingamerica.loc.gov/lccn/sn83025121/1901-06-07/ed-1/.

118. By 1908, $3 million had been approved by Congress for the construction of a dry dock, barracks, warehouses, an ammunition depot, a submarine base, a radio center, and a hospital. See Van Dyke, *Who Owns the Crown Lands of Hawai'i?*, 221. For $3 million, see Stephanie Hinnershitz, "The Key to the Pacific: The Construction of the Pearl Harbor Naval Base," *The National World War II Museum*, October 6, 2021, https://www.nationalww2museum.org/war/articles/construction-pearl-harbor-naval-base.

119. "Kapakuiki Hae Hawai'i," https://hawaiialive.org/kapakuiki-hae-hawaii/.

120. The inclusion of the United Kingdom's Union Jack acknowledges the British Royal Navy's historical relations with the Hawaiian Kingdom. In 1793, Captain George Vancouver from Great Britain presented the Union Jack to King Kamehameha I. The Union Jack was used as the unofficial Hawaiian flag until 1816.

121. "Kapakuiki Hae Hawai'i," https://hawaiialive.org/kapakuiki-hae-hawaii/.

122. Joyce D. Hammond, "Hawaiian Flag Quilts: Multivalent Symbols of a Hawaiian Quilt Tradition," *Hawaiian Journal of History* 27 (1993), 1.

123. Hammond, "Hawaiian Flag Quilts," 2.

124. Ibid.

125. "1898 Rosina Kalanikauwekiulani Ayers's "Hawaiian Coat-of-Arms" Quilt," https://americanhistory.si.edu/collections/search/object/nmah_556599.

126. Hammond, "Hawaiian Flag Quilts," 12.

127. Hammond, "Hawaiian Flag Quilts," 11.

128. Hammond, "Hawaiian Flag Quilts," 7.

129. Ibid.

130. Kalākaua wrote the original Hawai'i Pono'i in 1874. See Williams, "Ke Ko'o o Hawai'i," 51.

131. "Hawaiian National Anthem," https://www.hawaiiankingdom.org/national-anthem.shtml.

132. The earliest examination of the Hawaiian flag quilt embodying a resistance movement was in 1933. That year the Mokihana Club, a Kaua'i women's literary, civic, and social club, mounted an exhibition of the Hawaiian flag quilts. See Hammond, "Hawaiian Flag Quilts," 15.

133. Scholars today are working to "write back" against the traditional national narrative that erased Hawaiian resistance and contention from the record. This roster includes but is not limited to Carlos Andrade, Noelani Arista, Leilani Basham, Noelani Goodyear Ka'ōpua, Lilikalā Kame'eleihiwa, Jonathan Kamakawiwo'ole Osorio, Davianna McGregor, Donovan Preza, David Keanu Sai, and Ronald C. Williams Jr. See Williams, "Aole Hoohui ia Hawaii," 153–79.

134. Kualapai, "The Queen Writes Back," 46.

135. Kualapai, "The Queen Writes Back," 47.

136. Ibid.

137. Queen Lili'uokalani to William Lee, January 31, 1898, HM59570, Huntington Library.

138. Coffman, *Nation Within*, 317.

"CUBA AND PUERTO RICO: TWO WINGS OF A BIRD?"

1. See "Trans-Atlantic Slave Trade – Database," https://www.slavevoyages.org/voyage/database and "Intra-American Slave Trade – Database," https://www.slavevoyages.org/american/database.

ON THE VERGE OF SOVEREIGNTY: CUBA AND PUERTO RICO AT THE TURN OF THE TWENTIETH CENTURY

1. "The Antilles for the sons of the Antilleans" was a rallying cry uttered by Puerto Rican physician and revolutionary Ramón Emeterio Betances in a speech he gave at the Masonic lodge of Port-au-Prince in Haiti, probably during his longest stay there, between February 1870 and December 1871. The militant slogan is thought to have been in circulation since 1867 and to have originated among New York-Antillean revolutionary circles, but Betances popularized it. See Ramón Emeterio Betances, *Las Antillas para los antillanos*, ed. Carlos M. Rama (San Juan: Instituto de Cultura Puertorriqueña, 2001), v–vi. The slogan was Betances's direct response to the U.S. imperialist tenet "America for the Americans" that came to summarize the Monroe Doctrine. See Kahlila Chaar-Pérez, "'The Antilles for the sons of the Antilles': On Translating Ramón Emeterio Betances," *Small Axe* 25, no. 3 (November 2021): 160–65.

2. Christopher Columbus arrived in Cuba in 1492 and in Puerto Rico in 1493, on his first and second voyages, respectively. On both islands, Columbus and his crew encountered Indigenous populations who descended from the Arawak people from the Orinoco basin in today's Venezuela and Guyana, and who peopled the Caribbean in a series of migration waves starting before the Christian era. By the fifteenth century, Taínos inhabited both islands. Cuba's aboriginal name was Cubanascan, and Puerto Rico's Borikén, from which derives today's demonym "Boricua," which is used as synonym for Puerto Rican and carries a strong identification with the island's cultural identity. Juan Ponce de León began the formal Spanish colonization of Puerto Rico in 1508, and Diego Fernández de Cuellar did the same in Cuba in 1511. During the first years of colonization, Spaniards organized Taínos in the *encomienda* system, which involved missionizing them and exploiting their labor in agriculture and mining for the benefit of the colony. This caused the decimation of the Indigenous people. Others fled and formed families in places that were difficult for the Spanish to access. See Louis A. Pérez, *Cuba: Between Reform and Revolution* (Oxford, UK: Oxford University Press, 2006), 9. Fernando Picó, *Historia general de Puerto Rico* (Río Piedras, Puerto Rico: Ediciones Huracán, 1986), 20–35.

3. José Trías Monge, *Puerto Rico: The Trials of the Oldest Colony in the World* (New Haven, CT: Yale University Press: 1997), 12–13; Marta Bizcarrondo and Antonio Elorza, *Cuba / España. El dilema autonomista, 1878–1898* (Madrid: Editorial Colibrí, 2001), 389.

4. Trías Monge, *Puerto Rico*, 12–13.

5. In Cuba the Autonomist government would be effective on January 1, and in Puerto Rico on February 9, when a provisional autonomic cabinet was constituted to organize elections. Approving an autonomic charter for Cuba and Puerto Rico through royal decree bypassed the parliamentary process in order to avoid the opposition of the general public in Spain. Trías Monge, *Puerto Rico*, 150.

6. The concept of "sovereignty" in this essay refers to Merriam-Webster's second definition of "one who exercises supreme authority within a limited sphere." This notion of sovereignty allows for different political models, including independence, and also autonomy, which encompasses self-government while remaining associated to the metropolitan power of Spain.

7. The Spanish word *criollo*, or Creole, was used throughout the Spanish empire to refer to the descendants of Spanish colonists, or *peninsulares*, born in the New World.

8. Jorge Duany, "Introduction: A Movable Nation," *Picturing Cuba: Art, Culture, and Identity in Cuba and the Diaspora*, ed. Jorge Duany (Gainesville: Florida University Press, 2019), 1–4. Silvia Álvarez Curbelo, "Caribbean Siblings: Sisterly Affinities and Differences Between Cuba and Puerto Rico in the Nineteenth Century," in *The Routledge Hispanic Studies Companion to Nineteenth-Century Spain* (London: Routledge, 2022), 6.

9. René Taylor, "José Campeche (1751–1809)," in *Puerto Rico: Arte e identidad* (San Juan: Editorial de la Universidad de Puerto Rico, 1998), 17–27.

10. Taylor, "José Campeche (1751–1809)," 17.

11. Lizette Cabrera Salcedo, *Reflejos de la historia de Puerto Rico en el arte: 1751–1950* (Río Piedras, Puerto Rico: Museo de Historia, Antropología y Arte, 2015), 25–27.

12. Cabrera Salcedo, *Reflejos de la historia de Puerto Rico en el arte: 1751–1950*, 25. See also Álvarez Curbelo, "Caribbean Siblings," 5.

13. This was the first such invitation in three hundred years of Spanish colonization of the New World. See Álvarez Curbelo, "Caribbean Siblings," 6.

14. For detailed analysis of the most important sessions of the *Cortes* involving New Spain, see Rafael Marquese, Márcia Berbel, and Tâmis Parron, *Slavery and Politics: Brazil and Cuba* (Albuquerque: University of New Mexico Press, 2016), 76–86. For a discussion on the question of citizenship, naturalization, and race at the *Cortes de Cádiz*, see David Sartorius, *Ever Faithful: Race, Loyalty, and the Ends of Empire in Spanish Cuba* (Durham, NC: Duke University Press, 2014), 22–27.

15. See Álvarez Curbelo, "Caribbean Siblings," 6. María de los Ángeles Castro, "Ramón Power en las Cortes de Cádiz," *EnciclopediaPR,* September 12, 2014, https://enciclopediapr.org/content/ramon-power -en-las-cortes-de-cadiz/.

16. María de los Ángeles Castro, "Ramón Power en las Cortes de Cadiz." See also Picó, *Historia general de Puerto Rico*, 126–29.

17. Álvarez Curbelo, "Caribbean Siblings," 6. See also Fernando Picó, *Historia general de Puerto Rico*, 128–29.

18. Álvarez Curbelo, "Caribbean Siblings," 6.

19. In Cuba and Puerto Rico, some people also favored separatism, as they saw reason for the transformation from colony to province. However, they were outnumbered by the reformist sector, which saw an opportunity for the socioeconomic advancement of the islands in remaining under Spanish dominion. Luis Mattei Filardi, *En las tinieblas del colonialismo: "cien metros" de historia puertorriqueña* (Puerto Rico: Ediciones Nóema, 2014), 57–65. With the Constitución de Cádiz, free Cubans and Puerto Ricans also received Spanish citizenship and the right to create local councils of officials elected by universal male suffrage. The reforms articulated by the *Junta* that Fernando VII had to sign upon his restoration in 1812 were ahead of his time. To date, no other European power had extended so many rights to its New World colonies. Trías Monge, *Puerto Rico*, 9.

20. A year later, in 1822, Santo Domingo was occupied by Haiti. See Álvarez Curbelo, "Caribbean Siblings," 7.

21. For an analysis of Puerto Rico's socio-political context during the nineteenth century and the reasons why the island did not join the countries of Spanish America in fighting for its independence during the first quarter of the nineteenth century, see Silvia Álvarez Curbelo, "La patria criolla," in *Puerto Rico: arte e identidad* (Río Piedras: Editorial de la Universidad de Puerto Rico, 1998), 33–36; see also Álvarez Curbelo,

"Despedidas," *Revista de Indias* 57, no. 211 (1997): 783–99; Pérez, *Cuba: Between Reform and Revolution*, 9–10.

22. Trías Monge, *Puerto Rico*, 6.

23. Between 1584 and 1808, the Spanish Crown's *Situado mexicano* sent a periodic transfer of money generated from Mexican silver mining to Puerto Rico to aid its military buildup. The subsidy did not arrive as regularly as promised, which in part accounted for the island's economic underdevelopment. See Jorge Duany, *Puerto Rico: What Everyone Should Know* (New York: Oxford University Press, 2017), 17. By contrast, twice a year, Havana was the final stop of treasure ships arriving from the Mexican port of Veracruz and the Panamanian port of Portobelo, and provided them with escort ships to sail through the Bahamas Channel as they harnessed the powerful current of the Gulf Stream on their way back to Spain. The periodic event, which brought hundreds of sailors to Havana for several weeks while they waited for their ships to depart for Spain, functioned as an economic engine for Cuba. Hugh Thomas, *Cuba: A History* (London: Penguin Books, 1971), 7. See also Pérez, *Cuba: Between Reform and Revolution*, 26.

24. While the islands' economies relied on sugar production as early as the sixteenth century, it was not until the late eighteenth century that their respective industries prospered. César J. Ayala, *American Sugar Kingdom: The Plantation Economy of the Spanish Caribbean, 1898–1934* (Chapel Hill: University of North Carolina Press, 1999), 16. In Cuba and Puerto Rico, an influx of planters fleeing the revolution in Saint-Domingue aided in this development. Cuba was on a faster track than Puerto Rico, due to its broader upper class and the lobbying of Francisco Arango y Parreño (1765–1837), a *criollo* planter and representative to the *Cortes*. Arango y Parreño advocated successfully for the expansion of the slave trade and for tax exemptions and technological investments to expand the sugar economy in Cuba. See Ada Ferrer, *Cuba: An American History* (New York: Scribner, 2022), 67–77. In Puerto Rico, the sugar economy did not take off until 1815, thanks to the *Cédula de Gracias* (Writ of Grace), a royal order encouraging white immigration and protections to the slave trade. See Álvarez Curbelo, "Caribbean Siblings," 5.

25. On the racialization of insurgency by Spanish authorities in Cuba, see Ada Ferrer, *Insurgent Cuba: Race, Nation, and Revolution, 1868–1878* (Chapel Hill: University of North Carolina Press, 1999), 111. In Cuba, according to the census of 1861, among the 1,396,000 persons who made up the island's population, 370,000, or 26 percent, were enslaved. See Adelaida Zórina, "On the Genesis of Capitalism in Nineteenth-Century Cuba," *Latin American Perspectives* 2, no. 4 (December 1995): 7–20. An unprecedented number of enslaved individuals from Africa and the Lesser Antilles were also brought into Puerto Rico, but that island's enslaved population never reached the density of Cuba's. At its height in the 1850s, it comprised 11 percent of the population. See Jorge Duany, *Puerto*

Rico: What Everyone Needs to Know, 15; and José Manuel García Leduc, *Apuntes para una historia breve de Puerto Rico: desde la prehistoria hasta 1898* (San Juan: Isla Negra, 2002), 191.

26. Fernando VII's death in 1833 led to wars of succession, referred to as the "Carlist Wars," between the conservative camp that favored his brother Carlos, and those who favored his daughter Isabel II, who courted the liberals to gain their support. After four years, she prevailed, and a new liberal constitution was passed in 1837. Between 1833 and 1892, Spain had seventy-five governments, of which the majority were in power for less than two years. Trías Monge, *Puerto Rico*, 9.

27. García Leduc, *Apuntes para una historia breve de Puerto Rico*, 213. See also Álvarez Curbelo, "Caribbean Siblings," 8.

28. Pressured by England, Spain had been signing treaties to prohibit the slave trade since 1807. The local planters in Cuba and Puerto Rico, however, ignored those agreements.

29. In 1838, Puerto Rico's Governor General Miguel López de Baños penalized vagrants, which he defined as people who were not formally employed by patrons. In 1849, Governor Juan de la Pezuela established the *Régimen de la libreta de jornaleros*, or "Regime of the day laborer passbook," which forced laborers without property to carry a passbook specifying their employer and place of work at all times. See García Leduc, *Apuntes para una historia breve de Puerto Rico*, 196. These laws were established to create a class in permanent servitude. We are grateful to Silvia Álvarez Curbelo for this last observation.

30. Several factors contributed to this slowdown in the sugar economy. Puerto Rico endured a cholera epidemic between 1855 and 1859 that killed many enslaved plantation workers. It also increased the price of enslaved people, making it more profitable for Puerto Rican planters to sell them to Cuba than to keep them. At the same time, there was scarce capital for the modernization of plantation technology. This situation made plantations more dependent on *jornaleros*. See García Leduc, *Apuntes para una historia breve de Puerto Rico,* 196–97.

31. Following a trajectory well-established since colonization, Cuba began to modernize at a much faster pace than Puerto Rico. The printing press arrived in Cuba in at the end of the seventeenth century, almost a century earlier than in Puerto Rico. In 1837, Cuba inaugurated the fourth railway in the Americas. Time and again through the nineteenth century, the Spanish Crown denied Puerto Rico's request for the establishment of a university, such as the one that existed in Havana since 1728. Álvarez Curbelo, "Caribbean Siblings," 9. For an extended analysis of the role of modernity in the social, political, and intellectual development of Puerto Rico, see Silvia Álvarez Curbelo, *Un país del porvenir: el afán de modernidad en Puerto Rico* (San Juan: Ediciones Callejón, 2001).

32. Ferrer, *Insurgent Cuba*, 17.

33. Álvarez Curbelo, "Caribbean Siblings," 11.

34. Ibid.

35. Ferrer, *Insurgent Cuba*, 17.

36. In 1868, this was more strongly the case in Puerto Rico than in Cuba, where slave society was more ingrained.

37. I borrow this expression from late historian Fernando Picó, who used it in relation to Puerto Rico. Picó, *Historia General de Puerto Rico*, 192.

38. *La Gloriosa*, the "Glorious Revolution," also took place in Spain that year. This revolution opened the political debate on individual freedoms and civil rights. It yielded the creation of two constitutions: a monarchic constitution in 1869 and a republican constitution in 1873. The latter abolished the monarchy for one brief year, establishing the First Spanish Republic (1873–1874). In any event, the liberal triumph that *La Gloriosa* represented in Spain only extended in very limited ways to Cuba and Puerto Rico, which had their representation in the *Cortes* restituted. Under very limited circumstances, they also received the recognition of the right of assembly. Other freedoms recognized in Spain, such as the right to strike, were not recognized in the Antilles. See García Leduc, *Apuntes para una historia breve de Puerto Rico*, 218.

39. This moment witnessed the rise of a national portraiture distinct from the one serving the Spanish authorities. Some leaders, such as Betances, Martí, and Maceo, were aware of the power of portraiture and sat for studio photographs at different times of their life. Martí had an oil portrait made from life by Herman Norman in 1891. A portrait from life of Betances by a painter identified as "F. Domingo" is in the collection of the Ateneo Puertorriqueño. From a reference by Betances's biographer Luis Bonafoux to a portrait of his from life exhibited at the Paris Universal Exposition of 1900, it is possible to deduce that the portrait was painted by the Spanish artist Francisco Domingo Marqués (1842–1920). But in general, it was the posthumous circulation of photographs as well as engraved and painted portraits that consecrated these figures within the national pantheons of Cuba and Puerto Rico. For the references to the portrait from life of Betances by F. Domingo, see Vicente Géigel Polanco, "Mis recuerdos del Ateneo" in *Revista del Instituto de Cultura Puertorriqueña* 29, no. 73 (October–December 1976): 6. See also Luis Bonafoux quoted by F. Manrique Cabrera, "Aproximaciones a Betances" in *Betances* (San Juan: Casa Nacional de la Cultura, Instituto de Cultura Puertorriqueña, 1980), 14. The rise of a national portraiture tradition is also linked to the cultural institutions that supported it. Cuba could support its own portraiture after independence, as its cultural institutions had the backing of the state and sought to establish an iconography of nationhood. By contrast, the Ateneo Puertorriqueño is the only institution in Puerto Rico that supported the commissioning of portraits of Puerto Rican cultural and political figures. During the 1960s and 1970s, with the rise of a modern art movement that directly addressed Puerto Rico's colonial situation, figures such as Betances, Hostos, and others re-emerged in art as symbols of the fight for independence.

40. Betances's activism was truly Pan-Caribbean and included the Dominican Republic and Haiti. See Kahlila Chaar-Pérez, "'The Antilles for the sons of the Antilles,'" 160–65; and Kahlila Chaar-Pérez, "A Revolution of Love: Ramón Emeterio Betances, Anténor Firmin, and Affective Communities in the Caribbean," *The Global South* 7, no. 2 (Fall 2014): 11–36.

41. "El Honorable Dr. Betances, murió este Noble Filantropo Puerto Rriqueño siendo el Ilustre Delegado del P. R. C. en Paris, Francia," Schomburg Center for Research in Black Culture, Manuscripts, Archives and Rare Books Division, New York Public Library Digital Collections.

42. For a background on Betances's Antillean self-identification and its relation to his political thinking, see Paul Estrade, "La nación antillana: sueño y afán de 'El Antillano' (Betances)," in *La nación soñada: Cuba, Puerto Rico y Filipinas ante el 98*, ed. Consuelo Naranjo, Miguel A Puig-Samper, and Luis Miguel García Mora (Madrid: Doce Calles, 1996), 25–36.

43. Betances and Eugenio María de Hostos developed the idea of the Antillean Confederation, which was never fully fixed. Betances included Haiti. Sometimes Betances and Hostos also included Jamaica in the confederation. Ibid., 28–36.

44. Betances cofounded the *Comité Revolucionario de Puerto Rico* with abolitionist leader Segundo Ruiz Belvis and José Francisco Basora. Lizette Cabrera Salcedo, "Segundo Ruiz Belvis," *EnciclopediaPR*, April 30, 2021, https://enciclopediapr.org/content/segundo-ruiz-belvis/.

45. The word "borinqueño" is the demonym corresponding to Borikén, the Indigenous Taíno name for Puerto Rico, or Borinquen, the Spanish adaptation of the Taíno name.

46. Rodríguez de Tió penned the lyrics to be sung to a well-known melody composed by amateur musician Francisco Ramírez and arranged into a *danza* by Spanish tenor Félix Astol Artés. According to Cuban historian Josefina Toledo, Rodríguez de Tió composed the poem at the urging of Betances himself. Toledo explains that the song to which the poem was arranged was already known as *La Borinqueña*, although its original lyrics were romantic. At a gathering in San Germán with other independentists, Rodríguez de Tió decided to turn the song into a call to arms. Josefina Toledo, *Lola Rodríguez De Tió*. Colección Clío (Havana: Ediciones Unión, 2007), 38–39.

47. Mackenna's portraits of other Puerto Rican political and cultural figures include José de Diego, Federico Degetau, and Luis Muñoz Rivera. He is also known as a prolific landscape painter. Adlín Ríos Rigau, *Fernando Díaz Mackenna*, exhibition brochure (Santurce, Puerto Rico: Galería Sagrado Corazón, 2008).

48. Josefina Toledo, *Lola Rodríguez de Tió*, 38–39.

49. Olga Jiménez de Wagenheim, *Puerto Rico's Revolt for Independence: El Grito de Lares* (New York: Routledge, 2019), 57–77.

50. Jiménez de Wagenheim, *Puerto Rico's Revolt for Independence*, 1; 82–96.

51. Jiménez de Wagenheim, *Puerto Rico's Revolt for Independence*, 84.

52. Mattei Filardi, *En las tinieblas del colonialismo: "cien metros" de historia puertorriqueña*, 92.

53. See Jiménez de Wagenheim, *Puerto Rico's Revolt for Independence,* 89–96. Rodríguez de Tió's connections to the leaders of the uprising made her the source of constant surveillance by Spanish authorities thereafter. Josefina Toledo, *Lola Rodríguez de Tió*, 43–44.

54. Colonial authorities used *mambí* (or the plural, *mambises*) as a pejorative term for insurgents. The members of the Cuban Liberation Army then claimed it as a badge of honor, using it to refer to themselves. Ada Ferrer, *Insurgent Cuba*, 210n63.

55. The *trocha* ran from north to south, from Júcaro to Morón.

56. Jesse Hoffnung-Garskof, *Racial Migrations: New York City and the Revolutionary Politics of the Spanish Caribbean* (Princeton, NJ: Princeton University Press, 2019), 270.

57. Only a year after settling in the United States, Martí positioned the countries of Latin America as the ideal breeding ground for a hemispheric vision of solidarity and racial equality in "Nuestra América" (Our America), which remains his most-read text. Additionally, he warned Latin Americans of the rising imperial power of the northern nation. José Martí, "Nuestra América," *La Revista Ilustrada de Nueva York*, January 10, 1891.

58. Emilio Bejel, "José Martí: iconografía y memoria," *La Habana elegante: Revista semestral de literatura y cultura cubana, caribeña, latinoamericana, y de estética.* Segunda época no. 46 (Autumn/Winter 2009), http://www.habanaelegante.com/Fall_Winter_2009 /Invitation_Bejel.html.

59. Emilio Bejel, *José Martí: Images of Memory and Mourning* (London: Palgrave McMillan, 2012), 3. Throughout the twentieth century and until the present, Martí's image was instrumentalized to different ideological ends by the Cuban government and various sectors of society. Lillian Guerra, *The Myth of José Martí: Conflicting Nationalisms in Early Twentieth-Century Cuba* (Chapel Hill: University of North Carolina Press, 2005), 1–21.

60. Jorge R. Bermúdez, *Martí en Salinero: 155 aniversario del natalício de José Martí*, exhibition brochure (Havana: Casa Natal José Martí, 2008).

61. Cited in Ferrer, *Insurgent Cuba*, 1999, 143.

62. "Costa Rica: Bureau of the American Republics," in *The Executive Documents of the Senate of the United States for the First Session of the Fifty-Second Congress, 1891–1892* (Washington, DC: Government Printing Office, 1892), 83. See also Armando Vargas Araya, *La huella imborrable: las dos visitas de José Martí a Costa Rica. 1893 y 1894* (San José, Costa Rica: Editorial EUNED, 2008), 1–2.

63. Because he was Black, Maceo had endured resistance to his leadership during the Ten Years' War. Yet two decades later, and almost nine years after the abolition of slavery, Maceo led the insurgent western invasion. Ferrer, *Insurgent Cuba*, 144.

64. Pérez, *Cuba: Between Reform and Revolution*, 125.

65. Martí's ideological influence over the rebel cause was so singular and powerful that the Spanish believed his loss would lead to the revolution's collapse, but the memory of his revolutionary ideals and sacrifices only strengthened the struggle. See Philip S. Foner, *Antonio Maceo: The "Bronze Titan" of Cuba's Struggle for Independence* (New York: Monthly Review Press, 1977), 169–70.

66. Ada Ferrer, *Insurgent Cuba*, 142–45.

67. Ibid., 143.

68. General Bens of the Spanish forces claimed that the Spanish won the combat of the *Potrero de Saratoga*. See General Bens, *Mis memorias: veintidos años en el desierto* (Madrid: Ediciones del Gobierno del África Occidental Española, 1944), 34–35. General Máximo Gómez claimed that the Cuban Liberation Army won, and the Spaniards retreated. See Máximo Gómez, *Diario de campaña, 1868-1897* (Oviedo, Spain: Universidad de Oviedo, 1998), 146–47.

69. Pérez, *Cuba: Between Reform and Revolution*, 127.

70. Pérez, *Cuba: Between Reform and Revolution*, 130–31.

71. Menocal's soldiering is discussed in "Forces at Play: War and Empire in the Art of Winslow Homer and Armando García Menocal," in this volume, pp. 183–203.

72. Kristin L. Hoganson, *American Empire at the Turn of the Twentieth Century: A Brief History with Documents* (Boston: Bedford/St. Martins, 2017), 12.

73. Hostos, who initially believed in reform and autonomy, only gradually embraced independence. See María Dolores González-Ripoll Navarro, "Independencia y antillanismo en la obra de De Hostos," in *La nación soñada: Cuba, Puerto Rico y Filipinas ante el 98*, ed. Consuelo Naranja Orovio, Miguel A. Puig-Samper, and Luis Miguel García Mora (Madrid: Doce Calles, 1996), 37–47.

74. García Leduc, *Apuntes para una historia breve de Puerto Rico*, 227.

75. Álvarez Curbelo, "Caribbean Siblings," 14.

76. Ibid., 14.

77. Palacio was removed by Spain's overseas minister thanks to an autonomist who was able to secretly board a ship to Spain and denounce his abuse of power. Ibid., 14.

78. Another model of autonomy, proposed by the Cuban Rafael María de Labra, was limited to internal administrative affairs. García Leduc, *Apuntes para una historia breve de Puerto Rico*, 225.

79. Once war broke out in Cuba, Muñoz Rivera capitalized on the Spanish government's precarious situation there, condemning the revolutionaries and insisting that autonomist reform was the solution to the war. César Ayala and Rafael Bernabe, *Puerto Rico in the American Century: A History since 1898* (Chapel Hill: University of North Carolina Press, 2007), 23.

80. The idea of making a pact with a monarchist party was for some autonomists a betrayal of their republican ideas. José Celso Barbosa, another prominent figure in the party, therefore, branched out and founded the Partido Autonomista Ortodoxo. Bernabe and Ayala, *Puerto Rico in the American Century*, 24.

81. Scholars have disagreed over the reach of its content, as some of its text is unclear and contradictory. More importantly, with the U.S. invasion, it was impossible to test its practicality. Indeed, the most important was the creation of an Insular Parliament, the first state legislature in Puerto Rican history with a simple majority of members elected by Puerto Ricans. Mattei Filardi, *En las tinieblas del colonialismo*, 85.

82. While Louis A. Pérez and Ada Ferrer assert that Cuba was close to winning the war against Spain, John Lawrence Tone disputes this thesis, arguing that although Cuban insurgents fought an outstanding guerrilla campaign, they were not able to retain the territory they gained, and thus progress was slippery and victory over Spain dubious. See Louis A. Pérez, *Cuba: Between Reform and Revolution*, 139. Ada Ferrer, *Cuba: An American History*, 153. John Lawrence Tone, *War and Genocide in Cuba* (Chapel Hill: University of North Carolina Press, 2006), chapter 18.

83. Cited in Pérez, *Cuba: Between Reform and Revolution*, 142.

84. Clay Risen, *The Crowded Hour: Theodore Roosevelt, the Rough Riders, and the Dawn of American Democracy* (New York: Scribner, 2019), 151.

85. Cited in Daniel Immerwahr, *How to Hide an Empire: A History of the Greater United States* (New York: Farrar, Straus and Giroux, 2019), 68.

86. Roosevelt ordered a water-repellent uniform in cravenette from Brooks Brothers clothiers. See Thomas Bailey and Katherine Joslin, *Theodore Roosevelt: A Literary Life* (Lebanon, NH: ForeEdge, an imprint of University Press of New England, 2018), 117. Although the Rough Riders were privately outfitted, the rest of the U.S. forces were poorly clothed. See Ivan Musicant, *Empire by Default* (New York: Henry Holt, 1998), 252.

87. *The Rough Riders* was one of numerous books published immediately during and after the war. The demand for books about the war was so great that in early 1898 the Library of Congress composed a bibliography of works relating to Cuba, to be sent free of charge to any library. Requests poured in from libraries across the country, and by the end of 1898, similar bibliographies on Hawai'i, Spain, and the Philippines were also offered. See Ellen E. Adams and Joshua F. Beatty, "'The Foundation of Naval Science': Alfred Thayer Mahan's *The Influence of Sea Power on History* and the Library of Congress Classification System." Paper presented at the Canadian Association of Professional Academic Librarians conference, Calgary, Canada, May 30, 2016.

88. Musicant, *Empire by Default*, 189.

89. Musicant, *Empire by Default*, 340.

90. Sampson ordered the collier USS *Merrimac* to be sunk on purpose, even though a crew of eight sailors remained on board. His intention was to use the *Merrimac* as a blockship placed between mines, so that there was no way for the Spanish to sail out of the narrow, approximately 180-foot-wide harbor. On June 3, the ship's captain, Richmond P. Hobson (1837–1930), scuttled the ship, but it did not sink in the right place. The *Merrimac* foray failed, and Hobson and his seven men, moderately wounded, were taken prisoner by the Spanish. See M. J. Rosenau and John H. Beacom, "Report on the City and Harbor of Santiago de Cuba and Arrangements for a Quarantine," *Public Health Reports (1896–1970)* 14, no. 11 (1899): 373–77.

91. Daniel Immerwahr, *How to Hide an Empire*, 69.

92. Tomás Pérez Vejo, *El 3 de julio de 1898: El fin del imperio español* (Barcelona: Penguin Random House Grupo Editorial España, 2020), n.p.

93. Ibid.

94. Ibid.

95. By 1922 that definition of pansy was obsolete, and the word was used as a derogatory term to refer to "weak and effeminate" men. See Oxford English Dictionary, online.

96. Angel Rivero Méndez, *Crónica de la Guerra Hispanoamericana en Puerto Rico* (Madrid: Sucesores de Rivadeneyra, 1922), 40.

97. Enrique Vivoni Farage, "San Juan de Puerto Rico: de plaza fuerte a ciudad bella," in *Los arcos de la memoria: el '98 de los pueblos puertorriqueños*, ed. Silvia Álvarez Curbelo, Mary Frances Gallart, and Carmen I. Raffucci (San Juan: Postdata, 1998), 30–33.

98. Fernando Picó, *Puerto Rico, 1898: The War After the War* (Princeton, NJ: Markus Wiener Publishers, 2004), 21; Héctor Andrés Negroni, *Historia Militar de Puerto Rico* (San Juan: Sociedad Estatal Quinto Centenario, 1992), 321.

99. Angel Rivero Méndez, *Crónica de la Guerra Hispanoamericana en Puerto Rico*, 157–68. Mark Barnes, *The Spanish-American War and Philippine Insurrection: An Annotated Bibliography* (Abingdon, Oxford: Taylor and Francis, 2010), 195.

100. Héctor Andrés Negroni, *Historia Militar de Puerto Rico*, 323.

101. Fernando Picó, *1898: The War after the War*, 28. The warships were the *Massachusetts, Gloucester, Columbia, Yale*, and *Dixie*. Héctor Andrés Negroni, *Historia Militar de Puerto Rico*, 329.

102. Ponce historian Jorge Figueroa has examined forty-five of Ballell's photographs of the arrival of the U.S. military into the southern city, and they coincide in their point of view of the ships. Figueroa's research was cited by Silvia Álvarez Curbelo in her lecture "Ponce, ciudad abierta: la ciudad y el puerto en tiempos de la invasión (1898)," which she presented on March 19, 2015, at Museo de Arte de Ponce, on the occasion of the acquisition of the painting by Cuyàs-Agulló and the photograph on which it is based. We are grateful to Álvarez Curbelo for her generosity in sharing her lecture with us.

103. Silvia Álvarez Curbelo, "Ponce, ciudad abierta: la ciudad y el puerto en tiempos de la invasión (1898)," 3.

104. In Puerto Rico, the conflict lasted seventeen days and resulted in 157 casualties: 105 were Spaniards and 52 were from the United States. Of these, 24 (17 Spaniards and 7 from the United States) died from combat wounds. Jiménez de Wagenheim, *Puerto Rico's Revolt for Independence*, 208. On the support of Puerto Rican society for the occupation of the island by the United States' military, see Fernando Picó, *1898: The War after the War*, 31–33.

105. Yoel Cordoví Núñez, *Máximo Gómez Utopía y Realidad de una República* (Havana: Editorial Historia, 2014), 147.

106. Howard Gillette Jr. "The Military Occupation of Cuba, 1899–1902: Workshop for American Progressivism," *American Quarterly* 25, no. 4 (October 1973): 410–25.

107. Yoel Cordoví Nunez, *Liberalismo, crisis e independencia en Cuba, 1880–1904* (Coral Gables, FL: Editorial Letra Viva, 2013), 175–76.

108. Pérez, *Cuba: Between Reform and Revolution*, 145.

109. Khary Oronde Polk, *Contagions of Empire: Scientific Racism, Sexuality, and Black Military Workers Abroad* (Chapel Hill: University of North Carolina Press, 2020), 27–34.

110. Havana was the principal source of the yellow fever epidemics that plagued the southern United States in the nineteenth century. See Mariola Espinosa, "The Threat from Havana: Southern Public Health, Yellow Fever, and the U.S. Intervention in the Cuban Struggle for Independence, 1878–1898," *Journal of Southern History* 72, no. 3 (August 2006): 541–68. See also Fernando Güereña-Burgueño, "The Centennial of the Yellow Fever Commission and the Use of Informed Consent in Medical Research," *Salud Pública México* 44, no. 2 (March 2002):140–44.

111. Finlay had not been able to prove his hypothesis and the subjects on whom he experimented were not asked for their consent. Vincent J. Cirillo, *Bullets and Bacilli: The Spanish-American War and Military Medicine* (New Brunswick, NJ: Rutgers University Press, 2004), 115–16.

112. *The History of Vaccines: An Educational Resource by the College of Physicians from Philadelphia*, https://www.historyofvaccines.org/content/jesse-lazear. Lazear trained in entomology with famed malariologist Giovanni Battista Grassi at the University of Rome. Lazear was responsible for the group's mosquito experiments in Cuba. Another test case, James Carroll, died in 1907 from a heart valve sequela he sustained during this experiment. See Vincent J. Cirillo, *Bullets and Bacilli*, 113–14.

113. As a result of this discovery, Dr. Finlay was elected president of the 31st Meeting of the APHA in 1904 and honored at the subsequent annual meeting in recognition of his scientific work. See Fernando Güereña-Burgueño, "The Centennial of the Yellow Fever Commission and the Use of Informed Consent in Medical Research," 140.

114. José Amador, *Medicine and Nation Building in the Americas, 1890–1940* (Nashville, TN: Vanderbilt University Press, 2015), 2.

115. Jack C. Lane, *Armed Progressive: General Leonard Wood* (Lincoln: University of Nebraska Press, 2009), 111.

116. Pérez, *Cuba: Between Reform and Revolution*, 147.

117. Pérez, *Cuba: Between Reform and Revolution*, 148.

118. In June 1901, the Cuban constituent convention acquiesced and accepted the amendment by a margin of one vote. Pérez, *Cuba: Between Reform and Revolution*, 149.

119. Pérez, *Cuba: Between Reform and Revolution*, 149.

120. Sargent reportedly described Wood's face as "a magnificent head." See Charles Merrill Mount, "The Rabbit and the Boa Constrictor: John Singer Sargent at the White House," in *Records of the Columbia Historical Society, Washington, DC*, 71/72 (1971): 631.

121. Henna had differing political views from Hostos as a separatist from Spain, but a supporter of annexation to the United States. See Ayala and Bernabe, *Puerto Rico in the American Century*, 24.

122. We are grateful to Silvia Álvarez Curbelo for driving the point that examining the history of the Puerto Rican response to 1898 requires thinking beyond the twenty-first-century Puerto Rican party lines.

123. Others include the teacher Rafael Cordero, the poets José Gautier Benítez and José Gualberto Padilla, and the abolitionist José Julián Acosta. See Edward J. Sullivan, *From San Juan to Paris and Back: Francisco Oller and Caribbean Art in the Era of Impressionism* (New Haven, CT: Yale University Press, 2014); *Francisco Oller: Un Realista del Impresionismo* (Ponce, Puerto Rico: Museo de Arte de Ponce, 1983).

124. Osiris Delgado Mercado, *Francisco Oller (1833–1917): Pintor de Puerto Rico* (San Juan: Centro de Estudios Avanzados de Puerto Rico y el Caribe, 1983), 160. We are grateful to Flavia Marichal for pointing us to this reference.

125. See "1898: A Contest in Memory," pp. 163–81 in this volume.

126. E. Fernández García, Francis W. Hoadley, and Eugenio Astol, eds., *El libro de Puerto Rico / The Book of Porto Rico* (San Juan: El libro azul publishing, 1923), 1,035.

127. Olga Jiménez de Wagenheim, *Puerto Rico: An Interpretive History from Pre-Columbian Times to 1900* (Princeton, NJ: Markus Wiener Publishers, 1998), 213.

128. Fernández García, Hoadley, and Astol, eds., *El libro de Puerto Rico*, 1,035.

129. Ayala and Bernabe, *Puerto Rico in the American Century*, 52.

130. Ibid., 26.

131. Forced to contend with the limits of government established by Washington, DC, the Republican Party, which was allied with large propertied interests and the professional classes, decided not to criticize the U.S. administration, hoping that its position would garner the authorities' favor and eventually lead to annexation. Ibid., 53.

132. "Luis Muñoz Rivera (1859–1916)," in *Hispanic Americans in Congress, History, Art and Archives*, United States House of Representatives, https://history.house.gov/People/Detail/20429.

133. Fernández García, Hoadley, and Astol, eds., *El libro de Puerto Rico*, 1035.

134. On the social changes brought on by the change of sovereignty, see Picó, *Historia general de Puerto Rico*, 234–55; Ayala and Bernabe, *Puerto Rico in the American Century*, 14–24. Beginning in 1900, the colonial government expanded the public school system and established English as the language of instruction. The imposition of English in schools and the use of education as a tool for Americanization caused great malaise and debate. Yet between 1900 and 1940, the children of workers and small merchants, particularly from urban areas, received unprecedented access to education. For different perspectives on the history of education in Puerto Rico and the changes established in the first decades of the U.S. colonial administration, see Pablo Navarro-Rivera, "Acculturation Under Duress: The Puerto Rican Experience at the Carlisle Indian Industrial School 1898–1918," *Centro Journal* 18, no. 1 (Spring 2006): 222–59; Fernando Picó, *Historia general de Puerto Rico*, 254–55.

"FORGETTING EMPIRE, REMEMBERING RESISTANCE"

1. Ernest Renan delivered the lecture on March 11, 1882. For a translated transcription of the lecture, see Ernest Renan, *What Is a Nation? And Other Political Writings*, trans. and ed., M. F. N. Giglioli (New York: Columbia University Press, 2018), 251.

2. Edward W. Said, *Beginnings: Intention and Method* (New York: Basic Books, 1975), xvi.

3. Luis H. Francia, *Enrique El Negro / Black Henry*, unpublished manuscript, n.d.

4. Republic of the Philippines, Philippine National Police, "PNP Seal & Badge," https://pnp.gov.ph/pnp-seal-badge/

CUTTING A PATH TO SOVEREIGNTY: THE COMPLEX POLITICAL LANDSCAPES OF THE PHILIPPINES AND GUAM

1. Moorfield Storey, "The Neutralization of the Philippines as a Peace Measure: From the Recent Annual Address of Moorfield Storey, President of the Anti-Imperialist League of Boston." *The Advocate of Peace (1894-1920)* 70, no. 1 (1908): 19–20.

2. *Harper's Weekly* was first published in 1857 and quickly rose to prominence for its quality illustrations and editorial content. By 1874, the magazine had a circulation of 160,000, its readership building up to around 200,000 at the turn of the century. It remained an important publication until it ceased in 1916. See Frank Luther Mott, *A History of American Magazines*, vol. 2, 1850–1865 (Cambridge, MA: Harvard University Press, 1938), 469–87.

3. The "Boys in Blue" references the blue shirts and, sometimes, the blue tunics or coats that were worn by U.S. Army soldiers.

4. On January 28, 1897, Remington wrote to Poultney Bigelow about his first trip to Cuba, "Just home from Cuba—saw more hell there than I ever read about. Went for New York Journal—smallpox—typhoid—yellow jack—dishonesty—suffering beyond measure." See Allen P. Splete and Marilyn D. Splete, eds., *Frederic Remington—Selected Letters* (New York: Abbeville Press, 1988), 218–19.

5. Scholars have been at odds over the debates about racism involved in the war, as well as about the Filipino nationalism that it fostered. Brian Linn's foundational work on the conflict is the most accurate in its assessment of the war through a lens of military history. See Brian McAllister Linn, *The Philippine War, 1899–1902* (Lawrence: University Press of Kansas, 2000). Paul Kramer addresses the Philippine-American War as a "race war," a characterization that is contested by some military historians. The term "race war" specifies how conflict emerges from two or more ethnicities. See Paul A. Kramer, *The Blood of Government: Race, Empire, the United States and the Philippines* (Chapel Hill: University of North Carolina Press, 2006). Filipino scholars use the war to designate the start of the national revolution and Philippine independence, yet they frame the war as a national event rather than one of regional warfare, an approach contested by military historians. See Renato Constantino and Letizia R. Constantino, *The Philippines: A Past Revisited* (Quezon City, Philippines: Tala Publishing Services, 1975).

6. Remington was commissioned by Richard Watson Gilder, editor of *Century* magazine. He was originally instructed to report on Native Americans but focused instead on the Black soldiers of the Tenth Cavalry. See Roscoe L. Buckland, *Frederic Remington: The Writer* (New York: Twayne Publishers, 2000), 19.

7. See John Langellier, *Scouting with the Buffalo Soldiers: Lieutenant Powhatan Clarke, Frederic Remington, and the Tenth U.S. Cavalry in the Southwest* (Denton: University of North Texas Press, 2020), 5.

8. In the summer of 1888, Remington had traveled to Arizona, where he accompanied Powhatan Clarke and six Black cavalry soldiers for twelve days on their scouting trips near Fort Grant and the San Carlos Reservation.

9. Albert J. Beveridge, "The March of the Flag," *Chicago Tribune*, September 19, 1898. Kristin Hoganson explains the fearmongering by the era's white supremacists, who sowed the seeds against Filipinos. See Kristin L. Hoganson, *Fighting for American Manhood: How Gender Politics Provoked the Spanish-American and Philippine-American Wars* (New Haven, CT: Yale University Press, 1998), 134–39.

10. In some Muslim areas, however, the U.S. Army met little resistance prior to 1902 because locals did not support the insurgents. See Linn, *The Philippine War*, 226–28.

11. This is according to a survey by the Episcopal Commission on Indigenous Peoples from 1993. See James F. Eder, "The Future of Indigenous Peoples in the Philippines: Sources of Cohesion, Forms of Difference," *Philippine Quarterly of Culture and Society* 41, nos. 3–4 (September/December 2013): 274.

12. Most of the U.S. troops sent to the Philippines were drawn from state militia volunteers, and their national service was supposed to end when the treaty was signed with Spain on December 10, 1898. However, under the Constitution's Article 1, Section 15, the militia can be called into federal service *to suppress insurrection*. Had it been declared a "war," and especially a foreign war, then the majority of militia would have been discharged. Note that the National Defense Act of 1916 has since changed the parameters under which the president can call up state militias. See Allan R. Millett and Peter Maslowski, *For the Common Defense: A Military History of the United States of America*, 2nd. ed. (New York: Free Press, 1994), 341–42.

13. See Linn, *The Philippine War*, 32.

14. As explained below, this battle of August 13 was a mock battle, as the Spanish allowed the U.S. bombardment of Fort San Antonio Abad so they could surrender Manila to the United States, rather than to the Filipinos who had surrounded Intramuros (the fortified part of Manila) and cut off supplies.

15. David J. Silbey, *A War of Frontier and Empire: The Philippine-American War, 1899–1902* (New York: Hill and Wang, 2007), xi–xvi.

16. For the population of 1898, see Frank T. Reuter, "William Howard Taft and the Separation of Church and State in the Philippines," *Journal of Church and State* 24, no. 1 (Winter 1982): 105.

17. See Linn, *The Philippine War*, 75. The people of Negros sent a petition to Captain Henry Glass, who had recently arrived from Guam.

18. The definition of war is a legal term and refers to organized armed violence under a recognized authority and thus is different from criminal or communal violence. David J. Silbey outlines Filipino sovereignty and discusses the question of terminology. See Silbey, *A War of Frontier and Empire*, xi–xv.

19. The writings and publications of the Propagandists were not allowed to be openly circulated in the Philippines.

20. The Rizal family were tenants of a Dominican hacienda. The authors thank Ambeth Ocampo for this information.

21. Rizal copied Antonio de Morga's *Sucesos de las Islas Filipinas* (1609) while he was researching in the British Museum. The text, which had been published in Mexico, served as the basis for Rizal's arguments against Spain's racist attacks on Filipino history, culture, and character. See Kramer, *The Blood of Government*, 5–6, 64. See also Ambeth R. Ocampo, "Rizal's Morga and Views of Philippine History," *Philippine Studies* 46, no. 2 (1998): 184–214; and John N. Schumacher, *The Propaganda Movement, 1880-1895* (Manila: Ateneo de Manila University Press, 1997).

22. Kramer, *The Blood of Government*, 73.

23. Ambeth R. Ocampo, *101 Stories on the Philippine Revolution* (Pasig City, Philippines: Anvil, 2009), 38.

24. Rizal and Luna probably knew each other through Luna's younger brother, José, who was Rizal's classmate at the Ateneo municipal high school of Manila. Although Rizal was based in Brussels in 1891, he traveled to Paris in April and October of that year. Thank you to Ambeth Ocampo for this research.

25. Luna apprenticed with Alejo Vera and accompanied him to Rome, where Luna was loosely associated with the city's Spanish Academy. Thank you to Ambeth Ocampo for this information.

26. The source for this painting is suspected to be a popular book by Charles Louis Dezobry, *Rome au siècle d'August, ou voyage d'un Gaulois à Rome à l'époque du règne d'August et pendant une partie du règne de Tibèr* (Rome in the Time of Augustus, Adventures of a Gaul in Rome). Luna won the First Equal Prize in Madrid's Exposición General de Bellas Artes, one of three First Class medals but not the more significant Medal of Honor, which would have placed him above Spaniards. See John Clark, *The Asian Modern*, vol. 1 (Singapore: National Gallery Singapore, 2021), 90. This was the same exhibition where Cuban artist Armando García Menocal won second prize for his work *Generosidad Castellana* (Castilian Generosity); see p. 308 in this volume.

27. Prior to this, in the 1881 Exposición General de Bellas Artes, Luna was awarded a Second Class medal for his painting *Death of Cleopatra*. For both competitions, he had to submit a historical painting on Ancient Rome or Greece to please the jurors from the Academy. Rizal, Graciano López Jaena, and other propagandists first interpreted Luna's painting as representative of the Philippine condition. Luna's extant correspondence does not indicate his intent.

28. See Clark, *The Asian Modern*, 90; and Santiago Albano Pilar, *Juan Luna: The Filipino as Painter* (Manila: Eugenio López Foundation, 1980), 59. Rizal made the toast at a party hosted by Pedro Paterno. See Kramer, *The Blood of Government*, 56. See also Leon Ma. Guerrero, *The First Filipino: A Biography of José Rizal* (Manila: Advocate Book Supply Co., 1963), 112–13. Ambeth Ocampo describes this toast as perhaps the first instance of art criticism by a Filipino. See correspondence with the author, February 2, 2022.

29. Guerrero, *The First Filipino*, 116.

30. Guerrero, *The First Filipino*, 274. *Noli me tangere* is also Latin for the words Jesus Christ spoke to Mary Magdalene when she recognized him after the resurrection, according to John 20:17. In 1892, Luna sent Rizal twenty-one illustrations for a new Tagalog edition of *Noli me tangere*, translated by Rizal's elder brother Paciano and edited by Rizal. See Guerrero, *The First Filipino*, 307. Unfortunately, the manuscript and most of these illustrations were destroyed during World War II. Author's correspondence with Ambeth Ocampo, September 14, 2022. Rizal was completing a specialization in ophthalmology at the University of Heidelberg in Germany when he wrote *Noli me tangere*, which was banned in the Spanish colonies upon its publication. See "José Rizal," Religion and Public Life, Harvard Divinity School, https://rpl.hds .harvard.edu/faq/jos%C3%A9-rizal. Since 1957, it has been required reading in the Filipino university system. See Filomeno V. Aguilar Jr., Ma. Elizabeth J. Macapagal, and Christian Jil R. Benitez, "Learning without Reading *Noli me tangere*: The Rizal Law in Two Public High Schools," *Philippine Studies: Historical and Ethnographic Viewpoints* 69, no. 3 (2021): 325–60.

31. Guerrero, *The First Filipino*, 123–24.

32. Luna made this work, as well as a portrait of Miguel López de Legazpi, as part of an agreement he had in receiving a scholarship from the Ayuntamiento (City Hall) of Manila. See Filomeno V. Aguilar Jr., "The *Pacto de Sangre* in the Late Nineteenth-Century Nationalist Emplotment of Philippine History," *Philippine Studies* 58, nos. 1–2 (June 2010): 98.

33. Thank you to Ambeth Ocampo for this information.

34. Aguilar, "The *Pacto de Sangre*," 81.

35. They are dressed in a cuirass (breastplate) mimicking the period-fashionable silhouette of the male peascod doublet (jacket). Those with helmets wear variations of the cabasset, characterized by its flat brim and light weight. See Herbert W. Krieger, *The Collection of Primitive Weapons and Armor of the Philippine Islands in the United States National Museum* (Washington, DC: Government Printing Office, 1926), 109–10.

36. Pre-colonial Filipino armor was usually made from leather or other natural materials, such as water buffalo horn, and it weighed around twenty to twenty-five pounds. See Krieger, *Primitive Weapons and Armor of the Philippine Islands*, 107.

37. Thank you to E. Tory Laitila for his consultation on this painting.

38. Thank you to Brian Linn for pointing out how the painting addresses different religions in the Filipino collective identity.

39. In 1889, Marcelo Del Pilar (who died in 1896) credited Luna's role in "rekindling the memory of the Pacto de Sangre": "*La paleta de Luna ha revivido del pacto de sangre entre Legazpi y Sicatuna.*" See Marcelo Del Pilar, *La soberanía monacal en Filipinas: Apuntes sobre la funesta preponderanci del fraile en las islas, así en lo politico, como en lo económico y religioso* (Manila: Imprenta de Don Juan Atayde, 1889; reprinted 1898), 3; and Aguilar, "The *Pacto de Sangre*," 98. Aguilar also credits Ambeth Ocampo for interpreting the painting as a representation of "the first international treaty between the Philippines and a foreign country." See Ibid., 83.

40. Kramer, *The Blood of Government*, 59.

41. See John Clark, "3.2 Juan Luna (1857–1899) Notes, Chronology, Bibliography," 2013, John Clark Archive, Asia Art Archive, Hong Kong, https://cdn.aaa.org.hk.

42. The short-lived group embraced and enhanced the masculinity of their bodies through fencing, gymnastics, martial arts, and weightlifting as a means to differentiate themselves from the menacing androgyny they perceived in the Spanish friars. See Vicente L. Rafael, "Nationalism, Imagery, and the Filipino Intelligentsia in the Nineteenth Century," *Critical Inquiry* 16, no. 3 (Spring 1990): 594.

43. See Stephen Hong Sohn, "Los Indios Bravos: The Filipino/American Lyric and the Cosmopoetics of Comparative Indigeneity," *American Quarterly* 62, no. 3 (September 2010): 552–55; and Ambeth R. Ocampo, "The 'Barkada' brouhaha," *Philippine Daily Inquirer*, August 14, 2020.

44. Thank you to Ambeth Ocampo for pointing out these nuances.

45. Sitting Bull had led warriors of the Lakota Sioux, Northern Cheyenne, and Arapaho tribes in the Battle of the Little Bighorn and defeated the U.S. federal troops commanded by George Custer. After his defeat and capture, he was cast in the touring show in 1885. Although technically he remained a prisoner of war, Sitting Bull gained international fame in his reenactments of attacks on white settlers. See Sohn, "Los Indios Bravos," 554–55.

46. Rosemarie Bank, "Representing History: Performing the Columbian Exposition," *Theatre Journal* 54, no. 4 (2002): 589–606, esp. 603. See also Sohn, "Los Indios Bravos," 554–55n29.

47. Glenn Anthony May, *Inventing a Hero: The Posthumous Re-Creation of Andres Bonifacio* (Madison: University of Wisconsin, Center for Asian Studies, 1996), 12–13.

48. Rafael, "Nationalism, Imagery, and the Filipino Intelligentsia in the Nineteenth Century," 594.

49. May, *Inventing a Hero*, 12–13. Bonifacio modeled the Katipunan on Masonic lodges, and its members were organized into ranks or degrees, with each having different colored hoods, passwords, and formulas. A rigorous initiation concluded with the *sandugo,* or blood compact. According to Ambeth Ocampo, they drank only blood, not blood mixed with wine.

50. May notes that the Katipunan grew in membership slowly until 1896, when its numbers reached the thousands, but he specifies that it is unlikely its membership ever totaled thirty thousand, which was claimed in a memoir by Pio Valenzuela. See May, *Inventing a Hero*, 12–13, and 170n30.

51. May, *Inventing a Hero*, 13–14.

52. At this time, Juan Luna was imprisoned in Fort Santiago with his brother Antonio for complicity in the 1896 revolution. Rizal was held separately on a ship in Manila Bay when the revolution began. Under interrogation, Antonio Luna gave information on people he thought implicated him in the revolution, including Rizal, which likely resulted in Rizal's being condemned to death. Thank you to Ambeth Ocampo for this information.

53. May, *Inventing a Hero*, 14.

54. Carlos Quirino, "The Spanish Colonial Army: 1878–98," *Philippine Studies* 36, no. 3 (Third Quarter 1988): 382–83.

55. The warships *Cristina, Castilla,* and *Don Juan de Austria* were positioned to fire upon Bacoor and Noveleta, whereas the gunboats *Leyte, Bulosan, Villalobos,* and the transport ship *Cebu* fired upon Rosario and San Francisco de Malabon. Meanwhile, Aguinaldo had numerically inferior forces. See Quirino, "The Spanish Colonial Army," 382–84. Women sometimes played major roles in the fighting. Aguinaldo assigned Gregoria "Gloria" P. Montoya command of several units to delay Spanish reinforcements. She dismantled the wooden bridge across Imus River that connects the town of Bacoor to Cavite Viejo. See Rafaelita Hilario Soriano, ed., *Women in the Philippine Revolution* (Quezon City: Printon Press, 1995), 88–89; and D. J. Walker, *Spanish Women and the Colonial Wars of the 1890s* (Baton Rouge: Louisiana State University Press, 2008), 14.

56. Glenn May outlines scholarly debates on the Tejeros Convention during which Aguinaldo was elected the new president of the governmental structure of the Katipunan. See May, *Inventing a Hero*, 16; 82–111. Paul Kramer explains that Bonifacio had suffered numerous military defeats. Further, Bonifacio represented an egalitarian—and radical—approach to Filipino independence. Aguinaldo represented the *principal* class, and was more conservative, endorsing elites as the leaders of the new independent Philippines. See Kramer, *The Blood of Government*, 81. Bonifacio did not recognize that by accepting hospitality in the home of his wife's relations, who were associated with the Magdiwangs, and being related by marriage to Magdiwangs, he was not seen as impartial. Thank you to Ambeth Ocampo for this information.

57. May, *Inventing a Hero*, 16; Linn, *The Philippine War*, 17.

58. Thank you to Ambeth Ocampo for pointing out these nuances.

59. The Katipunan's infighting had taken a toll, however. By February 1897, the Spanish, assisted by thousands of Filipino volunteers, had captured every rebel-held town in Cavite Province. Much of the area was destroyed, and the population dropped from 135,000 to 97,000. See Linn, *The Philippine War*, 17. As Linn points out, these are Spanish figures and likely low. For Filipinos fighting with Spanish soldiers, see Quirino, "The Spanish Colonial Army," 381. Filipinos also were employed by the U.S. Army. See Linn, *The Philippine War*, 127; and Silbey, *A War of Frontier and Empire*, 113–14.

60. See Linn, *The Philippine War*, 109.

61. Silbey, *A War of Frontier and Empire*, 15. Paul Kramer cites 1.7 million pesos. See Kramer, *The Blood of Government*, 81. Christopher Capozzola notes the amount paid as 400,000 pesos, and the full sum was not paid. See Christopher Capozzola, *Bound by War: How the United States and the Philippines Built America's First Pacific Century* (New York: Basic Books, 2020), 19. Aguinaldo was paid in installments, and never received the last one. The Spanish never carried out the reforms. Thank you Ambeth Ocampo for this information.

62. The American consul, E. Spencer Pratt, met with Aguinaldo in Singapore. See Linn, *The Philippine War*, 20–21.

63. Aguinaldo and Dewey later published memoirs with different accounts of the conversation. See Aguinaldo, *My Memoirs* (Manila: Cristina Aguinaldo Suntay, 1967) and George Dewey, *The Autobiography of George Dewey, Admiral of the Navy* (New York: Charles Scribner's Sons, 1913).

64. See Ocampo, *101 Stories on the Philippine Revolution*, 205–6.

65. Ibid.

66. An Englishman, Howard W. Bray, interpreted the conversation between Aguinaldo and Dewey. See Ocampo, *101 Stories on the Philippine Revolution*, 186; 225.

67. The prewar decision to concentrate all the Regular army units for operations against Cuba meant that only the 14th Infantry Regiment, recently arrived from Alaska, was ready for immediate deployment. Fourteen thousand volunteers were in the initial wave that was sent to the Philippines in June 1898. See Linn, *The Philippine War*, 6; 12–14.

68. Some scholars feel that this declaration of independence was illegitimate because Aguinaldo was not supported by Filipinos throughout the archipelago.

69. Capozzola, *Bound by War*, 22.

70. Dewey had cut the telegraph cable to Hong Kong and did not know that the United States and Spain had declared a cease-fire on August 12, 1898.

71. Fermín Jaudenes, Spain's last governor of the Philippines, negotiated with Dewey through British and Belgian diplomats. See Ronald E. Dolan, ed., *Philippines: A Country Study,* 4th ed. (Washington, DC: Federal Research Division, 1993), 23. On the mock battle, see Theodore S. Gonzalves, *The Day the*

Dancers Stayed: Performing in the Filipino/American Diaspora (Philadelphia: Temple University Press, 2009), 29–61.

72. Linn, *The Philippine War*, 5; 27.

73. For more on the Krag-Jorgensen rifle, see Linn, *The Philippine War*, 13. The Krag-Jorgensen was an impressive firearm, but it had to be loaded slowly, by hand. The Mauser rifle could be loaded through the top of the magazine with a stripper clip, which is much faster and smoother than loading by hand. See David J. Silbey, *A War of Frontier and Empire*, 73.

74. Linn, *The Philippine War*, 30.

75. See Olga Jiménez de Wagenheim, *Puerto Rico: An Interpretive History from Pre-Columbian Times to 1900* (Princeton, NJ: Markus Wiener Publishers, 1998), 221; Louie Pérez Jr., *Cuba Between Reform and Revolution*, 5th edition (New York: Oxford University Press, 2014), 143. The notion that people could not rule themselves as a rationalization for colonization goes beyond the United States in the Caribbean and the Pacific—Europeans also used it to justify intervention all over the world.

76. Kramer, *The Blood of Government*, 15, 88. On the term, "insurrection," David J. Silbey writes, "Though there was no Filipino nation in the conflict, the Filipino nation could not have existed without war. To label it an insurgency ignores that foundational importance." See Silbey, *War of Frontier and Empire*, xv. In 1998, on the centennial anniversary of the conflicts of 1898, the Library of Congress changed the subject classification for materials on the period from Philippine Insurrection to Philippine-American War, thereby acknowledging the conflict as one between two states, rather than as an uprising against an established power.

77. Linn, *The Philippine War*, 125.

78. Silbey, *War of Frontier and Empire*, 53.

79. Linn, *The Philippine War*, 3.

80. W. E. B. Du Bois, "Of Mr. Booker T. Washington and Others," in *The Souls of Black Folk* (Chicago: A. C. McClurg, 1903; New York: Penguin, 1989), 45.

81. The joint resolution to annex Hawai'i was signed into law on July 7, 1898. See page 76 in this volume.

82. "Excerpts from the Speech of Moorfield Storey at Faneuil Hall, June 15, 1898," in *Save the Republic, Anti-Imperialist Leaflet*, no. 11 (Washington, DC, 1898–99): 21.

83. Cited by Mark Antony De Wolfe Howe, *Portrait of an Independent, Moorfield Storey, 1845–1929* (New York: Houghton Mifflin, 1932), 317. Also see Richard Ormond, *John Singer Sargent: Portraits in Charcoal* (New York: Morgan Library and Museum; Washington, DC: National Portrait Gallery, Smithsonian Institution; Lewes, UK: D. Giles Limited, 2019), 159.

84. See Robert L. Beisner, *Twelve against Empire: The Anti-Imperialists, 1898–1900* (New York: McGraw-Hill, 1968), 98. Edward Atkinson, a Boston businessman who had advocated against annexing Hawai'i, held the first AIL meeting in his Boston office. For a statistical study of the membership of the AIL, see E. Berkeley Tompkins, *Anti-Imperialism in the United States: The Great Debate, 1890–1920* (Philadelphia: University of Pennsylvania Press, 1970), 126–60.

85. Elizabeth Cobbs Hoffman, *American Umpire* (Cambridge, MA: Harvard University Press, 2013), 171.

86. Richard Seymour, *American Insurgents: A Brief History of American Anti-Imperialism* (Chicago: Haymarket Books, 2012), 41–42.

87. Kristin L. Hoganson, "'As Badly off as the Filipinos': U.S. Women's Suffragists and the Imperial Issue at the Turn of the Twentieth Century," *Journal of Women's History* 13, no. 2 (Summer 2001): 9–33. Recall that the Nineteenth Amendment was not ratified until 1920, and even then, it did not extend the vote to all women. See Kate Clarke Lemay, *Votes for Women: A Portrait of Persistence* (Washington, DC: National Portrait Gallery, Smithsonian Institution; Princeton, NJ; Princeton University Press, 2019).

88. Her speech was called "What Peace Means." Cited by Louise W. Knight, *Citizen: Jane Addams and the Struggle for Democracy* (Chicago: University of Chicago Press, 2005), 395.

89. Jane Addams wrote of her portrait sitting, "We finally took my party dress waist, took off all the lace, made a V front & I am to leave it and then Mr B. will [fresco] it into the color he likes—that is he takes a squirter and squirts the color on it. Pretty idea isn't it? but at least it fits." See Jane Addams to Mary Rozet Smith, August 28, 1906. JAP-PSC-P – Jane Addams Papers. See digital.janeaddams.ramapo.edu.

90. Jane Addams to Walter Hines Page, undated, between July 21 and August 15, 1906. HDLP-WHI – Henry Demarest Lloyd Papers. See digital.janeaddams.ramapo.edu.

91. Jane Addams to Selma Rosenwald Eisendrath, June 7, 1916. JAP-PSC-P – Jane Addams Papers.

92. Extracts from a speech of October 18, 1898, by Samuel Gompers, president of the American Federation of Labor, were published as "Imperialism: Its Dangers and Wrongs: Mr. Samuel Gompers," in *Save the Republic: Anti-Imperialist Leaflet*, no. 11 (Washington, DC: Anti-Imperialist League, 1899), n.p.

93. Ann Gibson Winfield, *Eugenics and Education in America: Institutionalized Racism and the Implications of History, Ideology, and Memory* (New York: Peter Lang Publishers, 2007), 56.

94. Ambeth Ocampo, email correspondence with the author, September 13, 2022.

95. While a few were elected representatives from their own regions, many were appointed by decree to places they had probably never been. Most of the Mindanao representatives were appointed. Thank you to Ambeth Ocampo for this information.

96. The First Philippine Republic was formally ended on April 1, 1901, when Aguinaldo swore allegiance to the United States.

97. See Linn, *The Philippine War*, 33–35.

98. Mabini was ousted by moderates during negotiations for a cease-fire in May 1899. Linn, *The Philippine War*, 34; 109.

99. Reynaldo Ileto argues that the U.S. health measures taken as a campaign against cholera and other diseases actually helped the military defeat the Philippine "Insurrection," as burning homes and fields was also a way to starve the Filipino fighters. See Reynaldo Ileto, "Cholera and the Origins of The American Sanitary Order in the Philippines," in *Imperial Medicine and Indigenous Societies*, ed. David Arnold (Manchester, UK: Manchester University Press, 2017), 125–48.

100. For portraiture and Filipino nationalism at the turn of the century, see Resil B. Mojares, "Guillermo Tolentino's 'Grupo de Filipinos Ilustres' and the Making of a National Pantheon," *Philippine Studies* 58, nos. 1–2 (June 2010): 169–84.

101. "Memorial to the Senate of the United States, presented by D. Felipe Agoncillo to the U.S. Secretary of State, January 30, 1899," The Law Library of Jeffrey Roden, https://rodenlaw.wordpress.com/2009/01/22/memorial-to-the-senate-of-the-united-states-presented-by-don-felipe-agoncillo-to-the-us-secretary-of-state/. See also Felipe Agoncillo, *Memorial to the Senate of the United States* (Washington, DC, 1899).

102. Reflections from the National Museum of the Philippines on Hidalgo's Portrait of Felipe Agoncillo, *Together Apart: Art World Voices that Connect Us Now*, The British Council and the National Museum of the Philippines, 2020, https://sway.office.com/kIIWfMygKjBhZj8g.

103. The fighting involved all or part of thirteen U.S. regiments along a sixteen-mile front during a two-day battle. U.S. casualties totaled 238, of whom forty-four were killed in action or later died of wounds. The U.S. Army reports estimated that the Philippine Army of Liberation suffered four thousand casualties, of whom seven hundred were killed. See Linn, *The Philippine War*, 42–52.

104. Aguinaldo was away on February 4 and 5, attending a ball in Malolos, and most of his officers were also absent. Apolinario Mabini, who headed Aguinaldo's cabinet, criticized him for micromanaging all military decisions—and then ignoring the army. See Linn, *The Philippine War*, 54–55.

105. Kenneth E. Hendrickson, "Reluctant Expansionist: Jacob Gould Schurman and the Philippine Question," *Pacific Historical Review* 36, no. 4 (November 1967): 405–21.

106. Under Taft's leadership, a judicial system was established; a civil service organized; popular elections were held; and municipal boards were maintained. Elected officials in towns were given considerable freedom in planning projects and appropriating funds. See Norman G. Owen, *Compadre Colonialism: Studies in the Philippines under American Rule* (Ann Arbor: University of Michigan Press, 2020), 17. See also Paul D. Hutchcroft, "Colonial Masters, National Politicos, and Provincial Lords: Central Authority and Local Autonomy in the American Philippines, 1900–1913," *Journal of Asian Studies* 59, no. 2 (2000): 277–306. The American occupation also reformed the Philippine tax system and the legal system, including 110 articles of law and a new Philippine Supreme Court. See Silbey, *A War of Frontier and Empire*, 136.

107. Oscar M. Alfonso, "Taft's Views on 'The Philippines for the Filipinos,'" *Asian Studies* 6, no. 5 (1969): 239.

108. Telegram to President Roosevelt from officials in Manila, January 7, 1903. Theodore Roosevelt Papers: Series 1: Letters and Related Material, 1759–1919, Jan. 1–Feb. 11. The Library of Congress, Manuscript Division. See also Alfonso, "Taft's Views on 'The Philippines for the Filipinos,'" 237–38.

109. As cited in "Islands for Filipinos," *New York Times*, January 30, 1904, 5.

110. Alfonso, "Taft's Views on 'The Philippines for the Filipinos,'" 241.

111. "Historical Perspective of The Philippine Educational System," Republic of the Philippines, Department of Education, https://www.deped.gov.ph/about-deped/history/.

112. See Silbey, *A War of Frontier and Empire*, 211.

113. McKinnon soon quintupled the number of open schools in Manila. See Linn, *The Philippine War*, 31. McKinnon was with the First California Volunteers and after the capture of Manila, he was appointed superintendent of the schools and cemeteries of Manila. See "Priest on the Philippines," *New York Times*, October 30, 1899, 3.

114. Henry Gilford, "William Seraile, Voice of Dissent: Theophilus Gould Steward (1843–1924) and Black America," *Afro-Americans in New York Life and History* 18, no. 2 (July 31, 1994): 60.

115. For the experiences of African Americans during the Philippine-American War, see Willard B. Gatewood, *"Smoked Yankee" and the Struggle for Empire: Letters from Negro Soldiers, 1898–1902* (Champaign: University of Illinois Press, 1971) and Willard B. Gatewood, *Black Americans and the White Man's Burden, 1898–1903* (Champaign: University of Illinois Press, 1975).

116. Over six thousand African American soldiers arrived in the Philippines in August 1899. There were six African American regiments, including two Regulars: the 24th and 25th Infantry, the 9th and 10th Cavalry, and the 48th and 49th Infantry U.S. Volunteers. See Timothy D. Russell, "'I Feel Sorry for These People': African American Soldiers in the Philippine-American War, 1899–1902," *Journal of African American History* 99, no. 3 (Summer 2014): 201; 205.

117. Thank you to Jean Parker Vail for sharing her family history, especially that of her grandmother, Ida Burr Parker.

118. Cited by Linn, *The Philippine War*, 203. John H. Parker was an innovator of the strategic use of modern weaponry during the War of 1898 in the Cuban campaign.

119. Linn, *The Philippine War*, 284.

120. Vito Belarmino's forces were the only ones to remain. In May 1901, Belarmino launched a three-week offensive in Sorsogon but surrendered on July 4. See Linn, *The Philippine War*, 285–86.

121. See Glenn A. May, "Why the United States Won the Philippine-American War, 1899–1902," *Pacific Historical Review* 52 (1983) 353–77. Captain John R. M. Taylor kept track of captured correspondence and records of the Army of Liberation in the Bureau of Insurgent Records, whose papers are now in the National Archives. These papers are also published in a five-volume manuscript, *The Philippine Insurrection against the United States: A Compilation of Documents with Notes and Introduction* (Pasay City, Philippines: Eugenio Lopez Foundation, 1971). See John T. Farrell, "An Abandoned Approach to Philippine History: John R. M. Taylor and the Philippine Insurrection Records," *The Catholic Historical Review* 39, no. 4 (January 1954): 385–407.

122. "General Orders No. 100: Instructions for the Government of the Armies of the United States in the Field," known as the Lieber Code, was the first modern codification of the laws of war. First issued on April 24, 1863, by President Abraham Lincoln, it was primarily written by Francis Lieber. See Vanya Eftimova Bellinger, "Lieber and Clausewitz: The Understanding of Modern War and the Theoretical Origins of General Orders No. 100," *Journal of the Civil War Era* 12, no. 1 (March 2022): 28–53.

123. For example, Article 17 declares that it is lawful to starve civilians. Historians today recognize the major flaws in its implementation during the Philippine-American War. As David J. Silbey points out, "GO 100 forbade 'wanton' destruction, but what constituted 'wanton' destruction?" See Silbey, *War of Frontier and Empire*, 163.

124. Linn, *The Philippine War*, 277–78.

125. The commanders were Major General John C. Bates, and his successor, Major General James F. Wade. Bates negotiated the Bates Agreement, effectively keeping war out of the southernmost islands of Sulu, but he was relatively passive in all other areas of leadership. See Linn, *The Philippine War*, 277.

126. Trías focused on Manila and mishandled the defense of Cavite. By late 1901, the resistance in Cavite and Tayabas had ended. See Linn, 277.

127. Linn, *The Philippine War*, 278.

128. Malvar especially was an effective organizer of resistance, as he had personally selected the best Filipinos to be officers in his troops, and established shadow governments in most towns. See Linn, *The Philippine War*, 287.

129. Linn, *The Philippine War*, 288.

130. Cited in Linn, *The Philippine War*, 286.

131. Paterno worked with Trinidad H. Pardo de Tavera and Benito Legarda, among others. See Michael Cullinane, *Ilustrado Politics: Filipino Elite Responses to American Rule, 1898–1909* (Manila: Ateneo University Press, 2003), 5. Taft did not care for Paterno, however, and so Paterno's political power waned in the period of U.S. control.

132. Constantly hunted by soldiers of the United States, Aguinaldo was forced to be on the move and his role as leader of the Army of Liberation was mostly symbolic. See Linn, *The Philippine War*, 136–38.

133. Aguinaldo later collaborated with Japanese forces during World War II, which drove the United States out of the Philippines. See Walter LaFeber, *The American Age: U.S Foreign Policy at Home and Abroad, 1750 to the Present*, 2nd ed. (New York: W. W. Norton, 1994), 217.

134. Cailles was also appointed governor of Laguna by the U.S. occupation administrators. See Linn, *The Philippine War*, 297. Between February and June 1902, about two hundred former *principales* surrendered intelligence in exchange for a pardon of all assistance that they had given to Malvar's forces during the war. See May, "Resistance and Collaboration in the Philippine-American War," 74–75.

135. Linn, *The Philippine War*, 302–3.

136. May used parish records from 1902 to evaluate the human cost of reconcentration. See Glenn A. May, "'The Zones' of Batangas," *Philippine Studies* 29, no. 1 (1981): 99. Katherine Bjork estimates that some towns in the zones with a normal population of 3,000 swelled to over 30,000. See Bjork, *Prairie Imperialists: The Indian Country Origins of American Empire* (Philadelphia: University of Pennsylvania Press, 2019), 166.

137. Linn explains how Captain Henry C. Hale, under Bell's command, carefully attempted to "reduce to a minimum the hardships of the common people." Cited by Linn, *The Philippine War,* 303.

138. See Linn, *The Philippine War*, 304; Glenn A. May, "Resistance and Collaboration in the Philippine-American War: The Case of Batangas," *Journal of Southeast Asian Studies* 15, no. 1 (May 1984): 72.

139. For more information on these debates, see Linn, *The Philippine War,* 304.

140. Linn, *The Philippine War*, 311.

141. The stolen bells became a symbol of painful memory and irreconciliation between the Philippines and the United States. They were returned on December 11, 2018.

142. Linn, *The Philippine War*, 312.

143. Ibid.

144. Linn, *The Philippine War*, 312–21.

145. Afterward, nearly all the *ilustrados* and their descendants were appointed to the American colonial government. See Rafael, "Nationalism, Imagery, and the Filipino Intelligentsia in the Nineteenth Century," 594n2.

146. Silbey, *A War of Frontier and Empire*, 207. Interestingly, Trías, Cailles, and others took up arms to help suppress the U.S. Army.

147. See Lanny Thompson, "The Imperial Republic: A Comparison of the Insular Territories under U.S.

Dominion after 1898," *Pacific Historical Review* 71, no. 4 (November 2002): 571–72.

148. Twenty-six of the thirty generals in service in the Philippines between 1898 and 1902 had some experience in West during the campaigns of territorial expansion. See pp. 33–36 in this volume. See Walter L. Williams, "United States Indian Policy and the Debate over Philippine Annexation: Implications for the Origins of American Imperialism," *Journal of American History* 66, no. 4 (1980): 828n105. Such generals include Wesley Merritt, Nelson Miles, and Leonard Wood. Katherine Bjork analyzes the pre-1898 experiences that shaped military leaders such as William Bullard, John J. Pershing, and Hugh Lennox Scott. See Bjork, *Prairie Imperialists*, 205–42.

149. Wood was part of the campaign in Cuba. During the summer of 1898, he commanded the 1st U.S. Volunteer Cavalry Regiment, popularly known as the Rough Riders, and later served as governor there from 1899 to 1902.

150. See Kramer, *The Blood of Government*, 218–20; note 220.

151. Cited by Capozzola, *Bound by War*, 67.

152. George C. Shaw served under Pershing's command in Mindanao was given the Medal of Honor for gallantry in action on May 4, 1903. He donated this kris to the Smithsonian Institution in 1922. Krieger writes, "The collection of Col. George C. Shaw, United States Army . . . is noteworthy in that it was accumulated during the punitive expedition under Capt. J. J. Pershing against Lake Lanao Moros in Mindanao in 1903." See Krieger, *Primitive Weapons and Armor of the Philippine Islands*, 5. Pershing wrote of the weapon, "They sold many of their knives to Americans, but not these heirlooms. These keen-edged weapons of warfare were well-calculated to do effective work in hand-to-hand combats when wielded by a skillful fighter." See John J. Pershing, *My Life Before the World War, 1860–1917: A Memoir, General of the Armies, John J. Pershing*, ed. John T. Greenwood (Lexington: University of Kentucky, 2013), 146–47. For more on U.S. soldiers' acquisitions of Filipino weapons, see Paul A. Kramer's essay, "New Possessions: Colonial Curios, Trophies, Weapons, and Museum Collections from the Philippine-American War," in this volume, pp. 205–217.

153. Krieger explains that Filipino metalsmiths in Borneo, which had an older iron industry, were particularly skilled at creating beautiful shapes. However, Sulu and western Mindanao produced fine metal blades with rich ornamentation in gold, silver, ivory, and brass. See Krieger, *Primitive Weapons and Armor of the Philippine Islands*, 10, 15, 67.

154. Krieger, *Primitive Weapons and Armor of the Philippine Islands*, 67.

155. Donald Smythe, "Pershing and the Disarmament of the Moros," *Pacific Historical Review* 31, no. 3 (1962): 242. All weapons longer than fifteen inches were seized, including agricultural tools. See Capozzola, *Bound by War*, 85. Katharine Bjork offers an in-depth scholarly account of Pershing in the Philippines. See Bjork, *Prairie Imperialists*, 169–203.

156. See Capozzola, *Bound by War*, 13–16.

157. Pershing formed two companies of Moro Scouts, the Fifty-First and the Fifty-Second. The first was made up of Maguindanaos from Cotbato, and the latter was comprised of Maranaos from Lanao. See Bjork, *Prairie Imperialists,* 255n24. For battle deaths, see Capozzola, *Bound by War*, 85.

158. These numbers were concluded by Richard E. Welch Jr., in 1979, in what John M. Gates refers to as "judicious scholarship." Gates outlines how the original debates in 1901 over the number of the war's civilian casualties included misquotes (attributing a statement by James F. Bell to J. Franklin Bell, for example) that led to a misinterpretation of the deaths caused by the Philippine-American War. In the Philippines, there was a cholera epidemic from 1902 to 1903 that Gates argues was not necessarily related to the war. See John M. Gates, "War-Related Deaths in the Philippines, 1898–1902," *Pacific Historical Review* 53, no. 3 (August 1984): 370; 374–76.

159. However, subsequent events challenged U.S. power, including Japan's stunning victory in the Russo-Japanese War in 1905. Tensions between the United States and Japan simmered until World War II.

160. Kramer, *The Blood of Government,* 353–54.

161. Kramer, *The Blood of Government*, 355.

162. See Thompson, "The Imperial Republic," 573.

163. In 1668, Spain established a Catholic mission in Hagåtña (formerly known as Agaña). The first school for boys, San Juan de Letrán, opened in the early seventeenth century. See Pilar C. Lujan, "The Role of Education in the Preservation of the Indigenous Language of Guam," in *Issues in Guam's Political Development: The Chamorro Perspective* (Agaña, Guam: The Political Status Education Coordinating Commission, 1996), 18. During the Spanish period of Guam's history, a proclamation of ownership of land, and its occupancy, established a title. Despite the new social structures, CHamoru social and cultural interactions were able to find a place within the Catholic frameworks. Importantly, CHamoru systems of reciprocity, referred to as *chenchule,* were able to subsist. See Anne Perez Hattori, "Colonialism, Capitalism and Nationalism in the U.S. Navy's Expulsion of Guam's Spanish Catholic Priests, 1898–1900," *Journal of Pacific History* 44, no. 3 (December 2009): 284–85.

164. Public Law 33-236 (2016) established the Commission on CHamoru Language and the Teaching of the History & Culture of the Indigenous People of Guam with the responsibility of standardizing CHamoru alphabet, spelling, and orthography. This essay follows the recommendations recorded in "Guam CHamoru Orthography," last revised and updated in September 2020 by the Commission on CHamoru Language and the Teaching of the History & Culture of the Indigenous People of Guam, https://

kumisionchamoru.guam.gov/sites/default/files/utugrafihan_chamoru_guahan.pdf.

165. Carmen Artero Kasperbauer, "The Chamorro Culture," in *Issues in Guam's Political Development: The Chamorro Perspective*, 33.

166. Theodore Roosevelt and the Rough Riders sighted Santiago de Cuba in the Caribbean on the same day, June 20, 1898.

167. See Robert F. Rogers, "The Anglo-Saxon Way, 1898–1903," in *Destiny's Landfall: A History of Guam* (Honolulu: University of Hawai'i Press, 2011), 103.

168. The governor wrote to Glass, "I am under the sad necessity of being unable to resist such superior forces and I respectfully accede to your demands." See Rogers, "The Anglo-Saxon Way," 105.

169. Glass was the first officer ever to seize an overseas territory for the United States. See Stephen Kinzer, *The True Flag: Theodore Roosevelt, Mark Twain, and the Birth of American Empire* (New York: Henry Holt, 2017), 50–51.

170. Rogers, "The Anglo-Saxon Way," 104.

171. After the United States signed the treaty with Spain, Germany signed its treaty with Spain to purchase the Marshall and Caroline Islands, and all the Marianas except Guam. The Germans paid 18 million German marks ($4.2 million at the time). Rogers, "The Anglo-Saxon Way," 106; 108. In 1899, Germany and the United States divided Samoa, with the Germans occupying the western nine islands of the archipelago and the U.S. occupying the eastern six.

172. See Jillette Leon-Guerrero, "Guam Leaders from 1899–1904," Guampedia, https://www.guampedia.com.

173. Rogers, "The Anglo-Saxon Way," 108–9. Known locally as Pale` Enko`, Palomo was the only Indigenous CHamoru priest in the entire Spanish colonial period. Anne Perez Hattori, "Colonialism, Capitalism and Nationalism in the U.S. Navy's Expulsion of Guam's Spanish Catholic Priests, 1898–1900," *Journal of Pacific History* 44, no. 3 (December 2009): 285.

174. "Rev Jose Bernardo Torres Palomo," Find a Grave, https://www.findagrave.com/memorial/118305019/jose-bernardo_torres-palomo.

175. "Padre Palomo," *The Pacific Daily News* (Hagåtña, Guam), September 17, 2006, 18.

176. Diana L. Ahmad, "Two Captains, Two Regimes: Benjamin Franklin Tilley and Richard Phillips Leary, America's Pacific Island Commanders, 1899–1901," *International Journal of Naval History*, October 10, 2013.

177. Palomo, however, was allowed to stay.

178. Rogers, "The Anglo-Saxon Way," 112–13.

179. Hattori, "Colonialism, Capitalism and Nationalism," 299.

180. Rogers, "The Anglo-Saxon Way," 114. Note that prior to 1998, Hagåtña, the capital of Guam, was referred to as Agana. However, in 1998, the name changed to the CHamoru name, Hagåtña.

181. These were orders 1, 2, 8, 11, and 14. See Lanny Thompson, *Imperial Archipelago*, 230–35.

182. Ibid.

183. Thank you to Kristin L. Hoganson for pointing out this nuance.

184. Rogers, "The Anglo-Saxon Way," 114. Nicholas J. Goetzfridt, "William Safford," Guampedia, https://www.guampedia.com.

185. Rogers, "The Anglo-Saxon Way," 114.

186. During August 1901, Schroeder conducted a census of Guam. Those listed include fourteen U.S. civilians, 9,630 citizens, presumably CHamorus, and 32 aliens (mostly Spanish) for a total of 9,676 people on the island. See Rogers, "The Anglo-Saxon Way," 117. But in 2020, it was estimated that CHamorus made up 36 percent of Guam's population of 263,925. See "Introduction," in *Issues in Guam's Political Development: The Chamorro Perspective*, 11.

187. Additionally, Guamanians and CHamorus became sickened with diseases that the newcomers from the United States brought with them. By December 1899, typhoid fever was widespread, and six U.S. marines died, along with a number of CHamorus. See Rogers, "The Anglo-Saxon Way," 114.

188. Rogers, "The Anglo-Saxon Way," 116. See also Christine Taitano DeLisle, *Placental Politics: CHamoru Women, White Womanhood, and Indigeneity under U.S. Colonialism in Guam* (Chapel Hill: University of North Carolina Press, 2022).

189. Cited by Carlos P. Taitano, "Political Development," in *Issues in Guam's Political Development: The Chamorro Perspective*, 58.

190. Taitano, "Political Development," 58.

191. Bernard T. Punzalan, "Atanasio Taitano Perez," Guampedia, https://www.guampedia.com.

192. 8 U.S.C. 1407: Persons Living in and Born in Guam, United States Code, Office of the Law Revision Counsel, https://uscode.house.gov.

193. Anne Perez Hattori, "Righting Civil Wrongs: The Guam Congress Walkout of 1949," *ISLA: A Journal of Micronesian Studies* 3, no. 1 (Rainy Season, 1995): 8.

194. Hattori, "Righting Civil Wrongs: The Guam Congress Walkout of 1949," 1.

195. Valerie Solar Woodward, "'I Guess They Didn't Want Us Asking Too Many Questions': Reading American Empire in Guam," *The Contemporary Pacific* 25, no. 1 (2013): 67–91.

196. Julian Aguon, *The Properties of Perpetual Light* (Mangilao: University of Guam Press, 2021), 9.

"AMERICA HAS A COLONIES PROBLEM"

1. Declaration of Independence, July 4, 1776.

2. Sam Erman, *Almost Citizens: Puerto Rico, the U.S. Constitution, and Empire* (Cambridge, UK: Cambridge University Press, 2019), 8.

3. Daniel Immerwahr, *How to Hide an Empire: A History of the Greater United States* (New York: Farrar, Straus and Giroux, 2019), 80.

4. Adriel I. Cepeda Derieux and Neil Weare, "After Aurelius: What Future for the *Insular Cases*?," *Yale Law Journal* 130 (2020), 284, https://www.yalelawjournal.org/forum/after-aurelius-what-future-for-the-insular-cases.

5. *Downes v. Bidwell*, 182 U.S. 244, 287 (1901) (Brown opinion).

6. *DeLima v. Bidwell*, 182 U.S. 1, 181 (1901) (McKenna dissent).

7. *Downes*, 182 U.S. at 306 (White concurrence).

8. Boumediene v. Bush, 553 U.S. 723, 757 (2008).

9. *Downes*, 182 U.S. at 380 (Harlan dissent) ("The idea that this country may acquire territories anywhere upon the earth, by conquest or treaty, and hold them as mere colonies or provinces—the people inhabiting them to enjoy only such rights as Congress chooses to accord to them—is wholly inconsistent with the spirit and genius as well as with the words of the Constitution.").

10. Juan R. Torruella, "The Insular Cases: A Declaration of Their Bankruptcy and My Harvard Pronouncement," in *Reconsidering the Insular Cases: The Past and Future of the American Empire*, ed. Gerald L. Neuman and Tomiko Brown-Nagin (Cambridge, MA: Human Rights Program, Harvard Law School, 2015), 62.

11. Juan R. Torruella, *The Supreme Court and Puerto Rico: The Doctrine of Separate and Unequal* (Río Piedras: University of Puerto Rico, 1988).

12. Juan R. Torruella, "The Insular Cases: The Establishment of a Regime of Political Apartheid," *University of Pennsylvania Journal of International Law* 29, no. 2 (2007): 284–347.

13. Gonzales v. Williams, 192 U.S. 1 (1904). The Supreme Court misspelled González's name (as Gonzales) in their records.

14. Jess Zalph and Nina Totenberg, "Supreme Court Declines to Consider Challenge to Racist Citizenship Laws," NPR, October 17, 2022.

15. Adam Liptak, "Gorsuch Calls for Overruling 'Shameful' Cases on U.S. Territories," *New York Times*, May 2, 2022.

1898: A CONTEST IN MEMORY

1. *The President's Policy: War and Conquest Abroad, Degradation of Labor at Home* (Chicago: American Anti-Imperialist League, 1900), 7–8.

2. See "Treaty of Peace between the United States of America and the Kingdom of Spain, signed in Paris on December 10, 1898," Office of Insular Affairs, U.S. Department of the Interior: https://www.doi.gov/oia/about/treaty1898.

3. Rick Baldoz, "Racial Vectors of Empire: Classification and Competing Master Narratives in the Colonial Philippines" in *Du Bois Review* 5, no. 1 (2008): 70. See also José Trías Monge, *Puerto Rico: The Trials of the Oldest Colony in the World* (New Haven, CT: Yale University Press, 1997), 31.

4. See "Treaty of Peace between the United States of America and the Kingdom of Spain."

5. For instance, Article 3 of the treaty with France for the 1803 Louisiana Purchase stated: "That the inhabitants of the ceded territory shall be incorporated in the union of the United States, and admitted as soon as possible according to the principles of the Federal Constitution to the enjoyment of all rights, advantages, and immunities of the citizens of the United States [. . .]," cited in Trías Monge, *Puerto Rico*, 28. Following this precedent were the 1819 treaty with Spain for the cession of Florida, the 1848 Treaty of Guadalupe Hidalgo for the acquisition of the northern half of Mexico, and the 1867 Treaty for the purchase of Alaska.

6. The McKinley–Roosevelt ticket won both the electoral vote with 65.3 percent and the popular vote with 51.7 percent. It was the largest popular plurality any president had ever polled. See "Statistics: 1900," The American Presidency Project, University of Santa Barbara, https://www.presidency.ucsb.edu/statistics/elections/1900, and Thomas A. Bailey, "Was the Presidential Election of 1900 A Mandate on Imperialism?" *The Mississippi Valley Historical Review* 24, no. 1 (1937): 43–52.

7. The popular magazine *Harper's Weekly* distinguished itself for the quality of its illustrations and editorial content.

8. *Harper's Weekly* was one of the most influential periodicals in the United States. By 1874, the magazine reached a circulation of 160,000. See Frank Luther Mott, *A History of American Magazines*, vol. 2, 1850–65 (Cambridge, MA: Harvard University Press, 1938), 469–87.

9. The artist of the drawing, William Allen Rogers, was chief illustrator of *Harper's Weekly* from 1877 through 1902. See "Artist Biography: William Allen Rogers," Smithsonian Libraries, https://www.sil.si.edu/ondisplay/caricatures/bio_rogers.htm.

10. For a comparative analysis of the racist and gendered ways in which the "new possessions" were represented, and the relationship of these stereotypes to the colonial administrations established on each island, see Lanny Thompson, *Imperial Archipelago: Representation and Rule in the Insular Territories under U.S. Dominion after 1898* (Honolulu: University of Hawai'i Press, 2010).

11. Louis A. Pérez Jr., *Cuba: Between Reform and Revolution* (New York: Oxford University Press, 2014), 141.

12. Cited in Pérez, *Cuba: Between Reform and Revolution*, 144.

13. Ada Ferrer, *Cuba: An American History* (New York: Scribner, 2021), 178–79. There is disagreement among scholars about the Platt Amendment's main strategist. Louis A. Pérez Jr. designates Elihu Root as the mastermind who devised the amendment's four main provisions. See Pérez, *Cuba Under the Platt Amend-ment, 1902–1934* (Pittsburgh: University of Pittsburgh Press, 1986), 45. Walter LaFeber, however, designates both President William McKinley and Leonard Wood as the main strategists. See Walter LaFeber, *The American Age: U.S. Foreign Policy at Home and Abroad, 1750 to the Present* (New York: W. W. Norton, 1994), 210.

14. Pérez, *Cuba Under the Platt Amendment*, 45–46.

15. "Treaty between the United States and the Republic of Cuba Embodying the Provisions Defining Their Future Relations as Contained in the Act of Congress Approved March 2, 1901," May 22, 1903; Perfected Treaties, 1778–1945; General Records of the United States Government, Record Group 11; National Archives Building, Washington, DC.

16. Louis A. Pérez Jr., *The War of 1898: The United States and Cuba in History and Historiography* (Chapel Hill: University of North Carolina Press, 1998), 33–35.

17. They protested while in front of Wood's residence the evening of March 2, 1901. See Pérez, *Cuba: Between Reform and Revolution*, 144.

18. Ferrer, *Cuba: An American History*, 180.

19. Louis A. Pérez Jr., *Cuba Between Empires, 1878–1902* (Pittsburgh: University of Pittsburgh Press, 1998), 355–56.

20. Scholars disagree about the margin of the vote. According to Pérez, the vote passed by one. See Pérez, *Cuba: Between Reform and Revolution*, 144. However, Walter LaFeber writes that the Cuban constitutional convention accepted the Platt Amendment by a vote of 15 to 11. See LaFeber, *The American Age*, 210. Ada Ferrer reports the vote was 16 to 11. See Ferrer, *Cuba*, 140. For abstainers, see James H. Hitchman, "Negotiat-ing the Platt Amendment, March Through April 15, 1901," *Leonard Wood and Cuban Independence, 1898–1902* (Holland: The Hague, 1971), 135–48; 274, 269; and "The Platt Amendment Is Accepted by Cuba," *New York Times,* June 13, 1901.

21. Most of the provisions of the Platt Amendment were repealed in 1934. See Pérez, *The War of 1898*, 34.

22. This happened in the town of Ciales, where *criollos* disaffected by the Spanish government occupied the city hall and raised the U.S. flag on August 13, 1898. The neighboring town of Manatí sent volunteers to reoccupy Ciales, and the ensuing skirmish left eight people dead. See Fernando Picó, *1898: The War after the War* (Princeton, NJ: Markus Wiener Publishers, 2004), 48.

23. Noenoe Silva, *Aloha Betrayed: Native Hawaiian Resistance to American Colonialism* (Durham, NC: Duke University Press, 2004), 161. Trumbull White, an ardent annexationist described the ceremony as one in which "there were more tears than cheers." According to him, of the twenty-six members of the Hawaiian Band, the fifteen who were Native Hawaiians requested to be excused from playing their country's national anthem for the last time. Cited in Thompson, *Imperial Archipelago*, 112.

24. General Nelson Miles had originally planned to invade Puerto Rico at Fajardo. Per Puerto Rican accounts, U.S. ships debarked in Fajardo on August 2, 1898. The Spanish momentarily took back the city in early August, but U.S. soldiers left behind this flag hoisted at the lighthouse on the estate of Las Cabezas de San Juan in Fajardo. This was the property of the descendants of Juan Becerril Bermúdez, who owned several plantations in the east of Puerto Rico. His late granddaughter married Juan Euclides de Acosta y Calbo. The flag and other belongings from the hacienda have survived in the Acosta Family Collection of San Juan. See Robert Stolberg Acosta, *Retablos, joyas, platería y arte: Colección Acosta de San Juan, Puerto Rico (1695–2010)* (San Juan: self-published, 2011), 102–18. On the U.S. evacuation, see Ángel Rivero Méndez, "Capítulo XXII: Sucesos de Fajardo," in *Crónica de la Guerra Hispanoamericana en Puerto Rico* (Madrid: Sucesores de Rivadeneyra, 1922), 353–78; Coll y Toste, "Documentos referentes a la guerra hispanoamericana en Puerto Rico, del Archivo Particular de Coll y Toste," 76. See also "On the Verge of Sovereignty: Cuba and Puerto Rico at the Turn of the Twentieth Century" in this volume, pp. 82–113.

25. Mark Twain, "To the Person Sitting in Darkness," *North American Review* 172, no. 2 (February 1, 1901): 176.

26. The Northwest Ordinance of July 13, 1787, essentially established a model for becoming a state of the federal union through a three-step process. First, Congress would create a temporary district govern-ment for a designated region. Second, upon achieving a specified white, Euro-American population, Congress would organize a territorial government with an appointed governor, an appointed legislative council, and elected legislative assembly. Third, the process culminated with the incorporation of the territory as a state of the federal union with full representation in Congress. While the Ordinance underwent changes throughout the nineteenth century, it remained a primary model for the path to statehood. See Thompson, *Imperial Archipelago*, 186; 218n8; Arnold H. Leibowitz, *Defining Status: A Comprehensive Analysis of the United States Territorial Relations* (Dordrecht, Netherlands: Martinus Nijhoff, 1989), 6; and Jack Ericson Eblen, *The First and Second United States Empires: Governors and Territorial Government, 1784–1912* (Pittsburgh: University of Pittsburgh Press, 1968).

27. Lanny Thompson, *Imperial Archipelago*, 184.

28. However, Filipinos were not considered "alien" until 1934.

29. See Tom Coffman, *Nation Within: The History of the American Occupation of Hawaii* (Durham, NC: Duke University Press, 2016), 64. See also General Superin-tendent of the Census and Hawaii Board of Education, *Census of the Hawaiian Islands, Taken December 27* (Honolulu: 1879); and Alatau T. Atkinson, *Report of the General Superintendent of the Census, 1896* (Honolulu: Hawaiian Star Press, 1897), 34–37.

30. Upon annexation, McKinley appointed a Hawaiian Commission to study the best alternatives for the administrative framework in the archipelago. According to Thompson, the commission concluded that because of its advanced state of Americanization, Hawai'i was ready for a territorial government. See Thompson, *Imperial Archipelago*, 186.

31. Coffman, *Nation Within*, 321.

32. Thompson, *Imperial Archipelago*, 189.

33. The first article addressing this topic, authored by Carman F. Randolph, argued that, as in the case of previous continental territorial acquisitions, the Constitution applied to these territories and their inhabitants. Upon annexation, Randolph contended, the peoples of these territories owed allegiance to the United States and automatically became citizens. In another article, Judge Simeon E. Baldwin of Connecticut—who founded the American Bar Association and taught for fifty years at Yale Law School—held that it would not be wise to give such privileges to the "half-civilized Moros . . . or the ignorant and lawless brigands that infest Puerto Rico." See Juan R. Torruella, "The Insular Cases: The Establishment of a Regime of Political Apartheid," *University of Pennsylvania Journal of International Law* 29, no. 2 (Winter 2007): 291–92.

34. Abbott Lowell, "The Status of Our New Possessions: A Third View," *Harvard Law Review* 13, no. 3 (1899): 176, cited in Thompson, *Imperial Archipelago*, 190. See also Juan Torruella, "The Insular Cases," 297. For a discussion of the various approaches adopted by legal scholars, see Thompson, *Imperial Archipelago*, 189–90.

35. See Thompson, *Imperial Archipelago*, 183–245; Rick Baldoz and César Ayala, "The Bordering of America: Colonialism and Citizenship in the Philippines and Puerto Rico," *Centro Journal* 25, no. 1 (Spring 2013): 76–105.

36. Baldoz and Ayala, "The Bordering of America," 83.

37. Baldoz, "The Racial Vectors of Empire," 73.

38. James H. Blount, officer of the United States Volunteers in the Philippines (1899–1901) and United States District Judge in the Philippines (1901–1905), relayed Roosevelt's characterization of Filipinos as "a jumble of savage tribes" in James H. Blount, *The American Occupation of the Philippines, 1898–1912* (New York: G. P. Putnam's Sons, 1912), 297. Roosevelt's rationale that Anglo-Americans were as morally bound to govern the Apaches as the Filipinos can be found in Roosevelt to Charles Joseph Bonaparte, March 30, 1901, in Theodore Roosevelt, *The Letters of Theodore Roosevelt*, ed. Elting Morison, vol. 3, *The Square Deal, 1901–1905* (Cambridge, MA: Harvard University Press, 1951), 36–37.

39. Baldoz, "The Racial Vectors of Empire," 73.

40. Baldoz and Ayala, "The Bordering of America," 80.

41. Days after the Treaty of Paris was ratified, the U.S. Senate passed the McEnery Resolution stating that the treaty did not intend to "incorporate the inhabitants of the Philippine Islands into citizenship of the United States, nor [was] it intended to annex said islands as an integral part of the territory of the United States." The resolution passed the Senate but did not make it to the floor of the House of Representatives before the session expired. Baldoz and Ayala, "The Bordering of America," 80 and note 7.

42. McKinley assigned the first Philippine Commission on January 20, 1899, headed by Jacob Schurman. The second Philippine Commission, also known as the Taft Commission, was a body appointed by the president to exercise legislative and limited executive powers in the Philippines. It was first appointed by President McKinley in 1900. For more, see "Cutting a Path to Sovereignty: The Complex Political Landscapes of the Philippines and Guam," in this volume.

43. In contrast to Torruella, Thompson argues that the government model that was finally established in Puerto Rico was not the one "territorial government similar to Oklahoma" proposed by Carroll, but one proposed by General George Davis. See Torruella, "The Insular Cases," 297. See also Henry K. Carroll, *Report on the Island of Porto Rico* (Washington, DC: Government Printing Office, 1899).

44. Congressman Newlands of Nevada argued, "[T]he establishment of a precedent which [would] be invoked to control our action regarding the Philippines later on; such action embracing not simply one island near our coast, easily governed, its people friendly and peaceful, but rather embracing an archipelago of seventeen hundred islands, seven thousand miles distant, having different customs, and ranging all the way from absolute barbarism to semi civilization." See Torruella, "The Insular Cases," 298. Note that Newlands presented an inaccurate count of the islands in the Philippine archipelago, which number more than seven thousand.

45. The Foraker Act stated that the island's inhabitants were "citizens of Porto Rico" [*sic*]. This designation did not clarify whether they were also citizens of the United States, implying that the federal government did not view them as citizens. We are thankful to Neil Weare for his insight on this aspect of citizenship.

46. We are grateful to Lanny Thompson for underscoring how the appointed upper house, comprising the governor's cabinet (who were also agency secretaries), constituted another level of U.S. control over the island.

47. United States Philippine Commission (1899–1900), Jacob Gould Shurman, George Dewey, Elwell Stephen Otis, Charles Denby, and Dean Conan Worcester, *Report of the Philippine Commission to the President* (Washington, DC: U.S. Government Printing Office, 1900), 104.

48. While the Organic Act was inspired by the Northwest Ordinance, it also had important differences. For example, its legal and economic system were discontinuous with the U.S. federal system. The Philippines was categorized as a foreign port, and customs and tariffs were established. See Julian Go,

"Introduction: Global Perspectives on the U.S. Colonial State in the Philippines," in *The American Colonial State in the Philippines*, ed. Julian Go and Anne L. Foster (Durham, NC: Duke University Press, 2003), 7.

49. Thompson, *Imperial Archipelago*, 212.

50. Thompson, *Imperial Archipelago*, 211–12.

51. Thompson, *Imperial Archipelago*, 212–15. See also Paul A. Kramer, *The Blood of Government: Race, Empire, the United States and the Philippines* (Chapel Hill: University of North Carolina Press, 2006), chapter 3.

52. See Torruella, "The Insular Cases," 298, and Bartholomew Sparrow, *The Insular Cases and the Emergence of the American Empire* (Lawrence: University of Kansas Press, 2006), chapter 4.

53. There is inconsistency among legal scholars as to which Supreme Court cases constitute the *Insular Cases*. Juan R. Torruella, the recently deceased jurist and authority on the topic, considered six of the nine cases debated in 1901: *De Lima v. Bidwell* (182 U.S. 1 1901), *Goetze v. United States* (182 U.S. 221 1901), *Dooley v. United States* (182 U.S. 222 1901), *Armstrong v. United States* (182 U.S. 243 1901), *Downes v. Bidwell* (182 U.S. 244 1901), and *Huss v. N.Y. & Puerto Rico S.S. Co.* (182 U.S. 392 1901). Torruella referred to subsequent cases as the "progeny" of the *Insular Cases*. See Torruella, "The Insular Cases," 284. Efrén Rivera Ramos, professor at the University of Puerto Rico School of Law, extends the designation to twenty-three cases between 1901 and 1922. These include nine cases debated in 1901, thirteen cases debated between 1903 and 1914, and a culminating case in 1922. For a detailed list see Efrén Rivera Ramos, "Deconstructing Colonialism: "The Unincorporated Territory" as a Category of Domination," in *Foreign in a Domestic Sense: Puerto Rico American Expansions and the Constitution*, eds. Christina Duffy Burnett and Burke Marshall. (Durham/London: Duke Univerisity Press, 2001), https://doi.org/10.2307/j.ctv1134g0r; and Efrén Rivera Ramos, "The Legal Construction of American Colonialism: An Inquiry into the Constitutive Force of Law," PhD diss., (University College London, 1994), 163.

54. For example, in *De Lima v. Bidwell* (182 U.S. 1 1901), the first case that the Court addressed, the Supreme Court opinion found that goods from Puerto Rico could not be taxed as if they were from a foreign country. A majority of five justices stated that upon the ratification of the Treaty of Paris, Puerto Rico became a territory of the United States, and that Puerto Rico was not "foreign" for purposes of the statute at issue. For a summary of the cases, see Efrén Rivera Ramos, "The Legal Construction of American Colonialism: The Insular Cases," *Revista Jurídica Universidad de Puerto Rico* 65, no. 2 (1996): 225, 236–71; Krishanti Vignarajah, "The Political Roots of Judicial Legitimacy: Explaining the Enduring Validity of the Insular Cases," *University of Chicago Law Review* 77, no. 2 (2010): 781–845; and Thompson, *Imperial Archipelago*, 205–11.

55. Justice Henry B. Brown led the majority. See Article 1, Section 8. On the Uniformity Clause and Puerto Rico, see Philip Joseph Deutch, "The Uniformity Clause and Puerto Rican Statehood," *Stanford Law Review* 43, no. 3 (1991): 685–732, https://doi.org/10.2307/1228916. See also Thompson, *Imperial Archipelago*, 206–7.

56. Cited in Thompson, *Imperial Archipelago*, 208.

57. See Torruella, "The Insular Cases," 308–9.

58. Justice Henry Brown delivered the majority opinion that the Constitution applied primarily to the states, their citizens, and their representatives. The plenary power of Congress to acquire and govern territories derived from its authority to make treaties, declare war, and conquer territories. The United States had national sovereignty over its territories. In the process of western expansion, annexation treaties had included provisions to guarantee citizenship in contiguous territories, where Euro-Americans would displace and dominate Native peoples. The new insular possessions were non-contiguous and inhabited by "alien races" with different habits and laws. Thus, citizenship status for these possessions was not to be taken for granted. Justice Brown's opinion also stated that certain constitutional rights were "natural" because they coincided with universal rights. Therefore, they were applicable to new territories. But the implementation in the territories of "remedial rights," such as citizenship and suffrage, was up to Congress. See Thompson, *Imperial Archipelago*, 206–9.

59. Baldoz and Ayala, "The Bordering of America," 84.

60. Torruella, "The Insular Cases," 302.

61. Ibid. Six of the seven Justices deciding *Downes v. Bidwell* decided *Plessy v. Ferguson.* See Baldoz and Ayala, "The Bordering of America," 85.

62. Baldoz and Ayala, "The Bordering of America," 85.

63. Sam Erman, "Meanings of Citizenship in the U.S. Empire: Puerto Rico, Isabel Gonzalez, and the Supreme Court, 1898–1905," *Journal of American Ethnic History* 27, no. 4 (Summer 2008): 5–33.

64. Baldoz and Ayala, "The Bordering of America," 85.

65. In light of all the racism directed in the U.S. toward Filipinos, the "nationals" status left them particularly vulnerable to citizen and state discrimination as immigrants. Anti-miscegenation laws that forbid intermarriage between Filipinos ("Malays") and white people was one arena of discrimination. See Rick Baldoz, *The Third Asiatic Invasion: Empire and Migration in Filipino America, 1898–1946* (New York: New York University Press, 2011), 1–8. This legal condition, a vestige of the *Insular Cases*, still applies to American Samoans and is the basis for the case *Fitisemanu v. U.S.* See also Robert Barnes, "Biden Administration Urges Supreme Court Not to Take Citizenship Case," *Washington Post*, August 29, 2022.

66. The chairman of the House of Insular Affairs Committee, Democrat William Atkinson Jones, played a key role in shaping the second organic acts of the Philippines and Puerto Rico, as did the influential

Democrat from Colorado John F. Shafroth, who chaired the Senate Committee on Pacific Islands and Porto Rico.

67. Baldoz and Ayala, "The Bordering of America," 96.

68. See "Philippine Constitutions: The Jones Law of 1916," *Official Gazette*, August 29, 1916.

69. Baldoz and Ayala, "The Bordering of America," 95–96. At the same time, the extension of citizenship to Puerto Rico was seen by some U.S. politicians, such as Arthur Yager, governor of Puerto Rico from 1913 to 1921, as essential to stopping the rise of the independence movement on the island as a consequence of inconformity with the Foraker Act. See Trías Monge, *Puerto Rico*, 70.

70. The Act also limited Filipino immigration to the United States to fifty per year, and it allowed the United States to keep military forces in the Philippines. Between 1902 and 1934, Filipinos were counted as U.S. Nationals and were not subject to immigration laws. See Cathy J. Schlund-Vials, K. Scott Wong, and Jason Oliver Chang, eds., *Asian America: A Primary Source Reader* (New Haven, CT: Yale University Press, 2017), 81–85.

71. César J. Ayala and Rafael Bernabe, *Puerto Rico in the American Century: A History since 1898* (Chapel Hill: University of North Carolina Press, 2007), 57–59.

72. Ayala and Bernabe, *Puerto Rico in the American Century*, 57–59. For more on the Jones-Shafroth Act, see Trías Monge, *Puerto Rico,* 67–87. See also Albin J. Kowalewski, Laura Turner O'Hara, and Terrance Rucker, eds., "Foreign in a Domestic Sense: 1898–1945," in *Hispanic Americans in Congress 1822–2012* (Washington, DC: U.S. Government Printing Office, 2013), 156–58.

73. Muñoz Marín was the son of Luis Muñoz Rivera, the most prominent political figure in Puerto Rico in the late years of Spanish colonial rule in the nineteenth century and the first two decades of the twentieth century under U.S. rule. See "On the Verge of Sovereignty: Cuba and Puerto Rico at the Turn of the Twentieth Century," pp. 89–117 in this volume. See also Taína Caragol, "Meaningful (Dis)placements: The Portrait of Luis Muñoz Marín by Francisco Rodón at the National Portrait Gallery," in *Beyond the Face: New Perspectives on Portraiture*, ed. Wendy Wick Reaves (Washington, DC: National Portrait Gallery, in association with D. Giles Limited, 2018), 302–17. The possibility of choosing their governor in open elections concretized thanks to an amendment to the Jones-Shafroth Act proposed by Rexford G. Tugwell, who served as governor of Puerto Rico from 1941 to 1946 and aspired to give greater self-government to Puerto Rico.

74. Under this interpretation, Puerto Ricans were no longer governed by federal laws by virtue of the "territorial clause" of the Constitution, but due to the consent to the law P.L. 600, which allowed for Puerto Rico to have its own constitution, foregrounding the notion of a government by consent. Ayala and Bernabe, *Puerto Rico in the American Century*, 164. Recent legislation has shown clearly that the territorial clause,

which grants Congress plenary powers over its territories, still applies to Puerto Rico, see note 75 below.

75. The new status also established that in case of conflict between the United States and Puerto Rico, U.S. federal law would prevail over Puerto Rican law. To the benefit of the United States, the establishment of the ELA resulted in the removal of Puerto Rico from the United Nations' list of colonies. The establishment of the ELA faced opposition from radical nationalists, who staged armed attacks in Puerto Rico and Washington, DC, to create a crisis that would bring international attention to what they saw as Puerto Rico's continuing political powerlessness. Ayala and Bernabe, *Puerto Rico in the American Century*, 175. See also Trías Monge, *Puerto Rico*, 112–14.

76. In response to Puerto Rico's $72 million debt and $49 million in unfunded pension obligations, as the island was about to default in payments, President Barack Obama signed in 2016 the Law PROMESA, which stands for Puerto Rico Oversight, Management, and Economic Stability Act. The law's acronym translates into "promise" in Spanish. While federal law prohibits all branches of Puerto Rican government from declaring bankruptcy, PROMESA provided a debt-restructuring framework. The legislation put Puerto Rico's finances under the supervision of a federal fiscal oversight board, comprised of seven members appointed by Obama. While the law protected Puerto Rico from lawsuits for not being able to pay $2 billion in bonds that were due in June 2016, it also effectively voided the constitutional powers of Puerto Rico's political branches, ceding the oversight to the board members appointed by the U.S. president. Islanders have protested and heavily criticized the board since its inception, because it established severe austerity measures in an economy that had been in crisis for a decade and then suffered through Hurricane Maria in 2017, prioritizing payment to debt-collecting agencies over public services and infrastructure on the island. See Elizabeth Whiting "Puerto Rico Debt Restructuring: Origins of a Constitutional and Humanitarian Crisis," *University of Miami Inter-American Law Review* 50, no. 1 (2019): 237–75.

77. Daniel Immerwahr, *How to Hide an Empire: A History of the Greater United States* (New York: Farrar, Straus and Giroux, 2019), 155.

78. Immerwahr, *How to Hide an Empire*, 202–3.

79. The first election was in 1970, when Carlos G. Camacho became the first elected Governor of Guam. See "Appointed Governor Wins First Election," *Hartford Courant*, November 4, 1970.

80. The federal government uses 30 percent of the island for its military base. Although people living in Guam enjoyed more jobs because of the base's expansion, they strongly objected to the enlargement because it subsumed the ancient village of Pågat. See Julian Aguon, "In Guam, Even the Dead are Dying: The U.S. Military Is Building on the Graves of Our Ancestors," *The Guardian,* September 16, 2022. See also Immerwahr, *How to Hide an Empire*, 387.

81. Cited in Immerwahr, *How to Hide an Empire*, 387.

82. See Gina E. Taitano, "Kumision I Fino' Chamorro/ Chamorro Language Commission," *Guampedia,* https://www.guampedia.com/kumision-i-fino -chamorrochamorro-language-commission/; and Department of Chamorro Affairs, "About Us," https:// dca.guam.gov/about-us/.

83. For more on the anarchist, Leon Czolgosz, see Robert W. Merry, *President William McKinley: Architect of the American Century* (New York: Simon and Schuster, 2017), 618–19.

84. See, for example, "Skirmish of Rough Riders," 1899, which can be viewed on the Library of Congress's website: https://www.loc.gov/item/98501105/.

85. The canal had been discussed for decades, beginning with President Ulysses S. Grant's first address to Congress in 1869. For more information, see Christine Keiner, "Canalizing and Colonizing the Isthmus," in *Deep Cut: Science, Power, and the Unbuilt Interoceanic Canal* (Athens: University of Georgia Press, 2020), 24–26.

86. See Ariana A. Curtis, "Becoming More and More Panamanian: Contemporary Constructions of West Indian Identity in Urban Panama," (PhD dissertation, American University, 2012), 87–89.

87. Roosevelt's encouragement to Panamanians to secede was backed by New York lawyer William Nelson Cromwell and French engineer Philippe Bunau-Varilla, both investors in the canal project, and they worked with him to achieve it. See Juan Gonzalez, *Harvest of Empire: A History of Latinos in America*, rev. ed. (London: Penguin Books, 2011), 66–68.

88. The Hay–Bunau-Varilla Treaty came after the Herran–Hay Treaty, which the Columbian government had rejected. See Marixa Lasso, *Erased: The Untold Story of the Panama Canal* (Cambridge, MA: Harvard University Press, 2019). See Curtis, "Becoming More and More Panamanian," 89.

89. Thank you to Rolando de la Guardia and Ana Elizabeth González of the Museo del Canal Intero-ceánico de Panamá for their consultation about the history of the Panama Canal.

90. Curtis, "Becoming More and More Panamanian," 90.

91. Only those who lived in the Zone could purchase items from its stores, visit its recreational facilities, and be treated in its hospitals, among other restrictions. See Curtis, "Becoming More and More Panamanian," 92.

92. Julie Greene, "A Modern State in the Tropics," in *The Canal Builders: Making America's Empire at the Panama Canal* (New York: Penguin Press, 2009), 115–16.

93. More than 55,000 people were employed by the U.S. government, and an estimated 5,600 died of injury and disease. See Byron Breedlove, "Special Wonders of the Canal," *Emerging Infectious Diseases* 27, no. 8 (August 2021): 2,244–46. doi:10.3201/eid2708.ac2708 and Keiner, "Canalizing and Colonizing the Isthmus," 29. See also "The Portraits in the Gallery Have Never

Been Only National" by Kristin Hoganson in this volume, pp. 22–29.

94. Breedlove, "Special Wonders of the Canal," 2,244–46.

95. President Roosevelt appointed U.S. Army doctor William Gorgas to lead the sanitation effort in Panama. Gorgas had worked in Cuba alongside research scientist Walter Reed to help eradicate the spread of yellow fever with sanitation methods. See Greene, "A Modern State in the Tropics," 69–71.

96. According to the 1912 census, the 553 square miles comprising the Panama Canal Zone had a population of 61,279, or 14 percent of Panama's total population. See Marixa Lasso, "From Citizens to 'Natives': Tropical Politics of Depopulation at the Panama Canal Zone," *Environmental History* 21, no. 2 (2016): 240–49.

97. Tammy La Gorce, "His Greatest Subject? The Panama Canal: Jonas Lie made Roughly 30 Paintings in the Three Months He Spent at the Site in 1913," *New York Times,* February 28, 2016.

98. Gustavo Gelpí, "An Experiment in U.S. Territorial Government: The District of the Canal Zone and Its Federal Court (1904–1979)," *The Constitutional Evolution of Puerto Rico and other U.S. Territories (1898–Present)* (Colombia: Editorial Nomos, S.A., 2017), 165.

99. The Torrijos–Carter Treaties were the result of negotiations to ease the tensions between Panamani-ans and the U.S. government over the control of the Zone. These tensions reached a climax in 1964, when protests broke out over Panamanians hoisting their national flag in the Canal Zone. The demonstration turned deadly as U.S. troops fired on the protesters, killing twenty-four of them and wounding hundreds. See Gonzalez, *Harvest of Empire*, 155.

100. Kris James Mitchener and Marc Weidenmier, "Empire, Public Goods, and the Roosevelt Corollary," *Journal of Economic History* 65, no. 3 (September 2005): 661–62.

101. Mitchener and Marc Weidenmier, "Empire, Public Goods, and the Roosevelt Corollary," 680.

102. *Theodore Roosevelt's Annual Message to Congress for 1904*; House Records HR 58A–K2; Records of the U.S. House of Representatives; Record Group 233; Center for Legislative Archives; National Archives.

103. For more information, see Ellen D. Tillman, *Dollar Diplomacy by Force: Nation-Building and Resistance in the Dominican Republic* (Chapel Hill: University of North Carolina Press, 2016). President Franklin Delano Roosevelt distanced his administration from the policy of U.S. interventionism in Latin America through his Good Neighbor policy established in 1933, which emphasized trade and collaboration. Under his direction, a year later, the Platt Amendment was also abrogated. See "Good Neighbor Policy, 1933," U.S. Department of State, Office of the Historian, https:// history.state.gov/milestones/1921-1936/good-neighbor.

104. No photographers were present the day of the signing of the protocol. The following day, the DC-based photographer Frances Benjamin Johnston

staged the representatives and signatories in a corner of the White House's Treaty Room. By contrast, Chartran repositioned the sitters against a window overlooking the South Portico of the executive mansion. In a published interview in the *New York Mail*, Chartran explained that Johnston was unable to take the photograph against the glaring light coming through the window, and therefore had to reposition the officials against the corner. See Sue Morris, "The Art of Politics and the Politics of Art: Part Two," The Frick Pittsburgh, December 10, 2020, https://www .thefrickpittsburgh.org/Story-The-Art-of-Politics-and -the-Politics-of-Art-Part-Two.

105. "Picture for the White House: M. Chartran's Commission from Mr. Frick," *New York Times*, December 5, 1899.

106. Kenneth Warren, *Triumphant Capitalism: Henry Clay Frick and the Industrial Transformation of America* (Pittsburgh: University of Pittsburgh Press, 1995), 336.

107. See "Picture for the White House."

108. For example, the president's policies to increase tariffs benefitted Frick's finances enormously. In July 1897, the Dingley Tariff Act increased duties on a range of goods and products by an average of 57 percent, effecting trade protectionism legislation that protected domestic manufacturing from foreign competition. See "Dingley Tariff," in *Gale Encyclopedia of U.S. Economic History*, ed. Thomas Carson and Mary Bonk (Detroit: Gale Group, 1999), 245.

109. Samuel Schreiner, *Henry Clay Frick, Gospel of Greed* (New York: St. Martin's, 1996), 271–72.

110. William Jennings Bryan ran again against McKinley in 1900. During the War of 1898, Bryan had become a leading member of the Anti-Imperialist League and ran on an anti-imperialist platform. After the Treaty of Paris, U.S. policy in the new territories, especially in the Philippines, was central to the 1900 presidential campaign. See Edward S. Kaplan, *U.S. Imperialism in Latin America: William Jennings Bryan's Challenges and Contributions* (Westport, CT: Greenwood Press, 1998), 12.

111. Mark Schiebe, "The Rembrandts of Investment: Collecting Art and Money in the Trilogy of Desire," *Studies in American Naturalism* 13, no. 2 (2018): 165–81. For the campaign donation, see Sue Morris and Clayton Docent, "Henry Clay Frick, The Art of Politics and the Politics of Art," *Frick Pittsburgh*, December 3, 2020.

112. For more information on the U.S. and Spanish members of the commission, see "Protocol of Agreement between the United States and Spain, Embodying the Terms of a Basis for the Establishment of Peace between the Two Countries," in U.S. Congress, *Papers Relating to the Foreign Relations of the United States with the Annual Message of the President Transmitted to Congress December 5, 1898* (Washington, DC: U.S. Government Printing Office, 1901), 828–30.

113. On the Cuban commission's visit to Washington, DC, in late 1898, see Pérez, *Cuba Between Empires, 1878–1902*, 255–56.

114. The Puerto Rico Commission called itself *La liga de patriotas*, or the League of Patriots. It was led by Hostos, a sociologist and educator known throughout Latin America, and included the physician José Julio Henna, also known as J. Julio Henna, a renowned advocate of Puerto Rico's annexation to the United States, as well as the physician and novelist Manuel Zeno Gandía, who was not a spokesperson for any particular status solution, but who seemed to bridge the opposed preferences between Hostos and Henna. See Vivian Auffant Vázquez, "Puerto Rico, Eugenio María de Hostos y Manuel Zeno Gandía en la Comisión a Washington," *Biblioteca Virtual Miguel de Cervantes*, www.cervantesvirtual.com. On Hostos, see pp. 98 and 111 in this volume.

115. On Juan Luna and Felipe Agoncillo, see pp. 129–32 in this volume.

116. The first letter, dated January 20, 1899, enumerated a total of fifteen reforms for Puerto Rico. These included the establishment of a civil government, application of the civil rights as contained in paragraphs two to seven in Article 1, Section 9 of the Constitution, application of Amendments 1 to 10 of the Constitution, and free trade with the United States. See J. Julio Henna and M. Zeno Gandía, *The Case of Puerto Rico* (Washington, DC: W. F. Roberts, 1899), 11–13. According to archival documents in the Library of Congress, Hostos, Zeno Gandía, and Henna met with McKinley on January 21, 1899. See *Eugenio María de Hostos and Eugenio Carlos de Hostos Papers*, Manuscript Division, Library of Congress.

117. "Porto Ricans Want a Vote," *Washington Post*, January 25, 1899, p. 1. For more on the change from "Porto Rico" to "Puerto Rico," see Gervasio Luis García, "I Am the Other: Puerto Rico in the Eyes of North Americans, 1898," *Journal of American History* 87, no. 1 (June 2000): 39–40.

118. "Felipe Agoncillo: Plea of the Filipinos. Full Text of the Protest against Our Taking the Island. Agoncillo Raises an Issue," *New York Times,* December 25, 1898.

119. Carolina Maestre identified the photograph of the commissioners in the papers of Eugenio María de Hostos and Eugenio Carlos de Hostos at the Library of Congress. The photograph also appeared in a publication commemorating the 150th anniversary of Hostos's birth. See *Imágenes de Hostos a través del tiempo* (Río Piedras: Museo de Historia, Antropología y Arte de la Universidad de Puerto Rico, 1988).

FORCES AT PLAY: WAR AND EMPIRE IN THE ART OF WINSLOW HOMER AND ARMANDO MENOCAL

1. The author would like to thank Bárbara Omaira Argüelles Almenares, Sarah Lea Burns, Rich Denis, Jorge Duany, and Kristin Hoganson for their feedback on early drafts of this essay.

2. Admiral Pascual Cervera and his squadron arrived in Santiago on May 19, 1898, to gather coal for fuel. There was almost no coal available, but he and his officers decided to stay in the harbor to perform necessary maintenance. They were trapped beginning on May 27, when the U.S. North Atlantic Fleet began its blockade of the coast of Cuba.

3. Neither Winslow Homer nor Armando García Menocal left extensive, explicit commentary about their wartime experiences. Compared to Homer, who hailed from a solidly middle-class New England family, little has been written about Menocal, a member of the elite creole bourgeoisie. There is no biography on Menocal, whereas scholars have dedicated their careers to exploring Homer's life and art. Some of Menocal's oeuvre is held in private collections, but the majority is at the Museo Nacional de Bellas Artes in Havana, Cuba. See https://www.bellasartes.co.cu /artistas/armando-garcia-menocal.

4. Menocal was wounded sometime between August 12 and 16, 1895, during the Battle of El Ciego in Camagüey Province. See Bernabé Boza, *Mi diario de la guerra desde Baire hasta la intervención americana* (Havana: La Propagandista, 1900), 40; and *Diccionario Enciclopédico de Historia Militar de Cuba, Parte Uno (1510–1898), Volume II Acciones Combativas* (Havana: Verde Olivo, 2003), 47–50.

5. Born to a prominent Cuban family whose wealth stemmed from the sugar industry, Menocal attended the best art schools in Cuba and Spain. In the 1870s and 1880s, many white members of the middle and upper classes left Cuba and spent most of their adult lives in exile in Europe or in United States. Menocal's family was no different. In 1866, when Menocal was three, his father died. Thereafter, he was raised by his maternal uncle, Gabriel García Menocal y Martín de Medina (1833–1905), the administrator of the sugar plantation Australia, in the province of Matanzas. Gabriel was the father of Mario García Menocal, who was elected as the president of Cuba in 1913. Once exiled, Gabriel García Menocal became a sugar planter at San Juan Bautista, State of Tabasco, Mexico. However, the Spanish exiled Gabriel García Menocal and his family to Mexico sometime after the first Cuban war of independence, the Ten Years' War, began in 1868 because he sympathized and plotted with the Cuban revolutionaries, the *mambises*. Consequently, Armando García Menocal spent time in Mexico, the United States, Spain, and Cuba. See http://www. latinamericanstudies.org/menocal-bio.htm. On the Cuban bourgeoisie's transition from sugar planting to administration in the 1880s, see: Louis A. Pérez, *Cuba: Between Reform and Revolution* (New York: Oxford University Press, 2006), 102–4.

6. Homer reported that his 1864 painting *Skirmish in the Wilderness* "was painted from sketches made on the spot at the time of the battle." See Lloyd Goodrich, *Winslow Homer* (New York: Whitney Museum of American Art; Macmillan Company, 1944), 230. These sketches were from 1862 and 1864. Abigail Booth Gerdts relays that Charles B. Curtis's undated manuscript catalogue of the Union League Club's collection is the source for this statement. See Abigail Booth Gerdts and Lloyd Goodrich, eds., *Record of Works by Winslow Homer*, vol. 1 (New York: Spanierman

Gallery, 2005), 314–15. The Artist Files on Winslow Homer confirm the statement to Charles B. Curtis. See Miscellaneous, Winslow Homer, Art and Artist Files, Smithsonian American Art and Portrait Gallery Library, Smithsonian Libraries and Archives, Washington, DC.

7. See A. Wilson Greene, *Fredericksburg Battlefields: Fredericksburg and Spotsylvania County Battlefields Memorial National Military Park* (Harpers Ferry, WV: United States Park Service, Division of Publications, 2000), 62.

8. Thank you to Sarah Lea Burns for her insightful reading of Winslow Homer and history painting, especially her analysis *Trooper Meditating beside a Grave* and *Prisoners from the Front*, which we discussed during the NEH Summer Seminar in the Visual Culture of the Civil War, held in July 2021.

9. Dorothy Mahon, conservator, and Evan Read, manager of technical documentation, both in the department of paintings conservation at the Metropolitan Museum of Art, discovered this painted-out figure. Homer often reworked his paintings. Thank you to Stephanie Herdrich, Sylvia Yount, and Dorothy Mahon for relaying this information during the study day for the exhibition *Winslow Homer: Crosscurrents* at the Metropolitan Museum of Art, held on June 29, 2022. See also Stephanie L. Herdrich and Sylvia Yount, eds., *Winslow Homer: Crosscurrents* (New York: Metropolitan Museum of Art, with Yale University Press, 2022), 190n81.

10. The naval ship's positions were normally between 3,000 and 8,000 yards from the coast of Cuba. The presence of two searchlights is likely inaccurate. According to sketches published in 1900, only one ship had the searchlight. See Severo Gomez Nunez, "The Spanish-American War: Blockades and Coastal Defense, in U.S. Navy, Office of Naval Intelligence," in *Notes on the Spanish-American War* (Washington, DC: Government Printing Office, 1900), 77. The ships' distances from the coast are illustrated in the colored pen-and-ink map on tracing linen, "Approaches and Entrance to Santiago Harbor," U.S. Hydrographic Office, July 1898. Collection of Maps and Geography, Library of Congress. G4922 . S3R3 1898 .A6 Vault, Santiago, Cuba/Cuba–South Coast.

11. History painting is grounded in the representation of the figure and reflects larger intellectual and cultural traditions. The French Royal Academy in the seventeenth century introduced the term "history painting" to describe paintings with subjects addressing ancient Greek and Roman narratives and classical mythology, as well as the Bible. In the late eighteenth century, battle scenes and other modern historical subjects also became enveloped in the genre.

12. Translation by Rich Denis. See *El Figaro*, December 1902. Cited by Luz Merino Acosta, "Aquel Cambio de Siglo," in Acosta et al., eds., *Menocal y Romañach: Maestros cubanos del cambio de siglo* (Salamanca, Spain: Gráficas Varona, S.A., 2003), 11. Interestingly, Menocal became the director of the Academy of San Alejandro in 1927. His leadership likely helped form the

Cuban National School, the Afro-Cuban movement led by artists such as Wifredo Lam. Like Menocal, they trained at the Academy of San Alejandro in Havana and Academy of San Fernando in Madrid.

13. The mayor likely invited Menocal to make the painting. See Actas Capitulares del Cabildo of Havana, book 258, invoice 277–87. Act session of Feb. 3 of 1909.

14. The Spanish-American Light and Power Company was founded in 1883 and headquartered in New York City. See "Caused by The Cuban War: The Troubles of the Spanish-American Light Company," *New York Times,* December 8, 1896, 16.

15. See "1898: A Contest in Memory," pp. 163–80 in this volume.

16. For more on the Platt Amendment, see Louis A. Pérez Jr., *Cuba Under the Platt Amendment, 1902–1934* (Pittsburgh, PA: University of Pittsburgh Press, 1986); and Ada Ferrer, *Cuba: An American History* (New York: Scribner, 2021).

17. The term "neocolonial" acknowledges that from 1898 to 1933, Cuba's economy and infrastructure was greatly influenced by the power and influence of the United States. See Juan C. Santamarina, "The Cuba Company and the Expansion of American Business in Cuba, 1898–1915," *Business History Review* 74, no. 1 (2000): 41–83.

18. See "Civil Orders and Circulars, Headquarters, 20 February 1900, Traducion no. 76, by Adna R. Chaffee," Armando García Menocal, faculty file, Academia San Alejandro, Cuba. In some ways, Menocal's experience dealing with patrons of the colonial regime was like that of the preeminent Puerto Rican artist Francisco Oller y Cestero, as discussed in "Prelude to Empire: Indian Wars and Sea Power," pp. 31–51 in this volume.

19. For citation, see José Martí Pérez, "Galería de Colón: Libro nuevo de Néstor Ponce de León," *Obras completas* (Havana: Editorial de Ciencias Sociales, 1975), 5, 203–8. For more about the "colony enchained," see Catherine Vallejo, "Seeing 'Spain' at the 1893 Chicago World (Columbian) Exhibition," in David R. Castillo and Bradley Nelson, eds., *Spectacle and Topophilia: Reading Early Modern and Postmodern Hispanic Cultures* (Nashville, TN: Vanderbilt University Press, 2011), 166.

20. When the painting was exhibited in Chicago, Menocal went to see it and ran into other Cubans, including Manuel Pichardo and Raimundo Cabrera, who sought out his painting. See M. Elizabeth Boone, *"The Spanish Element in Our Nationality": Spain and America at the World's Fairs and Centennial Celebrations, 1876–1915* (University Park: Penn State University Press, 2019), 98. Menocal's *Embarque de Cristóbal Colón por Bobadilla* was exhibited in the fair in the galleries devoted to Spain. See *World's Columbian Exposition, 1893* (Chicago: W. B. Conkey, 1893), 8; 181. Interestingly, Homer exhibited fifteen works in the U.S. galleries. The two artists both attended the exposition, and it is likely they saw each other's work.

21. See Bárbara Omaira Argüelles Almenares, "Armando García Menocal: Contribuciones a la imagen pictórica de Antonio Maceo y al tema histórico de la Guerra de Independica (1895–1915)," *Maceo en el tiempo: Acción, pensamiento y entorno histórico.* (Havana: Editorial de Ciencias Sociales, 2015), 199.

22. In a letter to Arthur Benson Homer, Homer's mother wrote that her son spent two months on the front. See Gordon Hendricks, *The Life and Work of Winslow Homer*, 50. Note that Hendricks cites letters by Henrietta Benson Homer as belonging to a private collection. Although he reproduced some of the letters as facsimiles in his book, no one has identified the "private collection." Thus, Hendricks is cited as the primary source in this note and hereafter.

23. See David Tatham, *Winslow Homer's Books: A Descriptive List of Books Once Owned by Winslow Homer, and Now the Property of the Margaret Woodbury Strong Museum, Rochester, New York* (Syracuse, NY: Syracuse University Department of Fine Arts, 1976), 14–15. This collection has since been dispersed, but much of it now resides in the Portland Museum of Art in Maine.

24. For an excellent account of Homer's time in Yorktown, see Lucretia Hoover Giese and Roy Perkinson, "A Newly Discovered Drawing of Sharpshooters by Winslow Homer: Experience, Image, and Memory," *Winterthur Portfolio* 45, no. 1 (Spring 2011): 61–90.

25. Sharpshooters served in the Second, Fifth, and Third Corps during the beginning of the Peninsula campaign. See Giese and Perkinson, "Newly Discovered Drawing," 61, 74n38, 86n78.

26. David Miller, curator of political and military history at the National Museum of American History, Smithsonian Institution, identified the rifle as a match rifle in email correspondence with the author on August 23, 2021. Match rifles were used in long-range shooting contests.

27. Homer made no preparatory drawings for the painting, although he made related drawings of sharpshooters. See Giese and Perkinson, "Newly Discovered Drawing," 78–84.

28. Experiments in telescopic sights had been conducted as far back as the 1600s, but effective telescopic sights were not developed until around 1840. Rifling also goes back as far as the 1600s, but it could not be mass produced until the nineteenth century. By 1861, sportsmen had been using telescopic sights in shooting matches, but the rifles required very heavy barrels to sustain a larger charge of black powder for long-range shooting.

29. "Report of Brig. Gen. Fitz John Porter, U.S. Army, commanding divisions, of operations April 4–6," in *War of the Rebellion: A Compilation of the Official Records of the Union and Confederate Armies, prepared under the direction of the Secretary of War, by Bvt. Lieut. Col. Robert N. Scott, Third U.S. Artillery*, ser. 1, vol 11., pt. 1:

"Reports" (Washington, DC: Government Printing Office, 1884), 286.

30. Earl J. Hess notes that the typical Civil War soldier did not know how to use the rifle musket to its greatest advantage. See Hess, *The Rifle Musket in Civil War Combat: Reality and Myth* (Lawrence: University of Kansas Press, 2016), 4.

31. Homer made this comment after receiving a book from George G. Briggs, C. A. Stevens's *Berdan's U.S. Sharpshooters in the Army of the Potomac, 1861–1865,* published in 1892. Homer to George G. Briggs, February 19, 1896, Archives of American Art.

32. Others, like Francis Channing Barlow, became impervious to death caused by war. In June 1862, Barlow wrote: "It is singular how soon men become used to such horrid scenes. We see the dead and wounded carried past without any emotion." Francis Channing Barlow to Edward Barlow, June 10, 1862, Francis C. Barlow Letters, 1861–1865, microfilm, Massachusetts Historical Society, Boston.

33. See Francis Channing Barlow to Edward Barlow, April 23, 1862, the Massachusetts Historical Society, Boston.

34. Henrietta Homer to Arthur Benson Homer, June 7, 1862, quoted in Hendricks, *The Life and Work of Winslow Homer,* 50.

35. His cousin, Mario García Menocal, was Major General in the V Corps and would be elected president of Cuba in 1913. Other cousins who fought include Tomás García Menocal (born 1875); Pedro Pablo García Menocal (life dates unknown), *Coronel;* Gustavo García Menocal (life dates unknown), *Comandante;* Juan Manuel García Menocal (life dates unknown) *Coronel.* See correspondence between the author and Bárbara Omaira Argüelles Almenares, November 19, 2021.

36. See John Lawrence Tone, *War and Genocide in Cuba, 1895–1898* (Durham: University of North Carolina Press, 2006),

37. In his survey of Cuban art, Esteban Valderrama acknowledged only that Menocal had participated in the Invasion "From Baraguá to El Mariel." See Valderrama and Benigno Vázquez Rodríguez, *La pintura y la escultura en Cuba* (Havana: Editorial Lex, 1952), 59. However, Menocal fought for most of the war and traveled from *Oriente* province to the western side during the Invasion. See *Diccionario Enciclopédico de Historia Militar de Cuba,* 47–50. Thank you to Bárbara Omaira Argüelles Almenares for her help in this research.

38. This was grueling soldiering for the four thousand men led by Gómez and his second in command, Maceo. During this time, the Cuban Liberation Army fought twenty-seven important battles and took control of twenty-two important towns. In doing so, the insurgents gained significant resources, including more than two thousand rifles, eighty thousand rounds of ammunition, and three thousand horses. See Ada Ferrer, *Insurgent Cuba: Race, Nation, and Revolution,*

1868–1898 (Chapel Hill: University of North Carolina Press, 2005), 193.

39. The inability to cross the *trocha*—the trench made by the Spanish that traversed the island from Morón in the north to Júcaro in the south—in the Ten Years' War (1868–1878) had ultimately doomed the island's earlier struggle for independence. In 1875, Cuban insurgents under the command of Máximo Gómez briefly crossed the *trocha.* By 1895, however, the *trocha* had lost much of its strength as an imposing defensive line. The Spanish rarely guarded what remained, as the jungle had taken over much of the line. See Tone, *War and Genocide in Cuba,* 1.

40. In addition to the Battle of Coliseo in Matanzas, Menocal's most notable battles include the Battle of Calimete in Matanzas (December 29, 1895) and the Battle of Finca La Chorrera, El Calvario in Havana (October 25, 1897). Having soldiered with distinction, Menocal was promoted to major and emerged from the war with deep connections to the Independence movement's leaders. After joining the Fifth Corps, Menocal served briefly under the Marquis de Santa Lucia (1828–1914), Salvador Cisneros Betancourt. Subsequently, he was aide-de-campe to Máximo Gómez. For Menocal's rank, see William Belmont Parker, ed., *Cubans of To-day* (New York: G. P. Putnam and Sons, 1919), 474.

41. Menocal made a pen drawing depicting machete warfare during the skirmish of Bacuino, in Las Villas in 1896. See artist's record, Center of Information, Museo Nacional de Bellas Artes.

42. Tone, *War and Genocide in Cuba,* 123–25.

43. Ibid.

44. Maceo was delayed by terrain and barbed-wire fencing. See Tone, *War and Genocide in Cuba,* 123–25.

45. José Miró Argenter, "Mal Tiempo," *Crónicas de la Guerra* (Havana: Editorial Letras Cubanas, 1981), 210.

46. Tone, *War and Genocide in Cuba,* 125. However, this number is debated. Cubans reported that the Spanish suffered more than three hundred casualties, including 147 dead. By comparison, forty-two Cubans were wounded, and only four were killed. See the *Diccionario Enciclopédico de Historia Militar de Cuba,* 370.

47. Menocal dedicated *Carga al Machete* to the Veterans Center of Sancti Spiritu, a town close to Bacuino in central Cuba. See Ricardo Villares, "Menocal, pintor mambí," *Bohemia* (December 2, 1977), 47.

48. Henri Bergson's philosophy of French élan is at the base of this argument. On Bergson, see Arnaud François, *Nietzsche, Schopenhauer, Bergson: Volonté et réalite* (Paris: Presses Universitaires de France, 2009) and Mark Sinclair, "Bergson's Philosophy of Will and the War of 1914–1918," *Journal of the History of Ideas* 77, no. 3 (July 2016): 467–87.

49. Although invented in 1861, the Gatling gun was not adopted by the U.S. Army until after the U.S. Civil War. It first saw regular use in the War of 1898.

50. Menocal reportedly made three murals for this house, including *Battle of San Juan* and *The Invasion.*

See Benigno Vázquez Rodríguez, "Biographies of Professors and Notes of Graduates," in *Painting and Sculpture in Cuba* (Havana: National School of Fine Arts San Alejandro, Presidential Palace and National Museum, 1952), 64. Abreu was a wealthy philanthropist whose private zoo cared for more than two hundred primates and forty other animal species. See Clive D. L. Wynne, "Rosalía Abreu and the Apes of Havana," *International Journal of Primatology* 29, no. 2 (April 2008): 289–302. Abreu and her sister Marta Abreu y Arencibia financed a large part of the Cuban Liberation Army. See Pánfilo D. Camacho, *Marta Abreu: una mujer comprendida* (Havana: Editorial Trópico, 1947); Juan Manuel Fernández Triana, *Marta Abreu: la dama todo corazón* (Havana: Publicaciones Acuario, Centro Félix Varela, 2010); Ovidio Cosme Díaz Benitez, *Santa Clara Nuestra* (Havana: Editorial Historia, 2016), 83; Josefina Toledo, *Marta Abreu: la caridad como energía creadora* (Havana: Editorial de Ciencias Sociales, 2014).

51. Hugh Thomas, *Cuba: The Pursuit of Freedom* (New York: Harper & Row, 1971), 322–24.

52. Philip S. Foner, *Antonio Maceo: "The Bronze Titan" of Cuba's Struggle for Independence* (New York: Monthly Review Press, 1977), 207–8.

53. Maceo rode one of the horses that was shot, but he miraculously survived. José Miró Argenter, an eyewitness to the battle, wrote, "General Maceo quickly organizes the attack from the front and throws himself over the Spanish lines at the gallop of his fiery Moorish horse, which seems not to touch the earth . . ." See Miró Argenter, "Mal Tiempo," 208.

54. Homer to M. Knoedler and Company, January 14, 1902: "That Santiago de Cuba picture *is not intended to be 'beautiful.'* There are certain things (unfortunately for critics) that are stern facts but are worth recording as a matter of history as in this case. This is a small part of Morro Castle & immediately over the Harbor entrance which is only about 400 feet wide—& from this point were seen all the stirring sights of June & July 1898. *I find it interesting.*" See microfilm NY 59–5, Archives of American Art, Washington, DC.

55. During the Battle of Santiago Bay, the Spanish suffered 323 men killed, 151 wounded, and 1,720 captured. See "Documentary Histories: Spanish-American War," https://www.history.navy.mil/research /publications/documentary-histories/united-states -navy-s/the-battle-of-santia.html. Others number the Spanish losses higher, at nearly five hundred killed. One U.S. sailor was killed. See Jerry Keenan, *Encyclopedia of the Spanish-American and Philippine-American Wars* (Santa Barbara, CA: ABC CLIO Press, 2001), 360.

56. Menocal, too, may have seen this display since he also visited the exposition in Chicago in 1893.

57. See Ivan Musicant, *Empire by Default: The Spanish-American War and the Dawn of the American Century* (New York: Henry Holt and Company, 1998), 347–49.

58. See William T. Sampson, "The Atlantic Fleet in the Spanish War," *Century Magazine* 57, no. 35 (April 1899): 901.

59. Ramey Mize explores this experimentation in "Battle Grounds: Painting, War and Witness in the Americas, 1861–1902," PhD diss., 2023, University of Pennsylvania.

60. Cited by Natalie Spassky, et al., *American Paintings in The Metropolitan Museum of Art: A Catalogue of Works by Artists Born between 1816 and 1845 American Paintings*, vol. 2 (New York: Metropolitan Museum of Art, in association with Princeton University Press, 1985), 490.

61. Thank you to Dana Byrd for leading a discussion comparing these two bodies of work during the Winslow Homer Study Day at the Metropolitan Museum of Art. The 1887 Cuban Census numbered the total Black population in Cuba at approximately one third, 32.4 percent. See the International Bureau of the American Republics, *Cuba: Population, History, and Resources* (United States: U.S. Bureau of the Census, Washington, DC, 1909), n.p.

62. Gerald Eugene Poyo, *With All and for the Good of All* (Durham, NC: Duke University Press, 1989), 64.

63. Winslow Homer to Charles Savage Jr., not dated, Bowdoin College Museum of Art. https://artmuseum. bowdoin.edu/objects-1/info/5789.

64. "The Cause of Cuba: Guerilla Warfare in the Ever Faithful Isle, Special Dispatch to The Boston Globe," *Boston Globe*, July 14, 1883, p. 4.

65. See "A New Cuban Revolution Proposed," *New York Herald,* July 14, 1883.

66. See Gerald E. Poyo, *"With All, and for the Good of All:" The Emergence of Popular Nationalism in the Cuban Communities of the United States, 1848–1898* (Durham, NC: Duke University Press, 1989), 64.

67. José Ramón Leocadio Bonachea, Colonel Porfirio Estrada, Captain Pedro Cestero, Lieutenant Cornelio Oropesa, and the pilot Bernardo Torres were sentenced to death for rebellion and filibustering. Miguel Suárez and Pedro Ros were sentenced to life imprisonment; the rest of the sailors were sentenced to twelve years in prison. Captain General Fajardo ratified the sentence. See Rolando Rodríguez, "Un héroe villaclareño casi olvidado," *Cuba Debate,* May 25, 2018. http://www.cubadebate.cu/especiales/2018 /05/25/un-heroe-villaclareno-casi-olvidado/.

68. Imilcy Balboa Navarro (Translated by Bonnie A. Lucero), "Bandits, Patriots or Delinquents? Social Protest in Rural Cuba (1878–1902)," *International Journal of Cuban Studies* 7, no. 1 (Spring 2015): 82.

69. The castle's first component was completed in 1643. See Flora Morcate, et al., *Santiago de Cuba y ses monumentos* (Havana: Editorial Oriente, 1996), 120–23. The castle itself was part of a Caribbean-wide defense system implemented by the Spanish but developed by the Italian architect Giovanni Battista Antonelli (1547–1616). See Elvis Fuentes, "Crossroads, Crossing and the Cross," in *Caribbean: Art at the Crossroads of the World*, ed. Deborah Cullen and Elvis Fuentes (New Haven, CT: Yale University Press, 2012), 61, 66.

70. It is not clear why Homer obscured the last digit, but perhaps he only knew rough dates for its rebuilding after the British naval officer Christopher Myngs sacked Santiago de Cuba, including Morro Castle, in 1662.

71. The execution by firing squad in the esplanade near Morro Castle of Bonachea, Bornello Oropita, Plutarco Estrada, Bernadia Torres and Pedro Cesteros was reported in March 1885. See "The Fate of The Cuban Patriots: Gen. Bonachea and Four of His Comrades," *Washington Post*, March 18, 1885.

72. Ada Ferrer coined the phrase "raceless nation" in *Insurgent Cuba*, 4–5.

73. See Foner, *Antonio Maceo: The "Bronze Titan" of Cuban's Struggle for Independence*, 241–51.

74. John Lawrence Tone describes Maceo's authoritative style of leadership and his forceful, deadly strategies of guerrilla warfare. See Tone, *War and Genocide in Cuba*, 90–91.

75. Antonio Álvarez Pitaluga, "La caída de un héroe y el secuestro de un mito," *Caliban: Revista Cubana de Pensamiento e Historia* (May–August, 2012), 31.

76. See, for example, Benjamin West's *Death of General Wolfe* (1770), collection of the National Gallery of Canada.

77. Ada Ferrer expounds on this idea of a raceless nation, explaining, "Thus the language of raceless nationality, a language of harmony and integration, became also a 'language of contention.'" See Ferrer, *Insurgent Cuba*, 9–10.

78. Ada Ferrer addressed the changing ideology about race, linking its foundations to the 1790s revolution in Haiti and tracing how the anticolonial movement in Cuba, especially in the 1890s, produced a different conception of race and nation. See Ferrer, *Insurgent Cuba*, 112–13.

79. See "Cutting a Path to Sovereignty: The Complex Political Landscapes of the Philippines and Guam" in this volume, pp. 125–55.

80. In 1908, the newspaper *Prevision*, the political organ for the Party of the Independence of Color, expressed its concern about the lack of Black men in the painting, "when the whole world knows that the Army of Liberation was mostly comprised of black soldiers in its battle lines." See *Prevision,* November 12, 1908. See also Argüelles Almenares, "Armando García Menocal," 194n36. Major General Pedro Díaz Molina (1850–1924), a Black soldier, witnessed the event and although he left quickly, his absence in the painting was a glaring omission. See Antonio Álvarez Pitaluga, "La caída de un héroe y el secuestro de un mito," 27–34.

81. In the session of November 13, 1908, the City Council appointed a commission made up of councilors Esteban Baguer and Coppinger, "so that, assisted by the technicians they deem appropriate,

examine said work, and report if it was acceptable." In the session of January 11, 1909, the aforementioned committee presented their report rendered about the opinion of the professors Manuel Lluch y Ramiro Triguero of Escuela de Pintura y Escultura de San Alejandro, who noted that "this work is inspirationally comprehended and it is as a whole made of a good artistic composition, congratulating the city hall for the ownership of the work." See *Actas Capitulares del Cabildo of Havana*, vol. 258, invoice 277–287. Act session of Feb. 3 of 1909. See also letter from Eugenio Léopoldo Aspiarzo, November 16, 1908, to Director of the Academy of Painting of the City, Armando García Menocal, faculty file, Academia San Alejandro, Cuba. Aspiarzo requested two professors from San Alejandro be appointed to evaluate the artistic merit of the painting.

82. For the investigation, see Argüelles Almenares, "Armando García Menocal," 193. The money was taken from the municipal budget. It was approved by vote in a session of the City Council, which recorded the proceeding in an agreement. See *Actas Capitulares del Cabildo of Havana*, B 258, Invoice 277–287. Act session of Feb. 3 of 1909.

83. Menocal won the Silver Medal for *La muerte de Maceo* and for *The Lady in Pink.* See John Ellingwood Donnell Trask and John Nilsen Laurvik, eds., *Catalogue de luxe of the Department of Fine Arts, Panama-Pacific International Exposition* (San Francisco: P. Elder and Company, 1915), 82, 155.

84. See letter from Eugenio Léopoldo Aspiarzo, November 16, 1908, to Director of the Academy of Painting of the City, Armando García Menocal, faculty file, Academia San Alejandro, Cuba.

85. Mario García Menocal made his first bid for the Cuban presidency in 1908, no doubt aided by his interests and friends in the United States. Family connections must have helped Menocal with this and subsequent commissions. The first large-scale decoration of the presidential palace was ordered by Mario García Menocal during his government, and Menocal painted at least two large murals, including *La Batalla Victoria de las Tunas.* See James Luby, "Havana, the New Monte Carlo of America," *Munsey's Magazine* 69, no. 2 (February–May 1920): 224–25.

86. Bárbara Omaira Argüelles Almenares also explains Menocal's commission and its contexts. See Argüelles Almenares, "Armando García Menocal," 189–92.

87. See Lillian Guerra, "Perceiving Populism: United States Imperialism and the Paradox of Labour Struggle in Cuba, 1906–1909," *The Journal of Caribbean History* 37, no. 1 (2003): 9.

88. See Lillian Guerra, *The Myth of José Marti: Conflicting Nationalisms in Early Twentieth-Century Cuba* (Chapel Hill: University of North Carolina Press, 2005), 13–21. Menocal probably fell somewhere between the first two ideological camps: the revolutionary nationalists and the pro-imperialist nationalists. His family was certainly pro-imperialist; beginning in 1899, his uncle, Aniceto, was employed by the U.S. Army Corps of Engineers as chief engineer in charge of construction at the waterworks of Havana. Menocal's first cousin (with whom he was raised), Mario García Menocal, was elected President of Cuba in 1913 and conducted a pro-U.S. government.

NEW POSSESSIONS: COLONIAL CURIOS, TROPHIES, WEAPONS, AND MUSEUM COLLECTIONS FROM THE PHILIPPINE-AMERICAN WAR

1. The anthropological collections that Herbert W. Krieger oversaw are now held by the Smithsonian's National Museum of National History. For more information on the history of the United States National Museum and its relationship to the larger Smithsonian, see "A Brief History of NMNH," National Museum of Natural History, https://naturalhistory.si.edu/about /brief-history-nmnh.

2. Herbert W. Krieger, *The Collection of Primitive Weapons and Armor of the Philippine Islands in the United States National Museum*, Smithsonian Institution, United States National Museum, *Bulletin* 137 (Washington, DC: Government Printing Office, 1926), 8.

3. "Herbert W. Krieger, 80, Curator at Smithsonian," *Washington Post, Times Herald*, July 3, 1970, B8.

4. "Crossbow," entry in Krieger, *Collection of Primitive Weapons*, 35; "Wooden Sword Club," in ibid., 47–48.

5. Krieger, *Collection of Primitive Weapons*, 6.

6. Krieger, *Collection of Primitive Weapons*, 1.

7. For "punitive expedition," see Krieger, *Collection of Primitive Weapons*, 3, 5, 107. For "invasion and occupation," see ibid., 4.

8. Krieger, *Collection of Primitive Weapons*, 1.

9. For some key works on this effort, see Amy Lonetree, *Decolonizing Museums: Representing Native America in National and Tribal Museums* (Chapel Hill: University of North Carolina Press, 2012); Amy Lonetree, "Decolonizing Museums, Memorials, and Monuments," *The Public Historian* 43, no. 4 (2021): 21–27; Bryony Onciul, *Museums, Heritage and Indigenous Voice: Decolonizing Engagement* (New York: Routledge, 2015); Susan Sleeper-Smith, *Contesting Knowledge: Museums and Indigenous Perspectives* (Lincoln: University of Nebraska Press, 2009); Katrin Sieg, *Decolonizing German and European History at the Museum* (Ann Arbor: University of Michigan Press, 2021).

10. Scholarship on the Philippine-American War is extensive and growing. For important, relatively recent PhD theses, see James Heberton Berkey, "Imperial Correspondence: Soldiers, Writing, and the Imperial Quotidian during the Spanish-American and Philippine-American Wars" (PhD, Indiana University, 2010); Rowena Quinto Bailon, "Battling Destiny: Soldiers' Letters and the Anti-Colonial Discourse in the Philippine-American War" (PhD, University of Texas at Dallas, 2014); Cynthia L. Marasigan, "'Between the Devil and the Deep Sea': Ambivalence, Violence, and African American Soldiers in the Philippine-American War and its Aftermath" (PhD, University of Michigan, 2010).

11. For the growing scholarship on the U.S. military and tourism outside the United States, see Scott Laderman, *Tours of Vietnam: War, Travel Guides, and Memory* (Durham: Duke University Press, 2009); Scott Laderman, "Tourists in Uniform: American Empire-Building and the Defense Department's Cold War Pocket Guide Series," *Radical History Review*, Issue 129 (October 2017): 74–102; Vernadette Vicuña Gonzalez, *Securing Paradise: Tourism and Militarism in Hawai'i and the Philippines* (Durham, NC: Duke University Press, 2013); David Farber and Beth Bailey, "The Fighting Man as Tourist: The Politics of Tourist Culture in Hawaii during World War II," *Pacific Historical Review* 65, no. 4 (November 1996): 641–66. See, especially, "Tours of Duty and Tours of Leisure" a special issue of *American Quarterly*, coedited by Jana K. Lipman, Vernadette Vicuña Gonzalez, and Teresia Teaiwa, which is dedicated to "militourism," *American Quarterly* 68, no. 3 (September 2016).

12. "Manila Notes," *Hartford Courant*, February 25, 1899, 9.

13. "Philippine Trophies," *Hartford Courant*, September 30, 1899, 8.

14. "Manila Notes," *Hartford Courant,* February 25, 1899, 9.

15. "Many Promotions for Worthy Volunteers from this State," *San Francisco Chronicle*, August 29, 1899, 12.

16. "Visitors to the *Raleigh*: Cruiser's Men Entertained 2,500 Guests during the Day," *New York Times*, April 18, 1899, 4.

17. "Visitors to the *Raleigh*."

18. "Many Promotions for Worthy Volunteers from this State," *San Francisco Chronicle*, August 29, 1899, 12.

19. "War Veterans," *Los Angeles Times*, February 5, 1903, 11.

20. "First Story of the 29th Regiment and Its Fine Work in the Philippines," *Atlanta Constitution*, May 5, 1901, 14.

21. See, for example, the section entitled "Headhunting and Associated Ceremonial Weapons," in Krieger, *Collection of Primitive Weapons*, especially 87–91.

22. "Curios of Philippines," *Washington Post*, October 27, 1903, 9.

23. Smithsonian National Museum of Natural History, catalogue record, Moro kris and sheath, catalogue number E311481-0, donated by Mrs. George F. Becker.

24. "Collection of Filipino Weapons: Among Them Are Many Queer Implements for Taking Life," *Detroit Free Press*, July 29, 1906, 8.

25. Ibid.

26. "Terrible Weapons Used by Filipinos," *Chicago Daily Tribune*, January 12, 1902, 38.

27. "History-Making Blades of the Knife-Fighting Orient," *San Francisco Chronicle*, August 28, 1904, 5.

28. "Collection of Filipino Weapons."

29. "Terrible Weapons Used by Filipinos."

30. See the Smithsonian's National Museum of National History catalogue records for: Bamboo Jewsharp; "Culaing" or "Culang," Moro, Philippines, collected and donated by Col. Paul E. Beckwith, catalogue no. E230143-0; Earring, Igarote, Philippines, collected and donated by Col. Paul E. Beckwith, catalogue no. E230144-0.

31. On these debates, see Paul A. Kramer, *The Blood of Government: Race, Empire, the United States and the Philippines* (Chapel Hill: University of North Carolina Press, 2006), esp. chapters 2, 3, and 5.

32. "Capt. Bordman's War Talk: Lectures at Concord Junction on His Philippine Experiences," *Boston Daily Globe,* September 21, 1901, 2.

33. "Queer Things Among Them," *Detroit Free Press*, May 28, 1899, D2.

34. "Shipload of Curios: Odd-Looking Products of Our New Possessions," *St. Louis Post-Dispatch*, May 21, 1899, 9.

35. "False Tales of Looting," *San Francisco Chronicle*, September 26, 1900, 9.

36. "Respectfully Referred to the Secretary of War," cover, *Collier's Weekly* 23, no. 23 (September 9, 1899).

37. On U.S. colonialism in the Philippines and Americans' perception of Catholic power in the islands, see Kate Moran, *The Imperial Church: Catholic Founding Fathers and United States Empire* (Ithaca, NY: Cornell University Press, 2020).

38. "Protest Filed by Catholics," *Chicago Daily Tribune*, September 17, 1899, 5.

39. Ibid.

40. Ibid.

41. "Church Looted: By Soldiers and Costly Paraphernalia of Priests Sent Home," *Cincinnati Enquirer*, September 18, 1900, 2.

42. See, for example, "Canards Refused: Father McKinnon Gives the Lie to Scandal Mongers," *Los Angeles Times*, October 22, 1899, A1; "Churches Were Not Looted," *New York Times*, October 25, 1899, 4.

43. See, for example, "Canards Refuted"; "Friars are All in Prisons," *Cincinnati Enquirer*, October 24, 1899, 3; "Archbishop Ireland Explains," *New York Times*, November 2, 1899, 2.

44. For more on anti-colonialists in the United States, see pp. 137–39 in this volume.

45. For anti-colonialist references to colonialism as involving the pursuit of "loot," see, for example, Charles A. Towne, "Lest We Forget," in *Republic or Empire?: The Philippine Question* (Chicago: The Independence Company, 1899), 325. For references to colonialism as involving "plunder," see, for example, Hon. John L. McLaurin, "Our New Colonial Policy," in *Republic or Empire?*, 586; Hon. Henry U. Johnson, "Imperial Splendor and Imperial Mistakes," in *Republic or Empire?*, 630.

46. Curtis Hinsley, *The Smithsonian and the American Indian: Making a Moral Anthropology in Victorian America* (Washington, DC: Smithsonian Institution Press, 1981).

47. W. J. McGee to S. P. Langley, September 7, 1898, McGee Letterbooks (microfilm), National Anthropological Archives, Smithsonian Institution.

48. For correspondence on McGee's arrangements between the Smithsonian and the Pan-American Exposition, see Smithsonian Institution Archives, RU 70, Series 14, Box 52.

49. "Had Seen Many Lands: Col. Hilder, Scientist, Soldier, and Lecturer, Dead," *Washington Post*, January 22, 1901, 2.

50. P. L. Sherman to F. W. True, May 31, 1900, SIA, RU 70, Series 14, Box 52, Folder "H-J."

51. P. L. Sherman to F. F. Hilder, May 14, 1900, SIA, RU 700, Series 14, Box 52, Folder "H-J."

52. "Many Filipino Curios: Col. Hilder Returns with Rich and Large Collection," *Washington Post,* June 7, 1900, 11.

53. F. F. Hilder to F. W. True, May 17, 1900, SIA, RU 70, Series 14, Box 52, Folder "H-J."

54. P. L. Sherman to F. F. Hilder, April 30, 1900, SIA, RU 70, Series 14, Box 52, Folder "H-J."

55. P. L. Sherman to F. F. Hilder, May 14, 1900, SIA, RU 70, Series 14, Box 52, Folder "H-J."

56. P. L. Sherman to F. F. Hilder, November 13, 1900, SIA, RU 70, Series 14, Box 52, Folder "P. L. Sherman."

57. For an account of the Pan-American Exposition with an emphasis on its hegemonic, racial-colonial imagery, see Robert Rydell, *All the World's a Fair: Visions of Empire at America's International Expositions, 1876–1916* (Chicago: University of Chicago Press, 1984), chapter 5. While Hilder's exhibit attracted attention, the press and public focused most on the "Philippine Village" set up under private auspices on the Exposition's midway.

58. William H. Swartout, "A Descriptive Story of the Philippine Exhibit," *World's Fair Bulletin* (June 1904), 49.

59. On Filipino objections to the display of "non-Christians" at an exposition held in Madrid in 1887, see Kramer, *The Blood of Government*, chapter 1.

60. [Gustavo Niederlein], *Carta Circular del Gobernador Taft: Invitación Solicitando Una Cooperación General* (Manila: Bureau of Printing, 1903). Translation by the author.

61. Swartout, 49.

62. Kramer, *The Blood of Government*, chapter 4.

63. "Philippine Show Has Cost $600,000," *St. Louis Post-Dispatch*, November 18, 1904, 4.

64. "Filipino Houses for Wealthy Only, Philippine Exhibits at the World's Fair to be Sold by Government Agents," *St. Louis Post-Dispatch*, November 2, 1904, 5.

65. "New York to Get Pick of Filipino Exhibit," *New York Times*, February 18, 1905, 6.

66. Ibid.

67. Ibid.

68. Merton Miller, "Report of the Ethnological Survey," Appendix M, Part 2, *Report of the Philippine Commission to the Secretary of War for 1905* (Washington, DC: Government Printing Office, 1906), 422.

69. Miller, "Report of the Ethnological Survey," 422.

70. See, for example, Trumbull White, *Our New Possessions: A Graphic Account, Descriptive and Historical, of the Tropic Islands of the Sea Which Have Fallen Under Our Sway* (St. Louis: J. H. Chambers and Co., 1898); Murat Halstead, *Our New Possessions: Natural Riches, Industrial Resources… of Cuba, Porto Rico, Hawaii, the Ladrones and the Philippine Islands, with Episodes of their Early History* (Chicago: Dominion Co., 1898); Thomas J. Vivian, *Everything about Our New Possessions: Being a Handy Book on Cuba, Porto Rico, Hawaii, and the Philippines* (New York: Fenno, 1899); John B. Devins, *An Observer in the Philippines; or, Life in Our New Possessions* (New York: American Tract Society, 1905).

71. See pp. 168–73 in this volume's conclusion, "1898: A Contest in Memory," for more on the uncertain legal and political status of the territories in the early twentieth century.

THE 1898 DIASPORAS: CONTEMPORARY ARTISTS REDEFINING PORTRAITURE

1. In his widely popular naval treatise, Alfred Thayer Mahan wrote extensively about the desirability that islands have for great nations. He offered a utilitarian view of them as connectors for commercial trade and as strategic military outposts, placing emphasis on harbors, fertile terrain, and tropical climate as further assets within them. Alfred Thayer Mahan, *The Influence of Sea Power in History, 1660–1783* (Boston: Little Brown and Company, 1890). On the general lack of knowledge in the United States about the unincorporated territories of Guam and Puerto Rico and the biases of contemporary media coverage, see Frances Negrón-Muntaner, "Why Does U.S. Media Insist on Describing Guam as Tiny?," *Columbia Journalism Review*, August 28, 2017, https://www.cjr.org/criticism/guam-media-military.php; Karishma Vanjani, "Journalists Reflect on Media Coverage of Puerto Rico and How the Media Can Do Better," *Craig Newmark Graduate School of Journalism*, January 28, 2020, https://www.journalism.cuny.edu/2020/01/panelists-reflect-medias-coverage-puerto-rico-can-better/.

2. See pp. 160–61 and 171–72 in this volume for a discussion of the *Insular Cases* and their impact on the governance of the lands seized by the United States in 1898. The judicial decision from which the phrasing "foreign in a domestic sense" originated with the case *Downes v. Bidwell* (1901).

3. The word *subaltern* was first used by historian Ranajit Guha in 1980 to refer to "the general attribute of subordination in South Asian society, whether this is expressed in terms of class, caste, age, or in any other way." Subaltern studies analyze the interplay of dominance and subordination in colonial systems. Originally pertaining to India, Subaltern studies have been widely influential and applied to other nations and regions of the world. See Ranajit Guha, preface to *Selected Subaltern Studies*, ed. Ranajit Guha and Gayatri Spivak (New York: Oxford University Press, 1988), 35.

4. Writing about the British empire, Edward Said affirmed that the universalizing discourses of European modernity assumed the silence—willing or forced—of the non-European world. This is true also of the discourses of modernity of the U.S. empire: they assume the silence of its colonies so that the discourse of freedom and democracy can remain unchallenged. Edward Said, *Culture and Imperialism* (New York: Knopf, 1993), 50–51.

5. I am borrowing the expression "imperial archipelago" from Lanny Thompson to refer to the islands claimed as U.S. territories in 1898. Thompson himself borrowed the term from Javier Morilla Alicea, who used it to describe the late nineteenth-century Spanish empire. Lanny Thompson, *Imperial Archipelago: Representation and Rule in the Insular Territories Under U.S. Dominion after 1898* (Honolulu: University of Hawai'i Press: 2010), 13n1.

6. In his 1997 essay "The Spectacle of the Other," Stuart Hall refers to the dominant "repertoires or regimes of representation" as racialized systems of representation established in the visual and discursive realms to demonstrate the "otherness" of a cultural or ethnic group. Stuart Hall, "The Spectacle of the Other," in *Representation: Cultural Representations and Signifying Practices,* ed. Stuart Hall (London: The Open University, 1997), 223–90.

7. Colonialism engenders patterns of migration that reverberate through generations, sometimes outliving colonial rule. See Lucy Mayblin and Joe Turner, *Migration Studies and Colonialism* (Cambridge, UK: Polity Press, 2021).

8. Besides those cited, some other key sources referring to these patterns of migration and their social and cultural implications include Theodore S. Gonzalves and Roderick N. Labrador, *Filipinos in Hawai'i* (Charleston, SC: Arcadia Publishing, 2011); and Jorge Duany, *Blurred Borders: Transnational Migration between the Hispanic Caribbean and the United States* (Chapel Hill: University of North Carolina Press, 2011).

9. Virginia Sánchez Korrol, *History of Puerto Ricans in the United States, Part Two. Labor Migration and U.S. Policies*, https://centropr-archive.hunter.cuny.edu/education/story-us-puerto-ricans-part-two.

10. Ibid.

11. According to Jorge Duany, at least 31,000 Puerto Ricans moved to these islands between 1898 and 1930. Until 1910, Puerto Rican migrants in Hawai'i numbered 3,510, making the Pacific archipelago the U.S. jurisdiction with the highest population of Puerto Rican migrants. Jorge Duany, *Puerto Rico: What Everyone Needs to Know* (Oxford, UK: Oxford University Press, 2017), 134–35.

12. Approximately 835,000 people left Puerto Rico for the continental United States between 1940 and 1970.

See Virginia Sánchez Korrol and Pedro Juan Hernández, *Pioneros II: Puerto Ricans in New York City, 1948–1998* (Charleston, SC: Arcadia Publishing, 2010), 8.

13. The Puerto Rican presence in the United States dates back to the nineteenth century, when many of them organized from New York, together with the Cubans, against Spanish colonial rule. After the transfer of sovereignty from Spain to the United States, and once Puerto Ricans were granted U.S. citizenship in 1917, they started to migrate to the United States in sustained flows. See Virginia Sánchez Korrol, *From Colonia to Community: The History of Puerto Ricans in New York City* (Oakland: University of California Press, 1994). A distinctive trait of the Puerto Rican diaspora is its *vaivén*, its movement back and forth between Puerto Rico and the continental United States, as theorized by Jorge Duany. Jorge Duany, *The Puerto Rican Nation on the Move: Identities on the Island and in the United States* (Chapel Hill: University of North Carolina Press, 2002). The most recent migration climax has been exacerbated by a series of natural disasters, including Hurricanes Irma and Maria and a series of earthquakes in 2020 in the south of the island.

14. CHamorus also came to the continental United States in search of higher education and as a result of the destruction caused by Typhoon Karen in 1962. See Faye F. Untalan, "CHamoru Migration to the United States," *Guampedia*, https://www.guampedia.com /chamorro-migration-to-the-u-s/.

15. The U.S. Census of 2020 marked the first decade in which the population of all the U.S. island territories declined. The trend was most dramatically reflected in Puerto Rico, where the population decreased 11.8 percent over the past decade, to 3.3 million. See Jens Manuel Krogstad, "Puerto Ricans Leave in Record Numbers for the US," Pew Research Center, October 14, 2015, https://www.pewresearch.org/fact-tank/2015/10 /14/puerto-ricans-leave-in-record-numbers-for -mainland-u-s/; and Antonio Flores and Jens Manuel Krogstad, "Puerto Rico's Population Declines Sharply after Hurricanes Maria and Irma," Pew Research Center, July 26, 2019. In Guam, it decreased 3.5 percent since 2010. Suzanne Gamboa, "Puerto Rico's Population Fell 11.8 percent to 3.3 million, Census Shows," *NBC News*, April 26, 2021, https://www.nbcnews.com/news /latino/puerto-ricos-population-fell-118-33-million -census-shows-rcna767; D'Vera Cohn, Eileen Patten, and Mark Hugo López, "Puerto Rican Population Declines on Island, Grows on U.S. Mainland," *Pew Research Center*, August 11, 2014, https://www .pewresearch.org/hispanic/2014/08/11/puerto-rican -population-declines-on-island-grows-on-u-s -mainland/; Lily Schlieman, "American Samoa, Commonwealth of the Northern Marianas, Guam See Population Decreases in 2020 Census," *Asia Matters for America*, November 29, 2021, https:// asiamattersforamerica.org/articles/american-samoa -commonwealth-of-the-northern-marianas-guam-see -population-decreases-in-2020-census.

16. See "Selected Population Profile in the United States" for Puerto Ricans, *United States Census Bureau*, https://data.census.gov/cedsci/table?q=s0201&t =402%20-%20Puerto%20Rican&tid=ACSSPP1Y2019 .S0201; "Quick Facts, Puerto Rico," *United States Census Bureau*, https://www.census.gov/quickfacts/fact/table /PR/POP010220#POP010220.

17. See "Asian American and Pacific Islander Heritage Month: May 2021," *United States Census Bureau*, April 19, 2021, https://www.census.gov/newsroom /facts-for-features/2021/asian-american-pacific -islander.html; Steven Wilson, William Koerber, and Evan Brassell, "2020 Population of U.S. Island Areas Just Under 339,000," United States Census Bureau, October 28, 2021, https://www.census.gov/library /stories/2021/10/first-2020-census-united-states -island-areas-data-released-today.html.

18. Rick Baldoz, *The Third Asiatic Invasion: Empire and Migration in Filipino America, 1898–1946* (New York: New York University Press: 2011), 114.

19. U.S. planters recruited Filipino workers in a ratio of fourteen men to one woman. This dramatic disparity led to intense racist backlash when Filipino men entered into relationships with Euro-American women. Filipinos in the 1930s were at the center of a profoundly racist and nativist U.S. discourse, referred to as "the Filipino problem," which accused them of stealing jobs, practicing substandard hygiene, being dependent on public assistance, and exhibiting high rates of criminality. Baldoz, *Third Asiatic Invasion*, 16.

20. Baldoz, *Third Asiatic Invasion*, 18. Jeanne Batalova and Luis Hassan Gallardo, "Filipino Immigrants in the United States," *Migration Policy Institute*, July 14, 2020. https://www.migrationpolicy.org/article/filipino -immigrants-united-states-2020.

21. The Filipino immigrant population increased fivefold from 105,000 to 501,000 between 1960 and 1980. From there, it nearly tripled to almost 1.4 million by 2000. Batalova and Gallardo, "Filipino Immigrants in the United States."

22. According to the American Community Survey, in 2019 there were 1.7 million people born in the Philippines living in the United States. This number increases to 2.9 million if we count people of Filipino origin. See https://data.census.gov/cedsci/table?q =filippinos&tid=ACSSPP1Y2019.S0201.

23. Homi K. Bhabha, *The Location of Culture* (London: Routledge, 1994), 2.

24. Ibid.

25. The validation of empire through the representation of colonial subjects in photographs, prints, and world expositions has been a growing field of scholarship since the mid-1980s. A germinal study of this field is Robert Rydell, *All the World's a Fair: Visions of Empire at American International Expositions, 1876–1916* (Chicago: University of Chicago Press, 1985). For an in-depth study of the relationship between the U.S. representation of Puerto Rico after 1898 and the visual rhetoric of imperialism, see Lanny Thompson, *Nuestra isla y su gente: la construcción del "otro" puertorriqueño en Our Islands and Their People* (Río

Piedras: Centro de Investigaciones Sociales y Departamento de Historia, Universidad de Puerto Rico, 1995). Thompson expands that study to the whole U.S. "imperial archipelago" and deepens it by studying the relation between visual and discursive representation of the colonial subject and the kind of governance established on each territory in his *Imperial Archipelago: Representation and Rule in the Insular Territories under U.S. Dominion after 1898.* Libia González analyzes U.S. photography and travelogues in Puerto Rico at the turn of the century in "La ilusión del paraíso: fotografías y relatos de viajeros sobre Puerto Rico," in *Los arcos de la memoria: el '98 de los pueblos puertorriqueños*, ed. Silvia Álvarez Curbelo, Mary Frances Gallart, Carmen I. Raffucci (San Juan: Asociación Puertorriqueña de historiadores, 1998), 273–304. Through a comparative approach that takes into account the U.S. imperial archipelago but focuses more closely on Puerto Rico, Jorge Duany examines the representation of the colonial subjects at the turn of the century in stereographs published by Underwood & Underwood, lantern slides from the collection of Helen Hamilton Gardener at the National Anthropological Archives of the Smithsonian Institution, the displays of the Pan-American Exposition of Buffalo in 1901, and the Louisiana Purchase Exposition in 1904, curated by anthropologists of the U.S. National Museum, now Smithsonian Institution. See Duany, *Puerto Rican Nation*, chapters two and four. For an analysis of the representation of Filipinos in the Pan-American Exposition of Buffalo and the Louisiana Purchase Exhibition, and the role of the Smithsonian Institution as a producer of colonial ethnographic knowledge, see Paul A. Kramer, *The Blood of Government: Race, Empire, the United States, and the Philippines* (Chapel Hill: University of North Carolina Press, 2006), esp. chapter four.

26. Preface, *Our Islands and Their People*, 1899, 1.

27. Esther Gabara, "Cannon and Camera: Photography and Colonialism in the Américas," in *English Language Notes,* 44, no. 2 (Fall/Winter 2006): 45–64.

28. Ibid.

29. Stephanie Syjuco's artistic practice does not revolve exclusively around the theme of colonialism. Other topics she frequently addresses include systems of exchange and circulation of knowledge and goods, the impact of technology on life, and craft aesthetics, among others. The renewed sense of urgency for exploring imperialism as a result of the 2016 presidential campaign was something Syjuco expressed. Stephanie Syjuco, Zoom interview with author, February 14, 2022.

30. "Stephanie Syjuco: Artist's Talk," moderated by Anne Goodyear, Bowdoin College, November 18, 2021, https://www.youtube.com/watch?v=Xyn6PNtTfeQ.

31. Syjuco, interview with author.

32. See Paul A. Kramer's essay "New Possessions: Colonial Curios, Trophies, Weapons, and Museum Collections from the Philippine-American War" in this volume, pp. 205–17.

33. The first objects and natural specimens from the Philippines that entered into Smithsonian collections were acquired during the United States South Seas Exploring Expedition, led by naval officer Charles Wilkes from 1838 to 1842. This expedition constituted an attempt from the United States as a budding nation to establish a stronger diplomatic presence in the Pacific and to position itself in the scientific community by joining the competition to explore the Arctic Circle and the Pacific. The expedition covered California's San Francisco Bay—still part of Mexico then—Manila, Singapore, the Fiji Islands, and the Cape of Good Hope, among other places. Wilkes's expedition yielded over 4,000 artifacts, which entered the collections of the Smithsonian in 1858, helping establish its scientific reputation. See Nathaniel Philbrick, "The Scientific Legacy of the U.S. Exploring Expedition," Smithsonian Institution Libraries Digital Collections, https://www.sil.si.edu/DigitalCollections/usexex/learn/Philbrick.htm

34. Syjuco, interview with author.

35. Photographs of unnamed Filipinos killed during the War of 1898 and the Philippine-American War, lying dead in trenches circulated widely in the United States in 1899 and are still accessible in historical archives around the country. The 1899 publication *Neely's Photographs: Fighting in the Philippines* is an infamous example of a book gathering disturbing graphic images of the Filipino victims of the war.

36. Stephanie Syjuco, email message to author, March 1, 2022.

37. Worcester's archive encompassed more than 15,000 ethnographic photographs, the majority of which were divided among the Bentley Historical Library at the University of Michigan in Ann Arbor; the Newberry Library and the Field Museum in Chicago, Illinois; and the Peabody Museum of Archaeology and Ethnology at Harvard University in Cambridge, Massachusetts. Mark Rice, *Dean Worcester's Fantasy Islands: Photography, Film, and the Colonial Philippines* (Ann Arbor: University of Michigan Press, 2014), 2–3. On Damián Domingo, see Florina H. Capistrano-Baker, "Trophies of Trade Collecting Nineteenth-Century Sino-Filipino Export Paintings," in *Archives of Asian Art* 67, no. 2 (October 2017): 237–56.

38. The 1889 expedition lasted two years and yielded a collection of three thousand birds, mammals, reptiles, butterflies, and ethnographic objects. See "Dean Conant Worcester Biography," *The Dean C. Worcester Photographic Collection at the University of Michigan, Museum of Anthropology*, https://webapps.lsa.umich.edu/umma/exhibits/Worcester%202012/biography.html.

39. Ibid.

40. Rice, *Dean Worcester's Fantasy Islands*, 1. Baldoz, *Third Asiatic Invasion,* 23.

41. Thompson, *Imperial Archipelago*, 121.

42. Rice, *Dean Worcester's Fantasy Islands*, 33. See also Gerald R. Gems, *Sport and the American*

Occupation of the Philippines: Bats, Balls, and Bayonets (Lanham, MD: Lexington Books, 2016), 112.

43. Maia Cruz Palileo, interview by Cheryl Sim in conjunction with *RELATIONS: la diaspora et la peinture*, Fondation PHI pour l'art contemporain, July 17, 2020, https://www.youtube.com/watch?v=pvwLMS3HXo8&t=261s.

44. For Palileo, the interest in understanding where they come from, "the motherland," is a motivation for their identity-based work. Maia Cruz Palileo, "Becoming the Moon," *In the Making: American Masters*, PBS, October 10, 2020, https://www.youtube.com/watch?v=ZHUWGOg0kxQ.

45. Ibid.

46. Maia Cruz Palileo, conversation with author during studio visit, September 19, 2019.

47. Ibid.

48. As a movement, "primitivism" emerged in the early 1900s and was fostered by European artists, such as Pablo Picasso, Maurice de Vlaminck, Henri Matisse, and André Derain, who championed a reinvigoration of Western art through motifs appropriated from the arts of Africa and Oceania, regions considered uncorrupted by European modernity. With his late nineteenth-century paintings of placid Tahitian landscapes and half-dressed figures, Gauguin was a forebear to these artists. Gauguin and his successors projected onto Africa and Oceania a Eurocentric vision of those regions as primitive, pure, and unbound by the insincere morals of bourgeois Western society. They believed that their appropriation of aesthetic elements from those "untouched" regions would transform European art and restore its vitality. Within the context of European colonialism at the turn of the century, the incorporation of Oceanian and African motifs into their art was an anticolonial gesture. However, it was one that was steeped in colonialism and exoticizing fantasies of the "other." See Mark Antliff and Patricia Leighten, "Primitivism," in *Critical Terms for Art History*, ed. Robert S. Nelson and Richard Shiff (Chicago: University of Chicago Press, 1996), 170–84. See also Patricia Leighten, "The White Peril and L'Art Nègre," *The Art Bulletin* 72, no. 4 (December 1990): 609–30.

49. Paul Gauguin spent two long sojourns in Tahiti, the first from 1891 to 1893 and the second from 1895 to 1901. From 1901 to 1903, he lived in the Marquesas Islands. See Colta Feller Ives, *The Lure of the Exotic: Gauguin in New York Collections* (New York: Metropolitan Museum of Art, 2002), 77–79; 139. Jean-François Staszak, "Primitivism and the Other: History of Art and Cultural Geography," *Geojournal* 60, no. 4 (2004): 353–64.

50. Elizabeth C. Childs, "The Colonial Lens: Gauguin, Primitivism, and Photography in the Fin de Siècle," in *Antimodernism and Artistic Experience*, ed. Lynda Jessup (Toronto: University of Toronto Press, 2001), 52.

51. Even during his time, Gauguin was the object of criticism by peers for his seemingly opportunistic appropriation of the ostensibly virtuous and pure cultures from outside Paris and other European metropolitan centers. Commenting on Gauguin's 1893 exhibition in Paris, after his first stay in Tahiti, Camille Pissarro wrote to his son: "He is always poaching on another's fields; today he is robbing from the savages of the South Sea Islands!" Camille Pissarro, *Camille Pissarro: Lettres à son fils Lucien* (Paris: Albin Michel, 1950), 126.

52. Staszak, "Primitivism and the Other," 353–64.

53. The oval shape of the seal references the CHamoru sling stone, the palm tree symbolizing sustenance, and a flying *proa* that served as the means of transportation of early CHamorus. The river meeting the sea in the design is a reference to Hagåtña River, and the distant cliff references Two Lovers' Point, where, according to legend, a forbidden romance led to the couple tying their hair together and jumping to their death. The seal is the centerpiece of Guam's flag, which is flown alongside the U.S. flag. It was first raised on July 4, 1918. Leslie Reynolds and Deniz Smith, "Guam Seal and Flag," *Guampedia*, https://www.guampedia.com/guam-seal-and-flag/.

54. Gisela McDaniel, Zoom interview with author, February 24, 2022.

55. This body of work was exhibited under the title *Manhaga Fu'una* at Pilar Corrias Gallery in London, from January 27 to February 26, 2022.

56. This excerpt was part of the sound component featured in *Manhaga Fu'una* at Pilar Corrias Gallery in London, from January 27 to February 26, 2022.

57. Ferdinand Magellan and his naval crew arrived in Guam on March 6, 1521, but the island was claimed by Miguel López de Legazpi for Spain in 1565. Robert F. Rogers, *Destiny's Landfall: A History of Guam*, rev. edition (Honolulu: University of Hawai'i Press, 2011), 47.

58. Between 1940 and 2000, the CHamorus went from comprising 90 percent to 40 percent of the population. See Untalan, "CHamoru migration to the United States."

59. Jonathan K. Noel, Sara Namazi, and Robert L. Haddock, "Disparities in Infant Mortality Due to Congenital Anomalies on Guam," *Hawai'i Journal of Medicine and Public Health* 74, no. 12 (December 2015): 397–402.

60. Frantz Fanon, *Black Skin, White Masks*, trans. Richard Philcox (New York: Grove Press, 2008).

61. Miguel Luciano, phone conversation with author, February 2, 2022.

62. For a recount of the U.S. invasion on July 25, 1898, see "On the Verge of Sovereignty: Cuba and Puerto Rico at the Turn of the Twentieth-Century," in this catalogue, pp. 106–11. In 1998, at the demonstration in Guánica, Lolita Lebrón was a headlining speaker. Lebrón was then known as a former political prisoner, having spent twenty-five years in prison for the 1954 armed attack against Congress to highlight Puerto Rico's colonial situation.

63. The Associated Press, "Navy Attributes Fatal Bombing to Mistakes," *New York Times*, August 3,

1999, https://www.nytimes.com/1999/08/03/us/navy-attributes-fatal-bombing-to-mistakes.html. After three years of protests and civil disobedience that garnered international support, 70 percent of Puerto Ricans voted in a referendum for the immediate departure of the Navy from Vieques, instead of accepting President Bill Clinton's offer to prolong the Navy's stay in exchange for $90 million in economic incentives. In 2003 President George W. Bush ordered the immediate halt of military exercises and the closing of the two naval bases on the island. "Puerto Ricans Force United States Navy Out of Vieques Island, 1999–2003," *Global Non-violent Action Database*, Swarthmore College, https://nvdatabase.swarthmore.edu/content/puerto-ricans-force-united-states-navy-out-vieques-island-1999-2003.

64. Luciano, cited in Don Rauf, *Schwinn: The Best Present Ever* (Lanham, MD: Rowman and Littlefield, 2007), 129.

65. See Suset Laboy, "Meet Felicitas 'La Prieta' Mendez: Pioneer in Struggles for Desegregation," *Centro Voices e-Magazine,* Center for Puerto Rican Studies, February 4, 2015, https://centropr-archive.hunter.cuny.edu/centrovoices/chronicles/meet-felicitas-la-prieta-mendez-pioneer-struggles-desegregation.

66. Felícita Méndez was born Felícita Gómez Martínez. It is unclear why, during her lifetime, Felícita began to be referred to as Felícitas, with an "s" at the end. In this essay, I refer to her as Felícita to correspond with how her name appears in Luciano's artwork.

67. The labor shortages were caused by the 1924 Immigration Act, which limited the annual number of immigrants of any nationality and excluded immigrants from Asia, except Filipinos, who were deemed U.S. colonial subjects. Choosing 1890 as the base year for the quotas drastically reduced the entry of immigrants from Southern and Eastern Europe, including Jews. See "The Immigration Act of 1924 (The Johnson-Reed Act)," Office of the Historian, https://history.state.gov/milestones/1921-1936/immigration-act. See also Elliott Young, "Beyond Borders: Remote Control and the Continuing Legacy of Racism in Immigration Legislation," in *A Nation of Immigrants Reconsidered: US Society in an Age of Restriction 1924–1965*, ed. Magdalena Marinari, Madeline Y. Hsu, and María Cristina García (Chicago: University of Illinois Press, 2019), 28–44. Workers traditionally employed by the agricultural sector were funneled toward more profitable urban industries. The Arizona Cotton Growers Association worked with the U.S. Bureau of Insular Affairs to recruit Puerto Ricans to do field work. Their situation as colonial U.S. citizens made them a seemingly convenient work force. See Jennifer McCormick and César Ayala, "Felícita 'La Prieta' Méndez (1916–1998) and the End of Latino School Segregation in California," *Centro Journal* 19, no. 2 (Fall 2007): 13–35.

68. Refusing to work under such conditions, the laborers were quartered in the State Fairgrounds in Phoenix, without shelter or sufficient food, as a coercion mechanism. See George Perry, "Imported Porto Rican Laborers Suffering at Hands of Arizona Cotton Growers' Combine," *Pittsburgh Courier*, October 9, 1926, 13; see also Linda C. Noël, "Strange Bedfellows: American Growers and Mexican Immigrants in the United States, 1926–1930," *Monde(s)* 1, no. 3 (2013): 213–35.

69. McCormick and Ayala, "Felícita 'La Prieta' Méndez," 21.

70. Ibid., 16.

71. McCormick and Ayala document how Puerto Ricans working in the cotton fields of Arizona were racialized as "negroes," while in California, they were racialized as "Mexicans" and assigned the negative stereotypes that academic and legal discourse used to keep African American, Mexicans, and Mexican American populations at the bottom of the social and economic ladder. The authors propose that this experience was formative in Felícita's shaping of her multiracial rationale for defending the equal right to education for children of all races. McCormick and Ayala, "Felícita 'La Prieta' Méndez,"13–35.

72. Ibid., 27.

73. Méndez v. Westminster School Dist., 64 F. Supp. 544, 549 (C.D.Cal.1946), cited in McCormick and Ayala, "Felícita 'La Prieta' Méndez," 28.

74. Ed Morales, "Classic Schwinn Bike Helps Tell a Tale of Puerto Rican Migrants," *New York Daily News*, October 19, 2011, https://www.nydailynews.com/latino/classic-schwinn-bike-helps-tale-puerto-rican-migrants-article-1.964119.

75. The title *Freedom Rider Vest* symbolically ties Felícita Méndez's struggle to the African American and white activists who, in 1961, risked their lives and participated in Freedom Rides through the bus system of the American South to protest racial segregation in bus terminals. The Freedom Rides were organized by the Congress of Racial Equality (CORE).

76. For a study of national galleries as institutions of nation-building and carriers of political and cultural ideologies, see Simon Knell, *National Galleries: The Art of Making Nations* (London: Routledge, 2016).

77. The missions of the National Portrait Gallery in London, the National Portrait Gallery of Australia, the National Portrait Gallery of Scotland, and the National Portrait Gallery of the Smithsonian Institution, as stated on their websites, emphasize the potential for portraiture to further understanding national history and identity. See https://www.npg.org.uk/about/organisation/; https://www.portrait.gov.au/portraits/; https://www.portrait.gov.au; https://www.nationalgalleries.org/visit/scottish-national-portrait-gallery#the-gallery; https://npg.si.edu.

Bibliography

Abbot, Willis J. *Blue Jackets of '98: A History of the Spanish-American War*. New York: Dodd, Mead, and Company, 1910.

Abellán, José Luis. *El 98 cien años después*. Madrid: Alderabán, 2000.

Abinales, P. N., and Donna J. Amoroso. *State and Society in the Philippines*. Second edition. Lanham, MD: Rowman and Littlefield Publishers, 2017.

Abinales, Patricio N. *Making Mindanao: Cotabato and Davao in the Formation of the Philippine Nation-State*. Quezon City, Philippines: Ateneo de Manila University Press, 2000.

Acosta, Luz Merino et al., eds. *Menocal y Romañach: Maestros cubanos del cambio de siglo*. Salamanca, Spain: Gráficas Varona, S.A., 2003.

Agoncillo, Teodoro A., and Oscar M. Alfonso. *History of the Filipino People*. Quezon City, Philippines: Malaya Books, 1967.

Aguilar, Filomeno V. "The 'Pacto de Sangre' in the Late Nineteenth-Century Nationalist Emplotment of Philippine History." *Philippine Studies* 58, no. 1/2 (2010).

Aguinaldo, Emilio. *My Memoirs*. Translated by Luz Colendrino-Bucu. Manila, 1967.

Ahmad, Diana L. "Two Captains, Two Regimes: Benjamin Franklin Tilley and Richard Phillips Leary, America's Pacific Island Commanders, 1899–1901." *International Journal of Naval History* 10, no. 1 (October 2013).

Akiboh, Alvita. "Pocket-Sized Imperialism: U.S. Designs on Colonial Currency." *Diplomatic History* 41, no. 5 (November 2017): 874–902.

Alger, Russell Alexander. *The Spanish-American War*. New York: Harper and Bros., 1901.

Allen, Charles H. *First Annual Report of Charles H. Allen, Governor of Porto Rico: Covering the Period from May 1, 1900, to May 1, 1901*. San Juan: Ediciones Puerto, 2005.

Allen, Helena G. *The Betrayal of Liliuokalani: Last Queen of Hawaii, 1838–1917*. Honolulu: Mutual Publishing, 1982.

Allendesalazar, José Manuel. *El 98 de los americanos*. Madrid: Ministerio de Asuntos Exteriores, 1997.

Almenares, Bárbara Omaira Argüelles. "Armando García Menocal: Contribuciones a la imagen pictórica de Antonio Maceo y al tema histórico de la Guerra de independencia (1895–1915)." In *Maceo en el tiempo: acción, pensamiento y entorno histórico*, edited by Ibarra Guitart and Jorge Renato. Havana: Editorial de Ciencias Sociales, 2015.

Álvarez Curbelo, Silvia, Mary Frances Gallart, and Carmen I. Raffucci, eds. *Los arcos de la memoria: el '98 en los pueblos puertorriqueños*. San Juan: Universidad de Puerto Rico, Recinto de Río Piedras, 1998.

Álvarez Curbelo, Silvia, "Caribbean Siblings: Sisterly Affinities and Differences between Cuba and Puerto Rico in the Nineteenth Century." In *The Routledge Hispanic Studies Companion to Nineteenth Century*

Spain, edited by Yolanda Martínez San Miguel and Santa Arias, 4–18. London: Routledge, 2022.

——. *Un país del porvenir: el afán de modernidad en Puerto Rico.* San Juan: Ediciones Callejón, 2001.

Amorsolo, Fernando, and Santiago Albano Pilar. *Fernando Amorsolo Seven-Museum Exhibition.* Rizal, Philippines: CRIBS Foundation, 2008.

Anderson, Benedict. *The Age of Globalization: Anarchists and the Anticolonial Imagination.* New York: Verso, 2013.

Andrew, John A. "Betsey Stockton: Stranger in a Strange Land." *Journal of Presbyterian History* 52, no. 2 (Summer 1974): 157–66.

Apostol, Gina. *Insurrecto.* New York: Soho Press, 2018.

Aragunde, Rafael. *Hostos: ideólogo inofensivo y moralista problemático.* Hato Rey, Puerto Rico: Publicaciones Puertorriqueñas, 1998.

Argenter, José Miró. "Mal tiempo." In *Crónicas de la guerra.* Havana: Editorial Letras Cubanas, 1981.

Arista, Noelani. *The Kingdom and the Republic: Sovereign Hawaiʻi and the Early United States.* Philadelphia: University of Pennsylvania Press, 2019.

——. "Moʻolelo and Mana: The Transmission of Hawaiian History from Hawaiʻi to the United States, 1836–1843." *Journal of the Early Republic* 38, no. 3 (Fall 2018): 415–43.

Armáiz, Jorge L. Crespo. "De la prosperidad a la resistencia: La representación de Puerto Rico en la revista *National Geographic* (1898–2003)." *Caribbean Studies* 42, no. 1 (January–June, 2014): 3–43.

Arndt, Matthias, ed. *Wasak! Filipino Art Today.* Berlin: Distanz, 2016.

Ashburn, Percy Moreau. *The Elements of Military Hygiene: Especially Arranged for Officers and Men of the Line.* Boston: Houghton Mifflin, 1909.

Auffant Vázquez, Vivian. *La liga de patriotas puertorriqueños de Eugenio María de Hostos.* San Juan: Publicaciones Gaviota, 2012.

Ayala, César J. *American Sugar Kingdom: The Plantation Economy of the Spanish Caribbean, 1898–1934.* Chapel Hill: University of North Carolina Press, 1999.

Ayala, César J., and Rafael Bernabe. *Puerto Rico in the American Century: A History Since 1898.* Chapel Hill: University of North Carolina Press, 2007.

Bahamonde Magro, Angel, and José G. Cayuela Fernández. *Hacer las Américas: las Elites Coloniales Españolas en el siglo XIX.* Madrid: Alianza Ed., 1992.

Balce, Nerissa S. *Body Parts of Empire: Visual Abjection, Filipino Images, and the American Archive.* Ann Arbor: University of Michigan Press, 2016.

Baldoz, Rick. *The Third Asiatic Invasion: Empire and Migration in Filipino America 1898–1946.* New York: New York University Press, 2011.

——. "The Racial Vectors of Empire: Classification and Competing Master Narratives in the Colonial Philippines." *Du Bois Review* 5, no. 1 (2008): 69–94.

Baldoz, Rick, and César Ayala, "The Bordering of America: Colonialism and Citizenship in the Philippines and Puerto Rico." *Centro Journal* 25, no. 1 (Spring 2013): 76–105.

Barrenechea, Francisco J. *Campeche, Oller, Rodón: tres siglos de pintura puertorriqueña.* San Juan: Instituto de Cultura Puertorriqueña, 1992.

Basson, Lauren. "Fit for Annexation but Unfit to Vote? Debating Hawaiian Suffrage Qualifications at the Turn of the Twentieth Century." *Social Science History* 29, no. 4 (Winter 2005): 575–98.

Bataller, Carmen Alborgh, and José Martí. *José Martí: obra y vida.* Madrid: Ministerio de Cultura, 1995.

Bateman, Fiona, and Lionel Pilkington, eds. *Studies in Settler Colonialism: Politics, Identity and Culture.* London: Palgrave MacMillan, 2011.

Bautista, Jay Giovanni, Lourd Ernest de Verya, Patrick Flores, Tessa Maria Guazon, and Alice Guillermo. *Alfredo Esquillo.* Makati City, Philippines: Eskinita Art Gallery, 2018.

Beadles, John A. "The Debate in the United States Concerning Philippine Independence, 1912–1916." *Philippine Studies* 16, no. 3 (July 1968): 421–41.

Bejel, Emilio. *José Martí: Images of Memory and Mourning.* London: Palgrave McMillan, 2012.

Beisner, Robert L. *Twelve against Empire: The Anti-Imperialists, 1898–1900.* New York: McGraw-Hill, 1968.

Belmont, Perry. *Republic or Empire?* New York City: Allied Printing Trades Council, 1900.

Benítez, Marimar. *Francisco Oller un realista del Impresionismo: Exposición organizada por el Museo de Arte de Ponce en conmemoración del sesquicentenario del natalicio del pintor puertorriqueño Francisco Oller, 1833–1917.* Ponce, Puerto Rico: Museo de Arte de Ponce, 1983.

Benitez-Johannot, Purissima, and Joselina Cruz. *Unfolding Half a Century: The López Memorial Museum & Library.* Pasig City, Philippines: Eugenio López Foundation, 2009.

Benítez Rojo, Antonio. *The Repeating Island: The Caribbean and the Postmodern Perspective.* Durham, NC: Duke University Press, 1992.

Benson, Lee. "The Historical Background of Turner's Frontier Essay." *Agricultural History* 25, no. 2 (April 1951): 59–82.

Berman, Avis, ed. *William Glackens.* New York: Skira Rizzoli; Philadelphia: Barnes Foundation, 2014.

Betances, Ramón Emeterio, and Félix Ojeda Reyes. *La manigua en París: Correspondencia diplomática de Betances.* San Juan de Puerto Rico: Centro de Estudios Avanzados de Puerto Rico y El Caribe en colaboración con el Centro de Estudios Puertorriqueños. Hunter College, City University of New York, 1984.

Biaggi, Ingrid M. Vila. "El país desfigurado: una mirada a los problemas estructurales que impiden el progreso congruente y sustentable de Puerto Rico." *Revista Jurídica UPR* 85, no. 3 (2016): 769–817.

Bigelow, Poultney. "A Yankee in Spain: On the Spanish Frontier." *Harper's Weekly* 42, no. 2160 (May 14, 1898): 465–70.

Bjork, Katherine. *Prairie Imperialists: The Indian Country Origins of American Empire.* Philadelphia: University of Pennsylvania Press, 2019.

Blackford, Mansel. "Guam, the Philippines, and American Samoa." In *Pathways to the Present: U.S. Development and its Consequences in the Pacific*, 166–202. Honolulu: University of Hawai'i Press, 2007.

Blasco Ibáñez, Vicente L. *Artículos Contra la Guerra de Cuba*. Valencia, Spain: León Roca, 1978.

Blow, Michael. *A Ship to Remember: The* Maine *and the Spanish-American War*. New York: William Morrow and Company, 1992.

Bonsal, Stephen. "The Fight for Santiago: The Account of an Eye-Witness." *McClure's Magazine* 11, no. 6 (October 1898): 499–518.

Boone, Mary Elizabeth. *Vistas de España: American Views of Art and Life in Spain, 1860–1914*. New Haven, CT: Yale University Press, 2007.

———. *"The Spanish Element in Our Nationality": Spain and America at the World's Fairs and Centennial Celebrations, 1876–1915*. University Park: Penn State University Press, 2019.

Bosch, Juan. *Hostos, el sembrador*. Santo Domingo, Dominican Republic: Ediciones Fundación, 2013.

Boza, Bernabé. *Mi diario de la guerra desde Baire hasta la intervención americana*. Havana: La Propagandista, 1900.

Bradford, James C., ed. *Crucible of Empire: The Spanish-American War and Its Aftermath*. Annapolis, MD: Naval Institute Press, 1993.

Brannen, Daniel E., Julie Carnagie, and Allison McNeill. *Spanish-American War*. Detroit, MI: UXL, 2003.

Breitbart, Eric. *A World on Display: Photographs from the St. Louis World's Fair, 1904*. Albuquerque: University of New Mexico Press, 1997.

Bretos, Miguel A. "Imaging Cuba under the American Flag: Charles Edward Doty in Havana, 1899–1902." *Journal of Decorative and Propaganda Arts* 22 (1996): 82–103.

———. *Matanzas: The Cuba Nobody Knows*. Gainesville: University Press of Florida, 2010.

Briggs, Laura. *Reproducing Empire: Race, Sex, Science, and U.S. Imperialism in Puerto Rico*. Berkeley: University of California Press, 2003.

Brinton, Christian. *Catalogue of Paintings by Ignacio Zuloaga: Exhibited by the Hispanic Society of America March 21 to April 11, 1909*. New York: Hispanic Society of America, 1909.

Brody, David. *Visualizing American Empire: Orientalism and Imperialism in the Philippines*. Chicago: University of Chicago Press, 2010.

Brown, Steve. "Archaeology of Brutal Encounter: Heritage and Bomb Testing on Bikini Atoll, Republic of the Marshall Islands." *Archaeology in Oceania* 48, no. 1 (April 2013): 26–39.

Burnett, Christina Duffy, and Burke Marshall. *Foreign in a Domestic Sense: Puerto Rico, American Expansion, and the Constitution*. Durham, NC: Duke University Press, 2001.

Burns, Adam D. "Retentionist in Chief: William Howard Taft and the Question of Philippine Independence, 1912–1916." *Philippine Studies: Historical & Ethnographic Viewpoints* 61, no. 2 (June 2013): 163–92.

Cabrera Salcedo, Lizette. *Reflejos de la historia de Puerto Rico en el arte: 1751–1950*. Río Piedras, Puerto Rico: Museo de Historia, Antropología y Arte, 2015.

Campomanes, Oscar V. "Casualty Figures of the American Soldier and the Other: Post-1898 Allegories of Imperial Nation-Building as "Love and War." In *Vestiges of War: The Philippine-American War and the Aftermath of an Imperial Dream, 1899–1999*, edited by Angel Velasco Shaw and Luis H. Francia, 134–62. New York: New York University Press, 2004.

———. "Images of Filipino Racialization in the Anthropological Laboratories of the American Empire: The Case of Daniel Folkmar." *PMLA* 123, no. 5 (October 2008): 1629–99.

———. "Two Bulosan Letters from America." *Philippine Studies* 39, no. 3 (Third Quarter 1991): 337–50.

Campomanes, Oscar V., and Todd S. Gernes. "Carlos Bulosan and the Act of Writing." *Philippine Studies* 40, no. 1 (First Quarter 1992): 68–82.

Capistrano-Baker, Florina H. "Trophies of Trade: Collecting Nineteenth-Century Sino-Filipino Export Paintings." *Archives of Asian Art* 67, no. 2 (October 2017): 237–56.

———. "Whither Art History? Whither Art History in the Non-Western World: Exploring the Other('s) Art Histories." *Art Bulletin* 97, no. 3 (September 2015): 246–57.

Capistrano-Baker, Florina H., Antonia C. Ortigas, Mabi David, and Leslie Espino. *Pioneers of Philippine Art*. Makati City, Philippines: Ayala Foundation, 2006.

Capozzola, Christopher. *Bound by War: How the United States and the Philippines Built America's First Pacific Century*. New York: Basic Books, 2020.

Cariño, José María Ancheta. *Álbum: Islas Filipinas, 1663–1888*. Manila: Ars mundi Philippinae, 2004.

Carlstrom, Oscar E. "The Spanish-American War." *Journal of the Illinois State Historical Society (1908–1984)* 16, no. 1/2 (April–July 1923): 104–10.

Caron, James E. "The Blessings of Civilization: Mark Twain's Anti-Imperialism and the Annexation of the Hawaiian Islands." *The Mark Twain Annual*, no. 6 (2008): 51–63.

Caronan, Faye C. "Colonial Consumption and Colonial Hierarchies in Representations of Philippine and Puerto Rican Tourism." *Philippine Studies* 53, no. 1 (2005): 32–58.

Carpenter, Brian B., Donald H. Dyal, and Mark A. Thomas, *Historical Dictionary of the Spanish-American War*. Westport, CT: Greenwood Press, 1996.

Casanova de Villaverde, Emilia. *Apuntes biográficos de Emilia Casanova de Villaverde*. New York, 1874.

Caswell, Lucy Shelton. "Drawing Swords: War in American Editorial Cartoons." *American Journalism* 21, no. 2 (Spring 2004): 13–45.

Cayuela Fernández, José G. *España en Cuba: Final de siglo*. Zaragoza, Spain: Institución Fernando el Católico, 2000.

Chang, David A. *The World and All the Things upon It: Native Hawaiian Geographies of Exploration*. Minneapolis: University of Minnesota Press, 2016.

Chang, Williamson. "Darkness Over Hawaii: The Annexation Myth Is the Greatest Obstacle to

Progress." *Asian-Pacific Law & Policy Journal* 16, no. 2 (Spring 2015): 70–115.

———. "'A Rope of Sand': A Documentary History of the Failure of the United States to Annex the Hawaiian Islands." SYS Law 530-006. https://kipdf.com/a-rope-of-sand-a-documentary-history-of-the-failure-of-the-united-states-to-anne_5ac71fe61723dd349641765c.html.

———. "Hawai'i's Ceded Lands: The Ongoing Quest for Justice in Hawai'i," William S. Richardson School of Law, University of Hawai'i at Manoa, Faculty Lecture Series, October 1, 2014. https://www.academia.edu/62576921/Hawaii_s_Ceded_Lands_and_the_Ongoing_Quest_for_Justice_in_Hawai_i.

Chaar-Pérez, Kahlila. "'The Antilles for the Sons of the Antilles': On Translating Ramón Emeterio Betances." *Small Axe* 25, no. 3 (November 2021): 160–165.

———. "'A Revolution of Love': Ramón Emeterio Betances, Anténor Firmin, and Affective Communities in the Caribbean." *The Global South* 7, no. 2 (Fall 2013): 11–36.

Cirillo, Vincent J. *Bullets and Bacilli: The Spanish-American War and Military Medicine.* New Brunswick, NJ: Rutgers University Press, 2003.

Clark, John. *The Asian Modern.* University Park: Penn State University Press, 2021.

Coffman, Tom. *Nation Within: The History of the American Occupation of Hawai'i.* Durham, NC: Duke University Press, 2016.

Coll, Edna. *Cayetano Coll y Toste: síntesis de estímulos humanos.* Río Piedras: Editorial Universitaria, Universidad de Puerto Rico, 1970.

Comité del Sesquicentenario de Eugenio Maria Hostos. *Imágenes de Hostos a través del tiempo: exposición itinerante en conmemoración del ciento cincuenta aniversario de su natalicio.* Recinto de Rio Piedras: Museo de la Universidad de Puerto Rico, 1988.

Constantino, Renato, and Letizia R. Constantino. *The Philippines: A Past Revisited.* Quezon City, Philippines: Tala Publishing Services, 1975.

Corazon, Villareal, ed. *Back to the Future: Perspectives on the Thomasite Legacy to Philippine Education.* Manila: American Studies Association of the Philippines, 2003.

Cordoví Núñez, Yoel. *Máximo Gómez: utopía y realidad de una República.* Havana: Editorial Historia, 2014

Corry, John A. *1898: Prelude to a Century.* New York: Fordham University Press, 1998.

Coston, William Hillary. *The Spanish-American War Volunteer: Ninth United States Volunteer Infantry.* Harrisburg, PA: Mount Pleasant Printery, 1899.

Crawford, Michael J., Mark L. Hayes, and Michael D. Sessions. *The Spanish-American War: Historical Overview and Select Bibliography.* Washington, DC: Naval Historical Center, Dept. of the Navy, 1998.

Cueto, Emilio, and Julio Larramendi. *Inspired by Cuba!: A Survey of Cuba-Themed Ceramics.* Gainesville: University Press of Florida, 2018.

Cullen, Deborah, and Elvis Fuentes, eds. *Caribbean: Art at the Crossroads of the World.* New Haven, CT: Yale University Press, 2012.

Cullinane, Michael. *Illustrado Politics: Filipino Elite Responses to American Rule, 1898–1908.* Quezon City, Philippines: Ateneo de Manila University Press, 2003.

Curtis, Ariana A. "Becoming More and More Panamanian: Contemporary Constructions of West Indian Identity in Urban Panama," PhD diss. American University, 2012.

Davis, Charles A., Bess Davis, and Walker B. Davis. *Charles A. Davis Papers, 1854–1901.* Newberry Library, Chicago.

De las Casas, Bartolomé. *A Brief Account of the Destruction of the Indies.* 1552. Project Gutenberg eBook, 2007.

De Hostos, Eugenio Carlos. *Eugenio María de Hostos: Promoter of Pan Americanism.* Madrid: Imprenta Litografía y Encuadernación Juan Bravo, 1954.

De Olivares, José, and William Smith Brian. *Our Islands and Their People as Seen with Camera and Pencil.* St. Louis: Thompson Publishing, 1899.

del Valle, Teresa. *The Importance of the Manila Islands to Spain at the Beginning of the Nineteenth Century.* Mangilao: University of Guam, 1991.

DeLisle, Christine Taitano. *Placental Politics: CHamoru Women, White Womanhood, and Indigeneity under U.S. Colonialism in Guam.* Chapel Hill: University of North Carolina Press, 2022.

Despierto, Juan Pando. *El Sueño de Ultramar.* Madrid: Ministerio de Educación y Cultura, Biblioteca Nacional, 1998.

DeTemple, Jill. "Singing the *Maine*: The Popular Image of Cuba in Sheet Music of the Spanish-American War." *The Historian* 63, no. 4 (Summer 2001): 715–29.

Devine, Michael J. "John W. Foster and the Struggle for the Annexation of Hawaii." *Pacific Historical Review* 46, no. 1 (February 1977): 29–50.

Diamond, Heather A. *American Aloha: Cultural Tourism and Negotiation of Tradition.* Honolulu: University of Hawai'i Press, 2008.

Díaz, José O. "Puerto Rico, the United States, and the 1993 Referendum on Political Status." *Latin American Research Review* 30, no. 1 (1995): 203–11.

Díaz Quiñonez, Arcadio. *El arte de bregar.* San Juan: Ediciones Callejón, 2000.

———. *Once tesis sobre un crimen de 1899.* San Juan: Luscinia C.E., 2021.

Diccionario Enciclopédico de Historia Militar de Cuba, Parte Uno (1510–1898), Volume II. Havana: Ediciones Verde Olivo, 2003.

Díez García, José Luis. *Cánovas y la Restauración.* Madrid: Centro Cultural del Conde Duque, 1997.

Dphrepaulezz, Omar H. "Genesis of Genocide? Leonard Wood, Theodore Roosevelt and the White Man's Empire in the Southern Philippines." *Theory in Action* 9, no. 4 (October 2016): 65–89.

Drinnon, Richard. *Facing West: The Metaphysics of Indian-Hating and Empire Building.* Norman: University of Oklahoma Press, 1997.

Driver, Marjorie G., and Omaira Brunal-Perry. *Chronicle of the Mariana Islands: Recorded in the Agaña Parish Church 1846–1899.* Mangilao: University of Guam, 1998.

Duany, Jorge. *The Puerto Rican Nation on the Move: Identities on the Island and in the United States.* Chapel Hill: University of North Carolina Press, 2002.

———. *Puerto Rico: What Everyone Needs to Know.* Oxford: Oxford University Press, 2017.

Duany, Jorge, ed. *Picturing Cuba: Art, Culture, and Identity on the Island and in the Diaspora.* Gainesville: University of Florida Press, 2019.

Dye, Ryan D. "Irish American Ambivalence toward the Spanish-American War." *New Hibernia Review* 11, no. 3 (Autumn 2007): 98–113.

Eblen, Jack Ericson. *The First and Second United States Empires: Governors and Territorial Government, 1784–1912.* Pittsburgh: University of Pittsburgh Press, 1968.

Eder, James F. "The Future of Indigenous Peoples in the Philippines: Sources of Cohesion, Forms of Difference." *Philippine Quarterly of Culture and Society* 41, no. 3/4 (September/December 2013): 273–94.

Elorza, Antonio, and Elena Hernández Sandoica. *La Guerra de Cuba (1895–1898): historia política de una derrota colonial.* Madrid: Alianza, 1998.

Erman, Sam. *Almost Citizens: Puerto Rico, the U.S. Constitution, and Empire.* New York: Cambridge University Press, 2019.

———. "Meanings of Citizenship in the U.S. Empire: Puerto Rico, Isabel González, and the Supreme Court, 1898–1905." *Journal of American Ethnic History* 27, no. 4 (Summer 2008): 5–33.

Etemad, Bouda. *Possessing the World: Taking the Measurements of Colonisation from the 18th to the 20th Century.* Translated by Andrene Everson. New York: Berghahn Books, 2007.

Eugenio López Foundation. *A Guide to Luna and Hidalgo Paintings in the López Memorial Museum.* Pasay City, Philippines: Eugenio López Foundation, 1979.

Farrell, Don A. *The Pictorial History of Guam: The Americanization, 1898–1918.* Edited by Phyllis Koontz. Tamuning, Guam: Micronesian Productions, 1986.

Farrell, John T. "An Abandoned Approach to Philippine History: John R. M. Taylor and the Philippine Insurrection Records." *The Catholic Historical Review* 39, no. 4 (January 1954): 385–407.

Fee, Mary H. *A Woman's Impressions of the Philippines.* Chicago: A. C. McClurg and Company, 1910.

Fermin, Jose D. *1904 World's Fair: The Filipino Experience.* Quezon City: University of the Philippines Press, 2004.

Ferrer, Ada. *Insurgent Cuba: Race, Nation, and Revolution, 1868–1898.* Chapel Hill: University of North Carolina Press, 1999.

———. *Cuba: An American History.* New York: Scribner, 2021.

Feuer, A. B. *The Santiago Campaign of 1898: A Soldier's View of the Spanish-American War.* London: Praeger, 1993.

———. "The Sinking of the *Merrimac* in Santiago Bay." In *The Spanish-American War at Sea: Naval Action in the Atlantic.* Westport, CT: Praeger, 1995.

Field, Ron. *Spanish-American War, 1898.* London: Brassey's, 1998.

Finaldi, Gabriele et al. *Sorolla: Spanish Master of Light.* New Haven, CT: Yale University Press, 2019.

Fisher, Louis. "Destruction of the *Maine* (1898)." The Law Library of Congress, 2009. http://www.loufisher.org/docs/wi/434.pdf.

Fojas, Camilla, and Rudy P. Guevarra, eds. *Transnational Crossroads: Remapping the Americas and the Pacific.* Lincoln: University of Nebraska Press, 2012.

Foner, Philip S. *Antonio Maceo: "The Bronze Titan" of Cuba's Struggle for Independence.* New York: Monthly Review Press, 1977.

Font, Mauricio, and Alfonso Quiroz, eds. *The Cuban Republic and José Martí: Reception and Use of a National Symbol.* Lanham, MD: Lexington Books, 2006.

Francia, Luis. *A History of the Philippines: From Indios bravos to Filipinos.* New York: Overlook Press, 2014.

Fuchs, Miriam. "The Diaries of Queen Lili'uokalani." *Profession* (1995): 38–40.

Fujikane, Candace, and Jonathan Y. Okamura, eds. *Asian Settler Colonialism: from Local Governance to the Habits of Everyday Life in Hawaii.* Honolulu: University of Hawai'i Press, 2009.

Fulton, Robert A. *Moroland: The History of Uncle Sam and the Moros, 1899–1920.* Bend, OR: Tumalo Creek Press, 2007.

Fundación la Caixa. *Exposición: España fin de siglo 1898.* Barcelona: Fundación la Caixa, 1997.

Gabara, Esther. "'Cannon and Camera'—Photography and Colonialism in the Americas." *English Language Notes* 44, no. 2 (September 2006): 45–64.

Gannon, Barbara A. "'They Call Themselves Veterans:' Civil War and Spanish War Veterans and the Complexities of Veteranhood." *Journal of the Civil War Era* 5, no. 4 (December 2015): 528–50.

García Leduc, José Manuel. *Apuntes para una historia breve de Puerto Rico.* San Juan: Ediciones Isla Negra, 2003.

García Mora, Luis Miguel, Consuelo Naranjo Orovio, and Miguel Ángel Puig-Samper. *La nación soñada: Cuba, Puerto Rico y Filipinas ante el 98: actas del congreso internacional celebrado en Aranjuez del 24 al 28 de abril de 1995.* Madrid: Doce Calles, 1996.

Gates, John M. "War-Related Deaths in the Philippines, 1898–1902." *Pacific Historical Review* 53, no. 3 (August 1984): 367–78.

Gatewood, Willard B. *"Smoked Yankees" and the Struggle for Empire: Letters from Negro Soldiers, 1898–1902.* Fayetteville: University of Arkansas Press, 1987.

———. *Black Americans and the White Man's Burden, 1898–1903.* Champaign: University of Illinois Press, 1975.

Gelpí, Gustavo A. *The Constitutional Evolution of Puerto Rico and Other U.S. Territories (1898–Present).* San Juan: Inter American University of Puerto Rico, 2017.

Gerdts, Abigail Booth, and Lloyd Goodrich, eds. *Record of Works by Winslow Homer*. New York: Spanierman Gallery, 2005.

Geissler, Suzanne. *God and Sea Power: The Influence of Religion on Alfred Thayer Mahan*. Annapolis, MD: Naval Institute Press, 2015.

Gessner, Ingrid. "Epidemic Iconographies: Toward a Disease Aesthetics of the Destructive Sublime." *American Studies* 58, no. 4 (2013): 559–82.

Gilmore, N. Ray. "Mexico and the Spanish-American War." *Hispanic American Historical Review* 43, no. 4 (November 1963): 511–25.

Gleijeses, Piero. "1898: The Opposition to the Spanish-American War." *Journal of Latin American Studies* 35, no. 4 (November 2003): 681–719.

Go, Julian, and Anne L. Foster. *The American Colonial State in the Philippines*. Durham, NC: Duke University Press, 2003.

Gobierno de España. *Constitución colonial de las islas de Cuba y Puerto Rico, y leyes complementarias del régimen autonómico establecido por los Reales decretos de 25 de noviembre de 1897*. Havana: Imprenta del Gobierno y Capitanía General, 1897.

Goldstein, Alyosha, ed. *Formations of United States Colonialism*. Durham, NC: Duke University Press, 2014.

Gómez, Luis Ángel Sánchez. *Un imperio en la vitrina: el colonialismo español en el Pacífico y la Exposición de Filipinas de 1887*. Madrid: Consejo Superior de Investigaciones Científicas, 2003.

González, Juan. *Harvest of Empire: A History of Latinos in America*. New York: Viking, 2000.

González, Libia M. "La ilusión del paraíso: fotografías y relatos de viajeros sobre Puerto Rico." In *Los arcos de la memoria: el '98 de los pueblos puertorriqueños*, edited by Silvia Álvarez Curbelo, Mary Frances Gallart, and Carmen I. Raffucci, 273–304. San Juan: Asociación Puertorriqueña de historiadores, 1998.

Gonzalves, Theodore S., and Roderick N. Labrador. *Filipinos in Hawai'i*. Charleston, SC: Arcadia Publishing, 2011.

Gonzalves, Theodore S. *The Day the Dancers Stayed: Performing in the Filipino/American Diaspora*. Philadelphia: Temple University Press, 2009.

Gonschor, Lorenz. *A Power in the World: The Hawaiian Kingdom in Oceania*. Honolulu: University of Hawai'i Press, 2019.

Goodrich, Lloyd. *Winslow Homer*. New York: Whitney Museum of American Art; Macmillan Company, 1944.

Greene, Julie. *The Canal Builders: Making America's Empire at the Panama Canal*. New York: Penguin Press, 2009.

Guampedia Foundation. *101 Amazing Facts about Guam: Tåno' I Chamorro*. Hong Kong: Guampedia Foundation, 2014.

Guerra, Lillian. "Perceiving Populism: United States Imperialism and the Paradox of Labour Struggle in Cuba, 1906–1909." *The Journal of Caribbean History* 37, no. 1 (2003): 45–69.

———. *The Myth of José Martí: Conflicting Nationalisms in Early Twentieth-Century Cuba*. Chapel Hill: University of North Carolina Press, 2005.

Guerrero, Marcela, ed. *No existe un mundo poshuracán: Puerto Rican Art in the Wake of Hurricane Maria*. New York: Whitney Museum of American Art, 2022.

Guerrero, Milagros C. *Under Stars and Stripes*. Vol. 6 of *Kasaysayan: The History of the Filipino People*, edited by Jose Y. Dalisay. New York: Asia Publishing Company, 1998.

Guzmán, Amanda J. "Collecting the Puerto Rican Colony: Spanish-American War Material Encounters between Officer-Wives and Puerto Ricans." *Museum Anthropology* 41 (March 2018): 76–92.

Hall, Lisa Kahaleole. "Strategies of Erasure: U.S. Colonialism and Native Hawaiian Feminism." *American Quarterly* 60, no. 2 (June 2008): 273–80.

Hammond, Joyce D. "Hawaiian Flag Quilts: Multivalent Symbols of a Hawaiian Quilt Tradition." *Hawaiian Journal of History* 27 (1993): 1–26.

Mrs. A. Chester Hanford Collection of Materials Concerning Hawaii, 1882–1889. Houghton Library, Harvard University.

Harris, Susan K. *God's Arbiters: Americans and the Philippines, 1898–1902*. New York: Oxford University Press, 2011.

Hattendorf, John. *Faces of the Naval War College*. Newport, RI: Naval War College Press, 2009.

Hattendorf, John B. and William P. Leeman, eds. *Forging the Trident: Theodore Roosevelt and the United States Navy*. Annapolis, MD: Naval Institute Press, 2021.

Hattori, Anne Perez. *Colonial Dis-Ease: US Navy Health Policies and the Chamorros of Guam, 1898–1941*. Honolulu: University of Hawai'i Press, 2004.

———. *I Magobetnå-ña Guam; Governing Guam: Before and After the Wars*. Agaña, Guam: Political Status Education Coordinating Commission, 1994.

———. "'The Cry of the Little People of Guam': American Colonialism, Medical Philanthropy, and the Susana Hospital for Chamorro Women, 1898–1941." *Health and History* 8, no. 1 (2006): 4–26.

———. "Colonialism, Capitalism and Nationalism in the U.S. Navy's Expulsion of Guam's Spanish Catholic Priests, 1898–1900." *The Journal of Pacific History* 44, no. 3 (December 2009): 281–302.

———. "Righting Civil Wrongs: The Guam Congress Walkout of 1949." *ISLA: A Journal of Micronesian Studies* 3, no. 1 (Rainy Season 1995), 1–28.

Hawkins, Hunt. "Mark Twain's Anti-Imperialism." *American Literary Realism, 1870–1910* 25, no. 2 (Winter 1993): 31–45.

Hawkins, Michael C. *Making Moros: Imperial Historicism and American Military Rule in the Philippines' Muslim South*. DeKalb: Northern Illinois University Press, 2013.

Hemment, John C. *Cannon and Camera: Sea and Land Battles of the Spanish-American War in Cuba, Camp Life, and the Return of the Soldiers*. New York: D. Appleton and Company, 1898.

Hendricks, Gordon. *The Life and Work of Winslow Homer*. 1st ed. New York: H. N. Abrams, 1979.

Hendrickson, Kenneth E. *The Spanish-American War*. Westport, CT: Greenwood Publishing Group, 2003.

Herdrich, Stephanie and Sylvia Yount, eds., *Crosscurrents: Winslow Homer*. New York: The Metropolitan Museum of Art, with Yale University Press, 2022.

Herman, R. D. K. "Coin of the Realm: The Political Economy of 'Indolence' in the Hawaiian Islands." *History and Anthropology* 11, nos. 2 and 3 (1999): 387–416.

——. "In the Canoe: Intersections in Space, Time, and Becoming." In *A Deeper Sense of Place: Stories and Journeys of Indigenous-Academic Collaboration,* edited by Jay T. Johnson and Soren C. Larsen, 55–72. Corvallis: Oregon State University Press, 2013.

——. "Out of Sight, Out of Mind, Out of Power: Leprosy, Race, and Colonization in Hawai'i." *Journal of Historical Geography* 27, no. 3 (January 2001): 319–37.

——. "Pu'u Kohola: Spatial Genealogy of a Symbolic Landscape." In *Symbolic Landscapes*, edited by Gary Backhaus and John Murungi, 91–108. Lanham, MD: Lexington Books., 2009.

——. "The Aloha State: Place Names and the Anti-Conquest of Hawai'i." *Annals, Association of American Geographers* 89, no. 1 (1999): 76–102.

Hess, Stephen, and Sandy Northrop. *Drawn & Quartered: The History of American Political Cartoons.* Montgomery, AL: Elliott and Clark Publishing, 1996.

Hoffnung-Garskof, Jesse. *Racial Migrations: New York City and the Revolutionary Politics of the Spanish Caribbean, 1850–1902.* Princeton, NJ: Princeton University Press, 2019.

Hoganson, Kristin L. *Fighting for American Manhood: How Gender Politics Provoked the Spanish-American and Philippine-American Wars.* New Haven, CT: Yale University Press, 1998.

——. *Consumers' Imperium: The Global Production of American Domesticity, 1865–1920.* Chapel Hill: University of North Carolina Press, 2007.

——. *American Empire at the Turn of the Twentieth Century: A Brief History with Documents.* Boston: Bedford/St. Martins, 2017.

——. "'As Badly off as the Filipinos': U.S. Women's Suffragists and the Imperial Issue at the Turn of the Twentieth Century." *Journal of Women's History* 13, no. 2 (Summer 2001): 9–33.

Winslow Homer collection, 1863, 1877–1945. Archives of American Art, Smithsonian Institution.

Winslow Homer collection, Bowdoin College Museum of Art.

Winslow Homer letters to M. Knoedler and Company, 1900–1904. Archives of American Art, Smithsonian Institution.

Winslow Homer. Art and Artist Files, Smithsonian American Art and Portrait Gallery Library, Smithsonian Libraries and Archives, Washington, DC.

Hong Sohn, Stephen. "Los Indios bravos: The Filipino/American Lyric and the Cosmopoetics of Comparative Indigeneity." *American Quarterly* 63, no. 3 (September 2010): 547–68.

Howard, Woodford. "Frank Murphy and the Philippine Commonwealth." *Pacific Historical Review* 33, no. 1 (1964): 45–68.

Howells, William Dean. "Editha." *Harper's Monthly* 110, no. 656 (January 1905): 214–24.

Hulme, Peter. "'The Silent Language of the Face': The Perception of Indigenous Difference in Travel Writing about the Caribbean." In *Perspectives on Travel Writing*, edited by Glenn Hooper and Tim Youngs, 85–98. Burlington, VT: Ashgate, 2004.

Hutchcroft, Paul D. "Colonial Masters, National Politicos, and Provincial Lords: Central Authority and Local Autonomy in the American Philippines, 1900–1913." *The Journal of Asian Studies* 59, no. 2 (May 2000): 277–306.

Iaukea, Sydney L. *The Queen and I: A Story of Dispossessions and Reconnections in Hawai'i.* Berkeley: University of California Press, 2012.

Ibañez del Carmen, Aniceto, and Francisco Resano del Corazón de Jesús. *Chronicle of the Mariana Islands.* Translated by Marjorie G. Driver. Edited by Omaira Brunal-Perry. Mangilao: Micronesian Area Research Center, University of Guam, 1976.

Icasiano, Carmita Eliza de Jesus. "Philippine Traditional Crafts in Discipline-Based Art Education: A New Prospect." *Asian Studies* 45, nos. 1 and 2 (2009): 57–82.

Ignacio, Abe, Enrique de la Cruz, Jorge Emmanuel, and Helen Toribio. *The Forbidden Book: The Philippine-American War in Political Cartoons.* San Francisco: T'Boli Publishing and Distribution, 2004.

Ileto, Reynaldo Clemeña. *Pasyon and Revolution: Popular Movements in the Philippines, 1840–1910.* Quezon City, Philippines: Ateneo de Manila University Press, 1997.

——. "Cholera and the Origins of The American Sanitary Order in the Philippines." In *Imperial Medicine and Indigenous Societies,* edited by David Arnold, 125–148. Manchester: Manchester University Press, 2017.

Imada, Adria L. "Hawaiians on Tour: Hula Circuits through the American Empire." *American Quarterly*, 56 (March 2004): 117, 144–45.

Issues in Guam's Political Development: The Chamorro Perspective. Guam: The Commission, 1996.

Immerwahr, Daniel. *How To Hide an Empire: A History of the Greater United States.* New York: Farrar, Straus and Giroux, 2019.

Jackson, F. E. *The Representative Men of Porto Rico.* F. E. Jackson & Son, 1910.

Jaena, Graciano López. "Tribute to Juan Luna and Félix Resurrección Hidalgo." In *Graciano López Jaena: Speeches, Articles and Letters*, translated by Encarnación Alzona, edited by Teodor Agoncillo. Manila: National Historical Commission, 1974.

James, Arthur Curtiss. "Advantages of Hawaiian Annexation." *North American Review* 165, no. 493 (December 1897): 758–60.

Jane, Fred T. *Jane's All the World's Fighting Ships, 1898.* New York: Arco Publishing Company, Inc., 1969.

Johnston, Healoha, ed. *Ho'oulu Hawai'i: The King Kalākaua Era.* Honolulu: Honolulu Museum of Art, 2018.

Jones, Willis Knapp. "The Martí Centenary." *Modern Language Journal* 37, no. 8 (December 1953): 398–402.

Kagan, Richard L. *The Spanish Craze: America's Fascination with the Hispanic World, 1779–1939*. Lincoln: University of Nebraska Press, 2019.

Kapur, Nick. "William McKinley's Values and the Origins of the Spanish-American War: A Reinterpretation." *Presidential Studies Quarterly* 41, no. 1 (March 2011): 18–38.

Kame'elehiwa, Lilikala. *Na Wahine Kapu*. Honolulu: Ai Pohaku Press, 1999.

Kamehiro, Stacy L. *The Arts of Kingship: Hawaiian Art and National Culture of the Kalākaua Era*. Honolulu: University of Hawai'i Press, 2009.

——. "Featherwork in the Hawaiian Monarchy Period." In *Royal Hawaiian Featherwork: Nā Hulu Ali`i*, edited by Leah Caldeira, et al., 89. Honolulu: University of Hawai'i Press, 2015.

——. "Worlding the Kingdom of Hawai'i." In *Ho'oulu Hawai'i: The King Kalākaua Era*, edited by Healoha Johnston, 93–96. Honolulu: Honolulu Museum of Art, 2018.

Kaplan, Amy. *Anarchy of Empire in the Making of U.S. Culture*. Cambridge, MA: Harvard University Press, 2005.

——, and Donald E. Pease. *Cultures of United States Imperialism*. Durham, NC: Duke University Press, 1994.

Kashay, Jennifer Fish. "Agents of Imperialism: Missionaries and Merchants in Early-Nineteenth-Century Hawaii." *New England Quarterly* 80, no. 2 (June 2007): 280–98.

Katzman, Laura, ed. *The Museum of the Old Colony: An Art Installation by Pablo Delano*. Charlottesville: University of Virginia Press for the Duke Hall Gallery of Fine Art, James Madison University, 2022.

Katzman, Laura, and Cameron Seglias. "1898: Imag(in)ing the Caribbean in the Age of the Spanish-American War." *H-Soz-Kult: Kommunikation und Fachinformation für die Geschichtswissenschaftenin* (January 1, 2020). https://www.hsozkult.de/conferencereport/id/tagungsberichte-8595.

Kauanui, J. Kēhaulani. *Paradoxes of Hawaiian Sovereignty: Land, Sex, and the Colonial Politics of State Nationalism*. Durham, NC: Duke University Press, 2018.

Keenan, Jerry. *Encyclopedia of the Spanish-American and Philippine-American Wars*. Santa Barbara, CA: ABC CLIO Press, 2001.

Keiner, Christine. *Deep Cut: Science, Power, and the Unbuilt Interoceanic Canal*. Athens: University of Georgia Press, 2020.

Kinzer, Stephen. "Cruel Realities: The American Conquest of Guam." *World Policy Journal* 23, no. 2 (Summer 2006): 100–4.

——. *The True Flag: Theodore Roosevelt, Mark Twain, and the Birth of American Empire*. New York: St. Martin's Griffin, 2017.

Kramer, Paul A. *The Blood of Government: Race, Empire, the United States, & the Philippines*. Chapel Hill: University of North Carolina Press, 2006.

Krieger, Herbert W. *The Collection of Primitive Weapons and Armor of the Philippine Islands in the United States National Museum*. Washington, DC: Government Printing Office, 1926.

Krueger, David. "The Red Cross, the Daughters of the American Revolution, and the Origins of the Army Nurse Corps in the Spanish-American War." *Journal of Military History* 83, no. 2 (April 2019): 409–19.

Kualapai, Lydia. "The Queen Writes Back: Lili'uokalani's Hawaii's Story by Hawaii's Queen." *Studies in American Indian Literatures*, Series 2, 17, no. 2 (Summer 2005): 32–62.

LaFeber, Walter. *The American Age: United States Foreign Policy at Home and Abroad*. New York: W.W. Norton, 1994.

——. *The New Empire: An Interpretation of American Expansion, 1860–1898*. Ithaca, NY: Cornell University Press, 1963.

Langellier, John. *Scouting with the Buffalo Soldiers: Lieutenant Powhatan Clarke, Frederic Remington, and the Tenth U.S. Cavalry in the Southwest*. Denton: University of North Texas Press, 2020.

Lasso, Marixa. *Erased: The Untold Story of the Panama Canal*. Cambridge, MA: Harvard University Press, 2019.

Leary, John Patrick. "America's Other Half: Slum Journalism and the War of 1898." *Journal of Transnational American Studies* 1, no. 1 (2009): 1–33.

Leeke, Jim. *Manila and Santiago: The New Steel Navy in the Spanish-American War*. Annapolis, MD: Naval Institute Press, 2009.

Legarda, Benito J., Jr. *After the Galleons: Foreign Trade, Economic Change and Entrepreneurship in the Nineteenth-Century Philippines*. Manila: Ateneo de Manila University Press, 1999.

Leibowitz, Arnold H. *Defining Status: A Comprehensive Analysis of the United States Territorial Relations*. Dordrecht, Netherlands: Martinus Nijhoff, 1989.

Levine, Emily and Candace Greene, eds. *A Pictographic History of the Oglala Sioux: Drawings by Amos Bad Heart Bull*. 50th Anniversary Edition. Lincoln: University of Nebraska Press, 2017.

Levy, Teresita A. *Puerto Ricans in the Empire: Tobacco Growers and U.S. Colonialism*. New Brunswick, NJ: Rutgers University Press, 2014.

Ley Foraker. Aguadilla, Puerto Rico: El Criollo, 1900.

Lili'uokalani. *Hawaii's Story by Hawaii's Queen*. Annotated by David W. Forbes. 1898. Honolulu: Hui Hānai, 2013.

Link, Arthur Stanley. *Wilson the Diplomatist: A Look at His Major Foreign Policies*. Chicago: Quadrangle Books, 1963.

Linn, Brian McAllister. *The Philippine War, 1899–1902*. Lawrence: University Press of Kansas, 2000.

Lockmiller, David A. *Magoon in Cuba: A History of the Second Intervention, 1906–1909*. New York: Greenwood Press, 1969.

Lodge, Henry Cabot. "The Spanish-American War: I – The Unsettled Question." *Harper's New Monthly Magazine* 98, no. 585 (February 1899): 449–64.

——. "The Spanish-American War: II – The Coming of War." *Harper's New Monthly Magazine* 98, no. 586 (March 1899): 505–23.

———. "The Spanish-American War: III – The Blockade of Cuba and Pursuit of Cervera." *Harper's New Monthly Magazine* 98, no. 587 (April 1899): 715–33.

López, Alfred J. *José Martí: A Revolutionary Life.* Austin: University of Texas Press, 2014.

López Jaena, Graciano. "Tribute to Juan Luna and Félix Resurrección Hidalgo." In *Graciano López Jaena: Speeches, Articles and Letters*, translated by Encarnación Alzona, edited by Teodor Agoncillo. Manila: National Historical Commission, 1994.

Lugo-Ortiz, Agnes. *Identidades Imaginadas: Biografía y nacionalidad en el horizonte de la Guerra (Cuba 1860–1898).* San Juan: Universidad de Puerto Rico, 1999.

MacLennan, Carol A. *Sovereign Sugar: Industry and Environment in Hawai'i.* Honolulu: University of Hawai'i Press, 2014.

Madrid, Carlos. *Seráphico: The Franciscan Missionaries in the Aurora Region, 1609–1899.* Manila: National Historical Commission of the Philippines, 2017.

Mahan, Alfred Thayer. *The Influence of Sea Power Upon History, 1660–1783.* Boston: Little, Brown and Company, 1890.

———. *Retrospect and Prospect: Studies in International Relations, Naval and Political.* Boston: Little, Brown and Company, 1902.

Maldonado-Denis, Manuel. *Visiones sobre hostos.* Caracas, Venezuela: Biblioteca Ayacucho, 1988.

Mancini, J. M. *Art and War in the Pacific World: Making, Breaking, and Taking from Anson's Voyage to the Philippine-American War.* Oakland: University of California Press, 2018.

Marković, Miodrag. *From Timisoara to Hawaii: Paul Petrovits—A Forgotten Serbian Painter.* Belgrade: The Belgrade Institute for the History of Art, 2015.

Martí, José. *Our America: Writings on Latin America and the Struggle for Cuban Independence.* New York: Monthly Review Press, 1977.

Martinez-Novillo, Alvaro, and Javier Tusell. *Paisaje y figura del 98.* Madrid: Fundación Central Hispano, 1997.

Matos Rodríguez, Félix V. "Their Islands and Our People: U.S. Writing About Puerto Rico, 1898–1920." *CENTRO Journal of the Center for Puerto Rican Studies* 11, no. 1 (1999): 3–49.

Mattei Filardi, Luis. *En las tinieblas del colonialismo: "cien metros" de historia puertorriqueña.* San Juan: Ediciones Nóema, 2014.

Maxwell, Anne. *Colonial Photography and Exhibitions: Representations of the "Native" and the Making of European Identities.* London: Leicester University Press, 1999.

———. "Framing the Asia-Pacific: The Gerhard Sisters at the St. Louis World's Fair." *History of Photography* 39, no. 3 (2015): 227–41.

May, Glenn A. *Inventing a Hero: The Posthumous Recreation of Andres Bonifacio.* Madison, WI: New Day Publishers, 1996.

———. "Why the United States Won the Philippine-American War, 1899–1902." *Pacific Historical Review* 52, no. 4 (November 1983): 353–377.

———. "The 'Zones' of Batangas." *Philippine Studies* 29, no. 1 (First Quarter 1981): 89–103.

———. "Resistance and Collaboration in the Philippine-American War: The Case of Batangas." *Journal of Southeast Asian Studies* 15, no. 1 (March 1984): 69–90.

McCaffrey, James M. "Texans in the Spanish-American War." *Southwestern Historical Quarterly* 106, no. 2 (October 2002): 254–79.

McCoy, Alfred, and Francisco A. Scarano, eds. *Colonial Crucible: Empire in the Making of the Modern American State.* Madison: University of Wisconsin Press, 2009.

McCullough, Matthew. *The Cross of War: Christian Nationalism and the U.S. Expansion in the Spanish-American War.* Madison: University of Wisconsin Press, 2014.

Medak-Saltzman, Danika. "Transnational Indigenous Exchange: Rethinking Global Interactions of Indigenous Peoples at the 1904 St. Louis Exposition." *American Quarterly* 62, no. 3 (September 2010): 591–615.

Medel, José Antonio. *The Spanish-American War and its Results.* Havana: P. Fernandez and Co., 1932.

Merina, Anita. "Filipiniana Treasures in the Smithsonian." *Filipinas Magazine* 2, no. 18 (October 1993): 5–8, 66.

Merry, Robert W. *President William McKinley: Architect of the American Century.* New York: Simon and Schuster, 2017.

Merry, Sally Engle. *Colonizing Hawai'i: The Cultural Power of Law.* Princeton, NJ: Princeton University Press, 2000.

Metropolitan Museum of Manila. *Unang pambansang eksibisyon sa paggunita kina: Juan Luna and Félix Resurrección Hidalgo: First national Juan Luna and Félix Resurrección Hidalgo Commemorative Exhibition.* Manila: Metropolitan Museum of Manila, 1988.

Miller, Albert George. *Elevating the Race: Theophilus G. Steward, Black Theology, and the Making of an African American Civil Society, 1865–1924.* Knoxville: University of Tennessee Press, 2003.

Miller, Bonnie M. *From Liberation to Conquest: The Visual and Popular Cultures of the Spanish-American War of 1898.* Amherst: University of Massachusetts Press, 2011.

Miller, Stuart Creighton. *Benevolent Assimilation: The American Conquest of the Philippines, 1899–1903.* New Haven, CT: Yale University Press, 1982.

Millis, Walter. *The Martial Spirit: A Study of Our War with Spain.* Boston: Houghton Mifflin Company, 1931.

Mingote Calderón, José Luis, and María José Suarez Martínez. *Imágenes de una exposición: Filipinas en el Parque de El Retiro, en 1887.* Madrid: Museo Nacional de Antropología, 2017.

Mirabal, Nancy Raquel. "Melba Alvarado, El Club Cubano Inter-Americano, and the Creation of Afro-Cubanidades in New York City." In *The Afro-Latin@ Reader: History and Culture in the United States*, edited by Miriam Jiménez Román and

Juan Flores, 120–126. Durham, NC: Duke University Press, 2010.

———. "'No Country but the One We Must Fight For': The Emergence of an Antillean Nation and Community in New York City, 1860–1901." In *Mambo Montage: The Latinization of New York*, edited by Agustín Laó-Montes and Arlene Dávila, 57–72. New York: Columbia University Press, 2001.

Mize, Ramey. "Battle Grounds: Painting, War and Witness in the Americas, 1861–1902," PhD dissertation in progress, University of Pennsylvania.

Mojares, Resil B. *Brains of the Nation: Pedro Paterno, T. H. Pardo de Tavera, Isabelo de los Reyes and the Production of Modern Knowledge.* Quezon City, Philippines: Ateneo de Manila University Press, 2006.

———. "Guillermo Tolentino's *Grupo de Filipinos Ilustres* and the Making of a National Pantheon." *Philippine Studies* 58, no. 1/2 (June 2010): 169–84.

Mora Postigo, Concha. "Restos humanos antiguos en el Museo Nacional de Antropología." In *Anales del museo nacional de antropología: 1998 número V*, 255–272. Madrid: Ministerio de Educación y Cultura, 1998.

Morey, Michael. *Fagen: An African American Renegade in the Philippine-American War.* Madison: University of Wisconsin Press, 2019.

Morillo-Alicea, Javier. "Uncharted Landscapes of 'Latin America': The Philippines in the Spanish Imperial Archipelago." In *Interpreting Spanish Colonialism: Empires, Nations, and Legends,* edited by Christopher Schmidt-Nowara and John M. Nieto-Phillips, 25–53. Albuquerque: University of New Mexico Press, 2005.

Morrow, Prince A. "Leprosy and Hawaiian Annexation." *North American Review* 165, no. 492 (November 1897): 582–90.

Mount, Charles Merrill. "The Rabbit and the Boa Constrictor: John Singer Sargent at the White House." *Records of the Columbia Historical Society, Washington, DC* 71/72 (1971/72): 618–656

Muñoz Rivera, Luis, ed. *Puerto Rico Herald* 1, no. 11, Sep. 21, 1901.

———, ed. *Puerto Rico Herald* 1, no. 12, Sep. 28, 1901.

———, ed. *Puerto Rico Herald* 1, no. 14, Oct. 12, 1901.

———, ed. *Puerto Rico Herald* 1, no. 16, Oct. 26, 1901.

Murolo, Priscilla. "Wars of Civilization: The US Army Contemplates Wounded Knee, the Pullman Strike, and the Philippine Insurrection." *International Labor and Working-Class History,* no. 80 (Fall 2011): 77–102.

Musicant, Ivan. *Empire by Default: The Spanish-American War and the Dawn of the American Century.* New York: H. Holt, 1998.

Navarro, Mireya. "Uproar Against Navy War Games Unites Puerto Ricans." *New York Times,* July 10, 1999.

Negrón-Muntaner, Frances, ed. *Sovereign Acts: Contesting Colonialism across Indigenous Nations and Latinx America.* Tucson: University of Arizona Press, 2017.

Negrón-Muntaner, Frances. "Here Is the Evidence: Arturo Alfonso Schomburg's Black Countervisuality." *African American Review* 54, no. 1–2 (Spring/Summer 2021): 49–71.

Niedermeier, Silvan. "Intimacy and Annihilation: Approaching the Enforcement of U.S. Colonial Rule in the Southern Philippines through a Private Photograph Collection." *InVisible Culture: An Electronic Journal for Visual Culture* 25 (April 2017): 1–28.

Ninkovich, Frank. *The United States and Imperialism.* Malden, MA: Blackwell Publishers, 2001.

Nofi, Albert. *The Spanish-American War, 1898.* Conshohocken, PA: Combined Books, 1996.

Noyes, Martha. *Then There Were None.* Honolulu: Bess Press, 2003.

O'Brien Galleries records, 1811–1970. Archives of American Art, Smithsonian Institution.

Ocampo, Ambeth R. "Rizal's Morga and Views of Philippine History." *Philippine Studies* 46, no. 2 (Second Quarter 1998): 184–214.

———. *101 Stories on the Philippine Revolution.* Pasig City: Anvil Publishing, 2009.

Ojeda Reyes, Félix. *Peregrinos de la Libertad: Documentos y fotos de los exiliados puertorriqueños del siglo XIX localizados en los archivos y bibliotecas de Cuba.* Río Piedras: Editorial de la Universidad de Puerto Rico, 1992.

Oshima, Neal M. *Images from Sheer Realities: Clothing and Power in Nineteenth Century Philippines.* Manila: Bookmark, 2000.

Osorio, Jon. *Dismembering Lāhui: A History of the Hawaiian Nation to 1887.* Honolulu: University of Hawai'i Press, 2002.

Owen, Norman G. *Compadre Colonialism: Studies in the Philippines under American Rule.* Ann Arbor: University of Michigan Press, 2020.

Palma, Rafael. *Biografía de Rizal.* Manila: Bureau of Printing, 1949.

Pan-Montojo, Juan, and José Álvarez Junco. *Más se perdió en Cuba: España, 1898 y la crisis de fin de siglo.* Madrid: Alianza Editorial, 1998.

Paquette, Gabriel. "Enlightened Narratives and Imperial Rivalry in Bourbon Spain: The Case of Almodóvar's "Historia Política De Los Establecimientos Ultramarinos De Las Naciones Europeas" (1784–1790)." *The Eighteenth Century* 48, no. 1 (Spring 2007): 61–80.

Paras-Perez, Rod, Santiago Albano Pilar, and Emmanuel Torres. *Pioneers of Philippine Art: Luna, Amorsolo, Zobel.* Maktai City, Philippines: Ayala Foundation, 2004.

Partridge, Scott H. "Two Early Missionaries in Hawaii: Mercy Partridge Whitney and Edward Partridge Jr." *BYU Studies Quarterly* 52, no. 1 (2013): 136–47.

Pearlman, Michael D. "Spanish-American War: Stumbling into the Way to Fight a Limited War." In *Warmaking and American Democracy: The Struggle over Military Strategy, 1700 to the Present.* Lawrence: University Press of Kansas, 1999.

Pérez, Louis A. Jr. *Cuba: Between Reform and Revolution*, 3rd ed. New York: Oxford University Press, 2006.

———. *Cuba in the American Imagination: Metaphor and the Imperial Ethos.* Chapel Hill: University of North Carolina Press, 2008.

———. *On Becoming Cuban: Identity, Nationality, and Culture*. Chapel Hill: University of North Carolina Press, 2008.

———. *The War of 1898: The United States and Cuba in History and Historiography*. Chapel Hill: University of North Carolina Press, 1998.

Philippine Map Collectors Society. *The First Philippine Republic and the United States, 1898–1907: Philippine-American Friendship Day*. Makati City: Philippine Map Collectors Society, Inc. and Yuchengco Museum, 2015.

Phinney, A. H. "The First Spanish-American War." *Florida State Historical Society Quarterly* 4, no. 3 (January 1926): 114–29.

Picó, Francisco. *Puerto Rico 1898: la guerra después de la guerra*. Río Piedras, Puerto Rico: Ediciones Huracán, 1984.

———. *Cada guaraguao: galería de oficiales norteamericanos en Puerto Rico (1898–1899)*. Río Piedras, Puerto Rico: Ediciones Huracán, 1998.

———. *Historia general de Puerto Rico*. Río Piedras, Puerto Rico: Ediciones Huracán, 1986.

Pierson, Ruth Roach, and Nupur Roach Chaudhuri, eds. *Nation, Empire, Colony: Historicizing Gender and Race*. Bloomington: Indiana University Press, 1998.

Pilar, Santiago Albano, Juan Luna, and Nick Joaquin. *Juan Luna: The Filipino as Painter*. Manila: Eugenio López Foundation, 1980.

Pitaluga, Antonio Álvarez. "La caída de un héroe y el secuestro de un mito." *Caliban: Revista Cubana de Pensamiento e Historia* (May–August, 2012): The Political Status Education Coordinating Commission. *Kinalamten Pulitikåt: Siñenten I Chamorro (Issues in Guam's Political Development: The Chamorro Perspective)*. Aguña, Guam: Department of Chamorro Affairs, 2002.

Post, Charles Johnson. *The Little War of Private Post*. Boston: Little, Brown and Company, 1960.

Poyo, Gerald E. *"With All, and for the Good of All": The Emergence of Popular Nationalism in the Cuban Communities of the United States, 1848–1898*. Durham, NC: Duke University Press, 1989.

Pratt, Julius W. *Expansionists of 1898: The Acquisition of Hawaii and the Spanish Islands*. 1936. Chicago: Quadrangle Books, 1964.

Proto, Neil Thomas. *The Rights of My People: Liliuokalani's Enduring Battle with the United States, 1893–1917*. New York: Algora Publishing, 2009.

Quanchi, Max. "Imaging the USA's Pacific Empire." *History of Photography* 39, no. 3 (July 2015): 213–26.

Quirino, Carlos. "The Spanish Colonial Army 1878–98." *Philippine Studies* 36, no. 3 (Third Quarter 1988): 381–86.

Rafael, Vicente L. "White Love: Surveillance and Nationalist Resistance in the U.S. Colonization of the Philippines." In *Cultures of United States Imperialism*, edited by Amy Kaplan and Donald E. Pease. Durham, NC: Duke University Press, 1994.

Rafael, Vicente L. "Nationalism, Imagery, and the Filipino Intelligentsia in the Nineteenth Century." *Critical Inquiry* 16, no. 3 (Spring 1990): 591–611.

Redford, Audrey, and Benjamin Powell. "Dynamics of Intervention in the War on Drugs: The Buildup to the Harrison Act of 1914." *The Independent Review* 20, no. 4 (Spring 2016): 509–30.

Reece, Kilin. "A Royal Quartet: Charting the Martin Guitars that Left the Mainland." *Fretboard Journal* (June 2018): 88–97.

Report of the Philippine Exposition Board in the United States for the Louisiana Purchase Exposition. Washington, DC: Bureau of Insular Affairs, War Department, 1905.

Rice, Mark. *Dean Worcester's Fantasy Islands: Photography, Film, and the Colonial Philippines*. Ann Arbor: University of Michigan Press, 2014.

Richardson, Jim. *The Light of Liberty: Documents and Studies on the Katipunan, 1892–1897*. Quezon City, Philippines: Ateneo de Manila University Press, 2013.

Rickover, H. G. *How the Battleship* Maine *Was Destroyed*. Annapolis, MD: Naval Institute Press, 1994.

Rivero Méndez, Ángel. *Crónica de la Guerra Hispano-Americana en Puerto Rico*. Madrid: Sucesores de Rivadeneyra, 1922.

Roces, Alfredo R. *Félix Resurrección Hidalgo and the Generation of 1872*. Pasay City, Philippines: Eugenio López Foundation, 1995.

———. *Filipino Heritage: The Making of a Nation*. Manila: Lahing Pilipino Publishing, 1978.

Rodríguez-Silva, Ileana M. *Silencing Race: Disentangling Blackness, Colonialism, and National Identities in Puerto Rico*. New York: Palgrave Macmillan, 2012.

Rogers, Robert F. *Destiny's Landfall: A History of Guam*. Honolulu: University of Hawai'i Press, 2011.

Roggenkamp, Karen. "The Evangelina Cisneros Romance, Medievalist Fiction, and the Journalism that Acts." *Journal of American and Comparative Cultures* 23, no. 2 (Summer 2000): 25–37.

Rosaldo, Renato. *Cultural Citizenship in Island Southeast Asia: Nation and Belonging in the Hinterlands*. Berkeley: University of California Press, 2003.

Rosenfeld, Harvey. *Richmond Pearson Hobson: Naval Hero of Magnolia Grove*. Las Cruces, NM: Yucca Tree Press, 2001.

Rotter, Andrew J. *Empires of the Senses: Bodily Encounters in Imperial India and the Philippines*. New York: Oxford University Press, 2019.

———. "Empires of the Senses: How Seeing, Hearing, Smelling, Tasting, and Touching Shaped Imperial Encounters." *Diplomatic History* 35, no. 1 (January 2011) 2–19.

Ruiz, Ramón Eduardo. Review of *Inside the Monster: Writings on the United States and American Imperialism* by José Martí. *Pacific Historical Review* 46, no. 1 (February 1977): 141.

Russell, Timothy D. "'I Feel Sorry for These People': African American Soldiers in the Philippine-American War, 1899–1902." *Journal of African American History* 99, no. 3 (Summer 2014): 197–222.

Roberts, Brian Russell, and Michelle Ann Stephens. *Archipelagic American Studies*. Durham, NC: Duke University Press, 2017.

Rodríguez Orellana, Manuel. "Vieques: The Past, Present, and Future of the Puerto Rico–U.S. Colonial Relationship." *Berkeley La Raza Law Journal* 13, no. 2 (2002): 425–39.

Safford, William Edwin. *A Year on the Island of Guam, 1899–1900: Extracts from the Notebook of Naturalist William Edwin Safford*. Edited by Jillette Torre Leon-Guerrero. Agaña Heights, Guam: Guamology Publishing, 2016.

Sai, David Keanu. "American Occupation of the Hawaiian State: A Century Unchecked." *Hawaiian Journal of Law and Politics* 1 (Summer 2004): 47–82.

———. "Hawaiian Neutrality: From the Crimean Conflict through the Spanish-American War." Paper presented at the University of Cambridge, UK Centre for Research in the Arts, Social Sciences and Humanities. *Sovereignty and Imperialism: Non-European Powers in the Age of Empire*, September 10–12, 2015.

Salazar, María José. *José Gutiérrez Solana: Colección Banco Santander*. Madrid: Museo Nacional Centro de Arte Reina Sofía, 1998.

Samonte, Cecilia. "Obtaining 'Sympathetic Understanding': Gender, Empire, and Representation in the Travel Writings of American Officials' Wives, 1901–1914." *Journal of Transnational American Studies* 3, no. 2 (December 2011): 2–15.

Samson, Ditas R. "History in Art: The Ayala Museum's Fine Arts Collection." *Arts of Asia* 43 (January/February 2013): 94–101.

Sandburg, Carl. *Always the Young Strangers*. New York: Harcourt, Brace and World, 1953.

Santamarina, Juan C. "The Cuba Company and the Expansion of American Business in Cuba, 1898–1915." *The Business History Review* 74, no. 1 (Spring 2000): 41–83.

Sarnecky, Mary T. *A History of the U.S. Army Nurse Corps*. Philadelphia: University of Pennsylvania Press, 1999.

Sartorius, David. *Ever Faithful: Race, Loyalty, and the Ends of Empire in Spanish Cuba*. Durham, NC: Duke University Press, 2014.

Scarano, Francisco A. *Puerto Rico: Cinco siglos de historia*. San Juan: McGraw-Hill, 1993.

Schoonover, Thomas David. *Uncle Sam's War of 1898 and the Origins of Globalization*. Lexington: University Press of Kentucky, 2003.

Schubert, Frank N. *Voice of the Buffalo Soldier: Records, Reports, and Recollections of Military Life and Service in the West*. Albuquerque: University of New Mexico Press, 2003.

Schumacher, John N. *The Propaganda Movement, 1880–1895: the Creation of a Filipino Consciousness, the Making of the Revolution*. Manila: Ateneo de Manila University Press, 1997.

Scott, Edward Van Zile. *The Unwept: Black American Soldiers in the Spanish-American War*. Montgomery: Black Belt Press, 1996.

Scott, Phoebe. "Authority and Anxiety." In *Between Declarations and Dreams: Art of Southeast Asia since the 19th Century*, edited by Low Sze Wee, 16–30. Singapore: National Gallery Singapore, 2015.

Seager, Robert. *Alfred Thayer Mahan: The Man and His Letters*. Annapolis, MD: Naval Institute Press, 1977.

Seraile, William. *Voice of Dissent: Theophilus Gould Steward (1843–1924) and Black America*. Brooklyn: Carlson, 1991.

Serra Montalvo, Rafael. *Ensayos políticos: Segunda serie*. New York: P. J. Díaz, 1896.

Sexton, Jay. *The Monroe Doctrine: Empire and Nation in Nineteenth-Century America*. New York: Hill and Wang, 2011.

Seymour, Richard. *American Insurgents: A Brief History of American Anti-Imperialism*. Chicago: Haymarket Books, 2012.

Shaw, Angel Velasco, and Luis H. Francia, eds. *Vestiges of War: The Philippine-American War and the Aftermath of an Imperial Dream 1899–1999*. New York: New York University Press, 2004.

Sierra de la Calle, Blas. *Hazañas Yankees: diseños satíricos de 1898*. Valladolid, Spain: Museo Oriental, 1998.

———. *Ilustración Filipina, 1859–1860*. Valladolid, Spain: Museo Oriental, Caja España, 2003.

Silbey, David. *A War of Frontier and Empire: The Philippine-American War, 1899–1902*. New York: Hill and Wang, 2007.

Siler, Julia Flynn. *Lost Kingdom: Hawaii's Last Queen, the Sugar Kings, and America's First Imperial Adventure*. New York: Atlantic Monthly Press, 2012.

Silva, Noenoe K. *Aloha Betrayed: Native Hawaiian Resistance to American Colonialism*. Durham, NC: Duke University Press, 2004.

Sinopoli, Carla M., and Lars Fogelin, eds. *Imperial Imaginings: The Dean C. Worcester Photographic Collection of the Philippines, 1890–1913*. Ann Arbor: University of Michigan, Museum of Anthropology, 1998.

Sneider, Allison L. *Suffragists in an Imperial Age: U.S. Expansion and the Woman Question, 1870–1929*. New York: Oxford University Press, 2008.

Soriano, Rafaelita Hilario, ed. *Women in the Philippine Revolution*. Quezon City, Philippines: Printon Press, 1995.

Sparrow, Bartholomew. *The Insular Cases and the Emergence of the American Empire*. Lawrence: University of Kansas Press, 2006.

Spassky, Natalie. "Winslow Homer at the Metropolitan Museum of Art." *Metropolitan Museum of Art Bulletin* 39, no. 4 (Spring 1982): 1–49.

Sta. María, Felice, and Santiago Albano Pilar. *Discovering Philippine Art in Spain*. Manila: Department of Foreign Affairs, National Centennial Commission, Committee on International Relations, 1998.

Stevens, Joseph Earle. "An American in Manila." *McClure's Magazine* 11, no. 2 (June 1898): 186–92.

Steward, T. G. *The Colored Regulars in the United States Army*. Philadelphia: A. M. E. Book Concern, 1904.

Stewart, Charles, and William Ellis. *Journal of a residence in the Sandwich Islands, during the years 1823, 1824, and 1825: including descriptions of the natural scenery, and remarks on the manners and customs of the inhabitants; an account of Lord*

Byron's visit in the British frigate Blonde, and of an excursion to the great volcano of Kirauea in Hawaii, 2nd ed. New York: J. P. Haven, 1828.

Stolberg Acosta, Robert. *Retablos, joyas, platería y arte: Colección Acosta de San Juan, Puerto Rico (1695–2010)*. Self-published, 2011.

Stoler, Laura Ann. *Carnal Knowledge and Imperial Power: Race and the Intimate in Colonial Rule*. Berkeley: University of California Press, 2002.

——, ed. *Haunted by Empire: Geographies of Intimacy in North American History*. Durham, NC: Duke University Press, 2006.

Storer, Rusell, Clarissa Chikiamco, and Muhammad Hafiz Syed. *Between Worlds: Raden Saleh and Juan Luna*. Singapore: National Gallery Singapore, 2017.

Stricklin, Krystle. "Grave Visions: Photographs, Violence, and Death in the American Empire, 1898–1913." PhD diss. University of Pittsburgh, 2021.

Sullivan, Edward J. *From San Juan to Paris and Back: Francisco Oller and Caribbean Art in the Era of Impressionism*. New Haven, CT: Yale University Press, 2014.

Tabor, Brenda Kean. "Spotlight: 'Beyond the *Maine*' Sunset of Old Spanish Empire." *Dialogo* 3, no. 1 (Fall 1997): 23.

Taft, Helen Herron. *Recollection of Full Years*. New York: Dodd, Mead and Company, 1914.

Tate, Merze. "Slavery and Racism as Deterrents to the Annexation of Hawaii, 1854–1855." *Journal of Negro History* 47, no. 1 (January 1962): 1–18.

Taviel de Andrade, Enrique. *Historia de la exposición de las islas Filipinas en Madrid el año de 1887*. Madrid: Ulpiano Gómez y Pérez, 1887.

Taylor, John R. M. *The Philippine Insurrection against the United States: A Compilation of Documents with Notes and Introduction*. Pasay City, Philippines: Eugenio López Foundation, 1971.

Terra, Jun. *Juan Luna Drawings: The Paris Period*. Edited by Marita Pascual Nuque. Makati, Philippines: E. M. Pascual, 1998.

Thiessen, Thomas D. "The Fighting First Nebraska: Nebraska's Imperial Adventure in the Philippines, 1898–1899." *Nebraska History* 70 (1989): 210–72.

Thomas, Megan C. *Orientalists, Propagandists, and Ilustrados: Filipino Scholarship and the End of Spanish Colonialism*. Minneapolis: University of Minnesota Press, 2012.

Tillman, Ellen D. *Dollar Diplomacy by Force: Nation Building and Resistance in the Dominican Republic*. Chapel Hill: University of North Carolina Press, 2016.

Thompson, Lanny. *Nuestra isla y su gente: la construcción del "otro" en Our Islands and Their People*. Río Piedras, Puerto Rico, 1995.

——. *Imperial Archipelago: Representation and Rule in the Insular Territories under U.S. Dominion after 1898*. Honolulu: University of Hawai'i Press, 2010.

——. "The Imperial Republic: A Comparison of the Insular Territories under U.S. Dominion after 1898." *Pacific Historical Review* 71, no. 4 (November 2002): 535–74.

Tompkins, E. Berkeley. *Anti-Imperialism in the United States: The Great Debate, 1890–1920*. Philadelphia: University of Pennsylvania Press, 1970.

Tone, John Lawrence. *War and Genocide in Cuba, 1895–1898*. Chapel Hill: University of North Carolina Press, 2008.

Torre Leon-Guerrero, Jillette, Jan S. N. Furukawa, and Diane Aoki, eds. *A Year on the Island of Guam 1899–1900: Extracts from the Notebook of Naturalist William Edwin Safford*. Agana Heights, Guam: Guamology Publishing, 2016.

Torres, Emmanuel. *One Hundred Years of Philippine Painting*. Burbank, CA: Westland Graphics, 1984.

Torres-Cuevas, Eduardo. *Antonio Maceo: las ideas que sostienen el arma*. Havana: Ciencias Sociales, 1995.

Torruella, Juan R. *Global Intrigues: The Era of the Spanish-American War and the Rise of the United States to World Power*. Río Piedras: Editorial de la Universidad de Puerto Rico, 2007.

——. "The Insular Cases: The Establishment of a Regime of Political Apartheid." *University of Pennsylvania Journal of International Law* 29, no. 2 (Winter 2007): 238–348.

Traxel, David. *1898: The Birth of the American Century*. New York: A. A. Knopf, 1998.

Trías Monge, José. *Puerto Rico: The Trials of the Oldest Colony in the World*. New Haven, CT: Yale University Press, 1997.

Troutman, Charles H. *The Organic Act of Guam and Federal Laws Affecting the Governmental Structure of Guam (through June 11, 2001)*. Mangilao: University of Guam and the Government of Guam, 2002.

Tse, Nicole, Maricor Soriano, Ana Labrador, and Robert A. Balarbar. "Decision Making, Materiality and Digitisation: Esteban Villanueva's *Basi Revolt Paintings of Ilocos*." *AICCM Bulletin* 39, no. 1 (November 2018): 42–54.

Tse, Nicole, Ana P. Labrador, and Robyn Slogget. "Painting Practice in the Philippines: Two Institutionalized Practices and their Materials and Techniques." *CIHA* (January 2008): 590–98.

Tse, Nicole, Ana Maria Theresa Labrador, Marcelle Scott, and Roberto Balarbar. "Preventive Conservation: People, Objects, Place and Time in the Philippines." *Studies in Conservation* 63, no. 2 (September 2018): 274–81.

Tunc, Tanfer Emin. "Manifest Destiny's Child: Mary Hazleton Blanchard Wade and the Literature of American Empire." *Children's Literature in Education* 48, no. 3 (September 2017): 245–61.

Twigg-Smith, Thurston. *Hawaiian Sovereignty: Do the Facts Matter?* Honolulu: Goodale Publishing, 1998.

Underwood, Robert. *Unfinished Business: The Meaning of 1898: Statement at the Centennial Commemoration, Piti, Guam*. Micronesia Area Research Center, University of Guam. June 1998. https://issuu.com/guampedia/docs/unfinished_business_the_menaing_of_1898

Utley, Robert J. *Sitting Bull: The Life and Times of An American Patriot*. New York: Henry Holt and Company, 1993.

Valdés, Vanessa K. *Diasporic Blackness: The Life and Times of Arturo Alfonso Schomburg.* Albany: State University of New York, 2017.

Vallejo, Catherine. "Seeing 'Spain' at the 1893 Chicago World (Columbian) Exhibition." In *Spectacle and Topophilia: Reading Early Modern and Postmodern Hispanic Cultures,* edited by David R. Castillo and Bradley Nelson, 155–172. Nashville, TN: Vanderbilt University Press, 2011.

Van Dyke, Jon M. *Who Owns the Crown Lands of Hawai'i?* Honolulu: University of Hawai'i Press, 2008.

de Varigny, C. "L'Insurrection Cubaine." *L'illustration* 54, no. 2808 (December 19, 1896): 483–84.

Vergara, Benito M. *Displaying Filipinos: Photography and Colonialism in Early 20th Century Philippines.* Quezon City: University of the Philippines Press, 1998.

Verhaeren, Émile and Darío de Regoyos. *España Negra.* Palma de Mallorca, Spain: José J. de Olañeta, 1999.

Vieyra, Natalia Angeles. "Fragmentary Impressions: Camille Pissaro and Francisco Oller in the Americas, 1848–1898." PhD diss. Temple University, 2021.

———. "Problem Portraits: Francisco Oller in the Age of U.S. Imperialism." *Panorama: Journal of the Association of Historians of American Art* 7, no. 2 (Fall 2021).

Villareal, Corazon D. *Back to the Future: Perspectives on the Thomasite Legacy to Philippine Education.* Manila: American Studies Association of the Philippines in Cooperation with the Cultural Affairs Office, U.S. Embassy, 2003.

Von Holst, H. E. "The Annexation of Hawaii." *The Advocate of Peace (1894–1920)* 60, no. 3 (March 1898): 63–70.

de Wagenheim, Olga Jiménez. *Puerto Rico: An Interpretive History from Pre-Columbian Times to 1900.* Princeton, NJ: Markus Wiener Publishers, 1998.

Walker, D. J. *Spanish Women and the Colonial Wars of the 1890s.* Baton Rouge: Louisiana State University Press, 2008.

Warren, Kenneth. *Triumphant Capitalism: Henry Clay Frick and the Industrial Transformation of America.* Pittsburgh: University of Pittsburgh Press, 1995.

Weare, Neil. "Why the *Insular Cases* Must Become the Next Plessy." *Harvard Law Review* (blog), March 28, 2018, https://blog.harvardlawreview.org/why-the-insular-cases-must-become-the-next-plessy/.

Weare, Neil, and Adriel Cepeda Derieux. "After *Aurelius*: What Future for the *Insular Cases*?" *The Yale Law Journal* 130, (2020–2021), https://www.yalelawjournal.org/forum/after-aurelius-what-future-for-the-insular-cases.

Welch, Richard E., Jr. *Response to Imperialism: The United States and the Philippine-American War, 1899–1902.* Chapel Hill: University of North Carolina Press, 1987.

Wexler, Laura. *Tender Violence: Domestic Visions in an Age of U.S. Imperialism.* Chapel Hill: University of North Carolina Press, 2000.

Whyte, Kenneth. *The Uncrowned King.* Berkeley, CA: Counterpoint, 2009.

Williams, Riánna M. "Hawaiian Ali'i Women in New York Society: The Ena-Coney-Vos-Gould Connection," *Hawaiian Journal of History* 38 (2004): 147–64.

Williams, Ronald C., Jr. "'Aole Hoohui ia Hawaii': U.S. Collegiate Teams Debate Annexation of Hawai'i and Independence Prevails, 1893 to 1897." *Hawaiian Journal of History* 43, (2009): 153–79.

———. "Race, Power, and the Dilemma of Democracy: Hawai'i's First Territorial Legislature, 1901." *Hawaiian Journal of History* 49, (2015): 1–46.

———. "To Raise a Voice in Praise: The Revivalist Mission of John Henry Wise, 1889–1896." *Hawaiian Journal of History* 46, (2012): 1–35.

Williams, William Appleman. "The Frontier Thesis and American Foreign Policy." *Pacific Historical Review* 24, no. 4 (November 1955): 379–95.

———. *The Tragedy of American Diplomacy.* New York: W. W. Norton, 2009.

Wilson, William P. *Official Catalogue, Philippine Exhibits: Universal Exposition, St. Louis, U.S.A., 1904.* St. Louis: Published for the Committee on Press and Publicity by the Official Catalogue Company, 1904.

Witherbee, Sidney A., ed. *Spanish-American War Songs: A Complete Collection of Newspaper Verse During the Recent War with Spain.* Detroit: Sidney A. Witherbee, 1898.

Wolters, Timothy S. "Recapitalizing the Fleet: A Material Analysis of Late-Nineteenth-Century U.S. Naval Power." *Technology and Culture* 52, no. 1 (January 2011): 103–126.

Woodward, Valerie Solar. "'I Guess They Didn't Want Us Asking Too Many Questions': Reading American Empire in Guam." *The Contemporary Pacific* 25, no. 1 (January 2013): 67–91.

"Would Annex Isle of Pines: Residents Renew Agitation in View of Danish Project." *New York Times*, August 18, 1916.

Zimmerman, Warren. *First Great Triumph: How Five Americans Made Their Country a World Power.* New York: Farrar, Straus and Giroux, 2002.

Chronology

CAROLINA MAESTRE WITH SHANNON NEAL

1787

Ka'iana'ahu'ula (c. 1755–1795), generally referred to as Ka'iana, accompanies Captain John Meares (c. 1756–1809) on his travels of the world.

1803

To support a decimated French army fighting in the Haitian Revolution (1791–1804) and military campaigns in Europe, Napoleonic France sells the Louisiana Territory to the United States for $15 million, doubling the size of the country.

1804

After more than twelve years of revolution, Haiti gains independence from France and becomes the first Black republic. Enslavers in Latin America and the United States fear that enslaved people in other regions will follow Haiti's example.

1808

Napoleonic France occupies Spain, resulting in the abdication of King Charles IV (1748–1819) and his son Fernando VII (1784–1833). Political instability in Spain fuels the Latin American Wars of Independence (1809–1826).

1811

German scientist and geographer Alexander von Humboldt (1769–1859) publishes the best-selling book *Political Essay on the Kingdom of New Spain*, in which he discusses nine potential routes for an isthmian canal in Central America.

1812

March 19

In opposition to Napoleonic rule, representatives from the Spanish Provinces, the Spanish Americas, and the Philippines approve a liberal constitution known as the Constitución de Cádiz. The constitution grants the Philippines and the Spanish Americas parliamentary representation in the Spanish *Cortes*. The short-lived constitution is abrogated in 1814 with Fernando VII's return to power.

June 18

The U.S. Congress declares war on Great Britain, initiating the War of 1812 (1812–1815).

1815

The Manila–Acapulco galleon trade route, an important trans-Pacific commercial circuit for the Spanish Empire since 1565, comes to an end in part due to instability in Mexico during the Mexican War of Independence (1810–1821).

1817

September 23

Spain submits to British pressure and agrees to abolish the slave trade by May 1820 for an indemnity of 10 million pesetas. Due to ineffective enforcement, the trade persists via clandestine networks.

1820

March 30

The first company of the American Board of Commissioners for Foreign Missions (ABCFM) arrives in Hawai'i.

1821

September 27

Mexico gains independence from Spain. Colonial administrators in the Philippines now report directly to Madrid.

1823

December 2

In his annual message to Congress, President James Monroe (1758–1831) introduces the Monroe Doctrine in opposition to the extension of European colonialism in the Americas. The doctrine warns European powers not to reconquer newly independent republics or seek future colonies in the Western Hemisphere. Any intention to do so would be perceived as an act of aggression to the United States.

1830

May 28

President Andrew Jackson (1767–1845) signs the Indian Removal Act into law, forcing the removal of Cherokee, Chickasaw, Choctaw, Creek, and Seminole, among other Indigenous Nations, from their homelands to the west of the Mississippi River.

1840

October 8

King Kamehameha III (1814–1854) promulgates the first constitution of the Hawaiian Kingdom, establishing a constitutional monarchy.

1842

December 30

President John Tyler (1790–1862) sends a message to Congress recognizing the independence of the government of Hawai'i and opposing any attempt by another power to take control of the archipelago. This message, known as the Tyler Doctrine, extends the Monroe Doctrine to the Pacific.

1845

March 1

President Tyler signs a joint resolution to annex the Republic of Texas to the United States, setting a precedent that later would be used to justify the annexation of Hawai'i. Texas is admitted as a slave state.

July

U.S. columnist John O'Sullivan (1813–1895) coins the term "Manifest Destiny" in an article for the *Democratic Review* (fig. 1).

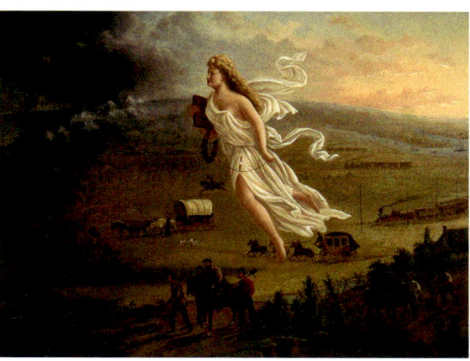

Fig. 1 *American Progress*, John Gast (1842–1896), 1872. Oil on canvas; 29.2 × 40 cm (11½ × 15¾ in.). The Autry Museum of the American West

1846

President James K. Polk (1795–1849) sends an envoy to Mexico offering $20,000,000 to buy present-day California and New Mexico. Upon refusal, Polk sends General Zachary Taylor (1784–1850) to the Nueces Strip, a disputed boundary between Mexico and the United States. On May 13, 1846, the United States declares war on Mexico, starting the Mexican-American War (1846–1848).

December 12

The United States and New Granada (present-day Colombia and Panama) sign the New Granada Treaty, also known as the Mallarino-Bidlack Treaty, granting the United States transit rights across the Isthmus of Panama.

1847

Unsatisfied with the arbitrary rule of *peninsulares,* or Spaniards born on the Iberian Peninsula, and encouraged by the admittance of Texas to the Union as a slave state, Cuban Creole enslavers establish El Club de la Habana to organize against Spanish colonial rule and pursue annexation to the United States.

1848

February 2

The signing of the Treaty of Guadalupe Hidalgo ends the Mexican-American War (1846–1848) and results in the U.S. annexation of present-day California, New Mexico, and parts of Nevada and Utah.

Fig. 2 Winslow Homer (1836–1910), Oliver Ingraham Lay (1845–1890), 1865. Oil on canvas; 51.1 × 41 cm (20⅛ × 16⅛ in.). National Academy of Design, New York

March 8

In what was known as the Great Māhele, or the great land division, King Kamehameha III and aliʻi members redistribute Hawaiian lands between the mōʻī (king, monarch, or ruling chief), the aliʻi (high-born elite) and the makaʻāina (common people), abolishing the feudal land system.

June

President Polk offers $100 million to Spain to purchase Cuba, without success.

Between 1848 and 1850, Narciso López (1797–1851), with the support of El Club de la Habana, leads several armed expeditions to Cuba in support of Cuban annexation to the United States as a slave state, but they fail.

1854

June

While pursuing U.S. interests in the Caribbean, President Franklin Pierce (1804–1869) sends instructions to negotiate the recognition of the Dominican Republic in exchange for rights to a coaling station in Samaná Bay.

June 8

The Gadsden Purchase Treaty is ratified by the U.S. Senate and signed by President Pierce. The agreement stipulates that the United States will pay Mexico $10 million for 29,670 square miles of land near the Mexico border with Arizona and southwestern New Mexico. This is the final territorial acquisition made within the continental United States.

October 18

Eager to acquire Cuba as a slave state, President Pierce sends emissaries to Ostend, Belgium, with a mission to negotiate a $130 million offer to Spain to purchase Cuba. The aims of this mission, articulated in the Ostend Manifesto, failed.

1857

Europe's declining purchase of U.S. agricultural products triggers the 1857 Financial Panic.

1860

November 6

Abraham Lincoln (1809–1865) wins the U.S. presidency.

1861

April 12

Confederate forces fire on Fort Sumter in Charleston, South Carolina, marking the beginning of the U.S. Civil War (1861–1865).

October 15

Harper's Weekly sponsors an artist correspondent pass for Winslow Homer (1836–1910) to document the front lines of the U.S. Civil War.

1862

May 20

President Lincoln signs the Homestead Act, a federal incentive for Euro-Americans to populate the continental West.

March

Winslow Homer is granted a second pass and spends about two months embedded with the 61st New York Volunteer Infantry, as part of the Second Corps of the Army of the Potomac.

1863

January 1

Nearing the third year of the U.S. Civil War, President Lincoln issues the Emancipation Proclamation, declaring all enslaved people free within the rebellious states.

Winslow Homer finishes his first oil painting, *The Sharpshooter*, based on his experience on the front lines of the U.S. Civil War (fig. 2).

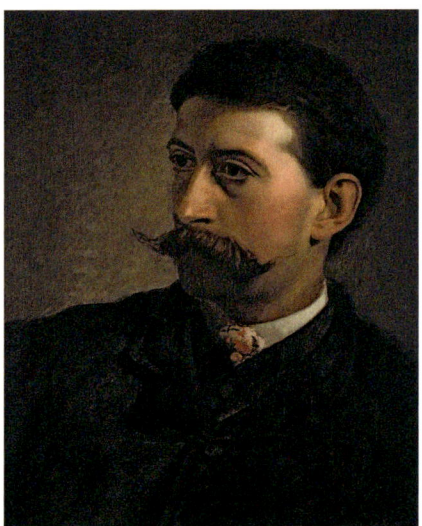

1865

After the U.S. Civil War ends on April 9, Cuban enslavers relinquish efforts toward U.S. annexation because it is no longer possible for Cuba to become a slave state.

November 25

The Ministerio de Ultramar, the Spanish entity overseeing colonial governance, issues a call to representatives from Cuba and Puerto Rico to discuss colonial reforms. While the Junta Informativa de Ultramar (Overseas information summit) began the following year, their proposals did not materialize.

1867

Lola Rodríguez de Tió (1843–1924) writes the Puerto Rican revolutionary anthem, "La Borinqueña," with lyrics that incite Puerto Ricans to take up arms against the Spanish.

March 30

The United States reaches an agreement with Russia to purchase the territory of Alaska for $7.2 million.

1868

January 6

In Santo Domingo, Ramón Emeterio Betances (1827–1898), José Francisco Basora (life dates unknown), and Segundo Ruiz Belvis (1829–1867) found the Comité Revolucionario de Puerto Rico, or Puerto Rican Revolutionary Committee, to plot a revolt for Puerto Rican independence.

September 23

Members of the Comité Revolucionario de Puerto Rico stage an uprising against Spanish rule and proclaim Puerto Rican independence. Known as the *Grito de Lares*, the uprising is suppressed by Spanish authorities.

October 10

Led by Carlos Manuel de Céspedes (1819–1864), the *Grito de Yara* proclaims Cuban independence and initiates the Ten Years' War (1868–1878).

1869

After studying in Spain, Puerto Rican educator, lawyer, and journalist Eugenio María de Hostos (1839–1903) moves to New York City and becomes an activist for Puerto Rican and Cuban independence.

November 17

The Suez Canal opens to navigation, connecting the Mediterranean with the Red Sea.

1871

January 15

Cuban independence advocate José Martí (1853–1895) is exiled to Spain, serving only a fraction of an initial sentence of six years of hard labor in the Isle of Pines for conspiracy against the Spanish.

1872

March 3

By royal decree of Amadeo I (1845–1890), king of Spain from 1870 to 1873, the Puerto Rican artist Francisco Oller y Cestero (1833–1917) is named Painter of the Royal Court.

1875

January 2

After completing his legal studies, José Martí leaves Europe to meet with his family in Mexico City.

January 30

The United States and the Kingdom of Hawai'i sign the Reciprocity Treaty, which allows certain Hawaiian goods, particularly sugar and rice, to enter U.S. markets tariff-free for a period of seven years.

1876

June 25–26

The combined forces of the Lakota Sioux, Northern Cheyenne, and Arapaho tribes defeat the Seventh Cavalry Regiment in the Battle of Greasy Grass, also known as the Battle of Little Bighorn.

1877

Filipino artist Juan Luna (1857–1899) travels to Spain and attends the Academy of San Fernando in Madrid.

1878

February 10

The Pact of Zanjón ends the Ten Years' War in Cuba, promising administrative reforms and freedom to the enslaved people registered in the insurgent army.

March

Unsatisfied with the Pact of Zanjón, General Antonio Maceo Grajales (1845–1896) assembles 1,500 armed men to protest the agreement. The Protest of Baraguá extends the armed conflict in Cuba for another ten weeks.

July

The Partido Liberal Autonomista, the autonomist faction in Cuba, is established to defend the reforms and promises outlined in the Pact of Zanjón. Many disillusioned separatists join the autonomist faction.

In response to the formation of the Partido Liberal Autonomista in Cuba, *peninsulares* create the Partido Unión Constitucional to protect their interests.

1879

General Calixto García (1839–1898) organizes the Cuban Revolutionary Committee in New York City and leads a separatist expeditionary force to Cuba, launching the short-lived war known as *La Guerra Chiquita* (1879–1880).

April

William Cogswell (1819–1903) travels to Honolulu to paint the first of several portraits of King David Kalākaua (1836–1891).

1880

Armando García Menocal (1863–1942) moves to Madrid to study at the Academy of San Fernando with Francisco Jover y Casanova (1836–1890).

January 3

José Martí arrives in New York City and joins the efforts of the Cuban Revolutionary Committee in support of *La Guerra Chiquita*.

1882

May 6

President Chester A. Arthur (1829–1886) signs the Chinese Exclusion Act, which initially prohibits immigration of Chinese laborers for ten years. It is the first federal law to deny entry to a specific ethnic group.

1884

During the winter months, Winslow Homer travels to Florida, Cuba, and the Bahamas.

Juan Luna wins the First Equal prize at the National Exposition of Fine Arts in Madrid for his painting *Spoliarium* (see p. 129). Armando García Menocal wins the second prize at the exposition for his painting *Generosidad Castellana* (Castilian Generosity).

October 20

José Martí meets with General Máximo Gómez (1836–1905) and General Antonio Maceo Grajales (1845–1896) in New York, and splits with the generals over differing views for attaining Cuban independence.

1886

September 24

In response to a dwindling native Hawaiian population and increasing foreign presence, King David Kalākaua (1836–1891) revives the Hale Nauā Society, with the aim of collecting, studying, and preserving Native Hawaiian culture and practices.

1887

March

José Rizal (1861–1896) publishes *Noli me tangere* (Touch me not), a critique of the Catholic Church and Spanish governance in the Philippines.

Román Baldorioty de Castro (1822–1889) becomes the first chairman of the newly founded Partido Autonomista Puertorriqueño, which sought self-rule under the Spanish Crown.

The Reciprocity Treaty between Hawaiʻi and the United States is renewed. To the dismay of Kānaka Maoli, or Native Hawaiians, the United States is granted exclusive rights to Pearl Harbor for the building of a coaling station.

July 6

The Hawaiian League, led by Lorrin Thurston (1858–1931), and with the support of the Honolulu Rifles militia, forces King Kalākaua to sign a new constitution. Referred to as the Bayonet Constitution, this document rendered the monarch nearly powerless over government affairs.

1888

Kānaka Maoli organize the Hui Kālaiʻāina, a political organization to protest the Bayonet Constitution and restore the Hawaiian monarch's power within the government.

1890

Alfred Thayer Mahan (1840–1914) publishes *The Influence of Sea Power Upon History, 1660–1730,* theorizing that a modern navy is the key to U.S. global hegemony.

The McKinley Tariff Act of 1890, sponsored by then-senator of Ohio William McKinley (1843–1901), raises protective tariffs by nearly 50 percent on certain imports and eliminates tariffs for others such as sugar and coffee. The act disadvantaged the Hawaiian sugar trade, which had benefitted from its own reciprocity treaty with the United States since 1875.

1891

Armando García Menocal becomes chair of elementary drawing at the Academia de San Alejandro in Havana.

January 20

King Kalākaua dies in San Francisco following a trip to Washington, DC, to discuss the 1890 McKinley Tariff. Queen Liliʻuokalani (1838–1917) begins her rule of Hawaiʻi.

1892

January

José Martí founds the Partido Revolucionario Cubano, or Cuban Revolutionary Party, in Key West, Florida, with the aim of organizing and securing Cuban independence.

March 14

The first issue of *Patria,* the ancillary newspaper of the Partido Revolucionario Cubano, is printed.

July 7

In Manila, Andrés Bonifacio (1863–1897) founds the Katipunan, a secret revolutionary society, with the aim of overthrowing Spanish colonial rule.

October 19

William Cogswell (1819–1903) sells his posthumous portrait of King Kalākaua and a portrait of Queen Liliʻuokalani to the queen for $1,500 each.

1893

Frederick Jackson Turner (1861–1932) first publishes "The Significance of the Frontier in American History" in *Proceedings of the State Historical Society of Wisconsin,* claiming the close of the United States' western frontier.

January 16

U.S. Minister to the Hawaiian Kingdom, John L. Stevens (1820–1895), yields to the Committee of Safety's request and orders marines from the USS *Boston* to land in Honolulu. The troops position themselves near government buildings and the ʻIolani Palace.

January 17

The Committee of Safety successfully stages a coup against Queen Liliʻuokalani, aided by the intimidating presence of the marine detachment from the USS *Boston*. The Provisional Government of Hawaiʻi (1893–1894) is established.

March 4

President Grover Cleveland (1837–1908) is inaugurated. He does not recognize the Provisional Government of Hawaiʻi, withdraws the annexation treaty from Congress, and sends Congressman James Blount (1837–1903) to Honolulu to investigate the circumstances of the overthrow and the opinion of the Hawaiian people toward annexation.

July 17

Known as the Blount Report, Congressman James Blount's investigation finds that the Hawaiian coup was motivated by white colonials' economic and racist interests, and that the "undoubted sentiment of the people is for the queen, against the Provisional Government, and against annexation," with the exception of the extremely small minority white population.

Armando García Menocal exhibits *La muerte de Maceo* in the Spanish rooms in the World's Columbian Exposition of 1893 in Chicago from May 1 through October 30.

1894

July 4

The Constitution of 1894, drafted by Lorrin A. Thurston and Sanford B. Dole (1844–1926), takes effect, establishing the Republic of Hawaiʻi with Dole as president.

1895

Pale` Enko`, or Padre José Torres Palomo (1836–1919), becomes Guam's first CHamoru to be ordained as a Catholic priest.

Lola Rodríguez de Tió moves to New York City and collaborates with Cuban and Puerto Rican expatriates to support the revolutionary cause.

January

Hawaiian royalists stage a failed armed counterrevolution against the Republic of Hawaiʻi. The government finds Queen Liliʻuokalani guilty of treason and sentences her to house arrest.

February 24

The Grito de Baire declares Cuban independence and initiates the third War of Cuban Independence (1895–1898), also known as *La guerra necesaria*, or the Necessary War.

May 19

José Martí is killed by Spanish troops at the Battle of Dos Ríos.

June 5

Armando García Menocal enlists in the third War of Cuban Independence and becomes General Máximo Gómez's aide.

1896

February 16

General Valeriano Weyler (1838–1930) enforces the reconcentration policy in Cuba to prevent the civilian population from aiding rebels.

August 23

A revolution against Spanish rule, known as the "Cry of Balintawak," initially led by Andrés Bonifacio, begins in the Philippines.

October 23

Queen Liliʻuokalani receives a full pardon. She immediately makes plans to travel to Washington, DC, to advocate for the restoration of her sovereignty.

December 7

General Antonio Maceo Grajales dies during a Spanish ambush in Havana province.

December 30

The Spanish colonial government executes José Rizal for sedition in Luneta Park, Manila.

1897

January 23

Queen Liliʻuokalani arrives in Washington, DC.

March 4

President William McKinley (1843–1901) is inaugurated.

May 10

After being sentenced to death by a military court, Andrés Bonifacio is executed.

June 16

Three months after President McKinley is inaugurated, a new treaty for the annexation of Hawaiʻi is drafted and submitted to the U.S. Senate. Without majority support, the treaty is later voted down.

August 8

Conservative Spanish prime minister Antonio Cánovas del Castillo (1828–1897) is assassinated by an Italian anarchist. Liberal Práxedes Mateo Sagasta (1825–1923) succeeds him.

September 14

Pro-annexationist senator John Morgan (1824–1907) and four other U.S. congressmen arrive in Honolulu to investigate the events surrounding the overthrow of Queen Liliʻuokalani.

October 6

The Spanish Government replaces controversial General Valeriano Weyler with General Ramón Blanco (1833–1906) as governor of Cuba.

Fig. 3 Front page of *La Correspondencia de Puerto Rico,* December 12, 1897, featuring an outline of the decrees of the Autonomic Charter, which were first published in *La Gaceta de Madrid* on November 26 and 27, 1897. Library of Congress, Chronicling America: Historic American Newspapers, Washington, DC

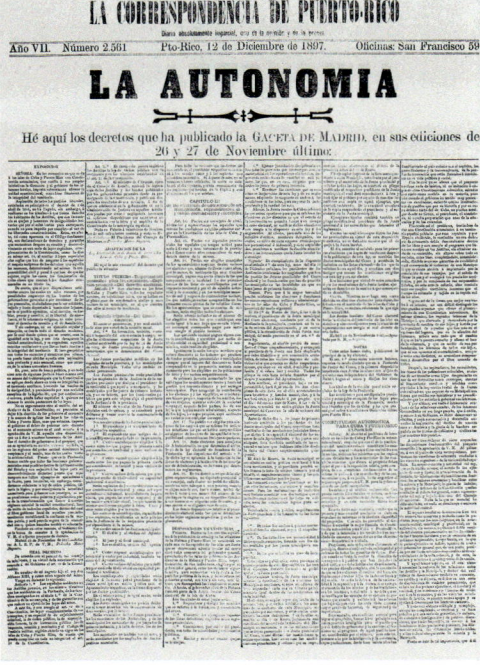

Fig. 4 Group of U.S. Army female nurses on duty at First Reserve Hospital, Manila, Philippines, Unidentified photographer, 1898. Albumen silver print; 33 × 38.1 cm (13 × 15 in.). National Museum of Health and Medicine

October 8

Hawaiian royalist groups organize a rally in Honolulu.

November 1

Emilio Aguinaldo declares the Philippines independent at Biak-na-Bato. A new constitution is drafted.

November 20

Hawaiian royalist groups, the Hui Aloha 'Āina and the Hui Kālai'āina, travel to Washington, DC, to deliver their petitions to protest annexation.

November 25

Spain grants Cuba and Puerto Rico the Autonomic Charter, increasing self-government under Spanish rule (fig. 3).

December 14

The Spanish colonial government in the Philippines and Emilio Aguinaldo negotiate the end of the conflict with the signing of the Treaty of Biak-na-Bato. Aguinaldo and other revolutionaries go into exile in Hong Kong.

December 22

U.S. consul general of Havana, Fitzhugh Lee (1835–1905), writes to the U.S. State Department, requesting naval vessels be sent to Havana to protect U.S. citizens in Cuba during the third War of Cuban Independence.

1898

January

Queen Lili'uokalani publishes *Hawaii's Story by Hawaii's Queen,* in which she describes her upbringing, rule, and dethronement.

January 25

The USS *Maine* anchors to buoy in Havana Harbor.

February 9

The *New York Journal* publishes Spanish Ambassador Enrique Dupuy de Lôme's (1851–1904) letter criticizing President McKinley.

February 15

The USS *Maine* explodes in Havana Harbor.

March 29

The U.S. government presses the Spanish government to declare an armistice in the Cuban conflict.

April 19

The U.S. Congress passes a joint resolution authorizing war with Spain. The resolution included the Teller Amendment, named after Senator Henry M. Teller (1830–1914) of Colorado, stating that the United States would not retain permanent control of Cuba.

April 22

The U.S. fleet leaves Key West to initiate a blockade of Cuba.

April 25

The United States formally declares war on Spain.

April 28

After the declaration of war, U.S. Surgeon General George Miller Sternberg (1838–1915) receives congressional authority to appoint female nurses under contract (fig. 4).

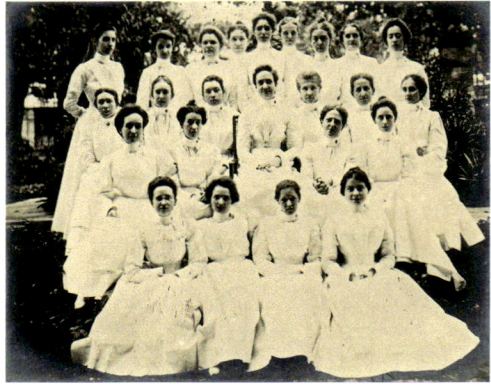

May 1

Under the command of U.S. Navy Commodore George Dewey (1837–1917), the Asiatic Squadron defeats the Spanish fleet in Manila Bay, the first U.S. victory of the War of 1898.

May 10

Secretary of the Navy John Davis Long (1838–1915) issues orders to Captain Henry Glass (1844–1908), commander of the cruiser USS *Charleston*, to take control of the port of Guam.

May 12

A U.S. naval fleet under the command of Rear Admiral William T. Sampson (1840–1902) bombards the city of San Juan, Puerto Rico (fig. 5).

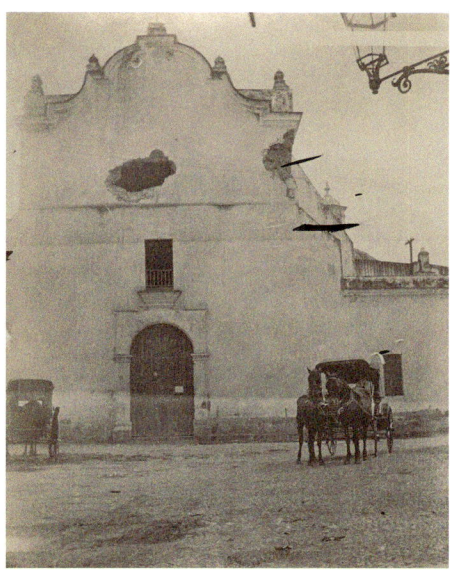

May 19

Carried by a U.S. naval vessel, Emilio Aguinaldo returns to the Philippines from exile in Hong Kong.

June 12

Emilio Aguinaldo proclaims Philippine independence at a ceremony in Cavite.

June 21

Spanish authorities in Guam surrender and U.S. forces raise the American flag.

June 24

Lieutenant Colonel Theodore Roosevelt (1858–1919) and the Rough Riders encounter Spanish troops in the Battle of Las Guásimas, near Santiago de Cuba.

June 30

The U.S. Army arrives in the Philippines, under the command of Brigadier General Thomas M. Anderson (1836–1917).

July 1

In battle, U.S. and Cuban troops take El Viso Fort, the town of El Caney, and San Juan Heights. The Rough Riders also take San Juan Hill during the Battle of Kettle Hill.

July 3

Under the command of Rear Admiral William T. Sampson and Commodore Winfield Scott Schley (1839–1911), the U.S. squadron destroys the Spanish flotilla, under the command of Admiral Pascual Cervera y Topete (1839–1909), in Santiago de Cuba (fig. 6).

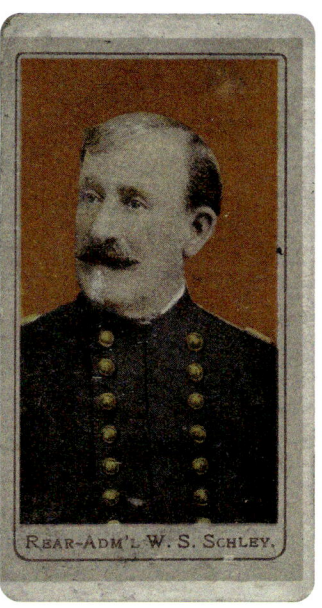

July 4

Known as the Newlands Resolution, the annexation of Hawai'i is approved by both the House and the Senate. President McKinley signs it into law on July 7, 1898.

July 13–17

After the Siege of Santiago, Spanish forces led by José Toral y Velázquez (1832–1904) surrender Santiago de Cuba to Generals Nelson Miles (1839–1925), William Shafter (1835–1906), and Joseph Wheeler (1836–1906).

July 25

The U.S. Army lands in Guánica, Puerto Rico, under the command of General Nelson Miles.

August 7

Emilio Aguinaldo appoints lawyer Felipe Agoncillo (1859–1941) to travel to Washington, DC, and secure Filipino participation in the peace negotiations between Spain and the United States, but is denied.

August 12

In Washington, DC, Spanish and U.S. officials sign a cease-fire agreement, putting an end to hostilities (fig. 7).

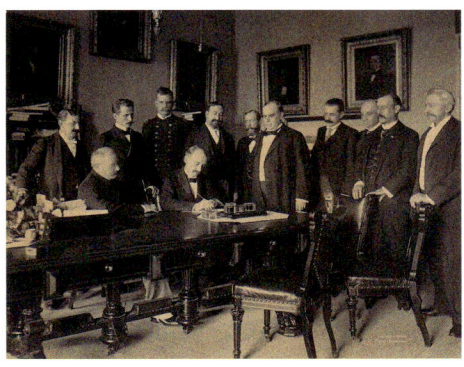

Fig. 5 *San José Church after the U.S. Bombardment of San Juan on May 12, 1898*, Unidentified photographer, 1898. Gelatin silver print; 11.9 × 9.4 cm (4⅝ × 3¾ in.). Archivo General de Puerto Rico

Fig. 6 *Rear Admiral W. S. Schley (1839–1911)*, from the *Heroes of the Spanish War* series, American Tobacco Company, c. 1901. Commercial color lithograph; 6.6 × 3.7 cm (2⅝ × 1⁷⁄₁₆ in.). The Metropolitan Museum of Art; The Jefferson R. Burdick Collection, gift of Jefferson R. Burdick

Fig. 7 *Signing of the Peace Protocol*, Frances Benjamin Johnston (1864–1952), August 12, 1898. Gelatin silver print; 31 × 41.1 cm (12³⁄₁₆ × 16³⁄₁₆ in.). National Portrait Gallery, Smithsonian Institution

Fig. 8 *School Begins*, Louis Dalrymple (1866–1905) for *Puck* magazine, January 25, 1899. Chromolithograph, Library of Congress, Washington, DC

August 13

After the Battle of Manila, also known as the Mock Battle, Spanish forces led by Fermín Jáudenes y Álvarez (1836–1915) concede defeat to the U.S. Army led by Generals Wesley Merritt (1836–1910) and Arthur MacArthur (1845–1912), and Commodore George Dewey, rather than to Aguinaldo's forces.

September

Aguinaldo convenes the first Filipino parliament, the Malolos Congress.

October 1

Representatives of Spain and U.S. commissioners convene in Paris to negotiate the details of the Treaty of Paris.

October 16

Felipe Agoncillo arrives in Paris but is denied participation in the peace treaty negotiations between the United States and Spain. During his stay, his friend, the Filipino artist Félix Resurrección Hidalgo (1855–1913), paints his portrait. Agoncillo also meets with artist Juan Luna, who was also in Paris hoping to participate in the peace negotiations.

October 18

The last Spanish troops leave Puerto Rico. Under the command of General John R. Brooke (1838–1936), the U.S. military government in the island begins.

Puerto Rican painter Francisco Oller y Cestero signs and dates his portrait of President McKinley.

November 19

The Anti-Imperialist League is founded in opposition to territorial expansion, on the grounds that it runs counter to U.S. democratic principles.

December 10

Representatives of Spain and the United States sign the Treaty of Paris. Spain agrees to cede Puerto Rico and Guam, sell the Philippines to the United States for $20 million, and relinquish claims to Cuban sovereignty. After the signing of the treaty, Felipe Agoncillo and Juan Luna travel to Washington, DC, to secure Filipino sovereignty.

December 21

President McKinley issues the Benevolent Assimilation Proclamation, outlining U.S. governmental policy in the Philippines (fig. 8).

1899

January 1

The U.S. military occupation of Cuba begins.

January 20

Eugenio María de Hostos, José Julio Henna (1848–1924), and Manuel Zeno Gandía (1855–1930) arrive in Washington, DC, to negotiate the terms of annexation for Puerto Rico with President McKinley.

January 21

The First Philippine Republic is established with the promulgation of the Malolos Constitution.

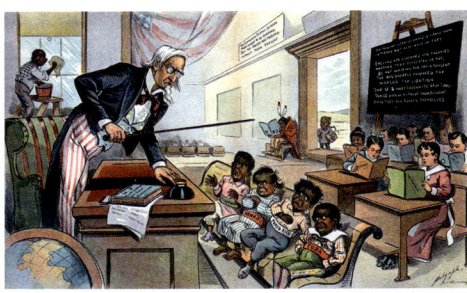

January 23

Emilio Aguinaldo is inaugurated as the president of the First Philippine Republic.

February 4–5

Filipino revolutionaries and U.S. forces engage in battle at Manila for two days. The Philippine-American War begins.

February 6

The Treaty of Paris is ratified by the U.S. Congress.

1900

April 12

The U.S. Congress passes the Foraker Act, establishing a civilian government in Puerto Rico under U.S. control. The act provides for an elected house of representatives on the island, but not for voting representation in Congress.

April 17

The United States annexes the eastern islands of the Samoan archipelago in the South Pacific Ocean, which became known as American Samoa.

September

The Second Philippine Commission, led by William Howard Taft (1857–1930), begins its administration in the Philippines, lasting until 1916.

November 7

The Treaty of Washington is signed to clarify Article III of the Treaty of Paris, which traced the Philippine Archipelago's demarcation coordinates for the land to be ceded to the United States. The treaty specifies that all islands in the archipelago, even those that fall outside of the demarcation coordinates, including the islands of Cagayan Sulu and Sibutu, are to be ceded to the United States. For this, the United States agrees to pay $100,000 within six months after the exchange of ratification.

1901

In 1901, thirty-two CHamorus, including Atanasio Taitano Perez (1874–1950), propose self-governance and U.S. citizenship.

January

A series of U.S. Supreme Court decisions known as the *Insular Cases* introduce the doctrine of unincorporated territories, determining that the U.S. Constitution was not fully applicable to the people living in the territories annexed through the Treaty of Paris.

March 2

The U.S. Congress passes the Platt Amendment, stipulating the conditions of U.S. withdrawal from Cuba, giving the United States power to intervene in Cuban affairs and to lease land on the island.

March 4

President McKinley begins his second term as president.

March 23

Macabebe Scouts, guided by a former Filipino insurgent, Cecilio Segismundo (life dates unknown), and commanded by Brigadier General Frederick Funston (1865–1917), capture Emilio Aguinaldo on Palanan, Isabela Province, Philippines.

April 1

Aguinaldo declares allegiance to the United States. Eighteen days later he issues a formal surrender.

September 14

On the grounds of the Pan-American Exposition in Buffalo, New York, President McKinley dies from a gunshot by an anarchist (fig. 9). Theodore Roosevelt becomes president.

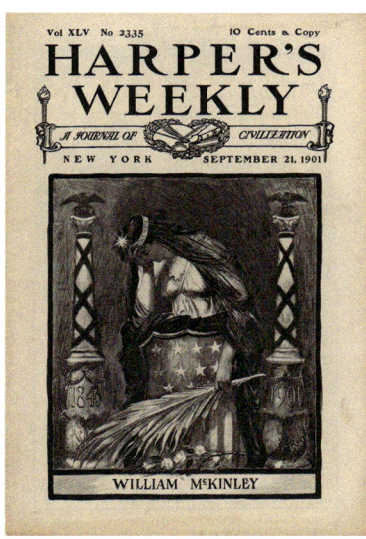

September 28

Known as the "Balangiga Massacre," Filipino guerrilla soldiers led by Lieutenant Colonel Eugenio Daza (1870–1954), attack Company C of the 9th U.S. Infantry at Balangiga, the worst defeat of the U.S. military since the Battle of Little Bighorn in 1876.

1902

Winslow Homer finishes *Searchlight on Harbor Entrance, Santiago de Cuba* (see p. 184).

April 16

The Batangas leader, General Miguel Malvar (1865–1911), surrenders. Around a thousand Batangas residents die during the U.S. Army's use of reconcentration camps to counter guerrilla warfare in the Philippines.

May 20

The Cuban Republic is established under the 1901 Constitution with Tomás Estrada Palma (1835–1908) as president.

June 28

The U.S. Congress passes the Spooner Act, authorizing a canal to be built across the Isthmus of Panama.

July 1

The Organic Act of 1902 ends military government in the Philippines.

1903

February 16

Tomás Estrada Palma signs an agreement to lease Guantánamo Bay to the United States.

November 18

The Hay–Bunau-Varilla Treaty is signed, granting the United States permission to build a canal through Panama and the cession of a land area thirty miles long and five miles wide on each side of the canal where the United States could govern as sovereign. Construction on the canal starts the next year and is completed in 1914.

1904

Zoraida Valdezate, from Puerto Rico, graduates from the Carlisle Indian Industrial School (fig. 10).

February 19

Luis Muñoz Rivera (1859–1916) and José de Diego (1866–1918) found the Partido Unión de Puerto Rico, or the Union Party of Puerto Rico, in opposition to the government established under the Foraker Act.

March 2

U.S. Secretary of State, John Hay (1838–1905), and Ambassador of Cuba Gonzalo Quesada, sign the Hay-Quesada Treaty, which recognizes Cuba's sovereignty over the Isle of Pines (today called the Isle of Youth), an island located south of Havana and Pinar del Río. U.S. business interests established on the isle since 1898 opposed the treaty. The U.S. Congress only ratified the Hay-Quesada Treaty in 1925, when it determined that the Isle of Pines was of no maritime value for the United States.

April 30–December 1

The St. Louis World's Fair includes displays of Filipino and other Native peoples.

Fig. 9 *Assassination of William McKinley*, Cover of *Harper's Weekly*, September 21, 1901, William Allen Rogers (1854–1932). Halftone on paper; 41.1 × 29 cm (16³⁄₁₆ × 11⁷⁄₁₆ in.). National Portrait Gallery, Smithsonian Institution

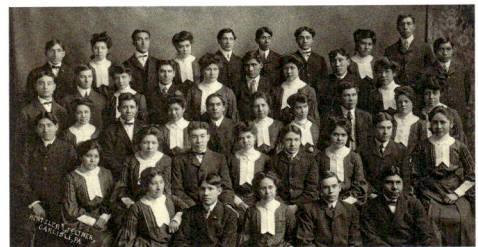

Fig. 10 Carlisle Indian Industrial School class of 1904, Unidentified photographer. Gelatin silver print; 16.5 × 30.5 cm (6½ × 12 in.). Cumberland County Historical Society, Carlisle, Pennsylvania

1905

Fighting in Leyte and Samar Provinces in the Philippines concludes.

1906

Armando García Menocal finishes the mural *Batalla de Coliseo* in Las Delicias, the estate of sugar plantation owner and philanthropist Rosalía Abreu (1862–1930).

March 5–8

Nearly 800 U.S. soldiers and Philippine Constabulary forces, fighting under Governor Leonard Wood (1860–1927), defeat Tausug Muslims in the Battle of Bud Dajo, in Sulu Province. Over 1,000 Tausugs are killed, including women and children.

1908

Armando García Menocal (fig. 11) completes the commissioned painting *La muerte de Maceo* for the Ayuntamiento, or city hall, of Havana (see p. 185).

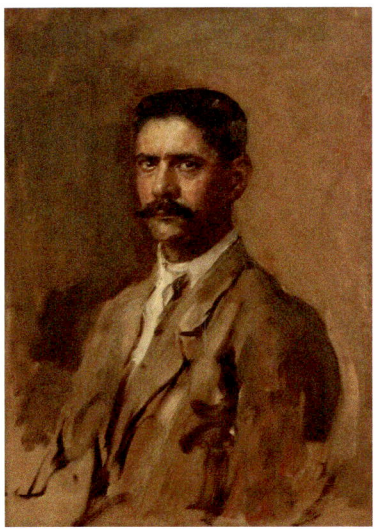

Fig. 11 *Self-Portrait*, Armando García Menocal (1863–1942), date unknown. Oil on canvas; 75.5 × 54 cm (29¾ × 21¼ in.). Museo Nacional de Bellas Artes de Cuba, Havana

1913

June 11–15

Brigadier General John J. Pershing (1860–1948), commander of Moro Province, sends Moro and Philippine Scouts to fight and kill 500 Tausug warriors at the Battle of Bud Bagsak on the island of Jolo.

December 13

Fighting concludes in Moro Province, marking the end of the Philippine-American War.

1916

August 29

The Jones Law of the Philippines establishes a new constitution that creates an elected Philippine legislature, with Manuel Quezón (1878–1944) as senate president, but maintains a U.S.-appointed executive branch. Importantly, it promises eventual independence. It remains in effect until 1934, with the passing of the Tydings-McDuffie Act.

1917

March 2

The Jones Act of Puerto Rico, officially known as the Jones-Shafroth Act, grants Puerto Ricans U.S. citizenship and limited internal civil self-government while maintaining the island's colonial status.

Index

Meares, John, 60, 304; *Ka'iana*, 60, *60*

Mechanics and Workingmen's Political Protective Union, 63

Melville, George W., *Panorama of the World's Fair, St. Louis, 1904*, *216–17*

Méndez, Felícita, 236, 238–39, *238*

Méndez, Gonzálo, 238

Méndez v. Westminster, 238

Menocal, Armando García, 17, 98, 101, 180, 183–84, 187, 192–95, 200, 202–3, 278n5, 280n40, 307, 308, 309; *Batalla de Coliseo* (Battle of Coliseo), *182* (detail) 183–84, *185*, 194–95, *194* (detail), *195* (detail), 314; *Boceto de La muerte de Maceo* (Study for *The death of Maceo*), 187, *188* (detail); *Campesino y soldado español* (Peasant and Spanish soldier), *100*, 101; *Carga al Machete* (Charge with machetes), 193, *193*; *Embarque de Cristóbal Colón por Bobadilla* (Embarkation of Christopher Columbus by Order of Bobadilla), 189, *189*; *Generosidad Castellana* (Castilian Generosity), 308; *Ingenio con carruaje* (Sugar mill with carriage), 36, *37*; *La muerte de Maceo* (The death of Maceo), 183–84, *185*, 187–88, 200, 202–3, 309, 314; *Self-Portrait*, *314*

Menocal, Mario García, 202, 278n5

Menocal y Martín de Medina, Gabriel García, 278n5

Merritt, Wesley, 127, 136, 312

Metropolitan Truth Society, 211

Mexican-American War (1846–1848), 32–33, 305

migrations of 1898, 220–22

Miles, Nelson, 17, 31, 33, *33*, 35, 47, 108, 110, 114, 311

Military Order of the Loyal Legion of the United States, 190

Mindanao Island, Philippines, 126, 128, 130, 132, 146

Miró Argenter, José, 187, 202

missionaries, 17, 42, 60–61, 75

Monroe, James, 17, *18*, 31, 176, 305

Monroe Doctrine, 17, 31–32, 45, 117, 167, 176, 242n28, 243n8, 248n92, 251n30, 305

Montoya, Gregoria "Gloria" P., 16

Morand, Augustus, 61

Morgan, John T., 72

Morgan, J. P., 178, 309

Morgan Report, 72, 79

Moro, Philippines, 114, 145–46

Moro Scouts, 146

Moses Taylor & Co., 36

Mosher, Charles D., *John Marshall Harlan*, *171*

Muñoz Marín, Luis, 86, 117, 275n73

Muñoz Rivera, Luis, 102, 115, *116*, 117, 275n73, 313

museum collections, critical appraisal of, 12–13, 205–9, 212–17

Muslims, in the Philippines, 128, 130, 145–46, 170, 314

Napoleon. *See* Bonaparte, Napoleon

National Anthropological Archives, 222, 226

National Association for the Advancement of Colored People (NAACP), 137

National Geographic (magazine), 227

National Museum of American History, Washington, DC, 222

National Museum of Asian Art, Washington, DC., 222, 226

National Museum of Natural History, Washington, DC, 222, 226

National Portrait Gallery, 12–13, 221, 239, 241n7

National Reform Party (Hawai'i), 63

Native Americans: cultural artifacts from, 212; displacement of/violence against, 17, 31–33, 243n5

Natividad, Lisa Linda, 173

nativism, 165, 220, 222

Nāwahī, Joseph, 75

Negros, Philippines, 126–28, 140

Newberry Library, Chicago, 227

New Granada Treaty (1846), 305

New Mexico, 32

USS *New Orleans*, 108

New Spain, 91

New York Journal (newspaper), 39, 41, 310

New York Times (newspaper), 50, 207, 216

Nicaragua, 45, 176

Nicoya, 98

Nodarse Bacallao, Alberto, 187, 202

Northern Mariana Islands, 24, 159

Northwest Ordinance (1787), 168, 272n26

Obama, Barack, 122

Olivares, José de, *Our Islands and Their People as Seen with the Camera and Pencil*, 221, *222*

Oller y Cestero, Francisco, 47, 94, 108, 249n107, 307; *Eugenio María de Hostos*, 115, *115*; *President William McKinley*, 31, 47, *48*, 49, *49* (detail), 180, 312

USS *Olympia*, 46, 135

USS *Oregon*, 24

Oregon Statesman (newspaper), 210

Oregon Territory, 32

Organic Act of Guam (1950), 155, 173

Organic Act of the Philippines (1902), 170, 273n48, 313

Osbourne, Guy R., 210

Ostend Manifesto, 306

O'Sullivan, John, 305

Otis, Elwell Stephen, 136, 140, 153, 170, 213

Pacific Islanders, 232

Pact of Biak-na-bato, 139

Pact of Zanjón (1878), 96, 307

Padre José Torres Palomo (unidentified photographer), *150*

Palacio, Romualdo, 102

Palomo, José Torres, 16, 149, *150*, 152–53, 309

Panama, 174, 176, 276n99

Panama Canal, 19, 24, 25, 36, 45, 114, 174, 240n5, 276n99, 313

Pan-American Exposition (Buffalo, New York, 1901), 212–14, *213*, 216, 313

Pan-American Exposition (San Francisco, 1915), 202

Panay, Philippines, 126, 127, 135, 139–40

USS *Paragua*, 210

Pardo de Tavera, Trinidad H., 130

Paret y Alcázar, Luis, 89

Parker, Ida Burr, 142, *144*

Parker, John H., 142, *144*

Parker, Samuel, 70

Partido Autonomista (Autonomist Party) [Puerto Rico], 102, 308

Partido Liberal (Spain), 102

Partido Revolucionario Cubano (Cuban Revolutionary Party), 96, 308

Partido Unión (Union Party) [Puerto Rico], 117, 172, 313

Paterno, Pedro, 135, 145

Patria libre, La (The free land) [newspaper], 96

Paulet, George, 79

Pearl Harbor, Hawai'i, 24, 45, 63, 76, 308

Perez, Atanasio Taitano, 16, 153, *154*, 155, 312

Pershing, John J., 146, *147*, 314

Philadelphia Commercial Museum, 216

Philippine-American War, 12, 18; American opposition to, 13, 24, 136–39, 146, 168, 210; casualties in, 12, 29, *29*, 146, 241n6; conduct of, 139–47; cultural artifacts obtained from, 205–17; duration of, 126, 128; ending of, 314; origin of, 136, 312; population of the Philippines during, 242n14; representations of, 122, 125; U.S. troops in, 127–28, 136, 263n12

Philippine Commonwealth and Independence Act. *See* Tydings-McDuffie Act

Philippine National Police, 123

Philippines: banknote issued by, *123*; cultural artifacts from, 205–17; education in, 141–43; geography and population of, 126, 128; guerrilla warfare in, 128, 143–46, 208; independence movement in, 12, 14, 16, 128, 132–35, 139, 146, 172; Japan and, 16, 146; migration from, 220–21; and race, 125–26, 128, 136, 138–39, 169–70, 262n5, 286n19; reconcentration in, 145; Spanish sovereignty over, 127–35, 248n95; U.S. sovereignty over, 12, 128, 136, 169–72; war casualties of, 241n6; in War of 1812, 46

Philippine Scouts, 146

Pierce, Franklin, 245n44, 247n86, 306

Pissarro, Camille, 47

Platt, Orville H., 167

Platt Amendment (1902–1934), 12, 16, 86, 114, *167*, 167–68, 188, 271n13, 313

Plessy v. Ferguson, 160, 165, 171

Polk, James, 32–33, 245n44, 305, 306

Ponce de León, Juan, 243n4, 243n5

popular culture, 11, 19, 27–28, 103, 105, 177–78, 260n87

Acknowledgments

This publication and the related exhibition at the National Portrait Gallery evolved from discussions we had with each other. With our expertise in Latino art and history (Taína Caragol) and in the intersection of U.S. art and military history (Kate Clarke Lemay), we first drew upon our individual and personal experiences. We compared notes about the relationships the United States has had with lands under its sovereignty. We realized that the histories of Cuba, Guam, Hawai'i, Puerto Rico, and the Philippines, despite the vast oceans between them, are interconnected. We began to see how portraiture and biography had the potential to narrate the history of the events that occurred during the flashpoint year of 1898. And finally, we traced how the arc of history extends to this day, with the continued debates in the Supreme Court regarding the 1901 *Insular Cases*; the ever-evolving political relationship between the United States and Cuba; and the continued coalition between the United States and the Philippines, especially around the security of the South China Sea. From these conversations, an exhibition was born.

A project of this scale addressing the history of imperialism and the United States is a major endeavor, demonstrating the commitment of the National Portrait Gallery's director, Kim Sajet, to addressing difficult chapters of history. Due to the COVID-19 pandemic, this exhibition faced challenges beyond the normal scope, and we deeply admire her leadership. Simply put, Dr. Sajet's belief in this project made it possible.

The research and travel involved to develop *1898* posed a great number of logistical challenges and required meticulous planning, innumerable meetings, and an extraordinary amount of airplane miles. We could not have managed to execute this exhibition without Carolina Maestre, whose steady focus was critical to the project's success. From conducting research to helping with image licensing and editing captions, Carolina offered key assistance. The publication of this beautiful, rich, and extensive catalogue was guided by Rhys Conlon, head of publications, and Sarah McGavran, editor, both of whom spent countless hours working with us on this project. Without them, this book would never have crossed the finish line, and we cannot thank them enough for their generosity as colleagues. They were joined by the talented copyeditor Martin Fox and our fantastic collaborators at Marquand Books: Adrian Lucia, Melissa Duffes, Ryan Polich, Leah Finger, Jeremy Linden, and Kestrel Rundle. We are ever grateful to the gifted Michelle Komie, Jodi Price, and the entire Princeton University Press team. Special thanks also go to Laura Eichorn, Tori Garnett, Michele Jarrouj, and Maia Puryear of the Smithsonian.

We extend our gratitude to the entire staff at the National Portrait Gallery for their dedication to this exhibition, which is among the largest and most challenging the museum has undertaken. The *1898* project manager, Allison Keilman, deserves a medal for the numerous details she tracked. She licensed nearly two hundred images for this book, and she helped manage numerous loans and contracts. Registrars Marissa Olivas and Sophia Brocenos, under the leadership of Jennifer Wodzianski, beautifully managed the shipping of the loans, handling complications imposed by the pandemic with enviable ease. Their work arranging the shipment of the portrait of Queen Lili'uokalani was especially commendable. Conservators Lou Molnar, Im Chan, and Christina Finlayson ensured the safety of the objects in the exhibition. We depended on our colleague Mark Gulezian, photographer, to ensure that the book's illustrations were beautiful. Marlene Harrison, head of exhibitions, oversaw the financial obligations of the show by assessing the budget and identifying necessary changes, resolving complications with loans, and shepherding communications. The ever-important work by our colleagues in advancement, including Usha Subramanian, Lindsay Gabryszak, Raven Bradburn, Megan Beck, and Matt Gray, raised the funds to make this exhibition possible and helped us establish new networks with donors. Kristy Snaman, Sara Mazzoleni, and V. A. Falzon created the most wonderful opening celebration of the exhibition. Rich Reichley and his staff worked miracles for the budget, which enabled us to travel across the world to complete necessary research. Our talented colleagues in design and production, including Tibor Waldner, Peter Crellin, Adam Ressa, Laura Thornton, Anne Wilsey, Sally Kim, Alex Cooper, Luke Moses, Grant Lazer, and Michael Baltzer; as well as Wayne Long, Dale Hunt, and Todd Gardner, made the exhibition's presentation both stunning and seamless. For their unyielding support of this show, we thank our curatorial colleagues Robyn Asleson, Charlotte Ickes, and Ann Shumard; Hallie Kroll and Casey Magrys; as well as our former colleagues Dorothy Moss and Leslie Ureña. For their impactful educational initiatives and public programs, thank you to Rebecca Kasemeyer, Clara de Pablo, Erin Beasley, Kaia Black, Beth Evans, Vanessa Jones, Elisabeth Kilday, Jocelyn Kho, Shirlee Lampkin, Geraldine Provost Lyons, Irina Rubenstein, and Briana Zavadil White. Deb Sisum, head of new media, helped us create a website for this exhibition and did not blink an eye when we asked her to include texts in four languages. Our communications team worked tirelessly to promote the exhibition, and we are glad to be able to count on Concetta Duncan, Gabbie Obusek, Ada Hinton, and Madison Hayes. Librarians Anne Evenhaugen and Alexandra Reigle hunted down sources that seemed nearly impossible to locate, and they also facilitated our research during the trying period of the pandemic. Former colleagues Carolyn Carr, Claire Kelly, Gwendolyn DuBois Shaw, Lou Molnar, Patricia Svoboda, and David C. Ward helped this project in its initial stages. For his encouragement from the beginning, we thank Eduardo Díaz, deputy director of the National Museum of the American Latino. And finally, we thank Brandon Brame Fortune, chief curator emerita, Michael Hussey, director of history, restorative history, and research, and Rhea Combs, director of curatorial affairs, for their unwavering support of this exhibition.

In order to look their best, several artworks in the exhibition required conservation. We thank Sol Rivera for treating the works from Puerto Rican private and public collections. We also thank William Adair of Gold Leaf Studios for restoring the frame of Queen Lili'uokalani's portrait by William Cogswell. Audio producer Ruth Morris crossed time zones and technological barriers to create a wonderful audio component for the exhibition with expert voices from all the lands addressed. We are grateful to María Eugenia Hidalgo for her translations of all exhibition content into Spanish. Special thanks to the network of Hawaiians fluent in ʻŌlelo Hawaiʻi for their editing of the translations. Over our six years curating this show, a multitude of interns assisted us in conducting research. We extend our gratitude to Mayela Caro, Suny Cárdenas-Gómez, Alba Gabriela Gómez-Valentín, Pauline Fleury, Emily Jeong, Alexandria Lybbert, Grace Marra, Shannon Neal, Gloria Ortega, Juliette Pasquini, Darcy Phillips, Matthew Phillips, Frances Poole-Crane, Katie Prinkey, Calder Sharp, Moises Severino, Madi Shenk, Gabrielle Robinson Tillenburg, and Jane Wilde. Special thanks among the interns go to Rich Denis for his outstanding research and help facilitating our visit to Cuba.

During the fateful year of 1898, peoples of Micronesia, the Caribbean, the North Pacific Ocean, the Philippine Sea, and the South China Sea witnessed the expansion of United States' rule into their lands. We were curious about the history of U.S. imperialism as told from the points of views of these groups, and we sought to engage with scholars, archivists, curators, and other representatives from these islands. Some of these conversations were critical to securing essential loans, including that of the portrait of Queen Lili'uokalani. For his work on this loan, we thank Adam Jansen, State Archivist of Hawaiʻi. We also thank the members of the Benevolent Royal Hawaiian Societies, including the Royal Order of Kamehameha I, ʻAhahui Kaʻahumanu, Hale O Na Aliʻ O

Hawaiʻi, and the Daughters and Sons of Hawaiian Warriors–Mamakakaua. For his help with the loans from the Philippines, thank you to José Victor Chan-Gonzaga, Assistant Secretary of the Office of American Affairs of the Philippine government's Department of Foreign Affairs. Carlos Ruiz Cortés, Executive Director of the Instituto de Cultura Puertorriqueña, as well as Freddy Vélez, María del Mar Caragol, Carmen Torres, and María Isabel Rodríguez facilitated research visits and loans from their institution. We are grateful to Flavia Marichal, Director of Museo de Historia, Antropología y Arte for guiding us to crucial artworks in public and private collections in Puerto Rico. Cheryl Hartup, Director, Museo de Arte de Ponce, Iraida Rodríguez-Negrón, Grace M. Cay Castañón, generously opened the doors of their museum and art storage for a study visit. María Molina, Head of the Cultural Office of the Embassy of Spain, and Gabriel Alou Forner, Political Counselor of the Embassy of Spain in the United States, facilitated connections and research visits in Spain. National Portrait Gallery commissioner Eduardo Rabassa, former commissioner Anna Chavez, also shared advice and contacts in anticipation of research trips to Spain. Sulia Páez and Manuel Menocal of the Cuban Embassy in the United States made our trip to Cuba logistically possible. In the City of Havana's Jean Baptiste Vermay conservation laboratory, Juan Carlos Bermejo, director of painting conservation, provided access to the monumental *La muerte de Maceo*. Studio visits and conversations with Reynier Leyva Novo, Miguel Luciano, Gisela McDaniel, José Manuel Mesías, Maia Cruz Palileo, Aryam Rodriguez, Juan Sánchez, Ranfis Suárez Ramos, and Stephanie Syjuco were crucial to our understanding of the impact of 1898 in contemporary art.

Other people shared their knowledge and helped us better understand the very difficult and nuanced history of 1898. We thank Bárbara Arguelles Almenares, Marga Binamira, David Aiona Chang, Alice Christophe, Silvia Álvarez Curbelo, Gustavo Gelpí, Monica Guzman, Jorge Duany, Stephanie Herdrich, Kristin Hoganson, Healoha Johnston, Ana Theresa Labrador, Tory Laitila, Jillette Leon-Guerrero, Brian Linn, Delia María López Campistrous, José Manuel Mesías, Ramey Mize, Carlos Madrid, Ambeth Ocampo, E. Carmen Ramos, Noenoe Silva, Lanny Thompson, Neil Weare, and Ron Williams Jr. We also thank our colleagues at the Smithsonian for their consultation, including Carrie Beauchamp, Bethany Bentley, Cécile Ganteaume, Theodore S. Gonzalves, Candace Greene, Alexandra Harris, Fernanda Luppani, Ann McMullen and Tanya Thrasher. We are grateful to our Smithsonian Advisory Committee, including Joshua Bell, Kālewa Correa, Ariana Curtis, Michelle Anne Delaney, Paul Gardullo, Jake Homiak, Adrienne Kaeppler, Steve Velasquez, Cynthia Vidaurri, Sam Vong, and Ranald Woodaman.

Curators, archivists, librarians, and institutional directors around the globe facilitated our research. Our thanks go to María Isabel Rodríguez, Archivo General de Puerto Rico; Juan Carlos Fernández Borroto, Biblioteca Nacional José Martí; Yoel Cordoví Núñez and Belkis Quesada, the Instituto de Historia de Cuba; Manuel Álvarez Casado, Archivo de Indias; José María Moreno Martín, Museo Naval, Madrid; Severiano Hernández Vicente, Subdirector of State Archives, Spain; Encarnación Hidalgo Cámara, Museo de América; Paz Castillo Lojendío, Museo Nacional del Prado; and Sara Duke, the Library of Congress.

We are grateful to the lenders of this exhibition, including the Archdiocese of New Orleans; the Army and Navy Club; Ateneo Puertorriqueño; the Brooklyn Museum; the Claude Moore Health Sciences Library, University of Virginia; the National Museum of Natural History, Smithsonian Institution; Dr. Eduardo Pérez, Dr. Robert Stolberg Acosta, Eliezer Aldarondo Ortiz, Emilio Cueto, Emilio M. Ortiz; the Hawaiʻi State Archives; History Nebraska; Instituto de Cultura Puertorriqueña; Laura Katzman; Library of Congress; Luis Antonio and Cecile Gutierrez; Miguel B. Fernández; Museo de Arte de Ponce; Museo de Historia, Antropología y Arte, Universidad de Puerto Rico; the National Archives and Records Administration; National Library of the Philippines; the National Museum of American History, Smithsonian Institution; the National Museum of Health and Medicine; the National Museum of the Philippines; the New-York Historical Society; Smithsonian Institution Libraries; Green Library, Florida International University; the Metropolitan Museum of Art; the White House; U.S. House of Representatives; the U.S. Naval Academy Library; the U.S. Naval War College; University of Notre Dame Libraries; and the West Point Museum.

We acknowledge the funders of *1898: U.S. Imperial Visions and Revisions* with our deepest gratitude, including the Andrew W. Mellon Foundation; Ann S. and Samuel M. Mencoff; Luis A. Miranda, Jr., the Miranda Family Foundation; the Terra Foundation for American Art; Ann E. Roulet, Laura Roulet, and Rafael Hernández;

Kate Kelly and George Schweitzer; Gretchen Sierra-Zorita and Peter B. Hutt II; and M. Salomé Galib y Duane McLaughlin. The publication was supported by Furthermore, a program of the J. M. Kaplan Fund; and Fred M. Levin and Family, the Shenson Foundation, in memory of Nancy Livingston Levin. The project received federal support from the Latino Initiatives Pool, administered by the National Museum of the American Latino, and the Asian Pacific American Initiatives Pool, administered by the Smithsonian Asian Pacific American Center. Special thanks are due to those who helped facilitate this support, including Jorge Zamanillo, Diana Bossa, Deborah Cullen-Morales, Carrie Haslett, and Yao-Fen You.

Curating an exhibition that significantly restores chapters of history is no small task, and we are very grateful to our families and friends for their support. Taína Caragol would like to thank her husband Marc Neumann and her son, Karlo Neumann-Caragol, for being emotional pillars through this process, as well as Migdalia Barreto and Alberto Caragol, and Ri Caragol and Liliana Pérez. She also extends her gratitude to Miriam Basilio, Emanuel Bravo, María del Mar Caragol Rivera, Rafael Díaz Casas, Ramón Cernuda, Ingrid Elliott, Joanne Flores, María Judith Feliciano, Salomé Galib, Marcela Guerrero, Libia González, Rafael Hernández, Laura Katzman, Kate Clarke Lemay, Carolina Maestre, Pipía Marzo, Laura Roulet and her late mother Ann Roulet, Ana María Reyes, Natalia Salazar, Gretchen Sierra-Zorita, Jorge Sobredo, Edward J. Sullivan, and Natalia Ángeles Vieyra. Kate Clarke Lemay would like to thank her brothers, John Clarke Lemay and Lee Clarke Lemay, for their love and support. She also honors the enduring memory of her parents, J. A. Leo Lemay and Ann Clarke Lemay. For their enriching and steadfast friendship, she thanks Sarah Lea Burns, Raven Bradburn, Taína Caragol, Colin Colbourn, Michelle Ewy, Lindsay Gabryszak, Diana Greenwold, Jason Horner, Natalie Howe, Miranda Summers Lowe, Carolina Maestre, Julissa Marenco, Wanda McDonald, Colleen Martucci, Dorothy Moss, Lisa Olson, Melinda Rolph, Danielle Salley, Devereaux Salley, Romi Sloboda, Lisa Tetrault, and Ryan Wadle.

Credits

Excerpts of "Mutiny," by Craig Santos Perez, are featured on p. 123 with permission from the author.

Artists' Copyrights
© 'Au'a, 2019, Kapulani Landgraf: pp. 54–56.
© Miguel Luciano: p. 237, p. 238.
© Gisela McDaniel: p. 233, p. 234.
© Maía Cruz Palileo: p. 227, p. 229 (bottom), p. 230, p. 231.
© Stephanie Syjuco: p. 223, 224, and 225.

Cover: *President William McKinley* by Francisco Oller y Cestero, 1898 (detail). See p. 48.
Back Cover: *Queen Lili'uokalani* by Harris & Ewing Studio, 1908 (detail). See pp. 80–81.
Endsheets: "Acquisitions of Territory" in *McConnell's Historical Maps of the United States*, 1919 (detail). See p. 32. "The Spanish-American War 1898" in *The Comprehensive series, Historical-Geographical Maps of the United States*. Chicago: Modern School Supply Company, 1919.

DETAILS: pp. 2–3 (see p. 46); pp. 4–5 (see p. 106); p. 6 (see p. 164): pp. 22–23 (see p. 314), p. 30 (see p. 34); p. 58 (see p. 67); pp. 84–85 (see p. 110), p. 88 (see p. 99), pp. 120–21, p. 124 (see p. 128); pp. 158–59 (see p. 312); p. 162 (see p. 176), p. 182 (see p. 185, top), and p. 218 (see p. 233).

Unless otherwise noted, all images are courtesy of the National Portrait Gallery, Smithsonian Institution, Washington, DC (Photographer: Mark Gulezian).

PHOTOGRAPHY CREDITS
Albright-Knox Art Gallery: p. 232.
Archbishopric of San Juan Collection: p. 90.
Office of Archives and Records, Archdiocese of New Orleans, photo by Frank Aymami: p. 152.
Architect of the Capitol: p. 177.
Archives of American Art, Smithsonian Institution: p. 192 and p. 196.
Archivo General de Indias: p. 132 and p. 135.
Archivo General de Puerto Rico: p. 311 (top left).
Courtesy of the Army and Navy Club Library Trust, Washington, DC: p. 46.
Ateneo Puertorriqueño, photo by John Betancourt: p. 95.
Autry Museum of the American West: p. 305.
Bangko Sentral NG Pilipinas: p. 123.
Biblioteca Nacional de España: p. 98 and p. 99.
Bowdoin College Museum of Art: p. 190.
Casaquinta Las Delicias del Palatino, Havana: p. 185 (top).
Center of Military History, Museum Division, U.S. Army: p. 126.
Cooper Hewitt, Smithsonian Institution: p. 198 (top).
Courtesy of Emilio Cueto, photo by Mark Gulezian: p. 10 and p. 101.
Cumberland County Historical Society, Carlisle, PA: p. 314 (top).
Davis Museum at Wellesley College / Art Resource, NY: p. 191 (bottom).

District of Puerto Rico: p. 160.
Courtesy of Mr. and Mrs. Mike Fernandez, photo by Mark Gulezian: p. 97 (right).
Courtesy of Luis Antonio and Cecile Gutierrez, photo by Mark Gulezian: p. 128.
Hawaiian Mission Houses Historic Site and Archives: p. 72.
Hawai'i State Archives: p. 16, p. 66, p. 68, p. 73, p. 77, and p. 80; photo by David Franzen: p. 67; photo by Mark Gulezian: p. 58.
History Nebraska: p. 29 and p. 134.
Illinois State Library: p. 127 (right).
Instituto de Cultura Puertorriqueña, photo by John Betancourt: p. 108 and p. 116.
Joslyn Art Museum: p. 186.
Keil Creations: p. 161 (right).
KHM-Museumsverband: p. 202.
Courtesy of Laura Katzman, photo by Alex Jamison: p. 222.
Courtesy of Kapulani Landgraf: pp. 54–56.
Library of Congress, Washington, DC: p. 32, p. 39, p. 49 (fig. 15), p. 51, p. 63, p. 105, p. 107, p. 172, p. 173, p. 179, p. 197, p. 213, p. 215, p. 216, p. 217, p. 310, and p. 312.
Courtesy of Aldarondo and López-Bras, LLC, photo by John Betancourt: p. 110.
Courtesy of Miguel Luciano: p. 237, p. 238.
Courtesy of Gisela McDaniel and Pilar Corrias, London, photo by Trever Long: p. 218, p. 233, and p. 234.
© The Metropolitan Museum of Art. Image source: Art Resource, NY: p. 175, p. 184, p. 187, and p. 311 (top right).
Museo de Arte de Ponce: p. 111.
Museo de la Ciudad, Havana: p. 188.
Museo de Historia, Antropología y Arte, Universidad de Puerto Rico: p. 96; photo by John Betancourt: p. 115.
Museo Nacional de Bellas Artes de Cuba, Havana: p. 189, p. 193 (bottom), and p. 314 (bottom).
Museo Naval, Madrid: p. 104.
© National Academy of Design, New York / Bridgeman Images: p. 306.
National Archives and Records Administration: p. 25, p. 74, and p. 167.
National Gallery of Art, Washington: p. 198 (bottom).
National Library of the Philippines: p. 140.
National Museum of American History, Smithsonian Institution: p. 78, p. 122, p. 133, and p. 136.
National Museum of Health and Medicine: p. 310.
National Museum of Natural History, Department of Anthropology, Smithsonian Institution: p. 71, p. 87, and p. 221; photo by Donald E. Hurlbert: p. 65; photos by Greg Staley: p. 131, p. 146, and p. 209; photos by Victor Krantz: p. 35.
National Museum of the Philippines: p. 141; photo by Bengy Toda: p. 129.
Naval Academy Library: p. 150 (right) and p. 151.
Naval History and Heritage Command: p. 149.
Naval War College, Newport, RI: p. 15.
Newberry Library, Chicago: p. 228.
Newspapers.com: p. 38.
New-York Historical Society: p. 40.
Courtesy of Emilio and Sylvia M. Ortiz, photo by Daniella Piantini: p. 37 and p. 100.

Palacio de la Presidencia, República de Cuba; photo by José Manuel Mesías: p. 185 (bottom).
Courtesy of Maía Cruz Palileo and Monique Meloche Gallery, Chicago: p. 227, p. 229 (bottom), p. 230, and p. 231.
Courtesy of Dr. Eduardo Pérez and family, photo by John Betancourt: cover, p. 48 and p. 49 (fig. 16).
© Trustees of the Portland Museum of Art, Maine; courtesy of Meyersphoto.com: p. 191 (top).
Private collection, photo by Mark Gulezian: p. 106, p. 109, p. 166, and p. 211.
Presidential Museum and Library, Malacañan Palace: p. 130.
© RMN-Grand Palais / Art Resource, NY: p. 69 (left).
David Rumsey Collection: p. 92 and p. 93.
Schomburg Center for Research in Black Culture, The New York Public Library: p. 94 and p. 97 (left).
Smithsonian Libraries and Archives: p. 153 (right), p. 204, p. 206, p. 208, and p. 214.
Courtesy of Robert von Stolberg de Acosta Foundation, photo by John Betancourt: p. 168.
Courtesy of Stephanie Syjuco and Catharine Clark Gallery, San Francisco: p. 223, p. 224, and p. 225.
Richard F. Taitano Micronesian Area Research Center: p. 150 (left), p. 153 (left), p. 154.
Taft Museum of Art, photo by Tony Walsh Photography: p. 142.
Courtesy of Belinda Torres-Mary, great grand-daughter of Isabel González: p. 161 (left).
University of British Columbia: p. 60.
University of Hawai'i at Mānoa Library: p. 27.
University of Miami Libraries, Cuban Heritage Collection: p. 112.
University of Michigan Museum of Anthropological Archaeology: p. 229 (top).
University of Virginia, Claude Moore Health Sciences Library: p. 113.
U.S. House of Representatives: p. 164.
West Point Museum Collection, United States Military Academy: p. 201.
White House Historical Association: p. 176.

This book is published in conjunction with the exhibition *1898: U.S. Imperial Visions and Revisions*, presented at the National Portrait Gallery, Smithsonian Institution, Washington, DC., from April 28, 2023, to February 25, 2024.

Funding was provided by:

The Andrew W. Mellon Foundation
Ann S. and Samuel M. Mencoff
Luis Miranda, Jr., the Miranda Family Foundation
Terra Foundation for American Art
Ann E. Roulet, Laura Roulet, and Rafael Hernández
Kate Kelly and George Schweitzer
Gretchen Sierra-Zorita and Peter B. Hutt II
M. Salomé Galib y Duane McLaughlin

Furthermore: a program of the J. M. Kaplan Fund

This publication has been supported by Fred M. Levin and Family, The Shenson Foundation, in memory of Nancy Livingston Levin.

The project received federal support from the Latino Initiatives Pool, administered by the National Museum of the American Latino, and the Asian Pacific American Initiatives Pool, administered by the Smithsonian Asian Pacific American Center.

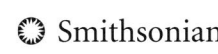
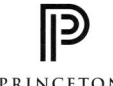

National Portrait Gallery

Smithsonian

PRINCETON

Library of Congress Control Number: 2023931755
ISBN 978-0-691-24620-8

British Library Cataloging-in-Publication Data is available

Published by National Portrait Gallery, Smithsonian Institution, Washington, DC
npg.si.edu

In association with Princeton University Press
41 William Street, Princeton, New Jersey 08540
99 Banbury Road, Oxford OX2 6JX
press.princeton.edu

Produced by Marquand Books, Seattle
marquandbooks.com

Copyedited by Martin Fox
Designed by Ryan Polich
Typeset in Roslindale and Acumin Pro by Tina Henderson
Proofread by Ted Gilley
Indexed by Dave Luljak
Color management by I/O Color, Seattle
Printed and bound in Italy by Graphicom

10 9 8 7 6 5 4 3 2 1

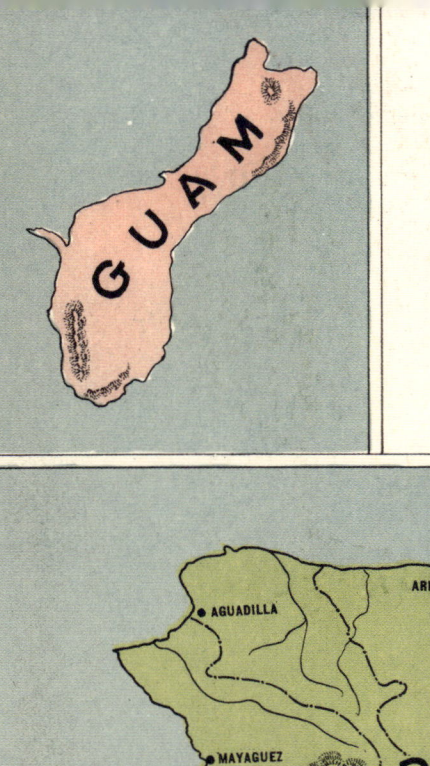

GUAM

At various times there had been friction between United States merchants and Spanish officers in Cuba, owing to the evasion of neutrality laws or to trade regulations. In 1895 the Cubans rebelled against Spain and the cruel treatment of the Cubans by the Spanish during the next three years aroused general indignation. In 1898 the United States battleship Maine was blown up in Havana harbor. War was declared.

The chief events of the war were the battle of Manila Bay, the sinking of the Merrimac, the battles near Santiago, the destruction of Cervera's fleet, the invasion of Porto Rico, and the capture of Manila. By the treaty of peace signed in Paris in December, 1898, the territory of the United States was enlarged by:

(1) Porto Rico and the Philippine Islands, conquests of war.

(2) The Island of Guam, purchased from Spain. Cuba became an independent republic.

Through an effort on the part of Aguinaldo, a Philippine Native, to make himself head of a Philippine state, insurrection against the United States troops began in 1899.

After two years of scattered fighting in which the native troops were defeated, Aguinaldo was taken prisoner and the insurrection was stamped out.

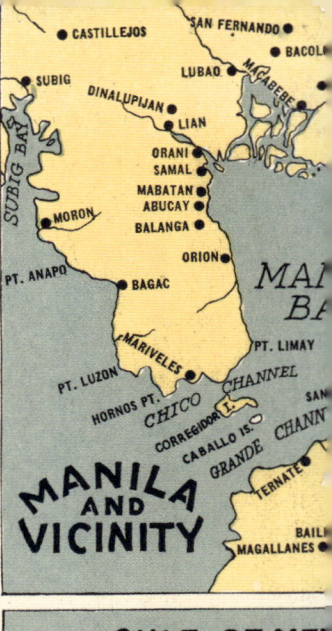

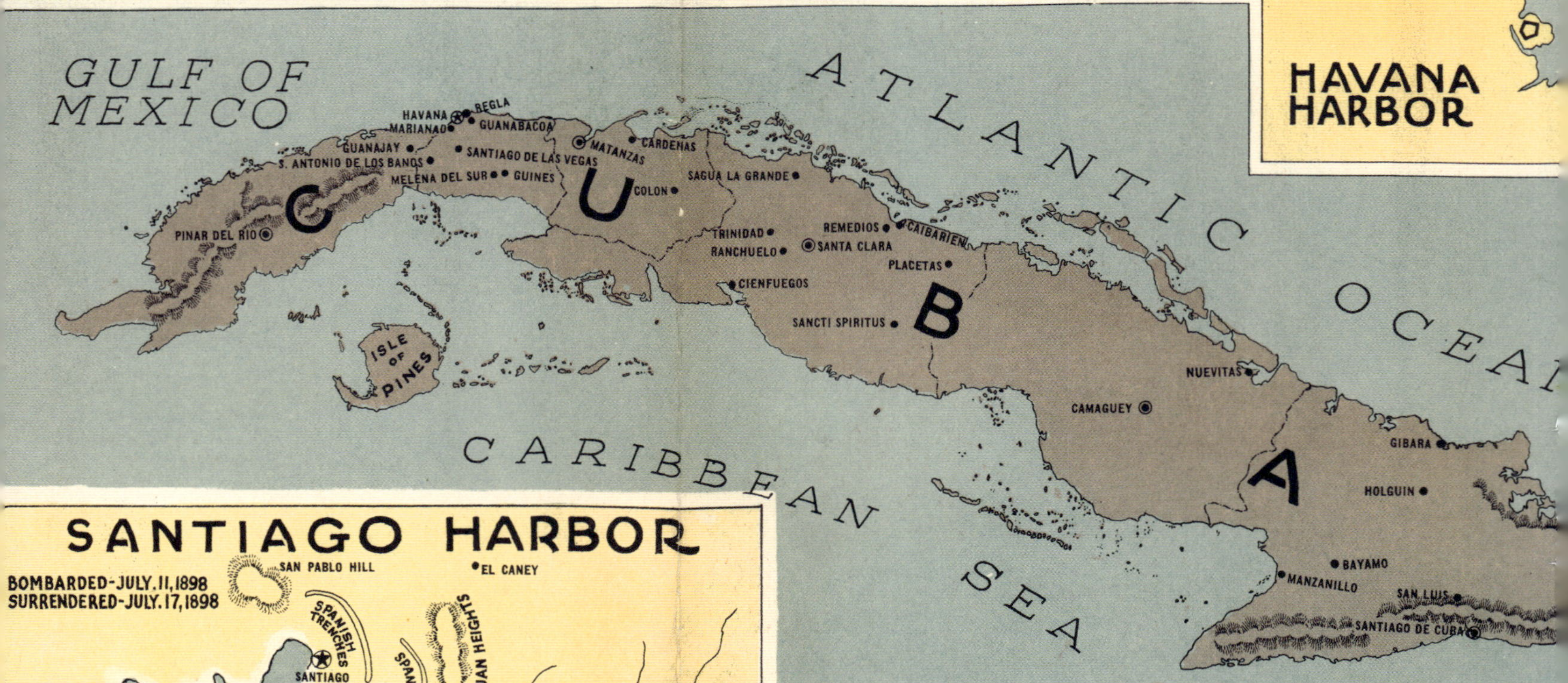

MANILA AND VICINITY

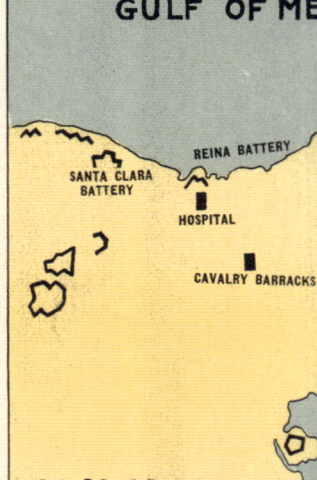

GULF OF MEX

HAVANA HARBOR

PORTO RICO

- AGUADILLA
- ARECIBO
- SAN JUAN
- BAYAMO
- FAJARDO
- MAYAGUEZ
- CAGUAS
- HUMACAO
- YAUCO
- PONCE
- GUAYAMA

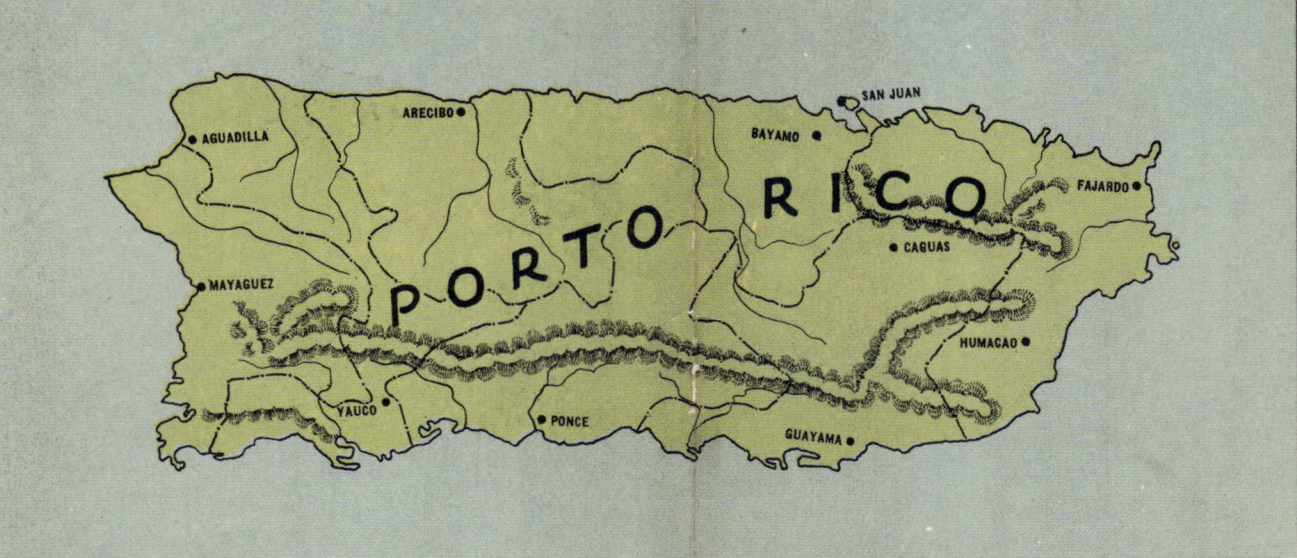

GULF OF MEXICO

ATLANTIC OCEAN

CUBA

CARIBBEAN SEA

ISLE OF PINES

- HAVANA
- REGLA
- MARIANAO
- GUANABACOA
- GUANAJAY
- SANTIAGO DE LAS VEGAS
- MATANZAS
- CARDENAS
- S. ANTONIO DE LOS BAÑOS
- MELENA DEL SUR
- GUINES
- COLON
- SAGUA LA GRANDE
- PINAR DEL RIO
- TRINIDAD
- REMEDIOS
- CAIBARIEN
- RANCHUELO
- SANTA CLARA
- PLACETAS
- CIENFUEGOS
- SANCTI SPIRITUS
- NUEVITAS
- CAMAGUEY
- GIBARA
- HOLGUIN
- BAYAMO
- MANZANILLO
- SAN LUIS
- SANTIAGO DE CUBA

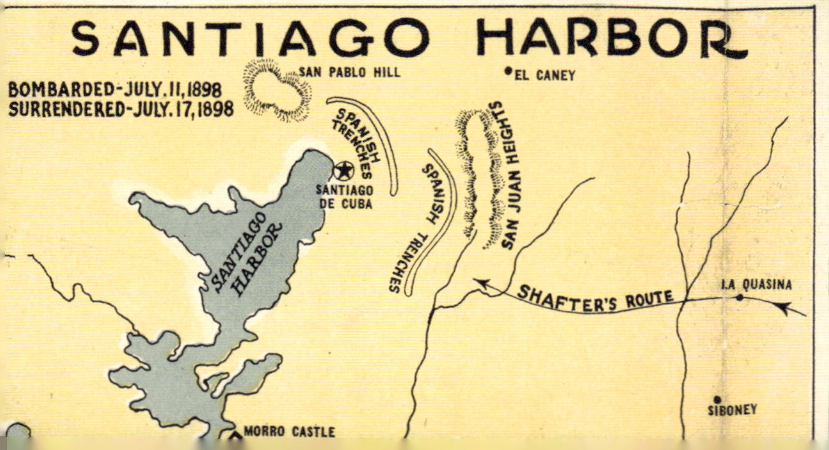

SANTIAGO HARBOR

BOMBARDED-JULY 11, 1898
SURRENDERED-JULY 17, 1898

- SAN PABLO HILL
- EL CANEY
- SPANISH TRENCHES
- SANTIAGO DE CUBA
- SAN JUAN HEIGHTS
- SHAFTER'S ROUTE
- LA QUASINA
- SANTIAGO HARBOR
- SIBONEY
- MORRO CASTLE